REWRITING NATURE

History will mark the twenty-first century as the dawn of the age of precise genetic manipulation. Breakthroughs in genome editing are poised to enable humankind to fundamentally transform life on Earth. Those familiar with genome editing understand its potential to revolutionize civilization in ways that surpass the impact of the discovery of electricity and the development of gunpowder, the atomic bomb, or the Internet. Significant questions regarding how society should promote or hinder genome editing loom large in the horizon. And it is up to humans to decide the fate of this powerful technology. *Rewriting Nature* is a compelling, thought-provoking interdisciplinary exploration of the law, science, and policy of genome editing. The book guides readers through complex legal, scientific, ethical, political, economic, and social issues concerning this emerging technology, and challenges the conventional false dichotomy often associated with science and law, which contributes to a growing divide between both fields.

Paul Enríquez, JD, LLM, PhD, is an intellectual property attorney and scientist who researches and writes at the intersection of law, science, and policy. He holds doctoral degrees in law and structural and molecular biochemistry. His research on law, science, and technology, genome editing, biochemistry, and the regulation of biotechnology, has been published in numerous scientific, legal, and popular-media publications, and has been presented at national and international conferences. He currently serves as a judicial clerk at the United States Court of Appeals for the Federal Circuit.

Rewriting Nature

THE FUTURE OF GENOME EDITING AND HOW TO BRIDGE THE GAP BETWEEN LAW AND SCIENCE

PAUL ENRÍQUEZ
United States Court of Appeals for the Federal Circuit

CAMBRIDGE
UNIVERSITY PRESS

CAMBRIDGE
UNIVERSITY PRESS

University Printing House, Cambridge CB2 8BS, United Kingdom

One Liberty Plaza, 20th Floor, New York, NY 10006, USA

477 Williamstown Road, Port Melbourne, VIC 3207, Australia

314–321, 3rd Floor, Plot 3, Splendor Forum, Jasola District Centre,
New Delhi – 110025, India

103 Penang Road, #05–06/07, Visioncrest Commercial, Singapore 238467

Cambridge University Press is part of the University of Cambridge.

It furthers the University's mission by disseminating knowledge in the pursuit of education, learning, and research at the highest international levels of excellence.

www.cambridge.org
Information on this title: www.cambridge.org/9781108475709
DOI: 10.1017/9781108598897

First published 2021

A catalogue record for this publication is available from the British Library.

ISBN 978-1-108-47570-9 Hardback
ISBN 978-1-108-46879-4 Paperback

For Lourdes Renée Vinueza

The most courageous, generous, noble, loving, and hardest-working person I will ever know.

Summary of Contents

Contents

Figures

Foreword

The White House's announcement that the President of the United States had nominated me to serve as a circuit judge on the U.S. Court of Appeals for the Federal Circuit set off a memorable and intense period in my life. I had already undergone thorough vetting by the U.S. Department of Justice's Office of Legal Counsel, White House Counsel, the FBI, the American Bar Association, and several other bar associations. So I was not surprised to receive an extensive questionnaire from the staff of the U.S. Senate Judiciary Committee.

The Judiciary Committee's questionnaire signaled a milestone in my path to the Federal Circuit because it brought me closer to a Senate confirmation hearing. Around that time I became aware of discussions within circles of the patent bar concerning the need for judges on the Federal Circuit who possessed scientific or technical backgrounds, which I lacked. Certain members of the community believed that cases before the Federal Circuit are so imbued with science and advanced technologies that only judges with a scientific background can understand them.

The discourse was disturbing. I imagined Senator Grassley or Senator Leahy asking me during the confirmation hearing, "Is it true you have no scientific background?" I raised this prospect during a meeting with two friends who were members of the patent bar. One responded that the issue was a red herring. According to her, no person alive has expertise and formal education in all the technological nuances that come before the Federal Circuit. She was right.

Indeed, one of my first cases involved DNA technology. Late one night as I lay in bed, I read the petitioner's principal brief. I saw a couple of figures of the double helix, one of which was broken. Gulp! I vividly recall that the brief began with the statement, "In order to understand the issues in this case, you must understand a few basic principles of DNA technology." I read the brief cover to cover, some parts several times, and eventually I was fully confident that I understood the DNA technology involved in the case. Importantly, I understood the relationship between that technology and the law involved in the case. Although I cannot be expert in all the technologies in the patent cases that come before me, I expect the lawyers to be experts at explaining the technology in their case. And invariably they are. After all, the Federal Circuit is not a scientific laboratory, but a court of law. Even with the lawyers' technological guidance, I find my cases challenging, exciting, and incredibly interesting, whether they involve DNA, fruit-tree varieties, a blender, a chemical compound, or the tire skirt of a semi-tractor trailer rig. Perhaps the most exciting and challenging aspect of my work on the court is the understanding that my judgment has the potential to greatly impact the intersection of the sciences and arts and law.

In this book, Paul Enríquez, takes us on an exciting tour of that intersection. He starts by providing a fresh and unique perspective on the impact that nascent scientific and technological developments can have on society. Starting with Johannes Gutenberg's stunning invention, the mechanical, movable-type printing press, Enríquez explores how some innovations and discoveries can have a ripple effect across all levels of society. In Gutenberg's case, the printing press opened vast windows of communication with the common person about inventions and discoveries, new expressions of thought, and groundbreaking discoveries of celestial bodies orbiting and spinning across an infinite universe. As a result, the work of scientists and mathematicians like Copernicus spread rapidly and unstoppably.

But discoveries like the Gutenberg press also bring conflict. Long-held religious beliefs are shaken at their core, and governments slowly lose their grip because of new societal enlightenment. Another example is the internet. The world is forever changed as enlightenment brings man closer to heaven, or in other cases nearer to the bowels of hell.

Enríquez believes we are at the brink of another global threshold much like that heralded by the Gutenberg printing press. Only this time, the sea change is made possible by genome editing. Enríquez calls the genome the book of life, and he sees genome editing as rewriting that book. The thought of rewriting the book of life should give everyone pause. But Enríquez believes that too many will not pause, whether out of disregard for the elements of human life or out of sheer intellectual negligence.

In particular, Enríquez shows why we should all be concerned with the system of *Clustered, Regularly Interspaced, Short, Palindromic Repeats*, commonly called CRISPR. This gene-editing tool has taken the scientific community by storm. Over 17,000 scientific publications have appeared that cover gene editing in a wide swath of subjects including plants, animals, insects, and, yes, humans. Enríquez stresses that we do not yet understand the types of broad global changes that CRISPR could initiate. The problem is not CRISPR itself but that those having influence do not appreciate the scientific and moral implications of gene editing.

This is particularly true in the legal profession and, more specifically, the judiciary. Enríquez cites legal cases that demonstrate how a faulty understanding, or blatant disregard, of scientific facts ultimately results in bad law. My sense is that he is correct. There is a gap between the law and scientific and technological changes.

The law lags. I suppose many judges feel that lag is inevitable, for how can judges opine on the scientific foundations of future innovations? We accept that first comes innovation, followed by conflict, then the legal case followed by the decision. Is it possible or desirable to change that order?

Enríquez courageously explores new ways to equip judges with a higher level of scientific understanding to meet these challenges. Perhaps a primer of sorts would work, as suggested by Judge Neuberger, former President of the UK Supreme Court. Or perhaps a "normative structural legal framework" is required as Enríquez discusses, or a form of "scientific empiricism that is broadly adaptable to addressing questions of science in law." I do not have a crystal ball to forecast the future. But I am reminded that I often voluntarily participate in scientific forums and conferences designed especially for judges. There is no doubt that such conferences enable me and many other judges to "grasp the key scientific concepts related to transformative technologies" that come before me in patent cases. There is hope in the good news that judges, in my experience, are eager to learn.

The real surprise, and great value, of the book is that Enríquez takes the reader on a chapter-by-chapter tour on the interdependencies of science, philosophy, sociology, ethics, and law with an eye toward understanding key issues in those disciplines as they relate to genome editing. We no longer have to search for a primer. This book helps bridge the gap between science and the law on the issue of genome editing. What makes Enríquez's contribution valuable is that in addition to being a scientist, scholar, and intellectual property attorney, Enríquez proves to be a great teacher. He is a maestro, one who masters the craft and its related art of communication. I applaud him for this wonderful scholarly work of law and science.

Honorable Jimmie V. Reyna
Circuit Judge, United States Court of Appeals for the Federal Circuit

Acknowledgments

Living organisms need water and nutrients to thrive. That simple biological axiom captures both the extent and essence of what is needed to support life. And then there are writers—arguably the neediest creatures on Earth. Beyond the basics, writers have a fair litany of other extravagant needs: supporters, believers, access to reference materials, stimulating environments conducive to creativity, ice cream—the slowly hand-churned type with fruit chunks in it. The list goes on.

Writing this book has been an incredibly exhilarating, fun, stimulating, demanding, and labor-intensive experience from professional and personal standpoints. I have benefited immensely from the kindness of many people without whom this book would not exist.

I owe gratitude to Matt Gallaway, my editor extraordinaire at Cambridge University Press, for believing in this project and masterfully guiding it to publication. This book had been brewing in my mind for some time, until Matt serendipitously reached out to me about bringing it to fruition. He embodies all the good qualities of an editor—supportive, talented, perceptive, and enthusiastic. Most of all, I thank Matt for being flexible and understanding as I endured the countless pressures of myriad other work commitments, including writing and defending a PhD dissertation, performing scientific research in the laboratory, working at a law firm, and more—all while pursuing this intellectually rewarding endeavor. Many thanks also to the magnificent, world-class staff at Cambridge University Press (and its network of partners, affiliates, and anonymous peer reviewers), who have been terrific to work with and helped to make this project a reality. I wish to acknowledge Laura Blake, Helen Kitto, Akash Datchinamurthy, Cameron Daddis, Heather Mackay, Doreen Anderson, and the entire publication staff involved in this project for all the diligent work behind the scenes.

I have been incredibly fortunate to count on inordinately generous readers, colleagues, and friends, who provided thoughtful, eloquent, and insightful feedback on various chapters of the book. For taking the time to read, comment, and challenge my ideas at various stages, I kindly thank Michael Abramowicz, Terri

Beiner, Michael Byrne, John Conley, Jason Delborne, Dov Fox, Fred Gould, Dmitry Karshtedt, Sean Murphy, Rick Peltz-Steele, Robert Rose, Nicole Salamander, Steve Spiker, Anna Stepanova, and Patricia Zettler. I am filled with deep gratitude to each for their invaluable comments and conversations, which often led me to refine and strengthen my arguments. This book bears the mark of their collective wisdom and expertise; it is unquestionably better because of their input.

During the last three years, I also had the opportunity to test and present some of the ideas in this book at several scholarly conferences. In particular, I wish to express my heartfelt appreciation and gratitude to John Conley and Gary Marchant, for inviting me to present my work at the University of North Carolina at Chapel Hill School of Law and the Arizona State University Sandra Day O'Connor College of Law, respectively. Many thanks to Tanuja Koppal for inviting me to present at conferences organized by the Cambridge Healthtech Institute. I also wish to acknowledge the Volkswagen Foundation for supporting and hosting a superb international genome-editing workshop convened by the InterAcademy Partnership (the global network of academies of sciences and medicine), the US National Academies of Sciences, Engineering, and Medicine, the European Academies' Science Advisory Council, and the German National Academy of Sciences Leopoldina, to which I was invited as a participant. The workshop took place in Hanover, Germany and received additional support from the Gordon and Betty Moore Foundation. I thank audiences at these and other conferences for their comments and questions, as well as their commitment and contributions to facilitate conversations about science, law, and technology. Lastly, some of the chapters in this book expand upon ideas I published in earlier works, including *Editing Humanity: On the Precise Manipulation of DNA in Human Embryos*, 97 N.C. L. REV. 1147 (2019), *Genome Editing and the Jurisprudence of Scientific Empiricism*, 19 VAND. J. ENT. & TECH. L. 603 (2017), *CRISPR GMOs*, 18 N.C. J.L. & TECH. 432 (2017), *GM-Food Regulations: Engage the Public*, 548 NATURE 31 (2017), and *CRISPR-Mediated Epigenome Editing*, 89 YALE J. BIOLOGY & MED. 471 (2016). I wish to acknowledge the journals and the work of their editorial staffs.

For contributing to my professional development during the writing of this book, I also thank the organizers and sponsors of ComSciCon 2017—a national science-communication workshop hosted by Harvard University that aims to empower future leaders in science communication—for selecting and inviting me as a participant. Many thanks also to the Hispanic National Bar Association and Microsoft Corporation for their splendid partnership and for selecting me as a 2018 Intellectual Property Law Scholar.

Many generous and kind individuals I have encountered throughout my adult life have been active participants in my professional growth and have made all the difference. I am indebted to the Hons. Jimmie V. Reyna, Philip R. Martínez, and Richard D. Taylor for being wonderful teachers, role models, and even better persons; John Whealan and Lisa Blacker, who cook the best-tasting meat-and-potatoes recipe in the US Eastern Seaboard, for their wisdom, kindness, and selfless generosity; as well as Terri Beiner, Susan Karamanian, Jeff Kushan, Sean Murphy, Robert Rose, Gail Rosenthal, Bobby Royal, and Brian Strahl for all the grace and goodwill they have shown me. My deepest thanks to Michael Byrne for his acumen, good humor, friendship, intelligence, and enviable editorial skills. When I lacked institutional support, he provided pivotal access to research materials. I could not have begun to write this monograph without his help. More importantly, he offered his gift of time and was always willing to lend an ear (even if the subject matter was outside his areas of expertise) and offer suggestions when an idea was brewing but became stuck in transit out of the corners of my mind. I can only repay him with gratitude because there is simply no monetary value that can be ascribed to his assistance during the writing of this book.

My desire to thank some people who have also had a profound impact on my professional life is unfortunately foreclosed by the space–time continuum. As such, the best I can do is acknowledge the contributions of Thaddeus Stevens, Martin Luther King, Jr., Thurgood Marshall, and the many leaders who fought tirelessly for equality and the advancement of education, as well as the contributions of Nicolaus Copernicus, Marie Curie, Albert Einstein, and numerous other brilliant scientists who dedicated their professional lives to the advancement of science, knowledge, and truth. My appreciation for these trailblazers goes beyond mere admiration of their work; it is deeply personal. I stand on the shoulders of these inspirational giants and I am a beneficiary of their legacies.

Marshall's advocacy and championing of education and civil rights as a lawyer, for example, paved the way for me to attend a desegregated school when I arrived to the United States as a minor. When he later became a Justice of the US Supreme Court, he cast a fifth vote for the 5–4 majority in *Plyler v. Doe*, 457 U.S. 202 (1982), which has been—hands down—the most consequential court decision in my life.

Plyler struck down a Texas statute enacted for the purpose of denying immigrant children access to a public education on the basis of prejudice and hostility toward their immigration status. At the time, the State had implemented a scheme whereby so-called migrant recruiters would knock on residential doors in immigrant communities and recruit impoverished and neglected migrant children with limited or no English-speaking ability. The State would then fill out and submit slips to the federal government to procure funds—hundreds of millions of dollars—for migrant and bilingual education programs, all while callously denying school admission to the very children used to acquire said federal funds, and so doing it on the basis of their immigration status. Worse, the State—under the guise of maintaining fiscal integrity—excluded these marginalized children even though their parents owned or rented property and paid taxes that financed the schools. Recognizing that the denial of opportunity of a basic education relegated this group of children to second-class social status and posed significant barriers to their advancement on the basis of individual merit, the Court held that the statute was unconstitutional and violated the Equal Protection Clause. *Plyler* was decided before I was even born, yet I bear witness to its legacy. Had the Court upheld the discriminatory policies pursued by the State, this book would never have been written.

I relied on no institutional support in bringing this book to print, which made it all the more challenging. I had no research assistant, no secretary, no access to a librarian or resource-acquisition personnel, no institutional grant, and no sabbatical leave with which to carve time for this project. I did, however, benefit greatly from the company of Calvin, my angelic sidekick, standby research assistant, and sweet four-legged child. He filled in all those roles and provided more emotional support than I could ever have imagined. Calvin has more patience than any creature on Earth, if only because he puts up with all my antics. He tolerates my existence when I morph into a real-life Pepé Le Pew hoping he will not rebuff a hug and kiss. He also exercises lenity when I force him to wear a Halloween costume or disturb an occasional siesta because he is barking extra loud in his sleep. Most of all, he provided myriad times of levity during much of the writing of this book—especially when he sensed my stress and lack of sleep—for which I am infinitely thankful. Nothing like squeaking toys and playing chase with a gentle soul to make the world right all over again.

* * *

Finally, on a more personal note:

A project like this, born in the midst of intense personal and professional times, was bound to inconvenience many people. None more so than my mother Lourdes Renée Vinueza, a superhuman warrior and tower of strength, to whom this book is dedicated in its entirety.

My mother was born and raised in Ecuador into poverty as one of six siblings. Her grandmother was once a slave, her mother was a street merchant, and her father worked street gigs involving the delivery of heavy cargo, which he carried on his back. As a child, my mom and all her siblings shared the same bed and experienced constant food insecurity. Through grit and self-determination, she managed to leave that environment and carve a career for herself. After I was born, she had saved enough money for the down payment of the house in which I grew up. I use the word house liberally because it comprised four brick and cinder-block walls with asbestos-cement corrugated-roofing sheets. It was built in a new rural pueblo surrounded by dirt roads located several miles outside the capital city.

The village had no potable water, and so among my earliest memories are the walking trips we used to make to collect water from tank trucks that would visit weekly or bimonthly. Each family could collect a large barrel of water; I would help by carrying back one full pot or bucket of water, roughly three-quarters of which would miraculously survive the trip. Those walks back home were never fun. Budgeting water was key and one quickly learned creative ways to make a barrel last. I learned that mixing two pots of water—one boiled and another cold—was just the right amount to shower using a plastic cup. Over the years, the village grew in population. Paving of roads and access to potable water eventually followed. My mom worked a full-time job and ran a part-time business so I would never go hungry. As time went by, her hard work allowed her to save enough money to buy a beat-up, 1970s mini-pickup and install a roof that eliminated the need to set pots and pans to collect water that leaked when it rained.

To my beautiful, brave, sweet mom, who has lived through more hardships than I can possibly bear to share in these pages. She endured domestic violence and left an abusive household and marriage. She then had the courage and strength to give up her family, home, job, possessions, and everything she knew so I could have a shot at a better life in a foreign land. She is my heroine because she saved me from abject poverty and an alcoholic father. And she rescued me from others who subjected me to sexual abuse, before I even knew or understood what sex is. I owe my life to her, and not merely because she gave birth to me. My greatest and everlasting fortune has been that I am her son.

Predictably, life did not get any easier for her in the United States. We arrived without possessions. We spoke no English. And she confronted a whole new set of challenges with a teenage son by her side. She often cried at night to spare me her suffering. I can only imagine how hard the transition must have been for her. We learned to be afraid of speaking up when encountering injustice, because for those with no voice, the cost of speaking can be great. No matter how difficult things got, she supported me through it all and was a constant source of patience, encouragement, and strength. She is simply the best person and role model I know. She constantly pushes herself and seeks new learning opportunities. When she became a US citizen, she attended college because she wanted to challenge herself. I am so proud of her and all that she has accomplished and overcome.

To the greatest, most courageous person I will ever know: Mom, this book is yours! It represents a celebration of your triumphs. One of my missions in life is to make you proud. I hope this book lives up to that task. Thank you for loving me and all you have ever done. I love you.

Table of Cases

Abigail Alliance for Better Access to Developmental Drugs v. von Eschenbach, 495 F.3d 695 (D.C. Cir. 2007)
Adoptive Couple v. Baby Girl, 570 U.S. 637 (2013)
Alberty Food Products v. United States, 194 F.2d 463 (9th Cir. 1952)
Alliance for Bio-Integrity v. Shalala, 116 F. Supp. 2d 166 (D.D.C. 2000)
Association for Molecular Pathology v. Myriad Genetics, Inc., 569 U.S. 576 (2013)
Auer v. Robbins, 519 U.S. 452 (1997)
Bartels v. Iowa, 262 U.S. 404 (1923)
Beal v. Doe, 432 U.S. 438 (1977)
Bowers v. Hardwick, 478 U.S. 186 (1986)
Broad Institute, Inc., Junior Party v. Regents of the University of California, Senior Party, Patent Interference No. 106,048, 2017 WL 657415 (P.T.A.B. Feb. 15, 2017)
Brown v. Board of Education, 347 U.S. 483 (1954)
Buck v. Bell, 274 U.S. 200 (1927)
Burwell v. Hobby Lobby Stores, Inc., 573 U.S. 682 (2014)
Cabell v. Markham, 148 F.2d 737 (2d Cir. 1945)
Califano v. Jobst, 434 U.S. 47 (1977)
Carey v. Population Services International, 431 U.S. 678 (1977)
Case C-528/16, *Confédération Paysanne v. Premier Ministre*, ECLI:EU:C:2018:583 (July 25, 2018)
Chevron, U.S.A., Inc. v. Natural Resources Defense Council, Inc., 467 U.S. 837 (1984)
City of Cleburne v. Cleburne Living Center, Inc., 473 U.S. 432 (1985)
County of Sacramento v. Lewis, 523 U.S. 833 (1998)
Craig v. Boren, 429 U.S. 190 (1976)
Daubert v. Merrell Dow Pharmaceuticals, Inc., 509 U.S. 579 (1993)
Davis v. Berry, 216 F. 414 (S.D. Ia. 1914)
Diamond v. Chakrabarty, 447 U.S. 303 (1980)
Diamond v. Diamond, 283 P.3d 260 (N.M. 2012)
District of Columbia v. Heller, 554 U.S. 570 (2008)

Dred Scott v. Sandford, 60 U.S. (19 How.) 393 (1857)
Eisenstadt v. Baird, 405 U.S. 438 (1972)
Ekedahl v. COREStaff, Inc., 183 F.3d 855 (D.C. Cir. 1999)
Foundation on Economic Trends v. Heckler, 587 F. Supp. 753 (D.D.C. 1984)
Foundation on Economic Trends v. Heckler, 756 F.2d 143 (D.C. Cir. 1985)
General Medical Co. v. FDA, 770 F.2d 214 (D.C. Cir. 1985)
Gitlow v. New York, 268 U.S. 652 (1925)
Goesaert v. Cleary, 335 U.S. 464 (1948)
Grayned v. City of Rockford, 408 U.S. 104 (1972)
Griswold v. Connecticut, 381 U.S. 479 (1965)
Harris v. McRae, 448 U.S. 297 (1980)
Haynes v. Lapeer, 166 N.W. 938 (Mich. 1918)
Honeywell Inc. v. Sperry Rand Corp., No. 4–67 Civ. 138, 1973 WL 903 (D. Minn. Oct. 19, 1973)
Howard v. Ferrellgas Partners, L.P., 92 F. Supp. 3d 1115 (D. Kan. 2015)
In re Moore, 306 N.C. 394 (1982)
Jackson v. Pollion, 733 F.3d 786 (7th Cir. 2013)
Jacobson v. Massachusetts, 197 U.S. 11 (1905)
Johnson v. Zimmer, 686 F.3d 224 (4th Cir. 2012)
Kumho Tire Co. v. Carmichael, 526 U.S. 137 (1999)
Lawrence v. Texas, 539 U.S. 558 (2003)
Meyer v. Nebraska, 262 U.S. 390 (1923)
Meyer v. State, 187 N.W. 100 (Neb. 1922)
Michael H. v. Gerald D., 491 U.S. 110 (1989)
Moore v. City of East Cleveland, 431 U.S. 494 (1977)
Nix v. Hedden, 149 U.S. 304 (1893)
Nix v. Hedden, 39 F. 109 (C.C.S.D.N.Y. 1889)
Obergefell v. Hodges, 576 U.S. 644 (2015)
Parham v. J.R., 442 U.S. 584 (1979)
Perrin v. United States, 444 U.S. 37 (1979)
Pierce v. Society of Sisters, 268 U.S. 510 (1925)
Planned Parenthood of Southeastern Pennsylvania v. Casey, 505 U.S. 833 (1992)
Plessy v. Ferguson, 163 U.S. 537 (1896)
Plyler v. Doe, 457 U.S. 202 (1982)
Poe v. Ullman, 367 U.S. 497 (1961)
Poelker v. Doe, 432 U.S. 519 (1977)
Prince v. Massachusetts, 321 U.S. 158 (1944)
Raffles v. Wichelhaus, 2 H. & C. 906, 159 Eng. Rep. 375 (Ex. 1864)
Regents of the University of California v. Bakke, 438 U.S. 265 (1978)
Regents of the University of California v. Broad Institute, Inc., 903 F.3d 1286 (Fed. Cir. 2018)

Regents of the University of California, Junior Party v. Broad Institute, Inc., Senior Party, Patent Interference No. 106,115 (P.T.A.B. Sept. 10, 2020)
Reno v. Flores, 507 U.S. 292 (1993)
Roe v. Wade, 410 U.S. 113 (1973)
Skinner v. Oklahoma, 316 U.S. 535 (1942)
Smith v. Board of Examiners of Feeble-Minded, 88 A. 963 (N.J. 1913)
Steele v. Harrison, 220 Kan. 422 (1976)
Tan v. Phelan, 333 U.S. 6 (1948)
Tileston v. Ullman, 318 U.S. 44 (1943)
Troxel v. Granville, 530 U.S. 57 (2000)
United States v. An Article of Drug . . . Bacto-Unidisk . . ., 394 U.S. 784 (1969)
United States v. Cardiff, 344 U.S. 174 (1952)
United States v. Johnson, 221 U.S. 488 (1911)
United States v. Lexington Mill & Elevator Co., 232 U.S. 399 (1914)
United States v. Regenerative Sciences LLC, 741 F.3d 1314 (D.C. Cir. 2014)
United States v. Regenerative Sciences LLC, 878 F. Supp. 2d 248 (D.D.C. 2012)
United States v. Rutherford, 442 U.S. 544 (1979)
United States v. Sullivan, 332 U.S. 689 (1948)
United States v. Windsor, 570 U.S. 744 (2013)
Washington v. Glucksberg, 521 U.S. 702 (1997)
Wickard v. Filburn, 317 U.S. 111 (1942)
Wisconsin v. Yoder, 406 U.S. 205 (1972)
Zablocki v. Redhail, 434 U.S. 374 (1978)

Abbreviations

A	Adenine
Å	Ångström
AAV	Adeno-associated virus
ACA	Patient Protection and Affordable Care Act (also known as Obamacare)
ADHD	Attention Deficit Hyperactivity Disorder
AIDS	Acquired Immunodeficiency Syndrome
ALS	Amyotrophic Lateral Sclerosis
AMA	American Medical Association
APA	Administrative Procedure Act
APHIS	Animal and Plant Health Inspection Service
AUMF	Authorization for Use of Military Force
BLA	Biologics License Application
BRAG	Biotechnology Risk Assessment Research Grants (program)
Bt	*Bacillus thurigiensis*
C	Cytosine
ca^5C	5-carboxylcytosine
CAA	Consolidated Appropriations Act of 2016
Cas	CRISPR-associated (also CRISPR-associated sequences)
CBER	Center for Biologics Evaluation and Research
CBI	Confidential business information
CCR5	C-C Chemokine Receptor Type 5
CD4	Cluster of Differentiation 4
CF	Cystic fibrosis
cfDNA	Cell-free DNA (also known as circulating free DNA)
cffDNA	Cell-free fetal DNA
CFTR or CFTCR	Cystic Fibrosis Transmembrane Conductor Receptor
CGR	Cognitive Genomics Research
ChIP-Seq	Chromatin immunoprecipitation followed by sequencing

CJD	Creutzfeldt–Jakob disease
COVID-19	Coronavirus disease 2019
CPU	Central-processing unit
CRISPR	Clustered, Regularly Interspaced, Short, Palindromic Repeats
crRNA	CRISPR RNA
dCas9	Deactivated ("dead") Cas9 (a catalytically inactive or nuclease-null Cas9 protein)
dES	Diethyl sulfate
DHHS	Department of Health and Human Services
DMD	Duchenne muscular dystrophy
DNA	Deoxyribonucleic acid
eccDNA	Extrachromosomal circular DNA
EI	Ethyleneimine
EMS	Ethyl methanesulfonate
ENIAC	Electronic Numerical Integrator and Computer
EPA	Environmental Protection Agency
EPO	European Patent Office
EU	European Union
EUP	Experimental use permit
f^5C	5-formylcytosine
FAO	United Nations Food and Agriculture Organization
FDA	United States Food and Drug Administration
FDCA or FFDCA	Federal Food, Drug, and Cosmetic Act
FIFRA	Federal Insecticide, Fungicide, and Rodenticide Act
G	Guanine
GCA	General cognitive ability
GGE	Germline genome editing
GIF	Graphics-interchange format
GM	Genetically modified (crops)
GMO	Genetically modified organism
GRAS	Generally recognized as safe
GWAS	Genome-wide association studies
HCT/P	human cells, tissues, and cellular and tissue-based product
HDR	Homology-directed repair
HFEA	UK Human Fertilization and Embryology Authority
HGH	Human growth hormone
HIV	Human Immunodeficiency Virus
hm^5dC	5-hydroxymethyldeoxycytosine
HR	Homologous recombination
HSC	Hematopoietic stem cell
IAV	Influenza A virus
IND	Investigational New Drug Application

iPSC	Induced pluripotent stem cell
IQ	Intelligence quotient
IRODaT	International Registry in Organ Donation and Transplantation
IVF	In Vitro Fertilization
LCMV	Lymphocytic choriomeningitis virus
lncRNA	Long noncoding RNA
LRRK2	Leucine-Rich Repeat Kinase 2
m^5dC	5-methyldeoxycytosine
MCR	Mutagenic Chain Reaction
MECD	Meesmann's Epithelial Corneal Dystrophy
miRNA	MicroRNA
mRNA	Messenger RNA
MSC	Mesenchymal stem cell
MTD	Maximum-tolerated dose
NASEM	National Academies of Sciences, Engineering, and Medicine
NATO	North Atlantic Treaty Organization
NBFDS	National Bioengineered Food Disclosure Standard
NBS	Nicolaides-Baraitser syndrome
ncRNA	Noncoding RNA
NEPA	National Environmental Policy Act of 1969
NHEJ	Nonhomologous End Joining
NIH	United States National Institutes of Health
NTD	Neglected tropical diseases
OMIM	Online Mendelian Inheritance in Man®
ORF	Open reading frame
OSTP	White House Office of Science and Technology Policy
OTC	Ornithine transcarbamylase
PAM	Protospacer-adjacent motif
PERV	Porcine endogenous retrovirus
PFDA	Pure Food and Drug Act
PGD	Preimplantation genetic diagnosis
PHSA	Public Health Service Act
PIP	Plant-incorporated protectants
piRNA	piwi-interacting RNA
PNA	Peptide nucleic acid
PPA	Plant Protection Act
Pre-crRNA	Precursor CRISPR RNA
PTAB	Patent Trial and Appeal Board
PTM	Post-translational modification
RAC	Recombinant DNA Advisory Committee
rbGH	Recombinant bovine growth hormone
RFRA	Religious Freedom Restoration Act of 1993

RNA	Ribonucleic acid
rRNA	Ribosomal RNA
RVD	Repeat-variable diresidue
SAFLA	Safe and Accurate Food Labeling Act of 2015
SARS-CoV-2	Severe acute respiratory syndrome coronavirus-2
SCD	Sickle-cell disease
SCID-X1	X-linked Severe Combined Immunodeficiency Syndrome
SEC	Securities and Exchange Commission
sgRNA	Single-guide RNA
siRNA	Small interfering RNA
snoRNA	small nucleolar RNA
SNP	Single-nucleotide polymorphisms
snRNA	Small nuclear RNAs
STS	Science and Technology Studies
T	Thymine
TALE	Transcription activator-like effector
TALEN	Transcription activator-like effector nuclease
T-DNA	Transfer DNA
Ti	Tumor-inducing (plasmid)
tracrRNA	Trans-activating crRNA
tRNA	Transfer RNA
TSA	Transportation Security Agency
TSNA	Tobacco-specific nitrosamines
U	Uracil
UN	United Nations
USA PATRIOT Act	Uniting and Strengthening America by Providing Appropriate Tools Required to Intercept and Obstruct Terrorism Act
USDA	United States Department of Agriculture
USPTO	United States Patent and Trademark Office
UV	Ultraviolet
V3	Hypervariable region 3 (loop)
VSV	Vesicular stomatitis virus
vWD	von Willebrand Disease
WGS	Whole-genome sequencing
WHO	World Health Organization
ZFN	Zinc-finger nuclease

1

A Momentous Time for Humankind

Human ingenuity is marvelous. It boils down to an impeccable and often ethereal balance among its constituent elements, including knowledge, curiosity, creativity, and action. When the magnitude of each element expands in harmony, human ingenuity becomes transformative. It translates to power—the kind that transforms the world!

This book is a testament to that power. Whether you are holding it in your hands or scrolling through pages on a touchscreen, you and I are able to communicate through this medium because, once upon a time, human ingenuity led to the creation of one of the most significant and consequential inventions of all time: the printing press.

Johannes Gutenberg, a German goldsmith who lived in the early to mid-fifteenth century, is generally credited with inventing the printing press circa 1436.[1] Gutenberg did not invent books. In fact, he did not even invent printing. Long before the Renaissance, woodblock printing had already been customary during the seventh and eighth centuries in China, Korea, and Japan.[2] And the metal, movable-type system of printing, which originated in Korea, had been used since the eleventh century.[3] Gutenberg's contribution rested on his ability to concoct a novel mechanical contraption to mediate ink transfer between the movable type and paper. He used prior knowledge to adapt screw mechanisms found in antecedent inventions—namely, the wine, papermaker, and linen presses of the time—as the basis to create the mechanical, movable-type printing press.[4] But he did not stop there. When he realized that the conventional water-based ink was not durable for printing purposes, he developed oil-based ink, which, as it turned out, bonded more effectively with the types.[5]

The amalgam of knowledge, curiosity, creativity, and action aimed at speeding up the printing process, which culminated in the ingenious design of the first movable-type printing press, fundamentally transformed the world. By the end of the fifteenth century, Gutenberg's invention had spread all over Europe. For the first time in history, books could be produced en masse and at a low cost relative to other printing methods. Indeed, more than twenty million books had been printed by the year 1500.[6]

FIGURE 1.1 The Gutenberg printing press, circa 1440

The printing press ushered in a new revolution in mass communication and dissemination of information that contributed to the rise of public literacy and the end of the Dark Ages. Although the Gutenberg printing press did not jumpstart the Renaissance, it undoubtedly fueled its swift progression.

Nicolaus Copernicus, the revered Renaissance mathematician and astronomer, as well as other scientists and scholars of the time benefited directly from the printing press. Copernicus, for instance, profited greatly from the printing of various astronomical tables that began to appear in the late fifteenth century—including the Alfonsine Tables, which date back to the year 1252.[7] Astronomical tables contained data to calculate ecliptic longitudes—as well as the position of celestial bodies, including the Sun, Moon, and other planets—that were useful in maritime navigation during the fifteenth and sixteenth centuries when Spain, Portugal, England, France, and other wealthy nations ventured out to sea in search of new lands. Copernicus built upon data from these tables in his groundbreaking book *De Revolutionibus Orbium Coelestium* (*On the Revolutions of the Heavenly Spheres*), which set off the scientific revolution.[8] The book conceptualized his elegant and controversial theory of heliocentricism, which postulated that the Sun—not the Earth—was at the center of the Universe, and that Earth and other known planets actually revolved around the Sun.

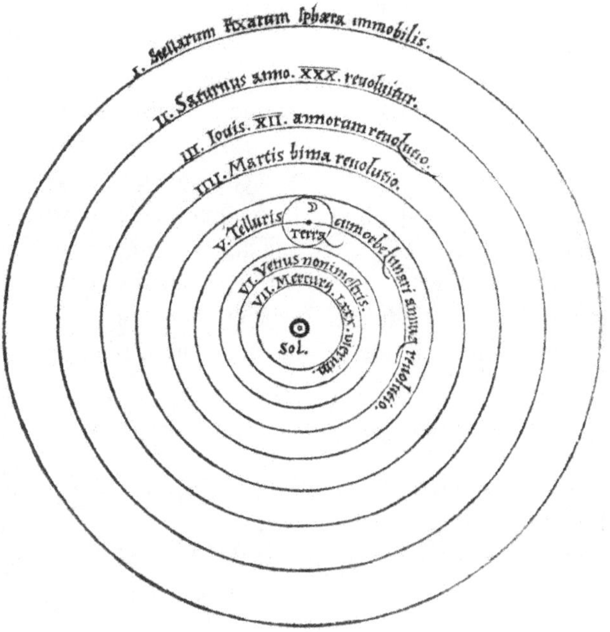

FIGURE 1.2 Copernican model of heliocentrism as originally depicted in 1543

The heliocentric theory published in Copernicus's revolutionary book *De Revolutionibus Orbium Coelestium* (*On the Revolutions of the Heavenly Spheres*) positioned the Sun at the center of the Universe, with Earth and the other planets rotating around the Sun in circular paths.

As time went on, printing became more widespread. Cambridge University Press, the oldest publishing house in the world and publisher of this book, was established in 1534.[9] Other publishers soon followed. With the advent of an increased flow of information, however, literature that contradicted religious teachings was subject to bans by the Roman Catholic Church. In 1559, the Church published the *Index Librorum Prohibitorum* (*Index of Prohibited Books*), comprising a list of condemned works.[10] According to legislation of the Catholic Church, no person could read any book on the list unless explicitly granted permission to do so.[11] Copernicus's book eventually became part of that list.[12]

The aforementioned history surrounding the invention of the printing press is not unique, at least insofar as it represents the fate of a powerful, revolutionary, technological agent that induces a tectonic shift in culture and society. Transformative technologies seem to share a common modus operandi. Nearly six centuries after the printing press, for example, the Internet brought about another modern era of information reminiscent of centuries past.

This book is about a new truly remarkable transformative technology: genome editing. The volume aims to explore interdisciplinary inquiries of science, law, technology, ethics, philosophy, and policy. In so doing, it seeks to demonstrate how modern genome-editing technologies are unique disruptors that open infinite opportunities to venture into areas completely unknown to humans. These new disruptors possess the power to push humanity past knowledge and information boundaries—as was once the case for the printing press, the Internet, and other transformative technologies. But the stakes are higher now. This emerging breed of genome-editing disruptors goes much further into virgin territory than any of its predecessors, propelled by the fact that genome editing holds the power to not only transform the world we live in, but change humanity and every living organism from within.

I A NEW REVOLUTION

For the first time in the nearly two hundred millennia since *Homo sapiens* first appeared on Earth, humankind has procured the power to rewrite nature's book of life. Following key scientific developments at the dawn of the twenty-first century, we have—for better or worse—reached the Rubicon of precise genetic manipulation, which until now has existed only in science fiction.

Leading this revolution is the most significant technological breakthrough of our generation. It concerns the discovery of an atomic, programmable, macromolecular machine comprising a pair of precision scalpels that shear DNA molecules known colloquially as "CRISPR," an acronym that refers to the system of *Clustered, Regularly Interspaced, Short, Palindromic Repeats* and CRISPR-associated (Cas) proteins, which has now been repurposed for genome editing. Only on rare occasions does a technology with such far-reaching implications appear, while holding the power to forever change the world and humankind. Those familiar with this emerging genome-editing technology understand its colossal power and potential to become a global transformative agent, on par with—and arguably surpassing the impact of—the discovery of electricity, or the development of gunpowder, the printing press, the atomic bomb, and the Internet.

A *Antecedent Disruptors*

More than eight decades ago, for instance, scientific inquiry conceptualized nuclear fission[13] as a theoretical explanation for the recondite empirical evidence that ^{239}U, an isotope of uranium produced by the neutronic irradiation of ^{238}U, could have its nucleus split into highly radioactive fragments.[14] That theory was ultimately supported by experimental observations showing the enormous release of ionization energy resulting from nuclear fragmentation,[15] thereby confirming a decades-old relationship between mass and energy—$E = mc^2$—first formulated by Albert Einstein.[16] With remarkable speed, the newfangled knowledge covertly served as the basis for the Manhattan Project, the research program that ultimately developed the atomic bomb through nuclear fission.[17]

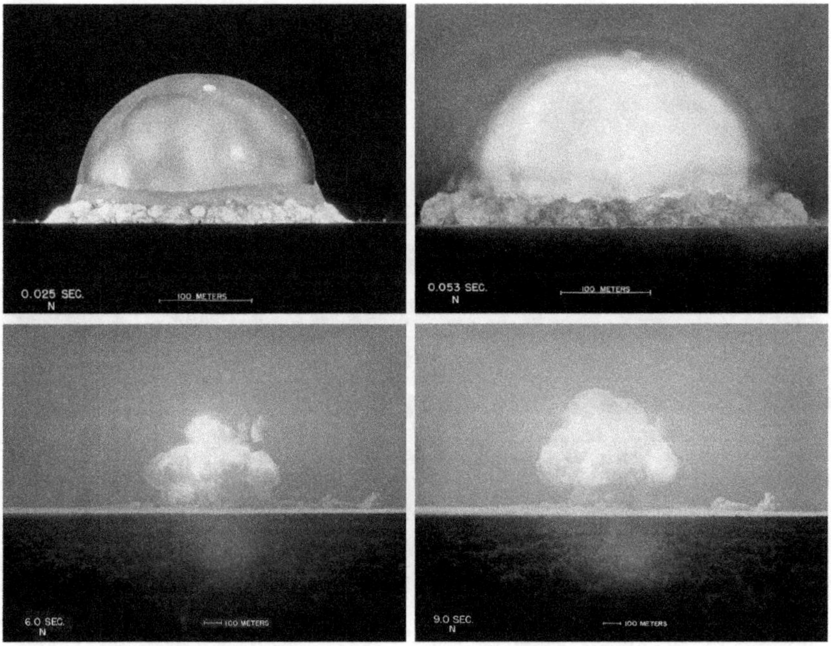

FIGURE 1.3 The first atomic explosion

The Manhattan Project's Trinity Test detonated the first nuclear device in the Jornada del Muerto desert near Socorro, New Mexico on July 16, 1945.

The genesis of modern computing too had its principles neatly packaged in a seminal paper authored by the mathematician Alan Turing.[18] The revolutionary notion that a machine could imitate computations performed by humans spawned the first "Turing-complete," programmable, general-purpose, Electronic Numerical Integrator and Computer (ENIAC).[19] Unpredictably, the technology evolved into personal computers and smartphones, and enabled the ensuing development of the Internet.[20] Other fundamental discoveries over the past few centuries—in mathematics, physics, chemistry, and biology—have facilitated our ability to harness the power of natural phenomena in space travel, wireless communications, medicine, and a myriad of other applications.

The advent of the atomic bomb and the Internet have transformed the world in both positive and negative ways. For example, some argue that the development of the atomic bomb changed the world for the better because it brought an end to the bloodiest conflict the world has ever witnessed.[21] Others decry the nuclear bomb as an instrument that led to utter destruction in the Japanese cities of Hiroshima and Nagasaki, nearly a half-million deaths, and political instability for decades after War World II.[22] Computers and the Internet too have changed how humans communicate, access information, shop, and even perceive reality.[23] At the same time, the

FIGURE 1.4 Technicians operating the ENIAC, circa 1943–1946

The ENIAC was the first Turing-complete, electronic, programmable, digital computer capable of being reprogrammed to solve a full range of computing problems.

technology has enabled an entire slew of new cybercrimes and other internet-based antisocial behaviors.[24] Genome editing is no different in this sense. Its impact has become well-nigh indisputable in the last few years. This book explores the disruptive nature of the technology, as well as its potential benefits and perils.

B *Who Owns CRISPR?—A Bitter Fight*

The ability to manipulate genomes at will harbingers a new era in world history with far-reaching implications for the future of every living organism. Since the debut of CRISPR–Cas9 as a genome-editing tool in 2012, laboratories around the world have adopted CRISPR systems with unparalleled speed. Roughly 17,000[25] scientific publications to date feature theory, empirical observations, and description of applications related to genome editing in organisms spanning nearly every biological kingdom from bacteria and fungi, to plants, animals, and now even humans.[26] Stratospheric expectations for CRISPR systems have already attracted more than $1 billion in venture capital[27] in a brief period of time. In 2016, Editas Medicine, Inc., a pioneer CRISPR-based company, became the first to file the requisite paperwork for an initial public offering with the Securities and Exchange Commission (SEC).[28] Within months, CRISPR Therapeutics AG also filed for an initial public offering.[29] And other companies specializing in a wide variety of genome-editing technologies have since debuted, including Intellia Therapeutics, Horizon Discovery, Caribou Biosciences, Synthego, GenEdit, Beam Therapeutics, Precision Biosciences, LogicBio, Locus Biosciences, Inscripta, and many others.

To date, the genome-editing revolution has largely encompassed the province of scientific discovery. In the last few years, however, scientific progress through research and development, as well as an increased demand for technology commercialization —thanks in large part to procurement of intellectual property rights—have summoned the law to become an active and prominent participant. A high-stakes, intellectual property dispute over rights to the first patents related to CRISPR systems ended—at least for now—when the United States Court of Appeals for the Federal Circuit decided *Regents of the University of California v. Broad Institute, Inc.* in 2018[30]

The case was a highly publicized legal dispute between the University of California, Berkeley, the University of Vienna, and Emmanuelle Charpentier (collectively the "University of California") on one side, and the Broad Institute of the Massachusetts Institute of Technology (MIT) and Harvard University (collectively the "Broad Institute") on the opposite side. In early 2016, the US Patent and Trademark Office (USPTO) Patent Trial and Appeal Board (PTAB) declared an interference proceeding, which is a type of patent legal contest under the old, first-to-invent patent system that existed before the enactment of the America Invents Act.[31] An interference is typically declared to determine priority between parties that claim a common invention. In the context of the CRISPR dispute, therefore, declaring an interference would concern the determination of priority for the first CRISPR patents[32]—namely, whether the Broad Institute or the University of California were first to invent CRISPR–Cas9 under United States patent law.[33]

The PTAB, however, did not rule on the issue of priority and found instead that there was no interference-in-fact between the University of California's patent application and the Broad Institute's patent claims in twelve issued patents and one pending patent application.[34] The University of California appealed that decision to the Federal Circuit, which ultimately ruled in favor of the Broad Institute and concluded that substantial evidence supported the PTAB's findings that (1) the parties' claims were not drawn to the same patentable subject matter—in other words, that the claims were directed to different inventions—and (2) the University of California's claims did not render the Broad Institute's claims obvious.[35]

Notably, the litigation did not lead to a decision that any of the parties' claims were unpatentable, and the Federal Circuit abstained from ruling on the validity of either set of claims. But the bitter fight continues. The PTAB has redeclared an interference proceeding,[36] which will likely set the stage for an award of priority to either party and the resolution of other patentability issues unless the parties settle their dispute out of court.

The battle for patent rights has not been confined to the United States. Early in 2020, the European Patent Office (EPO) Board of Appeal upheld an earlier revocation of a foundational CRISPR–Cas9 patent[37] that had been granted to the Broad Institute on grounds that the issued European patent lacked novelty in view of prior art.[38] And in a separate proceeding, the EPO Opposition Division announced that another European patent on CRISPR–Cas9[39] granted to the University of California, the University of Vienna, and Emmanuelle Charpentier survived a patentability challenge and required only minor amendments.

Litigation in these cases has been contentious and with good reason. The companies and interested parties battling over the technology seek dominance in an emerging industry with a multibillion-dollar valuation. As is evident from the litigation history, however, the legal disputes exclusively concern the fight for foundational intellectual property rights over CRISPR–Cas systems. The law has been largely absent outside the intellectual property realm.

II THE GROWING GAP BETWEEN LAW AND SCIENCE

Despite the recent and constant stream of breakthroughs in the field of genome editing and CRISPR's renown in science,[40] discussions about the technology in the legal and policy realms continue to lag behind the pace of scientific progress. In the absence of on-point law, the scientific community has attempted to reach some consensus to preempt antagonistic regulation and prescribe subjective standards of use. However, significant and complex political, societal, and legal issues concerning this emerging technology are beginning to surface. A considerable bulk of current laws and regulations are not well equipped to address many of those issues, which must be examined within the framework of law and policy, rather than science. Undoubtedly, scientific progress has come at an astounding pace, but uncertainty about how the law will treat this emerging technology looms in the horizon.

A *Corrosive Insularism and the Pursuit of Knowledge*

Many members of the legal community, including jurists, legal scholars, and practitioners, have either largely ignored this field or kept a distance from it, presumably due, in part, to the challenges that complex scientific principles often pose to nonscientists in the legal and legislative arenas. A concurring opinion penned by the late Justice Antonin Scalia, in *Association for Molecular Pathology v. Myriad Genetics, Inc.* (*Myriad*),[41] notoriously illustrated the degree of scientific antipathy among some members of the legal community.

In *Myriad*, a unanimous US Supreme Court ruled that a naturally occurring DNA segment—such as a gene—constitutes a product of nature that cannot be patented merely because it has been isolated by a researcher.[42] All Justices endorsed this principle in unison. Scalia, nevertheless, found it imperative to qualify his vote by issuing a short, one-paragraph concurrence, which included the following statement:

I join the judgment of the Court . . . except Part I-A and some portions of the rest of the opinion going into fine details of molecular biology. I am unable to affirm those details *on my own knowledge or even my own belief*. [43]

Exercising great candor, Scalia thus conceded his lack of knowledge of relevant scientific details in the case before him. At the same time, he disturbingly remarked he did not even believe in scientific facts that have been well established for decades. Indeed, the text Scalia quibbled about concerned scientific facts that every student in the fifth grade—and possibly even earlier in today's primary-education curricula—becomes acquainted with. Genes are made up of DNA. DNA forms a double helix. Mutations are changes in a DNA sequence. Genes encode genetic information to make proteins. And so on. Scalia's demurral of uncontroversial facts found in every fifth-grade biology textbook is puzzling to many in the scientific community. His statement manifests scientific apathy at best, and utter disbelief at worst.

To some extent, Scalia's admission is commendable. A person in a position of great power should not be afraid to admit knowledge gaps. After all, no human holds absolute knowledge in any area. Conversely, it is worrisome that a powerful person may be called to decide pivotal questions with broad societal implications when that person makes no effort whatsoever to close self-perceived knowledge gaps. Expressing disbelief in science is not sufficient. Those with power to delineate the contours of what constitutes the rule of law ought to educate themselves about matters before them.

To better perform the functions associated with the judicial branch, judges "need[] to develop an informed—although necessarily approximate—understanding of the state of [the] relevant scientific art."[44] *Myriad* was true to this aphorism for the role of science in the judiciary. The Supreme Court's effort to preface its decision with relevant scientific facts should be commended. And despite some minor inaccuracies related to protein synthesis,[45] RNA processing,[46] and DNA noncoding regions,[47] which we will discuss in greater detail in Chapter 2, the Court more or less accurately described the science—certainly enough to competently rule on the merits.

Scalia's brand of scientific aversion has corrosive effects. It ultimately hinders the sort of interdisciplinary dialogue and insight required to fully understand and address significant problems in an increasingly interconnected world.[48] To be fair, scientific aversion among members of the judiciary is not a new phenomenon. But, as retired Judge Richard Posner put it, "it [is] increasingly concerning, because of the extraordinary rate of scientific and other technological advances that figure increasingly in litigation."[49]

In the near future, law and policy makers will be confronted with many questions related to genome editing and CRISPR, and the legal community must proactively take steps to familiarize itself with this new technology. Given the rapid expansion of CRISPR-based applications, the gap between science and the law is becoming increasingly problematic.

As a testament to this growing problem, Judge David Neuberger, former President of the UK Supreme Court, published a commentary in the journal *Nature* calling attention to the scientific community and arguing that scientific primers would be "hugely beneficial" for the legal community.[50] Such primers, he contended, would save money and time, help assess the reliability of expert witnesses, and increase the proportion of cases that are settled without trial. Specifically, he singled out genetic engineering as an area in which a primer would be useful to jurists given that legal controversies in the field are likely to proliferate and recur.

In the absence of on-point law, some in the scientific community have campaigned, in arguably self-serving ways,[51] for a consensus to preempt antagonistic regulation and prescribe subjective standards of use under the misguided auspices of a priori scientific empiricism. This must give us pause. Einstein memorably remarked, "[T]he man of science is a poor philosopher."[52] Most scientists—by training—are unfamiliar with intricate legal principles, constitutional doctrine, regulatory processes, and policy making; likewise, most lawyers are oblivious to scientific theory, physicochemical laws, and cellular and macromolecular processes. Given these vastly different realms of knowledge, it is understandable that many scientists and lawyers often pursue insularism by academic discipline. Surely, there is comfort in academic seclusion, but isolation is often dangerous to learning and the pursuit of knowledge. "People do not learn very much when they are surrounded only by the likes of themselves."[53] Interdisciplinary colloquy, therefore, is the most sensible approach to bridge the current chasm between science and the law surrounding this momentous technology.

A blueprint for genome-editing science and the law is sorely overdue. This timely monograph addresses the urgent and fundamental need to close critical knowledge gaps among the fields of law, science, and policy relating to emerging genome-editing technologies. To that end, the research presented herein employs both descriptive and normative interdisciplinary tools to foster an understanding of genome editing and propose a legal framework for its use.

B A *Jurisprudence of Scientific Empiricism to Bridge the Gap between Law and Science*

Broadly speaking, the book challenges conventional views regarding the false dichotomy frequently associated with mutually exclusive normative roles for science and law—the proximate cause driving laissez-faire attitudes[54] of deference to elude questions of "law in science and science in law."[55] It proposes a normative structural legal framework, namely, a *jurisprudence of scientific empiricism* that is broadly adaptable to addressing questions of science in law. The scientific empiricism referred to in this book specifically concerns the natural sciences—for example, physics, chemistry, biology, and other disciplines of the life and physical sciences—and not the social sciences—such as sociology, psychology, economics, political science, and so forth. This distinction is mainly due to discrete research methodologies and analytical tools endogenous to each discipline.[56]

In particular, the above point revolves around the fact that, whereas the natural sciences rely extensively on quantitative methods, the social sciences depend, to a great extent, on qualitative research. The proposed framework in this book is exclusively concerned with scientific empirical data that is reproducible and quantifiable. Hence, for example, a jurisprudence of scientific empiricism would seek to answer whether genome editing may lawfully, in the context of a clinical trial, be used to correct a genetic mutation associated with a disease given the existence of empirical data demonstrating that such genetic corrections are feasible, safe, effective, and reproducible (or not) under controlled experiments. The approach, however, would not apply to deciding the legal status of such a clinical trial by studying the decision-making processes and attitudes that patients undergoing treatment have toward genome-editing technologies. The primary empirical data acquired from social scientists in the latter scenario would largely depend on interviews and other qualitative research that may be considered ontologically subjective.

The kind of empirical-based framework for jurisprudence advocated in this book seeks to facilitate solving challenging questions of science and law and, thus, is primarily concerned with closing gaps between the two fields. Accordingly, the focus of a jurisprudence of scientific empiricism is, for example, not to inject social science into the analysis of scientific dilemmas. Nor is it to lay out criticisms of certain scientific narratives. In many respects, the field of Science and Technology Studies (STS), also known as Science and Society or Social Studies of Science, already concerns itself with the gamut of those topics. STS is an established field that relates to the study of scientific and technological innovation through the lens of sociology, anthropology, philosophy, history of science, social justice, and other fields of the humanities and social sciences. In the last few decades, significant and meaningful contributions have certainly come from such research. But STS and other similarly situated disciplines have ultimately been limited by efforts to cabin discussions of science and technology through a social lens.

The normative approach proposed in this book goes beyond those limitations. Indeed, the book contends that core scientific principles and themes are often lacking in existing nonscientific literature and scholarship in many fields. While it is important for scientists to understand the importance of public engagement, science communication and governance, and other social factors, it is equally—and arguably more—important that social scientists, lawyers, and policy makers grasp key scientific concepts related to transformative technologies they must regulate, examine, or comment on. It is time for the legal profession, as Posner put it, to "get over its fear and loathing of science."[57]

No framework exists in our current legal system with which to address the aforementioned complex nature for questions of science in law, especially when scientific inquiry plays important or dispositive roles beyond the interests of litigant parties. Let me be clear here. Our legal system has in place a robust and influential methodology, known as the *Daubert* standard, that addresses the admissibility of expert witness testimony under the Federal Rules of Evidence.[58] The *Daubert* standard, which the United States Supreme Court articulated in the landmark case *Daubert v. Merrell Dow Pharmaceuticals, Inc.*, is therefore based on evidentiary rules and highlights the gatekeeping role that judges play in the legal system. *Daubert* governs the admission of evidence—including that which is scientific in nature—and allows the trier of fact to assess the value of said evidence in the courtroom. Expert testimony under *Daubert* must always be based on professional studies or personal experience, and must be the product of reliable principles and methods.[59]

The *Daubert* standard has certainly revolutionized the way we treat scientific evidence in the legal system. But *Daubert* does not extend beyond the admissibility of expert testimony and has failed to facilitate the application of scientific principles in areas of jurisprudence in which science and scientific analysis are arguably needed the most. As Judge David Tatel of the US Court of Appeals for the DC Circuit—and cochair of the Committee on Science, Technology, and Law at the National Academies of Sciences, Engineering, and Medicine—observed in an essay that he recently coauthored, "the law has few systems designed to take advantage of the evolving nature of scientific knowledge."[60]

Consider, for instance, the US Supreme Court's ruling in *Burwell v. Hobby Lobby Stores, Inc.*, a 2014 case that contemplated whether the Religious Freedom Restoration Act of 1993 (RFRA) prohibits the federal government from requiring that closely held corporations provide health-insurance coverage for contraception methods that run counter to the religious beliefs of the companies' owners.[61] The *Hobby Lobby* Court held that closely held corporations may be exempt from the contraceptive mandate in the Patient Protection and Affordable Care Act of 2010 on the basis of sincerely held religious beliefs. In other words, a closely held, for-profit corporation need not comply with governmental regulations that its private owners find morally objectionable from a religious standpoint.

Yet *Hobby Lobby*'s majority opinion erroneously presumed that all four contraception methods at issue were abortifacients that "may operate after the fertilization of an egg."[62] Such a stance contradicts the scientific empirical evidence available at the time the case was decided and today.[63] On this point, an amici curiae brief in support of the petition for a writ of certiorari penned by the Physicians for Reproductive Health (PRH), the American College of Obstetricians and Gynecologists, the Association of Reproductive Health Professionals, the American Society for Reproductive Medicine, and numerous other professional medical entities communicated eloquently with the Court to bring awareness to certain scientific facts. Importantly, the brief pointed to the respondents' unsupported characterization of the FDA-approved contraceptives under review as abortifacients. As noted in the brief, the term "[a]bortifacient has a precise meaning in the medical and scientific community and it refers to the termination of a pregnancy. Contraceptives that prevent fertilization from occurring, or even prevent implantation, are simply not abortifacients regardless of an individual's personal or religious beliefs or mores."[64]

Despite the existence of scientific evidence that squarely rejected the abortifacient categorization for the contraceptives discussed in the case, the Court either completely dismissed or chose to ignore the information. Indeed, *Hobby Lobby* cited at least eight other amicus curiae briefs. The opinion, however, neither cited to the PRH brief nor distinguished the meaning of abortifacient substances from the contraceptive methods under review.

Even more interesting is the analytical path that the majority opinion followed. *Hobby Lobby* found unpersuasive the petitioners' argument that the contraception mandate did not substantially burden the free exercise of religion because providing the coverage would not itself lead to the destruction of embryos.[65] According to the majority, the central question presented was whether the RFRA protected the owners' religious beliefs—whatever they may be—against a substantially burdensome contraception mandate. The majority expressly indicated that federal courts have no business whatsoever in evaluating the *reasonableness* of any religious beliefs.[66] So long as the owners sincerely believed that the contraception methods were directly linked to the destruction of human embryos, the Court would not dare call into question the veracity or even reasonableness of their beliefs—even if scientific facts and evidence directly contradicted them.

But that line of reasoning is susceptible to fatal flaws from a logical standpoint. What ought to happen when the owner of a closely held corporation refuses to hire women based on a sincerely held religious belief that the female gender comprises intellectually inferior human beings who ought to revere men, or perhaps the employer who refuses to hire lesbian and gay prospective employees because of a deeply held religious belief that homosexuality is both unnatural and a direct manifestation of mental illness? What about an employee who refuses to work in the mornings because of a sincerely held religious belief that the sun will incinerate her as a result of having a vampire bloodline? What shall courts make of arguments based on sincerely held religious beliefs that surmise the Earth is flat; darker human skin tones reflect disease; the sun in Washington, DC rises at the exact same time every day of the year; certain people born with deformities are really extraterrestrial beings devoid of human DNA; or a respiratory disease caused by a virus can be cured by ingesting bleach? It is difficult to conceive that courts would be deferential toward one or more of these purported religious beliefs.

"[I]t is not for [courts] to say that [an individual's] religious beliefs are mistaken or insubstantial."[67] Rather, the judiciary's "narrow function" involves the determination of whether the belief represents "an honest conviction."[68] These basic tenets for reviewing cases involving the free exercise of religion may provide a working model for sincerely held religious beliefs based on *faith* or other *unfalsifiable precepts*. Surely, no amount of logic or empirical data can conclusively establish, beyond a reasonable doubt, the existence of all the numerous deities attributable to the world's religions. When it comes to beliefs that depend entirely on a *scientific fact*, however, the law exhibits an awkward relationship with science.

The *Hobby Lobby* Court was free to ignore dispositive *scientific facts* as it pleased because no current framework or standard exists for binding judges to consider highly relevant scientific evidence that is likely to be dispositive in a case. This deficiency in our system of jurisprudence is a major contributing factor to the lack of scientific knowledge among jurists and other law and policy makers who often eschew scientific evidence. Unless litigants raise an issue that depends on a scientific principle and offer expert testimony to address it during trial, courts are simply free to ignore or even dismiss any potentially relevant and material scientific evidence, which may be dispositive to the adjudication of a case. Judge Tatel, for example, has taken notice of this alarming deficit in our legal system. During a panel discussion about the role of science in law, he raised an open-ended question concerning how the judiciary ought to deal with scientific evidence that is not presented by litigants.[69] This book contributes to that significant conversation.

A jurisprudence of scientific empiricism advocates for the adoption of a standard that permits a more systematic method to address questions of science in law, at least insofar as it pertains to scientific evidence that has been well established over time. In cases where science may be debated—namely, where "different experts ... can interpret the same data differently"[70]—courts would be free to revert back to *Daubert*, which allows triers of fact to evaluate the relevant scientific evidence presented. Simply put, a jurisprudence of scientific empiricism follows on *Daubert*'s footsteps, builds upon the interdependence of law and science, and expands the scope of scientific evidence in the legal system.

The *Hobby Lobby* discussion in the preceding paragraphs is but a mere example of the types of dialogues embedded throughout this book. In the coming chapters, we will reflect on a range of issues that showcase the role of scientific empiricism in the adjudication of legal disputes. Some of the issues will be examined retroactively, so as to analyze whether the application of a jurisprudence of scientific empiricism would have impacted the final result. For instance, Chapter 10 discusses *Buck v. Bell*,[71] the 1927 case that legalized the involuntary sterilization of individuals deemed "mental defectives" in state institutions. The question surrounding the constitutionality of compulsory sterilizations may appear to be strictly legal in nature at first glance. But we will discuss the role of deference to a state's erroneous scientific assertions, which ultimately opened the gates for the use of pseudoscientific principles surrounding heredity as a pivotal factor in the purported transmission of insanity and imbecility. The chapter, therefore, argues that the use of established scientific evidence would have proved dispositive in that case.

Other examples in the book will be forward-looking. Should an administrative agency exercise its jurisdictional powers to regulate an emerging technology for which safety and efficacy have yet to be established? Should society allow humans to engineer crops intended for human consumption? Does a cognizable right to select uses of germline genome editing in human embryos exist? These are just some of the questions that the book will address in subsequent chapters.

As you made your way through this section, it may already have become apparent to you that examining issues of science and law primarily from the vantage point of sociology, philosophy, anthropology, religion, and other fields of social science will simply not contribute to making progress toward resolving controversies related to scientific and technological advances such as genetic engineering. Decades of fervid debate about genetically modified organisms, designer babies, and other controversial topics support that proposition.

The controversy surrounding "designer babies" is, for instance, particularly illustrative in this discussion. Frivolous enhancement of human traits—including, intelligence, height, beauty, athleticism, and more—are commonly cited by many social scientists as major concerns about the use of modern biotechnologies. However, knowledge of the genetics of such complex traits, which are determined by the collective contribution of many genes—and possibly hundreds or even thousands in many cases—is vastly incomplete. Even with the advent of genome editing, the notion that scientists can tinker with a multitude of genes simultaneously and know how such manipulation will affect an individual is preposterous at this time. And it will likely remain so during our lifetimes. That scientific fact favors gradual and thoughtful measures, including legislation and policy making, to address actual concerns raised by new technologies.

Entertaining dubious hypotheticals is a dangerous endeavor. Before a discussion about the ethics and social implications of creating an army of "tall, beautiful, and hyperintelligent babies" can take place, it should be incumbent upon experts in all fields to ensure that scientific facts are firmly embedded in the conversation, so that participants do not misrepresent or oversell what is technologically feasible. The need for a resource that examines the science of genome editing free from the rampant sensationalism that characterizes popular discussions of this field is high.

Finally, anchoring discussions on a jurisprudence of scientific empiricism can also help us to minimize the likelihood that personal views will dominate a range of conversations. My belief is that an individual's personal views—mine included—on a range of highly diverse issues concerning genome editing, are of less import than facilitating the exchange of information and critical thinking tools that will promote a thoughtful debate on what should or should not be done with transformative technologies. Too often, our society has grown accustomed to reducing discussion of complex issues to an *are-you-for-or-against-[insert any topic]* narrative. This book rejects that oversimplification and aims to present scientific evidence in an impartial and unbiased manner, so that you may consider the facts and use your critical thinking skills to form your own opinions.

III THE MISSION

At the outset, it is important to recognize that "[a] judge is not a scientist, and a courtroom is not a scientific laboratory."[72] Law and policy makers need not become scientific experts or "amateur scientists"[73] in order to make significant contributions to the field of genome editing. Nor does the general public. And the pages in this volume should not be construed to imply either proposition. This book, however, insists that we *all* must become engaged and proactively seek to develop an informed understanding of the core elements of significant technologies that can transform the world, such as genome editing.

One major aspiration of this book is to facilitate building a system structured in a manner that encourages people and institutions to weld scientific empiricism and jurisprudence. Such a system would greatly benefit society. Uprooting old and monistic conventions in the path toward building that system, however, is a challenging endeavor that requires interdisciplinary cooperation.

Challenging as it may be, we must strive to bridge the gap between science and law because the cost of doing nothing is great. The success of the eugenics movement of the early twentieth century, for example, came on the heels of entrenched insularism. Scientists with the most relevant knowledge were largely confined to a life of research and failed to effectively communicate with the public to correct scientific misperceptions. Disengagement and scientific apathy within the legal community led to serious errors that institutionalized pseudoscientific principles.

Beyond facilitating the fusion of law and science, this book's other overarching goals are to (1) ignite a measured and fruitful conversation about the current and prospective uses of genome-editing technologies, stripped of illusory conjectures, and (2) provide a primer on genome editing to facilitate an interdisciplinary exchange of ideas. There is much the scientific, legal, and policy communities can contribute and achieve by working together.

In furtherance of these goals, the volume makes three essential contributions. First, it serves as a comprehensive resource on the science of gene editing and its legal implications for law and policy makers. This type of resource is crucial now more than ever, particularly in light of recent scientific advances that introduce great complexity to the field of genetic engineering. Misinformation about the science abounds in the public domain, which in turn encourages unfounded controversies and impedes development of rational science-based policies.

Second, the book seeks to promote a measured and thoughtful dialogue—stripped of illusory conjectures—about the current and prospective uses of technology in the realm of gene editing. This requires a twofold approach: (1) the volume must adhere closely to core scientific principles and facts that form the foundation of technological applications, and (2) such scientific principles must be communicated in an accessible format to audiences lacking a scientific background. Thus, Chapters 2 through 5 provide a robust and comprehensive epistemic foundation of the history and current state of the scientific literature in the field of genome editing, and propound positive claims for prospective applications of genome editing that are firmly grounded in empirical evidence.[74]

These introductory chapters are descriptive and technical, but written in a format suitable for general audiences. They are essential because, without a detailed explanation and coherent understanding of the nuts and bolts of relevant scientific principles, the reader may extrapolate unfounded notions of the immediate, short-term, and long-term prospects and limitations of the technology. Simply put, a solid foundation of key genome-editing scientific principles offers the structural scaffolding—an insurance policy, so to speak—for a fruitful dialogue grounded in reason rather than baseless conjecture.

Third, this book aims to highlight key areas in which law can be used to promote, tweak, or hinder development of this nascent scientific field. One substantial predicament about technologies that are powerful, yet not popularly understood, is that they are often prone to having their capabilities overstated or even misrepresented to be well beyond what they actually are. Impractical and sensationalist claims about issues raised by technological advances, which I collectively characterize as "deceptive simplicity,"[75] often pose substantive impediments to constructive debate. By anchoring prospective technological applications in a jurisprudence of scientific empiricism, the book minimizes the risk of technological misinterpretation by speculators. And in so doing, it advocates for a flexible normative framework that fuses law and scientific empiricism; one which consolidates genome-editing applications into a uniform doctrinal structure unencumbered by deceptive simplicity. The proposed paradigm would also be applicable to other fields of law in which scientific inquiry may play important or dispositive roles.

The synergism between the foregoing contributions underscores the importance of interdisciplinary efforts to prevent, mitigate, and resolve future "global problems"[76] raised by technological progress. Thus, the jurisprudence of scientific empiricism proposed in this book offers a flexible, normative framework rooted in the notion that "[c]ritical thinking . . . cannot possibly be restricted to the examination of the concepts of [one's] own specific field."[77].

IV THE ROADMAP

As laid out throughout this chapter, the book focuses on themes and discussions that converge at the intersection of the core science of gene editing, the law and areas thereof that are likely to exert significant pressures on further scientific development, and informed policy making to address future challenges brought on by genome-editing technological applications. Each chapter, therefore, tackles a discrete set of topics derived from one or more of these pillars to propel your understanding of the synergy and interdependence of law, science, and policy.

Put simply, this book is your vessel. Each chapter represents a unique destination in the voyage through a conceptual genome-editing archipelago of law, science, and policy.

We start our journey by traveling back in time to elucidate how the idea of genetic manipulation, and later genome editing, became a reality. Chapter 2 sets the milieu—a historical mise-en-scène, so to speak—that provides context for the origins of primeval DNA tinkering. Although the wave of recent breakthroughs concerning gene editing has propelled the field to the forefront of science, the concept itself is not new. And contrary to what you may have heard in some popular media outlets, scientists have actually long recognized the value of developing methods to induce modifications in DNA sequences. Chapter 2 explains the origins of genome editing and argues that the concept of genetic manipulation is rooted in popular culture. The chapter begins by introducing you to Gregor Mendel's groundbreaking pea-plant experiments in the mid-1800s, which gave rise to modern genetics. The chapter then provides a concise overview of the origins of the concept of genetic manipulation, and how the discovery of two critical elements—restriction enzymes and DNA-repair mechanisms—in the second half of the twentieth century marked the genesis of modern molecular biology and biotechnology. Importantly, this chapter will acquaint you with fundamental concepts in molecular biology and genetics—including gene expression, DNA replication, RNA transcription, protein translation, DNA repair, the structure of DNA, the rise of genetic mutations, the flow of genetic information through the central dogma of molecular biology, and more—and explains important scientific terminology in a clear and accessible format with the aid of illustrations.

The next destination is a chapter replete with syntactical, rhetorical, scientific, and legal discussions concerning meaning and interpretation. Socrates, the renowned philosopher, famously averred that "the beginning of wisdom is the definition of terms." The veracity of that ageless quip is, of course, debatable from a rhetorical standpoint. The definition of terms may or may not mark the genesis of wisdom but, rest assured, conceptual reflection of term definitions indisputably constitutes a crucial early step in legal construction and interpretation. Chapter 3 focuses on a simple, yet fundamental, question that remains unaddressed in modern literature: *What exactly is genome editing?* To that end, the chapter lays an interpretive and normative foundation that imports meaning into the term's scope. It starts by highlighting how scientific literature has remarkably devoted substantial efforts to discuss ways to develop, use, improve, and expand genome-editing technologies without actually attaching a particular meaning to the term genome editing.

At a high level, Chapter 3 thus advocates for the adoption of a unified definition of genome editing primarily aimed at building a science-, legal-, and policy-based framework to address current and future predicaments within the ambit of genome-editing technologies. It examines common and general limitations that stem from the use of specific definitions or terminologies, including overreliance on dictionary definitions, which some courts are using more frequently as interpretive tools to adjudicate cases and controversies. After exposing limitations associated with the use of dictionaries in legal analysis, the chapter argues that congruity and uniformity on genome-editing terminology is sorely needed now due to the increasing interdisciplinary reach of the technology. The chapter further explores the integral role of compromise in the formal codification and promulgation of rules and definitions and, more broadly, in active law and policy making. The proposed definition undergoes rigorous analysis and, along the way, the chapter dispels the myth that law generally lags behind scientific progress.

Chapter 4 spotlights the tools of genome editing. In recent years, CRISPR systems—and CRISPR–Cas9 in particular—have risen to prominence for their use in genome editing. Undoubtedly, CRISPR systems are democratizing scientists' access to new tools required for uncovering future significant scientific, medical, and technological advances. But these are not the only tools being used to edit DNA sequences. Much like the use of different types of airplanes and vehicles for human transportation, so too can different tools be used for gene editing. This chapter examines the evolution and development of the different types of modern genome-editing tools that have enabled the targeted manipulation of genetic sequences. In so doing, it elucidates how genome editing is a logical extension of the genetic manipulation enabled by pioneer recombinant-DNA techniques. The chapter argues that genome editing exists today because recombinant-DNA technology and molecular cloning were developed, promoted, and refined to give rise to avant-garde molecular tools. Venturing further into this chapter will allow you to rummage through the genome-editing toolbox and examine the advantages and disadvantages of four distinct categories of genome-editing systems: (1) chemistry-based systems; (2) viral-based editing systems; (3) nucleases that rely on protein-DNA interactions for DNA targeting—such as meganucleases, zinc-finger nucleases, and TALE nucleases; and (4) RNA-guided, DNA nuclease systems, which comprise CRISPR–Cas systems.

Widespread use of a biotechnology often does not occur for years after it is first introduced to the scientific community. Yet CRISPR–Cas systems, unlike their predecessor technologies, have been adopted by laboratories all around the world with unprecedented speed and used to edit the genomes of virtually every living organism. As discussed earlier in this chapter, powerful technologies are often misrepresented by speculative agents who—knowingly or not—extrapolate unfounded notions of, and spread misinformation that oversells, what is technologically feasible. Chapter 5 provides a comprehensive, yet nonexhaustive, survey of the current and prospective applications of genome-editing technologies that faithfully tracks primary scientific sources and, thus, is firmly grounded in a jurisprudence of scientific empiricism. The chapter examines applications of genome editing in myriad fields ranging from stem-cell research, pest-population control, viral diagnostics, biofuel production, and agriculture to synthetic biology, animal research, human therapeutics, epigenome editing, digital-data recording in living organisms, and more. This exposition underscores two main points. First, genome-editing technologies are not mere tools for basic research, but rather epitomize prolific mines for future significant scientific breakthroughs. Second, every technology endowed with awe-inspiring powers should be handled responsibly and with respect.

Having laid out a broad foundation of how genome editing arose, what it is, and what it can be used for, the book veers from the general and dives deeply into select uses of genome editing.

Chapter 6 sets a backdrop for subsequent discussions about the rationale behind the use of genome-editing biotechnologies in crops intended for human consumption. Feeding the world and achieving food security, for example, have become significant goals of biotechnology. The United Nations estimates that the world population will rise to nearly ten billion people by 2050. To confront challenges in global agriculture, scientists have engineered crops with specific traits—including pest, chemical, and drought resistance—to improve crop nutritional content and yields, and minimize the impact of suboptimal environmental conditions. These strategies led to the development and global commercialization of genetically modified (GM) crops, which in turn ignited fervid opposition to genetically modified organisms (GMOs) by many groups worldwide. To elucidate the basis of GMO controversies, this chapter dives into the science of GMOs. It offers a detailed account of the numerous techniques scientists use to make GMOs and examines the advantages, limitations, and potential risks associated with each technique. The chapter further undertakes a comprehensive examination of the current state of the primary scientific literature concerning perceived health and environmental risks commonly associated with GMOs. The chapter's primary aim is to furnish a succinct resource that renders dense scientific information related to GMOs accessible to all readers.

Building upon the science related to GMOs, Chapter 7 then investigates the regulatory implications of gene-edited crops. The chapter reexamines some of the general concerns about the use of novel biotechnologies that arose with the advent of recombinant DNA technology in the 1970s, along with legislative and judicial developments in the early to mid-1980s that began to exert pressure on the executive branch to act. To assuage these concerns, the Reagan Administration created the Coordinated Framework for the Regulation of Biotechnology. This 1986 policy document avowed that existing health and safety laws could provide adequate regulatory oversight for biotechnology products under a product-based, rather than a process-based, approach and assigned broad federal jurisdiction to the Food and Drug Administration (FDA), the Environmental Protection Agency (EPA), and the United States Department of Agriculture (USDA). Chapter 7 examines how novel genome-editing technologies will test the limits of the Coordinated Framework, which is largely limited in scope by older genetic-engineering methods. The chapter analyzes the regulatory status of gene-edited crops and how, under specific circumstances, these crops can escape regulatory oversight due to the Coordinated

Framework's focus on the use of transgenic DNA to carry out the intended genetic manipulations. The chapter explores current regulatory gaps and argues that, in the near future, it will likely be increasingly cumbersome to distinguish genome-edited crops and naturally occurring crops. The technology, therefore, is likely to challenge the very essence of what constitutes a GMO and extends opportunities to help allay controversies surrounding GM crops.

The next three chapters take on topics related to human genome editing. Chapter 8 will introduce you to the science of engineering complex traits in humans, which will assist your understanding of how to separate truth from hype. A new age began in November 2018, when the world learned shocking news about the birth of the first gene-edited babies in China. He Jiankui, an unseasoned researcher who performed haphazard and surreptitious experiments on viable human embryos using CRISPR–Cas9, confirmed he had manipulated the *CCR5* gene, which plays a role in resistance to the Human Immunodeficiency Virus (HIV). Calls for bans on such uses of genome-editing technology surfaced immediately. Some critics claim that human germline (sperm, eggs, zygotes, and embryos) editing is immoral, unethical, and will push society down a dangerous eugenic path. A common concern is that genome-editing technologies are inherently insidious because they will lead to "designer babies" with a panoply of artificial traits, including superior intelligence, athleticism, or even beauty. Uncertainty in this emerging field of law and science is further compounded by the dual lack of scientific knowledge among the general public and international norms in a globalized world. Chapter 8 examines the myth of designer babies, as well as the dissonance between public opinion and the science of complex human traits. In so doing, it grounds the conversations on scientific facts to elucidate whether intelligence and other complex traits can really be engineered in a test tube.

Chapter 9 pivots from the science onto administrative law. Human genome editing has become a reality and is here to stay. A logical question that follows, therefore, is whether the government should regulate the technology and, if so, what precise measures should be adopted to promote or hinder technological development. This chapter focuses on those questions at the intersection of human genome editing—specifically, germline genome editing (GGE)—and administrative law. The chapter highlights the FDA's role as the agency in charge of protecting the public health by ensuring the safety and efficacy of human drugs and biological products, and shepherding scientific discoveries into the clinical realm. By examining precedents in gene therapy and stem-cell interventions, which are likely relevant to GGE, the chapter identifies regulatory gaps and proposes a novel regulatory framework for future GGE interventions. The chapter further frames the regulatory discussion in the context of an existing de facto legislative GGE ban, which prohibits the FDA from reviewing investigational uses of GGE technology in human embryos. After analyzing the legislative ban, the chapter concludes that the ban creates more societal costs than benefits and increases the likelihood that GGE technologies will be forced to develop in jurisdictions where regulatory systems may be inadequate from social and ethical standpoints.

Chapter 10 begins with the premise that administrative law is pivotal to delineating the limits of governmental regulation of technological advances. Indeed, courts grant administrative agencies vast deference on matters related to the agencies' expertise and jurisdiction. The administrative state, however, is not the sole source of law in our democratic system.

The constitutional structure that supports our democratic system recognizes certain fundamental rights involving human liberties. These rights are considered so important that any governmental action impinging on them warrants examination under strict scrutiny, a legal standard that imposes a high bar for the government. Under strict scrutiny, the government must articulate a compelling purpose for enforcing a law encroaching fundamental rights and prove there are no less restrictive means to accomplish the law's purpose. Some fundamental rights are explicitly enumerated in the Constitution. For instance, freedom of speech is protected under the First Amendment. Similarly, the right to vote—at least insofar as the prohibition of the abridgment of the right to vote on account of race, gender, age, failure to pay poll taxes, or previous condition of servitude—is protected explicitly by the Fifteenth, Nineteenth, Twenty-Fourth, and Twenty-Sixth Amendments, and also implicitly protected under the Fourteenth Amendment. Other fundamental rights, including the rights to procreate, marry, exercise parental autonomy, make medical care decisions, engage in consensual sexual activity among adults, travel, use contraception, express a sexual orientation, have custody of one's children, among others, are unenumerated yet also recognized as fundamental under the Constitution.

But where do these rights come from? And, more importantly, what—if anything—do they have in common with genome-editing technologies? Guided by these questions, Chapter 10 examines novel issues related to genome editing and constitutional law. It surveys modern-day substantive due process and equal protection jurisprudence to evaluate whether existing precedents define a cognizable fundamental right to select uses of germline genome editing. The chapter explores constitutional issues related to genome editing by faithfully adhering to the book's overarching theme of invoking a jurisprudence of scientific empiricism, and highlighting the synergy between science and the law. Within that framework, the chapter illustrates the catastrophic dangers of ignoring or misinterpreting science in constitutional law, and analyzes the involuntary sterilization of "mentally defective" individuals legalized under *Buck v. Bell*. The chapter uses *Buck* as a stern cautionary tale to warn about the failures to ground legal- and policy-based determinations firmly on scientific facts, especially when such determinations concern issues for which substantive scientific principles or elements may be dispositive.

Chapter 11 then applies some of the lessons from previous chapters and introduces normative recommendations for developing legal and science-based policy frameworks to address some of the genome-editing issues discussed throughout the book. The chapter, for instance, builds upon discussions in Chapters 8 through 10 to propose a system to demarcate foundational rights and uses of germline genome editing on the basis of four categories: (1) therapeutic uses to remedy disease; (2) prophylactic purposes, which may or may not be therapeutic; (3) cosmetic or enhancement purposes; and (4) uses involving modification of traits that raise concerns of unlawful discrimination. In so doing, the chapter explores conceptual and structural approaches to GGE clinical interventions and promotes dialogues about the extent to which editing the genetic composition of the human germline should be permitted and, in some instances, protected. Furthermore, to expand on concepts introduced in Chapters 6 and 7, this chapter focuses on strategies to promote research- and science-based policy development related to GMOs and genetically modified crops. Within that backdrop, the chapter elucidates policy development as an inherently complex process that depends not only on strict science-based evidence, but on a multitude of legal, economic, social, political, and other factors that ultimately shape law and policy.

Lastly, Chapter 12 reflects on the book's interdisciplinary journey through the realm of genome editing. This reflection is forward-looking and underscores the need for cooperation between lawyers, scientists, and policy makers as genome-editing technologies continue to develop and mature in an increasingly globalized and interconnected world. The chapter reminds us that genome-editing technologies belong to all of humankind and must be nurtured and developed in ways that will serve future generations as an agent for good. The chapter further encourages and challenges all of us to become more engaged in shaping the future of genome editing through the exercise of basic civic duties, and provides a high-level perspective of significant factors that play a role in shaping legal- and scientific-based public policy.

So let us venture beyond the cloud of headlines and talking points, and travel far away from the shallow waters of uncritical discussions. It is my sincere hope that this volume will give you an opportunity to develop a deep, interdisciplinary understanding and appreciation for genome editing, as well as its prospects and challenges. I welcome you to this exciting intellectual journey!

Notes

1 *See* Sue Vander Hook, Johannes Gutenberg: Printing Press Innovator 45 (2010).

2 *See* Jixing Pan, *On the Origin of Printing in the Light of New Archaeological Discoveries*, 42 Chinese Sci. Bulletin 976, 977, 979–81 (1997).

3 William E. Burns, *Technologies of the Word—Movable Type and the Printing Press, in* SCIENCE AND TECHNOLOGY IN WORLD HISTORY 411 (William E. Burns ed. 2020).

4 *See* JAMES MORAN, PRINTING PRESSES: HISTORY AND DEVELOPMENT FORM THE FIFTEENTH CENTURY TO MODERN TIMES 20 (1973).

5 Burns, *supra* note 3, at 411.

6 VANDER HOOK, *supra* note 1, at 91.

7 *See generally* Siebren van der Werf, *History and Critical Analysis of Fifteenth and Sixteenth Century Nautical Tables*, 48 J. HISTORY OF ASTRONOMY 207, 207–08 (2017).

8 NICOLAUS COPERNICUS, DE REVOLUTIONIBUS ORBIUM COELESTIUM [ON THE REVOLUTIONS OF THE HEAVENLY SPHERES] (Charles Glenn Wallis trans., Prometheus Books 1995) (1543).

9 *See* A Brief History of Cambridge University Press, https://www.cambridge.org/about-us/who-we-are/history/brief-history-press.

10 *See, e.g.*, Francis J. Connell, *Censorship and the Prohibition of Books in Catholic Church Law*, COLUM. L REV. 699, 700 (1954).

11 *Id.* at 703.

12 *See, e.g.*, Domenico Bertoloni Meli, *Leibniz on the Censorship of the Copernican System*, 20 STUDIA LEIBNITIANA 19, 19 (1988).

13 Lise Meitner & O. R. Frisch, *Disintegration of Uranium by Neutrons: A New Type of Nuclear Reaction*, 143 NATURE 239, 239 (1939).

14 Von O. Hahn & F. Strassmann, *Über den Nachweis und das Verhalten der bei der Bestrahlung des Urans Mittels Neutronen Entstehenden Erdalkalimetalle* [*Concerning the Existence of Alkaline Earth Metals Resulting from Neutron Irradiation of Uranium*], 27 DIE NATURWISSENSCHAFTEN 11 (1939), *translated in* Hans G. Graetzer, *Discovery of Nuclear Fission*, 32 AM. J. PHYSICS 9, 10 (1964).

15 O. R. Frisch, *Physical Evidence for the Division of Heavy Nuclei Under Neutron Bombardment*, 143 NATURE 276, 276 (1939).

16 A. Einstein, *Ist die Trägheit Eines Körpers von Seinem Energieinhalt abhängig? [Does the Inertia of a Body Depend upon its Energy-Content?]*, 18 ANNALEN DER PHYSIK 639 (1905), *translated in* THE COLLECTED PAPERS OF ALBERT EINSTEIN, VOL. 2, THE SWISS YEARS: WRITINGS, 1900–1909, at 172 (Anna Beck trans., 1989), http://einsteinpapers.press.princeton.edu/vol2-trans/1?ajax [https://perma.cc/K6TE-UP3M].

17 For a historical account of the origins and development of the US atomic bomb program of World War II, see generally F. G. GOSLING, THE MANHATTAN PROJECT: MAKING THE ATOMIC BOMB (U.S. Dep't of Energy ed. 1999).

18 A. M. Turing, *On Computable Numbers, with an Application to the Entscheidungsproblem*, 42 PROC. LONDON MATHEMATICAL SOC'Y 230, 230 (1937).

19 Electronic Numerical Integrator and Computer, U.S. Patent No. 3,120,606 (filed June 26, 1947) (issued Feb. 4, 1964). To this day, debate exists concerning

whether the first modern computer was the Atanasoff-Berry Computer (ABC) or the ENIAC. *See generally* ALICE ROWE BURKS, WHO INVENTED THE COMPUTER?: THE LEGAL BATTLE THAT CHANGED COMPUTING HISTORY 247–68 (2003). Honeywell Inc. v. Sperry Rand Corp., No. 4-67 Civ. 138, 1973 WL 903, at *7, *30–38, *90 (D. Minn. Oct. 19, 1973), invalidated the ENIAC patent on grounds that the ABC constituted prior art, which rendered the patent invalid and unenforceable. However, the ABC was neither programmable nor Turing-complete. *Atanasoff-Berry Computer*, COMPUTER HIST. MUSEUM, http://www.computerhistory.org/revolution/birth-of-the-computer/4/99 [https://perma.cc/MPU6-S6PX] (last visited Feb. 23, 2017). Indeed, the ABC may be considered the first electronic computer, while the ENIAC was the first general-purpose, programmable, electronic computer. BURKS, *supra*, at 247–49, 330–31. It is somewhat settled that ENIAC was the first Turing-complete, large-scale, electronic, programmable digital computer. *See* Michael R. Williams, *A Preview of Things to Come: Some Remarks on the First Generation of Computers, in* THE FIRST COMPUTERS: HISTORY AND ARCHITECTURES 3 (Raúl Rojas & Ulf Hashagen eds., 2000). Thus, the debate focuses on whether ENIAC's programmable and Turing-complete features qualify it as the direct precursor to modern computers. Ultimately, some dismiss the importance of whether the ABC, ENIAC, or other machines of the time constituted the "first" computer. *Id.* Others argue that the invention of the modern computer has ambiguous origins and involves contributions from scientists in at least three different countries. *See* Raúl Rojas, *Who Invented the Computer? The Debate from the Viewpoint of Computer Architecture, in* MATHEMATICS OF COMPUTATION 1943–1993: A HALF-CENTURY OF COMPUTATIONAL MATHEMATICS, 48 PROC. SYMPOSIA APPLIED MATHEMATICS 361, 364–65 (Walter Gautschi ed., 1993).

20 *See* BARRY M. LEINER ET AL., BRIEF HISTORY OF THE INTERNET 1 (2012), http://www.internetsociety.org/sites/default/files/Brief_History_of_the_Internet.pdf [https://perma.cc/ZL6B-37EP] (chronicling the origins and evolution of the Internet).

21 MICHAEL KORT, THE COLUMBIA GUIDE TO HIROSHIMA AND THE BOMB 8, 46–49 (2007); Winston Churchill, Leader of the Opposition, Where Do We Stand?, (Aug. 16, 1945), *in* 11 VITAL SPEECHES DAY 738 (1945), http://www.ibiblio.org/pha/policy/1945/1945-08-16c.html [https://perma.cc/7RS7-C76R].

22 GOSLING, *supra* note 17, at 51, 54, (stating that the bombs dropped on Japan eventually killed an estimated 340,000); KORT, *supra* note 21, at 76–78, 81 (describing political instability); Martin J. Sherwin, *The Atomic Bomb and the Origins of the Cold War: U.S. Atomic-Energy Policy and Diplomacy, 1941-45*, 78 AM. HIST. REV. 945, 945 (1973).

23 *See generally, e.g.*, Kaveri Subrahmanyam et al., *The Impact of Home Computer Use on Children's Activities and Development*, 10 CHILD. & COMPUTER TECH. 123 (2000).

24 *See generally* The Handbook of Internet Crime (Yvonne Jewkes & Majid Yar eds., 2010) (providing a collection of essays discussing various forms of internet crimes, including cyberterrorism, intellectual property theft, online child pornography and sexual exploitation, cyberbullying, identity theft and fraud, and others).

25 A search on the PubMed scientific database using the "CRISPR" acronym filtered by title and abstract returned 16,957 hits. PubMed.gov Search Results for CRISPR, PubMed.gov, http://www.ncbi.nlm.nih.gov/pubmed/?term=CRISPR[Title%2FAbstract] [https://perma.cc/7PC2-BNN8] (last visited Apr. 12, 2020) (search for CRISPR filtered by title and abstract by using the language "CRISPR[Title/Abstract]"). Note that the search does not include literature that refers to CRISPR in the body of the paper, which may return even more hits.

26 *See generally* Paul Enríquez, *Editing Humanity: On the Precise Manipulation of DNA in Human Embryos*, 97 N.C. L. Rev. 1147 (2019); Paul Enríquez, *Genome Editing and the Jurisprudence of Scientific Empiricism*, 19 Vand. J. Ent. & Tech. L. 603 (2017) [hereinafter Enríquez, *Genome Editing*]; Paul Enríquez, *CRISPR GMOs*, 18 N.C. J.L. & Tech. 432 (2017).

27 *See, e.g.*, John Carroll, *Bayer Bets $335M on CRISPR Therapeutics and the Future of Gene Editing*, FierceBiotech (Dec. 21, 2015), http://www.fiercebiotech.com/story/bayer-bets-335m-crispr-therapeutics-and-future-gene-editing/2015-12-21 [https://perma.cc/LU94-5MUF]; Caroline Chen, *Gene-Editing Drugmaker Backed by Google, Gates Files for IPO*, Bloomberg Bus. (Jan. 4, 2016), http://www.bloomberg.com/news/articles/2016-01-05/gene-editing-drugmaker-backed-by-google-gates-files-for-ipo [https://perma.cc/S47Q-8EK8]; Matthew Herper, *Bill Gates and 13 Other Investors Pour $120 Million into Revolutionary Gene-Editing Startup*, Forbes (Aug. 10, 2015), http://www.forbes.com/sites/matthewherper/2015/08/10/bill-gates-and-13-other-investors-pour-120-million-into-revolutionary-gene-editing-startup/#12f70a01664c [https://perma.cc/W7HL-7C5A]; Alex Lash, *CRISPR Cash: Intellia the Latest Gene-Editing Firm to Nab Big Money*, Xconomy (Sept. 1, 2015), http://www.xconomy.com/boston/2015/09/01/crispr-cash-intellia-the-latest-gene-editing-firm-to-nab-big-money/ [https://perma.cc/8CZ9-FBK5]; *Vertex and CRISPR Therapeutics Establish Collaboration to Use CRISPR-Cas9 Gene Editing Technology to Discover and Develop New Treatments for Genetic Diseases*, Bus. Wire (Oct. 26, 2015), http://www.businesswire.com/news/home/20151026005392/en/Vertex-CRISPR-Therapeutics-Establish-Collaboration-CRISPR-Cas9-Gene [https://perma.cc/4HYM-SE7F].

28 Editas Medicine, Inc., *Form S-1 Registration Statement Under the Securities Act of 1933*, U.S. Sec. & Exchange Commission (Jan. 4, 2016), http://www.sec.gov/Archives/edgar/data/1650664/000104746916009534/a2226902zs-1.htm [https://perma.cc/4F4E-TNRU].

29 *See* CRISPR Therapeutics AG, *Form S-1 Registration Statement Under the Securities Act of 1933*, U.S. Sec. & Exchange Commission (Sept. 9, 2016), http://www

.nasdaq.com/markets/ipos/filing.ashx?filingid=11077159 [https://perma.cc/KM9L-9YEH].

30 903 F.3d 1286 (Fed. Cir. 2018).

31 Pub. L. No. 112-29, 125 Stat. 284 (2011) (codified as amended in scattered sections of 35 U.S.C.).

32 *See, e.g.*, CRISPR-Cas Systems and Methods for Altering Expression of Gene Products, U.S. Patent No. 8,697,359 (filed Oct. 15, 2013) (issued Apr. 15, 2014); Engineering and Optimization of Systems, Methods and Compositions for Sequence Manipulation with Functional Domains, U.S. Patent No. 8,993,233 (filed Dec. 12, 2013) (issued Mar. 31, 2015).

33 *See* Heidi Ledford, *Bitter Fight over CRISPR Patent Heats up*, 529 NATURE 265, 265 (2016), http://www.nature.com/polopoly_fs/1.17961!/menu/main/topColumns/topLeftColumn/pdf/nature.2016.17961.pdf [https://perma.cc/6MGY-TLNA].

34 *See* Broad Inst., Inc., Mass. Inst. of Tech. & President & Fellows of Harvard Coll., (Patents 8,697,359; 8,771,945; 8,795,965; 8,865,406; 8,871,445; 8,889,356; 8,895,308; 8,906,616; 8,932,814; 8,945,839; 8,993,233; 8,999,641 & Application 14/704,551), Junior Party v. Regents of the Univ. of Cal., Univ. of Vienna & Emmanuelle Charpentier (Application 13/842,859), Senior Party, Patent Interference No. 106,048, 2017 WL 657415 (P.T.A.B. Feb. 15, 2017).

35 *See* 903 F.3d at 1296–97.

36 *See* Regents of the Univ. of Cal., Univ. of Vienna & Emmanuelle Charpentier (Applications 15/947,680; 15/947,700; 15/947,718; 15/981,807; 15/981,808; 15/981,809; 16/136,159; 16/136,165; 16/136,168;16/136,175; 16/276,361; 16/276,365; 16/276,368; and 16/276,374), Junior Party v. Broad Inst., Inc., Mass. Inst. of Tech. & President & Fellows of Harvard Coll., (Patents 8,697,359; 8,771,945; 8,795,965; 8,865,406; 8,871,445; 8,889,356; 8,895,308; 8,906,616, 8,932,814, 8,945,839, 8,993,233; 8,999,641, 9,840,713 & Application 14/704,551), Senior Party, Patent Interference No. 106,115 (P.T.A.B. Sept. 10, 2020).

37 *See* Engineering of Systems, Methods and Optimized Guide Compositions for Sequence Manipulation, Eur. Patent No. 2,771,468 (filed Dec. 12, 2013).

38 European Patent Office, *Decision in Case T 844/18 on the CRISPR Gene Editing Technology*, Jan. 17, 2020, https://www.epo.org/law-practice/case-law-appeals/communications/2020/20200117.html#:~:text=European%20patent%20EP%202771468%20relates%20to%20the%20CRISPR%20gene%20editing%20technology.&text=On%2016%20January%202020%2C%20the,the%20revocation%20of%20the%20patent.

39 *See* Methods and Compositions for RNA-Directed Target DNA Modification and for RNA-Directed Modulation of Transcription, Eur. Patent No. 2,800,811 (filed Mar. 15, 2013).

40 CRISPR earned the 2015 "Breakthrough of the Year" accolade awarded by the prominent *Science* journal. Marcia McNutt, *Breakthrough to Genome Editing*, 350 SCIENCE 1445, 1445 (2015).

41 569 U.S. 576 (2013).

42 *Id.* at 580.

43 *Id.* at 596 (Scalia, J., concurring in part and concurring in the judgment) (emphasis added).

44 Steven Breyer, *The Interdependence of Science and Law*, 280 SCIENCE 537, 537 (1998).

45 "Sequences of DNA nucleotides contain the information necessary to create strings of amino acids, which in turn are used in the body to build proteins." *Myriad*, 569 U.S. at 581. This statement is incorrect because amino acid "strings" are *not* used in the body to build proteins. Rather, amino acid "strings" are the proteins themselves in an unfolded state. We will discuss more about the process of protein synthesis in Chapter 2. As ribosomes synthesize polypeptide chains ("strings"), a series of intermolecular forces—such as ionic interactions, the hydrophobic effect, formation of hydrogen bonds, and more—begin the process of protein folding. Thus, the strings of amino acids *fold* into proteins. And proteins can come together to *form* ("build") complexes. Alternatively, the Court could have been referring to messenger RNA (mRNA) molecules, which are used by the ribosomes as *templates* to create ("build") the strings of amino acids. Enríquez, *Genome Editing*, *supra* note 26, at 692 n.608 (internal citations omitted).

46 "Transcription results in a single strand RNA molecule, known as pre-RNA." *Myriad*, 569 U.S. at 581. This statement refers to the transcription of DNA into *primary transcripts*—a single-stranded RNA molecule that has not been processed. As we will discuss in Chapter 2, a primary transcript is later processed to yield various forms of RNA molecules—such as mRNAs, piRNAs, miRNAs, tRNAs, lncRNAs, rRNAs, and more. The Court may have been referring to mRNA processing, in which a *pre-mRNA* (not pre-RNA) molecule undergoes processing to become a mature mRNA. Enríquez, *Genome Editing*, *supra* note 26, at 692 n.609 (internal citations omitted).

47 "Nucleotides that do not code for amino acids . . . are known as 'introns.'" *Myriad*, 569 U.S. at 581. This statement is factually inaccurate because many noncoding nucleotides exist in promoter, enhancer, silencer, and other regulatory regions of the genome that are not introns. The Court may have been referring to noncoding nucleotides within a gene's open reading frame (ORF) that are spliced out during processing. Enríquez, *Genome Editing*, *supra* note 26, at 692 n.610 (citation omitted); *see also infra* Chapter 2.

48 Paul Enríquez, *Deconstructing Transnationalism: Conceptualizing Metanationalism as a Putative Model of Evolving Jurisprudence*, 43 VAND. J. TRANSNAT'L L. 1265, 1269, 1336 (2010) [hereinafter Enríquez, *Metanationalism*].

49 Jackson v. Pollion, 733 F.3d 786, 788 (7th Cir. 2013).

50 David Neuberger, *Stop Needless Dispute of Science in the Courts*, 531 NATURE 9, 9 (2016).

51 *See* Edward Lanphier et al., *Don't Edit the Human Germ Line*, 519 NATURE 410, 410 (2015) (advocating for a complete ban of germline genome editing). Notably, this commentary coauthored by Edward Lanphier, former President and Chief Executive Officer of Sangamo BioSciences, highlights a meaningful need to elaborate on issues concerning competing financial interests. Sangamo BioSciences currently controls a vast intellectual property portfolio comprising twenty issued US patents encompassing the foundational technology of design, selection, and application of an older generation of genome-editing tools consisting of Zinc-Finger proteins, nucleases, and transcription factors. *See* Sangamo BioSciences, Inc., *Form 10-K Annual Report Under the Securities Act of 1933*, U.S. SEC. & EXCH. COMM'N (Dec. 31, 2014), https://www.sec.gov/Archives/edgar/data/1001233/000156459015000950/sgmo-10k_20141231.htm [https://perma.cc/N68E-4X64]. As of February 4, 2015, Sangamo had compiled "133 families of Sangamo-owned or co-owned patent filings," including 120 US and 437 foreign issued patents. *Id.* A few things are worth pointing out.

First, CRISPR-based biotechnologies may pose an economic threat to Sangamo's monopoly over genome editing using older Zinc Finger-based technologies. Although Sangamo has already hopped on the CRISPR wagon, *see, e.g.*, Screening Assays for Therapeutics for Parkinson's Disease, U.S. Patent Application No. 14/647,732 (filed Dec. 2, 2013), it lacks the commanding foundational intellectual property it enjoys in the Zinc-Finger field. Second, many of Sangamo's gene-editing biotechnologies, some of which are currently in clinical trials, are based on somatic-cell, rather than germ-cell, therapeutics. Correcting genomes in the germline is arguably more effective than doing so in somatic cells because germ cells are totipotent and give rise to all cell types. Accordingly, CRISPR–Cas9 germline editing could in theory, if proven safe, obviate resorting to a number of Sangamo's therapeutic tools, which would dilapidate more than a decade of capital investments in research and development. Third, Lanphier and colleagues' efforts to distinguish somatic and germline editing along with claims that germline therapeutic benefits are tenuous, and philosophically and ethically unjustifiable, *see* Lanphier et al., *supra*, at 411, inordinately approach the logical fallacy of a distinction without a difference, particularly given the commentary's moral-arbiter tone. The authors avoid acknowledging that, as with any incipient biotechnology, including Sangamo's own Zinc-Finger Nucleases at one point in time, safety and ethical concerns are always part of the calculus behind a cost-benefit analysis for clinical applications of a technology in its early developmental stages. For a more detailed discussion of Zinc-Finger

Nucleases and other older genome-editing technologies based on protein-DNA interactions, see *infra* Chapter 4.

52 Albert Einstein, *Physics and Reality*, 221 J. FRANKLIN INST. 349, 349 (Jean Piccard trans., 1936). Whether his assessment is correct is, of course, beyond the scope of this book.

53 Regents of the Univ. of Cal. v. Bakke, 438 U.S. 265, 312 n.48 (1978) (citing William G. Bowen, *Admissions and the Relevance of Race*, PRINCETON ALUMNI WKLY., Sept. 26, 1977, at 9).

54 *See, e.g.*, Craig v. Boren, 429 U.S. 190, 204 (1976) ("There is no reason to belabor this line of analysis. It is unrealistic to expect either members of the judiciary or state officials to be well versed in the rigors of experimental or statistical technique."); ROBIN FELDMAN, THE ROLE OF SCIENCE IN LAW 37–48 (2009) (discussing lawyers' proclivities to defer to scientific expertise).

55 This book adopts this phrase from the title of an article penned by Oliver W. Holmes, Jr. over a century ago. *See* Oliver Wendell Holmes, *Law in Science and Science in Law*, 12 HARV. L. REV. 443, 444 (1899). Ironically, the same Holmes authored the infamous *Buck v. Bell* decision upholding the constitutionality of sexual sterilization for the mentally disabled relying on dubious science. *See* discussion *infra* Chapter 10.

56 It bears noting that, although the notion of a jurisprudence of scientific empiricism has not previously been proposed as articulated in this book, in the past, scholars have discussed—amid great controversy—using empirical evidence from the *social sciences* to instruct legal analysis. *See, e.g.*, ANGELO N. ANCHETA, SCIENTIFIC EVIDENCE AND EQUAL PROTECTION OF THE LAW (2006); Joshua B. Fischman, *Reuniting 'Is' and 'Ought' in Empirical Legal Scholarship*, 162 U. PA. L. REV. 117 (2013); Tracey L. Meares, *Three Objections to the Use of Empiricism in Criminal Law and Procedure—and Three Answers*, 2002 U. ILL. L. REV. 851 (2002); Craig Allen Nard, *Empirical Legal Scholarship: Reestablishing a Dialogue Between the Academy and Profession*, 30 WAKE FOREST L. REV. 347 (1995); Steven R. Schlesinger & Janet Lesse, *Justice Harry Blackmun and Empirical Jurisprudence*, 29 AM. U. L. REV. 405 (1980); J. Alexander Tanford, *The Limits of a Scientific Jurisprudence: The Supreme Court and Psychology*, 66 IND. L.J. 137 (1990); Timothy Zick, *Constitutional Empiricism: Quasi-Neutral Principles and Constitutional Truths*, 82 N.C. L. REV. 115 (2003).

57 *Jackson*, 733 F.3d at 790.

58 *See* Daubert v. Merrell Dow Pharm., Inc., 509 U.S. 579 (1993).

59 *See* Kumho Tire Co. v. Carmichael, 526 U.S. 137 (1999).

60 David Baltimore, David S. Tatel & Anne-Marie Mazza, *Bridging the Science-Law Divide*, 147 DÆDALUS, J. AM. ACAD. ARTS & SCIS. 181, 185 (2018).

61 Burwell v. Hobby Lobby Stores, Inc., 573 U.S. 682 (2014).

62 *Id.* at 701, 723.

63 *See* Enríquez, *Genome Editing*, *supra* note 26, at 693 n.612; *see also* U.S. Food & Drug Admin., Birth Control: Medicines to Help You, FDA, https://www.fda.gov/forconsumers/byaudience/forwomen/freepublications/ucm313215.htm [https://perma.cc/X8RT-ZGPW] (last updated Sept. 8, 2016) (providing some information on FDA-approved and cleared methods for birth control).

64 Brief for Physicians for Reproductive Health et al. as *Amici Curiae*, No. 13-354, 10.

65 *Hobby Lobby*, 573 U.S. at 723.

66 *Id.* at 724.

67 *Id.* at 725.

68 *Id.*

69 *See* David Souter, Ruth Bader Ginsburg, David S. Tatel & Linda Greenhouse, 154 Proc. Am. Phil. Soc'y 294, 298–99 (2010).

70 Steven Breyer, *The Interdependence of Science and Law*, 280 Science 537, 538 (1998).

71 274 U.S. 200 (1927).

72 *Id.* at 538.

73 Daubert v. Merrell Dow Pharm., Inc., 509 U.S. 579, 601 (1993) (Rehnquist, C.J., concurring in part and dissenting in part).

74 A revolution is well underway in genome editing science with the potential to fundamentally reshape the way we approach agriculture, synthetic biology, ecosystems, bioterrorism, gene therapy, and biomedicine through law and policy. *See* discussion *infra* Chapter 5.

75 Enríquez, *Genome Editing*, *supra* note 26, at 614–16. Although this term has not been used in the context proposed in this book, it has appeared in legal scholarship, at least as early as 1937. *See The Availability of a Principal's Defense to His Uncompensated Surety*, 46 Yale L.J. 833, 839 (1937); *see also, e.g.*, Brief for Respondent, Tan v. Phelan, 333 U.S. 6 (1948) (No. 370), 1947 WL 44413, at *12; Georg Schwarzenberger, *The Inductive Approach to International Law*, 60 Harv. L. Rev. 539, 569 (1947); Frederick M. Rowe, Note, *Price Discrimination, Competition, and Confusion: Another Look at Robinson-Patman*, 60 Yale L.J. 929, 961 n.210 (1951); Note, *State Law and Uniformity in Federal Taxation*, 55 Harv. L. Rev. 255, 255 (1941).

76 Enríquez, *Metanationalism*, *supra* note 48, at 1269, 1336. CRISPR-based technologies are poised to raise ethical and social problems with global implications. *See, e.g.*, *UN Panel Warns Against 'Designer Babies' and Eugenics in 'Editing' of Human DNA*, U.N. News Ctr. (Oct. 5, 2015), http://www.un.org/apps/news/story.asp?NewsID=52172 [https://perma.cc/7YHS-9KQ4].

77 Einstein, *supra* note 52, at 349.

2

How an Idea Became a Reality

Genome, or gene, editing has become a fixture of modern discussions of science and technology. Today, it is nearly impossible to read the newspaper, watch television, listen to the radio, or surf the Internet without encountering a constant stream of news and developments related to gene editing. In recent years, every major newspaper—including the *New York Times*, the *Washington Post*, the *Wall Street Journal*, among others—has managed to put ink on paper to report on and discuss it. Public as well as commercial television and cable news networks—regardless of political inclination—have covered it. Commercial and noncommercial broadcasts transmitted via conventional, digital, and satellite types of radio have devoted ample airtime to it.

The latest information on gene editing—from reputable sources, or not—is now readily available on blogs, twitter feeds, and podcasts around the world; all at the click of a button or the swipe of a touchscreen. Genome editing no longer thrives exclusively in the esoteric corners of scientific literature. Even *60 Minutes*, America's oldest and most-watched television newsmagazine, which frequently features segments on presidents, foreign leaders, celebrities, and contemporaneous investigative reporting of social, political, and cultural significance, has recently allotted airtime for genome editing.[1] If the iconic tick-ticking of the *60 Minutes* stopwatch serves as a trope for the arrival of genome editing to mainstream popular culture, one can confidently say that this breakthrough technology has arrived and is here to stay.

The ubiquity of genome editing in the news and its accompanying "craze"[2] might suggest to those outside the scientific community that the technology is a recent phenomenon. The concept of genome editing, however, is not new. In fact, as I explain in this chapter, the notion of manipulating the genetic material of living organisms is deeply rooted in popular culture.[3]

I OF PEAS AND HEREDITY

For a long time in history, humans have loosely understood the concept of trait inheritance. Much like the passing of property, titles, rights, and duties from ancestors to descendants, humans realized that certain traits can often be "passed on" from parents to offspring and subsequent generations. Such inheritance of traits was recognized as common among all living organisms. Just as children could inherit their mother's smile or father's nose, so too could plants and animals inherit specific traits from their progenitors.

An empirical and philosophical exploration of this loose understanding of how living organisms could inherit traits from their ancestors gained momentum in the nineteenth century and, ultimately, gave rise to the dawn of the age of evolutionary and molecular biology. Alfred Russel Wallace and Charles Darwin's 1858 codiscovery of *natural selection*[4] described the principle by which individuals with certain traits can better adapt to their environments and, thus, be more successful at surviving, reproducing, and passing down those traits. The articulation of this survival-of-the-fittest principle prompted Darwin to publish his book *On the Origin of Species*,[5] which proposed that populations evolve naturally over time via the process of natural selection.

Around the same time that natural selection made its debut in the scientific world, Gregor Mendel, widely known as the founder of modern genetics, was conducting groundbreaking research on plant speciation and hybridization. His research would go on to transform the vague, centuries-old inkling of trait inheritance into the more concrete, empirical-based, Laws of Inheritance.[6] Mendel was an Augustinian friar from a modest background who taught science as a high school teacher in Moravia, a region of modern-day Czech Republic. Between the mid-1850s and mid-1860s, he performed research on pea plants focusing on seven specific characteristics: seed shape (round or wrinkled), pod color (yellow or green), plant height (tall—6 to 7 feet—or dwarf—0.75 to 1.5 feet), seed color (yellow or green), flower position (axial or terminal), pod shape (inflated or constricted), and flower color (red or white).[7] By focusing on these seven discrete traits, he circumvented a fundamental problem that other contemporary scientists faced.

Rather than trying to measure highly variable traits in a quantitative and statistical manner, Mendel used a clear-cut approach to determine whether or not simple traits were inherited in the next generation of pea plants. Thus, for example, Mendel noticed that his plants produced either yellow or green seeds. These traits were very specific. There was no in-between color, or worse, a series of gradient shades spanning a variable green and yellow spectrum. The certainty and simplicity of the two traits allowed Mendel to ask an equally simple question: If he mated a pea plant that yields yellow seeds with one that yields green seeds, which of the two traits will appear in the progeny?

What Mendel did not know at the time, was that the traits he chose to study were under the regulatory control of single genes, which rendered them perfect subjects for his experiments. After crossing the plants, Mendel could simply observe the results and definitively answer which characteristics had developed, or—as would later be described—been inherited. The offspring plants produced either yellow or green seeds, red or white flowers, and so on.

In contrast, other nineteenth-century researchers were attempting to answer similar questions by studying complex traits that are controlled by the combined effect of multiple genes, such as human height or skin color. No one had the slightest clue at the time that genes were responsible for the variability of these human traits. And those studying human height, for instance, could not mate a 6'5" tall man with a 5'2" woman and ask whether their child would be either 6'5" or 5'2". Such experiment would be replete with methodological obstacles. Never mind the fact that it would take at least two decades to complete the experiment—for the offspring would need to reach adulthood. The outcome would ultimately depend on whether the offspring was male or female, had adequate nutrition throughout various stages of development, or was exposed to a myriad of environmental factors that can induce effects on stature. In the end, even accounting for all these variables, the offspring's height could fall anywhere between the parents' respective heights or, more surprisingly, outside of the 5'2" to 6'5" range.

In a nutshell, the complexity of traits governed by multiple genes was the root of confusion experienced by nineteenth century scientists searching to concoct a unified theory of trait inheritance. And although our understanding of molecular genetics has come a long way, the specific contribution of multiple genes underlying many complex traits remains either a mystery or an intractable problem even in today's modern age of genome editing and other technological advances.

Whether by happenstance or design, the simplicity of Mendel's pea plant-hybridization experiments underscore the importance of his contribution to science. Before he presented his findings at meetings of the Brünn Natural History Society in early 1865, scientists—including Darwin—erroneously believed that the basis of inheritance consisted of the combination of parental traits blended together to yield the traits of the offspring. It is precisely this reasoning that purportedly explained how parents of different stature and skin color could engender offspring with unique stature and skin tone.

Mendel's seminal work was published in 1866, but it was largely overlooked for over thirty-five years—long after his death in 1884.[8] His work became the source of renewed interest in the scientific community after it was "rediscovered" at the turn of the twentieth century when three scientists independently verified some of his original findings.[9] Amid a fierce dispute for priority among the rediscoverers, Mendel's work became famous. William Bateson, a Cambridge zoologist, subsequently popularized Mendel's work and used it as a stepping stone to proclaim the birth of *genetics*[10]—a term derived from the Greek génos, which means birth—as a scientific discipline concerned with the study of heredity.

The implications of Mendel's findings eventually upended the conventional view of inheritance. Mendel compiled a record of detailed observations showing how traits—or peculiar "differentiating characters" as he called them—were passed down from progenitors to progeny. In so doing, he alluded that traits arise from the composition and grouping of certain elements that exist in the cellular foundation of organisms.[11] This idea became widely influential in the early to mid-twentieth century. Indeed, a new generation of scientists embraced it. As more research accrued, the scientific community eventually integrated and reconciled Darwinian evolutionary theory and the principles of Mendelian genetics into an interdisciplinary and unified concept that became known as the *modern synthesis*.[12]

Although Mendel was unaware of the notion of genes, and did not coin the term, his insights prompted subsequent researchers to formulate the concept of discrete inherited units or determinant factors that give rise to observable physical characteristics.[13] Today, we refer to these as genes.

II FROM GENES TO PROTEINS

Before embarking on a discussion about genome-editing science, law, and policy, it is imperative that certain scientific terminology and principles be explained. The basic background information covered below is essential because it will help you, the reader, to better understand the material found in subsequent chapters. For readers unfamiliar with fundamental concepts in molecular biology and genetics, the following sections are all the more important.

A *Constituent Elements*

A *gene* refers to a stretch of sequence of a *deoxyribonucleic acid* (DNA) molecule encoding biological information that can, in turn, be used in cells to make *ribonucleic acid* (RNA) molecules and proteins. Simply put, the gene is the basic functional unit of biological inheritance. Its primary role is to store genetic information that carries instructions—a blueprint, so to speak—that will direct the development of an organism's characteristics. A *genome* refers to an organism's complete set of DNA molecules. Thus, an organism's genome comprises all of its DNA, including all of its genes.

The size of an organism's genome varies greatly among living animals, plants, and microorganisms. For instance, scientists estimate that the bread wheat (*Triticum aestivum*) genome consists of approximately 95,000 genes.[14] The genome of the bacterium *Escherichia coli* (*E. coli*) has approximately 4,300 genes.[15] And although scientists debate about a definitive total count for the number of genes in the human (*Homo sapiens*) genome, current estimates report roughly between 19,000 to 22,000 protein-coding genes and 22,000 noncoding genes[16] (we will discuss more about coding and noncoding genes later in this chapter).

Both DNA and RNA are types of *nucleic acid* molecules. Nucleic acids were first discovered in 1869 by Friedrich Miescher, a Swiss physician who isolated DNA—which he referred to as nuclein at the time—from pus cell nuclei.[17] All nucleic acids are biological polymers. In general, *polymers* are large molecules made up of many repeating subunits called *monomers*, which are connected to each other via chemical bonds in chain-like arrangements. Thus, one can think of *poly*mers as the grouping of many *mono*mers. Polymers are ubiquitous in our world. Rubber, Teflon®, wool, silk, nylon, most plastics, DNA, RNA, proteins, cellulose, and numerous other materials are types of polymers.

Nucleic acids consist of monomers called *nucleotides*. Each nucleotide contains a *nitrogenous base*, which is, as its name alludes, a molecule bearing nitrogen atoms. In broad chemical terms, a *base* refers to a substance that donates hydrogen ions. In contrast, an *acid* refers to a substance that accepts hydrogen ions. It may be helpful to think of acids and bases as the yin and yang of chemical reactions; one complements and neutralizes the other.

In addition to nitrogenous bases, nucleotides also consist of a series of five-carbon (pentose) sugar molecules and phosphate groups. A phosphate group is a chemical moiety, or compound, comprised of one phosphorous and four oxygen atoms. In the context of nucleic acids, the phosphate groups are inherently acidic and bestow a net negative charge upon DNA and RNA molecules. This negative charge shields and overpowers the positive charge of the nitrogenous bases—hence the name nucleic *acids*.

In sum, DNA is a type of nucleic acid molecule made up of many nucleotides linked together. Each nucleotide contains a nitrogenous base, a sugar molecule, and a phosphate backbone. These constituent elements give DNA acidic properties and an overall net negative charge. And genes are long regions of DNA that store genetic information, which can be used to make RNA and protein molecules. So far, so good!

B *You Complement Me!*

There are five predominant types of nitrogenous bases found in nature. DNA features the bases Adenine (A), Cytosine (C), Guanine (G), and Thymine (T). These bases—and their one-letter abbreviations—constitute the renowned genetic alphabet of A, C, G, and T. RNA is also made up of A, C, and G bases, but the nitrogenous base Uracil (U) replaces Thymine in all RNA molecules.

The model depicting DNA's structure was published in a landmark one-page paper in 1953 by James Watson and Francis Crick.[18] The paper contained no experiments, but was published alongside two other articles[19] presenting experimental data upon which Watson and Crick largely relied on to create their model. In particular, data generated by Rosalind Franklin, a chemist and x-ray crystallographer, proved pivotal in understanding the structure of DNA. Franklin had been studying ways to visualize DNA using x-ray crystallography, a scientific technique used to determine the atomic and molecular arrangement of atoms in a molecule. A photograph she took in 1952 of the diffraction pattern generated from shooting a fiber of DNA with x-rays revealed an image of a simple, regular pattern of spots arranged in the shape of the letter X. The picture, which had strikingly similar features to diffraction patterns of other established helical molecules, suggested to her that DNA too was likely helical in structure.[20]

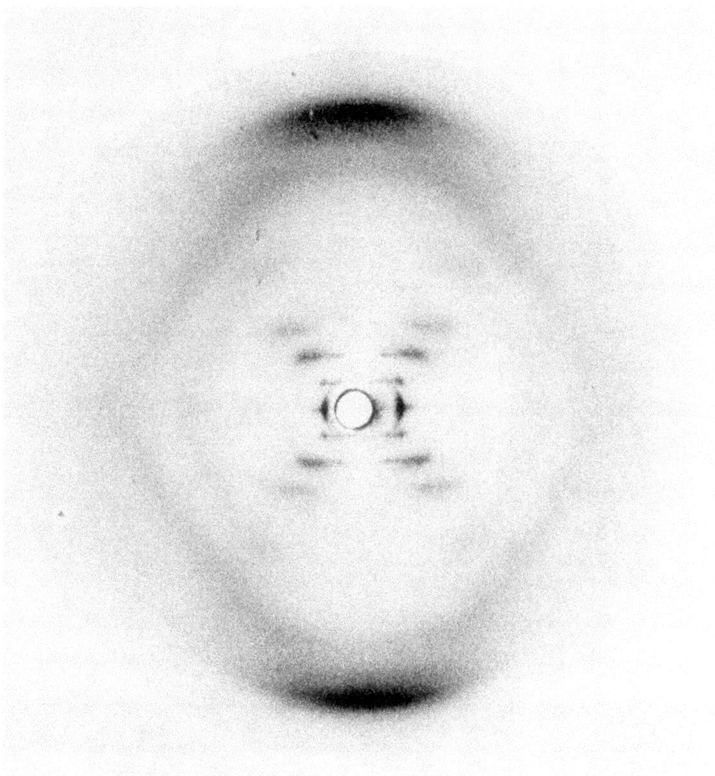

FIGURE 2.1 Photograph of the x-ray diffraction pattern of a DNA molecule

Rosalind Franklin captured this image of the beta form (B-form) of DNA in 1953, the year in which Watson and Crick unveiled the structure of DNA, aided by Franklin's work. The image results from a beam of x-rays being scattered onto a photographic plate by the DNA. The cross of bands indicates the helical nature of DNA.

Unbeknownst to Franklin, Watson had been shown her photograph before she submitted it for publication. Like Franklin, he understood the data revealed that DNA was probably helical. And he used that information to complete a model of the structure of DNA. Watson later acknowledged that seeing Franklin's photograph was "the key event"[21] that triggered publication of his paper, and that formulation of the Watson-Crick model would have been "most unlikely, if not impossible"[22] without the insights of Franklin's data.

The structural data provided essential insights that yielded an elegant model. We now know that DNA molecules adopt a simple, canonical, double helical structure. Specifically, DNA comprises two individual chains—or "*strands*"—that twist around each other repeatedly into a spiral-staircase shape. DNA is, thus, said to be a *double-stranded* molecule.

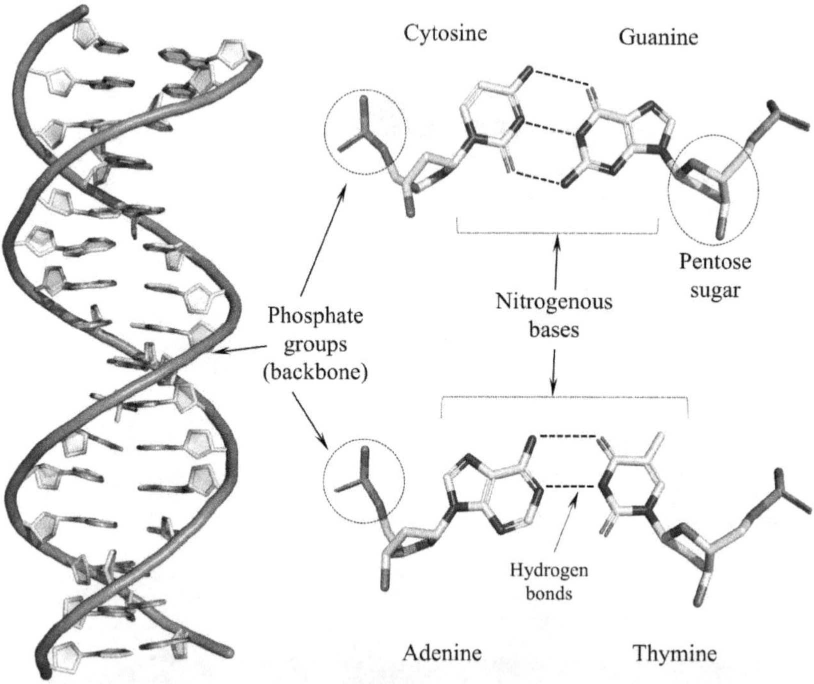

	U		C		A		G		
U	UUU	Phenylalanine	UCU	Serine	UAU	Tyrosine	UGU	Cysteine	U
	UUC	Phenylalanine	UCC	Serine	UAC	Tyrosine	UGC	Cysteine	C
	UUA	Leucine	UCA	Serine	UAA	STOP	UGA	STOP	A
	UUG	Leucine	UCG	Serine	UAG	STOP	UGG	Tryptophan	G
C	CUU	Leucine	CCU	Proline	CAU	Histidine	CGU	Arginine	U
	CUC	Leucine	CCC	Proline	CAC	Histidine	CGC	Arginine	C
	CUA	Leucine	CCA	Proline	CAA	Glutamine	CGA	Arginine	A
	CUG	Leucine	CCG	Proline	CAG	Glutamine	CGG	Arginine	G
A	AUU	Isoleucine	ACU	Threonine	AAU	Asparagine	AGU	Serine	U
	AUC	Isoleucine	ACC	Threonine	AAC	Asparagine	AGC	Serine	C
	AUA	Isoleucine	ACA	Threonine	AAA	Lysine	AGA	Arginine	A
	AUG	Methionine	ACG	Threonine	AAG	Lysine	AGG	Arginine	G
G	GUU	Valine	GCU	Alanine	GAU	Aspartic acid	GGU	Glycine	U
	GUC	Valine	GCC	Alanine	GAC	Aspartic acid	GGC	Glycine	C
	GUA	Valine	GCA	Alanine	GAA	Glutamic acid	GGA	Glycine	A
	GUG	Valine	GCG	Alanine	GAG	Glutamic acid	GGG	Glycine	G

FIGURE 2.2 Structure and constituent elements of the DNA double helix and the genetic code

The phosphate groups of DNA are on the outside of the double helix and form a backbone that represents the curving outer borders of the staircase. The nitrogenous bases of the DNA, on the other hand, are buried inside the double helix and represent the steps of the staircase. The bases are flat and stack on top of each other, much like a pile of pancakes.

The structure of DNA reveals important clues about its biological and physiological function. Recall earlier how chemical bases are substances that can donate hydrogen ions. The inward-directed orientation of each nitrogenous base in the double helix constrains them in a way that makes the bases from each strand face one another in close vicinity. This induced proximity facilitates the "donation" or exchange of hydrogens between the two strands. Such exchange leads to formation of *hydrogen bonds*, which are a type of chemical bond between two molecules.

Hydrogen bonds between opposite nitrogenous bases in the double helix guarantee that each base in the first strand is paired up with only one other base in the second strand. Thus, a *base pair* forms when two complementary bases bond together via hydrogen bonds. But bases do not pair up randomly; they follow specific rules.[23] An Adenine base only pairs up with a Thymine base via two hydrogen bonds (A–T). A Cytosine base only pairs up with a Guanine base, generally via three hydrogen bonds (C–G). These hydrogen bonds that form between the two DNA strands promote stability of the DNA double helix.

More importantly, because base-pairing only occurs between A–T and C–G complementary sequences, the individual DNA strands can be separated and used independently as new templates for DNA replication.[24] This is precisely what takes place during cell division. The hydrogen bonds between two parental DNA strands are broken by specific enzymes, and each strand can then be copied to produce complementary daughter strands. Accordingly, DNA complementarity is important because it ensures that the genetic information encoded in genes is heritable and stable through many generations.

C *The Same, But Different*

As outlined earlier in this chapter, genes are fragments of DNA molecules that encode biological information. Some genes can be very long fragments of DNA. The human dystrophin gene (symbol *DMD* – in standard genetic scientific nomenclature, gene names are italicized), for example, is over 2.3 million base-pairs long.[25] In contrast, other genes can be quite short. The *E. coli* methylcrotonyl-CoA carboxylase alpha chain (*mcc*A) gene is a mere twenty-one base-pairs long.[26]

Regardless of length, genes may exist in several alternative or variant forms known as *alleles*. The term allele is an abbreviation of the word allelomorph,[27] which first appeared in 1902 to refer to the source of other forms of an inherited trait in an organism.

Although genes are fragments of DNA, they do not exist in an isolated configuration within the cell nucleus. Rather, genes are grouped and sequentially aligned along extended threadlike structures called *chromosomes*, which are made up of nucleic acids that are often tightly packaged with proteins. In 1910, Thomas Hunt Morgan, a renowned American geneticist and embryologist, was the first to uncover empirical evidence to demonstrate the role of chromosomes as carriers of genes from one generation to the next.[28]

Broadly speaking, chromosomes are very long molecules of DNA comprising an array of many genes. It might help to visualize a chromosome as an unusually long freight train. Each freight wagon (gene) can carry a different type of cargo (genetic information), and each wagon is sequentially arranged along the railroad track. The freight train transports the cargo across two geographical locations—from the point of departure to the destination—much like the chromosome transports genes from the ancestral to the descendant generation.

No two freight wagons can occupy the same place along the railroad track; their location is unique. By analogy, every gene within a chromosome has a unique genetic position, or *locus*, relative to other genes. Different alleles of the same gene can be found at the same genetic locus of two individual chromosomes.

Let's say you have three friends—Adam, Beth, and Charlie. Assume the following sequence of DNA constitutes a complete gene, which we shall call *GENE1*, and is found on a specific genetic locus of chromosome number 5 of a human individual:

[1] ATGCGTCAGATGGGCAGTTGA

As pointed out earlier, *GENE1* may exist in variant forms called alleles.

[2] ATGCGTC**T**GATGGGCAGTTGA

[3] ATGCGTCAGATGG**AT**AGTTGA

The sequence [2] on the top is an allele of *GENE1*. It is still the same gene, but features a slight sequence variation (the underlined **T** was an A in the reference [1] version of the gene). The sequence [3] on the bottom is also an allele of *GENE1*, but features another sequence variation in a different part of the gene (the underlined **AT** was GC in the reference [1] version). All these sequences constitute the same *GENE1*, which may exist as three unique alleles—[1], [2], or [3]. Because humans are individuals of the same species, they will all have a copy of *GENE1*. However, each individual may carry a distinct *GENE1* allele. Thus, Adam, Beth, and Charlie may each have at least one of the alleles presented above. Regardless of which allele your friends carry, the version of *GENE1* they possess will always be found at the same locus of chromosome number 5.

D *Sex and Dominance*

Diploid organisms—namely, those that carry two sets of chromosomes and, thus, two sets of a particular gene—inherit one allele from each parent. Humans, for example, are diploid. Each individual possesses two sets of twenty-three chromosomes. They inherit one copy of a particular gene from the father and one copy from the mother.

All human *somatic* cells—namely, all of the body's cells except the reproductive cells—are diploid. By contrast, human *germ cells* are specialized reproductive cells that give rise to *gametes*. Gametes are *haploid* cells. That means each gamete carries only a single copy of a chromosome and, thus, contains only one copy of each gene.

An egg is a mature female gamete. A sperm cell is a mature male gamete. The lineage of an organism's germ cells, which hold the genetic information that is passed down to progeny, constitutes the *germline*.

During sexual reproduction and fertilization, each haploid gamete—one egg and one sperm—fuse together to produce a single diploid cell called a *zygote*. As development progresses, the single-cell zygote divides and differentiates many times, thereby giving rise to a multicellular *embryo*. The zygote has a complete duplicate set of parental chromosomes; one set from the mother and another set from the father.

When the parental alleles are the same, the organism is said to be *homozygous* because it carries two copies of the same allele. If the parental alleles are closely related but feature slight sequence variations (two different alleles), the organism is said to be *heterozygous* because it carries one copy of each distinct allele.

Imagine your diploid friends Adam and Beth decide to procreate. Both Adam and Beth have two copies of *GENE1* each. Adam has alleles [1] and [2], whereas Beth has alleles [2] and [3]. Because sperm and eggs are haploid cells, Adam can contribute sperm cells that have only either [1] or [2] *GENE1* alleles. Likewise, Beth can contribute eggs that have only either [2] or [3] alleles. Two offspring—Olivia and Oscar—are born. After examining Olivia and Oscar's genetic composition at the *GENE1* locus, we find the following as shown in Figure 2.3.

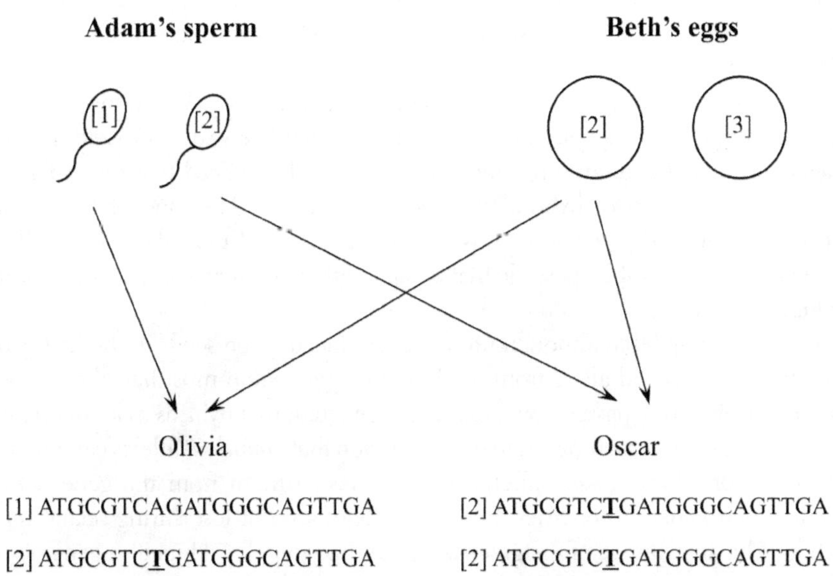

FIGURE 2.3 Allele inheritance via sexual reproduction

Adam and Beth carry haploid gametes (sperm and egg), which fuse together to form zygotes. Their offspring, Olivia and Oscar, each carry one copy of a *GENE1* allele from each parent. Oliva is heterozygous (she has two distinct alleles—[1] and [2]), while Oscar is homozygous (he has two copies of allele [2]) at the *GENE1* locus.

Both offspring inherited one allele from each parent. But notice how Olivia carries two distinct alleles of *GENE1*. She is, therefore, heterozygous at the *GENE1* locus. Oscar, on the other hand, has inherited two copies of the same *GENE1* allele from each of his parents. He is homozygous at the *GENE1* locus.

Let us take a mental stroll through Mendel's garden of peas once again to further illustrate the above concepts and introduce new ones.

Recall that Mendel mated pea plants that produced either yellow or green seeds. The seed-color trait in his plants was under the regulatory control of only one gene. In other words, whether the offspring plant would produce yellow or green seeds depended solely on which alleles were passed down from the progenitor plants. One —and only one—of the alleles gave rise to either yellow or green seeds. The seed color in Mendel's plants is therefore said to be a *monogenic* (one gene) trait because it is governed exclusively by a single allele. In contrast, when a particular trait is under the regulatory control of multiple alleles, it is said to be a *polygenic* (many genes) trait. Human height, skin color, eye color, intelligence, and many other human characteristics are in fact polygenic.

Mendel recognized that every time he mated a purebred yellow-seeded plant (that is, a homozygous plant having two yellow-seeded alleles) with a purebred green-seeded plant, the first generation of offspring hybrids would all produce plants with yellow seeds. It was as though the yellow-seed trait prevailed over and over. The green-seed trait just seemed to disappear. Accordingly, the yellow-seed trait was *dominant*.

But this is where Mendel's experiments get more interesting. When the first generation of yellow-seeded hybrids were allowed to self-fertilize—so as to yield a second generation of plants—a curious thing occurred. Mendel noticed that some plants in the second generation of hybrids produced green seeds. The ratio of hybrids that produced yellow and green seeds was approximately 3:1. If the yellow-seed trait was dominant, how could it be possible that a plant with two yellow-seeded parents would produce green seeds?

Mendel reasoned that although no plants produced green seeds in the first generation, the green-seeded allele from the founding generation must have been, somehow, inconspicuously passed down to the first generation of hybrids in an unchanged configuration. This reasoning led to the realization that *dominant* alleles can mask the appearance of other *recessive* alleles without erasing them from the gene pool or affecting their genetic properties. Recessive alleles are not lost during sexual reproduction. The appearance of the green-seed trait had merely "skipped" a generation.

This phenomenon can be explained by deconstructing the genetic contributions of the population of plants in each generation. For clarity and simplicity purposes, let us represent the dominant yellow-seeded allele with the letter "Y" and the recessive green-seeded allele with the letter "g" (in conventional genetics, however, the alleles would be represented by the same letter in capital and lower-case forms, for example, "Y" for yellow and "y" for green, to denote the dominant and recessive alleles).

The plants in the founding generation were diploid. Each parent was homozygous for yellow or green seeds—*YY* and *gg*. This *YY* and *gg* nomenclature is commonly used to represent an organism's *genotype*, which refers to the genetic makeup of said organism. The *YY* and *gg* diploid founding parents produced only *Y* haploid and *g* haploid gametes, respectively. When the *Y* and *g* haploid cells came together to form *Yg* diploid progeny cells, the resulting first generation of hybrids possessed the *Yg* genotype. As a result, the progeny exhibited the yellow-seed *phenotype*. The term phenotype refers to the visible characteristics—traits—that appear upon expression of an organism's genotype. Because the yellow-seed trait is the dominant allele, all *Yg* progeny in the first generation produced yellow seeds.

The first-generation *Yg* hybrids were heterozygous and subsequently used for self-fertilization to give rise to second-generation hybrids. Unlike the plants in the founding generation, each first-generation *Yg* parent produced both *Y* and *g* haploid gametes. Thus, the haploid cells could come together to form three distinct genotypes in the second generation: *YY*, *Yg*, or *gg* diploid cells. *YY* and *Yg* plants in the second generation had the yellow-seed phenotype due to the dominance of the *Y* allele. However, the *gg* plants exhibited the green-seed phenotype because they had two copies of the "*g*" recessive allele. And that is how the green-seed trait "reappeared" in the second generation.

First generation cross—parental genotypes *YY* and *gg*

Parental gametes	*g*	*g*
Y	*Yg*	*Yg*
Y	*Yg*	*Yg*

Yg = yellow

4/4 offspring

Second generation cross—parental genotypes *Yg* and *Yg*

Parental gametes	*Y*	*g*
Y	*YY*	*Yg*
g	*Yg*	*gg*

YY = yellow

Yg = yellow

gg = green

¾ yellow

¼ green

FIGURE 2.4 Punnett squares representing crosses between pea plants with yellow and green seeds in Mendel's hybridization experiments

In 1911, Reginald Punnett, a British geneticist, devised a simple and convenient method to predict the probability of possible genotypes that could arise from a given genetic cross using table diagrams called Punnett squares.[29] Mendel's experiments could be visualized as shown in Figure 2.4.

As demonstrated by the Punnett squares, there was a 100 percent probability that all of Mendel's first-generation hybrid plants would produce yellow seeds. In contrast, there was a 75 percent probability that the second-generation hybrid plants would produce yellow seeds, while only a 25 percent probability that the plants would yield green seeds. The Punnett squares, therefore, accurately predict Mendel's experimental 3:1 ratio of plants producing yellow and green seeds.

E *Life Is All About Expression*

The pivotal role of genes as repository sources of genetic information has been a recurring theme throughout this chapter. But the storage of information by itself is meaningless without something more.

Think about a library. In a strictly literal sense, a library is nothing more than a building where books are kept. The information that exists within the pages of those books may be of significant value, yet it cannot be appreciated and implemented unless people retrieve the information and use it for some specific purpose. The true value of the library, therefore, rests not on the fact that it is a refuge for knowledge, but rather on its function as a conduit of information that facilitates the *active* transfer, repurposing, application, and expression of knowledge.

Genes are no different in that respect. The information embedded in the genetic code must be retrieved and used—namely, *expressed*—in some specific manner. Thus, genes can be used as templates to create *gene products* such as other DNA and RNA molecules. And RNA molecules created from DNA templates can in turn be used as templates to create protein molecules, which are also gene products. The process of making gene products from select DNA sequences is known as *gene expression*. The flow and expression of genetic information from DNA to RNA and RNA to protein molecules applies to all living organisms and constitutes the *central dogma*[30] of molecular biology.

According to the central dogma, the information stored in DNA molecules can be perpetuated through the process of *replication*, which refers to the faithful copying of DNA sequences by a set of enzymes known as *DNA polymerases* prior to cell division. In addition, the information in DNA can be transferred —that is, used for gene expression—through the processes of transcription and translation.

Transcription involves the synthesis of a single-stranded RNA molecule from a double-stranded DNA molecule. During transcription, a set of enzymes called

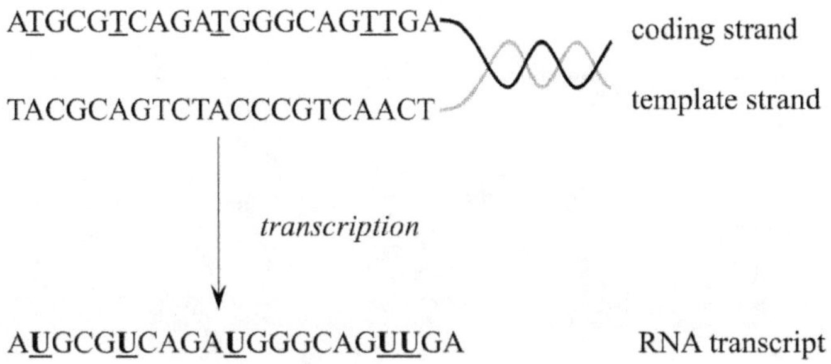

FIGURE 2.5 Transcription of *GENE1*

RNA polymerases synthesize a strand, or "*transcript*," of RNA. The transcript is complementary to one strand of DNA (the template strand) and identical to the other strand (the coding strand), except that Uracil replaces Thymine. Recall the *GENE1* sequence from earlier in this chapter. Figure 2.5 shows what *GENE1* looks like in its DNA double-stranded and transcribed RNA forms.

RNA transcript molecules are categorized according to their function and can be either *coding RNAs* or *noncoding RNAs* (ncRNAs). Coding RNAs, also known as *messenger RNAs* (mRNAs), are RNA transcripts that encode information to make proteins. Thus, mRNAs are intermediate nucleic acids. Their role is to bridge the transfer of genetic information from DNA to protein molecules.

Noncoding RNAs, as the name implies, are RNA molecules that do not encode genetic information to make proteins. They range in size from a few nucleotides to thousands of nucleotides long. There are many types of ncRNAs molecules, including ribosomal RNAs (rRNAs), transfer RNAs (tRNAs), microRNAs (miRNAs), small nuclear RNAs (snRNAs), long noncoding RNAs (lncRNAs), small interfering RNAs (siRNAs), piwi-interacting RNAs (piRNAs), small nucleolar RNAs (snoRNAs), CRISPR RNAs (crRNAs), and others, which we need not discuss here. Unlike mRNAs, whose primary role is to convey information for protein synthesis, ncRNAs perform a variety of other unique and important roles within cells.[31] They are fully functional on their own.

Translation refers to the process of protein synthesis using mRNA as the carrier of genetic information. During translation, the mRNA transcript is transported to a complex cellular particle called the *ribosome*, which is a molecular machine that reads and decodes the genetic information embedded in the mRNA and uses it to manufacture proteins.

Proteins, like nucleic acids, are a type of biological polymer. Proteins are made up of monomer subunits called *amino acids*. In essence, amino acids are to proteins what nucleotides are to DNA; they constitute the polymer's building blocks. A linear polymer chain of amino acids linked together is called a *polypeptide*, which arises when the amino acids are joined via peptide bonds. A *peptide bond*, is a type of chemical bond—it is much stronger than a hydrogen bond. When amino acids are

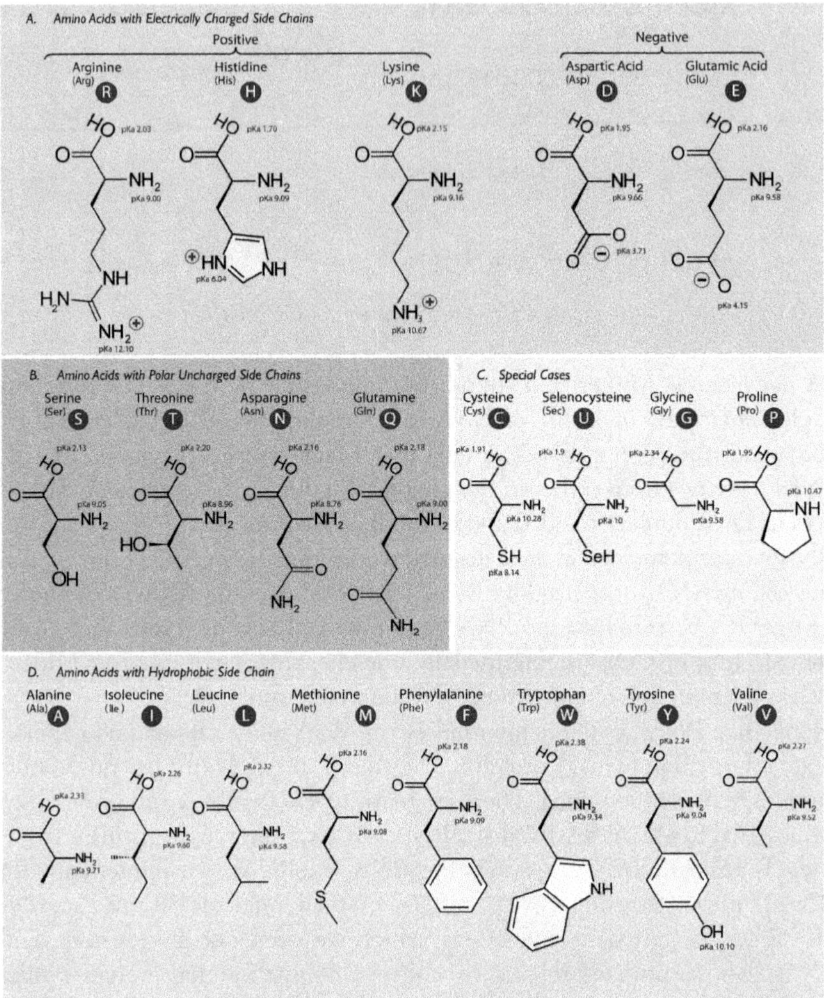

FIGURE 2.6 Chemical structures and abbreviations of the natural amino acids encoded by the eukaryotic genetic code for protein synthesis

linked together into a polypeptide chain, they are often referred to as "*residues*." All proteins comprise one or more polypeptide chains. Most genes encode the genetic information required to make at least one polypeptide.

The four letters of the genetic alphabet—A, T, C, G—encode twenty distinct amino acids. During translation, the ribosome reads the sequence of the mRNA molecule three bases at a time. Each coding triplet is called a *codon*,[32] which carries the genetic information necessary to incorporate any one of the twenty amino acids that can be used to make proteins. Because there are four letters in each type of nucleic acid, a total of sixty-four possible codons exist ($4^3 = 64$).[33] Sixty-one of those codons

AUG | CGU | CAG | AUG | GGC | AGU | UGA   mRNA transcript

↓ *translation*

Methionine—Arginine—Glutamine—Methionine—Glycine—Serine—STOP

M—R—Q—M—G—S   polypeptide

FIGURE 2.7 Translation of *GENE1*

encode one of the twenty amino acids, whereas the remaining three encode a stop codon that signals termination of the polypeptide chain. Correspondingly, the genetic code is truly a triplet code. Consider the *GENE1* transcript shown earlier, which we shall assume is an mRNA transcript for this exercise. Let us further break the molecule into triplets and translate it into a polypeptide as shown in Figure 2.7.

The end product of gene expression for the *GENE1* mRNA is MRQMGS, which represents the abbreviated sequence of a synthesized polypeptide consisting of six amino-acid residues. The UGA triplet at the end of the mRNA sequence encodes for a stop codon and, therefore, is not translated into a seventh residue. This process of translating mRNA transcripts into polypeptides is universal among all living organisms. As polypeptide chains are synthesized in the ribosome, they begin to fold into unique three-dimensional structures. The shape in which the protein folds is closely linked to how it functions.

Most proteins, like most genes, are relatively large molecules comprised of thousands of atoms. Due to their large molecular size, they are known as *macromolecules*. Genes, for example, are generally made up of thousands of nucleotides, while proteins typically range in size from a few hundred to thousands of amino acids.

Proteins are remarkable molecules. They perform an impressive array of unique and indispensable functions in living cells. Some, for instance, fulfill structural roles. Collagen is a type of structural protein that helps connective tissue—such as cartilage and bone tissue—maintain its shape and integrity.[34] Your hair and nails are made up of keratin—a tough, fibrous, structural protein.[35] Other proteins are involved in cellular transport. Hemoglobin transports oxygen in red blood cells throughout the body.[36] Transmembrane proteins facilitate the movement of small molecules and ions across cellular membranes.

Some proteins can also serve regulatory functions. For example, *transcription factors* are proteins that control gene expression by helping to turn genes on or off at appropriate times.[37] Other proteins may act as hormones that carry biological signals. Leptin, for example, is a hormone produced by fat cells that sends signals to the brain to help inhibit hunger when the body does not need energy.[38]

Furthermore, proteins may act as enzymes. An *enzyme* is a biological catalyst, namely, a molecule that can speed up the rate of, and catalyze, specific biochemical reactions. Enzymes are ubiquitous and perform countless biochemical reactions in all living organisms. We have already discussed a few in this chapter. For example, recall that RNA polymerases are enzymes that catalyze the synthesis of RNA molecules. And in the next chapter, we will discuss CRISPR–Cas9, an enzyme that triggers DNA double-stranded breaks.

In the early 1940s, scientists proposed the existence of a special relationship between genes and enzymes that became known as the one gene-one enzyme hypothesis.[39] The idea was that each gene encodes information needed to make only one enzyme. This has been proven partially correct, for we now know that some genes carry information to make one or more proteins that are not and do not act as enzymes, while other genes encode information to make ncRNA molecules that are not translated into proteins (in other words, they are not protein-coding genes).

To summarize, the process of gene expression involves the making of gene products. Transcription refers to the synthesis of various types of RNA transcripts from DNA molecules. And translation refers to the synthesis of polypeptides or protein molecules from mRNA transcripts. The flow of genetic information along these biological molecules implicates active cellular processes. Genes are repository sources of genetic information, but the information they carry must be actively expressed in order to fulfill their biological purpose.

A few caveats are worth mentioning. Generally speaking, the flow of information within the central dogma of molecular biology is unidirectional. This means that typically DNA is used to make RNA, and RNA is in turn used to make proteins. The direction of the flow of genetic information does not occur in reverse. Thus, proteins or RNA molecules cannot ordinarily be used as templates to make DNA. This principle is not absolute because in special cases involving *retroviruses*—a class of viruses that have RNA genes—it is possible indeed to make DNA molecules from RNA templates. HIV, the virus that causes AIDS, for instance, is a retrovirus that uses an enzyme called *reverse transcriptase* to literally reverse the process of transcription, so as to synthesize DNA molecules from its viral RNA genome.[40] Once the new DNA is made, the virus inserts it into the host-cell's genome, thereby forcing the infected cell to make new viral DNA copies. The retrovirus hacks the biological machinery of the host and uses it for its own benefit.

The foregoing overview of the central dogma of molecular biology will arm you with the knowledge requisite to navigate subsequent chapters of the book. I would be remiss, however, if I failed to note the vast complexity and depth of scientific knowledge beyond the surface we have scratched in this chapter. For purposes of our discussion, we need not venture into finer details of RNA splicing and processing, cell signaling, viral replication and integration, gene regulation, and a myriad of additional processes of molecular biology, genetics, biochemistry, and other related disciplines.

III NATURE IS NOT PERFECT

Despite the marvel and precision associated with replication, transcription, and other cellular processes involved in cell division and gene expression, nature is not perfect. These processes are sometimes error-prone. During DNA replication, for instance, mutations can rarely arise when the enzymes responsible for making copies of DNA introduce changes in the sequence of the newly synthesized DNA molecules. Alterations that occur in the sequence of molecules that carry genetic information are known as *mutations*. All living organisms—including humans—acquire mutations, which accumulate over time in the organisms' cells. Without doubt, you and I are both mutants!

The first empirical evidence for the existence of mutations dates back to the early twentieth century. In the early 1900s, Thomas H. Morgan and his team studied genetics in fruit flies. *Wildtype* fruit flies—the term "wildtype" refers to the most common phenotype for an organism in a natural breeding population—normally have brilliant red eyes. Morgan had been keeping a pedigree stock of fruit flies contained in his laboratory for over a year when he suddenly noticed that one white-eyed fly had inexplicably appeared among all the red-eyed flies.[41] To study the genetic basis of the white-eye trait, Morgan bred the white-eyed fly with other red-eyed flies and discovered that the trait was heritable. His experiments demonstrated that chromosomes carried the gene encoding the red-eye trait, which had been mutated into the allele encoding the white-eye trait—an entirely novel phenotype. Importantly, his experiments established that mutations can appear spontaneously and yet still be heritable.

A *The Good, the Bad, and the Middle Ground*

Most mutations are benign; that is, they do not cause harmful or deleterious effects on the survival of living organisms. In fact, your genome accumulates mutations every time your cells divide. The rate of mutation varies greatly among different types of organisms according to their genome size and other factors.[42]

Sometimes, mutations can have advantageous effects. For example, people carrying certain mutations in a gene called *SLC30A8* are almost two-thirds less likely to develop type-2 diabetes than those who carry the wildtype version of the gene.[43] A mutation in the *CCR5* gene, which we will discuss in more detail later in the book, has been shown to confer resistance to the HIV virus.[44] Mutations in the *EPAS1* and *MTHFR* genes have been associated with adaptation to high altitude in people from Tibet.[45] Beneficial genetic mutations can, thus, play a role in the adaption of living organisms to disease as well as environmental changes around them. Biological diversity depends greatly on mutations, which are critical for evolution.

But mutations can sometimes lead to serious harmful effects. Consider the molecular and genetic basis of Cystic Fibrosis (CF), a heritable genetic disease that progressively damages the lungs and digestive system in those affected by it. A mutation in the *CFTR* gene leads to the deletion of one amino acid—a phenylalanine residue at position 508, referred to as CFTRΔF508—from the protein receptor encoded by *CFTR*.[46] At the molecular level, the ΔF508 deletion causes the misfolding and premature degradation of the protein. It is the most common mutation associated with the disease in homozygous individuals suffering from the disease.

Sickle-cell disease (SCD) offers another example of the harmful physiological effects stemming from a mutation. SCD is a disease in which malfunctioning red blood cells lose the ability to carry oxygen properly, assume an abnormal shape, and die prematurely. A genetic basis for SCD involving the mutation of a hemoglobin-encoding gene was proposed in 1949.[47] Hemoglobin is the protein that carries oxygen in red blood cells. We now know that the disease is caused by a single Adenine to Thymine (A→T) substitution in the beta-globin gene that encodes for the sixth amino acid in the beta chain of a hemoglobin protein.[48] In individuals with SCD, the amino-acid sequence at position 6 of hemoglobin changes from a glutamate to a valine residue. Under low-oxygen conditions, such as during strenuous exercise or when performing activities that cause oxygen levels in the blood to drop, red blood cells can no longer assume a normal biconcave-disc shape; they instead become distorted, fragile, and change into a sickle-like form as shown in Figure 2.8. Red blood cells with the aberrant shape of the protein become hardened, often clog as they pass through small blood vessels, and rupture more easily. The cells are unable to fulfill their function of delivering oxygen to tissues and can lead to heart attack, stroke, and excruciating pain for those homozygous individuals suffering from the condition.

Sometimes mutations can have advantageous and harmful consequences simultaneously depending on how they are inherited. SCD, for instance, can be quite lethal for people who are homozygous for the faulty version of the gene. However, the same mutation that renders red blood cells unable to properly carry oxygen in blood can also confer protection against the parasite that causes malaria.[49] Due to this protective characteristic, the mutation is very common among certain human populations of African descent. Heterozygous individuals are, therefore, resistant to malaria and do not exhibit the health problems associated with SCD. The one normal copy of the hemoglobin-encoding gene they possess allows for sufficient production of normal red blood cells, while the mutant allele affords a level of natural protection against an infectious parasite.

B *Change Comes in Many Forms*

So, mutations occur rarely, are mostly benign, and can sometimes have beneficial or harmful effects, or both. But how exactly do mutations affect gene expression? To answer this question, let us return to our *GENE1* sequence.

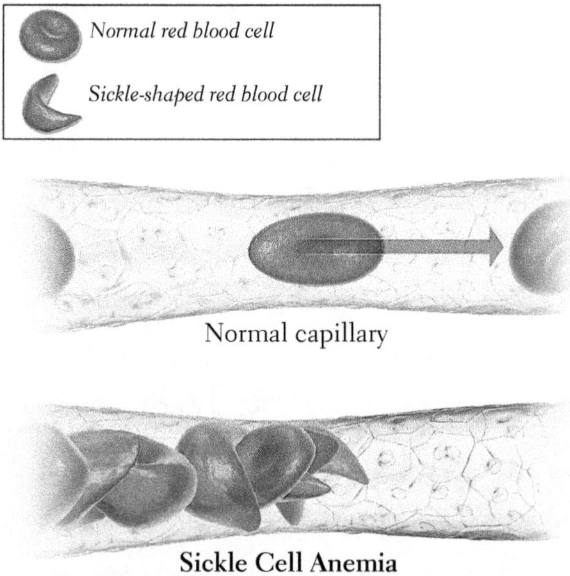

FIGURE 2.8 Red blood cells in Sickle-Cell Disease

Normal red blood cells (round) flow easily through capillaries (small blood vessels). In individuals with SCD, however, red blood cells that contain an abnormal form of hemoglobin (the blood oxygen-transport protein) become sickle-shaped. Sickle cells cannot move through capillaries as easily as normal cells and cause blockages, which prevent oxygen from reaching the tissues and cause severe pain and organ damage.

Assume that the *GENE1* allele [1] sequence came first into existence. As time passed, evolutionary forces introduced mutations that gave rise to alleles [2] and [3]. Figure 2.9 shows how the mutations affect the expression of *GENE1*.

As show in the left column of Figure 2.9, allele [2] acquired an A→T *point mutation* in the DNA sequence. A point mutation occurs when one base within a sequence of DNA is substituted with another base. The transcribed RNA is different from the allele [1] RNA transcript because the modified T became U during the process of transcription. The mutation in the RNA sequence also changed the codon from CAG in allele [1], which encodes for a glutamic acid (Q) residue, to CUG in allele [2], which encodes for the amino acid lysine (L) in the new polypeptide sequence. Thus, the A→T mutation in allele [2] results in a gene product that is different from that of the *GENE1* [1] allele.

Allele [3], as shown in the right column, acquired two distinct point mutations (GC→AT) at the underlined position during evolution. The RNA transcript sequence changed from GC→AU according to the rules of transcription we discussed earlier in the chapter. These two mutations also changed the codon from

***GENE1* allele [1]**

ATG | CGT | CAG | ATG | GGC | AGT | TGA	coding DNA
AUG | CGU | CAG | AUG | GGC | AGU | UGA	transcribed RNA
M—R—Q—M—G—S	translated polypeptide

***GENE1* allele [2]**	***GENE1* allele [3]**
ATGCGTC**T**GATGGGCAGTTGA	ATGCGTCAGATGG**AT**AGTTGA
AUGCGUCUGAUGGGCAGUUGA	AUGCGUCAGAUGGAUAGUUGA
M—R—L—M—G—S	M—R—Q—M—D—S

FIGURE 2.9 The effect of mutations on gene expression

Small sequence changes in the *GENE1* alleles can lead to different gene products.

GGC in allele [1], which encodes for a glycine (G) amino acid, to GAU, which encodes for an amino acid called aspartic acid (D). Thus, the GC→AT double mutation in allele [3] results in a gene product that is also different from those of the *GENE1* [1] and [2] alleles.

Now suppose a new fourth allele with the following sequence has evolved:

[4] ATGCGTCAGATGGGTAGTTGA

When compared to allele [3], this new allele [4] exhibits a single A→G substitution, which is underlined in the sequence. Nothing else has changed. However, when compared to allele [1], the A→G mutation actually reverted the sequence back to the original form at that position. The only difference between alleles [1] and [4] is now a C→T substitution, which was carried over from the double mutant [3] allele and is shown as T. How will gene expression of allele [4] fare in comparison to the others?

[4]	ATG | CGT | CAG | ATG | GGT | AGT | TGA	DNA
	AUG | CGU | CAG | AUG | GGU | AGU | UGA	RNA
	M–R–Q–M–G–S	polypeptide

Allele [4] acquired the A→G substitution relative to allele [3]. This mutation changed the RNA codon from GAU in allele [3], which encodes for an aspartic acid (D), to GGU, which encodes for the amino acid glycine (G). Thus, the A→G point mutation in allele [4] resulted in a gene product that is different from the *GENE1* [3] allele but, surprisingly, is exactly the same as the product of gene expression from the original [1] allele! This type of mutation, which reverses the effects of a prior mutation, is called a *reversion*.

The foregoing example illustrates why most mutations that occur in an organism's genome are benign. Although the DNA and RNA sequences in alleles [1] and [4] are different, the process of gene expression yields the same protein product. This phenomenon arises from the redundancy of the genetic code, which has evolved to encode only twenty amino acids from a repertoire of sixty-four unique triplet codons, as shown earlier in Figure 2.2. The repetitive nature of the genetic code guarantees that several codons can add the same amino acid in a polypeptide chain.

Mutations are not limited to base substitutions. Some mutations occur as *insertions*, in which one or more bases are added at a particular locus. Other mutations appear as *deletions*, in which one or more bases are removed from a given DNA sequence. Sometimes insertions and deletions can occur simultaneously—for example, when some bases are removed and replaced with new ones, or when bases at a particular site are removed and bases at another site are inserted. These mutations are called *indels*.

When a very large segment of DNA—such as a large region of a chromosome—is transferred from one locus to another, the mutation is called a *translocation*. Chromosomal translocations are frequently associated with leukemias, lymphomas, and other types of cancers that ensue following the fusion of a segment of one chromosome to another.[50] Mutations can also involve the *duplication* of certain DNA sequences. Huntington's disease is an example of a neurodegenerative disorder associated with a duplication repeat expansion in a region of the *HTT* gene, which encodes the huntingtin protein.[51] The more repeats that accumulate in the *HTT* locus, the more severe and life-threatening form of Huntington's disease that will develop in the individual.

Mutations can also be classified according to the effect they exert on gene expression. For instance, a *missense mutation* occurs when one or more base substitutions alter the sequence of a single codon, which in turn leads to a single amino-acid change in a polypeptide sequence. Alleles [2] and [3] of the *GENE1* exercise above involve missense mutations. Changes in the DNA sequence led to alterations in the synthesized polypeptide from MRQMGS in allele [1] to MRLMGS and MRQMDS in alleles [2] and [3], respectively. In contrast, a *silent mutation* refers to a change in a DNA sequence that otherwise yields the same amino-acid product as the unmodified DNA sequence and, therefore, has no discernible effect on an organism's phenotype. The case of the expression of allele [4] represents an example of a silent mutation. Although the DNA and RNA sequences of alleles [1] and [4] are different, the translated polypeptide for both allelic forms still ended up being MRQMGS.

A *null mutation* is an alteration in a DNA sequence that completely abolishes or inactivates the function of a gene. Such a mutation often results in what is known as a *gene knockout*, which is a term used to indicate that the function of a given gene has essentially been "knocked out" of the organism's genome. And a *frameshift mutation*, which we will discuss in more detail in the DNA repair section of this chapter, refers to an alteration that shifts the sequence arrangement of base triplets in a manner that changes the codons used during protein synthesis. Frameshift mutations can arise from insertions, deletions, or duplications and typically result in truncated or nonfunctional protein products.

Lastly, it is important to note that mutations can not only arise spontaneously or be inherited. They can also be induced via treatment or exposure to certain agents that damage DNA known as *mutagens*. Some toxic chemical mutagens react with DNA molecules to cause changes in the chemical structure of DNA. For example, tobacco products and smoke contain chemical mutagens known as tobacco-specific nitrosamines (TSNA).[52] TSNAs can wreak havoc in the cells of specific tissues and are well established as compounds that induce lung, oral, esophageal, and many other types of cancers.[53] Another chemical compound called ethyl methanesulfonate (EMS) also reacts with DNA to induce random genetic mutations.[54] EMS mutates primarily by targeting Guanine bases in DNA, which undergo EMS-induced alterations, but the mutagen is also capable of causing dangerous breaks in chromosomes.[55]

Radiation is also a powerful mutagen. High-frequency electromagnetic radiation,[56] x-rays,[57] gamma-rays, alpha particles, and ultraviolet (UV) radiation—also known as UV light[58]—are all types of radiation that act directly on DNA or interfere with the normal function of DNA-repair enzymes. High-energy radiation induces genetic lesions and other aberrations that lead to genomic instability, cancers, cell death, and other deleterious effects.[59]

IV A REVOLUTION OF MOLECULAR PROPORTIONS

Following the pivotal discovery of genes, DNA, and chromosomes as integral components of heredity during the late 1800s and early 1900s, the notion of manipulating genetic material took root in popular culture. Numerous works in scientific romance and science fiction began to incorporate peculiar themes of biological engineering and genetic manipulation during the 1910s, 1920s, and 1930s.[60] Some portrayals of genetic manipulation elicited innocuous sentiments. In the novel *The Blue Germ* (1918), a microscopic bacterium undergoes genetic manipulation of its chromosomes before spreading through an English population.[61] The engineered bacteria conferred immortality to humans exposed to it. Other portrayals, however, were ominous and instilled fears among the general public. In 1932, *Brave New World* famously depicted a dystopian society six centuries in the future where genetically modified humans are engineered and bred into social hierarchies.[62] Behavioral conditioning and eugenics are main themes in the novel, which warns of a future in which technological advances are misused to strip people of their freedom and humanity.

By the 1940s, the term *genetic engineering* was introduced in the scientific world, perhaps as early as 1941 during a lecture on sexual reproduction in yeast in Poland.[63] And genetic engineering—as a concept—was becoming more common in science fiction. For instance, human genetic engineering and selective breeding for eugenic purposes were main themes in *Beyond This Horizon* (1942), a narrative in which modified humans are the norm and nonmodified humans become the minority.[64] By the end of the decade, genetic engineering was evolving to denote the purposeful manipulation of genetic material.[65] At the time, the term referred to the molecular surgical cutting and stitching of chromosomes to remove or rearrange sets of genes. Soon thereafter, the term was incorporated into the science fiction genre via contemporary works such as *Dragon's Island* (1951).[66]

These works cemented the notion of genetic manipulation in science fiction and popular culture. But genetic engineering was an exclusive province of science fiction. That began to change with breakthrough discoveries that eventually allowed scientists to exercise more control over two critical elements: the ability to (1) cut DNA at desired sites and (2) repair the cuts. These two factors marked the genesis of modern molecular biology and biotechnology, which ultimately enabled gene editing.

A *Behold the Cutters*

Since long before humans inhabited the Earth, bacteria and viruses have been waging deadly wars against each other. Many viruses need to infect bacteria in order to survive. Viral infections, however, are too costly to bacteria, which often die as a result of viral invasion. Over millions of years of evolution, bacteria have thus developed defense mechanisms to stave off and destroy viruses.

This epic evolutionary war had gone unnoticed for the bulk of human history until bizarre findings concerning the apparent resistance or reduced efficiency of viral infection in some bacterial hosts were published in the early 1950s.[67] Somehow, bacteria had developed special mechanisms to adapt to viral attacks and degrade harmful viral DNA.[68] The findings led to the hypothesis of the existence of *restriction-modification* (RM) defense systems, which purportedly restricted the spread of viral infection and reprogrammed bacterial immunity by acting as effective barriers to viral DNA uptake into bacterial genomes.

As more scientists began to study RM systems, it became clear that bacteria produced certain enzymes that could detect and destroy viral DNA before it caused harmful effects. The enzymes were soon dubbed as *restriction enzymes*, or restriction endonucleases.

Nucleases are enzymes that degrade nucleic acids—either DNA or RNA. They do so, for instance, by breaking up the bonds that link nucleotides in a continuous double-stranded DNA molecule. They have the opposite role of polymerases. Nucleases are often grouped into two categories depending on how they cut up foreign DNA targets. An *endonuclease* is a type of nuclease that cuts within a DNA molecule. An *exonuclease*, on the other hand, is a type of nuclease that "chews up" DNA molecules from the ends.

Think back to the freight train illustration in the prior section. Let's say the train has one hundred wagons. Endonucleases could cut anywhere except at the corners; say between the nineteenth and twentieth wagons, or even between the ninety-third and ninety-fourth wagons—anywhere within the train. Exonucleases will instead target the wagons starting at the ends of the train; they could start by "chewing up" the first and one-hundredth wagons, then the second and ninety-ninth wagons, and so on. The exonuclease could cut from one end of the train or both ends, whereas the endonuclease always cuts DNA at an internal site.

The first restriction endonucleases were characterized in the late 1960s.[69] Unfortunately, those enzymes cut DNA at random sites and were not precise for any genetic sequences. The scientific community quickly realized the potential benefits of using more precise "cutter" DNA enzymes. A significant moment for the future of biotechnology came in 1970 when the first sequence-specific restriction enzyme was characterized.[70] The proof of concept that a protein can trigger sequence-specific, double-stranded cuts on DNA molecules truly changed the course of modern biotechnology.

Imagine you wish to sell your home. You have a spacious backyard with shrubs and a variety of other plants. The flora in your yard has become overgrown and diminishes your home's curb appeal, to the point where it detracts from the value of the property. You already envision how the yard should look, but you lack the tools to carry out that vision. You then stumble upon an invention that allows you to cut shrubbery and other plants, except the invention is not precise and will only cut the plants at random places. That tool would not be very useful to you because cutting the plants too short might kill them. In addition, if all of your plants are trimmed unevenly at random places, it will not do much to increase the home's curb appeal.

What you need is a tool that allows you to trim plants with precision so that you can carry out your vision. In a similar way, the discovery of restriction enzymes opened up an entire new world of possibilities for researchers who had been waiting eagerly for the molecular tools necessary to investigate the function of DNA sequences in all sorts of living organisms. Restriction enzymes finally enabled scientists to cut DNA molecules with more precision, which meant that researchers could, for the first time, isolate and study the role of specific fragments of DNA—such as genes—in the laboratory.

To date, nearly 4,000 restriction enzymes—with various specific recognition sequences—have been biochemically or genetically characterized.[71] Restriction enzymes have become indispensable tools for molecular biology. The enzymes enabled the development of methods to clone DNA and propelled a swift expansion of knowledge concerning molecular genetics and gene expression that swept through the 1970s and 1980s. For the discovery of restriction enzymes, three scientists shared the 1978 Nobel Prize in Physiology or Medicine.[72]

B *Heal Thy Cuts*

The restriction-enzyme quantum leap underscored the requirement of inducing DNA double-stranded breaks as the critical first step for targeted genetic manipulation. However, as time passed, it became apparent that these breaks in DNA were highly deleterious.[73]

As we discussed previously, DNA is constantly susceptible to all kinds of damage from spontaneous mutations, as well as physical, chemical, and a myriad of environmental factors. Double-stranded breaks on DNA—particularly in *eukaryotes* (organisms whose cells have a defined nucleus enclosed within a membrane, such as animals, plants, and humans)—are among the most hazardous type of DNA damage known.

From a cellular standpoint, a DNA break is not significantly different from a gunshot wound. Research into military combat zones, for example, has shown that approximately 90 percent of combat casualties occur before the injured individual reaches a medical treatment facility, and that the vast majority of those deaths stem primarily from severe loss of blood.[74] Hemorrhaging—not the bullet or shrapnel—is the major threat. Although the human body has developed mechanisms to repair wounds and prevent blood loss by assembling coagulant factors at a cut or puncture site, it is unfortunately unable to stop the bleeding when the wound is too large. Sustained hemorrhaging eventually lowers an individual's systolic pressure to critical levels, thereby depriving the body's organs of blood and oxygen. Death ultimately follows. Cells respond similarly to DNA breaks. Cuts in the DNA do not immediately lead to cell death. But the cuts must be repaired promptly or the cell will not survive.

Simply put, a broken DNA molecule is a peril to the genetic constitution and survival of the cell. DNA double-stranded breaks promote genome instability;[75] interfere with, or completely block, the pivotal processes of replication and transcription;[76] lead to chromosomal rearrangements—such as inversions and translocations—associated with cancers and other diseases;[77] and ultimately induce cell death, also known as *apoptosis*.[78] Accordingly, due to the highly hazardous nature of DNA double-stranded breaks, complex mechanisms to deploy specialized macromolecules for purposes of minimizing and repairing an injured DNA site have evolved within cells.

To date, numerous DNA repair mechanisms have been characterized. Some of these mechanisms—such as Base Excision Repair, Direct Reversal, Nucleotide Excision Repair, Mismatch Repair, and others—act on single-stranded DNA breaks, which we need not discuss throughout this book.[79] In the case of double-stranded breaks, DNA repair can follow two primary pathways: Homology-Directed Repair and Nonhomologous End Joining.

1 Striving for Precision

Homology-Directed Repair (HDR) is the most optimal type of DNA double-stranded break repair pathway. It is significantly more precise but requires the presence of an undamaged, homologous, donor template for repair.[80] The repair template must have substantial sequence identity to the region of damaged DNA. The most common form of HDR is *Homologous Recombination* (HR), which involves the genetic recombination, or "crossing-over,"[81] of regions of DNA that are exchanged between identical or highly similar DNA molecules.

As indicated earlier, the diploid cells of an organism have two sets of chromosomes—one *homologous chromosome* from each parent. The chromosomes are called homologous because they have the same number of genes at the same genetic loci (although each chromosome may have different alleles). Accordingly, before cell division takes place, a diploid cell has a homologous donor template—a chromosome—available for repair, in case one is needed. So, if the maternal chromosome breaks, the cell can repair the break using the paternal chromosome as template and vice-versa.

Following DNA replication, diploid cells have another potential template available for repair. As we discussed previously, the process of replication culminates in the formation of an identical copy of each parental chromosome. These identical copies are called *sister chromatids*. Both maternal and paternal chromosomes each have their own unique sister chromatids. Like homologous chromosomes, sister chromatids also have the same number of genes at the same genetic loci. However, because they are the product of DNA replication, they also carry the same alleles as their respective progenitor chromosomes. If the maternal chromosome breaks, the cell can repair the break using the maternal sister chromatid—an exact, instead of highly similar, replica!—as the template. Since sister chromatids have the same number of genes at the same genetic loci, *and* carry the same alleles as the progenitor chromosome, they are often preferred as templates for DNA repair.[82]

Due to the requirement of identical or near identical sequence homology between the template and the damaged DNA, the HDR pathway ensures highly accurate rates of double-stranded DNA repair. However, cells do not always have a sister chromatid or homologous chromosome available to serve as templates for DNA repair. In such cases, cells use an alternative mechanism to repair DNA double-stranded breaks known as Nonhomologous End Joining.

2 Repair at Any Cost

Nonhomologous End Joining (NHEJ), as the name implies, is a DNA repair mechanism that involves rejoining, or religating, the broken ends of a DNA molecule. Unlike HDR, NHEJ does not depend on sequence homology or a template to repair the injured site. The ends of the DNA fragments need not be complementary to each other.[83] The absence of a prerequisite of homology for repair means NHEJ can quickly and efficiently mend any type of DNA break when a template is not available.[84] But this characteristic also comes at a high cost because the process is inherently error-prone and can easily introduce small, random, insertion or deletion mutations that are capable of disrupting gene expression.

You may be asking: If HDR is more precise and the preferred mechanism for DNA repair, why might a cell choose the error-prone NHEJ repair pathway over HDR instead of just waiting until a homologous template becomes available? To answer that question, let us look back at the gunshot wound case that was introduced to discuss DNA repair at the beginning of Section IV.B.

Imagine a solider has just been shot in the leg during the course of a military combat operation. There is a high likelihood that the nearest medical treatment facility is far away and no practical means of transportation are available, especially as the battle continues to develop. An army medic immediately comes to the soldier's assistance and realizes that he is losing blood at an alarming rate. The medic understands that the soldier's life will be in serious peril, unless the bleeding can be kept under control. He proceeds to wrap his leg above the wound using a dirty rag as a tourniquet, while applying constant pressure with his fingers on the wound. The medic realizes that the circumstances render the soldier susceptible to bacterial infection, scarring, and other potential long-term consequences from using the unsterile rag and placing his fingers on the wound. However, the medic's top priority is to spare the soldier's life. Stopping the bleeding at any cost outweighs the risk of bacterial infection, which could be addressed at a later time.

Double-stranded breaks on DNA pose just as much of a threat to cellular life and function as does the bleeding to the soldier's life. Treating the gunshot wound in a hospital facility with the use of sterile equipment would be the best option. Unfortunately, the medic must do what is necessary to try to keep the soldier alive. In the same way, repairing a DNA break via the highly accurate HDR pathway would be the best possible option for the cell. But upon detection of a DNA break, the cell is in survival mode. Waiting for a homologous template to become available is far too risky, and the cell will repair the lesion via the NHEJ pathway to protect the broken DNA molecules from degradation, even if that leads to insertion and deletion mutations that could impact the process of gene expression.

Earlier in this chapter, we examined how different types of mutations can have various effects on gene expression, as well as why most mutations that are incorporated into a genome do not, in fact, lead to dangerous consequences. In addition, we introduced the concept of frameshift mutations, which refer to genetic alterations that shift the sequence arrangement of base triplets in a manner that changes the codons used during protein synthesis. DNA repair via the NHEJ pathway is a major source of frameshift mutations, which arise from base insertions or deletions at the site of injury. To illustrate how NHEJ can affect gene expression and lead to truncated or nonfunctional protein products, let us revisit our *GENE1* sequence.

Recall *GENE1* and its gene products, which result from the cellular processes of transcription and translation. We will use the gene expression of the wildtype allele [1] as a reference point in Figure 2.10.

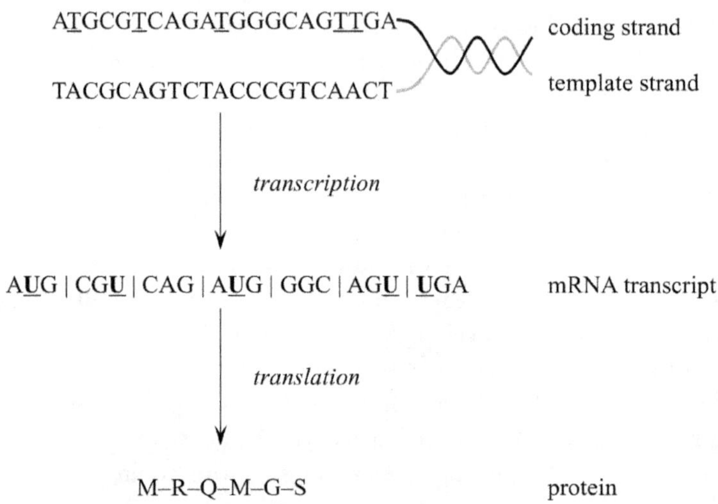

FIGURE 2.10 Expression of *GENE1* allele [1]

Now, imagine that a nuclease or some mutagen triggers a double-stranded break of the *GENE1* molecule. The break is staggered and renders the broken molecules susceptible to degradation. In fact, two bases (CT, represented by the double-strikethrough text in Figure 2.11) have already been degraded before the repair machinery arrived at the cut site. The cell senses danger and must repair the breaks.

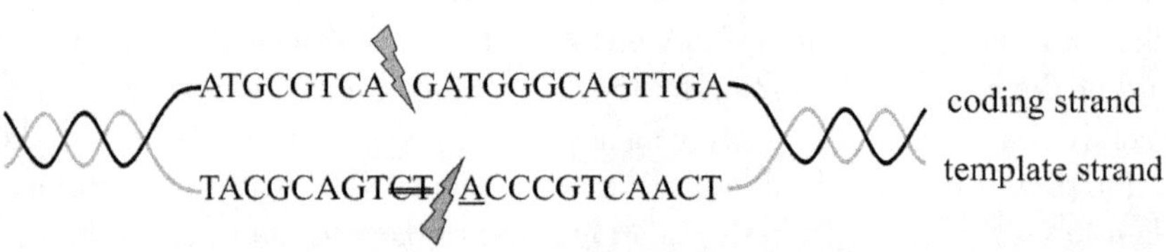

Following the double-stranded lesion, there are now two loose fragments of DNA.

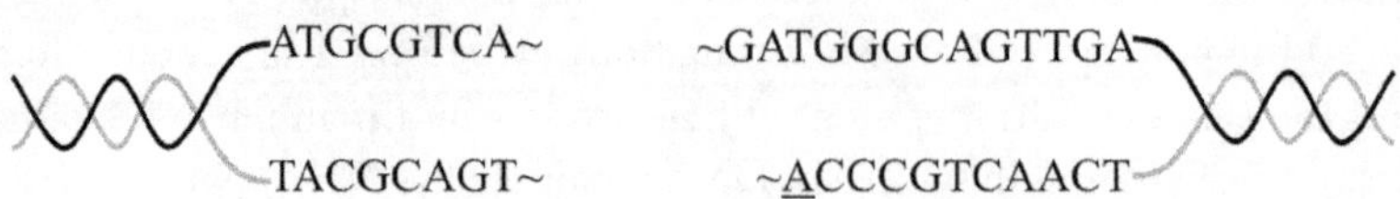

FIGURE 2.11 Repair of a double-stranded break at the *GENE1* sequence leads to mutations that give rise to a new allele

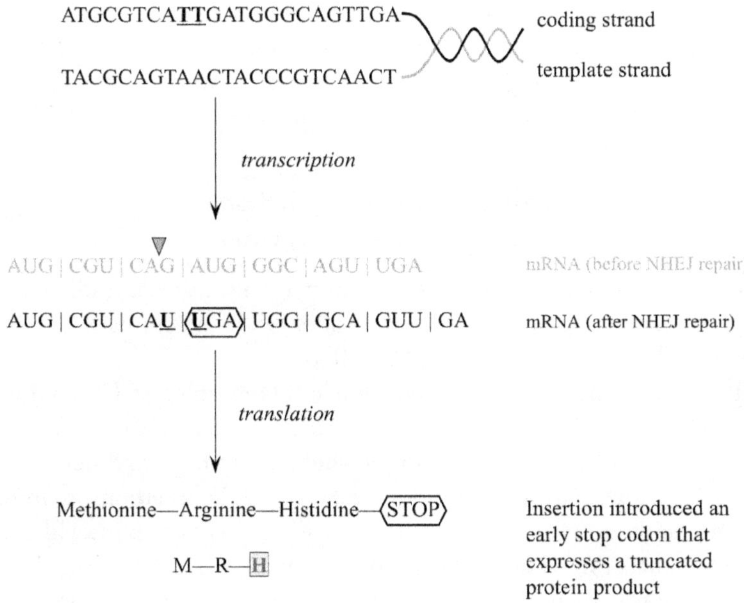

FIGURE 2.12 Expression of *GENE1* allele [5]

The new allele, which arose following NHEJ repair of a DNA break at the *GENE1* locus, encodes a truncated protein product that has lost its biological function.

The repair NHEJ machinery arrives and protects the ends from further degradation, except the ~~GT~~ bases from the template strand have now been deleted (in other words, degraded). Because there is no homologous template available, the cell cannot tell what the original sequence was before the break and tries to repair the lesion as best it can. It begins to bring the cut strands closer into proximity and is suddenly faced with the lack of base complementarity due to the ~~GT~~ deletion. As the cellular machinery scans the damage, it detects an Adenine at the end of one of the template fragments (underlined on the right in Figure 2.11) and so a Thymine is synthesized into the coding strand to complement the Adenine base. On the left side, the cell makes a mistake and introduces another Thymine on the coding strand and then begins to fill up the remaining gaps on the template strand based on the rules of base complementarity. After religation of the broken ends, the *GENE1* sequence has undergone genetic modification that led to insertion of two Thymine bases in the coding strand (shown as bold and underlined TT in Figure 2.12). This gives rise to a new *GENE1* allele [5] in the genetic pool. The allele must now undergo the process of gene expression, which is shown in Figure 2.12.

As shown above, the insertion of two bases (**TT**) that resulted from NHEJ repair altered the *GENE1 open reading frame* (ORF). An ORF refers to a continuous stretch of nucleic acid sequence that begins with a start codon, ends with a stop codon, and can be translated into a protein product. Every sentence, for instance, has a reading frame, which exists in the context of the arrangement of letters in the sentence and how that arrangement can be interpreted by the reader. Consider the following sentences. The first exhibits a proper reading frame, whereas the second has shifted one letter to the left:

(1) The cell needs to repair a break or risks cell death.
(2) Thec elln eedst or epaira b reako rr isksc elld eath.

Notice how the second sentence makes no sense just because the reading frame was shifted by one letter. Insertions and deletions alter ORFs in a similar way, which can yield gene products with altered or lost function.

The **TT** insertion in the above *GENE1* allele [5] introduced a Glutamine (Q) to Histidine (H) substitution mutation at the third amino-acid position (Q3H—this is the common scientific notation for amino-acid substitutions and denotes, in this case, that a Q residue at the third position became H). The insertion also introduced a premature stop codon (UGA) that led to translation of a polypeptide with sequence MRH, rather than the wildtype MRQMGS sequence. Thus, the small insertion resulted in a truncated protein product. Truncated proteins are often nonfunctional depending on how much of the protein sequence got cut off. If *GENE1* has an important functional role in the cell, the "loss of function" of the new polypeptide may have significant biological and physiological repercussions.

* * *

The scientific breakthroughs and insights from research into sequence-specific restriction enzymes and DNA repair mechanisms, which constitute the two critical elements that facilitated modern genome editing, marked the genesis of modern molecular biology and biotechnology. At last, researchers had stumbled upon the tools—although rudimentary at the time—that would allow them to manipulate DNA molecules in the lab and study the function of specific genetic sequences. Scientists built upon that research throughout the 1980s, 1990s, and 2000s and developed a set of primitive genome-editing tools, which we will examine in Chapter 4. But first, let us lay an interpretive foundation that will import meaning and clarity into the scope of the term genome editing.

Notes

1 *See* CRISPR: The Gene-Editing Tool Revolutionizing Biomedical Research, https://www.cbsnews.com/news/crispr-the-gene-editing-tool-revolutionizing-biomedical-research/.

2 *See* Elizabeth Pennisi, *The CRISPR Craze*, 341 SCIENCE 833 (2013).

3 Paul Enríquez, *Genome Editing and the Jurisprudence of Scientific Empiricism*, 19 VAND. J. ENT. & TECH. L. 603, 618 (2017) [hereinafter Enríquez, *Genome Editing*].

4 Charles Darwin & Alfred Wallace, *On the Tendency of Species to Form Varieties; and on the Perpetuation of Varieties and Species by Natural Means of Selection*, 3 J. Proc. Linnean Soc'y London Zoology 45 (1858). Over the years, controversy has surrounded the Wallace-Darwin codiscovery of the theory of evolution by natural selection, credit for which has been suggested to belong to Wallace alone. The controversy stems primarily from the fact that Wallace had sent a draft of an unpublished essay that laid out a version of the theory of evolution by natural selection to Darwin and asked for his review in confidence. Upon reviewing Wallace's essay, Darwin realized that Wallace's work, if published at the time, would have compromised the priority of some of his own work. Darwin had influential close friends in scientific circles, who ultimately convinced him to publish extracts of his work on evolution alongside Wallace's essay at a meeting of the Linnean Society of London. Whatever the case may be concerning Wallace and Darwin's contributions, there is no question that Wallace's essay triggered prompt publication of the theory of evolution in 1858 and Darwin's own book nearly a year later in 1859. For a more detailed account of this controversy, see Paul Enríquez, *CRISPR GMOs*, 18 N.C. J.L. & Tech. 432, 454–55 (2017).

5 Charles Darwin, On the Origin of Species by Means of Natural Selection, or the Preservation of Favoured Races in the Struggle for Life (1859).

6 *See* Gregor Mendel, *Versuche über Plflanzenhybriden* [*Experiments in Plant Hybridization*], Abhandlungen 3–47 (1866), Read at Meetings of the Brünn Natural History Society (Feb. 8 & Mar. 8, 1865), *reprinted in* Gregor Mendel, Experiments in Plant Hybridization 33–41 (1963).

7 *Id.*

8 Enríquez, *Genome Editing*, *supra* note 3, at 618.

9 Thomas H. Morgan, *The Relation of Genetics to Physiology and Medicine*, *in* Nobel Lectures, Physiology or Medicine 1922–1941, at 313–15 (Elsevier Publishing Co. 1965), http://www.nobelprize.org/nobel_prizes/medicine/laureates/1933/morgan-lecture.pdf (original lecture by Thomas H. Morgan delivered in 1934).

10 Randy Moore, *The "Rediscovery" of Mendel's Work*, Bioscene, May 2001, at 13.

11 Mendel, *supra* note 6, at 36.

12 *See, e.g.*, Julian Huxley, Evolution: The Modern Synthesis (1942).

13 Enríquez, *Genome Editing*, *supra* note 3, at 618.

14 *See* Rachel Brenchley et al., *Analysis of the Bread Wheat Genome Using Whole-Genome Shotgun Sequencing*, 491 Nature 705, 705 (2012).

15 *See* Frederick R. Blattner et al., *The Complete Genome Sequence of* Escherichia coli *K-12*, 277 Science 1453, 1453 (1997).

16 *See* Mihaela Pertea et al., *CHESS: A New Human Gene Catalog Curated from Thousands of Large-Scale RNA Sequencing Experiments Reveals Extensive Transcriptional Noise*, 19 Genome Biology art. 208, at 1 (2018).

17 Ralf Dahm, *Friedrich and the Discovery of DNA*, 278 DEVELOPMENTAL BIOLOGY 274 (2005). The first publications describing nuclein (DNA) appeared two years later in 1871. *Id.* at 284.
18 James D. Watson & Francis H. C. Crick, A *Structure for Deoxyribose Nucleic Acid*, 171 NATURE 737 (1953).
19 *See* Rosalind E. Franklin & R. G. Gosling, *Molecular Configuration in Sodium Thymonucleate*.171 NATURE 740 (1953); M. H. F. Wilkins, A. R. Stokes & H. R. Wilson, *Molecular Structure of Deoxypentose Nucleic Acids*, 171 NATURE 738 (1953).
20 Franklin & Gosling, *supra* note 19, at 740.
21 ANTOINETTE ROUVROY, HUMAN GENES AND NEOLIBERAL GOVERNANCE: A FOUCAULDIAN CRITIQUE 28 (2008).
22 Martin J. Tobin, *Three Papers, Three Lessons*, 167 AM. J. RESPIRATORY & CRITICAL CARE MED. 1047, 1048 (2003).
23 *See* Erwin Chargaff et al., *Composition of the Desoxypentose Nucleic Acids of Four Genera of Sea-Urchin*, 195 J. BIOLOGICAL CHEMISTRY 155 (1952).
24 Matthew Meselson & Franklin Stahl, *The Replication of DNA in Escherichia coli*, 44 PROC. NAT'L ACAD. SCI. U.S. 671 (1958).
25 *See* Christine N. Tennyson et al., *The Human Dystrophin Gene Requires 16 Hours to Be Transcribed and Is Cotranscriptionally Spliced*, 9 NATURE GENETICS 184 (1995); Dystrophin gene sequence, http://useast.ensembl.org/Homo_sapiens/Gene/Sequence?db=core;g=ENSG00000198947;r=X:31097677–33339441.
26 José E. González-Pastor et al., *The Smallest Known Gene*, 369 NATURE 281 (1994).
27 *See* William Bateson & E. R. Saunders, *The Facts of Heredity in the Light of Mendel's Discovery*, *in* REPORTS TO THE EVOLUTION COMMITTEE OF THE ROYAL SOCIETY, I. 125 (1902).
28 T. H. Morgan, *Sex Limited Inheritance in Drosophila*, 32 SCIENCE 120 (1910).
29 *See* R. C. PUNNETT, MENDELISM (3d ed. 1911); Lawrence C. Davis, *Origin of the Punnett Square*, 55 AM. BIOLOGY TEACHER 209 (1993).
30 *See* F. H. C. Crick, *On Protein Synthesis*, *in* SYMPOSIA OF THE SOC'Y FOR EXPERIMENTAL BIOLOGY, NUMBER XII: THE BIOLOGICAL REPLICATION OF MACROMOLECULES 138 (F. K. Sanders ed., 1958). Francis Crick originally used the phrase to explain that "the transfer of information from nucleic acid to nucleic acid, or from nucleic acid to protein may be possible, but transfer from protein to protein, or from protein to nucleic acid is impossible." *Id.* at 153.
31 For an overview of some noncoding RNAs and their biological functions, see Thomas R. Cech & Joan A. Steitz, *The Noncoding RNA Revolution—Trashing Old Rules to Forge New Ones*, 157 CELL 77 (2014).
32 The discovery of the first codon—for the amino acid phenylalanine—was reported in 1961. At the time, however, it was still not clear whether the code was singlet, triplet, or something else. *See* Marshall W. Nirenberg & J. Heinrich Matthaei, *The Dependence of Cell-Free Protein Synthesis in E. coli*

upon Naturally Occurring or Synthetic Polyribonucleotides, 47 Proc. Nat'l Acad. Sci. U.S. 1588 (1961).

33 By 1966, all 64 codons of the genetic code had been deciphered, revealing that each was a triplet codon. *See* Nat'l Human Genome Res. Inst., *1966: Genetic Code Cracked*, https://www.genome.gov/25520300/online-education-kit-1966-genetic-code-cracked.

34 For an overview of the cellular functions of collagen, see Structure and Function of Collagen Types (Richard Mayne & Robert E. Burgeson eds., 1987).

35 *See, e.g.*, Bin Wang et al., *Keratin: Structure, Mechanical Properties, Occurrence in Biological Organisms, and Efforts at Bioinspiration*, 76 Progress in Materials Sci. 229 (2016).

36 *See, e.g.*, A. J. Bellingham et al., *Regulatory Mechanisms of Hemoglobin Oxygen Affinity in Acidosis and Alkalosis*, 50 J. Clinical Investigation 700 (1971).

37 *See, e.g.*, Alan D. Frankel & Peter S. Kim, *Modular Structure of Transcription Factors: Implications for Gene Regulation*, 65 Cell 717 (1991).

38 *See, e.g.*, Faming Zhang et al., *Leptin: Structure, Function and Biology*, 71 Vitamins & Hormones 345 (2005).

39 *See, e.g.*, George Wells Beadle & Edward L. Tatum, *Genetic Control of Biochemical Reactions in Neurospora*, 27 Proc. Nat'l Acad. Sci. U.S. 499 (1941).

40 *See, e.g.*, Joseph M. Watts et al., *Architecture and Secondary Structure of an Entire HIV-1 RNA Genome*, 460 Nature 711 (2009).

41 *See* Morgan, *supra* note 28.

42 *See, e.g.*, John W. Drake et al., *Rates of Spontaneous Mutation*, 148 Genetics 1667 (1998); Robert E. Johnson et al., *Fidelity of Human DNA Polymerase η*, 275 J. Biological Chemistry 7447 (2000).

43 Jason Flannick et al., Loss-of-Function Mutations in SLC30A8 Protect Against Type 2 Diabetes, 46 Nature Genetics 357 (2014).

44 *See* Rong Liu et al., *Homozygous Defect in HIV-1 Coreceptor Accounts for Resistance of Some Multiply-Exposed Individuals to HIV-1 Infection*, 86 Cell 367 (1996).

45 *See* Jian Yang et al., *Genetic Signatures of High-Altitude Adaptation in Tibetans*, 114 Proc. Nat'l Acad. Sci. U.S. 4189 (2017).

46 Seng H. Cheng et al., *Defective Intracellular Transport and Processing of CFTR is the Molecular Basis of Most Cystic Fibrosis*, 63 Cell 827 (1990).

47 Linus Pauling et al., *Sickle Cell Anemia, a Molecular Disease*, 110 Science 543 (1949).

48 Brenda J. Conner et al., *Detection of Sickle Cell β^{S}-Globin Allele by Hybridization with Synthetic Oligonucleotides*, 80 Proc. Nat'l Acad. Sci. U.S. 278 (1983).

49 *See, e.g.*, A. C. Allison, *The Distribution of the Sickle-Cell Trait in East Africa and Elsewhere, and Its Apparent Relationship to the Incidence of Subtertian Malaria*, 48 TRANSACTIONS OF THE ROYAL SOC'Y TROPICAL MED. & HYGIENE 312 (1954).

50 *See, e.g.*, Peter D. Aplan, *Causes of Oncogenic Chromosomal Translocation*, 22 TRENDS IN GENETICS 46 (2006).

51 *See* Joost Schulte & J. Troy Littleton, *The Biological Function of the Huntingtin Protein and Its Relevance to Huntington's Disease Pathology*, 5 CURRENT TRENDS IN NEUROLOGY 65 (2011).

52 Stephen S. Hecht & Dietrich Hoffmann, *Tobacco-Specific Nitrosamines, an Important Group of Carcinogens in Tobacco and Tobacco Smoke*, 9 CARCINOGENESIS 875 (1988).

53 *See, e.g.*, Ruggero Montesano, *Alkylation of DNA and Tissue Specificity in Nitrosamine Carcinogenesis*, 17 J. CELLULAR BIOCHEMISTRY 259 (1981); Stephen S. Hecht et al., *Reaction of Nicotine and Sodium Nitrite: Formation of Nitrosamines and Fragmentation of the Pyrrolidine Ring*, 43 J. ORGANIC CHEM. 72 (1978).

54 *See* Anthony Loveless, *Increased Rate of Plaque-type and Host-range Mutation Following Treatment of Bacteriophage in Vitro with Ethyl Methane Sulphonate*, 181 NATURE 1212 (1958).

55 *See* Gary A. Sega, *A Review of the Genetic Effects of Ethyl Methanesulfonate*, 134 MUTATION RES. 113 (1984).

56 *See, e.g.*, Evelyne Sage & Naoya Shikazono, *Radiation-Induced Clustered DNA Lesions: Repair and Mutagenesis*, 107 FREE RADICAL BIOLOGY & MED. 125 (2017).

57 *See, e.g.*, H. J. Muller, *Artificial Transmutation of the Gene*, 66 SCIENCE 84 (1927); Karl Sax, *Chromosome Aberrations Induced by X-Rays*, 23 GENETICS 494 (1938).

58 *See, e.g.*, Hironobu Ikehata & Tetsuya Ono, *The Mechanisms of UV Mutagenesis*, 52 J. RADIATION RES. 115 (2011); L. J. Stadler & G. F. Sprague, *Genetic Effects of Ultra-Violet Radiation in Maize. I. Unfiltered Radiation*, 22 PROC. NAT'L ACAD. SCI. U.S. 572 (1936).

59 *See, e.g.*, R. B. Setlow, *The Wavelengths in Sunlight Effective in Producing Skin Cancer: A Theoretical Analysis*, 71 PROC. NAT'L ACAD. SCI. U.S. 3363 (1974); Sage & Shikazono, *supra* note 56.

60 For a list of some popular works related to genetic manipulation in science fiction in the twentieth century, see BRIAN STABLEFORD, SCIENCE FACT AND SCIENCE FICTION: AN ENCYCLOPEDIA 207 (Routledge 2006).

61 *See* MAURICE NICOLL, THE BLUE GERM (1918).

62 *See* ALDOUS HUXLEY, BRAVE NEW WORLD (1932).

63 *See, e.g.*, MARTINA NEWELL-MCGLOUGHLIN & EDWARD BRIAN RE , THE EVOLUTION OF BIOTECHNOLOGY: FROM NATUFIANS TO NANOTECHNOLOGY 47 (2006) (indicating that Danish microbiologist A. Jost coined the term during his lecture at the Technical Institute in Lwów, Poland).

64 *See* Robert A. Heinlein, *Beyond This Horizon, in* ASTOUNDING SCIENCE-FICTION, April 1942, at 9. Heinlein published the novel as a two-part series under the pseudonym Anson McDonald.
65 STABLEFORD, *supra* note 60, at 207.
66 *See* JACK WILLIAMSON, DRAGON'S ISLAND (1951).
67 *See, e.g.*, S. E. Luria & Mary L. Human, A *Nonhereditary, Host-Induced Variation of Bacterial Viruses*, 64 J. BACTERIOLOGY 557 (1952); E. S. Anderson & A. Felix, *Variation in Vi-Phage II of Salmonella typhi*, 170 NATURE 492 (1952); G. Bertani & J. J. Weigle, *Host Controlled Variation in Bacterial Viruses*, 65 J. BACTERIOLOGY 113 (1953); S. E. Luria, *Host-Induced Modifications of Viruses*, 18 COLD SPRING HARBOR SYMPOSIA ON QUANTITATIVE BIOLOGY 237 (1953).
68 *See, e.g.*, Daisy Dussoix & Werner Arber, *Host specificity of DNA produced by Escherichia coli: II. Control over acceptance of DNA from infecting phage λ*, 5 J. MOLECULAR BIOLOGY 37 (1962); Werner Arber, *Host-Controlled Modification of Bacteriophage*, 19 ANN. REV. MICROBIOLOGY 365 (1965).
69 *See* Stuart Linn & Werner Arber, *Host Specificity of DNA Produced by Escherichia coli, X. In Vitro Restriction of Phage Fd Replicative Form*, 59 PROC. NAT'L ACAD. SCI. U.S. 1300 (1968); Matthew Meselson & Robert Yuan, *DNA Restriction Enzyme from E. coli*, 217 NATURE 1110 (1968); Hamilton O. Smith & K. W. Wilkox, *A Restriction Enzyme from Hemophilus influenzae: I. Purification and General Properties*, 51 J. MOLECULAR BIOLOGY 379 (1970).
70 Thomas J. Kelly & Hamilton O. Smith, *A Restriction Enzyme from Hemophilus influenzae: II. Base Sequence of the Recognition Site*, 51 J. MOLECULAR BIOLOGY 393 (1970).
71 Richard J. Roberts, Tamas Vincze, Janos Posfai & Dana Macelis, *REBASE—Enzymes and Genes for DNA Restriction and Modification*, 38 NUCLEIC ACIDS RES. D234 (2010).
72 The Nobel Prize was awarded jointly to Werner Arber, Daniel Nathans, and Hamilton O. Smith "for the discovery of restriction enzymes and their application to problems of molecular genetics." The Nobel Prize in Physiology or Medicine 1978, https://www.nobelprize.org/prizes/medicine/1978/summary/.
73 *See, e.g.*, Thomas Bonura et al., *Enzymatic Induction of DNA Double-Strand Breaks in Gamma-Irradiated Escherichia coli K-12*, 72 PROC. NAT'L ACAD. SCI. U.S. 4265 (1975); Paul Howard-Flanders & Lee Theriot, *Mutants of Escherichia coli K-12 Defective in DNA Repair and in Genetic Recombination*, 53 GENETICS 1137 (1966); David O. Ferguson & Frederick W. Alt, *DNA Double Strand Break Repair and Chromosomal Translocation: Lessons from Animal Models*, 20 ONCOGENE 5572 (2001).
74 *See* Howard R. Champion et al., A *Profile of Combat Injury*, 54 J. TRAUMA S13 (2003); Russ S. Kotwal et al., *Eliminating Preventable Death on the Battlefield*, 146 ARCHIVES OF SURGERY 1350 (2011).

75 Cynthia J. Sakofsky et al., *Break-Induced Replication and Genome Stability*, 2 BIOMOLECULES 483 (2012).

76 Andriy Khobta & Bernd Epe, *Interactions Between DNA Damage, Repair, and Transcription*, 736 MUTATION RES. 5 (2012).

77 E.g., Giovanni Bosco & James E. Haber, *Chromosome Break-Induced DNA Replication Leads to Nonreciprocal Translocations and Telomere Capture*, 150 GENETICS 1037 (1998); Janet D. Rowley, *A New Consistent Chromosomal Abnormality in Chronic Myelogenous Leukaemia Identified by Quinacrine Fluorescence and Giemsa Staining*, 243 NATURE 290 (1973); L. Zech et al., *Characteristic Chromosomal Abnormalities in Biopsies and Lymphoid-Cell Lines from Patients with Burkitt and Non-Burkitt Lymphomas*, 17 INT'L J. CANCER 47 (1976); Chengming Zhu et al., *Unrepaired DNA Breaks in p53-Deficient Cells Lead to Oncogenic Gene Amplification Subsequent to Translocations*, 109 CELL 811 (2002).

78 *See* Anthony J. Davis & David J. Chen, *DNA Double Strand Break Repair Via Non-Homologous End-Joining*, 2 TRANSLATIONAL CANCER RES. 130, 130 (2013).

79 For a brief overview of the mechanisms, see generally GEOFFREY M. COOPER, THE CELL: A MOLECULAR APPROACH (2d ed. 2000).

80 *See, e.g.*, Feng Liang et al., *Homology-Directed Repair Is a Major Double-Strand Break Repair Pathway in Mammalian Cells*, 95 PROC. NAT'L ACAD. SCI. U.S. 5172 (1998); Xuan Li & Wolf-Dietrich Heyer, *Homologous Recombination in DNA Repair and DNA Damage Tolerance*, 18 CELL RES. 99 (2008).

81 *See* Harriet B. Creighton & Barbara McClintock, *A Correlation of Cytological and Genetical Crossing-Over in Zea Mays*, 17 PROC. NAT'L ACAD. SCI. U.S. 492 (1931).

82 *See, e.g.*, Lisa C. Kadyk & Leland H. Hartwel, *Sister Chromatids Are Preferred Over Homologs as Substrates for Recombinational Repair in Saccharomyces cerevisiae*, 132 GENETICS 387 (1992); Roger D. Johnson & Maria Jasin, *Sister Chromatid Gene Conversion Is a Prominent Double-Strand Break Repair Pathway in Mammalian Cells*, 19 EMBO J. 3398 (2000).

83 *See, e.g.*, Jeff S. King et al., *Noncomplementary DNA Double-Strand-Break Rejoining in Bacterial and Human Cells*, 21 NUCLEIC ACIDS RES. 1055 (1993); Wolfgang Goedecke et al., *Activation of a System for the Joining of Nonhomologous DNA Ends During Xenopus Egg Maturation*, 12 MOLECULAR & CELLULAR BIOLOGY 811 (1992).

84 For an overview of the molecular mechanisms of NHEJ repair, see Anthony J. Davis & David J. Chen, *DNA Double Strand Break Repair Via Non-Homologous End-Joining*, 2 TRANSLATIONAL CANCER RES. 130 (2013).

3

What Is Genome Editing?

Meaning is powerful. It brings ideas associated with simple letters, words, characters, sounds, or gestures to life. When fused with proper context, syntax, and structure, it ascribes significance to language. Without risk of hyperbole, meaning is perhaps the most integral element of communication.

Throughout civilizations and times of yore, humans have explored myriad ways to communicate and convey meaning explicitly or implicitly. History teaches that such tasks have frequently been carried out by using language as a conduit. The reason is quite simple: language lends itself to verbal, textual, and contextual nuance. The ideas through which meaning is conveyed can be grounded in language, qualified, and tinted with shades of meaning. Syntax can, in turn, be used to arrange words and terms in unique ways so that their meaning may be adequately defined, decoded, and interpreted. It is no surprise that when it comes to communicating new terms—including those used to describe novel inventions and technologies—humans often convey meaning through definitions. Indeed, an aphorism most commonly attributed to Socrates,[1] the renowned classical Greek philosopher and putative founder of western philosophy, famously avers that "the beginning of wisdom is the definition of terms."[2]

Whether defining terms truly gives rise to all wisdom as embodied in an ageless, two-and-a-half millennial quip is, of course, beyond the scope of this book. And we shall not embark on such a rhetorical and philosophical exploration here. The definition of terms may or may not mark the genesis of wisdom but, for purposes of our discussion, you can rest assured that conceptual reflection of the definition of terms constitutes a crucial early step in legal—namely, statutory, judicial, treaty, administrative agency, contractual, etc.—construction and interpretation.

Undoubtedly, striving to interpret before defining is as futile as putting the proverbial cart before the horse.

I PARSING WORDS

Suppose that two individuals—Calvin and Lulu—enter into an agreement requiring performance in exchange for money. Calvin is a herpetologist and keeps a cobra snake named Knoodles as a pet[3] in his home. He has grown very fond of Knoodles, takes great care of it, and even feeds it a special diet. One day, Calvin learns he must travel abroad for work for six months. Because he considers Knoodles to be a companion and it has become an important part of his life, Calvin wishes to hire the services of a company that will feed and care for it while he is gone. He finds an advertisement for a local company run by Lulu that employs staff certified in animal care and can provide luxury animal room and board to a range of pets for extended periods of times. After a brief conversation, Calvin and Lulu enter into a contract whereby "Calvin agrees to pay Lulu's company a down payment of 1,000 dollars plus a 400-dollar monthly fee to provide room, board, food, and care for his pet Knoodles for six months." As part of the down payment, Lulu agreed to pick Knoodles up from Calvin's home the day of his departure. When she arrives at Calvin's home and walks over to the room where Calvin keeps the cobra inside a secure enclosure, she witnesses Knoodles raising up from the ground to her eye level, flaring its neck to form an intimidating hood, and emitting a loud hiss. At that point, Lulu realizes that Knoodles is anything but a cuddly pet and she refuses to care for it. As a result of Lulu's apparent breach of contract, Calvin misses his flight and must find other accommodations for Knoodles. Calvin sues Lulu for breach of contract and costs incurred in excess of the contract.

Before Calvin can prevail in a court of law, the court must interpret what the parties meant when the contract was established. Assume, for the sake of discussion, that Calvin did not violate any laws by keeping a cobra in the jurisdiction in which he lives,[4] and that neither Calvin nor Lulu were intentionally misleading—that is, Lulu was unaware Knoodles was a cobra when she took the down payment and Calvin believed in good faith that Lulu's company would be able to care for his snake—during their brief discussion. The crux of the legal dispute between Calvin and Lulu will be whether the term "pet" encompasses elapid, venomous snakes such as Knoodles.

If an interpretive analysis reveals that cobra snakes constitute animals within the meaning of the word "pet," Calvin will likely prevail. Conversely, if the analysis shows the word "pet" does not encompass cobra snakes, Lulu will likely prevail. If, however, the analysis leads to the conclusion that the parties did not even have mutual assent upon contract formation, Lulu will not likely be held in breach of the contract because a "meeting of the minds"[5]—that is, a common understanding about what was bargained for—did not take place between the two parties.

Due to the ambiguity of the word "pet" in this scenario, the court might start by searching the general definition of "pet" in the dictionary. This is a thorny issue in legal interpretation for reasons we will discuss in more detail in Section VI below. Let us assume that the court turns to two English dictionaries: the Cambridge Dictionary and the Merriam-Webster Dictionary. As it relates to animals, the Cambridge Dictionary defines a pet as "an animal that is kept in the home as a companion and treated kindly."[6] Under this definition, which Calvin endorses,

Knoodles would probably qualify as a pet because (1) all snakes are animals, (2) it has become an important part of Calvin's life, (3) it was kept in Calvin's home, and (4) it was well-cared for, considered a companion, and even fed a special diet. The definition makes no mention of what types of animals, if any, should constitute pets. In fact, the Cambridge Dictionary entry for "pet" even makes mention of "a pet snake."[7]

As applicable to animals, the Merriam-Webster Dictionary, on the other hand, defines "pet" as "a domesticated animal kept for pleasure rather than utility."[8] Under this definition, which Lulu endorses, Knoodles is probably not a pet because, although its presence arguably brings Calvin companionship and pleasure, a cobra is a dangerous and potentially deadly wild animal that is not—and likely never will be—domesticated.

The outcome of the case might depend on which definition the court chooses to apply, how it construes the term, and whether the dictionary definition is considered determinant. But it cannot be denied that both definitions assign common and reasonable, yet distinct, meanings to the term pet. Had Lulu's company advertisement included a banner that mentioned the care of a range of animals including "exotic pets," Calvin's interpretation might prevail because Lulu could reasonably expect that many members of the community would infer or understand that snakes —venomous or not—are exotic animal pets. Absent such additional evidence that either Calvin or Lulu had knowledge of the other's intended meaning at the time the contract was formed, it would be impossible for the court to objectively choose one interpretation over the other. As a result, the court would likely hold that no contract was formed because there was no "meeting of the minds" between Calvin and Lulu. Their meaning of "pet" was, in essence, at polar opposites and they had vastly different expectations of the most essential element of the agreement, which concerned housing, feeding, and caring for an ambiguous animal pet named Knoodles over an extended period of time.

A dispute over the meaning of one single word in the foregoing illustration may appear insignificant at first glance, but the principle of mutual assent or "meeting of the minds" requirement has long been considered a cornerstone of contract law that has real life implications and consequences. A famous on-point case from the nineteenth century, *Raffles v. Wichelhaus*,[9] commonly known as the *Peerless* case, pertained to a mutual misunderstanding about a material element in a contract between two parties. The plaintiff and defendant in that case made a contract for the sale and purchase of cotton imported from India on a British ship named Peerless. Unbeknown to each party was the fact that, coincidentally, there were two cotton-carrying, British ships named Peerless traveling from Bombay to Liverpool—one sailing in October and the other in December. The parties had attached their own intended meaning to the term "Peerless" in the contract: the defendant intended to purchase the cotton on the *October* Peerless, whereas the plaintiff intended to sell the cotton on the *December* Peerless. The plaintiff sued for breach of contract when the defendant refused to accept delivery of, and pay for, the cotton on the December Peerless because the shipment was purportedly two months late and the defendant could no longer use the cotton. The central issue in that case was whether the contract concerned the Peerless ship that sailed in October or December. The plaintiff argued that the date of arrival was immaterial; mere delivery of cotton from India on a ship named Peerless would suffice. The defendant, on the other hand, argued that the contract was for the October shipment and the apparent latent ambiguity of the word "Peerless" meant that no binding contract was ever formed.

The court issued a per curiam decision—that is, a judgment collectively issued by the judges sitting in a judicial panel—in favor of the defendant. Notably, the court did not interpret the term Peerless in the contract to mean what either party had intended. Instead, judgment for the defendant was rendered because the argument that a contract was never formed resonated with the court. There was no mutual assent about a material component of the agreement. Thus, interpreting the term Peerless in the contract would have been futile given that the parties had not agreed on its meaning, or known or should have known about the other's intended meaning.

If we revisit the proverb attributed to Socrates—which we discussed at the beginning of this chapter—in light of *Knoodles* and *Peerless*, one might perhaps qualify Socrates's statement as "the beginning of litigation is the inadequate definition of terms." The aforementioned examples illustrate how a simple word or term can play pivotal roles in legal interpretation and construction. The significance of precision in language used to convey the meaning of terms—including those used to describe multibillion-dollar technological breakthroughs—cannot be underscored enough.

II THE NEED FOR A DEFINITION

The quest for meaning of a new term ought to start by exploring the scope, extent, and boundaries of its definition. This chapter sets out to do precisely that. It lays an interpretive and normative foundation that will be useful for discussions of genome editing in the chapters that follow—namely, the type of general discussions of genome editing that society will grapple in the near future.

Although the concept of "genome editing" is not new, there is surprisingly no unified or standard definition for the term. Indeed, scientific literature in prominent publications to date has devoted substantial ink to discussing how the technology was developed, its mechanisms of action, what it can be used for, how it can be improved to increase its efficient use, and so on without attempting to attach any specific or particular meaning to the term.[10] The lack of consensus on a definition or genome-editing terminology is even more perplexing considering the fact that genome editing has assumed a preeminent place—especially following the advent of the CRISPR–Cas9 system as a repurposed tool for programmable genome editing in 2012[11]—at the forefront of mainstream science among few and highly select, first-rate, technological breakthroughs.

Congruity and uniformity on genome-editing terminology is sorely needed at this point in time. The increasingly interdisciplinary expansion of genome editing in a wide range of academic fields—spanning scientific, legal, economic, social, ethical, philosophical, and policy-related areas of study—all but guarantee that inconsistent meanings, interpretations, and uses of genome-editing definitions and terminology will obfuscate future discussions regarding what measures, if any, society should implement to promote or hinder technological development.[12] It is difficult to avoid misunderstandings or worse, inadequate laws, regulations, and bad policies, when there is a failure to convey the meaning of that which is the subject of discussion. At a basic level, we should strive to communicate accurately, effectively, and efficiently across disciplines so that users of genome-editing information and the general public can discern the intended meaning that producers of genome-editing information wish to disseminate. And scientists—as the primary disseminators of such information—bear a large portion of the burden to ensure the roots of vagueness and ambiguity do not spread to other fields of study.

This chapter advocates for the adoption of a (more) uniform definition of genome editing primarily aimed at building a science-based, legal and policy framework to address current and future predicaments within the ambit of genome-editing technologies. It examines common and general limitations that stem from the use of specific definitions or terminologies, including overreliance on dictionary definitions, which some courts are using more frequently as interpretive tools to adjudicate cases and controversies. The chapter further explores the integral role of compromise in the formal codification and promulgation of rules and definitions and, more broadly, in active law and policy making. Appraisal of compromise as a factor in these processes aims to dispel the myth that law generally lags behind scientific progress. Lastly, the chapter analyzes the proposed definition of genome editing through an interpretive and pragmatic bifocal lens to reflect on the underlying question: What does it mean and, more importantly, what should it mean when people use the term genome editing?

III A PROPOSED DEFINITION

Genome editing, as referred to throughout this book, encompasses scientific, technological advances that enable the rational design of targeted genomic or genetic modifications—and, by logical extension, the process of bringing the design to fruition—at a local (for example, gene, regulatory region, etc.) or global (genome-wide) level with the aim of facilitating the precise insertion, addition, removal, conversion, or substitution of DNA molecules, comprising one or more nucleotides—such as those containing a nitrogenous base including, but not limited to, Adenine (A), Cytosine (C), Guanine (G), Thymine (T), and possibly others, which may be synthetically derived—into or from the cell(s) of a natural or semisynthetic living organism.[13]

There is a lot to unpack from the above definition, which we will do in Section VII momentarily. At the outset, it should be noted that no definition is perfect. This fact is, perhaps, most true and conspicuous under the probing light of litigation. Words that are otherwise clear to an ordinary reader may likely raise textual and interpretive issues for lawyers, who will parse through those words with fine-toothed syntactical combs.

That allegorical reflection is aptly memorialized in a statement made by former President Clinton while giving sworn testimony to a grand jury on August 17, 1998. At the time, he was embroiled in a scandal concerning multiple extramarital sex acts that took place between 1995 and 1997 in or around the Oval Office with Monica Lewinsky, a then-twenty-two-year-old White House intern. Ms. Lewinsky had filed a false affidavit in another case stating she "never had any sexual relationship with the President."[14] When asked whether his lawyer too made a false a statement to a federal judge by saying "there is absolutely no sex of any kind in any manner, shape or form, [between Clinton and Lewinsky]," the President chose his words carefully.[15] His response: "It depends on what the meaning of the word 'is' is." He went on to argue that the veracity of the statement hinged on whether the word "is" meant "is and never has been," as opposed to "there is none."[16] And so, because the affair did not constitute an *ongoing* relationship at the time of his lawyer's statement in January 1998, he told the grand jury that the statement was truthful under the latter interpretation of the word is.[17]

IV A SEMANTIC CONUNDRUM

Several limitations concerning the use of specific terminology exist. First, the meaning of words can be malleable and evolve over time and cultures. In the Renaissance period, for example, the term "sport" was often used by scientists to describe a spontaneous mutation or biological variation.[18] Today, one would be hard-pressed to find such a reference to sport apart from select niches of botany.[19]

During the fourteenth century, the term "cheater" was used to refer to a royal officer appointed to oversee the king's escheats[20]—namely, the land or real property subject to the escheat common law doctrine, which authorized the transfer of said land to the Crown or state upon the death of an heirless owner who died intestate (without a will). With the passage of time, the king's cheaters developed a tarnished reputation characterized by the unlawful confiscation and deprivation of people's property through fraudulent, unscrupulous means. By the 1600s, the term's meaning had morphed to describe the cheaters' behavior. To cheat became a synonym for to deceive and defraud by trickery. And William Shakespeare contemporaneously popularized that meaning in various plays.[21] Hence, it was the chicanery of the king's cheaters that spawned the modern vernacular meaning of cheater. Today, we reserve the term exclusively for swindlers, individuals who are dishonest and deceitful, or unfaithful adulterers and fornicators who engage in sexual activity behind their partners' backs.

The diachronic evolution of particular terms can, therefore, pose high barriers to understanding, inferring, or deciphering the meaning of language.

Second, a particular definition may be overly broad or restrictive. Suppose you are the first human to ever lay eyes on a felid as you stumble upon a domestic cat. She happens to have black fur and a relatively meek temperament toward humans—let's call her Kitty. To announce your discovery to the world, you begin to describe Kitty as a member of a new species of felid animal called "cat," which you define as a terrestrial, vertebrate, mammal that has four limbs and exhibits quadrupedal locomotion. That definition seems sound on its face, but would be far too expansive as it unmistakably applies to dogs, bears, cattle, rodents, elephants, many marsupials, and a myriad of ungulate animals, none of which could plausibly qualify as cats. The vast breadth and scope of the definition makes its meaning inherently ambiguous and, thus, it is difficult to critically distinguish and apply it in a uniform, logical, and systematic manner.

To address the shortcomings of your definition, you take another crack at it. This time you strive to be a bit more specific and define a cat as an animal belonging to a family of terrestrial, vertebrate, four-legged mammals with retractable—or more accurately, protractable—claws that exhibit quadrupedal locomotion, emit purr sounds, and can weigh up to thirty pounds. That new description seems more precise, but it falters too because it is plagued by its own stringency. Soon after the terminology is settled, you and others discover that additional Kitty-like animals exist, yet they cannot be classified as cats because they fail a particular element of the strict description. A lion, tiger, and jaguar would thus fall outside the scope of the term "cat" because, despite fulfilling most of the criteria, they all (1) weigh far more than thirty pounds, and (2) do not possess an ossified hyoid—the horseshoe-shaped bone at the base of the tongue that allows Kitty to purr—but rather an epihyoid elastic ligament that permits roaring instead of purring.[22] Similarly, a cheetah could not be classified as a cat. Unlike other big cats that roar, cheetahs can purr because they have bony hyoids, like domestic cats.[23] However, cheetahs do not possess fully retractable claws like Kitty and most other felids. So, even if the weight requirement is overlooked, a cheetah would not be considered a member of the cat family under this new stringent definition.

Simply put, if the scope is too broad, a term will be vague, ambiguous, and lack specificity, which may ultimately render it meaningless in practice. If the scope is too restrictive, a particular definition will impart rigidity, which may hinder its relevance and application to current and future problems that could not have been foreseen when first written.[24] This is a major concern for the use of terminology or particular definitions related to emerging technologies.

Third, law and policy makers often possess a shallow perception and knowledge-base of scientific and technological developments. Understandably, these knowledge gaps arise, in large part, from the challenges that complex scientific principles may pose on individuals without scientific training. Regardless of causal link, the knowledge gaps are at the root of law and policy makers' lack of foresight regarding the potential future derivations and applications of any given technology, as well as the ramifications of using terminology that may become rapidly outdated in the wake of scientific progress.

Consider the Coordinated Framework for the Regulation of Biotechnology (Coordinated Framework), the formal 1986 policy document that outlines the United States' federal scheme for regulating products derived from modern biotechnology.[25] The regulatory scheme concocted by the Coordinated Framework was largely driven by the scientific context of early genetic engineering methods that relied on recombinant DNA technologies.[26] Policy makers in the 1980s built the framework with that context in mind. Today, however, genome editing and other modern biotechnologies are testing the applicable limits of the Coordinated Framework to such an extent that it recently became necessary to launch an initiative to modernize the regulatory system for biotechnology.[27]

To be fair, the inability to anticipate the evolution of science and technology cannot be solely imputed to law and policy makers. Indeed, at the time the Coordinated Framework went into effect, it would have been virtually impossible even for scientists to predict all of the ways in which humans can now alter the genetic composition of living organisms at will.[28]

It is not the fault of humans to fall short of predicting the future. Nor can there be any doubt that a failure to neatly cabin the solution to every imaginable problem within specific terminology is, anything but, an immoderate challenge.

V THE POWER OF COMPROMISE

Fourth, it is worth remembering that the process of law and policy making is often a product of compromise. Legal definitions and terminology are, therefore, also the product of compromise. The intended meaning an individual member of a legislature, administrative agency, or policy making body ascribes to a term may not necessarily be shared by all other members. Moreover, a lawfully enacted and codified term may actually differ from the term's meaning in vernacular parlance. The fact that compromise is a significant factor throughout this process also underscores the influence that lobbyists and special interest groups can exert on creating a legal definition for a particular term. Such influence often leaves behind an invisible—yet indelible—mark on meaning.

It is not, as the conventional adage goes, that the law cannot keep pace with scientific progress. Rather, it is that law often stems from compromise. And compromise entails an arduous, political process that is seldom revisited for practical purposes.

A *A Proactive Instrument*

The one-dimensional sentiment that laws and policies always lag behind scientific and technological innovation erroneously implies that the law is predominantly reactive. But that cursory belief is not necessarily always congruent with reality. In fact, law and policy makers may already anticipate potential legal and policy challenges and choose to act proactively to address them.

On this point, consider the passage of the Dickey-Wicker Amendment, which is the United States law that prohibits the use of appropriated public funds on "research in which a human embryo or embryos are destroyed, discarded, or knowingly subjected to risk of injury or death greater than that allowed for research on fetuses in utero," including any embryos derived by fertilization or cloning.[29] The Amendment sought to indirectly preempt the cloning of a human being and became law on January 26, 1996,[30] more than one year before the reported birth of Dolly—the first mammal cloned from a differentiated cell (a somatic, mammary-gland cell) of an adult ewe[31]—and a wave of numerous other mammals that have been cloned since including cattle, sheep, dogs, cats, horses, rats, pigs, monkeys, and others.[32]

The case of Dolly, the sheep, demonstrates that law need not lag behind science and technology, *so long as* compromise can be attained. Between 1996 and 1998, for instance, the US House of Representatives and Senate introduced twenty bills directly targeting human cloning, none of which passed and became law due to lack of consensus and compromise.[33] And since 1999, every US Congress has introduced legislation to ban human cloning, which has also repeatedly failed to pass for various reasons including a failure to distinguish between therapeutic and reproductive cloning, the lack of market demands for cloning, opposition to regulation, a belief that cloning should be allowed, or other potential concerns held by law makers.[34] Keep in mind that these proposed bills in the last two decades were introduced proactively and without any credible and verifiable scientific evidence to corroborate even a single report of the existence of a cloned human.[35]

As noted above, human cloning provides two relevant examples of proactive law and policy making aimed at governing future uses of an emerging technology. The Dickey-Wicker Amendment, which prohibits human cloning indirectly, was enacted into law and remains in effect to this day. Conversely, efforts to ban human cloning directly have failed recurring attempts in the last two decades. Both examples underscore the fact that success or failure of law as a proactive tool hinge on whether compromise and consensus could be achieved, rather than an inherent inability to keep up with scientific progress.

But even during instances when the law is, in fact, reactive, it need not be laggard. Let's expand this thought next.

B A *Reactive Instrument*

Consider the aftermath of the devastating September 11, 2001 (9/11) attacks, the deadliest terrorist attacks on United States soil to date, which led to nearly 3,000 deaths, injured thousands of people, and cost billions of dollars in infrastructure and property damage. On Friday, September 14, 2001—a mere three days after the 9/11 attacks—Congress introduced and passed a joint resolution "[t]o authorize the use of United States Armed Forces against those responsible for the [9/11] attacks launched against the United States."[36] The joint resolution, which was subsequently enacted into law on Monday, September 18, 2001, passed both chambers of Congress with overwhelming bipartisan support. The law authorized the President:

> [T]o use all necessary and appropriate force against those nations, organizations, or persons he determines planned, authorized, committed, or aided the terrorist attacks that occurred on September 11, 2001, or harbored such organizations or persons, in order to prevent any future acts of international terrorism against the United States by such nations, organizations or persons.[37]

Of the 519 votes cast for the joint resolution, only one law maker—Barbara Lee, the US Representative for California's 9th District at the time—voted against the Authorization for Use of Military Force (AUMF),[38] which is still in effect today despite growing calls for its repeal.[39]

Shortly thereafter, the Uniting and Strengthening America by Providing Appropriate Tools Required to Intercept and Obstruct Terrorism (USA PATRIOT) Act was enacted into law on October, 26, 2001.[40] The Act expanded the government's authority to streamline measures—some of which have either been extoled or excoriated over the years—to investigate, deter, and punish terrorist activity in the United States and abroad. The USA PATRIOT Act garnered strong bipartisan support at the time and passed by wide margins in both the US House of Representatives (357–66)[41] and Senate (98–1).[42]

Perhaps the most salient legacy of the immediate aftermath of the 9/11 attacks are the reforms implemented to enhance airport security in the United States and many other countries. If you have traveled on an airplane in the last eighteen years, you know this all too well. Before 9/11, screening at airport security checkpoints was outsourced to private security companies. No one asked you to remove your shoes or take out your computer and pass them through an x-ray machine. Ordinary liquids did not set off security alerts—you need not chug your drink or dispose of it before going through security, and you did not have to part ways with your favorite bottle of perfume if it so happened to exceed the threshold volume limit of 3.4 ounces.[43] More shockingly, small knives detected via secondary screening—usually the result of passengers triggering metal detectors—would typically be returned to travelers.[44] In this new age of air travel, it is hard to fathom that the pre-9/11 airlines' checkpoint operations guide, which the Federal Aviation Administration (FAA) endorsed, explicitly allowed people to carry knives with blades up to four-inches long onboard a flight because the FAA did not consider them to be "menacing" items.[45] Once airborne, you could eat a meal with silverware and the airline carriers would provide a metal knife to cut meat. The world was different prior to the 9/11 attacks. Airline carriers—and sometimes airports—contracted with the private security companies to institute a derelict system under which moving passengers and aircraft, lowering control security costs, avoiding security-related congestions, and limiting the impact of security protocols on industry operations often took precedence over ensuring the safety and security of civil aviation.[46]

Long gone are those days. With the enactment of the Aviation and Transportation Security Act,[47] Congress swiftly authorized the creation of the Transportation Security Agency (TSA), which has replaced private security personnel with federal TSA employees at security checkpoints throughout all US airports. The Act passed with overwhelming bipartisan support, just like other 9/11-related legislative proposals at the time. Even in the few select airports that have privatized airport security through the Screening Partnership Program (SPP)—a federal program that allows qualified private companies to provide security screening services at select commercial airports[48]—the security screening providers must comply with all TSA policies and regulations, use TSA-approved equipment, and conduct their business subject to federal oversight and TSA monitoring.[49]

The expeditious response to the 9/11 attacks was not only confined to US domestic law. Less than twenty-four hours after the attacks, members of the North Atlantic Treaty Organization (NATO) invoked—for the first and only time ever—Article 5 of the Treaty,[50] which enshrines the collective-defense commitment of each member to stand by any other member in response to an armed attack.[51] The NATO members confirmed the invocation on October 2, 2001, after it was "clearly determined" that the 9/11 attacks had been perpetrated by Al-Qaeda, a terrorist organization headed by Osama bin Laden, with support from the Taliban regime in Afghanistan.[52] By October 7, 2001, less than one month after the 9/11 attacks, the United States and its NATO allies initiated military operations in Afghanistan as a concerted effort to cripple and ultimately defeat Al-Qaeda and the Taliban.[53]

The case of laws enacted in the wake of the 9/11 attacks suitably illustrates the significant role of compromise in using law as a reactive tool. Post 9/11 legislation was enacted quickly because there was consensus among law makers. Consensus formed for various reasons including, but not limited to, a wave of unity and solidarity in the face of a horrible national tragedy, as well as a sense of emergency to address legal and policy loopholes that enabled terrorists to perpetrate harm on American soil. Consensus, therefore, lowered the threshold needed to achieve compromise on how to adequately respond to the 9/11 attacks. With enough consensus geared toward securing compromise, entire financial, regulatory, and security systems can undergo reform in a matter of weeks. Even international communities comprised of countries that seldom agree on everything can galvanize behind a controversial issue such as the use of military force. Accordingly, it is clear that even when the law is reactive, it need not be laggard.

C *Proactive, Reactive, and Incomplete*

We have discussed instances in which law and policy makers may already anticipate potential legal and policy challenges and choose to act either proactively or reactively to address them. Occasionally, however, such challenges may already be anticipated but cannot be addressed because compromise eludes the process. The results are incomplete laws and policies that only partially tackle with a particular issue or problem. Yet, sometimes, having an imperfect law is better than having no law at all.

Contemplate, for example, the case of the recent federal requirement for a National Bioengineered Food Disclosure Standard (NBFDS), as mandated by amendments to the Agricultural Marketing Act of 1946 that went into effect in July 2016.[54] The law was enacted as a proactive and reactive measure to preempt the rise of a potential patchwork of conflicting state or local GMO labeling laws all over the country[55] and supersede a set of laws that had recently been enacted in a few states, such as Vermont's Act 120[56]—which was set to take effect on July 1, 2016 and mandated stringent labeling laws for all food produced via genetic-engineering technologies.

The NBFDS was first introduced as part of the Safe and Accurate Food Labeling Act of 2015 (SAFLA), which failed in the previous Congress—the bill passed in the House of Representatives but did not receive enough support in the Senate. Once Vermont's law went into effect on July 1, 2016, however, Congress scrambled to enact legislation that would ensure national uniformity of labeling laws for food derived from genetically engineered crops. Pressure began to mount and proposed amendments to the original SAFLA finally garnered the consensus required for compromise. Within two weeks, Congress reintroduced an amended version of the SAFLA as part of a bill to reauthorize and amend the National Sea Grant College Program Act—and for other purposes—which passed with bipartisan support and was enacted into law on July 29, 2016.[57]

Several concessions took place as a prerequisite for compromise on the path toward the NBFDS. Some supporters of strict GMO labeling laws had to step away from the establishment of rigid labeling standards and an overly broad definition of bioengineered foods that might have required virtually all processed foods that contains high-fructose corn syrup—a sweetener derived from corn starch that is ubiquitous in myriad prepackaged products including breakfast cereals, salad dressings, breads, snack foods, nutrition bars, coffee creamers, soft drinks, candies, and numerous other popular food items sold at every supermarket—to be labeled as containing genetically modified ingredients. By the same token, some opponents of GMO labeling laws had to agree to include on-package information featuring a telephone number or any electronic or digital link that could be scanned by a smartphone or a similar digital device for the purpose of obtaining more information about the bioengineered contents of food products.[58]

Compromise rendered the NBFDS incomplete insofar as it only partially addressed the issue of labeling bioengineered foods. Many law and policy makers are already aware of some gaps in the law. For instance, the definition of bioengineered food under the NBFDS is narrow and applies only to foodstuff containing "genetic material that has been modified through in vitro recombinant [DNA] techniques."[59] If "genetic material" means DNA under the statute—as it likely would—then most packaged products that contain ingredients derived from genetically engineered crops, which are sold at supermarkets everywhere, would not be considered bioengineered because they actually have no detectable DNA. Furthermore, scannable digital links are not qualitatively fungible with overt labels. Many consumers without access to digital devices in rural or poverty-stricken areas and the elderly may not have the means to access the information on the digital links. The gaps pointed out above may be completely anticipated, yet law and policy makers did not, and could not, address them because of lack of consensus surrounding some of these issues.

Imperfect as the NBFDS might be, it is better than having no federal law applicable to bioengineered food labeling. Federal jurisdiction over the regulation of food labeling ensures uniformity of the law. Without a uniform and consistent set of rules, each state would be free to set its own mandates, which could impose a heavy burden on interstate commerce activity.[60] A manufacturer would potentially have to comply with fifty different labeling requirements, each of which could be subject to change at any point in time. This, in turn, would likely make products more expensive, as manufacturers would pass down costs to consumers.[61] It is, therefore, no surprise that the food industry lobby spent millions of dollars aimed at preventing passage of state-mandated food labeling laws for bioengineered food.[62]

From a scientific standpoint, the rationale to impose mandatory label requirements for bioengineered foods is weak given that a scientific consensus has formed to support the health or environmental safety of genetically modified crops. That proposition is supported by investigations of the US National Academies of Science, Engineering, and Medicine[63] as well as scientific panels including the American Association for the Advancement of Science,[64] the American Medical Association, the European Commission,[65] the Royal Society of the United Kingdom,[66] and National Academies of Science in Australia, Brazil, China, France, Germany, India, and other countries.[67] Mandatory labels, therefore, could promote a misconception that bioengineered food is less safe than, or not nutritionally equivalent to, nonbioengineered food, which "can only serve to mislead and falsely alarm consumers."[68] Opponents of any mandatory labeling of bioengineered foods have already called for the repeal of the NBFDS citing the costs of implementation, the lack of scientific basis for the law, and the absence of any purported benefits to consumers, human health, and the environment.[69] A repeal scenario, however, is unlikely to occur given the contentious nature of bioengineered food among particular segments of the general public. The politically charged environment concerning genetically modified crops for human consumption and related laws make it difficult for law and policy makers to reach compromise. Accordingly, both supporters and opponents of mandatory labeling laws will likely have to get used to the narrow applicability and federal preemption features of the NBFDS.

* * *

The takeaway message from all the aforementioned cases concerning measures to address myriad issues ranging from human cloning and air travel to national security, bioengineered food, and more is that they are woven together by a common thread that has nothing to do with the conventional dogma associated with a presumed inability of the law to keep up with new developments—scientific or not. Rather, the common denominator is compromise. What those lessons teach us is that consensus breeds compromise. And there is hardly anything that the law cannot address—whether good or bad, fair or disproportionate, measured or ill-conceived—when compromise permeates, supports, and constitutes and integral part of active law and policy making.

Contrary to the conventional thinking that law always lags behind scientific progress, it is clear, as has been laid out in this chapter, that law can either precede or succeed relevant scientific or technological advances. Law can also be used either as a proactive or reactive instrument (or both). When used reactively, it may in fact be swift, and need not be laggard. Furthermore, even when legal gaps, challenges, and limitations are foreseen, the law may be left purposefully incomplete for good reasons—if the law is too proactive or reactive, it may hinder technological progress and innovation. Incompleteness may sometimes be advantageous because law ought to be a product of careful study and debate, not haphazard knee-jerk reactions and one-size-fits-all solutions. Significant potential gaps in the law are often the direct result of a collapse of the compromise process, rather than the rare but actual instances in which no one could have anticipated a particular outcome that tests the applicable limits of the law.

Understanding the role of compromise in law and policy making can help dispel the fog that often enshrouds the simplistic view that law cannot keep up with scientific innovation. A legislative, administrative, or judicial body that grapples for months or years with difficult issues about the contours of what should be permitted, prohibited, or regulated under the law is unlikely to have the political capital to revisit those issues on a whim every time new challenges arise. Working through and removing gridlock in the path toward compromise is a heavy task, which requires persuasion and building consensus on any given issue. That is partly why, despite nearly a decade of controversy following the enactment of the Patient

Protection and Affordable Care Act[70] (ACA)—also known as Obamacare—Congress is unable to pass legislation to overhaul the entire US healthcare system once again. It is why the NBFDS is unlikely to be repealed and replaced with an alternate bill that rehashes mandatory labeling of bioengineered food. It is also why the Supreme Court seldom grants a writ of certiorari to review legal questions concerning issues that have been recently litigated and adjudicated, particularly when the nine members of the Court—who sometimes approach judicial analysis and decision making from different perspectives—have devoted weeks and months of work and compromise to build enough consensus to issue a majority, or at least a plurality, opinion on a given case.

VI LOOK IT UP!—IN A CAN OF WORMS

Because compromise entails a demanding process, the particular meaning of terms as laid out in textual statutory, regulatory, and other legal language can often be obscure. Definitions, if any exist at all and garnered sufficient consensus to become law, may be riddled with vagueness, ambiguity, and incompleteness. That leaves to the judiciary the challenging task of interpreting terms that become the subject of disputes.

Without any clear guidance from the legal text to be interpreted, members of the judiciary have turned—with incremental frequency—to dictionaries as guides.[71] On its face, that is not an unreasonable thing to do. Who among us, after all, has not at some point used a dictionary as a compass in the search for meaning of a particular term we are unfamiliar with? In fact, we have learned and grown accustomed, from a very early age, to look up words we do not know in dictionaries.

While searching terms in dictionaries may be desirable for most common purposes, judicial reliance on dictionaries is controversial and problematic in many respects.[72] Critics of the usage of dictionaries in modern jurisprudence have pointed out that judges are regularly consulting dictionaries in highly subjective and result-oriented modes.[73] No discernible rules or patterns currently exist to forecast when and how judges may selectively use dictionaries as interpretive sources in the exercise of judicial duties. Selective dictionary use, or "cherry-picking," is therefore a growing concern in the legal community.

To add a layer of complexity, the cherry-picking may be twofold. First, judges may inconsistently cherry-pick and use different dictionaries sold by various publishing companies. To date, for example, more than 120 different dictionaries have been cited in opinions by Justices of the United States Supreme Court.[74] Second, judges may cherry-pick one or more specific entries among many others found for the same term in any given dictionary. For instance, recall the case of Knoodles earlier in this chapter. The entries (definitions) cited to interpret the meaning of the word "pet" in that example corresponded to one of ten different entries in the Cambridge Dictionary and one of eight entries in the Merriam-Webster Dictionary. In the

Cambridge Dictionary, the definition cited appeared first in the list. In the Merriam-Webster Dictionary, conversely, the definition cited appeared in second place after the use of the word pet to describe a spoiled child.[75] Thus, cherry-picking one single entry among a litany of others in the same dictionary introduces the issue of definitional priority, namely, whether the order in which an entry appears in a dictionary should indicate, from a legal standpoint, a more common—and, thus, purportedly more persuasive and significant—meaning for the searched term.[76]

The crux of the dilemma surrounding the use of dictionaries as authoritative sources in primary legal literature is not lost outside the legal community, particularly not on lexicographers. The bottom line is that "[a] dictionary is a collection of somebody's words in somebody's book. Whose words are collected and who collects them influence what kind of book a given dictionary turns out to be, and in turn, whose purposes it can best serve."[77]

A former Principal Editor at the Oxford English Dictionary opined in a *New York Times* piece that the use of dictionaries in the courtroom is "probably wrong, in almost all situations. Dictionary definitions are written with a lot of things in mind, but rigorously circumscribing the exact meanings and connotations of terms is not usually one of them."[78] The notion of dictionaries as instruments that present an exhaustive coverage of the language has become the lexicographical ethos of modern times. Yet, despite the implication of completeness that is general among dictionaries, the gathering of sources of meaning upon which dictionaries rely is anything but methodical or all-inclusive.[79] To the contrary, serendipity and bias permeate the search of sources covered, which depends on the "application of a delicate sensibility and years of educated subjectivity."[80]

Although modern lexicographers continue—to some extent—using techniques from the eighteenth and nineteenth centuries to collect lexicographical sources,[81] they are also increasingly relying on electronic searches of commercial online databases featuring full texts published by highly influential press or media outlets, starting with the *New York Times*, which currently stands as "the single most powerful influence in constituting the record of the English lexicon."[82] Thus, the unfettered use of dictionaries to interpret and construe legal text is a form of deference that grants power to a coterie of dictionary editors, who are chiefly concerned with broad meanings that may be inapposite to the particular subtleties and contexts that arise in specific cases and controversies where legal interpretation and construction have no substitute. As one commentator put it, it may come as a surprise to judges "who look to dictionaries as authorities in construing statutes, that in good measure they are interpreting law according to the *New York Times*."[83]

To be clear, dictionaries can be valuable tools in learning language, and perhaps even in the very early stages of legal interpretation. We must remember, however, that "it is one of the surest indexes of a mature and developed jurisprudence not to make a fortress out of the dictionary . . . ."[84] Laws and legal text "cannot be understood merely by understanding the words in [them]. . . . [D]ictionaries are like . . .

'word zoos.' One can observe an animal's features in the zoo, but one still cannot be sure how the animal will behave in its native surroundings. The same is true of words in a text."[85]

Ultimately, a profound discussion of whether the use of dictionaries is appropriate in legal interpretive analysis is beyond the scope of this chapter. And despite the aforementioned issues and limitations associated with defining specific terminology, as well as the use of dictionaries as sources of interpretive meaning that have been explored throughout this chapter, it is worth noting that specific, clear, adequate, and concise definitions are essential tools in effective legal interpretation and construction. In fact, one could go as far as asserting that such definitions are a necessity in the process of interpretive analysis. After all, how should we regulate or delineate legal boundaries for that which we cannot define?

A *Genome Editing and Ordinary Meaning*

A proper definition functions as a legal compass that can orient judges, scholars, and practitioners in their search for meaning of terms. When no definition is ascribed to a term, a fundamental canon of construction prescribes that "words will be interpreted as taking their ordinary, contemporary, common meaning."[86] And courts will generally turn to dictionaries to help ascertain if a particular word "has a plain or common meaning."[87] The problem with this approach is that it overlooks the fact that dictionaries rely largely on written sources created by and for the upper, educated classes and underrepresent the speech and writing created by and for people who are relatively uneducated.[88] Critics argue that, as a result, dictionaries speak only for an educated minority, which in turn calls into question whether the dictionary is a suitable medium to present ordinary and common language.[89]

The "ordinary and common meaning" canon of construction is also problematic as it applies to genome editing and other technical concepts. If genome editing is undefined, how can we expect judges to know the "ordinary meaning" of a term that is inherently scientific in nature? The general public, for example, is still largely unfamiliar with the concept of genome editing, which implies that an ordinary meaning for the term does not exist or has not yet formed. If legal disputes ensue, litigants may wish to introduce evidence of the meaning of genome editing that serves their specific purposes. Absent clear and concise definitions, courts may follow whatever rules of construction they see fit and continue to search for ordinary meaning in dictionaries. But current dictionary definitions of genome editing lack accuracy, specificity, and clarity.

Most contemporary dictionaries do not contain a definition for the term "genome editing." Some dictionaries, however, include a definition for the term "gene editing" (we will discuss, in Section VII next, why despite common interchangeable treatment of genome editing and gene editing, the two terms concern distinct concepts). Consider the following various dictionaries—some of which have been cited in opinions authored by Justices of the United States Supreme Court—that feature entries for genome editing or gene editing:

- Gene editing, as defined in the *Cambridge Dictionary*, relates to "the process of changing genes using scientific methods, in order to cure or prevent disease."[90]
- The *Merriam-Webster Dictionary* defines gene editing as "the use of biotechnological techniques to make changes to specific DNA sequences in the genome of a living organism."[91]
- The term genome or gene editing does not appear in the *Oxford English Dictionary*; however, a "draft addition" to the noun "editing" was added in March 2019, which defines gene editing in the context of molecular biology as "[t]he naturally occurring or artificial alteration of a gene or other nucleotide sequence, involving the insertion, deletion, or replacement of one or more nucleotides."[92]
- The *Oxford's Advanced Learner's Dictionary* includes a definition for the term gene editing that refers to "a treatment in which scientists remove, repair or replace genes that are not normal, using special enzymes."[93]
- The *Macmillan Dictionary* defines gene editing as "a type of genetic engineering in which DNA is inserted, replaced or removed from a genome using specially engineered enzymes called restriction enzymes or molecular scissors."[94]
- The *Collins English Dictionary*, unlike most other contemporary dictionaries, includes an entry for genome editing, which is defined as "the insertion or removal of DNA at a specific site on a genome using artificially engineered nucleases."[95]
- Other dictionaries such as *The American Heritage Dictionary*,[96] *Black's Law Dictionary*,[97] and *Merriam-Webster's Dictionary of Law*[98] do not have entries for the terms genome editing or gene editing. In the absence of such definitions, judges could potentially look for ordinary meaning by breaking up the term genome editing into two words and provide an interpretive analysis by examining the meaning of each constituent word. That, of course, is problematic as it would be somewhat akin to interpreting the term "cherry-picking" by looking at the words "cherry" and "pick" separately and without proper context. The former phrase may refer to a type of confirmation bias or the act of choosing things—data, evidence, facts, etc.—in a highly selective manner so as to present what is favorable and reject the unfavorable; the latter individual words used jointly may, conversely, refer to the literal act of picking cherries (the fruit).

As pointed out earlier, dictionary definitions may be desirable for most common purposes. However, in the realm of litigation and judicial interpretation, where outcomes may ultimately depend on nuanced interpretations of what constitutes genome editing under the law, the use of dictionary definitions possessing a dearth of substance can only lead to more confusion (see Section VII) rather than clarity. Worse still, even if litigants introduce evidence of particular meanings, courts are not bound to follow them. Dictionaries and other basic reference sources may be "admitted, not as evidence, but only as aids to the memory and understanding of the court."[99] Accordingly, courts may render interpretations and meanings that directly eschew scientific evidence.

B *Lessons from Tomatoes*

History teaches lessons that often fall on deaf ears. Consider *Nix v. Hedden*,[100] a case with a quirky set of facts in which a unanimous United States Supreme Court ruled that a tomato—notwithstanding its botanical classification as a fruit—is a vegetable as a matter of law.

Following the end of the Civil War, the United States favored protectionist measures aimed to benefit American commercial interests at the cost of free trade.[101] Criticisms on protectionist trade policies began to grow louder in the last quarter on the nineteenth century and led to the enactment of the Tariff Act of 1883. The Tariff Act reflected the compromise required to assuage disgruntled regional constituencies in support or opposition of the trade-policy status quo. The legislation increased tariff rates on some goods and reduced them marginally for others, but the net effect was minimal and protectionist policies remained in place.[102] The Tariff Act was not effective in reforming the tariff system and became unpopular to the point that no one wanted to claim credit for the law, which was colloquially dubbed the "Mongrel Tariff."[103]

To protect certain domestic agricultural interests, a provision of the Tariff Act of 1883 imposed a ten percent tariff on imported vegetables, but not on "[f]ruits, green, ripe, or dried."[104] John Nix & Co., a Manhattan wholesaler at the time, had begun importing produce from foreign lands, including tomatoes from the Caribbean. When one shipment of tomatoes from Bermuda arrived to the United States in the spring of 1886, the collector of the port of New York imposed a ten percent tariff under the Tariff Act. The owners of John Nix & Co., paid the tariff under protest and sued to recover the duties assessed on the shipment. They argued that the collector had wrongfully imposed the tariff because tomatoes are fruits and not vegetables.

During the trial, the owners introduced into evidence the definitions of the terms "fruit," "vegetables," and "tomatoes" found in the Webster's Dictionary, Worcester's Dictionary, and Imperial Dictionary.[105] The dictionaries concurred in defining fruit as "the seed of plaints [sic], or that part of plaints [sic] which contains the seed, and especially the juicy, pulpy products of certain plants, covering and containing the seed."[106] Notwithstanding the definitions cited, the lower court ruled against the owners and held that "the word 'fruit,' irrespective of what the dictionaries may lay down as to its botanical or technical meaning, is not in common speech used to cover tomatoes."[107] The owners then appealed the ruling to the Supreme Court. Their fate, nevertheless, had already been sealed at trial.

The Supreme Court acknowledged that "[b]otanically speaking, tomatoes are the fruit of a vine."[108] However, the Court went onto explain, "in the common language of the people" tomatoes are vegetables because people grow them in gardens, and are usually served cooked or raw during dinner—either with soup or an entrée course—but not alongside dessert in the way people generally serve fruits.[109]

That logic is, of course, somewhat perplexing. Never mind that people have been growing fruits in gardens for centuries. And although I cannot speak for the culinary proclivities of our nineteenth-century ancestors, it is difficult for my mind, at the moment, to block out visuals of a delicious kale salad with raw apple and strawberry slices, bacon bits, and sprinkled walnuts. Or the myriad entrée courses served with fruits—think of grilled pork chops with caramelized peaches, a roasted salmon with oranges and mandarins, a sweet potato-pineapple soup, a blueberry-mango risotto, and even the deeply controversial pineapple-on-pizza that embroils fierce passion among select groups of pizza aficionados. But I digress!

From a botanical standpoint, which concerns the scientific study of plants through various disciplines that have become integrated into plant biology, the meaning of "fruit" has remained unchanged despite the Supreme Court's ruling in *Nix*. Just as it did before *Nix* was decided, a fruit is "[s]trictly, the ripened ovary of a plant and its contents. More loosely, the term is extended to the ripened ovary and seeds together with any structure with which they are combined."[110]

Tomatoes fall squarely within the botanical definition of the term fruit. Yet, under the tariff laws of the United States, tomatoes are classified as vegetables because the Supreme Court says so.

It bears noting that the status of tomatoes as vegetables, however, extends only as far as the jurisdiction of the US Supreme Court. The European Union, for instance, has expressly declined to follow the law of the United States and instead defined tomatoes as fruits in its legislative acts.[111]

The key principle and lasting significance of *Nix*, for purposes of our discussion, is that the Supreme Court chose not to defer to the scientific meaning of the disputed term. Rather, the Court relied on the uncertain common language and knowledge of the people at the time to dictate the meaning of "fruit" under the Tariff Act.

The ruling raises two important considerations. First, just like tomatoes, genome editing may have one or more particular meanings in the language of science, but additional meanings—which may not be accurate or precise—could attach to the term in common parlance. And if that occurs, genome editing will be—for all practical purposes, including social, economic, regulatory, commercial, and more—whatever courts say it ought to be.

Second, to justify an ordinary-meaning interpretation, the *Nix* Court did not examine the properties and characteristics of tomatoes, but rather how and when they are used. In the same way, it is not far-fetched to foresee a scenario in which courts may interpret genome editing on the basis of how and when it is used, and what it is used for, rather than what it *actually* is. Law and policy makers must recognize that such an interpretive analysis increases the likelihood of confusion between genome editing and other scientifically distinguishable technological terms that involve genetic tinkering and manipulations such as gene therapy, genetic engineering, genome regulation, and others. On this point, there is evidence already that a variety of genome editing meanings are percolating into common language via dictionaries that explicitly define genome editing according to what it may be used for—for example, therapeutic and medicinal purposes—as opposed to its conceptual meaning.[112]

C *Sharing Responsibilities*

Scientists and interdisciplinary experts on genome editing bear a substantial burden to ensure that the principles and essence of what constitutes genome editing are communicated properly and effectively with law and policy makers, as well as general audiences. Law and policy makers, in turn, have a responsibility to become informed, heed the advice of scientists and other experts, and engage openly and transparently with experts and the general public when conflicting laws and policies that are inconsistent with science-based principles must be instituted. Accordingly, it is incumbent upon all interested parties to engage in timely discussions and debates about the role that genome editing should play in society.

If the goal is that such conversations or debates shall be productive, we ought to begin by laying principles and foundations about that which must be discussed, especially if the subject of discussion correlates with different contexts and multiple meanings. And that all starts with defining the contours of the subject matter under discussion. A suitable and robust definition can supply and facilitate a common understanding of a particular subject and, thus, help all participants to communicate more efficiently with each other. Even if individuals disagree on specific grounds, they will be more likely to engage in fruitful discussions if they possess a common understanding of the subject being discussed. It is, therefore, imperative that discussions about how best to define genome editing occur at this point in time before confusion and alternative meanings take root.

D *Not in the Abstract*

From a conceptual standpoint, drafting a well-thought-out definition entails a demanding task. Creating a robust definition, therefore, is inescapably a labor-intensive process. In carrying out that process, we must first and foremost acknowledge the inherent limitations of defining broad concepts, as has been laid out throughout this chapter. No one-size-fits-all definition that will apply perfectly to every situation exists. Nor will there ever be a definition that every genome-editing stakeholder endorses without reservations.

At a prefatorial level, crafting a genome-editing definition should not entail a process that examines genome editing in the abstract, so as to ascribe ontological properties to the term. The rationale against abstract conceptualization of the term is simple: Genome editing specifically concerns technological advances, scientific methods, and processes fit for particular and tangible purposes; the goal is to use the technology to bring about a downstream result, application, or product.

A definition of genome editing, therefore, should be as descriptive and as precise as reasonably possible, to facilitate uniformity and predictability in statutory and regulatory interpretation and construction. Abstract discussions about the virtue and rightness of using genome editing for specific purposes are surely proper through philosophical and ethical perspectives, but should not dictate how the term is defined. In other words, ontological assumptions, philosophical examinations, and abstract conceptualization of genome editing should apply only to matters concerning *how*, *where*, *when*, and *why* humans may promote or hinder—in various societal contexts—a given downstream use of genome-editing technology. Abstractions should neither govern nor define what genome editing *actually is* or what it *ought to be*.

Besides lacking abstract quality, a definition of genome editing should also strive to avoid vagueness and ambiguity. A definition, much like a law, "must provide explicit standards for those who apply [it]."[113] Just as "[a] vague law impermissibly delegates basic policy matters to policemen, judges, and juries for resolution on an ad hoc and subjective basis, with the attendant dangers of arbitrary and discriminatory applications,"[114] so too does a vague and ambiguous definition succumb to the same logical perils for any who must interpret it.

There are, of course, instances where vagueness and ambiguity can be useful. To illustrate this point, consider examples of renown terms found in the United States Constitution such as "cruel and unusual punishments,"[115] "due process,"[116] "freedom of speech,"[117] "unreasonable searches and seizures,"[118] "probable cause,"[119] "equal protection,"[120] among others. The Framers of the Constitution purposefully incorporated these vague and ambiguous terms in the document's text in order to help ratify and adopt it. Ambiguity and vagueness served an important purpose at the time, which was to facilitate compromise and avoid pugnacious dissension among the Founders, who often espoused incompatible political beliefs and diametric views about the type of nation the United States should become. As a result of their inherent vague and ambiguous nature, these constitutional terms require extensive interpretation, so much so that they fill entire volumes of the United States Reports—the official collection of bound decisions for the United States Supreme Court—as well as other legal treatises and encyclopedias.

Ambiguity and vagueness served a utilitarian purpose at the time the Constitution was drafted, but that purpose was specific to the fine details of a charter document that defined the creation and structure of a new government system. Genome editing, conversely, should not be defined as an abstract, vague, and ambiguous concept. Doing so would permit certain interested stakeholders to inject self-serving, arbitrary, and subjective interpretations that may be antithetical to the greater public good. Society as a whole—not select and powerful interest groups—should decide what genome editing is by following a rational and science-based approach.

The time has come to jumpstart the process of formally defining genome editing and fill this salient gap in the public sphere, as well as the scholarly literature. An avalanche of legal, social, economic, and ethical issues—many of which will be discussed throughout this book—is growing and accelerating rapidly as technological development matures. We can no longer afford to bear the cost of turning a blind eye or a deaf ear to this issue.

No formal genome editing definition currently exists. Neither Congress nor any administrative agencies have assumed leadership roles to address the need for a more concrete and standard definition. A congressional resolution, for example, was recently introduced by three law makers in the US Senate and called for international ethical standards in genome-editing research.[121] Yet, paradoxically, it did not even articulate a specific meaning for the use of the term genome editing beyond the fact that it can be used to change genetic material.[122] And as we saw earlier in this chapter, the international scientific community has not called, or expressed an appetite, for a uniform definition either.[123] Time is of the essence. If we fail to encourage ex ante analyses of the benefits of establishing a consensus toward a unified concrete meaning of genome editing at this point in time, we can expect inconsistent interpretations or arbitrary rulings when the issue becomes the subject of litigation. Let us learn from lessons of the past, lest genome editing share the same legal fate as the tomato in the wake of *Nix v. Hedden*.

Next, this chapter analyzes the proposed genome-editing definition by considering its constituent elements.

VII BREAK IT DOWN

Until now, this chapter has examined the need and rationale for developing a more uniform definition of genome editing, explored the pivotal role of compromise as a factor in establishing a definition, gauged limitations concerning the use of dictionaries as interpretive tools, and outlined strategies to overcome potential barriers imposed by vagueness and ambiguity in the path toward a unified definition. Having laid this conceptual foundation, let us now begin the analysis in this next section by reiterating the genome-editing definition proposed earlier in this chapter:

> ***Genome editing***, as referred to throughout this book, encompasses scientific, technological advances that enable the rational design of targeted genomic or genetic modifications—and, by logical extension, the process of bringing the design to fruition—at a local (for example, gene, regulatory region, etc.) or global (genome-wide) level with the aim of facilitating the precise insertion, addition, removal,

> conversion, or substitution of DNA molecules, comprising one or more nucleotides —such as those containing a nitrogenous base including, but not limited to, Adenine (A), Cytosine (C), Guanine (G), Thymine (T), and possibly others, which may be synthetically derived—into or from the cell(s) of a natural or semisynthetic living organism.[124]

The above definition appears straightforward on its face. However, as laid out at the beginning of this chapter, there is quite a bit of textual unpacking to do here. The most logical and efficient way to examine the language in the definition is, thus, to break it down into discrete portions so that we may assess and scrutinize the raison d'être for each of its constituent parts.

- ***Rational design***. A definition of genome editing that is legally meaningful should comprise the domain of working toward carrying out genomic modifications through cognitive means. This requires thinking and the conceptualization of a strategy about what DNA sequences are to be modified.

  Rational thus means, in this context, deliberate and intentional. To fall under the definition, DNA modifications cannot arise stochastically through sheer luck or happenstance. A rationality requirement ensures that the putative definition distinguishes between genome editing that occurs naturally from that which is caused by human intervention. Some retroviruses, for example, are capable of mediating natural genome editing. When the retrovirus infects a host organism, it inserts a copy of its genome into the DNA of the host's cells, thereby triggering changes in the genome of the host. But this type of naturally occurring genome editing cannot be deemed rational. Unlike humans, a virus does not think, is not self-aware, has no mind of its own, and does not resort to cognition to perform specific genetic changes.

  The rational-design limitation, in essence, confines genome editing to human activity and removes nature from the equation. It is possible that at some point in the future genome editing may be carried out through artificial intelligence, which will raise interesting questions related to whether future machine- or computer-mediated genome editing constitutes a rational enterprise. Until that time comes, if ever, a definition ought to focus exclusively on human-mediated genome editing.
- ***To fruition***. The rational design of genomic or genetic modifications implies intent, yet intent alone is not sufficient to induce genome editing. Bringing the design to fruition requires coupling intent with action—*think, then do*. Under the definition, merely designing an experiment would not constitute genome editing; the experiment needs to be carried out. This is a significant point because the law generally concerns conduct or actions, rather than thoughts.
- ***Technological advances***. The proposed definition encompasses scientific, technological advances as a tacit requirement for harnessing, repurposing,

adapting, or co-opting natural phenomena for genome-editing purposes. Under the definition, genome editing, therefore, depends on human ingenuity.

- ***Targeted***. Genome editing should be directed toward select, specific, target sites on an organism's genome. That focus would generally help to differentiate genome editing as a subset of the broader concept of genome engineering, which is often incorrectly used interchangeably and has generally been associated with the making of *untargeted* genetic changes. Prior generations of scientists, for example, have relied on first-generation genetic-engineering techniques to introduce genes or other genetic sequences of interest into living cells, but the problem is that they have not being able to control precisely where those changes are made. Genetic changes that land unexpectedly on a region of functional relevance can be highly deleterious to any organism. This is one of the primary reasons why scientists and researchers have, for roughly the past three decades, worried about the prospect of using gene therapy to correct genetic diseases while simultaneously introducing unintended changes capable of turning on oncogenes—a type of genes that when mutated or expressed at high levels predisposes cells to cancer—or disrupting the function of other genetic regions. Genome editing helps to turn the page on that narrative because it enables a more targeted manipulation of genetic sequences.
- ***Modification of DNA***. By specifying that genome editing involves the modification of DNA molecules, namely genetic sequences or fragments of DNA, the definition of genome editing excludes any other technologies that target modification of other bioorganic polymers such as RNAs, proteins, or polysaccharides—long chains of carbohydrates comprising chemically bonded sugar molecules. Hence, for example, modification of RNA molecules (RNA editing) would fall outside the province of genome editing, even though the process of making RNA modifications may share certain tools and mechanisms in common with the process of making DNA modifications.[125]

  Likewise, a genome-editing definition would exclude manipulation of the epigenome, which broadly refers to the layer of physical and chemical features that constitute the environment surrounding the genome. Alterations of the epigenome—including histone post-translational modifications, regulatory ncRNAs, and DNA epigenetic modifications that collectively regulate the genome and chromatin structure—belong to a separate category of techniques aimed at epigenome editing.[126]
- ***Precise***. The proposed definition includes an overarching "aim of facilitating" precise, targeted DNA modifications. Precise, under the definition, is a relative—not absolute—term and does not mean perfect. Rather, the term should be defined and analyzed from a vantage point of *aiming* to generate *substantially* accurate DNA modifications at a given target site.

  To illustrate this concept, consider precision in terms of sport. Archery and soccer, for instance, involve athletes or players attempting to hit a specific target in a particular location. Individuals must use an array of skills to estimate how much kinetic energy must be imparted on an arrow or ball, so as to propel the objects across a given distance toward the target site. The athletes must carefully consider the force, angle, and velocity required to accomplish the task, as well as many other variables ranging from the direction of the wind and other weather conditions to obstacles standing along the path toward the target. The athletes' cognitive determinations vis-à-vis the aforementioned factors are intentional and collectively performed in furtherance of the goal of hitting the desired target with high precision. To hit a bulls-eye or score a goal, the individual must be precise, and so doing constitutes a measure of the individual's skills. Perfection, however, is not a requirement for engaging in the sports of archery or soccer. And one would not consider an athlete to be engaging in either sport *only* when she hits the intended target, namely the bulls-eye or goal.

In a similar way, precision should be embedded in a formal definition of genome editing. A researcher must use cognitive skills to plan out how to precisely modify a DNA target by, among other factors, designing appropriate guide RNAs, considering potential off-target editing sites to minimize them, choosing a delivery method for the genome-editing tools of her choice, deciding what concentration of reagents to use, and timing the experiments accordingly. Each factor must be carried out deliberately and in furtherance of facilitating the goal of making precise DNA modifications at the target site. The degree of precision is likely to be directly proportional to how much thought, skill, and attention to detail went into the process. But as long as the researcher follows that cognitive process, she will have performed genome editing, even if the results of a given genome-editing experiment demonstrate the incidence of off-target editing.

In sum, one cannot perform genome editing without considering precision. An archer who shoots arrows toward a target with the intent to hit it and fails to do so can be considered imprecise, unskilled, or even unlucky, but still an archer nevertheless. In contrast, an individual who shoots arrows aimlessly at the sky or in random directions is, well, merely shooting arrows aimlessly as opposed to engaging in archery. Analogously, a researcher performs genome editing only when she aims to create precise DNA modifications and carries out experiments tailored specifically to such target sites. Conversely, a researcher who uses chemical or molecular tools to trigger random genetic modifications is merely performing random mutagenesis, not genome editing.

Lastly, one point deserves clarification in this discussion. Perfection is not an essential element of the proposed definition, but that should not translate into the notion that an exceptionally high or substantial degree of precision is irrelevant or inconsequential in genome editing. The benchmark for precision ought to be context-dependent. The threshold level of precision required for a genome-editing experiment may differ vastly depending on the purpose for which genome editing is performed. For example, genome editing aimed at probing genetic sequences for basic research purposes in vitro in a cell line or model organism may call for a lower standard of precision compared to genome editing performed for clinical purposes. The latter would call for highly accurate and precise genome editing because it involves research in human subjects.

- ***Local or global.*** Genome editing may be performed molecularly at a local or global scale. It should not exclusively apply to the sequences that make up genes—otherwise it would technically just be gene editing. The definition, thus, covers the modification of a range of noncoding DNA sequences, which constitute the majority of an organism's genome and may include intergenic regulatory regions, satellite DNA sequences, telomeric sequences, enhancer regions, silencer regions, centromeric sequences, transposons and retrotransposons, and others. Genome editing may be performed locally on any specific type of DNA sequence, or globally (genome-wide) to a multitude of DNA regions of the genome. Under the definition, therefore, genome editing encompasses DNA modifications via gene editing as well as noncoding DNA editing.
- ***Insertion, addition, removal, conversion, and substitution.*** It is important to distinguish and elaborate on these terms because they can often be used interchangeably in plain language. Insertion and addition, much like removal and substitution, can be synonymous depending on the context in which they are used.

  Removal within the meaning of genome editing may relate to excising or taking nucleotides out of a given target site only, whereas substitution may refer to taking nucleotides out and replacing them with one or more other nucleotides at the same locus.

  Conversion and substitution may lead to the same result, but they entail distinct processes. Consider the making of a targeted adenosine to guanosine modification, which is often represented as A→G in scientific notation, at a gene locus. Conversion may involve the hydrolytic deamination of adenosine to yield inosine, which is read or replicated as guanosine by certain polymerases and produces an A→G mutation at the target site, without the need to cleave the DNA phosphate backbone. Substitution, on the other hand, may implicate making a double-stranded break at the target DNA site, followed by homology-directed repair to generate the A→G mutation. Although the culmination of both processes may yield the same A→G modification, conversion would be mediated through what is now known as base editing,[127] whereas substitution would be established via gene editing. Accordingly, DNA modifications that fall under the proposed definition may originate from base editing or gene editing, both of which may be classified as subtypes of genome editing.

  Not all conversions, however, may constitute genome editing. Consider the conversion of cytosine into 5-methyldeoxycytosine (m^5dC) by a class of enzymes known as DNA methyltransferases, as well as the subsequent conversion of m^5dC into 5-hydroxymethyldeoxycytosine (hm^5dC), 5-formylcytosine (f^5C), and 5-carboxylcytosine (ca^5C) oxidation derivatives.[128] Each of these conversions occur on the cytosine base, but none of them substitute or change the cytosine into another nitrogenous base—in other words, m^5dC and hm^5dC can be thought of as merely different versions of the same cytosine. The conversions constitute DNA epigenetic modifications that regulate the target DNA without altering its sequence and relate exclusively to the province of epigenome editing,[129] which is outside the scope of the proposed genome-editing definition.

Lastly, although addition and insertion can sometimes be treated interchangeably, the terms may denote subtle differences in specific contexts under the proposed definition. To insert, for instance, means to put or introduce between or into something, whereas to add means to join or unite so as to increase in size or quantity. The use of either insertion or addition would properly describe the introduction of a short fragment of DNA between two adjacent genes. However, suppose a researcher seeks to extend the end of a telomere—a stretch of distal DNA sequence that protects the ends of chromosomes—by introducing a fragment of DNA at the end of a chromosome. Technically speaking, the DNA fragment in this scenario would be added, rather than inserted, at the telomere. To minimize the chance for ambiguity, the proposed definition therefore features both addition and insertion.

- ***Natural or synthetic nucleotides***. Recall from the previous chapter that DNA molecules consist of nucleotides linked together via chemical bonds. *Covalent* bonds—which refer to chemical bonds between atoms that share electron pairs—maintain the structure of the DNA sugar-phosphate backbone in place, while hydrogen bonds stabilize either A–T or C–G nitrogenous-base pairings. We learned that the naturally occurring A, C, G, and T nitrogenous bases constitute the renowned genetic alphabet, and that the nitrogenous base Uracil (U) replaces T in all RNA molecules.

  Although the overwhelming majority of DNA nucleotides exclusively comprise A, C, G, and T nitrogenous bases, evidence has shown that Uracil[130] and other natural, noncanonical nitrogenous bases such as Inosine[131] (I), Xanthine[132] (X), Oxanine[133] (O), and others can be incorporated into DNA. As more research on noncanonical nitrogenous bases accrues, scientists may uncover novel functional roles for these bases in DNA replication and repair, which in turn could lead to potential uses in genome-editing technologies. As a result, the proposed definition should not be limited to nucleotides containing the four canonical DNA nitrogenous bases.

  Nor should the genome-editing definition be constrained by the use of natural nucleotides. Indeed, synthetic nucleotides have, in recent years, expanded the canonical four-letter genetic alphabet.[134] And researchers have shown that these artificial nucleotides can be (1) incorporated into DNA by certain classes of DNA polymerases,[135] and (2) transcribed into RNA molecules by some RNA polymerases.[136] There may come a point in time in which already-existing or new synthetic nucleotides become common tools for editing the genomes of natural and semisynthetic living organisms. Accordingly, the proposed definition does not preclude the use of synthetic nucleotides in genome editing.

- ***In cells.*** Broadly speaking, this chapter recommends that genome editing should be limited to modifications of DNA within one or more cells from a living organism. This recommendation does not encompass circumscription to particular types of cells or even environments in which the genome editing takes place. Hence, genome editing may be performed *in vitro*, *in vivo*, or *ex vivo* on any type of cell—ranging from bacterial to plant, animal, etc.—so long as the cell(s) originated from a living organism. The proposed definition would therefore exclude potential modification of certain types of DNA molecules that may be found outside of living cells, including cell-free DNA[137] (cfDNA, also known as circulating free DNA), extrachromosomal circular DNA[138] (eccDNA), cell-free fetal DNA (cffDNA),[139] and other DNA molecules that may be circulating within a living organism but outside its living cells.

  By implication, the definition would also exclude modification of DNA molecules of inert agents or particles, and dead or extinct organisms. Let's explore that last sentence with two specific examples.

  DNA fragments from a fossil, for example, could be extracted, isolated, purified, and subsequently modified via genetic-engineering or even genome-editing tools in a test tube. However, the newly modified fossil DNA could not evolve into a stable and self-propagating configuration unless it was re-introduced into some type of living cell. If a case arose in which the fossil DNA fragment was introduced into a new living cell, there would be no fossil-DNA genome editing taking place. To the contrary, it is the genome of the *living recipient cell* that would, instead, be referred to as having been "*edited*" *with* fossil DNA. The new host cell would then go on to transcribe and translate the information encoded in the fossil DNA fragment.

  Viruses too require a host living cell to propagate. That is because a virus is not a living organism. Inert viral particles may exist outside living cells, but they can only replicate and assemble into more viral particles inside a host cell, which provides the cellular machineries necessary to support those processes. The viral genome—whether in DNA or RNA form—may be extracted, isolated, purified, and subsequently modified in a test tube. But the newly modified viral genome cannot self-propagate without the host cell. Under the proposed definition, viral genome editing would properly apply to targeted modifications of viral genomes that are triggered inside a living host cell, such as during lytic-phase viral proliferation or at latent stages after the viral genome has been integrated into the host-cell genome.[140]

- ***Natural or semisynthetic organisms.*** It almost goes without saying that genome editing, at its core, involves the targeted modification of genomes in *natural* living organisms. However, a definition of genome editing would be remiss without inclusion of *semisynthetic* living organisms, which can now be created —and also edited—using common tools in molecular biotechnology and genetic engineering.[141] Already, scientists are able to create fully recoded, synthetic genomes. And researchers across the world continue to design experiments and publish new work to expand the field of synthetic biology apace. There may come a time in the future in which researchers finally unveil a fully synthetic living organism. In this regard, the proposed definition is forward-looking and builds ample flexibility into the meaning of genome editing to conform to future advances and technologies.

* * *

This chapter has laid an important foundation for the rest of the book. As discussed above, the meaning of terms plays pivotal roles for construction and interpretation purposes. Inconsistent meanings, interpretations, and uses of genome-editing definitions and terminology can only obfuscate future discussions regarding what measures, if any, society should implement to promote or hinder technological development. The working definition proposed here is robust and precise, but also flexible. For example, the definition purposefully avoids incorporating a double-stranded-break limitation into the definition. In so doing, it leaves room for future discoveries and technological developments that may one day enable facile genome editing, writing, and rewriting.

Scientists, scholars, lawyers, and law and policy makers have thus far overlooked the importance of reaching consensus about what exactly genome editing is, and what it ought to mean. It is important that we, as a society, address this gap as we venture forward. For it is not sufficient to simply focus on what genome editing *can do*; we must concern ourselves with what genome editing *means* as well. As Desiderius Erasmus, the Renaissance philosopher and scholar, aptly articulated it:

> [S]ome, the "uninitiated" as the saying goes, while they hurry on to learn about things, neglect a concern for language and, striving after a false economy, incur a very heavy loss. . . . [A] person who is not skilled in the force of language is, of necessity, short-sighted, deluded, and unbalanced in his judgment of things as well. Finally you may observe that *none are more given to constant quibbling over the minutiae of language than those who boast that they pass over mere words and concentrate to the matter itself.*[142]

Notes

1 Scholars often debate whether Socrates in fact spoke the things that are commonly attributed to him. The consensus in the literature is that Socrates made no

philosophical writings in his lifetime. A. R. Lacey, *Our Knowledge of Socrates, in* THE PHILOSOPHY OF SOCRATES: A COLLECTION OF CRITICAL ESSAYS 22 (Gregory Vlastos ed., 1971). The bulk of what is known about Socrates comes from secondary sources regarding his life and thoughts that were written by many of his students, in particular Plato and—to some extent—Xenophon. *See, e.g., id.* at 23–24; Harold Sarf, *Reflections on Kierkegaard's Socrates*, 44 J. HISTORY IDEAS 255, 255 n.2 (1983). Accordingly, extricating concrete philosophical beliefs that belonged to Socrates from those held by his pupils who wrote about him has been a challenge for modern scholars of classical Greek philosophy. It may be the case that general ideas in Socrates's philosophical dialogues originated from Socrates but were subsequently recollected, modified, and recorded in written form from his students' perspectives, thereby muddling the specific contributions that are attributable to Socrates and giving rise to different Socratic versions and interpretations created by his tutees. It is also possible, as has been suggested before, that Socrates was merely a mouthpiece for Plato and others who wished to speak through the literary Socrates. *See, e.g.*, Joanne Waugh, *Socrates and the Character of Platonic Dialogue, in* WHO SPEAKS FOR PLATO?: STUDIES IN PLATONIC ANONIMITY 39 (Gerald A. Press ed., 2000); Debra Nails, *Mouthpiece Schmouthpiece, in* WHO SPEAKS FOR PLATO?: STUDIES IN PLATONIC ANONIMITY 16–17 (Gerald A. Press ed., 2000).

2 *See, e.g.*, Friedo J. W. Herbig, *The Phronesis of Conservation Criminology Phraseology: A Genealogical and Dialectical Narrative*, 15 PHRONIMON, no. 2, at 1 (2014).

3 Unusual as it might appear, reports of individuals keeping wild, venomous snakes as "pets" are not uncommon. *See, e.g.*, Dane Huffman, *Chapel Hill Man Bitten by Pet Cobra Appears in Court*, CBS17 NEWS, June 26, 2016, https://www.cbs17.com/news/chapel-hill-man-bitten-by-pet-cobra-appears-in-court/; Stephen Hudak, *Orlando King Cobra Handler Gives Up Elvis, Other Snakes*, ORLANDO SENTINEL, Jan. 27, 2017, https://www.orlandosentinel.com/news/breaking-news/os-orlando-king-cobra-case-reinstated-20170126-story.html; Ciaran Dunbar, *Cobras Among Northern Ireland's 'Wild Dangerous' Pets*, BBC NEWS, Jan. 28, 2018, https://www.bbc.com/news/uk-northern-ireland-42807970; Rick Miller, *Allegany Man Charged with Keeping Almost 300 Reptiles, Largest Seizure in State History*, OLEAN TIMES HERALD, July 3, 2019, http://www.oleantimesherald.com/olean/allegany-man-charged-with-keeping-almost-reptiles-largest-seizure-in/article_f27e6a46-c440-5190-b38b-525932ffe03b.html.

4 Laws regarding ownership, possession, or transport of venomous snakes vary among jurisdictions. *Compare, e.g.*, N.C. GEN. STAT. § 14–417 (2013) (allowing "any person to own, possess, use, transport, or traffic in any venomous reptile" so long as the animal is "housed in a sturdy and secure enclosure. Permanent enclosures shall be designed to be escape-proof, bite-proof, and have an operable lock. Transport containers shall be designed to be escape-proof and bite-proof.");

and TEX. PARKS & WILDLIFE CODE ANN. § 43.851 (Vernon 2008) (permitting persons to possess or transport live nonindigenous venomous snakes so long as they hold a valid permit), *with* IOWA CODE ANN. § 717F.1–F.3 (2019) (prohibiting persons to "own or possess a dangerous wild animal; [c]ause or allow a dangerous wild animal owned by a person or in the person's possession to breed; [and] [t]ransport a dangerous wild animal into [the] state." The statute explicitly includes cobras and other venomous snakes in the definition of "dangerous wild animals."). In some cases, there may be other municipal or county-specific ordinances that could potentially further restrict the ownership, possession, or transport of venomous snakes beyond the applicable state laws.

5 The phrase "meeting of the minds" refers to the parties' common understanding about the essential terms of the contract. *See, e.g.*, Ekedahl v. COREStaff, Inc., 183 F.3d 855, 858 (D.C. Cir. 1999) ("Proof of a meeting of the minds may be found either in the written agreement or, if the agreement is ambiguous, in the parties' actions at the time of contract formation." (citations omitted)). "Where the parties fail to agree to all material terms, no contract is formed." *Id.* (citations omitted). "[The] 'meeting of the minds' requirement is proved when the evidence shows 'with reasonable definiteness that the minds of the parties met upon the same matter and agreed upon the terms of the contract.'" Howard v. Ferrellgas Partners, L.P., 92 F. Supp. 3d 1115, 1124 (D. Kan. 2015) (quoting Steele v. Harrison, 220 Kan. 422, 428 (1976)).

6 *Pet*, CAMBRIDGE DICTIONARY, https://dictionary.cambridge.org/dictionary/english/pet (last visited Aug. 15, 2019).

7 *Id.*

8 *Pet*, MERRIAM-WEBSTER DICTIONARY, https://www.merriam-webster.com/dictionary/pet (last visited Aug. 15, 2019).

9 2 H. & C. 906, 159 Eng. Rep. 375 (Ex. 1864).

10 *See, e.g.*, Patrick D. Hsu, Eric S. Lander & Feng Zhang, *Development and Applications of CRISPR-Cas9 for Genome Engineering*, 157 CELL 1262 (2014); Jennifer A. Doudna & Emmanuelle Charpentier, *The New Frontier of Genome Engineering with CRISPR-Cas9*, 346 SCIENCE 1077 (2014).

11 *See* Martin Jinek et al., *A Programmable Dual-RNA–Guided DNA Endonuclease in Adaptive Bacterial Immunity*, 337 SCIENCE 816 (2012).

12 *See* Paul Enríquez, *Editing Humanity: On the Precise Manipulation of DNA in Human Embryos*, 97 N.C. L. REV. 1147, 1157 (2019).

13 *See* Paul Enríquez, *Genome Editing and the Jurisprudence of Scientific Empiricism*, 19 VAND. J. ENT. & TECH. L. 603, 617 (2017) [hereinafter Enríquez, *Genome Editing*].

14 *See* Affidavit of Jane Doe #6 signed by Monica S. Lewinsky on Jan. 7, 1998, THE OFFICE OF THE INDEPENDENT COUNSEL, VOL. III: DOCUMENT SUPPLEMENT, PART A, William J. Clinton Statements, Sep. 9, 1998, at 689.

15 *See* Grand Jury Testimony of President William Jefferson Clinton on Aug. 17, 1998, THE OFFICE OF THE INDEPENDENT COUNSEL, VOL. III: DOCUMENT SUPPLEMENT, PART A, William J. Clinton Statements, Sep. 9, 1998, at 509–10.

16 *Id.* at 510.
17 *Id.* at 511–13.
18 *See* THE BARNHART DICTIONARY OF ETYMOLOGY 1050 (Robert K. Barnhart ed., 1988). *See also* A. M. van Harten, *Mutation Breeding of Vegetatively Propagated Ornamentals, in* BREEDING FOR ORNAMENTALS: CLASSICAL AND MOLECULAR APPROACHES 107 (Alexander Vainstein ed., 2002).
19 And even for scientists in the field of botany, it is clear that, for most people, the term elicits the meaning associated with physical activity and recreation. *See, e.g.*, Toshi M. Foster & Maria José Aranzana, *Attention Sports Fans! The Far-Reaching Contributions of Bud Sport Mutants to Horticulture and Plant Biology*, 5 HORTICULTURE RES. 44 (2018) (using a cheeky reference to sports as a recreational activity in the article's title to draw readers into a discussion about traits caused by somatic mutations in plant cells).
20 *Cheater*, THE ONLINE ETYMOLOGY DICTIONARY, https://www.etymonline.com /word/cheater.
21 *See* WALTER WILLIAM SKEAT, AN ETYMOLOGICAL DICTIONARY OF THE ENGLISH LANGUAGE 105 (2d ed. 1884).
22 G. E. Weissengruber et al., *Hyoid Apparatus and Pharynx in the Lion (Panthera leo), Jaguar (Panthera onca), Tiger (Panthera tigris), Cheetah (Acinonyx jubatus) and Domestic Cat (Felis silvestris f. catus)*, 201 J. ANATOMY 195 (2002).
23 *See id*; Dawn E. Frazer Sissom, D. A. Rice, G. Peters, *How Cats Purr*, 223 J. ZOOLOGY 67 (1991).
24 *See* Paul Enríquez, *Deconstructing Transnationalism: Conceptualizing Metanationalism as a Putative Model of Evolving Jurisprudence*, 43 VAND. J. TRANSNAT'L L. 1265, 1270 (2010).
25 *See* Coordinated Framework for the Regulation of Biotechnology, 51 Fed. Reg. 23,302 (June 26, 1986).
26 Paul Enríquez, *CRISPR GMOs*, 18 N.C. J.L. & TECH. 432, 513 (2017) [hereinafter, Enríquez, *CRISPR GMOs*].
27 *See* Memorandum for Heads of Food and Drug Administration, Environmental Protection Agency, and Department of Agriculture: Modernizing the Regulatory System for Biotechnology Products, (July 2, 2015), https://obamawhitehouse .archives.gov/sites/default/files/microsites/ostp/modernizing_the_reg_system_ for_biotech_products_memo_final.pdf.
28 Enríquez, *CRISPR GMOs*, *supra* note 26, at 508.
29 Balanced Budget Downpayment Act, Pub. L. No. 104-99, § 128, 110 Stat. 26, 34 (1996).
30 *See id.*
31 *See* I. Wilmut et al., *Viable Offspring Derived from Fetal and Adult Mammalian Cells*, 385 NATURE 810 (1997). An earlier paper published in March 1996 reported the birth of lambs from an established cultured cell line derived from sheep embryos, as opposed to adult differentiated cells. *See* K. H. S. Campbell et al.,

Sheep Cloned by Nuclear Transfer from a Cultured Cell Line, 380 NATURE 64 (1996).

32 *See, e.g.*, Nat'l Human Genome Res. Inst., *Cloning Fact Sheet*, https://www.genome.gov/about-genomics/fact-sheets/Cloning-Fact-Sheet.

33 *See* Russell A. Spivak, I. Glenn Cohen & Eli Y. Adashi, *Germ-Line Gene Editing and Congressional Reaction in Context: Learning from Almost 50 Years of Congressional Reactions to Biomedical Breakthroughs*, 30 J.L. & HEALTH 20, 32–33 (2017).

34 *See id.* at 34.

35 Over the past two decades, there have been some controversial, but unproven claims related to human cloning. In 2002, Clonaid, a company associated with the Raëlist religious cult, which is based on the belief that extraterrestrial entities created life on Earth, claimed to have enabled the birth of the first cloned human. *See* Gina Kolate & Kenneth Chang, *For Clonaid, a Trail of Unproven Claims*, N.Y. TIMES, Jan. 1, 2003, at A13. The company, however, never substantiated the claims, which remain unproven to this day.

The closest scientific evidence for human cloning to date is, perhaps, the publication of two papers reporting the presumed cloning of human embryos in vitro—not the birth of cloned humans—in 2004 and 2005 in the journal *Science* by a team of researchers at Seoul National University in South Korea. *See* Woo Suk Hwang et al., *Patient-Specific Embryonic Stem Cells Derived from Human SCNT Blastocysts*, 308 SCIENCE 1777 (2005); Woo Suk Hwang et al., *Evidence of a Pluripotent Human Embryonic Stem Cell Line Derived from a Cloned Blastocyst*, 303 SCIENCE 1669 (2004). However, following an independent investigation by a scientific committee, the journal unconditionally retracted both papers because the investigation revealed that the scientists had engaged in widespread research misconduct and the data presented had been fabricated. Donald Kennedy, *Editorial Retraction*, 311 SCIENCE 335 (2006) (retracting the 2004 and 2005 papers). To this day, no credible and verifiable reports of human cloning have surfaced.

36 Authorization for Use of Military Force, Pub. L. No. 107–40, 115 Stat. 224 (2001).

37 *Id.* at § 2(a).

38 *See* U.S. House of Representatives, *Final Vote Results for Roll Call* 342, Sept. 14, 2001, http://clerk.house.gov/evs/2001/roll342.xml.

39 *See, e.g.*, Repeal of the Authorization for Use of Military Force, H.R. 1274, 116th Congress (2019); Alexandra Ocasio-Cortez (@AOC), TWITTER (Mar. 5, 2019, 6:38 AM), https://twitter.com/AOC/status/1102941524608860160; Ilhan Omar (@IlhanMN), TWITTER (MAY 26, 2019, 1:17 PM), https://twitter.com/ilhanmn/status/1132742450697523200. On June 19, 2019, the United States House of Representatives voted along party lines (226–203) to repeal the AUMF. *See* C-SPAN, *House Repeals 2001 AUMF in Trillion-Dollar Spending Bill*, June 19, 2019, https://www.c-span.org/video/?c4803662/house-repeals-2001-aumf-trillion-dollar-spending-bill. It is unknown, however, at the time of this writing, whether

the resolution will eventually garner enough support in both chambers of Congress.

40 UNITING AND STRENGTHENING AMERICA BY PROVIDING APPROPRIATE TOOLS REQUIRED TO INTERCEPT AND OBSTRUCT TERRORISM (USA PATRIOT ACT) ACT OF 2001, PUB. L. NO. 107–56, 115 STAT. 272 (2001).

41 U.S. HOUSE OF REPRESENTATIVES, *FINAL VOTE RESULTS FOR ROLL CALL* 398, OCT. 24, 2001, http://clerk.house.gov/evs/2001/roll398.xml.

42 U.S. SENATE, *ROLL CALL VOTE 107TH CONGRESS – 1ST SESSION*, OCT. 25, 2001, https://www.senate.gov/legislative/LIS/roll_call_lists/roll_call_vote_cfm.cfm?congress=107&session=1&vote=00313.

43 *See* TRANSPORTATION SECURITY ADMINISTRATION, *LIQUIDS RULE*, https://www.tsa.gov/travel/security-screening/liquids-rule.

44 NAT'L COMM'N ON TERRORIST ATTACKS UPON THE U.S., THE 9/11 COMMISSION REPORT 84 (2004), https://9-11commission.gov/report/911Report.pdf.

45 *Id.*

46 *Id.* at 84–85.

47 Aviation and Transportation Security Act, Pub. L. 107–71, 115 Stat. 597 (2001).

48 There are currently twenty-two airports that contract security screening services to private companies. For a list of the airports and the names of the private companies eligible to participate in the SPP, see Transportation Security Administration, *Screening Partnership Program*, https://www.tsa.gov/for-industry/screening-partnerships.

49 Transportation Security Administration, *Fact Sheet: Screening Partnership Program*, https://www.tsa.gov/sites/default/files/resources/spp_factsheet.pdf.

50 *See* North Atlantic Treaty Organization, *Statement by the North Atlantic Council*, Sept. 12, 2001, https://www.nato.int/docu/pr/2001/p01-124e.htm; North Atlantic Treaty Organization, *Collective Defence – Article* 5, June 12, 2018, https://www.nato.int/cps/en/natohq/topics_110496.htm#.

51 North Atlantic Treaty art. 5, Apr. 4, 1949, 63 Stat. 2241, 34 U.N.T.S. 243. Article 5 states, in part, that

> The Parties agree that an armed attack against one or more of them in Europe or North America shall be considered an attack against them all and consequently they agree that, if such an armed attack occurs, each of them, in exercise of the right of individual or collective self-defence recognised by Article 51 of the Charter of the United Nations, will assist the Party or Parties so attacked by taking forthwith, individually and in concert with the other Parties, such action as it deems necessary, including the use of armed force, to restore and maintain the security of the North Atlantic area.

Id.

52 North Atlantic Treaty Organization, *Invocation of Article 5 Confirmed*, Oct. 2, 2001, https://www.nato.int/docu/update/2001/1001/e1002a.htm.

53 C-SPAN, *Bush Announces the Beginning of the War in Afghanistan*, Oct. 7, 2001, https://www.c-span.org/video/?c4744362/bush-announces-beginning-war-afghanistan.

54 *See* Pub. L. No. 114–216, 130 Stat. 834 (2016). A prior version of the bill had been introduced in 2015 as the Safe and Accurate Food Labeling Act of 2015, which failed in the previous Congress.

55 Report of the Committee on Agriculture, U.S. House of Representatives, H.R. Rep. No. 114-896, 114th Cong., 2d Sess., at 24, Dec. 27, 2016.

56 9 V.S.A. § 3041–48 (2014). An Act Relating to the Labeling of Food Produced with Genetic Engineering, No. 120, 2014 Vermont Acts.

57 *See* Pub. L. No. 114–216, 130 Stat. 834 (2016).

58 *See* 130 Stat. 836–37, at § 293(d).

59 National Bioengineered Food Disclosure Standard, 7 U.S.C. § 1639(1) (2016).

60 *See* H.R. Rep. No. 114-896, *supra* note 55, at 24.

61 *See, e.g.*, William Lesser, *Costs of Labeling Genetically Modified Food Products in N.Y. State*, Dyson School of Applied Economics and Management, Cornell University (2014), http://publications.dyson.cornell.edu/docs/LabelingNY.pdf; Nicholas Kalaitzandonakes, Jayson Lusk & Alexandre Magnier, *The Price of Non-Genetically Modified (Non-GM) Food*, 78 FOOD POLICY 38 (2018). *But cf.*, Michael Hansen, *Consumers Union Critique of "Costs of Labeling Genetically Modified Food Products in N.Y. State" by Professor William Lesser*, CONSUMER REPORTS, May 29, 2014, https://advocacy.consumerreports.org/wp-content/uploads/2014/05/NY_GE_lbl_costs_5_14.pdf (arguing that the Lesser study makes broad and incorrect assumptions about potential increases in food prices as a result of food labeling, albeit without citing any sources in support of such criticisms of the Lesser study).

62 *See, e.g.*, The Takeaway, *GMO Lobbying Is a Booming Business as Labeling Laws Increase*, PUBLIC RADIO INT'L., Sept. 5, 2014, https://www.pri.org/stories/2014-09-05/gmo-lobbying-booming-business-labeling-laws-increase; Rob Coleman, *Food Lobby Spends $101 Million in 2015 to Avert GMO Labeling*, ENVTL. WORKING GROUP, Feb. 25, 2016, https://www.ewg.org/research/lobbying-anti-labeling-groups-tops-100m.

63 *See* COMMITTEE ON GENETICALLY ENGINEERED CROPS: PAST EXPERIENCE AND FUTURE PROSPECTS; BOARD ON AGRICULTURE AND NATURAL RESOURCES; DIVISION ON EARTH AND LIFE STUDIES; NATIONAL ACADEMIES OF SCIENCES, ENGINEERING, AND MEDICINE, GENETICALLY ENGINEERED CROPS: EXPERIENCES AND PROSPECTS 7 (2016) [hereinafter NASEM REPORT].

64 *See* AM. ASS'N FOR THE ADVANCEMENT OF SCI., STATEMENT BY THE AAAS BOARD OF DIRECTORS ON LABELING OF GENETICALLY MODIFIED FOODS, Oct. 20, 2012, http://www.aaas.org/sites/default/files/AAAS_GM_statement.pdf.

65 *See* EUROPEAN COMM'N, A DECADE OF EU-FUNDED GMO RESEARCH (2001-2010) 15 (2010), http://ec.europa.eu/research/biosociety/pdf/a_decade_of_eu-funded_gmo_research.pdf.

66 *See, e.g.*, The Royal Soc'y, *Is It Safe to Eat GM Crops?*, last updated May 2016, https://royalsociety.org/topics-policy/projects/gm-plants/is-it-safe-to-eat-gm-crops/; The Royal Soc'y, *Have GM Crops Caused Damage to the Environment?*, last updated May 2016, https://royalsociety.org/topics-policy/projects/gm-plants/have-gm-crops-caused-damage-to-the-environment/.

67 *See* Enríquez, *CRISPR GMOs*, *supra* note 26, at 472–76.

68 AM. ASS'N FOR THE ADVANCEMENT OF SCI., *supra* note 64.

69 *See, e.g.*, Henry I. Miller & Drew L. Kershen, *This May Be the Worst Regulation Ever*, Jan. 30, 2019, https://www.wsj.com/articles/this-may-be-the-worst-regulation-ever-11548890635.

70 Patient Protection and Affordable Care Act, Pub. L. No. 111–148, 124 Stat. 119 (2010).

71 *See, e.g.*, Jeffrey L. Kirchmeier & Samuel A. Thumma, *Scaling the Lexicon Fortress: The United States Supreme Court's Use of Dictionaries in the Twenty-First Century*, 94 MARQ. L. REV. 77, 84–85 (2010).

72 For an overview of some issues related to the use of dictionaries in legal contexts, see generally, James J. Brudney & Lawrence Baum, *Oasis or Mirage: The Supreme Court's Thirst for Dictionaries in the Rehnquist and Roberts Eras*, 55 WM. & MARY L. REV. 483 (2013); Samuel A. Thumma & Jeffrey L. Kirchmeier, *The Lexicon Has Become a Fortress: The United States Supreme Court's Use of Dictionaries*, 47 BUFF. L. REV. 227 (1999); Kirchmeier & Thumma, *supra* note 71; Ellen P. Aprill, *The Law of the Word: Dictionary Shopping in the Supreme Court*, 30 ARIZ. ST. L.J. 275 (1998); Kevin Werbach, Note, *Looking It Up: Dictionaries and Statutory Interpretation*, 107 HARV. L. REV. 1437 (1994); John Calhoun, Note, *Measuring the Fortress: Explaining Trends in Supreme Court and Circuit Court Dictionary Use*, 124 YALE L.J. 484 (2014).

73 *See, e.g.*, Brudney & Baum, *supra* note 72, at 483, 487 (pointing out that as many as one-third of statutory decisions in modern Supreme Court jurisprudence consult dictionaries in subjective ways).

74 Kirchmeier & Thumma, *supra* note 71, at 82. That number would likely be much higher if all lower court judges' use of dictionaries would be taken into consideration.

75 *See Pet*, MERRIAM-WEBSTER DICTIONARY, https://www.merriam-webster.com/dictionary/pet (last visited Aug. 15, 2019) (defining pet in the first entry as "(1) (a) a pampered and usually spoiled child, or (b) a person who is treated with unusual kindness or consideration: DARLING; and (2) a domesticated animal kept for pleasure rather than utility.").

76 *See* Brudney & Baum, *supra* note 72, at 514–15.

77 *See* John Willinsky, *Cutting English on the Bias: Five Lexicographers in Pursuit of the New*, 63 AM. SPEECH 44, 64 (1988) (quoting the definition of "dictionary" in CHERIS KRAMARAE & PAULA A. TREICHLER, A FEMINIST DICTIONARY 112 (1985)).

78 Adam Liptak, *Justices Turning More Frequently to Dictionary, and Not Just for Big Words*, N.Y. TIMES, June 14, 2011, at A11 (quoting Jesse Sheidlower, who was

the editor at large of the Oxford English Dictionary at the time the article was published).

79 *See* Willinsky, *supra* note 77, at 45.

80 *Id.* at 46.

81 *See id.* ("To systematically cover the principal publications in the language, lexicographers draw on four constituencies: an internal reading program led by the editors; an external reading program directed by the editors and consisting of part-time readers from across the English-speaking world; a systematic check of other lexicographical sources; and, finally, the unsolicited but welcomed contributions of interested readers of the dictionary.").

82 *Id.* at 46–48, 51, 53, 61.

83 Aprill, *supra* note 72, at 292.

84 Cabell v. Markham, 148 F.2d 737, 739 (2d Cir. 1945).

85 A. Raymond Randolph, *Dictionaries, Plain Meaning, and Context in Statutory Interpretation*, 17 Harv. J.L. & Pub. Pol'y 71, 73–74 (1994).

86 Perrin v. United States, 444 U.S. 37, 42 (1979).

87 Johnson v. Zimmer, 686 F.3d 224, 232 (4th Cir. 2012).

88 Aprill, *supra* note 72, at 292 (citing Sidney I. Landau, Dictionaries: The Art & Craft of Lexicography 164 (1984), and Deborah Cameron, Feminism and Linguistic Theory 84 (1985)).

89 *Id.*

90 *Gene editing*, Cambridge Dictionary, https://dictionary.cambridge.org/us/dictionary/english/gene-editing (last visited Aug. 22, 2019).

91 *Gene editing*, Merriam-Webster Dictionary, https://www.merriam-webster.com/dictionary/genome%20editing (last visited Aug. 22, 2019).

92 *Gene editing*, Oxford English Dictionary, https://www.oed.com/view/Entry/59547?redirectedFrom=gene+editing#eid1266627759 (last visited Aug. 22, 2019).

93 *Gene editing*, Oxford Advanced Learner's Dictionary, https://www.oxfordlearnersdictionaries.com/us/definition/english/gene-editing?q=gene+editing (last visited Aug. 22, 2019).

94 *Gene editing*, Macmillan Dictionary, https://www.macmillandictionary.com/dictionary/british/gene-editing (last visited Aug. 22, 2019).

95 *Gene editing*, Collins English Dictionary, https://www.collinsdictionary.com/us/dictionary/english/genome-editing (last visited Aug. 22, 2019).

96 *See* The American heritage Dictionary, https://ahdictionary.com/ (last visited Aug. 22, 2019) (returning a "no word definition found" for searches of the terms "gene editing" or "genome editing," https://ahdictionary.com/word/search.html?q=gene+editing, https://ahdictionary.com/word/search.html?q=genome+editing).

97 No entries for the terms "gene editing" or "genome editing" appear in the latest edition of Black's Law Dictionary. *See* Black's Law Dictionary (11th ed. 2019) (last visited Aug. 22, 2019).

98 No entries for the terms "gene editing" or "genome editing" appear in the Merriam-Webster's Dictionary of Law. *See* MERRIAM-WEBSTER'S DICTIONARY OF LAW (2d ed. 2011) (last visited Aug. 22, 2019).
99 Nix v. Hedden, 149 U.S. 304, 307 (1893).
100 *Id.* at 304.
101 *See* Scott A. Hendrickson & Jason M. Roberts, *Short-Term Goals and Long-Term Effects: The Mongrel Tariff and the Creation of the Special Rule in the U.S. House*, 28 J. POL'Y HISTORY 318, 320 (2016).
102 *See id.*, at 324 (citation omitted).
103 *See id.*, at 318.
104 *Nix*, 149 U.S. at 304.
105 Nix v. Hedden, 39 F. 109, 109 (C.C.S.D.N.Y. 1889), *aff'd*, 149 U.S. 304 (1893).
106 *Nix*, 149 U.S. at 306.
107 *Nix*, 39 F. 109, 109.
108 *Nix*, 149 U.S. at 307.
109 *Id.*
110 *See, e.g.*, A DICTIONARY OF PLANT SCIENCES 204 (Michael Allaby ed., 3d 2012). *See also, e.g.*, Harry J. Klee, *Ripening Physiology of Fruit from Transgenic Tomato (Lycopersicon esculentum) Plants with Reduced Ethylene Synthesis*, 102 PLANT PHYSIOLOGY 911 (1993) (studying some molecular aspects of tomato fruit ripening); Dean DellaPenna, Danny C. Alexander & Alan B. Bennett, *Molecular Cloning of Tomato Fruit Polygalacturonase: Analysis of Polygalacturonase mRNA Levels During Ripening*, 83 PROC. NAT'L ACAD. SCI. U.S. 6420 (1986)(same).
111 *See, e.g.*, Council Directive 2001/113, Annex III, 2002 O.J. (L 10) 67 (EC) ("for the purposes of this Directive, tomatoes, the edible parts of rhubarb stalks, carrots, sweet potatoes, cucumbers, pumpkins, melons and water-melons are considered to be fruit").
112 *See* dictionary definitions cited *supra* notes 90–95 and accompanying text.
113 Grayned v. City of Rockford, 408 U.S. 104, 108 (1972) (citations omitted).
114 *Id.* at 108–09.
115 U.S. CONST. amend. VIII ("Excessive bail shall not be required, nor excessive fines imposed, nor cruel and unusual punishments inflicted.").
116 U.S. CONST. amend. V ("[N]or shall any person . . . be deprived of life, liberty, or property, without due process of law . . . ."); *id.* amend. XIV, § 1 ("[N]or shall any State deprive any person of life, liberty, or property, without due process of law . . . .").
117 U.S. CONST. amend. I ("Congress shall make no law respecting an establishment of religion, or prohibiting the free exercise thereof; or abridging the freedom of speech, or of the press . . . .").
118 U.S. CONST. amend. IV ("[The right of the people to be secure in their persons, houses, papers, and effects, against unreasonable searches and seizures, shall not be violated, and no warrants shall issue, but upon probable cause,

supported by oath or affirmation, and particularly describing the place to be searched, and the persons or things to be seized.").

119 *Id.*

120 U.S. CONST. amend. XIV, § 1 ("[N]o state shall make or enforce any law which shall abridge the privileges or immunities of citizens of the United States; nor shall any state deprive any person of life, liberty, or property, without due process of law; nor deny to any person within its jurisdiction the equal protection of the laws.").

121 *See* S. Res. 275, 116th Cong. (2019), https://www.congress.gov/116/bills/sres275/BILLS-116sres275is.pdf. The resolution was introduced on July 15, 2019 by Senators Dianne Feinstein (Democrat—California), Marco Rubio (Republican—Florida), and Jack Reed (Democrat—Rhode Island). It was referred to the Committee on Foreign Relations, but was not agreed to in the Senate. The resolution did not garner enough support in the full chamber to pass, even though it is a written legislative motion that has no force of law.

122 *See id.* at 1 ("genome editing enables scientists to make changes to the genome in organisms by removing, adding, or replacing genetic material"). The resolution also stated that genome-editing technologies have promising therapeutic potential. *Id.*

123 *See, e.g.*, sources cited *supra* note 10.

124 *See* Enríquez, *Genome Editing*, *supra* note 13, at 617.

125 *See, e.g.*, David B. T. Cox et al., *RNA editing with CRISPR-Cas13*, 358 SCIENCE 1019 (2017); Julian Grünewald et al., *Transcriptome-Wide Off-Target RNA Editing Induced by CRISPR-Guided DNA Base Editors*, 569 NATURE 433 (2019).

126 *See, e.g.*, Paul Enríquez, *CRISPR-Mediated Epigenome Editing*, 89 YALE J. BIOLOGY & MED. 471 (2016) [hereinafter Enríquez, *Epigenome Editing*].

127 *See, e.g.*, Alexis C. Komor et al., *Programmable Editing of a Target Base in Genomic DNA Without Double-Stranded DNA Cleavage*, 533 NATURE 420 (2016); Nicole M. Gaudelli et al., *Programmable Base Editing of A•T to G•C in Genomic DNA Without DNA Cleavage*, 551 NATURE 464 (2017).

128 *See* Enríquez, *Epigenome Editing*, *supra* note 126, at 477–79.

129 *See generally id.*

130 *See, e.g.*, Hans E Krokan, Finn Drabløs & Geir Slupphaug, *Uracil in DNA – Occurrence, Consequences and Repair*, 21 ONCOGENE 8935 (2002); Bik-Kwoon Tye et al., *Uracil Incorporation: A Source of Pulse-Labeled DNA Fragments in the Replication of the Escherichia coli Chromosome*, 75 PROC. NAT'L ACAD. SCI. U.S. 233 (1978); Josephine Wardle et al., *Uracil Recognition by Replicative DNA Polymerases Is Limited to the Archaea, Not Occurring with Bacteria and Eukarya*, 36 NUCLEIC ACIDS RES. 705 (2008).

131 *See, e.g.*, Ingrun Alseth, Bjørn Dalhus & Magnar Bjørås, *Inosine in DNA and* RNA, 26 CURRENT OPINION GENETICS & DEV. 116 (2014); Manabu Yasui et al., *Miscoding Properties of 2'-Deoxyinosine, a Nitric Oxide-Derived DNA Adduct,*

During Translesion Synthesis Catalyzed by Human DNA Polymerases, 377 J. Molecular Biology 1015 (2008).

132 *See, e.g.*, Michael J. Lutz et al., *Differential Discrimination of DNA Polymerases for Variants of the Non-Standard Nucleobase Pair Between Xanthosine and 2,4-Diaminopyrimidine, Two Components of an Expanded Genetic Alphabet*, 24 Nucleic Acids Res. 1308 (1996); Viengsai Vongchampa et al., *Stability of 2'-Deoxyxanthosine in DNA*, 31 Nucleic Acids Res. 1045 (2003).

133 *See, e.g.*, Eui Kyoung Jang, Mi-Ran Ki & Seung Pil Pack, *Design of Reactive-End DNA Oligomers Via Incorporation of Oxanine into Oligonucleotides Using Terminal Deoxynucleotidyl Transferase*, 62 Process Biochemistry 99 (2017).

134 *See, e.g.*, Millie M. Georgiadis et al., *Structural Basis for a Six Nucleotide Genetic Alphabet*, 137 J. Am. Chemical Soc'y 6947 (2015); Denis A. Malyshev et al., *A Semi-Synthetic Organism with an Expanded Genetic Alphabet*, 509 Nature 385 (2014); Itaru Okamoto et al., *High Fidelity, Efficiency and Functionalization of Ds–Px Unnatural Base Pairs in PCR Amplification for a Genetic Alphabet Expansion System*, 5 ACS Synthetic Biology 1220 (2016); Joseph A. Piccirilli et al., *Enzymatic Incorporation of a New Base Pair into DNA and RNA Extends the Genetic Alphabet*, 343 Nature 33 (1990); Liqin Zhang et al., *Evolution of Functional Six-Nucleotide DNA*, 137 J. Am. Chemical Soc'y 6734 (2015).

135 *See, e.g.*, Tatiana Kent et al., *DNA Polymerase θ Specializes in Incorporating Synthetic Expanded-Size (xDna) Nucleotides*, 44 Nucleic Acids Res. 9381 (2016); Karin Betz et al., *Klentaq Polymerase Replicates Unnatural Base Pairs by Inducing a Watson-Crick Geometry*, 8 Nature Chemical Biology 612 (2012).

136 *See, e.g.*, Shuichi Hoshika et al., *Hachimoji DNA and RNA: A Genetic System with Eight Building Blocks*, 363 Science 84 (2019).

137 *See, e.g.*, P. Mandels & P. Métais, *Les Acides Nucléiques du Plasma Sanguin Chez l'Homme*, 142 Comptes Rendus des Séances de la Société de Biologie et de ses Filiales, 241 (1948); E. M. Tan et al., *Deoxybonucleic Acid (DNA) and Antibodies to DNA in the Serum of Patients with Systemic Lupus Erythematosus*, 45 J. Clinical Investigation 1732 (1966); Dominic G. Rothwell et al. *Genetic Profiling of Tumours Using Both Circulating Free DNA and Circulating Tumour Cells Isolated from the Same Preserved Whole Blood Sample*, 10 Molecular Oncology 566 (2016).

138 *See* Pankaj Kumar et al., *Normal and Cancerous Tissues Release Extrachromosomal Circular DNA (eccDNA) into the Circulation*, 15 Molecular Cancer Res. 1197 (2017).

139 *See* Y. M. Dennis Lo et al., *Presence of Fetal DNA in Maternal Plasma and Serum*, 350 Lancet 485 (1997).

140 *See, e.g.*, Yanwei Bi et al., *High-Efficiency Targeted Editing of Large Viral Genomes by RNA-Guided Nucleases*, 10 PLoS Pathogens e1004090 (2014);

Hyung Suk Oh et al., *Herpesviral Lytic Gene Functions Render the Viral Genome Susceptible to Novel Editing by CRISPR/Cas9*, 8 eLIFE e51662 (2019); Ke Zheng et al., *Highly Efficient Base Editing in Viral Genome Based on Bacterial Artificial Chromosome Using a Cas9-Cytidine Deaminase Fused Protein*, VIROLOGICA SINICA (2019), https://doi.org/10.1007/s12250-019-00175-4.

141 *See, e.g.*, Daniel G. Gibson et al., *Creation of a Bacterial Cell Controlled by a Chemically Synthesized Genome*, 329 SCIENCE 52 (2010); Julius Fredens et al., *Total Synthesis of Escherichia coli with a Recoded Genome*, 514 NATURE 569 (2019); Dennis A. Malyshev et al., A *Semi-Synthetic Organism with an Expanded Genetic Alphabet*, 509 NATURE 385 (2014); Aaron W. Feldman et al., *Optimization of Replication, Transcription, and Translation in a Semi-Synthetic Organism*, 141 J. AM. CHEM. SOC'Y 10644 (2019).

142 Desiderius Erasmus, *On the Method of Study*, *in* COLLECTED WORKS OF ERASMUS, VOL. 24: LITERARY AND EDUCATIONAL WRITINGS 2 669 (Craig Thompson ed., 1978) (emphasis added).

4

Molecular Paraphernalia

When Orville and Wilbur Wright flew the first successful airplane at Kill Devil Hills in Kitty Hawk, North Carolina on December 17, 1903, they realized they had changed the course of aviation history. It did not matter that the first flight lasted all but twelve seconds and covered a ground distance of 120 feet.[1] A method to effectively control the aerodynamic properties of a new type of flight machine had been invented.[2] And the future of human transportation forever changed trajectory.

Still, the Wright Brothers were acutely aware that technological development was necessary to improve controlled, powered-aircraft machines. After all, the *Flyer I*, their bicanard biplane prototype aircraft (in aeronautics, a canard refers to a small wing placed in front of a plane's main wing), required the pilot to lay flat on his stomach and steer the plane via movement of the hips. Needless to say, that model did not prove influential; no pilot steers any modern controlled aircraft with the hips! The significance of the *Flyer I*, however, rests in the pioneering theory behind its design and features. Without the prototype aircraft flown in 1903, commercial air travel across entire oceans would have never been possible.

In the early days of genetic engineering, scientists knew they had finally found the tools necessary to begin studying the function of specific genes or other DNA molecules of interest. But they were also fully aware that targeted experiments to edit specific sequences in the genomes of living organisms were still not anywhere within the realm of possibility. That, of course, has changed. This chapter examines the evolution and development of the different types of modern genome-editing tools at researchers' disposal that have enabled the targeted manipulation of genetic sequences. In so doing, it allows you to rummage freely through the genome-editing toolbox and focus on each category of genome editing. In order to appreciate these molecular tools, however, it is important to understand the rise of recombinant DNA technology, as it provides the proper context with which to examine the advent of modern genome editing. Much like interoceanic air travel, genome editing too did not materialize in a vacuum.

FIGURE 4.1 The Wright brothers, first flight of the Wright Flyer I at Kill Devil Hills, on 17 December 1903 (Pictorial Press Ltd / Alamy Stock Photo)

Succinctly, genome editing is a logical extension of the genetic manipulation enabled by pioneer recombinant DNA techniques. And it exists today because recombinant DNA technology was developed, promoted, and refined to give rise to avant-garde molecular tools.

I THE RISE OF RECOMBINANT DNA

The discovery of restriction enzymes capable of inducing DNA double-stranded breaks prone for repair via unique cellular mechanisms marked the genesis of modern molecular biotechnology and gave rise to the era of *recombinant DNA* technology.[3] The term recombinant DNA refers to any hybrid DNA molecule that is created by joining two or more pieces of DNA from multiple sources in combinations that cannot otherwise be found in nature. Although recombinant DNA material may—technically speaking—occur frequently in nature,[4] it has exclusively come to apply to DNA molecules that are engineered and produced through biotechnology.

As we discussed in the previous chapter, all living organisms have DNA comprising A, C, G, and T bases arranged in a double-helical structure. The only meaningful difference between the DNA in your genome and that of a plant, mouse, or even a bacterium rests in the sequence of said genomes. Due to the chemical resemblance of DNA among all living organisms, it is no surprise that DNA molecules from different sources can be combined inside a test tube. As strange as it may sound, humans routinely join DNA pieces from plant, animal, fungal, viral, and even human sources together, most commonly for purposes of performing basic research in laboratories all over the world.

The first recombinant DNA molecules debuted in the scientific literature in 1972—quickly after the characterization of the first restriction enzymes—when a team of researchers fused short DNA fragments from two viruses together.[5] Within months of that breakthrough, additional teams accomplished similar feats by publishing experiments that produced other recombinant DNA molecules.[6]

A *An Army of Clones*

The development of recombinant DNA technology swiftly enabled the first molecular cloning experiments. *Cloning* refers to the making of an identical copy of something. In the context of genetic engineering, it entails the insertion of a gene, or some other DNA fragment of interest, into a "carrier" DNA molecule known as a *vector*. Vectors are called carriers of genetic information because they allow the replication (cloning) of engineered recombinant DNA molecules in a given host organism.

Despite the negative connotations occasionally associated with cloning that have surfaced in the last few decades, molecular or genetic cloning has been an incredibly useful tool to understand the function of specific sequences of DNA. For instance, when a scientist wishes to study the function of a particular human gene, she typically begins by making lots of copies of the gene from isolated DNA found in human cells. She then clones the gene into a vector, such as a bacterial *plasmid*. A plasmid is a short, double-stranded, often circular, DNA molecule that has the ability to replicate independently inside a bacterial host. Once the human gene and the plasmid are joined together to form a new recombinant DNA molecule, she will insert the recombinant DNA into a host organism—for instance, the bacterium *Escherichia coli* (*E. coli*), which is perhaps the most common model organism used in basic research—via the process of genetic transformation.

Transformation refers to the incorporation, or uptake, of foreign DNA material—such as a recombinant DNA molecule—into a host organism of choice. Accordingly, an *E. coli* cell is said to be "transformed" (into a new genetically modified organism) when the recombinant DNA engineered by the scientist is incorporated into the cell. The new genetically modified bacterial host will then use its endogenous replicative machinery to propagate the plasmid carrying the recombinant DNA molecule, thereby making multiple clones of it. Each cloned recombinant DNA molecule can undergo gene expression to yield high quantities of its own gene products. For instance, the researcher may harvest *recombinant proteins*—namely, protein molecules synthesized from recombinant genes—that are manufactured by the transformed bacterial cells, and subsequently isolate them from other cellular components. She may then purify the recombinant proteins in the laboratory and use them for biochemical, genetic, structural, or medical analyses. The researcher may also purify the cloned DNA and use it for DNA sequencing analysis, or isolate recombinant RNA molecules to test whether they possess any regulatory functions. Recombinant DNA technology—and its infinite applications—has, therefore, embodied the cornerstone of scientific research since its inception in the 1970s.

The first cloning experiments were reported in late 1973 when a team of researchers introduced recombinant DNA into bacterial cells to create the first genetically modified organism via modern genetic engineering.[7] Following the establishment of those proof-of-concept experiments, the science advanced rapidly. The world's first transgenic animals—mice bearing DNA of viral origin—arrived a few months later in early 1974.[8] The term *transgenic* refers to the artificial introduction of genetic material belonging to one organism into the genome of another *unrelated* organism. The first genetically engineered plants were developed in the early 1980s by inserting antibiotic resistance genes into tobacco plant cells.[9] And a genetically modified bacterium capable of breaking down crude oil—which would eventually become the first patented genetically modified living organism—was developed for bioremediation purposes.[10] The fundamental knowledge derived from the applications of recombinant DNA research fueled innovation in genetic engineering and gave rise to new intellectual property.[11]

B *Naturally Artificial*

As recounted in this section, recombinant DNA has had a major and incalculable impact in biotechnology. Nearly every breakthrough of biomedical or biotechnological significance in the last few decades can be traced back to insights derived from research into recombinant DNA.

Consider insulin, a crucial protein hormone that regulates metabolism and is secreted by a specialized set of cells called *beta cells* within pancreatic islets. Insulin is commonly used to treat diabetes in patients with high blood glucose levels. Before recombinant DNA existed, insulin for use as a human medication was extracted from cow, sheep, or pig pancreatic glands. As a result, the meat industry played a key role in the commercial availability of insulin for diabetics. On average, for example, a cow weighing half-a-ton (1,000 lbs.) would produce one vial of insulin to supply less than a month's worth of medication for one individual with diabetes.[12]

To address an increase in the diabetic population and the potential threat of shortages from animal-derived insulin, researchers began to look for alternate sources of insulin. Emerging tools in recombinant DNA biotechnology provided a timely substitute means to achieve that goal. In the summer of 1978, a team of academic researchers published results of a study in which the gene encoding rat proinsulin—the insulin precursor—had been inserted into *E. coli* bacterial cells.[13] The study established proof of concept for a method to control the over expression and secretion of mammalian insulin inside a bacterial host using recombinant DNA techniques.

Shortly thereafter, on September 1978, scientists at Genentech, a biotech startup at the time, and Eli Lilly, which had contracted out research on insulin to Genentech, announced the successful expression of recombinant human insulin in *E. coli* cells.[14] The recombinant human insulin was, for all practical purposes, indistinguishable from naturally occurring human insulin. By 1982, the Food and Drug Administration (FDA) approved the use of recombinant human insulin and Eli Lilly began to market it under the brand name of Humulin®.[15] Humulin® became the first recombinant DNA product of modern genetic engineering to gain approval by the government for human consumption. Today, biosynthetic human insulin—which is functionally no different from the natural protein—constitutes the bulk of insulin sold for clinical use all over the world. Despite issues related to affordability and access, recombinant human insulin—including Novolin®, Insuman®, and Humulin®—continues to be manufactured by several pharmaceutical companies.[16]

The rational manipulation of genes and DNA sequences generated other important research data with pharmaceutical, medical, and biotechnological applications.

Large-scale production of human growth hormone (HGH), also known as somatotropin—a protein hormone secreted by the pituitary gland in the brain that stimulates growth during development, regulates various aspects of metabolism, maintains proper bone density, promotes cell regeneration, and contributes to cardiovascular function—was also recombinantly expressed in the late 1970s.[17] Biosynthetic HGH is commonly prescribed to individuals who are unable to produce enough endogenous HGH to support adequate growth and development. HGH deficiency in children and teenagers can lead to stunted stature and delayed sexual maturity, whereas in adults it contributes to weakening of bones, accumulation of fat, muscle mass loss, and energy deficits.

Before the recombinant version of the protein became available, HGH used to be extracted from the pituitary glands of human cadavers and given to HGH-deficient individuals for therapeutic purposes.[18] However, all cadaver pituitary-derived HGH was suddenly taken off the market following several case reports that linked the onset of Creutzfeldt–Jakob disease (CJD)—a fatal neurodegenerative disorder—to select patients who had received HGH extracted from human cadavers.[19] In the aftermath of revelations concerning this alarming mode of CJD transmission, recombinant HGH—marketed by Genentech under the name Protropin®—became the second genetic-engineering product approved by the FDA for the treatment of growth-hormone deficiency.[20] Human cadaver-derived HGH is no longer sold in the United States or the rest of the world, and has been replaced entirely by recombinant HGH.

Somatostatin, another short peptide hormone that regulates proper endocrine function and acts as a neurotransmitter, has also been recombinantly produced by fusing a chemically synthesized human gene with a bacterial gene.[21] But advances in recombinant DNA products have not only been confined to hormone analogs.

Vaccines and food-processing enzymes too have been formulated. The first vaccine derived from recombinant DNA technology in yeast cells was developed against the Hepatitis B virus, which causes a liver infection that can lead to liver failure, cirrhosis, and cancer of the liver.[22] Chymosin, an enzyme produced naturally in the stomach of young ruminant animals—including cattle, deer, goats, pigs, and others—has been recombinantly expressed in bacterial[23] and fungal[24] cells for purposes of curdling cheese. The enzyme no longer needs to be harvested from calves' stomachs, which required infant animals to be slaughtered for the sake of cheese-making. Instead, recombinant chymosin is now produced inside bacterial or yeast cell cultures. The cheese you purchase at the supermarket or eat at a restaurant —like the bulk of cheese manufactured everywhere—is most likely produced using recombinant microbes. Accordingly, recombinant chymosin has become an indispensable tool in the food processing industry.

C *Abstract Rights*

As the utility of recombinant DNA skyrocketed, uncertainty became associated with the legal status of new genetically modified organisms. In 1972, a microbiologist working for General Electric Corp. filed a patent application for an invention to clean up oil spills.[25] The invention concerned the development of a genetically engineered, recombinant bacterium that could metabolize several components of crude oil at significantly faster rates than any other naturally occurring bacteria.

The United States Patent and Trademark Office (USPTO) rejected the patent application reasoning that living organisms are products of nature and did not constitute patentable subject matter under 35 U.S.C. § 101, which states that "[w]hoever invents or discovers any new and useful process, machine, manufacture, or composition of matter, or any new and useful improvement thereof, may obtain a patent therefor, subject to the conditions and requirements of this title."[26]

The United States Supreme Court, however, disagreed with the USPTO rationale in the landmark case of *Diamond v. Chakrabarty*.[27] In a 5–4 majority ruling, the Court held that a human-made, living microorganism could be patentable subject matter within the purview of § 101 if it was the "product of human ingenuity," rather than "nature's handiwork."[28] So long as the invention concerned an organism with (1) markedly different characteristics from any other organism that could already be found in nature, and (2) had significant utilitarian properties, the invention could constitute a "manufacture" or "composition of matter" under the statute.[29] In essence, a patent could be granted for "anything under the sun that is made by man."[30]

The combined effects of scientific progress and law launched humanity into a new era of molecular exploration. The Supreme Court's decision to endorse intellectual property rights for living organisms in *Chakrabarty* triggered an avalanche of patent applications related to genetic-engineering inventions, which spawned a multibillion-dollar biotechnology industry.[31]

At the same time, trepidation about the potential repercussions[32] of manipulating the genetic composition of living organisms at will led to the famous *Asilomar Conference on Recombinant DNA Molecules*, which took place in Asilomar State Beach, California in February 1975. At the meeting, a group of 150 invitees, comprised mostly of scientists with expertise in molecular biology and a few lawyers, convened to discuss the potential safety hazards of emerging recombinant DNA biotechnologies.[33] In addition, sixteen members of the press representing major newspaper and scientific publications were invited for purposes of disseminating stories about the meeting to the general public. Overall, the conference participants agreed that most recombinant DNA research should proceed so long as certain safeguards related to containment of novel organisms were adopted.[34] However, there was also consensus about halting experiments involving cloning of recombinant DNA molecules derived from highly pathogenic organisms and toxin genes that could be used to harm humans, animals, or plants.[35]

Despite early public fears concerning recombinant DNA, genetic cloning, and controversies over the commercialization of living organisms, technological development continued apace. This was due in part to joint commercial ventures and an influx of capital that sought to refine the molecular tools assembled during the 1970s and 1980s. Thus, it was the combined effects of scientific progress, law, and the prospect of technological commercialization that launched humanity into the modern era of targeted genetic modification.

Over time, the rudimentary tools of first-generation genetic-engineering methods paved the way for a new group of molecular technologies that enabled genome editing. Next, this chapter introduces the transformative technologies of modern-day, programmable, genome editing that are shaking up biotechnology, medicine, agriculture, and many other fields.

II THE GENOME-EDITING TOOLBOX

As scientists began to unravel the molecular basis of restriction enzyme-mediated double-stranded breaks and DNA repair, it became possible for them to finally explore genome engineering as well. Such a molecular quest eventually led to the creation of tools for genome editing. The genome-editing toolbox comprises systems that fit four distinct categories: (1) chemistry-based synthetic DNA scission, (2) viral-based editing, (3) nucleases that rely on protein-DNA interactions for targeting DNA sequences, and (4) revolutionary RNA-guided DNA-nuclease systems.

A *Chemistry-Based Synthetic DNA Scission*

In the 1980s, scientists realized that making double-stranded breaks in DNA molecules could be accomplished not only with the use of restriction enzymes, but via various chemical reactions as well. Early methods of chemistry-mediated DNA scission involved the use of oligonucleotides—short fragments of DNA or RNA molecules—coupled to chemical reagents.[36] Researchers proved that these complexes could successfully induce site-specific cleavage of DNA molecules,[37] and activate DNA repair[38] in yeast and mammalian cells without the use of nucleases.

Alternative approaches to induce DNA double-stranded breaks have also emerged. One method involves the use of Cerium (atomic number 58, symbol "Ce"), the fifty-eighth element on the Periodic Table. Cerium is an iron-gray, malleable, lustrous, rare-earth metal that is susceptible to rapid oxidation at room temperature.[39] Reports that the Ce(IV) species is highly stable and capable of cutting DNA via hydrolysis[40] paved the way for more sophisticated artificial DNA-cutting methods involving complexation of Ce(IV) with Ethylenediaminetetraacetic acid (EDTA), a chelating reagent.[41]

The Ce(IV)–EDTA metal complex has also been coupled with pseudo-complementary Peptide Nucleic Acids (PNA) as a novel chemistry-based, artificial-restriction, DNA-cutter strategy for site-specific DNA cleavage.[42] PNAs are artificial molecules that resemble nucleic acids—such as DNA or RNA—but have a protein-like backbone instead of the canonical sugar-phosphate backbone that is characteristic among nucleic acids.[43] PNAs are capable of associating with Ce(IV)–EDTA and other metal complexes,[44] as well as nucleases,[45] and synthetic polyamides—a type of synthetic macromolecules comprising repeating units linked by amide bonds (such as nylons, aramids, and polyphthalamides)—that bind DNA's minor groove.[46] These synthetic DNA-scission platforms, which do not rely on restriction enzymes, have not been widely adopted by researchers. Nevertheless, they demonstrate the feasibility of using chemistry-based cutting tools for genome editing.[47]

B *Viral-Based Editing*

As we discussed in the previous chapters, some viruses are capable of integrating themselves into the host cell's genome. These viruses can cause DNA modifications, but the ensuing alterations are not targeted to specific genetic loci. Due to the propensity for random integration, viral-induced modifications of this sort cannot be considered gene editing as has been described in this book.

Nevertheless, researchers have used biotechnology to create vectors based on certain types of viruses that can trigger specific modifications at homologous target sequences without the need for nucleases.[48] One such type of viral-based system belongs to the category of adeno-associated viruses (AAV), which are nonpathogenic, nonenveloped viruses featuring a 4.7 kilobase-long, linear, single-stranded

DNA genome.[49] With this approach, scientists have demonstrated that engineered recombinant AAV vectors can replace some, or all, of the endogenous viral genes with packaged foreign DNA sequences of interest—that is, cargo DNA—for efficient cellular delivery.[50] Subsequent cargo release into the cell nucleus can mediate homologous recombination at selected loci and trigger AAV-based gene editing.

Gene targeting with AAV-based vectors has demonstrated promising therapeutic applications.[51] And because they have proven to be safe and effective, commercialization of AAV-based vectors and testing in clinical trials are underway. For instance, Horizon Discovery Group PLC, a biotechnology company based in Cambridge, UK, has marketed a proprietary version of nuclease-free, recombinant-AAV genome editing.[52] A clinical trial to assess the safety, tolerability, and efficacy of a recombinant AAV vector for use in human subjects led to the development of Luxturna®, the first in vivo, FDA-approved, gene-therapy treatment for a congenital disorder.[53] Despite a modest commercial performance, likely due to the platform's labor-intensive manufacturing and high costs, preliminary results from clinical testing showed significant improvement of patients with Leber Congenital Amaurosis, an incurable, inherited retinal disease.[54]

C *Nuclease Genome Editing Based on Protein-DNA Interactions*

1 Meganucleases

Meganucleases, also known as Homing Endonucleases, are naturally occurring DNA nucleases that mediate DNA double-stranded breaks and target relatively long DNA sequences ranging from twelve to forty base pairs.[55] Meganucleases have been instrumental in the study of DNA repair following double-stranded breaks.[56] They were initially identified as potential site-specific DNA nucleases for genome editing from the use of self-splicing[57] introns—an *intron* is a noncoding fragment of an RNA transcript, or its encoding DNA found within a gene, which is removed during RNA processing before translation of a gene into a protein.[58] Meganucleases were the first type of nucleases scientists used to prove that the mammalian genome could be modified with precision.[59]

One advantage of meganucleases is that they confer high target-DNA specificity due to having long, intrinsic recognition sequences. However, that very same feature often renders them futile for purposes of inducing programmable genome editing. That is mainly because lengthy target sequences in particular arrangements only occur rarely in a whole genome.[60]

To illustrate this point, consider the sequences that make up phone numbers. A phone number in the United States—for instance 202-479-3000, which is the United States Supreme Court's phone number—consists of a three-digit area code followed by a seven-digit number. Because each individual digit can be a number between 0 and 9, there is a one-in-ten chance that "4" will be the third number; a one-in-one-hundred chance that the sequence "47" will appear as the third and fourth numbers; a one-in-one-thousand chance the sequence "479" will appear as the third, fourth, and fifth numbers, respectively; and so forth. Longer-number sequences make phone numbers more unique because the likelihood that a particular sequence of ordered numbers will occur more than once decreases as you add more digits. The sequence 479-3000 may be a valid phone number in a different area code, but 202-479-3000 belongs to one phone number alone.

The same concept applies to sequences of DNA molecules. For instance, the sequence ATCGTAC may appear several hundred or thousand times in a genome comprising several billion DNA base pairs. But the likelihood that the sequence GAATATCGTACGCTTGATCGAATATGGTACGCCACTGCATTAAG will appear as often is very, very low. Meganucleases are very precise enzymes because they recognize long DNA sequences. The problem, therefore, is that a researcher might have a very specific nuclease at her disposal for a DNA sequence she has no interest in targeting.

Complex protein-engineering strategies to alter the DNA specificity of a meganuclease can ameliorate this problem.[61] However, due to inherent intricacies of protein engineering and the fact that meganuclease DNA-binding and DNA-cleavage functions are interlaced in a single domain,[62] this genome-editing platform has encountered numerous challenges that have precluded its widespread use in translational medicine.

2 Zinc-Finger Nucleases

Zinc-finger proteins are among the most characterized systems used for the manipulation of targeted, sequence-specific nucleic acids. Their discovery arose from research of transcriptional mechanisms in *Xenopus laevis*, the African clawed frog, oocytes—which refer to immature egg cells produced in the female ovaries—dating back to over three decades ago. At the time, scientists realized that a unique set of proteins, which were potentially looped into finger-like arrangements comprising repetitive, zinc-binding domains of roughly thirty amino-acid residues, were required for transcription factor-mediated gene regulation.[63]

Zinc-finger modules rely on interactions between Cysteine and Histidine residues with a zinc-ion ligand, which together form three-dimensional structures where one zinc finger recognizes three contiguous nucleotides of DNA.[64] It may help you to think of LEGO—which is an abbreviation of "leg godt," two Danish words meaning "play well"—pieces to visualize the DNA–zinc finger interaction. Assume that each stud in a given LEGO brick represents one DNA nucleotide. The brick itself (a DNA sequence) comprises three studs, which are arranged contiguously on top of the brick. Assume you also have one LEGO plate that fits perfectly on top of the brick because the plate's tubes can fit onto each stud like puzzle pieces. The LEGO

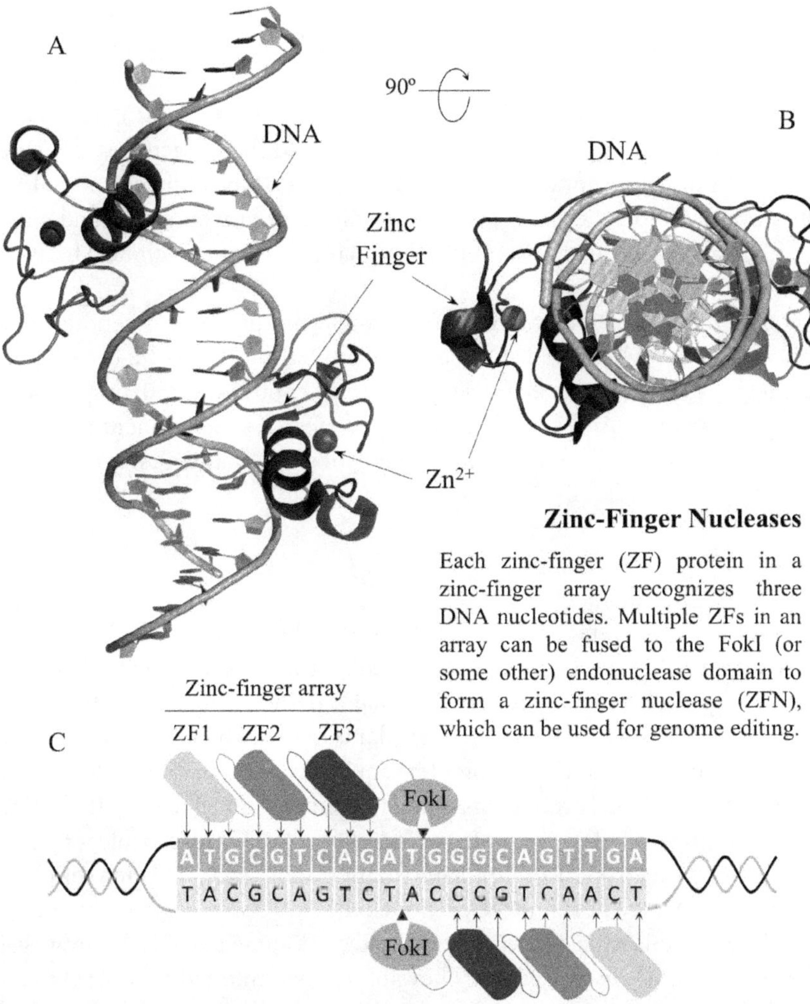

FIGURE 4.2 DNA recognition by zinc-finger proteins and zinc-finger nucleases (ZFN)

(A–B) Orthogonal views of target DNA recognition by zinc-finger proteins. A zinc ion (Zn^{2+}, sphere) stabilizes each zinc finger. (C) A zinc-finger array fused to the FokI nuclease domain forms a sequence-specific ZFN. [PDB 3DFX].

plate (a zinc finger) thus sits on top of (recognizes) the LEGO brick (a DNA sequence), which contains three contiguous studs (nucleotides).

Soon after scientists discovered zinc-finger proteins, they realized that the modular DNA recognition capabilities of each zinc-finger motif could be exploited by coupling it to the nuclease domain of FokI—a restriction endonuclease that was known at the time—to engineer artificial fusion proteins[65] called Zinc-Finger Nucleases (ZFN).[66] If you think back to the earlier LEGO example, the concept is akin to attaching the blade of a utility knife to the LEGO plate, so that when the plate recognizes the brick's studs, the blade will be available to cut a proximal LEGO brick.

Combining a nonspecific nuclease like FokI to zinc fingers capable of recognizing specific sequences of DNA provided a solution to the barriers posed by meganucleases. With that invention, ZFNs became the first biotechnological tools used to demonstrate the practicability of genome editing in human cells[67] and animals in vivo.[68] Decades after their discovery, ZFNs have now entered clinical trials amid high expectations.[69]

Although ZFNs have been critical to promote the progress of genome-editing technologies, their widespread use has been limited by the (1) high cost and (2) technical expertise needed to engineer and validate context-dependent specificity in zinc-finger proteins.[70] And adoption has lagged even despite frequent reporting of strategies designed to simplify and update engineering challenges associated with ZFNs.[71]

3 TALENs

For a number of years and despite their technical shortcomings, ZFNs and meganucleases dominated the budding genome-editing landscape. Then, in 2007, two research groups independently discovered that a particular bacterial strain, which appeared to be pathogenic to certain crop plants, secretes a certain type of effector proteins that bind specific DNA promoter sequences in eukaryotic cells.[72]

These newly identified proteins of bacterial origin became known as transcription activator-like effector (TALE) proteins. TALE proteins are capable of binding specific DNA sequences by mimicking transcription factors. Upon binding to DNA, the pathogenic effector proteins induce the expression of genes that promote the spread of bacterial infection in host cells. TALEs are secreted by Gram-negative bacteria of the *Xanthomonas* genus. They are injected into eukaryotic cells via the type III secretion system[73]—a unique secretion system that specifically evolved to deliver bacterial proteins into eukaryotic cells and is endogenous to some bacterial species from the *Salmonella*, *Chlamydia*, *Pseudomonas*, *Vibrio*, and other genera. Once inside the eukaryotic cell, TALEs translocate directly to the nucleus where they act as transcription factors to regulate the expression of genes that support bacterial infection.

The molecular basis for DNA recognition of each TALE comes from a central tandem amino-acid repeat domain of approximately thirty-three to thirty-five residues in length.[74] Each repeat folds into a V-like structure that features a short loop at the vertex, which contains two hypervariable amino-acid residues known as the repeat variable diresidues (RVD). Each TALE repeat recognizes only one specific nitrogenous base in a given DNA sequence. As a result, the DNA specificity of TALEs is modular and encoded in the RVDs of each tandem-repeat sequence. Both

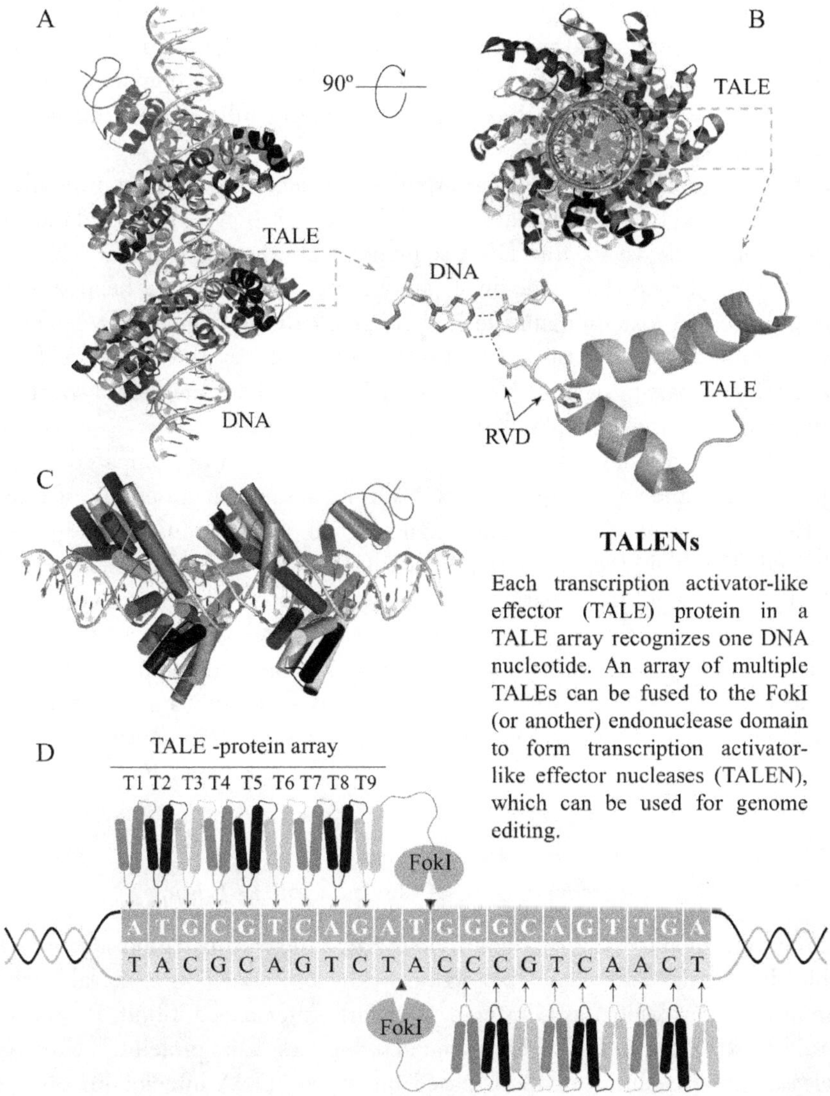

FIGURE 4.3 Target DNA recognition by TALE proteins and TALENs

(A–C) Orthogonal views of TALE tandem repeats bound to a target DNA sequence. An RVD recognizes one DNA base (close-up view). (D) A TALE array fused to the FokI nuclease domain forms a sequence-specific TALEN. [PDB 3UGM].

the mechanism and code responsible for DNA recognition of individual TALEs have been deciphered.[75]

Unlike zinc fingers, which require triplet sequence recognition sites, TALEs are able to target a single nucleotide at a time through RVD regions. This characteristic makes TALEs simpler to engineer and has enabled the rational design of artificial TALEs for biotechnological applications. Indeed, borrowing from principles of their ZFN predecessor, TALE proteins fused to the FokI nuclease domain gave rise to TALE nucleases (TALEN), which have been successfully utilized for genome-editing applications.[76]

TALENs and ZFNs share similar architectural features, most prominently the fusion of the FokI nuclease domain to the DNA recognition domain, and they both can be used to cleave specific DNA sequences. However, engineering of TALE arrays is less onerous than zinc-finger arrays, and TALENs have been shown to induce decreased toxicity thanks to higher specificity for cognate DNA targets.[77] Design simplicity has contributed to a relatively healthy expansion of TALENs in recent years, surpassing even ZFNs.[78] Indeed, TALENs have successfully been used to modify cells,[79] as well as plant[80] and animal[81] genomes.

Despite the advantages of possessing modular properties compared to zinc-finger proteins and the improvements made in design and assembly of custom TALE-based systems,[82] significant technological shortcomings remain to be addressed. The highly repetitive sequences associated with TALE tandem repeats make them susceptible to rearrangements when expressed in target cells due to recombination events that trigger deletions.[83] Moreover, the sheer size of TALE repeats creates obstacles to cellular delivery using some standard viral vectors—such as lentiviruses.[84] Construction of TALENs is also costly and can require up to four times the materials needed for comparable ZFN constructs.[85] Such limitations have precluded wider adaptability of TALE-based tools for genome editing.

D *Programmable, RNA-Guided, Genome Editing*

The most recent and versatile additions to the genome-editing toolbox are programmable, RNA-guided nucleases belonging to the bacterial and archaeal adaptive immunity system known as Clustered, Regularly Interspaced, Short, Palindromic Repeats (CRISPR) and CRISPR-associated sequences (Cas) proteins.[86] Unlike the nuclease genome-editing methods based on protein-DNA interactions discussed earlier in this chapter, RNA-guided, DNA nucleases circumvent the intricate and often cumbersome requirement of protein engineering to target DNA sequences. RNA-guided, DNA nucleases do not recognize cognate DNA targets via interactions between amino-acid residues in a protein and nitrogenous bases in a DNA sequence. Instead, these RNA-guided nucleases harness nature's principles of Watson-Crick nitrogenous base-pairing of nucleic acids to mediate DNA recognition (it may help you to recall from Chapter 2 that Watson-Crick base pairing refers to the principle through which nucleic-acid nitrogenous bases pair up—for example, A–T and C–G—with each other via hydrogen bonds to allow DNA to maintain its double-helical structure).[87]

1 CRISPR–Cas-Based Systems

The discovery of CRISPR systems can be traced back to more than three decades ago when a team of Japanese researchers published findings of a cryptic repeat cluster of unknown function in the bacterium *Escherichia coli* (*E. coli*).[88] Research on CRISPR systems remained mostly dormant until around the turn of the twenty-first century when advances in bioinformatics—alongside greater access to bacterial genomes in public databases—led to the realization that CRISPR sequences exist in a wide range of bacteria and archaea.[89]

Interest about the functional significance of the clusters grew steadily in small scientific niches. Soon thereafter, scientists coined the term CRISPR and identified a group of *Cas*[90] genes encoding proteins involved in catalyzing certain biochemical reactions using nucleic acids as substrates.[91] Bioinformatics analyses revealed that the *Cas* genes encoded regions associated with protein motifs that possess intrinsic nuclease and helicase catalytic activities (helicase refers to an enzyme that is able to separate annealed nucleic-acid strands by, for example, unwinding of the double helix that is characteristic of double-stranded DNA molecules).

By 2005, scientists reported that *CRISPR spacers*—the short intervening sequences of DNA flanked by CRISPR repeats—derive from preexisting sequences that belong to bacteriophages (a term that refers to the type of viruses that infect and replicate within bacteria and archaea) and conjugative plasmids (a type of small and circular extrachromosomal DNA molecule most often found among bacteria).[92] This remarkable insight led researchers to propose, for the first time, that *CRISPR arrays*, which contain alternating CRISPR repeat and spacer sequences, may play a functional role in conferring immunity against viral and plasmid foreign DNA. The CRISPR-immunity theory sparked a great deal of interest about CRISPR systems among wider circles of the scientific community.

Then in 2007, two decades after their discovery, key experiments performed at Danisco, the former Danish food and enzymes manufacturing company and now wholly owned subsidiary of DuPont, established the first empirical evidence that CRISPR was, in fact, an adaptive immunity system that bacteria and archaea use to protect themselves against attack by viruses and plasmids.[93]

To illustrate the adaptive immunity role of CRISPR systems, consider a scenario involving a police investigation to catch an arsonist on the run. Let's assume that an arsonist has just set fire to several government buildings located in a metropolitan area. Authorities were caught off-guard and the arsonist was able to get away without being arrested. Within a couple hours, detectives arrive at the crime scenes and begin to interview potential witnesses. As the investigation unfolds, it becomes apparent that the arsonist plans to strike again. In the meantime, rough sketches of the arsonist are distributed all over the city and the investigation eventually leads the police to locating a suspect. Video from a street camera in front of the crime scene proves that the suspect indeed set fire to one of the buildings, and the police bring the individual into custody. During processing, the police record vital information, take fingerprint impressions and a mug shot, and perform a full-body search of the alleged arsonist. The police creates a record of the incidents and the accused arsonist. All the information is then uploaded and stored into a large database. The accused arsonist, unfortunately, escapes jail before trial and is now on the run.

A few weeks later, another government building is set on fire in a nearby city. The police find an abandoned stolen car a few blocks away with several gallons of gasoline and a map of other targets across the city. Forensic investigators find fingerprints at the crime scene and in the abandoned car. They cross-check the fingerprints against other prints in several criminal databases. The fingerprints match those belonging to the arsonist on the run. Immediately, the police send the arsonist's mug shot and vital information to every police department in a 120-mile radius as well as all major news outlets. Within a matter of hours, police departments across three adjacent cities dispatch officers to search for the arsonist. He is spotted in a nearby town and subsequently brought into custody. This time, however, the police take extra security precautions and the arsonist, at last, stands trial a few weeks later. The arsonist is convicted and sent to a maximum-security prison for a term of thirty years. Good, old-fashioned police work thus prevented the arsonist from attacking other sites and causing further damage to government buildings.

Upon viral invasion, bacteria use CRISPR systems to create a molecular record of the viral attack, much like the police created a record of the arsonist in the example above. Small fragments of viral DNA are then inserted as spacer sequences into CRISPR arrays. Hence, the fragments of viral DNA become permanently stowed between CRISPR repeats and now constitute part of the bacterial genome. In other words, adaptive immunity to foreign nucleic acids is encoded in CRISPR arrays, which contain DNA sequences derived from the integration of invasive DNA as a new CRISPR spacer. The newly acquired spacers, therefore, act as fingerprints and mug shots that are stored in the bacterium's own database—its genome—for future reference.

When the same virus attacks the surviving bacteria once more, the bacteria can now use the information stored in its CRISPR array to defend itself against the new attack. To enable immunity against the virus, the bacterium transcribes the CRISPR array into a long transcript called the *precursor CRISPR RNA* (pre-crRNA), which is subsequently processed into multiple small, mature CRISPR RNAs (crRNA).[94] Each crRNA carries a single spacer sequence corresponding to a fragment of the viral DNA that was integrated into the CRISPR array. The bacterium also simultaneously expresses *cas* genes within the CRISPR locus, which encodes various Cas effector proteins.

To draw parallels to our earlier example, it may help you to think about the RNA-processing step as the downloading of the arsonist's full fifty-page report (the pre-crRNA) stored in the criminal database. The full report needs to be converted into a concise half-page description (the crRNA) of the arsonist for subsequent distribution to law enforcement agents (the Cas effector proteins) that will be dispatched to every town within the 120-mile radius.

Once the crRNAs have been fully processed and the CRISPR–Cas effector proteins are expressed, the crRNAs and Cas proteins assemble into various types of *ribonucleoprotein* complexes—a term that refers to molecular complexes comprising protein and nucleic acid components—that conduct surveillance throughout the cell. In essence, the crRNAs guide the Cas proteins as they scan nucleic acids and search for any foreign DNAs that may be complementary to each unique crRNA. The so-called guide RNAs thus help to recruit the Cas proteins to complementary nucleic acids from invasive genetic elements. The surveillance process outlined here is analogous to the vast deployment of police officers carrying the arsonist's description and photograph as they search for the arsonist across the 120-mile radius.

Upon encountering a complementary viral or plasmid foreign DNA sequence, also known as a *protospacer* sequence, the ribonucleoprotein surveillance complex recognizes a short sequence located directly upstream or downstream of the protospacer known as the *protospacer-adjacent motif* (PAM). The crRNA spacer sequence then anneals to the complementary protospacer sequence in the foreign DNA, which is held firmly in place by the Cas effector protein. The last step in targeted immunity involves the neutralization of the viral DNA via cleavage or degradation by the Cas effector protein. You may think of this step as the eventual arrest and incarceration of the arsonist, except that instead of sending the arsonist away to prison for thirty years, the bacteria gets rid of the viral DNA altogether. If the arsonist pulled a gun out and started shooting at police officers while trying to escape, he might be shot on site. Congruently, the Cas effector protein aims to neutralize the biological threat to the cell by cleaving or degrading foreign target nucleic acids.

Simply put, bacterial and archaeal CRISPR systems are akin to "a mnemonic—so to speak—designed to provide *immunological memory against viral infection*."[95] Bacteria and archaea use this mnemonic as a defense mechanism that allows the deployment of CRISPR machinery in order to wage war against viral invaders and ameliorate viral infection.

* * *

As research into CRISPR systems has accelerated, so too has our knowledge of the mechanistic details of the adaptive immunity phenomenon. CRISPR–Cas systems are currently classified, on the basis of phylogenetic analyses, into class 1 and class 2 groups, which are further divided into six different types and multiple subtypes.[96] And more CRISPR systems likely await characterization. Among CRISPR systems, CRISPR–Cas9 has emerged as the foremost genome-editing platform, partly due to being the first RNA-guided, DNA nuclease discovered. However, other CRISPR systems that target distinct types of nucleic acids—DNA or RNA—such as

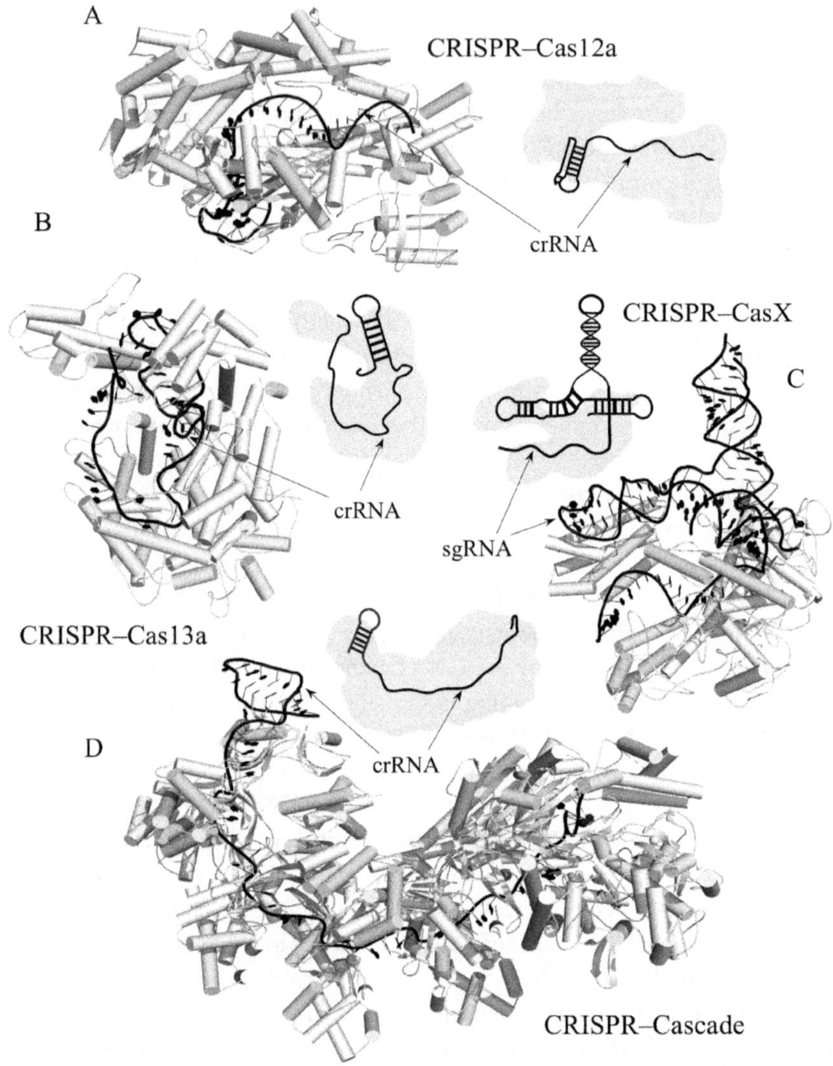

FIGURE 4.4 Structures of select CRISPR–Cas systems in complex with guide RNAs

(A) CRISPR–Cas12a. (B) CRISPR–Cas13a. (C) CRISPR–CasX. (D) CRISPR–Cascade. [PDBs 6I1K, 6VRC, 6NY2, 5H9F].

CRISPR–Cas12a[97] (formerly known as CRISPR–Cpf1[98]), CRISPR–CasX,[99] CRISPR–CasY,[100] CRISPR–Cas13,[101] CRISPR–Cascade,[102] CRISPR–Cas14,[103] CRISPR–Cas12b (as well as CRISPR–Cas12c, –12d, –12e, –12g, –12h, –12i),[104] and others have been identified and are likely to offer valuable future alternatives for nucleic-acid targeting.

2 CRISPR–Cas9

From a genome-editing standpoint, CRISPR–Cas9 has garnered worldwide attention largely because the Cas9 enzyme is part of the CRISPR type II system, which similar to types V and VI CRISPR systems only requires a single-effector Cas nuclease for RNA-guided cleavage of the target nucleic acid.[105]

The type II CRISPR–Cas9 system is the most characterized CRISPR–Cas system to date. To target specific DNA sequences and trigger DNA double-stranded breaks, the CRISPR–Cas9 complex requires dual RNA molecules that hybridize together and direct the Cas9 DNA endonuclease to the target DNA. One of the RNA molecules is a crRNA, which features the spacer region that recognizes the target DNA. The second RNA molecule is called a *trans-activating crRNA* (tracrRNA),[106] which seemingly acts as a scaffold linking the crRNA to Cas9 and facilitates the processing of pre-crRNAs that are transcribed from CRISPR arrays into mature crRNAs.

Upon assembly, the CRISPR–Cas9–crRNA–tracrRNA ternary complex seeks, recognizes, and cuts the target DNA a few nucleotides away from the PAM site—the very short trinucleotide sequence in the target DNA critical for the initial DNA binding of the CRISPR–Cas9 complex.[107] The Cas9 endonuclease cleaves double-stranded DNA via its RuvC and HNH nuclease domains, which are two conserved protein domains that form a compact Cas9 catalytic core.[108] Mutating two residues within the RuvC and HNH nuclease domains—Aspartate to Alanine at position 10 in the RuvC domain (D10A) and Histidine to Alanine at position 840 in the HNH domain (H840A) —is sufficient to deactivate the nuclease activity of the enzyme and turn it into a nuclease-null or "dead" Cas9 (dCas9).[109] These mutations allow CRISPR–Cas9 to target specific DNA sequences and bind to them without cleaving DNA.

A defining moment for the future of genome editing came in 2012 when an article published in the journal *Science* revealed that Cas9 is an RNA-guided, DNA endonuclease and the two small RNAs it associates with—the crRNA and tracrRNA—can be fused together into an engineered, synthetic, single-guide RNA (sgRNA) to direct Cas9 to any target DNA sequence of interest.[110] This finding earned two scientists—Jennifer Doudna, a biochemist, and Emmanuelle Charpentier, a microbiologist—$3 million each and the *Breakthrough Prize* for "harnessing an ancient mechanism of bacterial immunity into a powerful and general technology for editing genomes, with wide-ranging implications across biology and medicine."[111] In 2020, Charpentier and Doudna became the first women to share the Nobel Prize in Chemistry "for the development of a method for genome editing."[112]

The landscape of genome editing vastly changed with the advent of CRISPR systems and CRISPR–Cas9, in particular. Scientists are no longer confined to the tedious process of protein design inherent in other nuclease-based tools to target specific sequences of DNA molecules. Today, any researcher armed with an active Cas9, which may be readily purchased as part of a multitude of plasmids tailored to a researcher's needs, may perform genome editing to carry out a plethora of

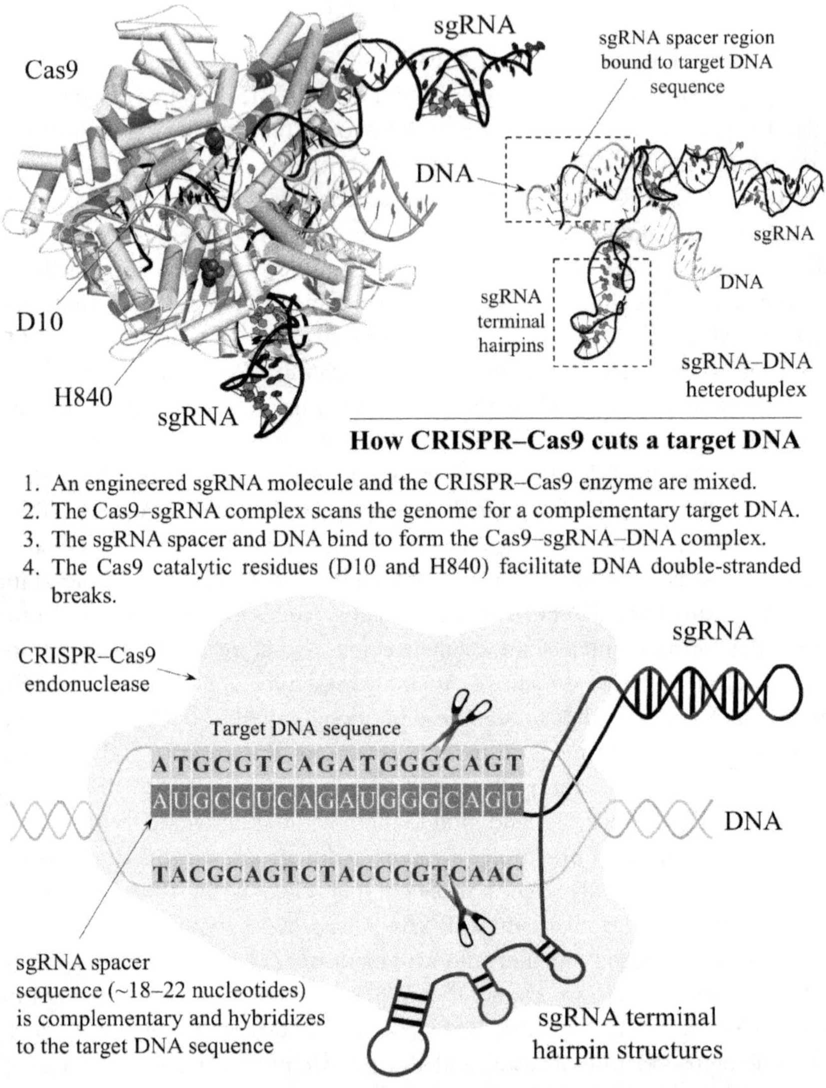

FIGURE 4.5 CRISPR–Cas9 in complex with an sgRNA and double-stranded target DNA

Atomic structure of the CRISPR–Cas9 enzyme primed for target DNA cleavage (top left). The two Cas9 residues that abolish Cas9 catalytic activity when mutated—D10A and H840A—are shown as spheres. The isolated sgRNA–DNA complex (top right without the Cas9) shows the sgRNA spacer region binding to the target DNA, as well as some sgRNA secondary structural features (hairpins). A cartoon representation of the CRISPR–Cas9–sgRNA–DNA complex is shown at the bottom. [PDB 5F9R].

experiments. Plasmids encoding Cas9 proteins, or any number of other Cas proteins, are widely available from commercial sources for as little as $65.00.[113]

Researchers can also design and order inexpensive sgRNAs, which may be synthesized for approximately $10.[114] Once the sgRNAs are ordered and delivered to the lab—voilà!—she may begin to edit her favorite genome for less than one hundred dollars. Even more striking, to edit additional sites, the researcher may use the same Cas9 with another made-to-order sgRNA. The inexpensive, accurate, and easy-to-use essence of CRISPR–Cas9 has changed the rules of the genome-editing game to such an extent that it has been hailed as a tool for the democratization of genome editing.

Widespread use of a biotechnology may not occur for years after it is first introduced to the scientific community. However, unlike its predecessor technologies, CRISPR–Cas9 has been adopted by laboratories around the world with unprecedented speed.[115] Within months of the *Science* publication, reports of genome editing in human cancer cells[116] and induced pluripotent stem cells[117] (iPSC) surfaced. And soon after, a flurry of publications followed detailing genome-editing studies on various organisms including mice,[118] nematodes,[119] fruit flies,[120] zebrafish,[121] frogs,[122] rabbits,[123] pigs,[124] goats,[125] cattle,[126] rice,[127] wheat,[128] tobacco,[129] thale cress,[130] sorghum,[131] and others. Since 2012, nearly 17,000 papers[132] referring to this nascent biotechnology have been published in the scientific literature. CRISPR systems have had a major impact on basic research, as well as on genome-editing research that is being adapted for translational applications in agriculture, synthetic biology, biomedicine, and human therapeutics.

The next chapter presents a survey of some of the current and prospective applications of genome-editing technologies. The overview is firmly grounded in empirical evidence and places particular emphasis on CRISPR-derived advances.

Notes

1 G. D. Padfield & B. Lawrence, *The Birth of Flight Control: An Engineering Analysis of the Wright Brothers' 1902 Glider*, 107 AERONAUTICAL J. 697 (2003).

2 *See* Flying-Machine, U.S. Patent No. 821,393 (filed Mar. 23, 1903).

3 Paul Enríquez, *Genome Editing and the Jurisprudence of Scientific Empiricism*, 19 VAND. J. ENT. & TECH. L. 603, 621 (2017) [hereinafter Enríquez, *Genome Editing*].

4 *See, e.g.*, Rafaelo M. Galvão et al., *A Naturally Occurring Recombinant DNA-A of a Typical Bipartite Begomovirus Does Not Require the Cognate DNA-B to Infect Nicotiana Benthamiana Systemically*, 84 J. GEN. VIROLOGY 715 (2003); Xiaorong Tao & Xueping Zhou, *Pathogenicity of a Naturally Occurring Recombinant DNA Satellite Associated with Tomato Yellow Leaf Curl China Virus*, 89 J. GEN. VIROLOGY 306 (2008); Kuniaki Nerome et al., *Antigenic Characteristics and Genome Composition of a Naturally Occurring Recombinant Influenza Virus Isolated from a Pig in Japan*, 64 J. GEN. VIROLOGY 2611 (1983); Jacqueline M. Burrows et al., *Identification of a Naturally Occurring Recombinant Epstein-Barr Virus Isolate from New Guinea*

that Encodes Both Type 1 and Type 2 Nuclear Antigen Sequences, 70 J. Virology 4829 (1996).

5 *See* David A. Jackson, Robert H. Symons & Paul Berg, *Biochemical Method for Inserting New Genetic Information into DNA of Simian Virus 40: Circular SV40 DNA Molecules Containing Lambda Phage Genes and the Galactose Operon of Escherichia coli*, 69 Proc. Nat'l Acad. Sci. U.S. 2904 (1972).

6 *See, e.g.*, Peter E. Lobban & Armin D. Kaiser, *Enzymatic End-to-End Joining of DNA Molecules*, 78 J. Molecular Biology 453 (1973); Janet E. Mertz & Ronald W. Davis, *Cleavage of DNA by R1 Restriction Endonuclease Generates Cohesive Ends*, 69 Proc. Nat'l Acad. Sci. U.S. 3370 (1972); Daniel Nathans & Hamilton O. Smith, *Restriction Endonucleases in the Analysis and Restructuring of DNA Molecules*, 44 Ann. Rev. Biochemistry 273 (1975).

7 Stanley N. Cohen et al., *Construction of Biologically Functional Bacterial Plasmids in Vitro*, 70 Proc. Nat'l Acad. Sci. U.S. 3240 (1973).

8 Rudolf Jaenisch & Beatrice Mintz, *Simian Virus 40 DNA Sequences in DNA of Healthy Adult Mice Derived from Preimplantation Blastocysts Injected with Viral DNA*, 71 Proc. Nat'l Acad. U.S. 1250 (1974).

9 Luis Herrera-Estrella et al., *Expression of Chimaeric Genes Transferred into Plant Cells Using a Ti-Plasmid-Derived Vector*, 303 Nature 209 (1983); Michael W. Bevan & Richard B. Flavell, *A Chimaeric Antibiotic Resistance Gene as a Selectable Marker for Plant Cell Transformation*, 304 Nature 184 (1983); Robert T. Fraley et al., *Expression of Bacterial Genes in Plant Cells*, 80 Proc. Nat'l Acad. Sci. U.S. 4803 (1983).

10 *See* Microorganisms Having Multiple Compatible Degradative Energy-Generating Plasmids and Preparation Thereof, U.S. Patent No. 4,259,444 (filed June 7, 1972).

11 *E.g.*, Process for Producing Biologically Functional Molecular Chimeras, U.S. Patent No. 4,237,224 (filed Jan. 4, 1979); *Id.*

12 *See* John A. Kehoe, *The Story of Biosynthetic Human Insulin*, *in* Frontiers in Bioprocessing 46 (Subhas K. Sikdar, Milan Bier & Paul W. Todd eds. 1990).

13 *See* Lydia Villa-Komaroff et al., *A Bacterial Clone Synthesizing Proinsulin*, 75 Proc. Nat'l Acad. Sci. U.S. 3727 (1978).

14 Irving S. Johnson, *Human Insulin from Recombinant DNA Technology*, 219 Science 632 (1983).

15 Lawrence K. Altman, *A New Insulin Given Approval for Use in U.S.*, N.Y. Times, Oct. 30, 1982, at A1.

16 *See, e.g.*, Ely Lilly & Co., *Patient Information, Humulin® R*, http://pi.lilly.com/us/humulin-r-ppi.pdf; Novo Nordisk Inc., *Highlights of Prescribing Information, Novolin® R*, https://www.novo-pi.com/novolinr.pdf; Sanofi India Ltd., *Insuman®*, https://www.sanofi.in/-/media/Project/One-Sanofi-Web/Websites/Asia-Pacific/Sanofi-IN/Home/science-and-innovation/for-healthcare-professionals/product-information/Insuman_PI.pdf.

17 *See* David V. Goeddel et al., *Direct Expression in Escherichia coli of a DNA Sequence Coding for Human Growth Hormone*, 281 NATURE 544 (1979).

18 *See, e.g.*, J. C. Beck et al., *Metabolic Effects of Human and Monkey Growth Hormone in Man*, 125 SCIENCE 884 (1957).

19 *See* Centers for Disease Control & Prevention, *Fatal Degenerative Neurologic Disease in Patients Who Received Pituitary-Derived Human Growth Hormone*, 34 MORBIDITY & MORTALITY WEEKLY REPORT 359 (1985); Elizabeth B. Rappaport & David J. Graham, *Pituitary Growth Hormone from Human Cadavers: Neurologic Disease in Ten Recipients*, 37 NEUROLOGY 1211 (1987).

20 Nell Henderson, *FDA Clears Use of Drug Made by Gene-Splicing*, WASH. POST, Oct. 19, 1985, https://www.washingtonpost.com/archive/politics/1985/10/19/fda-clears-use-of-drug-made-by-gene-splicing/98e8dd1d-02cb-4f67-8718-e94fdb4dcdd1/?noredirect=on&utm_term=.3204ffdfd4bd; Genentech Press Release, Oct. 18 1985, https://www.gene.com/media/press-releases/4235/1985–10-18/fda-approves-genentechs-drug-to-treat-ch.

21 *See* Keiichi Itakura et al., *Expression in Escherichia coli of a Chemically Synthesized Gene for the Hormone Somatostatin*, 198 SCIENCE 1056 (1977).

22 William J. McAleer et al., *Human Hepatitis B Vaccine from Recombinant Yeast*, 307 NATURE 178 (1984); H. Arimura et al., *Hepatitis B Vaccines Prepared from Yeast by Recombinant DNA Techniques: Memorandum from a WHO Meeting*, 63 BULLETIN WORLD HEALTH ORG. 57 (1985).

23 J. S. Emtage et al., *Synthesis of Calf Prochymosin (Prorennin) in Escherichia coli*, 80 PROC. NAT'L ACAD. SCI. U.S. 3671 (1983).

24 Nigel S. Dunn-Coleman et al., *Commercial Levels of Chymosin Production by Aspergillus*, 9 NATURE BIOTECHNOLOGY 976 (1991).

25 *See* U.S. Patent No. 4,259,444 (filed June 7, 1972).

26 35 U.S.C. § 101.

27 447 U.S. 303 (1980).

28 *Id.* at 309–10.

29 *Id.* at 310.

30 *Id.* at 309 (quoting Sen. Rep. No. 1979, 82d Cong., 2d Sess., 5 (1952); H.R. Rep. No. 1923, 82d Cong., 2d Sess., 6 (1952)).

31 Enríquez, *Genome Editing*, *supra* note 3, at 621.

32 *See, e.g.*, Paul Berg et al., *Potential Biohazards of Recombinant DNA Molecules*, 185 SCIENCE 303 (1974).

33 For a list of participants of the Asilomar International Conference on Recombinant DNA Molecules that took place on February 24–27, 1975, see Donald S. Fredrickson, *Asilomar and Recombinant DNA: The End of the Beginning*, *in* BIOMEDICAL POLITICS 258, app. at 293 (Kathi E. Hanna ed. 1991).

34 Paul Berg et al., *Summary Statement of the Asilomar Conference on Recombinant DNA Molecules*, 72 PROC. NAT'L ACAD. SCI. U.S. 1981 (1975).

35 *Id.* at 1983.

36 *See, e.g.*, Barbara C. F. Chu & Leslie E. Orgel, *Nonenzymatic Sequence-Specific Cleavage of Single-Stranded DNA*, 82 Proc. Nat'l Acad. Sci. U.S. 963 (1985).

37 Scott A. Strobel & Peter B. Dervan, *Site-Specific Cleavage of a Yeast Chromosome by Oligonucleotide-Directed Triple-Helix Formation*, 249 Science 73 (1990); Scott A. Strobel et al., *Site-Specific Cleavage of Human Chromosome 4 Mediated by Triple-Helix Formation*, 254 Science 1639 (1991).

38 A. Fawad Faruqi, et al., *Recombination Induced by Triple-Helix-Targeted DNA Damage in Mammalian Cells*, 16 Molecular Cell Biology 6820 (1996).

39 C. R. Hammond, The Elements 4–7 (n.d.), http://www-do.fnal.gov/hardware/cal/lvps_info/engineering/elements.pdf [https://perma.cc/986X-Z2L4].

40 Makoto Komiyama et al., *Catalytically Active Species for $CeCl_3$-Induced DNA Hydrolysis*, 115 J. Biochemistry 809 (1994).

41 Wen Chen & Makoto Komiyama, *Site-Selective DNA Hydrolysis by Ce^{IV}–EDTA with the Use of One Oligonucleotide Additive Bearing Two Monophosphates*, 6 ChemBioChem 1825 (2005); Jia-Ming Yan et al., *(Ethylenediaminetetraacetic Acid)cerium(IV) [Ce^{IV}(EDTA)] Complexes with Dual Hydrophobic Binding Sites as Highly Efficient Catalysts for the Hydrolysis of Phosphodiesters*, 85 Helvetica Chimica Acta 1496 (2002).

42 Makoto Komiyama et al., *Artificial Restriction DNA Cutter for Site-Selective Scission of Double-Stranded DNA with Tunable Scission Site and Specificity*, 3 Nature Protocols 655, 655 (2008).

43 *See* Peter E. Nielsen et al., *Sequence-Selective Recognition of DNA by Strand Displacement with a Thymine-Substituted Polyamide*, 254 Science 1497, 1498 (1991).

44 *See, e.g.*, Gilles Gasser, Anna M. Sosniak & Nils Metzler-Nolte, *Metal-Containing Peptide Nucleic Acid Conjugates*, 40 Dalton Transactions 7061 (2011).

45 Vadim Demidov et al., *Sequence Selective Double Strand DNA Cleavage by Peptide Nucleic Acid (PNA) Targeting Using Nuclease S1*, 21 Nucleic Acids Res. 2103 (1993).

46 *See* Joel M. Gottesfeld et al., *Regulation of Gene Expression by Small Molecules*, 387 Nature 202 (1997).

47 *See* Yuichiro Aiba, Jun Sumaoka & Makoto Komiyama, *Artificial DNA Cutters for DNA Manipulation and Genome Engineering*, 40 Chem. Soc'y Revs. 5657 (2011).

48 *See, e.g.*, David W. Russell & Roli K. Hirata, *Human Gene Targeting by Viral Vectors*, 18 Nature Genetics 325, 325 (1998). This study demonstrated that AAV-based viral vector transduction could generate higher frequencies of gene-targeting events in some cell populations than transfection and other methods.

49 David V. Schaffer et al., *Molecular Engineering of Viral Gene Delivery Vehicles*, 10 Ann. Rev. Biomedical Engineering 169, 171 (2008).

50 *See, e.g.*, Manuel A. F. V. Gonçalves, *Adeno-Associated Virus: From Defective Virus to Effective Vector*, 2 VIROLOGY J. 43, 49–50 (2005), http://virologyj.biomedcentral.com/articles/10.1186/1743-422X-2-43 [https://perma.cc/3J83-P674].

51 Russell & Hirata, *supra* note 48, at 328–29.

52 *See rAAV*, HORIZON, https://www.horizondiscovery.com/about-us/our-science/raav [https://perma.cc/Y3TZ-3APR] (last visited Feb. 25, 2017).

53 *See, e.g.*, SPARK THERAPEUTICS, A PHASE 1 SAFETY STUDY IN SUBJECTS WITH LEBER CONGENITAL AMAUROSIS (LCA) USING ADENO-ASSOCIATED VIRAL VECTOR TO DELIVER THE GENE FOR HUMAN RPE65 INTO THE RETINAL PIGMENT EPITHELIUM (RPE) [AAV2-HRPE65V2-101] (2007), https://clinicaltrials.gov/ct2/show/study/NCT00516477 [https://perma.cc/C8KS-W6TN].

54 *See, e.g.*, Artur V. Cideciyan et al., *Human RPE65 Gene Therapy for Leber Congenital Amaurosis: Persistence of Early Visual Improvements and Safety at 1 Year*, 20 HUM. GENE THERAPY 999 (2009); Albert M. Maguire et al., *Age-Dependent Effects of RPE65 Gene Therapy for Leber's Congenital Amaurosis: A Phase 1 Dose-Escalation Trial*, 374 LANCET 1597 (2009); Albert M. Maguire et al., *Safety and Efficacy of Gene Transfer for Leber Congenital Amaurosis*, 358 NEW ENG. J. MED. 2240 (2008).

55 The term "homing" refers to a gene conversion process, whereby a mobile sequence is copied and inserted into a new cognate site lacking the sequence. Maria J. Marcaida et al., *Homing Endonucleases: From Basics to Therapeutic Applications*, 67 CELLULAR & MOLECULAR LIFE SCI. 727, 727 (2010).

56 Tamas Lukacsovich et al., *Repair of a Specific Double-Strand Break Generated Within a Mammalian Chromosome by Yeast Endonuclease I-Scel*, 22 NUCLEIC ACIDS RES. 5649, 5650 (1994).

57 Steven Zimmerly et al., *A Group II Intron RNA Is a Catalytic Component of a DNA Endonuclease Involved in Intron Mobility*, 83 CELL 529, 529 (1995). *See generally* Bruce A. Sullenger & Thomas R. Cech, *Ribozyme-Mediated Repair of Defective mRNA by Targeted Trans-Splicing*, 371 NATURE 619 (1994).

58 *See Intron*, SCITABLE, http://www.nature.com/scitable/definition/intron-introns-67 [https://perma.cc/RZH2-DBNA] (last visited Feb. 25, 2017).

59 *See, e.g.*, Philippe Rouet et al., *Expression of a Site-Specific Endonuclease Stimulates Homologous Recombination in Mammalian Cells*, 91 PROC. NAT'L ACAD. SCI. U.S. 6064 (1994); R. Geoffrey Sargent, et al., *Repair of Site-Specific Double-Strand Breaks in a Mammalian Chromosome by Homologous and Illegitimate Recombination*, 17 MOLECULAR & CELLULAR BIOLOGY 267 (1997); Jian Yang et al., *Efficient Integration of an Intron RNA into Double-Stranded DNA by Reverse Splicing*, 381 NATURE 332 (1996).

60 Marcaida et al., *supra* note 55, at 727.

61 *See* Jordan Jarjour et al., *High-Resolution Profiling of Homing Endonuclease Binding and Catalytic Specificity Using Yeast Surface Display*, 37 NUCLEIC ACIDS

Res. 6871, 6878 (2009) (investigating DNA binding and catalysis for protein engineering); Pilar Redondo et al., *Molecular Basis of Xeroderma Pigmentosum Group C DNA Recognition by Engineered Meganucleases*, 456 Nature 107, 107 (2008) (engineering a meganuclease derivative to target a particular gene).

62 Julianne Smith et al., *A Combinatorial Approach to Create Artificial Homing Endonucleases Cleaving Chosen Sequences*, 32 Nucleic Acids Res. e149, 2, 6–7 (2006).

63 J. Miller et al., *Repetitive Zinc-Binding Domains in the Protein Transcription Factor IIIA from Xenopus Oocytes*, 4 EMBO J. 1609, 1612 (1985).

64 Nikola P. Pavletich & Carl O. Pabo, *Zinc Finger-DNA Recognition: Crystal Structure of a Zif268-DNA Complex at 2.1 Å*, 252 Science 809, 813 (1991).

65 Yang-Gyun Kim et al., *Hybrid Restriction Enzymes: Zinc Finger Fusions to Fok I Cleavage Domain*, 93 Proc. Nat'l Acad. Sci. U.S. 1156, 1156 (1996).

66 Although the name "zinc-finger nuclease" has become standard in biotechnology, in the past, the terms "chimeric-restriction enzyme" and "chimeric nuclease" have also been used. *See* Jeff Smith et al., *Requirements for Double-Strand Cleavage by Chimeric Restriction Enzymes with Zinc Finger DNA-Recognition Domains*, 28 Nucleic Acids Res. 3361, 3361 (2000).

67 *See, e.g.*, Matthew H. Porteus & David Baltimore, *Chimeric Nucleases Stimulate Gene Targeting in Human Cells*, 300 Science 763 (2003); Matthew H. Porteus, *Mammalian Gene Targeting with Designed Zinc Finger Nucleases*, 13 Molecular Therapy 438 (2006); Fyodor D. Urnov et al., *Highly Efficient Endogenous Human Gene Correction Using Designed Zinc-Finger Nucleases*, 435 Nature 646 (2005).

68 *See, e.g.*, Marina Bibikova et al., *Enhancing Gene Targeting with Designed Zinc Finger Nucleases*, 300 Science 764 (2003); Marina Bibikova et al., *Targeted Chromosomal Cleavage and Mutagenesis in Drosophila Using Zinc-Finger Nucleases*, 161 Genetics 1169 (2002).

69 *See generally Autologous T-Cells Genetically Modified at the CCR5 Gene by Zinc Finger Nucleases SB-728 for HIV (Zinc-Finger)*, ClinicalTrials.gov, https://clinicaltrials.gov/ct2/show/study/NCT00842634 [https://perma.cc/RB7E-VGE3] (last visited Feb. 13, 2017).

70 *See, e.g.*, Scot A. Wolfe et al., *DNA Recognition by Cys2His2 Zinc Finger Proteins*, 29 Ann. Rev. Biophysics & Biomolecular Structure 183, 199–201, 203–05 (2000); *see also infra* note 71 (reporting various ways to address challenges inherently associated with ZFNs).

71 *See, e.g.*, Ankit Gupta et al., *An Optimized Two-Finger Archive for ZFN-Mediated Gene Targeting*, 9 Nature Methods 588 (2012); Seokjoong Kim et al., *Preassembled Zinc-Finger Arrays for Rapid Construction of ZFNs*, 8 Nature Methods 7 (2011); Morgan L. Maeder et al., *Rapid "Open-Source" Engineering of Customized Zinc-Finger Nucleases for Highly Efficient Gene Modification*, 31 Molecular Cell 294 (2008); David A. Wright et al.,

Standardized Reagents and Protocols for Engineering Zinc Finger Nucleases by Modular Assembly, 1 NATURE PROTOCOLS 1637 (2006).

72 Sabine Kay et al., *A Bacterial Effector Acts as a Plant Transcription Factor and Induces a Cell Size Regulator*, 318 SCIENCE 648, 650 (2007); Patrick Römer et al., *Plant Pathogen Recognition Mediated by Promoter Activation of the Pepper Bs3 Resistance Gene*, 318 SCIENCE 645, 646 (2007).

73 Jorge E. Galán & Hans Wolf-Watz, *Protein Delivery into Eukaryotic Cells by Type III Secretion Machines*, 444 NATURE 567 (2006).

74 *See* Amanda Nga-Sze Mak et al., *The Crystal Structure of TAL Effector PthXo1 Bound to its DNA Target*, 335 SCIENCE 716 (2012); Dong Deng et al., *Structural Basis for Sequence-Specific Recognition of DNA by TAL Effectors*, 335 SCIENCE 720 (2012).

75 *See* Jens Boch et al., *Breaking the Code of DNA Binding Specificity of TAL-Type III Effectors*, 326 SCIENCE 1509, 1509 (2009); Matthew J. Moscou & Adam J. Bogdanove, *A Simple Cipher Governs DNA Recognition by TAL Effectors*, 326 SCIENCE 1501, 1501 (2009).

76 *See, e.g.*, Michelle Christian et al., *Targeting DNA Double-Strand Breaks with TAL Effector Nucleases*, 186 GENETICS 757 (2010); Ting Li et al., *TAL Nucleases (TALNs): Hybrid Proteins Composed of TAL Effectors and FokI DNA-Cleavage Domain*, 39 NUCLEIC ACIDS RES. 359 (2011); Magdy M. Mahfouz et al., *De Novo-Engineered Transcription Activator-Like Effector (TALE) Hybrid Nuclease with Novel DNA Binding Specificity Creates Double-Strand Breaks*, 108 PROC. NAT'L ACAD. SCI. U.S. 2623 (2011); Jeffrey C. Miller et al., *A TALE Nuclease Architecture for Efficient Genome Editing*, 29 NATURE BIOTECHNOLOGY 143 (2011).

77 Marine Beurdeley et al., *Compact Designer TALENs for Efficient Genome Engineering*, 4 NATURE COMMC'NS art. no. 1762, at 6 (2013), http://www.nature.com/ncomms/journal/v4/n4/pdf/ncomms2782.pdf [https://perma.cc/2QYH-YML5].

78 *Id.*

79 *See, e.g.*, Dirk Hockemeyer et al., *Genetic Engineering of Human Pluripotent Cells Using TALE Nucleases*, 29 NATURE BIOTECHNOLOGY 731 (2011); Deepak Reyon et al., *FLASH Assembly of TALENs for High-Throughput Genome Editing*, 30 NATURE BIOTECHNOLOGY 460 (2012).

80 *See, e.g.*, Ting Li et al., *High-Efficiency TALEN-Based Gene Editing Produces Disease-Resistant Rice*, 30 NATURE BIOTECHNOLOGY 390 (2012).

81 *See, e.g.*, Victoria M. Bedell et al., *In Vivo Genome Editing Using a High-Efficiency TALEN System*, 491 NATURE 114 (2012); Daniel F. Carlson et al., *Efficient TALEN-Mediated Gene Knockout in Livestock*, 109 PROC. NAT'L ACAD. SCI. U.S. 17382 (2012); Laurent Tesson et al., *Knockout Rats Generated by Embryo Microinjection of TALENs*, 29 NATURE BIOTECHNOLOGY 695 (2011).

82 *See, e.g.*, Tomas Cermak et al., *Efficient Design and Assembly of Custom TALEN and Other TAL Effector-Based Constructs for DNA Targeting*, 39 NUCLEIC ACIDS RES. e82 (2011).

83 *See, e.g.*, Maarten Holkers et al., *Differential Integrity of TALE Nuclease Genes Following Adenoviral and Lentiviral Vector Gene Transfer into Human Cells*, 41 NUCLEIC ACIDS RES. E63 (2013).
84 Jia Liu et al., *Cell-Penetrating Peptide-Mediated Delivery of TALEN Proteins via Bioconjugation for Genome Engineering*, 9 PLoS ONE e85755, e85755–56 (2014).
85 Beurdeley et al., *supra* note 77, at 6.
86 Ruud Jansen et al., *Identification of Genes That Are Associated with DNA Repeats in Prokaryotes*, 43 MOLECULAR MICROBIOLOGY 1565, 1565 (2002).
87 *See* discussion in Chapter 2, Part II.B.
88 Yoshizumi Ishino et al., *Nucleotide Sequence of the Iap Gene, Responsible for Alkaline Phosphatase Isozyme Conversion in Escherichia coli, and Identification of the Gene Product*, 169 J. BACTERIOLOGY 5429, 5432 (1987).
89 Francisco J. M. Mojica et al., *Biological Significance of a Family of Regularly Spaced Repeats in the Genomes of Archaea, Bacteria and Mitochondria*, 36 MOLECULAR MICROBIOLOGY 244, 244 (2000).
90 In standard genetic scientific nomenclature, gene names are generally italicized. In contrast, gene products such as proteins are designated using the same gene name, but in nonitalicized font.
91 Jansen et al., *supra* note 86, at 1568–69.
92 *See* Francisco J. M. Mojica et al., *Intervening Sequences of Regularly Spaced Prokaryotic Repeats Derive from Foreign Genetic Elements*, 60 J. MOLECULAR EVOLUTION 174 (2005).
93 Rodolphe Barrangou et al., *CRISPR Provides Acquired Resistance Against Viruses in Prokaryotes*, 315 SCIENCE 1709, 1711 (2007).
94 *See* Frank Hille & Emmanuelle Charpentier, *CRISPR-Cas: Biology, Mechanisms and Relevance*, 371 PHILOSOPHICAL TRANSACTIONS ROYAL SOC'Y B BIOLOGICAL SCI. 20150496, at 3 (2016), https://www.ncbi.nlm.nih.gov/pmc/articles/PMC5052741/pdf/rstb20150496.pdf.
95 Enríquez, *Genome Editing*, *supra* note 3, at 629 (emphasis added).
96 *See* Sergey Shmakov et al., *Discovery and Functional Characterization of Diverse Class 2 CRISPR-Cas Systems*, 60 MOLECULAR CELL 385 (2015); Kira S. Makarova et al., *An Updated Evolutionary Classification of CRISPR–Cas Systems*, 13 NATURE REVS. MICROBIOLOGY 722, 724 (2015).
97 *See, e.g.*, Janice S. Chen et al., *CRISPR-Cas12a Target Binding Unleashes Indiscriminate Single-Stranded DNase Activity*, 360 SCIENCE 436 (2018).
98 *See* Bernd Zetsche et al., *Cpf1 Is a Single RNA-Guided Endonuclease of a Class 2 CRISPR-Cas System*, 163 CELL 759, 760 (2015).
99 *See* Jun-Jie Liu et al., *CasX Enzymes Comprise a Distinct Family of RNA-Guided Genome Editors*, 566 NATURE 218 (2019).
100 *See* David Burstein et al., *New CRISPR–Cas Systems from Uncultivated Microbes*, 542 NATURE 237 (2017).

101 *See* David B. T. Cox et al., *RNA Editing with CRISPR-Cas13*, 358 SCIENCE 1019 (2017).

102 *See, e.g.*, Stan J. J. Brouns et al., *Small CRISPR RNAs Guide Antiviral Defense in Prokaryotes*, 321 SCIENCE 960 (2008); Joshua K. Young et al., *The Repurposing of Type I-E CRISPR-Cascade for Gene Activation in Plants*, 2 COMMUNICATIONS BIOLOGY Art. 383 (2019).

103 *See, e.g.*, Lucas B. Harrington et al., *Programmed DNA Destruction by Miniature CRISPR-Cas14 Enzymes*, 362 SCIENCE 839 (2018).

104 *See* Winston X. Yang et al., *Functionally Diverse Type V CRISPR-Cas Systems*, 363 SCIENCE 88 (2019).

105 Josiane E. Garneau et al., *The CRISPR/Cas Bacterial Immune System Cleaves Bacteriophage and Plasmid DNA*, 468 NATURE 67, 70 (2010) (discussing Cas9's involvement in DNA cleavage while it was still known as Cas5); Rimantas Sapranauskas et al., *The Streptococcus Thermophilus CRISPR/Cas System Provides Immunity in Escherichia Coli*, 39 NUCLEIC ACIDS RES. 9275, 9279 (2011).

106 *See, e.g.*, Krzysztof Chylinski, Anaïs Le Rhun & Emmanuelle Charpentier, *The TracrRNA and Cas9 Families of Type II CRISPR-Cas Immunity Systems*, 10 RNA BIOLOGY 726 (2013). Notably, unlike CRISPR–Cas9, the CRISPR–Cpf1 system does not require a tracrRNA. *See* Zetsche et al., *supra* note 98, at 760.

107 *See* Samuel H. Sternberg et al., *DNA Interrogation by the CRISPR RNA-Guided Endonuclease Cas9*, 507 NATURE 62, 63–64 (2014).

108 *See* Martin Jinek et al., *A Programmable Dual-RNA–Guided DNA Endonuclease in Adaptive Bacterial Immunity*, 337 SCIENCE 816, 816 (2012).

109 *See id.* at 817, 819.

110 *See generally id.*

111 *See Recipients of the 2015 Breakthrough Prizes*, BREAKTHROUGH PRIZE, https://breakthroughprize.org/News/21 [https://perma.cc/U7RY-79BK] (last visited Feb. 25, 2017). Their discovery may one day also earn them a Nobel Prize.

112 Press Release, The Nobel Prize in Chemistry 2020 (Oct. 7, 2020), https://www.nobelprize.org/uploads/2020/10/press-chemistryprize2020.pdf.

113 *See, e.g.*, *eSpCas9(1.1)*, ADDGENE, https://www.addgene.org/71814/ [https://perma.cc/8AT6-TK38] (last visited Feb. 25, 2017).

114 *See, e.g.*, Sathiji Nageshwaran et al., *CRISPR Guide RNA Cloning for Mammalian Systems*, 140 J. VISUALIZED EXPERIMENTS e57998 (2018).

115 Jacob Corn, *The Explosion of CRISPR/Cas9*, INNOVATIVE GENOMICS (July 18, 2015), https://innovativegenomics.org/blog/crispr-cas9-explosion/ [https://perma.cc/ZS4P-5C8B].

116 *See* Prashant Mali et al., *RNA-Guided Human Genome Engineering via Cas9*, 339 SCIENCE 823 (2013).

117 *E.g.*, *id.*; Martin Jinek et al., *RNA-Programmed Genome Editing in Human Cells*, 2 ELIFE e00471 (2013).

118 *See generally* Bin Shen et al., *Generation of Gene-Modified Mice via Cas9/RNA-Mediated Gene Targeting*, 23 CELL RES. 720 (2013).
119 *See generally* Ari E. Friedland, *Heritable Genome Editing in C. elegans via a CRISPR-Cas9 System*, 10 NATURE METHODS 741 (2013).
120 *See generally* Zhongsheng Yu et al., *Highly Efficient Genome Modifications Mediated by CRISPR/Cas9 in Drosophila*, 195 GENETICS 289 (2013).
121 *See generally* Li-En Jao et al., *Efficient Multiplex Biallelic Zebrafish Genome Editing Using a CRISPR Nuclease System*, 110 PROC. NAT'L ACAD. SCI. U.S. 13904 (2013).
122 *See generally* Takuya Nakayama et al., *Simple and Efficient CRISPR/Cas9-Mediated Targeted Mutagenesis in Xenopus tropicalis*, 51 GENESIS 835 (2013).
123 *See generally* Dongshan Yang et al., *Effective Gene Targeting in Rabbits Using RNA-Guided Cas9 Nucleases*, 6 J. MOLECULAR CELL BIOLOGY 97 (2014).
124 *See generally* Wenfang Tan et al., *Efficient Nonmeiotic Allele Introgression in Livestock Using Custom Endonucleases*, 110 PROC. NAT'L ACAD. SCI. U.S. 16526 (2013).
125 *Id.*
126 *Id.*
127 *See generally* Wenzhi Jiang et al., *Demonstration of CRISPR/Cas9/sgRNA-Mediated Targeted Gene Modification in Arabidopsis, Tobacco, Sorghum and Rice*, 41 NUCLEIC ACIDS RES. e188 (2013).
128 *See generally id.*; Qiwei Shan et al., *Targeted Genome Modification of Crop Plants Using a CRISPR-Cas System*, 31 NATURE BIOTECHNOLOGY 686 (2013).
129 *See generally* Jiang et al., *supra* note 127.
130 *Id.*
131 *Id.*
132 A search on the PubMed scientific database using the "CRISPR" acronym filtered by title and abstract returned 16,957 hits. PubMed.gov Search Results for CRISPR, PUBMED.GOV, http://www.ncbi.nlm.nih.gov/pubmed/?term=CRISPR[Title%2FAbstract] [https://perma.cc/7PC2-BNN8] (last visited Apr. 12, 2020) (search for CRISPR filtered by title and abstract by using the language "CRISPR[Title/Abstract]"). Note that the search does not include papers that refer to CRISPR in the body of the paper, which may return more hits.

5

What Can Genome Editing Be Used for?

As the previous chapters demonstrate, genome editing has revolutionized scientific research in the last few years. But you may be asking at this point: What exactly can humans do with this new technology? This chapter answers that question.

One substantial predicament about technologies that are powerful yet not popularly understood, such as genome-editing technologies, is that they are often prone to having their capabilities overstated or even misrepresented to be well beyond what they actually are. This chapter provides a comprehensive, albeit nonexhaustive, survey of the current and reasonably prospective applications of genome-editing technologies. The chapter faithfully tracks and explains primary scientific sources and is, thus, firmly grounded in a jurisprudence of scientific empiricism.

As we stroll through the chapter, we will examine applications of genome editing in fields ranging from stem-cell research, pest-population control, viral diagnostics, and agriculture to animal research, organ transplantation, synthetic biology, biofuel production, human therapeutics, epigenome editing, digital-data recording in living organisms, and more. The chapter underscores two main points. First, genome-editing technologies are not mere tools for basic research, but rather epitomize prolific mines for future significant scientific and medical breakthroughs. Second, every technology endowed with awe-inspiring powers should be handled responsibly and with respect. Using empirical scientific evidence as our guide, let us now embark on a journey to uncover just what genome editing is, and may be, good for.

I GENETIC DISORDERS AND EDITING OF SOMATIC CELLS AND STEM CELLS

Genetic disorders are medical conditions associated with genomic mutations that lead to health problems or disease in the individual bearing the mutations. Inheritable genetic disorders may be *monogenic*, which means they arise from mutations that affect a single gene, or *polygenic*, which relates to disorders based on mutations in multiple genes. To date, more than 6,500 genetic disorders of these sorts have been characterized,[1] and discovery of new disorders are continuously reported in the scientific literature. According to the Online Mendelian Inheritance in Man® (OMIM) database—a publicly available, comprehensive compendium of human genes and genetic phenotypes created by the National Institutes of Health's (NIH) National Library of Medicine, in collaboration with Johns Hopkins University—more than 15,000 genes with different variants are associated with the more than 6,500 genetic disorders currently known.[2]

In addition to the aforementioned types of known inheritable genetic disorders, there are also other diseases that have a genetic basis or association. Cancer, for example, includes a wide-ranging category of diseases caused by genetic mutations that accumulate over an individual's lifetime and are generally not inherited—although certain predispositions to some cancers have been identified in some individuals. And diseases caused by viral integration into an individual's genome may also be regarded as having genetic links. For example, HIV, the virus that causes AIDS, is able to integrate into the human genome and can proliferate when the encoding viral DNA at the integration locus is transcribed and subsequently translated into viral proteins. As the virus spreads to other cells and tissues, it leads to immunodeficiencies that disrupt the immune system's ability to defend itself against infections.

In recent years, genome editing of somatic cells[3]—that is, the nonreproductive, differentiated cells of the body (which do not include germline or undifferentiated stem cells)—has shown immense potential to address human suffering at the hands of genetic diseases. Let's discuss one noteworthy example of how somatic-cell genome editing is revolutionizing therapeutic approaches to HIV and AIDS.

A *A Molecular Battle against HIV*

A rationale for genome editing-based HIV treatment first appeared after an article in the journal *Cell* reported that some individuals' resistance to HIV-1, the most commonly transmitted strain of HIV, had a genetic basis.[4] To enter its host cells, the HIV virus requires the presence of a glycoprotein on the surface of certain immune cells—such as T cells, monocytes, macrophages, and dendritic cells—called Cluster of Differentiation 4 (CD4), which acts as a receptor for the HIV protein envelope. In addition to the CD4 receptor, the virus also requires a chemokine coreceptor, predominantly the cell-surface protein called C-C Chemokine Receptor Type 5 (CCR5). Approximately 1 percent of the Caucasian population carry a homozygous, 32-nucleotide deletion in the *CCR5* gene that renders the CCR5 coreceptor unable to recognize and bind to the HIV virus.[5] The effect of this mutation is that individuals who are homozygous—those who inherit the deletion from both parents—are virtually immune to HIV.

The potential for targeting CCR5 in the treatment of HIV infection was later clinically validated when Timothy Brown, an HIV-infected patient, received a bone marrow transplant from a donor who had the *CCR5* deletion.[6] The procedure led to restoration of normal CD4-positive ($CD4^+$) (a cell that is "positive" in this context refers to one that expresses the CD4 glycoprotein) T-cell counts and undetectable levels of HIV in Brown's body, even two years after transplantation. In fact, Timothy Brown has remained HIV free for over a decade after his bone marrow transplant.[7] This remarkable study, and its long-lasting effects, confirmed that conversion of a patient's genome—although not through genome editing—could potentially lead to a cure against the HIV virus and AIDS.

Inspired by the critical role of CCR5 in HIV infection, scientists at Sangamo Therapeutics, the California-based biopharmaceutical company, in collaboration with academic researchers, tested whether genome editing could be used to trim out a piece of the *CCR5* gene in human T cells and a mouse model of HIV infection.[8] Using ZFNs, they demonstrated the feasibility of this approach as a strategy to confer robust protection against HIV.[9]

A recent phase I clinical trial featuring this principle sought to remove $CD4^+$ T cells from HIV patients, edit them with ZFNs targeting the *CCR5* locus, and transplant the edited cells back into the patients.[10] Remarkably, results showed that infusion of autologously modified $CD4^+$ T cells in which the CCR5 receptor had been rendered dysfunctional by ZFN targeting is safe,[11] thereby paving the path for a phase II clinical trial[12] and potential cure in the near future. Furthermore, scientists have now successfully used the CRISPR–Cas9 system to (1) target and disrupt the expression of latently integrated HIV-1 provirus, and (2) excise it from the genome of T cells,[13] microglial cells,[14] promonocytic cells,[15] and human-induced pluripotent stem cells.[16] These studies are a vivid testament to the power of genome editing technologies to provide long-term immunity against viral infections by introducing disease-resistant alleles—as in the case of *CCR5*—or to deracinate a virus from its host genome completely. The implications of this research go far beyond HIV and could apply to other acquired diseases.

B *Congenital Disorders and Other Diseases*

Progress has not been confined to one disease. Genome editing has successfully corrected a mutation associated with hereditary tyrosinemia type I (HTI), a fatal genetic disorder, in the liver cells of a mouse model of the disease.[17] Cystic Fibrosis (CF)—a debilitating disease in which viscous mucus accumulates in the pulmonary and gastrointestinal tracts of patients, thereby leading to a life expectancy of approximately forty years—appears to be vulnerable to genome editing as well. CRISPR–Cas9 editing to modify the gene that encodes the Cystic Fibrosis Transmembrane Conductor Receptor (CFTCR or CFTR) protein in cultured intestinal stem cells isolated from CF patients successfully corrected a one-amino-acid deletion mutation associated with the most common form of the disease.[18]

Furthermore, a mutation in the Leucine-Rich Repeat Kinase 2 (*LRRK2*) gene, which is associated with a hereditary form of Parkinson's Disease, was rectified in induced pluripotent stem cells derived from patients afflicted with the disease, resulting in functional phenotypic rescue of differentiated neurons.[19] Correction of a mutation in the Interleukin-2 Receptor Subunit Gamma (*IL2RG*) gene, also known as Cytokine Receptor Common Subunit Gamma, in hematopoietic stem cells (HSC) derived from patients suffering from X-linked Severe Combined Immunodeficiency Syndrome (SCID-X1) gave rise to functional lymphoid cells.[20] Genome editing of HSCs is of particular significance given that they differentiate into all hematopoietic cell types and can be autologously transplanted.[21] Thus, genome editing using HSCs could open treatment avenues for many genetic blood disorders.

Efforts are underway to develop treatments for other types of monogenic diseases. For instance, an allele-specific editing strategy to combat Meesmann's Epithelial Corneal Dystrophy (MECD) demonstrates that a faulty allele can be ablated without affecting the healthy allele in a heterozygous disease.[22] Promising applications of genome editing could soon change therapeutic approaches in a multitude of hereditary disorders including Huntington's Disease, in which a single mutation repeat causes a devastating neurodegenerative disorder;[23] Achondroplasia, in which one of two mutations leads to dwarfism;[24] Amyotrophic Lateral Sclerosis (ALS), also known as Lou Gehrig's disease, in which certain point mutations trigger the death of neurons;[25] Nicolaides-Baraitser syndrome (NBS), in which mutations in a chromatin-remodeling gene lead to severe intellectual disability;[26] or Tay-Sachs disease, in which deleterious mutations prompt deterioration of nerve cells that render a child dead by age four.[27]

Due to the perception that targeting a single gene is inherently simpler than targeting multiple genes, it is likely that monogenic disorders will be the focus of early genome-editing therapies. In the long-run, however, genome-editing technologies will likely tackle more complex, polygenic and noninheritable conditions as well, such as cancer[28] and even aging.

Indeed, recent evidence in HSCs demonstrates that CRISPR–Cas9 can target noncoding regions—sections of chromosomal DNA lacking genes—of the genome to investigate the molecular regulation of the B-cell Lymphoma/Leukemia 11A (*BCL11A*) gene, which encodes a zinc-finger protein involved in normal lymphoid development.[29] A research group, for instance, examined a noncoding region known as the *BCL11A* erythroid enhancer (an *enhancer* generally refers to distal genetic regions found upstream or downstream of a gene that play a role in the regulation of gene expression by enhancing the rate of transcription of said gene), which is involved in regulation of hemoglobin disorders.[30] Proof of concept for this type of manipulation of noncoding regions of the genome suggests viable, alternative therapeutic strategies to treat sickle-cell disease and thalassemias.

Likewise, genome editing offers an opportunity to tackle other complex pathologies like Alzheimer's Disease,[31] HIV,[32] cardiovascular disease,[33] and Acute

Lymphoblastic Leukemia[34] by conferring protective mutations as treatment for affected patients or as prophylactic measures for those unaffected. These and numerous other examples demonstrate both the feasibility and inevitability of applying genome editing technologies to rid society of congenital disorders—whether recessive or dominantly inherited—and acquired diseases.

II GENE DRIVES

In what might seem like a concept straight out of a sci-fi script, reshaping entire populations of wild organisms with relatively short lifespans is now within technological reach thanks to a method coupling genome-editing technology with old-fashioned sexual reproduction. This method, called a *gene drive*, encompasses the alteration of traits in wild populations[35] via self-propagating, synthetic, genetic constructs that can artificially disseminate—hence the name "drive"—a gene modification through an organism's progeny with unprecedented speed. In essence, gene drives constitute a method to hijack evolution!

The notion of gene drives dates back to the late 1960s, when a theoretical comment published in the journal *Nature* proposed the hypothetical utility of chromosomal translocations as a way to control insect pest populations.[36] At the time, that possibility was merely hypothetical because the technology to test the hypothesis—namely, the tools and knowledge required for triggering translocations via enzyme-mediated genetic manipulation—simply did not exist. By the turn of the century, however, interest in gene drives resurfaced following insights that meganucleases could be used to create targeted DNA double-stranded breaks.[37] The premise of targeting the fertility genes of vermin species provided a roadmap to carry out population-wide genetic engineering. And by 2011, the first validation of a meganuclease-based gene drive—aimed at controlling the human malaria vector—established proof of principle for the genetic manipulation of an entire population starting from only a few laboratory individuals.[38]

A *Driving Evolution in Mosquitoes*

It was not long before others realized that the same concept could be used to engineer drives by integrating genes encoding the more efficient Cas9 enzyme alongside specific sgRNAs. In 2015, a group of US scientists repurposed the CRISPR–Cas9 system to develop the Mutagenic Chain Reaction (MCR).[39] In contrast to the classic laws of genetic inheritance, in which there is a 50 percent chance that a given offspring will inherit a modified allele, MCR-mediated gene drives introduced biased inheritance patterns to swiftly spread a select gene through an entire population of laboratory fruit flies. With an average 97 percent success rate—as opposed to 50 percent—gene drives can effortlessly convert heterozygous mutations into homozygous mutations in as few as two generations.[40]

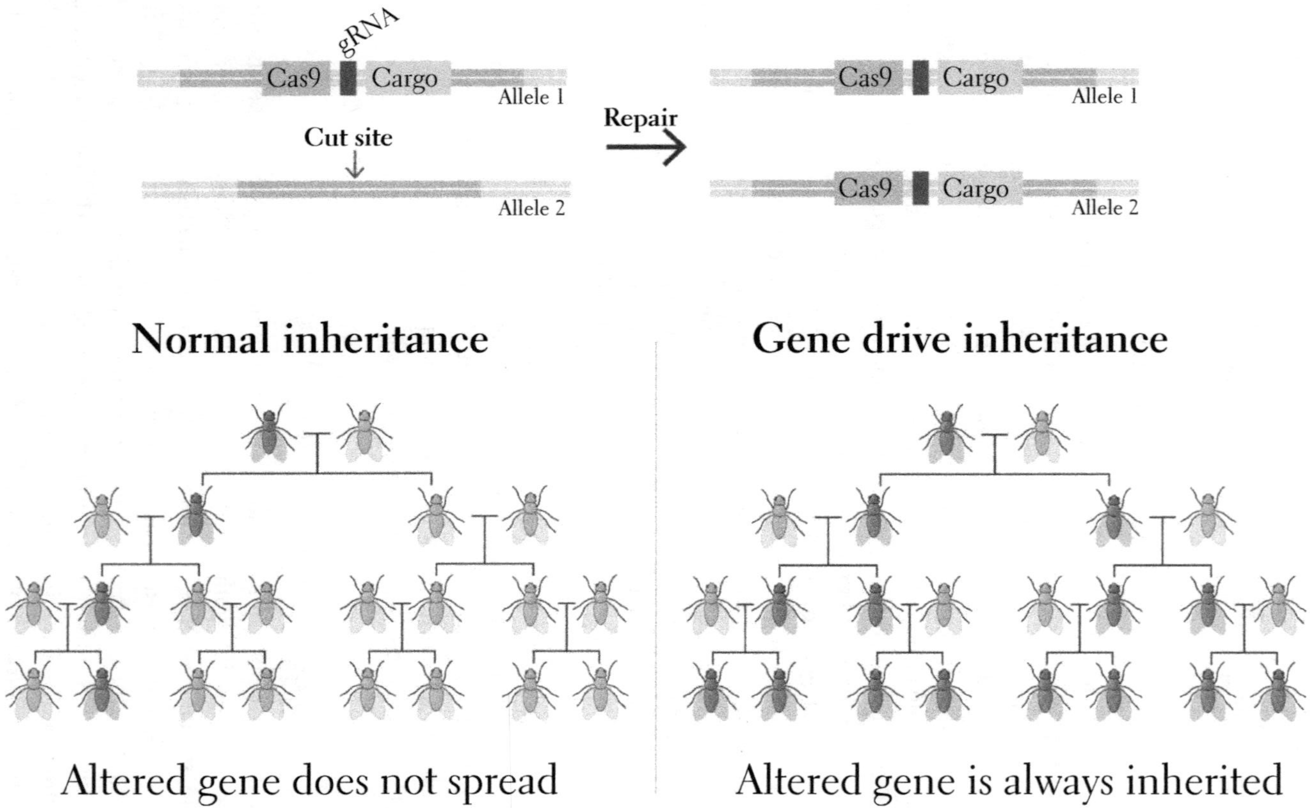

FIGURE 5.1 Model of gene-drive inheritance in a mosquito population (Mariuswalter)

Gene drives represent a novel technological tool to combat malaria—one of the deadliest diseases known to humankind. The World Health Organization estimates that as of 2013, ninety-seven countries had ongoing malaria transmission and approximately 3.4 billion people were at risk of contracting malaria, 1.2 billion of whom were at a high risk.[41] In 2018 alone, there were an estimated 228 million cases of malaria worldwide and more than 400,000 malaria-related deaths.[42]

To address this worldwide problem, researchers adapted the principles of MCR for CRISPR–Cas9-based gene drives to introduce genes that confer resistance to *Plasmodium falciparum*, the malaria parasite, into a South Asian mosquito species.[43] Shortly thereafter, an alternate approach to suppress a different species of mosquito vector for human malaria succeeded by targeting female mosquitoes that overwhelmingly—and helplessly—relinquished fertility by gene drive.[44] The former strategy seeks to spare mosquitoes by making them malaria-resistant and incapable of spreading the disease, whereas the latter aims to drastically reduce—or even wipe out—mosquito populations from an ecosystem. Ultimately, both strategies share the goal of suppressing a disease that places half the total world population at risk, particularly in low-income countries.

Yeast,[45] fruit flies,[46] and several mosquito species[47]—including the potent vector for the chikungunya, yellow fever, and dengue viruses[48]—have thus far been the subjects of CRISPR-mediated gene drive, or related, research. Although the technology remains, for the most part, enclosed within laboratory walls for now, some researchers have begun to study and model how releasing mosquitoes in the wild would spread certain engineered traits. One study, for example, demonstrated that alleles inserted at genetic loci that play significant roles in insect female fertility can spread rapidly in mixed caged populations, of roughly 600 mosquitoes per cage, with high gene-drive activity.[49] Others have used mathematical and quantitative modeling to estimate the rate of fixation of a mutant allele and caution against the release of gene drives in the wild.[50] Mathematical models based on some existing empirical data have, for instance, shown that gene-drive resistance can prevent the fixation of gene-drive alleles in large populations, but releasing even small numbers of organisms into a given local population can be highly invasive.[51]

Already, Oxitec, a British firm, has developed transgenic *Aedes aegypti* mosquitoes—through older technologies—and released them in field trials in Brazil, Malaysia, the Cayman Islands, and Panama with results showing up to a 90 percent reduction of insect populations.[52] Trial successes led to Brazilian approval of the first genetically modified insect for commercial use.[53] However, in the United States, Oxitec has faced intense criticism for releasing genetically modified moths in small outdoor trials in New York,[54] and Florida rejected a proposal to permit Oxitec to release mosquitoes in the wild without federal approval.[55]

B *Public Opinion in Times of Epidemic*

Diametric public views concerning the appropriate use of genetically modified insects highlight the pivotal role that public opinion will play in the development of gene-drive biotechnologies. Consider the recent threat to global human health posed by the Zika virus in 2015 and 2016. Zika virus outbreaks had been reported in more than fifty countries.[56] The World Health Organization declared a Public Health Emergency of International Concern as more than 4,000 microcephaly cases and neurological disorders had been documented in areas affected by the Zika virus.[57] The first case of Zika-related microcephaly in a new born baby in the United States surfaced in January 2016,[58] which prompted the Centers for Disease Control and Prevention to issue warnings for pregnant women to avoid traveling to countries with Zika virus outbreaks.[59] Fears were further augmented when studies revealed that, although mosquito bites are the main source of transmission, the virus can spread through sexual intercourse and blood transfusions.[60]

Throughout 2015 and 2016, the Zika virus brought panic to many areas of the world. Babies born with microcephaly and intracranial calcification became a fixture in the news.[61] Public support for the release of genetically modified insects as a method of mosquito population control would likely be low in areas unaffected, or rarely affected, by a mosquito-borne disease, such as in the United States.[62] However, the prospect of a local or national epidemic coupled with laggard progress in research toward development of a vaccine could awaken the public's appetite for drastic measures to prevent the spread of a virus transmitted by mosquitoes. That was precisely the case in Brazil, where a devastating wave of Zika virus infections swept across the northeastern region of the country.[63]

When faced with a public health crisis, groups that vehemently oppose genetic engineering under any circumstances may find themselves fighting a losing battle in the court of public opinion. Such an outlook is not hypothetical; other countries confronting mosquito-related health crises have weighed the social and economic costs and benefits of releasing bioengineered insects into the environment and opted to use biotechnology to allay the spread of disease.[64]

It is only a matter of time before the technological knack required for large-scale testing of a CRISPR gene drive is refined. Indeed, field trials could likely be ready to launch at a moment's notice if a general consensus to support them formed and gave the green light to proceed.[65] Genome-editing research now offers a meaningful opportunity to strike back at the mosquito, the deadliest animal in the world.[66]

These developments have prompted a debate about biosecurity and the benefits and harms of using gene drives to control certain species, including how to safeguard gene-drive testing in laboratory settings.[67] In fact, scientists wary of the potential consequences of unintended release of species carrying gene drives into the environment have already designed and tested *split drives*—to separate the elements of a gene drive—and *reversal drives*—to overwrite changes of the original gene drive—as molecular-confinement insurance strategies to guard against inadvertent escape of mutant organisms.[68]

C Neglected Tropical Diseases and Invasive Species

The wondrous capacity to circumvent Mendelian genetics constraints to guarantee that a gene can fix itself in a population is unprecedented. Regardless of the future regulatory decisions made to promote, control, or curtail gene drives altogether, no one can deny the power of the technology. The ability to hack genomes in pest organisms offers a weapon with the potential to help eradicate a long list of deadly and costly vector-borne diseases, including malaria, dengue, yellow fever, Zika virus, epidemic typhus, Lyme disease, Rocky Mountain spotted fever, and others.

Besides the potential eradication of vector-borne diseases, gene drives could also be used to combat certain neglected tropical diseases (NTD). NTDs are a group of parasitic and bacterial diseases affecting more than one billion people worldwide, predominantly in low-income countries.[69] They are considered neglected because they are largely nonexistent in developed nations, but persist only in the poorest, most marginalized areas of low-income countries. NTDs spread by parasitic organisms can cause substantial illness and death, impair physical and cognitive development, and limit productivity in the workplace.

Consider, for example, schistosomiasis, a predominantly snail-borne NTD caused by helminth parasites of the genus *Schistosoma*, which has brought suffering to hundreds of millions of people worldwide.[70] In terms of impact, schistosomiasis is second only to malaria as the most devastating parasitic disease.[71] It affects more than seventy-five countries spanning tropical and subtropical areas, in which 800 million people are at risk of contracting schistosomiasis, and more than 200 million people are infected with schistosomes.[72] Gene-drive technologies now offer a feasible way to address the disease burden associated with schistosomiasis.[73]

By the same token, science has produced a tool to reshape entire ecosystems. On one hand, given the reported success of gene drives to endow a species with anti-parasite resistance,[74] one can imagine possible scenarios where an endangered species could be generously armed with a gene drive to help it cope with changes in its habitat, or become immunized against parasites and opportunistic organisms driving it into extinction. On the other hand, CRISPR-based gene drives could be used to deliver a coup de grâce to invasive and noxious species like the Asian carp in the Great Lakes,[75] Argentine cactus moth in the Southern United States and Mexico,[76] cane toads in Australia,[77] tropical fire ants in the Galápagos Islands,[78] as well as a miscellany of other aquatic[79] and terrestrial[80] invasive plant and animal species, including the soybean cyst nematode, which affects soybean crops worldwide,[81] Giant African snails,[82] zebra mussels,[83] kudzu,[84] and others.

III ANIMALS IN BASIC AND TRANSLATIONAL RESEARCH

Animals have long played an integral role in scientific inquiry. From Aristotle's experiments on living animals[85] to Pasteur's groundbreaking studies on rabbits and dogs,[86] scientists have always sought animal models to explore biomedical research. Well over 100 million animals have been used for scientific research in Europe and the United States alone since governmental agencies began tracking animal studies.[87] In the United States, for example, 834,453 animals—excluding rats, mice, birds and other species not covered by the Animal Welfare Act—were used in research and teaching in 2014.[88]

A long list of model organisms[89] has helped to elucidate fundamental questions in science over many decades. Animal experimentation has provided insights into anatomy, physiology, genetics, behavior, development, and medicine that have dramatically transformed our ability to cope with and ameliorate human suffering.[90] It would be nearly impossible to establish safety measures and criteria prior to launching new human therapies and treatments without the use of animal models of human disease.[91]

A *Of Mice and Man*

In recent years, genome editing has routinely been utilized to edit a multitude of animal genomes. Of these, the mouse has become the foremost mammalian model organism for genetic and biomedical preclinical research, thanks in part to physiological similarities between mice and humans.[92] Genome editing studies in mice are instrumental for translational purposes and demonstrate great promise in forging a path toward human clinical applications. For instance, three independent US teams published proof-of-concept studies showing how CRISPR-based gene editing can be used to improve skeletal muscle function in adult and neonatal mice models of Duchenne muscular dystrophy (DMD), a fatal genetic disease that causes muscle degeneration, loss of mobility, and premature death.[93] One of the three teams had previously demonstrated the feasibility of preventing the disease by editing the germline—an organism's reproductive cells (eggs and sperm) that pass on genes from one generation to the next during sexual reproduction[94]—of mice models of DMD.[95]

Researchers have also corrected a mutation in the *Crygc* gene responsible for cataracts by editing the germline of mice, leading to the birth of fertile pups that went on to pass the corrected allele to their progeny.[96] A mouse model of mitochondrial disease demonstrated that germline genome editing can prevent transmission of faulty mitochondria—organelles that supply energy to cells[97]—to mice offspring.[98] CRISPR-mediated genome editing in postmitotic neurons of adult mice brains has been achieved in vivo.[99] And a separate team showed that Cas9-mediated germline multiplexing—the simultaneous disruption of multiple genes by gene editing—can be accomplished by targeting genes in zygotes, thereby producing animals with desired mutations in various genes.[100]

Despite the widespread use of mouse models of human disease, there are stark limitations associated with preclinical trials in rodents. First, the very characteristics that make mice useful models—relatively short life cycle compared to other mammals, physical size, short gestation periods, abundant progeny, etc.—can sometimes render them inadequate for validating the relevance of clinical findings.[101] Second, metabolic and physiological differences between mice and humans lead to differences in species-specific susceptibility to disease and pharmacological responses.[102] Third, mice models of disease often cannot recapitulate features associated with many human pathologies. A quintessential illustration of this phenomenon is the inability of mice to replicate the full panoply of neuropathologies—most notably, overt neurodegeneration in the human brain—that constitute the hallmark of many neurodegenerative diseases such as Parkinson's Disease,[103] Huntington's Disease,[104] and Alzheimer's Disease.[105] The same holds true for Cystic Fibrosis,[106] Lesch-Nyhan syndrome,[107] and many other conditions. The lack of accurate pathological reproducibility is problematic and may be linked to the meager impact these mouse models have had in clinical outcomes.[108]

B *Preclinical Use of Large Animal Models*

As a result of the natural constraints imposed by mice models of human disease, large animal models have become an increasingly attractive alternative for clinical investigation.[109] Indeed, as controversial as the research might be,[110] dogs,[111] cats,[112] pigs,[113] sheep,[114] rabbits,[115] goats,[116] horses,[117] nonhuman primates,[118] and other large animals have contributed greatly to our understanding of human pathologies. Advocates of research on large animals argue that using more complex mammalian species offers a more rigorous and reliable system to validate the efficacy of preclinical trials in small rodents.[119] Accordingly, a tide of experiments on large animals is surfing apace thanks to novel genome-editing technologies that have turned the unimaginable into a reality.[120]

In almost parallel studies, CRISPR systems have been effectively used to create muscular versions of pigs[121] and beagle dogs,[122] the canine breed most widely used in biomedical research, via engineering mutations in the myostatin (*MSTN*) gene. *MSTN*, also known as growth differentiation factor-8 (*GDF-8*), is a gene involved in regulation of skeletal muscle growth that has been linked to muscle hypertrophy.[123] At least nine genes, some of which are associated with lipid metabolism and cardiovascular conditions, have been targeted and mutated in rabbits.[124] Editing the *vWF* gene, responsible for von Willebrand Disease (vWD)—a bleeding disorder that prevents normal blood clotting[125]—led to a striking phenotype in mutant pigs; the animals exhibited prolonged bleeding that lasted nearly fifteen times longer than that of nonmutant pigs.[126] Because mice models cannot fully recapitulate the severe bleeding phenotype of vWD,[127] the ability of CRISPR-edited pigs to mimic human vWD is a major step toward developing a bona fide model to study the disease.

Similar phenotypic replication of pathologies that could not be established in mouse models has been accomplished in sheep,[128] pigs,[129] and other large animals,[130] lending credence to the hypothesis that large animal models constitute a more precise platform to study some human diseases. For example, a study in which scientists sought to introduce the most common Cystic Fibrosis-associated mutation of CFTR—the ΔF508 mutation—into transgenic mice could not accurately replicate the human Cystic Fibrosis pathology.[131] Yet, engineering pigs carrying the same mutation led to a range of clinical manifestations of Cystic Fibrosis seen in humans.[132] And studies have shown similar results in Amyotrophic lateral sclerosis (ALS) models, in which engineered mice did not exhibit human-like ALS pathologies, but engineered transgenic pigs displayed a range of ALS-related pathologies characteristic in some human ALS patient brains.[133] Now that CRISPR technologies and their applications are starting to become routine, we should fully expect numerous reports in the coming years establishing new large animal models for clinical research.

On this point, perhaps the most salient examples of the potential of genome editing for translational applications are proof-of-concept reports vis-à-vis CRISPR-edited nonhuman primates. In a world first, Chinese scientists used genome-editing technologies to modify the embryos of cynomolgus[134] and rhesus[135] monkeys and implant them into surrogate mothers, who subsequently delivered transgenic infant monkeys after full-term pregnancies. Proof that the genomes of nonhuman primates can, in fact, be modified at the embryonic stage to produce progeny with desired modifications turns the prospect of human germline modification from a forlorn aspiration into a feasible goal.

The race to produce monkeys with targeted genome modifications for more accurately modeling human diseases is now on full speed. Researchers have already reported the birth of monkeys with markedly depleted dystrophin and muscle degeneration seen in early human DMD.[136] A one-step method demonstrated successful embryonic editing and delivery of live monkeys carrying homozygous mutations in the tumor suppressor *p53* gene.[137] In 2016, a group of scientists published an article describing the creation of transgenic monkeys that exhibit autism-like behaviors and, remarkably, showed successful germline transmission of a modified gene by bringing their progeny into this world.[138] These findings demonstrate that, unlike mouse models lacking higher perceptual and cognitive function seen in primates,[139] studies using nonhuman primate genome editing are better equipped to provide models to further our understanding—and ultimately lead to treatments—of the cognitive, behavioral, anatomical, and emotional symptoms associated with a long list of neurological—autism spectrum disorder; behavioral—Attention Deficit Hyperactivity Disorder (ADHD), drug abuse, and alcohol abuse; psychiatric—schizophrenia, obsessive compulsive disorder, and depression;

and neurodegenerative disorders—Alzheimer's and Parkinson's Disease—that contribute to human suffering worldwide.

C *Genome Editing for Xenotransplantation Purposes*

Genome editing technologies can now be used to create useful animal models to interrogate the mechanisms of human diseases, which may lead to future diagnoses and treatments, as discussed above. However, other translational applications of animal genome editing are even closer on the horizon. A prime example is the field of xenotransplantation, which refers to the process of transplanting living cells, tissues, or organs from one species to another.[140]

1 In Dire Need of Organs

Organ donation and transplantation is the best, and often sole, form of treatment for end-stage organ failure.[141] In the United States alone, a shortage of organs for transplantation claims approximately twenty-two lives every day—over 8,000 annually.[142] Approximately 500,000 people die annually in India—which has a rate of less than 0.2 donors per one million population—due to a shortage of organs for transplantation.[143] Likewise, massive shortages of organ donors in China are estimated to contribute to tens-of-thousands of deaths every year.[144]

It is difficult to determine exactly how many people on organ waiting lists die every year globally due to the lack of reporting mechanisms in most of the developing world, but the worldwide death tolls from the shortage of organs likely reach the millions.

According to the International Registry in Organ Donation and Transplantation (IRODaT), only seventy-one countries currently report national data of donation and transplantation activity for database compilation on IRODaT.[145] In 2013, for example, the World Health Organization (WHO) reported 117,700 solid organ transplants.[146] In contrast, 29,532 individuals received organ transplants in 2014 in the United States, where over 123,000 people are currently on waiting lists for life-saving organ transplants.[147] Keep in mind that organ transplant statistics in the United States do not include transplantation of corneas, veins, heart valves, tendons, bones, skin, and other tissues. For example, 40,000 corneal transplants—the most routinely transplanted tissue—are performed every year in the United States.[148]

An overwhelmingly conservative and low-end estimate of worldwide deaths attributable to organ shortages may be derived from US statistics. If roughly 6.5 percent of people on waiting lists die every year (about 8,000 deaths per annum from a select population of 123,000), and approximately 24 percent of wait-listed individuals receive transplants (29,532 recipients from a 123,000 applicant pool), we can use the number of reported worldwide transplants (117,700 according to the WHO) and US-derived statistical rates to arrive at a baseline worldwide organ transplant waitlist population of nearly a half-million individuals (roughly 491,000 people), of which approximately 32,000 (or 6.5 percent) would die annually. This estimate would still be limited to less than half (recall that only seventy-one nations report data on IRODaT) of total countries in the world.

Yet, even this conservative figure likely grossly underestimates the actual number of deaths related to shortage of organs for transplantation given that there are nearly 200 countries in the world, and most of the nonreporting countries house low-income, poverty-stricken populations with limited access to healthcare and education. Current statistics on organ transplantation-related data exclude individuals in low-income regions of the world who are in dire need of access to life-saving organ transplantation. Furthermore, many people in both reporting and non-reporting countries may harbor long-held cultural apprehensions regarding transplantation, including distrust of the medical system and religious or ethnic myths and misbeliefs about diseased organ donation and transplantation.[149] Such ethnic, religious, and cultural limitations could even be responsible for under-reporting figures in developed countries with tightly clustered and self-isolating immigrant populations.

One might arrive at a closer estimate of total deaths using the above, or a similar, mathematical formulation with rates derived from developing countries like China and India where death rates are believed to be in the tens-of-thousands in China[150] and as high as 500,000 in India.[151] Combining figures stemming from much-needed independent statistical and mathematical modeling among developed and developing countries may shed more light on the actual state of organ transplantation needs worldwide.

Even setting aside the current incomplete state of global organ-transplantation statistics, it bears noting that individuals in need of organ transplantations in some parts of the world may not have the resources or capabilities to get on a waitlist—even if one were available in their country of origin—due to hurdles imposed by corrupt governments and international cartels engaged in organ trafficking.[152]

One last statistical caveat involves the likely existence of incomplete figures found on current waitlists across developed and developing nations. For instance, when the United States began tracking organ transplantation data in 1991, there were roughly 16,000 transplants performed and a little over 23,000 people on waitlists.[153] Since then, the number of transplants has less than doubled. Yet, remarkably, the number of patients waiting for transplants has increased by more than 530 percent over the past three decades.[154] It seems unlikely that so many more people today require transplants compared to years past. More likely, the ostensible increase is due to greater access to healthcare and well-trained physicians who can better identify patients as candidates for organ transplantation.

The take-home message from this section is that we do not yet know the precise extent of the global shortage of organs for transplantation, but we are certain that the need to address the shortage is dire all around the world.

2 A Long Way Forward

To mitigate the shortage of organs, scientists began to experiment, decades ago, with xenotransplantation to determine whether animals could provide a supply of organs to humans.[155] Animal kidney, heart, and liver organs were first in line, with catastrophic results for patients as a result of severe infection, immune reactions, and rejection of the organs.[156] However, after decades of research on xenotransplantation and the advent of genome-editing technology, researchers may now be on the verge of breaking through the nonhuman organ-donor glass ceiling.

In the last few years, research groups have published encouraging results from xenotransplantation of hearts[157] and a life-supporting kidney graft[158] from genetically modified pigs to baboons. One group, for example, used CRISPR–Cas9 to simultaneously eradicate all sixty-two copies of a porcine endogenous retrovirus (PERV)—a type of pig virus that could be transmitted to humans—in a pig kidney-cell line.[159] The genome-wide editing of every PERV copy in the genome of a pig-cell line prevented in vitro viral infection and transmission to human cells. And a subsequent research team, consisting of some of the same group members, generated PERV-inactivated pigs via somatic-cell nuclear transfer.[160] These studies demonstrated a valuable strategy to prevent cross-species viral transmission, which may help to allay safety concerns associated with the ultimate use of xenotransplantation in clinical settings in the near future.

These and other findings have spurred entrepreneurial interest in using synthetic biology and genome-editing methods to generate ready-for-transplant, human-compatible pig organs.[161] Backed by an infusion of venture capital, biotech companies are racing to get pig lungs in human clinical trials,[162] and academic researchers funded by the National Institutes of Health are working to carry out parallel studies that may bring clinical trials of pig kidney, heart, and liver transplantation in humans within the realm of possibility.[163] A hopeful preview came in 2015 when the Chinese Food and Drug Administration approved the sale of the world's first bioengineered—although without the use of gene editing—cornea derived from pig's eyes.[164] Within months, the first transplant was performed in an older patient suffering from a serious corneal ulcer with successful results.[165] As genome editing technologies mature, we should expect further developments in tissue and organ xenotransplantation,[166] as well as in other important fields of clinical relevance.

IV AGRICULTURE

A *Crops and Biofuels*

The United Nations projects the world population will rise from today's 7.2 billion to 9.6 billion by the year 2050.[167] This gargantuan increase in the human population will pose significant challenges to the world's ability to foster food security and meet nutritional needs using limited arable land and water available for irrigation.[168] As a result, sustainability and the contributions of rising agriculture-related pollution to climate change will become global problems.[169] Analyses for global crop demand forecast an increase between 100 percent and 110 percent from current levels by 2050.[170] Investment in biotechnologies aimed at increasing food yields and producing pest-resistant genetically modified (GM) crops have been proposed as a solution to the global food crisis.[171]

Fervid, and at times intemperate, controversy exists over the use of GM crops—colloquially known as GMOs—with supporters and critics constantly sparring about the perceived risks and benefits of GM crops to human health, the environment, and food security.[172] Although a minor potential for adverse events exists, to date, no overt or deleterious consequences have yet been documented in the scientific, peer-reviewed literature for the more than two decades that bioengineered foods have been available to consumers, with the exception of some highly contentious research from a French biologist and political activist.[173] This is not to say that the lack of current scientific evidence—even decades after introduction of GM crops—is prima facie evidence of a complete absence of risk. Conversely, at least some evidence suggests that adoption of GM crops reduces food insecurity, improves calorie consumption and dietary quality, and can be a key factor in a broader global food security strategy.[174]

Reports of the first GM plants—petunia, tobacco, sunflower, and carrot—appeared in the literature in 1983.[175] Within a decade, Calgene, a California-based firm, introduced the FLAVR SAVR tomato, the first GM crop product to be approved by the US Food and Drug Administration (FDA) for human consumption and commercialization.[176] Today, more than 200 GM crops ranging from fruits to grains and vegetables have been approved for human consumption in the United States and many more countries worldwide.[177] In 2014, a total of eighteen million farmers planted GM crops across 448 million acres of farmland in twenty-eight countries.[178] GM-crop arable land has swollen 10,000 percent since commercialization of GM crops commenced two decades ago.[179]

Scientists state that the exponential increase in farmlands devoted to GM crop agriculture is contributing to the global food crisis.[180] GM crop supporters point to these statistics to argue that GM crops and further development of biotechnologies are necessary to address population growth, climate change, and global demands for food and feed. In contrast, opponents argue that the impact of GM crops on human health and the environment is not well established and warrants more research. They perceive approval by regulatory agencies as a precocious exercise that sets dangerous precedents to the detriment of humankind.

Regulatory controversies notwithstanding, scientists have reported proof-of-concept experiments involving genome editing in many plants, including crops, since CRISPR systems became widely available to the scientific community in 2013. Among the CRISPR–Cas9-modified plants are wheat,[181] rice,[182] thale cress,[183] tobacco,[184] sweet orange,[185] sorghum,[186] maize,[187] barley,[188] wild cabbage,[189] tomato,[190] soybean,[191] liverwort,[192] potato,[193] and others.

Two particular studies illustrate well the prototypical uses of genome editing in crop cultivars. The first involves CRISPR-mediated endogenous disruption of the tomato *RIN* gene, which encodes a transcription factor that regulates fruit ripening.[194] RIN-defective mutations result in peculiar phenotypes in tomatoes including not turning to red color, maintaining flesh firmness for several months, and inhibiting other changes associated with fruit ripening. RIN-defective tomato cultivars are routinely bred with other tomato plant varieties to create tomatoes with an extended shelf life. These mutations occur naturally and, thus, mutant tomatoes are not considered to be transgenic or GMOs.

In the study, the authors used CRISPR–Cas9 to introduce single or few nucleotide changes in select regions of the *RIN* locus, which led to a truncated, nonfunctional RIN protein that mirrored the phenotype of the RIN-defective tomatoes. They also showed that the mutations could be passed on to the next generation of plants. Hence, this study shows the feasibility of extending the shelf life of a tomato fruit via genome editing without the use of transgenic constructs or selectable markers. In other words, the mutant tomato lines created in the experiments are, for all practical purposes, the equivalent of naturally occurring cultivars.

The second study concerns wheat resistance to the fungus *Blumeria graminis* f. sp. *tritici*, one of the world's most devastating plant pathogens and the culprit of powdery mildew disease.[195] The authors showed that small, single or few nucleotide, CRISPR- and TALEN-induced mutations targeting all six alleles of the mildew-resistance locus (*MLO*) gene in the hexaploid wheat genome are sufficient to knock out the function of the MLO protein. The mutations led to strong resistance to the powdery mildew fungal disease in wheat plants. Moreover, the mutations conferring broad spectrum resistance to the disease were also shown to be heritable, given that the genetic trait was stable in subsequent generations.

This remarkable study—the first of its kind—demonstrates the potential of genome-editing technologies to address global problems in agriculture via biotechnology. From a genetics standpoint, the *MLO* knock-out plants are practically indistinguishable from other *MLO*-mutant plants derived via conventional mutation breeding. Moreover, the fact that plants can now acquire disease resistance without the need to introduce DNA from other species or selectable markers highlights the advantages of using precise genomic targeting over traditional transgenesis methods.

Fruit ripening and disease resistance are merely the tip of the iceberg. Academic-industry partnerships will ensure a steady supply of scientific breakthroughs with commercial applications.[196] As more research unfolds, it may be possible in the future to cultivate crops without the use of pesticides and herbicides altogether by making plants emit endogenous, natural compounds that are not toxic to humans, to protect themselves against pathogenic organisms.[197]

Grain seeds needed to feed the world could be engineered to increase storage tolerance and avoid deterioration and premature spoiling,[198] which may help to ameliorate the ever-increasing need for arable lands. Production of allergen-free peanuts and other foodstuffs may now be possible by targeting and disrupting genes that encode allergens and other toxic cyanogens, which threaten the lives of millions of people with food sensitivities worldwide.[199] Salt-resistant crop plants could be introduced to permit seawater irrigation.[200] Drought-resistant crops could help to allay turmoil in water-poor regions of the world.[201]

Emergency biotechnological intervention could also be established to pioneer crop diversification efforts where needed, and could even save staple crops from extinction when deadly diseases threaten their existence. For instance, such intervention could be used to mitigate the threat to the Cavendish banana, which is currently in danger of extinction in some parts of the world due to the Tropical Race 4 fungus.[202]

Even biofuel production is on the horizon. Oilseeds from the plant *Camelina sativa*, and other plants, have in recent years been identified as promising sources of renewable biofuels, capable of reducing CO_2 emissions by 78.5 percent compared to petroleum diesel.[203] In fact, the US Navy, US Air Force, and many private entities have successfully tested *Camelina*-based fuel and announced plans to increase the use of biofuels to meet their energy requirements.[204] Renewable biofuels could not only benefit the domestic economy, but also help reduce US dependence on foreign petroleum, greenhouse gas emissions, and air pollution.[205] Genome-editing technologies may finally help to lower current barriers for production of renewable biofuels including yield requirements and commercial viability.

Unlike transgenic crops created with earlier genetic-engineering techniques, many new crop varieties derived via modern genome-editing biotechnologies require no introduction of any foreign DNA, are genetically indistinguishable from crops developed by mutation breeding protocols over the past three millennia, and bear no genetic-manipulation footprints in their progeny. The new era of genome editing offers powerful tools to protect and enhance important and desirable agronomic traits with vast repercussions for crop agriculture.

B *Animal Agriculture*

To satisfy the predicted food demand by 2050, global food production must increase by at least 70 percent from current levels, which translates into an additional—and quite staggering—400 billion pounds of meat worldwide.[206] In the United States alone, the production of red meat—which according to the USDA includes beef, veal, pork, lamb, and mutton—totaled 47.4 billion pounds in 2014.[207] More than 140 million livestock were slaughtered, including cattle, hogs, sheep, and lambs.[208] A total of 8.54 billion broiler chickens and nearly 100 billion eggs were produced in the United States in 2014.[209] Global agricultural activity, and livestock production in particular, is exerting a colossal impact on the environment and accounts for 22 percent of total greenhouse gas emissions—a greater percentage than the total contribution from the transportation sector (cars, trucks, airplanes, etc.).[210]

Aside from the translational and basic research purposes discussed earlier in this chapter, farm animals constitute an important source of commodities such as food nutrients,[211] natural fiber,[212] and labor.[213] A strategy to mitigate the current unsustainable rate of meat consumption involves genome editing in farm animals. One illustration concerns the objective of increasing the muscle mass of livestock for lean meat production by interfering with the *MSTN* gene responsible for muscle growth inhibition.[214]

Cases of naturally occurring mutations in the *MSTN* locus have been widely reported in animals that exhibit doubling of skeletal muscle mass.[215] Proof-of-concept, *MSTN*-editing studies aiming to increase mass yield in farm animals have been successfully established in pigs,[216] cattle,[217] goats,[218] and sheep.[219] More importantly, these methods of editing *MSTN* in livestock occur at native sites of the genome and abrogate the need to insert any foreign nucleotides that are not already found naturally inside the animals' genomes. This type of genome editing without the use of transgenes stands in contrast to the approval of transgenic salmon—genetically modified to grow at accelerated rates—by the FDA,[220] which, despite being labeled as safe for human consumption, has engendered controversy from anti-GMO groups.[221]

Another priority in animal agriculture is the development of methods to improve disease resistance to pathogens that threaten animal and human health. Substantial progress toward this goal has been documented by two recent studies. One demonstrated that minimal changes to the Cluster of Differentiation 163 (*CD163*) gene confer immunity in pigs against Porcine Reproductive and Respiratory Syndrome Virus, the most economically significant swine disease in North America, Europe, and Asia.[222] The other study targeted the *RELA* gene, which has been associated with the African Swine Fever Virus that triggers a deadly immune reaction in pigs.[223] Although the latter team did not expose edited pigs to the virus, the study showed that modern genome-editing biotechnologies can facilitate the delivery of live pigs without the use of older, often cumbersome, cloning technologies like somatic-cell nuclear transfer.

These scientific advances open the door for new strategies to combat other pathogenic organisms that affect important animals in agriculture. For example, the *SAL1* gene in chickens has been linked to resistance against certain *Salmonella* strains responsible for food-borne gastroenteritis in humans.[224] Genome editing now provides an opportunity to exploit this naturally occurring resistance to immunize chickens and avert serious economic losses stemming from human transmission events.[225]

Lastly, other potential uses of genome editing for animal agriculture range from the production of textiles (by triggering modifications in the Shannbei cashmere goat *FGF5*[226] gene that controls hair length[227]) to the development of safer dairy products (by generating animals that secrete milk with natural antibacterial properties[228]) and animal welfare (by creating hornless cattle breeds with naturally occurring mutations in the *POLLED* gene to avoid painful, costly, and inhumane dehorning of animals).[229] Like every other field mentioned above, genome-editing technologies are poised to revolutionize the optimization of livestock production to meet future demands for food and animal products that could affect human health, the environment, intellectual property,[230] the economy, and animal welfare.

V HUMAN GERMLINE EDITING

In 2015, a group of Chinese researchers launched humanity into uncharted territory. For the first time, the human germline—gamete cells (sperm or eggs), zygotes, and embryos—underwent endogenous genetic manipulation by the macromolecular CRISPR–Cas9 system.[231] Genome editing in human germ cells was largely predictable in light of the successes of germline editing in a plethora of animal and plant species, which had been reported since CRISPR–Cas9 became widely adapted by scientists. Predictability, however, did not allay the global shockwaves caused by the research.

In principle, manipulation of the human germline is not much different than germline manipulation in other species. Although humans are biologically more complex than other organisms, the process of CRISPR-mediated genome editing is virtually the same: concoct a lab recipe that combines specific types of three major bioorganic polymers—a target DNA, an sgRNA designed to hybridize with the DNA, and the Cas9 protein to trigger cuts in the DNA; allow the mix to form a complex inside the germ cells; and let science run its course. The group of Chinese researchers followed that precise formula and used the CRISPR–Cas9 system to investigate the feasibility and efficiency of genome editing coupled to DNA repair mechanisms in the human germline.

To establish proof of concept for human germline manipulation, the group chose to target the human β-globin (*HBB*) gene, the mutated form of which is linked to β-thalassemia, a debilitating and sometimes fatal blood disorder. A total of eighty-six nonviable human zygotes—the term *zygote* refers to the first cell formed upon a fertilization event—were injected with the CRISPR–Cas9 complex.[232] Seventy-one of those zygotes survived the microinjection process and fifty-four were tested to confirm correct editing.

Results revealed that only twenty-eight zygotes had their genome cleaved by the Cas9 enzyme, and a meager four zygotes (14 percent) had been successfully edited at the *HBB* locus using the template supplied by the scientists.[233] From the outset, the team preemptively clarified that the zygotes used were tripronuclear, that is, zygotes that carry an extra set of chromosomes due to fertilization of a single egg by two sperm. Tripronuclear zygotes are routinely generated during the process of in vitro fertilization (IVF), which typically leads to formation of approximately 5 percent tripronuclear zygotes from the total zygote pool. Because they cannot become viable embryos, the tripronuclear zygotes are usually discarded in IVF clinics. But they could be used to study human development where it is lawful for a simple reason: Having an extra set of chromosomes renders any subsequent tripronuclear embryos nonviable. The tripronuclear zygotes progress through the first stages of cell divisions in vitro, but eventually become arrested in development and cannot result in a live birth.

Three significant findings were identified in the experiment: (1) the editing and repair efficiency was dismally low (only 14 percent of embryos were successfully edited); (2) off-target mutations formed by cut-and-repair events in unintended DNA sites were detected, which resembled off-target events that typically occur in human cancer cells; and (3) the edited embryos were mosaic—that is, some of the embryo cells had the desired mutations while others did not.[234] The landmark study showed that CRISPR–Cas9 can mediate double-stranded breaks and DNA repair via homologous recombination in human embryos, but is replete with failures in terms of efficiency, specificity, and fidelity of the CRISPR–Cas9 system. More importantly, the data presented automatically precluded the potential clinical use of CRISPR–Cas9 in the reported form and demonstrated that human germline editing is not yet ready for primetime.

To be clear, the paper represents a somewhat outdated snapshot of the state of the art at the time of its publication. Other published research around the time had already shown some improvements on efficiency and specificity, and the Chinese team's results were consistent with already months-to-years-old CRISPR technology.[235] Scientists at the forefront of genome-editing technology were unimpressed with the results of the *Protein & Cell* paper—primarily because the research did not use the latest version of CRISPR–Cas9 technology—and called the attempt to edit human germ cells premature.[236] Furthermore, it appears that some of the lackluster results could be attributable to inexperience with using CRISPR protocols.[237] Palpably, the first try at human germline editing got off to a rocky start. But tweaks and improvements in the field are occurring at an astounding speed.[238]

From a scientific standpoint, the report did not contribute any novel understanding of the CRISPR–Cas9 system. Indeed, the authors pointed out that similar efficiencies had been reported in other organisms, including mice.[239] In effect, the paper was merely a clone of the same studies performed on other organisms. However, this time, the experiments were notable because they were conducted in human germ cells. The paper had first been submitted to *Nature* and *Science*, but was rejected by both journals in part because of ethical concerns.[240] Notwithstanding the article's scientific shortcomings, the true nuances of this momentous report lie in the ethical implications of the research and the subsequent consternation it spawned.

Rumors that Chinese scientists had performed experiments to edit the human germline, purportedly circulated by reviewers or parties privy to the manuscript's content at one or both of the journals to which it was initially submitted, reverberated with a loud echo among scientific circles. Alarmed scientists rushed to publish commentaries in response to the leak in both *Nature*[241] and *Science*[242] to criticize the experiments and preemptively call for either a ban or an outright moratorium on facets of human germline editing research.

The situation was reminiscent of some bygone controversies. Not since the days of IVF[243] and the birth of Dolly the sheep, the first animal cloned from an adult cell,[244] had clamor been so thunderous concerning an emerging technology.[245] A stentorian tone began to permeate news and media outlets within days of the published commentaries with several groups, including the Center for Genetics and Society in Berkeley, California,[246] the Society for Developmental Biology in Bethesda, Maryland,[247] and the International Society for Stem Cell Research[248] echoing calls to halt human germline editing research.[249] Declarations of an urgent need to organize meetings about the appropriateness of using CRISPR-like biotechnologies for human germline research led to meetings such as the International Summit on Human Gene Editing, which took place in December 2015 in Washington, DC.[250]

Just months earlier in September 2015, British scientists had promptly applied to the UK Human Fertilization and Embryology Authority (HFEA) for a license to edit genes in human embryos.[251] The license was granted in February 2016. It allowed biologists at the Francis Crick Institute in London to commence research on *healthy* human embryos younger than seven days, pending approval by a local research ethics board.

The HFEA approval marked the first time a national regulatory agency condoned investigations based on research involving human germline editing. It was also an important step toward elucidating more knowledge regarding CRISPR systems and their roles in genome editing within a more rigorous and developed framework than that of the research performed by the Chinese scientists, which involved nonviable human embryos and outdated versions of the CRISPR–Cas9 system. Findings derived from this type of research could not only have an immediate impact on current reproductive technologies and human development, but may provide clues that will be useful for future clinical applications of genome editing.

Genome editing technologies involving the human germline have far greater prospects for human health and welfare than somatic or stem cell gene-editing therapies. In addition to tackling acquired diseases, as well as monogenic and polygenic—dominant or recessive—congenital disorders in a particular individual, correcting gene errors or conferring prophylactic protection to diseases in the germline means the changes can be inherited in a firm and self-perpetuating configuration to subsequent generations. In essence, human germline editing is truly the holy grail of modern-day medicine.

The potential benefits are infinite. Further maturation and tweaking of genome-editing biotechnologies in combination with other foundational biotechnologies like genome sequencing and induced pluripotent stem cell (iPSC) biology may, sooner rather than later, enable us to ablate, mitigate, counteract, or safeguard against an extensive array of complex human ailments discussed throughout this chapter, including neurodegenerative disorders, congenital diseases, cognitive and behavioral anomalies, HIV and other viruses, obesity, cardiovascular disease, cancers, and more.

Contemplate, for a moment, the well-publicized dilemma of actress and director Angelina Jolie. In back-to-back op-eds in *The New York Times*, she shared with the world her decision to endure a preventive double mastectomy to remove her breasts[252] and a laparoscopic bilateral salpingo-oophorectomy to remove her ovaries and fallopian tubes.[253] Her decisions to undergo the procedures came following genetic testing via a blood test, which revealed she carried common mutations in the *BRCA1* gene that placed her at an 87 percent risk of developing breast cancer and a 50 percent risk of ovarian cancer. Jolie lost her grandmother, aunt, and mother to cancer, making her family history a cautionary tale that could likely have foreshadowed her own destiny. In the span of two years, she took a surgical plunge any woman would dread. Her journey rendered her a menopausal woman well before her natural time. At the same time, she also stood by her life-altering decision because she felt her children would no longer have to face losing their mother prematurely, as she did.

Jolie's remarkable story mirrors those of millions of women worldwide facing the deadly threat of cancer. The WHO estimates that breast cancer alone kills nearly 458,000 people each year, mainly in low- and middle-income countries. Men facing deadly prostate and testicular cancers are increasingly choosing to part ways with their prostates[254] or testes.[255] Millions of men and women all over the world face tough decisions because of various forms of pervasive cancers, which are among the leading causes of morbidity and mortality worldwide.[256] Indeed, the WHO estimates that new cancer cases are expected to increase by 70 percent in the next twenty years.[257] But what if such drastic choices could be avoided? In Jolie's case, the cancer risk was accentuated based on a familial history of cancer and mutations in the *BRCA1* gene. Had genome editing been safe and readily available to her, her decision to extirpate her breasts and ovaries might not even have been considered.

In the future, humans may be able to identify quantitative-trait loci linked to a genetic basis or predisposition to disease and proactively correct deleterious mutations that could pose grave threats to human life. Genome editing finally brings into the realm of reality clinical applications that had been unreachable for decades. It is quite likely that future generations of children and grandchildren may grow up in a CRISPR world, where they will no longer have to make Jolie-type choices due to cancers and numerous other human diseases. Even more remarkable is the notion that by correcting those mistakes in the germline DNA, new generations of would-be disease-prone mutation carriers may never have to witness the death of mothers, aunts, and grandmothers at the hands of the same killer.

Despite the vast potential for good by the use of genome-editing biotechnologies, to some the notion of human germline modification—no matter what the purpose—conjures up the insidious spirit of eugenics and other potential societal harms.[258] Frivolous enhancement of human traits, rising inequality, and a multitude of "designer babies" are commonly cited as major threats stemming from the use of genome-editing biotechnologies.[259] Others have chosen to either favorably cherry-pick or denounce certain applications of genome editing, as they worry that widespread opposition to the technology may curtail uses from which they stand to profit.[260] We will explore some of these themes arising from human germline editing in later chapters.

VI FIGHTING VIRUSES

Earlier in this chapter, we discussed the use of CRISPR–Cas9 genome editing to confer resistance to viruses by editing the host's virus-receptor genes, such as the case of targeting the human CCR5 receptor to prevent HIV infection.[261] Receptor targeting is not limited to human viral infections and has also been shown to establish resistance to viruses affecting other animals, such as porcine respiratory and reproductive syndrome virus in swine.[262] And we also discussed using CRISPR–Cas9 to eradicate multiple copies of a porcine endogenous retrovirus to prevent viral infection and transmission to human cells in the context of xenotransplantation.[263]

The concept of using vaccines against viruses has become widely known around the world. Conventional viral vaccines involve the adaptation of the immune system via exposure to viral proteins and fragments thereof, or attenuated viruses. Vaccines can be quite effective at treating infectious diseases, but they are hard to come by. Although vaccines constitute a prevalent strategy in the fight against viral diseases, to date, there are no antiviral drug or vaccine therapies for more than 200 infectious diseases affecting human populations worldwide.[264] In the last six decades, only ninety antiviral drugs have been formally approved for the treatment of a mere nine human infectious diseases. And the FDA has only approved vaccines for about sixteen viruses.

Recognizing the need for antiviral agents to combat viral diseases, researchers have recently began using CRISPR–Cas systems for research into vaccine development,[265] viral detection, and antiviral defense. Indeed, CRISPR-based antiviral and diagnostic strategies for the treatment and diagnosis of viral diseases are active areas of research.

Consider, for example, the ongoing global pandemic of coronavirus disease 2019 (COVID-19), which is caused by a novel strain of coronavirus from the *betacoronavirus* genus known as severe acute respiratory syndrome coronavirus-2 (SARS-CoV-2). The virus has wreaked havoc in many countries all over the world and paralyzed the world economy. On January 30, 2020, the World Health Organization (WHO) declared the SARS-CoV-2 outbreak a Public Health Emergency of International Concern.[266] By March 11, 2020, the WHO subsequently declared COVID-19 the first pandemic caused by a coronavirus.[267] The COVID-19 death toll reached 100,000 people in the United States[268] and nearly 400,000 worldwide[269] by the end of May 2020, with more than six million reported cases in over 200 countries.[270]

To address the COVID-19 pandemic, a recent study reported the use of the CRISPR–Cas13d system as a programmable, genetic, antiviral platform to directly recognize and degrade the SARS-CoV-2 single-stranded RNA viral genome and its resulting mRNAs in human lung epithelial cells, thereby inhibiting viral gene expression.[271] This strategy of triggering targeted-RNA cleavage that leads to restriction of viral gene expression has also been achieved with other variants of CRISPR–Cas13, including CRISPR–Cas13a and CRISPR–Cas13b, against lymphocytic choriomeningitis virus (LCMV), Influenza A virus (IAV), and vesicular stomatitis virus (VSV).[272] It bears noting that CRISPR–Cas13 technology does not involve traditional genome editing, but rather relies on the catalytic activity of the Cas13d effector enzyme, which involves the RNA-guided, RNA nuclease-mediated degradation of target RNA molecules.

To understand the difference between the use of Cas9 and Cas13, it may help you to recall that CRISPR–Cas9 is an RNA-guided, DNA endonuclease. In other words, CRISPR–Cas9 uses guide RNAs to cleave target DNA molecules. CRISPR–Cas13, on the other hand, uses guide RNAs to cleave target RNA molecules. And because the SARS-CoV-2 virus has a single-stranded RNA genome, CRISPR–Cas13 can be used to recognize and degrade viral RNA sequences of interest.

CRISPR–Cas systems can not only be used for potential treatment of a range of viral infections; they can also be used as a diagnostic tool. A CRISPR-based diagnostic platform using the Cas13a effector, for example, has been used as a molecular strategy to detect specific strains of the Zika and Dengue viruses.[273] Another study recently reported the use of a CRISPR–Cas12a-based assay for detection of SARS-CoV-2 from respiratory swab RNA extracts.[274]

The Cas12a study sought to accelerate clinical diagnostic testing for COVID-19 given the lack of testing kits available for the screening and diagnosis of patients suspected of having been infected with SARS-CoV-2. The study reported a visual and faster alternative to the current US Centers for Disease Control and Prevention SARS-CoV-2 real-time reverse transcriptase (RT)–PCR assay. Another platform that is suitable for point-of-care purposes using the CRISPR–Cas12b system reported similar results for detecting SARS-CoV-2 in about one hour.[275] The CRISPR–Cas12b-based SARS-CoV-2 testing kit, which is produced by Sherlock Biosciences for the detection of the virus that causes COVID-19, became the first FDA-authorized product using CRISPR technology after the company received Emergency Use Authorization from the US Food and Drug Administration.[276] These advances in testing capabilities may become critical as the COVID-19 pandemic continues to spread across the planet.

VII EPIGENOME EDITING — THE NEXT FRONTIER

Every cell in your body—and you have trillions of them—has the same genetic composition. In other words, the DNA sequences of your brain, bone, skin, eye, and reproductive cells are all genetically the same. You may be asking yourself, how then do cells with the same DNA become so specialized and different? That is a fascinating question that has captivated researchers for decades.

The answer lies in epigenetics, which is a complex scientific field that studies specific changes that happen on DNA or the environment around it. More specifically, epigenetics concerns the study of chemical changes that "adorn" the environment surrounding DNA sequences without altering them. Epigenetic regulation depends on dynamic and diverse combinations of covalent chemical modifications that occur on histone proteins—known as histone post-translational modifications (PTMs)—and DNA bases, as well as the expression of regulatory noncoding RNA (ncRNA) molecules.[277]

Histones are a type of proteins that associate with DNA and help to condense and pack it into chromatin.[278] The DNA wraps around histones so that it can fit inside the cell nucleus and form chromosomes. Think of yarn. When the yarn is loose, it can take up a lot of space and form tangles. But you can fit a lot of yarn in a small box when you pack it neatly into a small ball or loop. In a similar way, DNA can be neatly packed and condensed around histone proteins inside the cell nucleus. Histone proteins often bear chemical PTM marks—including methylation, acetylation, phosphorylation, ubiquitination, and many more—that help to create unique environments for the DNA in proximity. These marks that decorate histone proteins often act as a signaling platform for a repertoire of myriad proteins with diverse functional roles in gene expression.

In addition to histone PTMs, epigenetics concerns the study of DNA epigenetic modifications, which are chemical marks that can be added to DNA bases. A common epigenetic modification, for example, is the methylation of cytosine bases, which involves the addition of methyl groups on the cytosine base. When cytosine bases found in certain areas of the genome—such as in genetic promoter regions—are decorated with methylation marks, it can lead to the repression of gene transcription, which is also known as gene silencing.

The epigenetic signals from histone PTMs and DNA epigenetic modifications, as well as certain ncRNAs constitute a layer of information that controls the spatiotemporal regulation of gene expression patterns. To illustrate the significance of epigenetic marks, consider the use of makeup among actors. With the appropriate makeup and clothing, the same person can play multiple characters. Cate Blanchett, for instance, has played a homeless man (*Manifesto*,

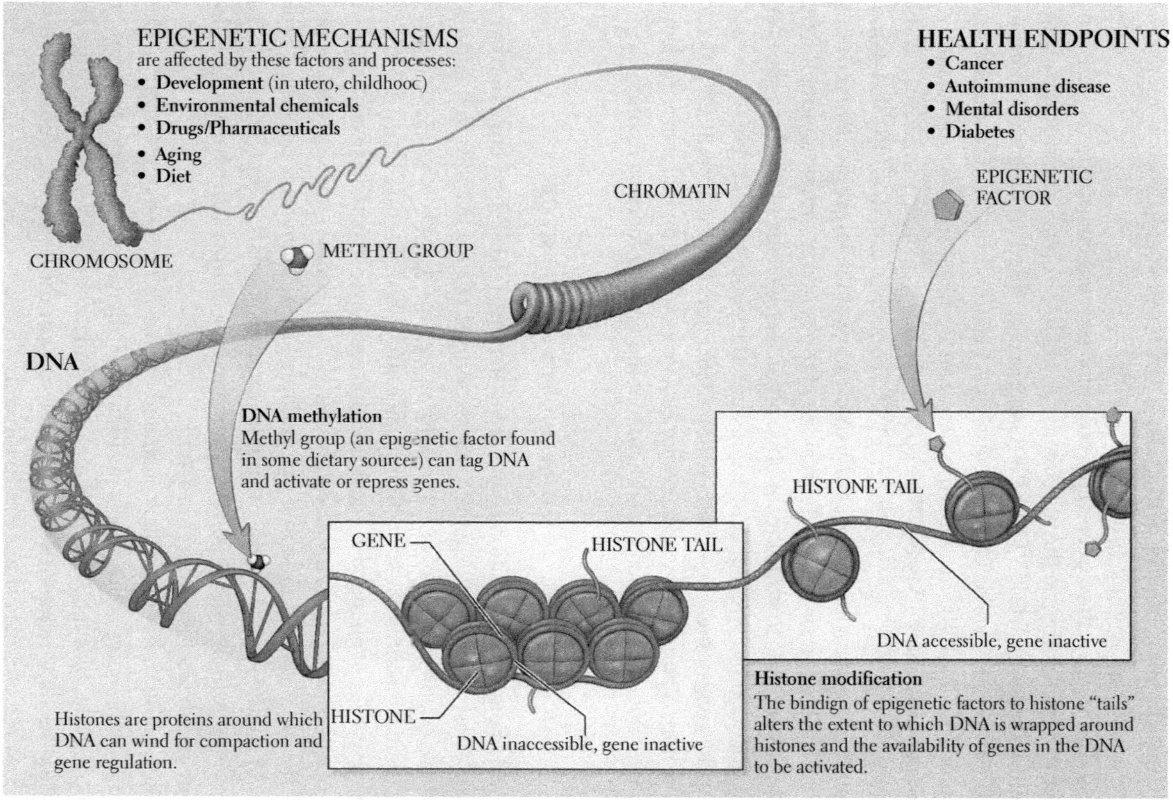

FIGURE 5.2 Epigenetics (The National Institutes of Health)

2015), a royal elf (*The Lord of the Rings*, 2001, 2002, 2003), a goddess of death (*Thor: Ragnarok*, 2017), Queen Elizabeth I of England (*Elizabeth: The Golden Age*, 2007), a neurotic former socialite (*Blue Jasmine*, 2013), and even Bob Dylan (*I'm Not There*, 2007). Blanchett played every single one of these characters using very specific makeup and clothes. In a similar way, cells with very specific epigenetic marks can assume multiple identities.

CRISPR–Cas systems have been repurposed for targeted epigenome editing, and can now be used to interrogate the functional roles of these epigenetic marks by using catalytically inactive or "dead" CRISPR–Cas proteins fused to epigenetic effector enzymes.[279] For instance, the Cas9 nuclease has been deactivated and turned into a dCas9 protein. The CRISPR–dCas9 system can be fused to enzymes capable of adding covalent histone PTMs or DNA epigenetic marks. These complexes can be subsequently recruited to specific target DNA sequences just like CRISPR–Cas9, except that dCas9 can no longer trigger DNA cleavage at the target site. By recruiting the CRISPR–dCas9 system to specific regions of the genome without cutting DNA, scientists have been able to study the function of some epigenetic marks, turn genes on or off, and fine-tune the levels of gene expression in specific types of cells.

Studying the epigenome is an extremely important endeavor. Epigenome editing can facilitate the understanding of gene expression at a deeper level, and offers a remarkable opportunity to unlock many secrets that represent the next engineering frontier.

VIII ARCHIVAL OF DIGITAL DATA IN LIVING CELLS

The archival of digital information is now feasible using CRISPR systems. In what is perhaps the most bizarre and quaint incarnation yet of all CRISPR applications, scientists have established proof of concept for using the CRISPR–Cas1–Cas2 system to record digital information in a biological format. For the first time, a team of American researchers encoded a short, five-frame movie at 36×26 pixels into the genomes of a population of living *E. coli* bacteria.[280] The short graphics-interchange format (GIF) file showed a galloping mare adapted from *Animal Locomotion*,[281] the collection of collotype prints featuring photographs of animals and people captured mid-movement, which was originally published by Eadweard Muybridge—the English-American photographer—in 1887.

In essence, humans have now demonstrated the feasibility of using CRISPR–Cas systems to modify living organisms so as to encode digital information that can be stored within their genomes. The rational manipulation of DNA as a medium for archiving digital data represents exciting new opportunities for the future of biological recordings and data storage in living cells.

* * *

The genome-editing applications described in this chapter constitute a comprehensive—yet nonexhaustive—representation of the potential uses of emerging genome-editing

FIGURE 5.3 Galloping mare in plate 626 of *Animal Locomotion*, Eadweard Muybridge, 1887 (Boston Public Library)

technologies. It is important to note, however, that many other uses of genome editing and CRISPR-based technologies currently exist, including development of new antibiotics and antimicrobials,[282] drug-target discovery,[283] systematic identification of gene and drug combinations,[284] live imaging to study conformational and cellular dynamics,[285] cell-lineage tracing,[286] whole-genome screening and labeling,[287] post-transplantation monitoring of graft rejection and common opportunistic viral infections,[288] digital-logic circuits in cells,[289] genetic central-processing units (CPU) for complex computation,[290] and more.[291]

Given the astounding rate at which new applications continue to emerge, it would be impossible to list every genome-editing application in this volume. Genome editing is by no means a panacea, but it has nevertheless proven to be a truly exceptional and transformative biotechnology. Unsurprisingly, such a significant and wide-ranging emerging technology presents new challenges for the development of cohesive and science-based law and policy, which we will discuss in the next chapters.

Notes

1 *See* OMIM Gene Map Statistics, https://omim.org/statistics/geneMap.

2 *See* OMIM® – Online Mendelian Inheritance in Man®, https://omim.org/about.

3 Somatic cells are all of the body's cells except the reproductive cells. *Somatic Cells*, BIOLOGY ONLINE, http://www.biology-online.org/dictionary/Somatic_cells [https://perma.cc/A8ZT-MRZ6] (last visited Feb. 13, 2017).

4 Rong Liu et al., *Homozygous Defect in HIV-1 Coreceptor Accounts for Resistance of Some Multiply-Exposed Individuals to HIV-1 Infection*, 86 CELL 367, 370 (1996).

5 Gero Hütter et al., *Long-Term Control of HIV by CCR5 Delta32/Delta32 Stem-Cell Transplantation*, 360 NEW ENG. J. MED. 692, 695 (2009).

6 *Id.* at 692.

7 *See Timothy Ray Brown*, FRED HUTCH, https://www.fredhutch.org/en/news/timothy-ray-brown.html [https://perma.cc/G42T-UKM7] (last visited Feb. 25, 2017).

8 *See* Elena E. Perez et al., *Establishment of HIV-1 Resistance in CD4⁺ T Cells by Genome Editing Using Zinc-Finger Nucleases*, 26 NATURE BIOTECHNOLOGY 808, 808 (2008).

9 *Id.*

10 *Autologous T-Cells Genetically Modified at the CCR5 Gene by Zinc Finger Nucleases SB-728 for HIV (Zinc-Finger)*, CLINICALTRIALS.GOV, https://clinicaltrials.gov/ct2 /show/study/NCT00842634 [https://perma.cc/RB7E-VGE3] (last visited Feb. 13, 2017).

11 Pablo Tebas et al., *Gene Editing of CCR5 in Autologous CD4 T Cells of Persons Infected with HIV*, 370 NEW ENG. J. MED. 901, 908 (2014).

12 *Sangamo BioSciences Presents Phase 2 Clinical Data from Two SB-728-T HIV Studies*, PR NEWSWIRE (Dec. 11, 2015), http://www.prnewswire.com/news-releases/sangamo-biosciences-presents-phase-2-clinical-data-from-two-sb-728-t-hiv-studies-300191693.html [https://perma.cc/G2X6-5AUF].

13 *E.g.*, Hirotaka Ebina et al., *Harnessing the CRISPR/Cas9 System to Disrupt Latent HIV-1 Provirus*, 3 SCI. REP. 2510 (2013).

14 *E.g.*, Wenhui Hu et al., *RNA-Directed Gene Editing Specifically Eradicates Latent and Prevents New HIV-1 Infection*, 111 PROC. NAT'L ACAD. SCI. U.S. 11461, 11462 (2014).

15 *Id.*

16 *E.g.*, Hsin-Kai Liao et al., *Use of the CRISPR/Cas9 System as an Intracellular Defense Against HIV-1 Infection in Human Cells*, 6 NATURE COMMC'NS 6413 (2015).

17 Hao Yin et al., *Genome Editing with Cas9 in Adult Mice Corrects a Disease Mutation and Phenotype*, 32 NATURE BIOTECHNOLOGY 551, 551 (2014).

18 Gerald Schwank et al., *Functional Repair of CFTR by CRISPR/Cas9 in Intestinal Stem Cell Organoids of Cystic Fibrosis Patients*, 13 CELL STEM CELL 653, 655 (2013).

19 Peter Reinhardt et al., *Genetic Correction of a LRRK2 Mutation in Human iPSCs Links Parkinsonian Neurodegeneration to ERK-Dependent Changes in Gene Expression*, 12 CELL STEM CELL 354, 354 (2013).

20 Pietro Genovese et al., *Targeted Genome Editing in Human Repopulating Haematopoietic Stem Cells*, 510 NATURE 235, 235 (2014).

21 *See generally* R. Aggarwal et al., *Hematopoietic Stem Cells: Transcriptional Regulation, ex Vivo Expansion and Clinical Application*, 12 CURRENT MOLECULAR MED. 34 (2012).

22 *See* D. G. Courtney et al., *CRISPR/Cas9 DNA Cleavage at SNP-Derived PAM Enables Both in Vitro and in Vivo KRT12 Mutation-Specific Targeting*, 23 GENE THERAPY 108, 108 (2016).

23 *See* Mahru C. An et al., *Genetic Correction of Huntington's Disease Phenotypes in Induced Pluripotent Stem Cells*, 11 CELL STEM CELL 253, 253 (2012).

24 *See* Douglas J. Wilkin et al., *Mutations in Fibroblast Growth-Factor Receptor 3 in Sporadic Cases of Achondroplasia Occur Exclusively on the Paternally Derived Chromosome*, 63 AM. J. HUM. GENETICS 711, 715 (1998).

25 *See* Thomas Gaj, *Therapeutic Genome Editing for Amyotrophic Lateral Sclerosis*, GRANTOME, http://grantome.com/grant/NIH/F32-GM113446-01A1 [https://perma.cc/JS5M-9ZC6] (last visited Feb. 25, 2017).

26 *See* Jeroen K. J. Van Houdt et al., *Heterozygous Missense Mutations in SMARCA2 Cause Nicolaides-Baraitser Syndrome*, 44 NATURE GENETICS 445, 448 (2012).

27 *See* Rachel Myerowitz, *Tay-Sachs Disease-Causing Mutations and Neutral Polymorphisms in the Hex A Gene*, 9 HUM. MUTATION 195, 196 (1997).

28 *See, e.g.*, B. Berdien et al., *TALEN-Mediated Editing of Endogenous T-Cell Receptors Facilitates Efficient Reprogramming of T Lymphocytes by Lentiviral Gene Transfer*, 21 GENE THERAPY 539 (2014); Elena Provasi et al., *Editing T Cell Specificity Towards Leukemia by Zinc Finger Nucleases and Lentiviral Gene Transfer*, 18 NATURE MED. 807 (2012).

29 *See, e.g.*, Yang-Jun Gao et al., *Expression of the B-Cell Lymphoma/Leukemia 11A Gene in Malignant Hematological Cell Lines Through Quantitative Reverse Transcription Polymerase Chain Reaction*, 8 CLINICAL ONCOLOGY & CANCER RES. 242, 242 (2011); Pentao Liu et al., *Bcl11a Is Essential for Normal Lymphoid Development*, 4 NATURE IMMUNOLOGY 525, 525 (2003).

30 *See* Matthew C. Canver et al., *BCL11A Enhancer Dissection by Cas9-Mediated in Situ Saturating Mutagenesis*, 527 NATURE 192, 192 (2015) (citing Julian Banerji et al., *Expression of a β-globin Gene Is Enhanced by Remote SV40 DNA Sequences*, 27 CELL 299 (1981)).

31 *See, e.g.*, Thorlakur Jonsson et al., *A Mutation in APP Protects Against Alzheimer's Disease and Age-Related Cognitive Decline*, 488 NATURE 96, 96 (2012).

32 *See* discussion *supra* notes 4–16 and accompanying text.

33 *See, e.g.*, Jonathan Cohen et al., *Low LDL Cholesterol in Individuals of African Descent Resulting from Frequent Nonsense Mutations in PCSK9*, 37 NATURE GENETICS 161, 162 (2005) (identifying two *PCSK9* mutations having a protective effect against hypercholesterolemia); The TG and HDL Working Group of the Exome Sequencing Project, National Heart, Lung, and Blood Institute, *Loss-of-*

Function Mutations in APOC3, Triglycerides, and Coronary Disease, 371 NEW ENG. J. MED. 22, 23 (2014) (identifying rare *APOC3* mutations associated with a lower risk of heart disease).

34 *See, e.g.*, Shannon L. Maude et al., *Chimeric Antigen Receptor T Cells for Sustained Remissions in Leukemia*, 371 NEW ENG. J. MED. 1507, 1512 (2014).

35 James E. DiCarlo et al., *Safeguarding CRISPR-Cas9 Gene Drives in Yeast*, 33 NATURE BIOTECHNOLOGY 1250, 1250 (2015).

36 Christopher F. Curtis, *Possible Use of Translocations to Fix Desirable Genes in Insect Pest Populations*, 218 NATURE 368, 368 (1968).

37 *See* Austin Burt, *Site-Specific Selfish Genes as Tools for the Control and Genetic Engineering of Natural Populations*, 270 PROC. ROYAL SOC'Y B: BIOLOGICAL SCI. 921, 921 (2003).

38 *See* Nikolai Windbichler et al., *A Synthetic Homing Endonuclease-Based Gene Drive System in the Human Malaria Mosquito*, 473 NATURE 212, 212 (2011).

39 *See* Valentino M. Gantz & Ethan Bier, *The Mutagenic Chain Reaction: A Method for Converting Heterozygous to Homozygous Mutations*, 348 SCIENCE 442, 442 (2015).

40 *Id.* at 443.

41 *Factsheet on the World Malaria Report 2013*, WORLD HEALTH ORG. (Dec. 2013), http://www.who.int/malaria/media/world_malaria_report_2013/en/ [https://perma.cc/Z2XH-JLPN].

42 *Malaria, Key Facts*, WORLD HEALTH ORG., https://www.who.int/news-room/fact-sheets/detail/malaria.

43 Valentino M. Gantz et al., *Highly Efficient Cas9-Mediated Gene Drive for Population Modification of the Malaria Vector Mosquito Anopheles stephensi*, 112 PROC. NAT'L ACAD. SCI. U.S. e6736 (2015).

44 *See* Andrew Hammond et al., *A CRISPR-Cas9 Gene Drive System Targeting Female Reproduction in the Malaria Mosquito Vector Anopheles gambiae*, 34 NATURE BIOTECHNOLOGY 78, 78 (2016).

45 *See* DiCarlo et al., *supra* note 35, at 1250 (reporting gene drive systems in wild and laboratory strains of the yeast *Saccharomyces cerevisiae*).

46 *See* Gantz & Bier, *supra* note 39, at 442 (testing a gene drive in *Drosophila melanogaster*).

47 *See, e.g.*, *id.* at e6736 (experimenting with *Anopheles stephensi*); Hammond et al., *supra* note 44, at 78 (targeting *Anopheles gambiae*); *see also* Andrea L. Smidler et al., *Targeted Mutagenesis in the Malaria Mosquito Using TALE Nucleases*, 8 PLoS ONE e74511, e74511 (2013) (using transgenic expression of TALENs for genetic manipulation of mosquitoes instead of CRISPR–Cas9).

48 Kathryn E. Kistler et al., *Genome Engineering with CRISPR-Cas9 in the Mosquito Aedes aegypti*, 11 CELL REP. 51, 51 (2015).

49 *See* Hammond et al., *supra* note 44, at 80.

50 *See, e.g.*, Robert L. Unckless et al., *Modeling the Manipulation of Natural Populations by the Mutagenic Chain Reaction*, 201 GENETICS 425, 427–28 (2015).

51 *See* Charleston Noble et al., *Current CRISPR gene drive systems are likely to be highly invasive in wild populations*, 7 eLife e33423 (2018).

52 *See United States*, Oxitec, http://www.oxitec.com/programmes/united-states/ [https://perma.cc/D2LH-7RF4] (last visited Feb. 9, 2017); *see also* Kerry Grens, *Mutant Mosquitoes Deployed to Stop Zika, Dengue*, Scientist (Jan. 19, 2016), http://www.the-scientist.com/?articles.view/articleNo/45128/title/Mutant-Mosquitoes-Deployed -to-Stop-Zika—Dengue/ [https://perma.cc/94DJ-AV9X].

53 Press Release, Oxitec, Oxitec's Solution for Controlling the Dengue Mosquito Is Approved by CTNBio (Apr. 10, 2014), http://www.oxitec.com/press-release-high-tech-solution-for-controlling-the-dengue-mosquito-is-approved-by-ctnbio/ [https://perma.cc/5MXV-XHQX].

54 Christina Sarich, *Genetically Modified Moths Released in New York*, Nat. Soc'y (June 19, 2015), http://naturalsociety.com/outrage-oxitecs-gm-moths-are-released -in-new-york/ [https://perma.cc/C4HB-SCA4].

55 William Axford, *Keys Bug Board Says No to Contract for Genetically Modified Mosquitoes Unless Feds Approve*, Miami Herald (Apr. 22, 2015), http://www.miami herald.com /news/local/community/florida-keys/article19207230.html [https://perma.cc/TJJ7-KGGH].

56 Sandee LaMotte, *Zika Around the World: Where Do We Stand?*, CNN, http://www.cnn.com/2016/08/30/health/zika-around-the-world/ [https://perma.cc /2AGH-CVXJ] (last updated Aug. 30, 2016, 7:54 AM).

57 *Public Health Emergency of International Concern (PHEIC) Declared for Zika and Clusters of Microcephaly and Neurological Disorders*, European Ctr. Disease Prevention & Control (Feb. 3, 2016), http://ecdc.europa.eu/en/activities/sciadvice /_layouts/forms/Review_DispForm.aspx?List=a3216f4c-f040-4f51-9f77-a96046dbfd72 &ID=790 [https://perma.cc/2KAD-HBXL]; *cf.* Dom Phillips & Lena H. Sun, *Brazil May Have Fewer Zika-Related Microcephaly Cases than Previously Reported*, Wash. Post (Jan. 29, 2016), https://www.washingtonpost.com/news/worldviews/wp/2016/01/29/brazil-may-have-fewer-zika -related-microcephaly-cases-than-previously-reported/ ?utm_term=.130b760628a2 [https://perma.cc/22HZ-3GXG] (reporting that many of the documented microcephaly cases in Brazil may not actually be microcephaly, nor related to the Zika virus).

58 Donald G. McNeil, Jr., *Hawaii Baby with Brain Damage Is First U.S. Case Tied to Zika Virus*, N.Y. Times (Jan. 16, 2016), https://www.nytimes.com/2016/01/17/health/hawaii-reports-baby-born-with-brain-damage-linked-to-zika-virus.html [https://perma.cc/2MD6-FXS3].

59 *See, e.g.*, Donald G. McNeil, Jr., *To Protect Against Zika Virus, Pregnant Women Are Warned About Latin American Trips*, N.Y. Times (Jan. 15, 2016), https://www .nytimes.com/2016/01/16/health/zika-virus-cdc-pregnant-women-travel-warning.html [https://perma.cc/K8DF-F63T].

60 *See, e.g.*, Adrija Hajra et al., *Zika Virus: A Global Threat to Humanity: A Comprehensive Review and Current Developments*, 8 N. Am. J. Med. Sci. 123 (2016).

61 *See, e.g.*, McNeil, *supra* note 58.
62 *See, e.g.*, Axford, *supra* note 55; Sarich, *supra* note 54.
63 *See, e.g.*, Oliver J. Brady et al., *The Association Between Zika Virus Infection and Microcephaly in Brazil 2015–2017: An Observational Analysis of over 4 Million Births*, 16 PLoS MED. e1002755 (2019).
64 *See, e.g.*, Kelly Servick, *Brazil will Release Billions of Lab-Grown Mosquitoes to Combat Infectious Disease. Will it Work?*, SCIENCE MAG., Oct. 13, 2016, https://www.sciencemag.org/news/2016/10/brazil-will-release-billions-lab-grown-mosquitoes-combat-infectious-disease-will-it.
65 Carl Zimmer, *A Call to Fight Malaria One Mosquito at a Time by Altering DNA*, N.Y. TIMES (July 17, 2014), http://www.nytimes.com/2014/07/17/science/a-call-to-fight-malaria-one-mosquito-at-a-time-by-altering-dna.html?_r=0 [https://perma.cc/D27C-K2MS] (quoting George Church, senior author of one of the papers targeting malaria mosquito vectors, as stating: "In a year or two, we could be doing field trials if there was a general consensus this was a good idea.").
66 Bill Gates, *The Deadliest Animal in the World*, GATES NOTES (Apr. 25, 2014), https://www.gatesnotes.com/Health/Most-Lethal-Animal-Mosquito-Week [https://perma.cc/7T6Z-L8F3].
67 *See, e.g.*, Omar S. Akbari et al., *Safeguarding Gene Drive Experiments in the Laboratory*, 349 SCIENCE 927 (2015); Keith G. Kozminski, *Biosecurity in the Age of Big Data: A Conversation with the FBI*, 26 MOLECULAR BIOLOGY CELL 3894 (2015); Bruce L. Webber et al., *Opinion: Is CRISPR-Based Gene Drive a Biocontrol Silver Bullet or Global Conservation Threat?*, 112 PROC. NAT'L ACAD. SCI. U.S. 10565 (2015); Katie Langin, *Genetic Engineering to the Rescue Against Invasive Species?*, NAT'L GEOGRAPHIC (July 18, 2014), http://news.nationalgeographic.com/news/2014/07/140717-gene-drives-invasive -species-insects-disease-science-environment/ [https://perma.cc/K9WH-EBH6]; *Gene Drive Research in Non-Human Organisms: Recommendations for Responsible Conduct*, NAT'L ACAD. SCIS., ENG'G & MED., https://www8.nationalacademies.org/cp/projectview.aspx?key=49717 [https://perma.cc/VAT3-WVPM] (last visited Feb. 26, 2017).
68 *See* DiCarlo et al., *supra* note 35, at 1252–53.
69 *Neglected Tropical Diseases*, CTRS. DISEASE CONTROL & PREVENTION, http://www.cdc.gov/globalhealth/ntd/ [https://perma.cc/TK9L-9LZ3] (last updated June 7, 2016). The list of common NTDs includes Buruli ulcers, Chagas disease, Cysticercosis, Dengue fever, Echinococcosis, Fascioliasis, Leprosy, Onchocerciasis, Rabies, Schistosomiasis, and others. *See Diseases*, CTRS. DISEASE CONTROL & PREVENTION, http://www.cdc.gov/globalhealth/ntd/diseases/index.html [https://perma.cc/BE7T-4HPN] (last updated Feb. 17, 2017), for a list and information about NTDs.
70 *See Chapter 3: Infectious Diseases Related to Travel*, CTRS. DISEASE CONTROL & PREVENTION, https://wwwnc.cdc.gov/travel/yellowbook/2016/infectious-diseases-

related-to-travel /schistosomiasis [https://perma.cc/2MM8-5C73] (last updated July 10, 2015).

71 *The Burden of Schistosomiasis (Schisto, Bilharzia, Snail Fever)*, Ctrs. Disease Control & Prevention, http://www.cdc.gov/globalhealth/ntd/diseases/schisto_burden.html [https://perma.cc/9MP3-LR7K] (last updated June 6, 2011).

72 Sutas Suttiprapa et al., *Genetic Manipulation of Schistosomes – Progress with Integration Competent Vectors*, 139 Parasitology 641, 641 (2012).

73 *See* Theresa Maier et al., *Gene Drives for Schistosomiasis Transmission Control*, 13 PLoS Neglected Tropical Diseases e0007833 (2019).

74 *See* Gantz et al., *supra* note 43 (using a gene drive to make the mosquito *Anopheles stephensi* resistant to the malaria parasite).

75 *See Asian Carp Threat to the Great Lakes*, Nat'l Wildlife Fed'n, https://www.nwf.org/Wildlife/Threats-to-Wildlife/Invasive-Species/Asian-Carp.aspx [https://perma.cc/6YHH-AE2D] (last visited Feb. 26, 2017); *see also Asian Carp Breed in Great Lakes, Threaten Fishing*, USA Today (Oct. 28, 2013), http://www.usatoday.com /story/news/nation/2013/10/28/asian-carp-great-lakes/3289387/ [https://perma.cc/R3MB-GPQJ].

76 *Argentine Cactus Moth (Cactoblastis cactorum)*, Desert Museum, http://www.desertmuseum.org/invaders/invaders_cactusmoth.php [https://perma.cc/KXA5-9RPZ] (last visited Feb. 26, 2017).

77 *Australian Government Policy on Cane Toads*, Australian Gov't: Dep't Env't & Energy, https://www.environment.gov.au/biodiversity/invasive-species/publications/cane-toad-policy#why [https://perma.cc/X8MQ-EKWN] (last visited Feb. 26, 2017).

78 *Managing Invasive Ants*, Galápagos Conservancy, http://www.galapagos.org/conservation/conservation/project-areas/ecosystem-restoration/managing-invasive-ants/ [https://perma.cc/GM2Z-2ABN] (last visited Feb. 26, 2017).

79 *Aquatic Species*, U.S. Dep't of Agric., Nat'l Invasive Species Info. Ctr., http://www.invasivespeciesinfo.gov/aquatics/main.shtml#aqan [https://perma.cc/P6SB-Y3EQ] (last visited Feb. 26, 2017).

80 *Animals*, U.S. Dep't Agric., Nat'l Invasive Species Info. Ctr., http://www.invasivespeciesinfo.gov/animals/main.shtml [https://perma.cc/54VY-A22R] (last visited Feb. 26, 2017).

81 Qing Yu, *Soybean Cyst Nematode* (Heterodera glycines *Ichinohe), in* Soybean Physiology and Biochemistry 461, 461 (Hany El-Shemy ed., 2011), http://cdn.intechopen.com/pdfs-wm/22782.pdf [https://perma.cc/8Q8G-JSES].

82 Darryl Fears, *This Invasive Giant Snail Is Spreading in Florida—and Bringing Nasty Parasites with It*, Wash. Post (July 10, 2015), https://www.washingtonpost.com /news/energy-environment/wp/2015/07/10/giant-land-snails-are-on-the-move-and-a-nasty-parasite-is-riding-them-like-a-bus/ [https://perma.cc/U286-35H2].

83 *The Lionfish Invasion!: Can We Stop the Invasion?*, Nat'l Oceanic & Atmospheric Admin., http://oceanservice.noaa.gov/education/stories/lion

fish/lion05_stop.html [https://perma.cc/P5HB-VCJN] (last visited Feb. 26, 2017).

84 *Kudzu, Control*, MO. DEP'T CONSERVATION, https://mdc.mo.gov/trees-plants/problem-plant-control/invasive-plants/kudzu-control [https://perma.cc/RGL2-NXEJ] (last visited Feb. 26, 2017).

85 Rachel Hajar, *Animal Testing and Medicine*, 12 HEART VIEWS 42, 42 (2011).

86 Kendall A. Smith, *Louis Pasteur, the Father of Immunology?*, 3 FRONTIERS IMMUNOLOGY, art. 68, 8 (2012).

87 Daniel Butzke et al., *The Advent of the Golden Era of Animal Alternatives, in* ANIMAL MODELS FOR THE STUDY OF HUMAN DISEASE 49–50 (P. Michael Conn ed., 2013).

88 *Animals Used in Research*, NAT'L ANTI-VIVISECTION SOC'Y, http://www.navs.org/the-issues/animals-in-research/#.WJ5to5KgQxU [https://perma.cc/9BSA-YVBJ] (last visited Feb. 25, 2017).

89 *See List of Model Organisms*, WIKIPEDIA, https://en.wikipedia.org /wiki/List_of_model_organisms [https://perma.cc/8T3Y-AXTA] (last updated Dec. 29, 2016).

90 For a works-in-collection featuring a thorough examination of the use of animal models for human disease in a wide array of fields ranging from ophthalmology and cardiology to genetics, behavior, cancer, and development, see ANIMAL MODELS FOR THE STUDY OF HUMAN DISEASE (P. Michael Conn ed., 2013).

91 *See, e.g.*, Lars Dalgaard, *Comparison of Minipig, Dog, Monkey and Human Drug Metabolism and Disposition*, 74 J. PHARMACOLOGICAL & TOXICOLOGICAL METHODS 80 (2015).

92 S. K. Chung et al., *Mouse Models for Human Diseases*, 3 H.K. MED. J. 201, 201 (1997); *Background on Mouse as a Model Organism*, NAT'L HUM. GENOME RES. INST. (Dec. 2002), http://www.genome.gov/10005834 [https://perma.cc/EJ85-MCV8] (last reviewed May 31, 2012).

93 *See* Chengzu Long et al., *Postnatal Genome Editing Partially Restores Dystrophin Expression in a Mouse Model of Muscular Dystrophy*, 351 SCIENCE 400, 400 (2016); Christopher E. Nelson et al., *In Vivo Genome Editing Improves Muscle Function in a Mouse Model of Duchenne Muscular Dystrophy*, 351 SCIENCE 403, 403 (2016); Mohammadsharif Tabebordbar et al., In *Vivo Gene Editing in Dystrophic Mouse Muscle and Muscle Stem Cells*, 351 SCIENCE 407, 407 (2016).

94 *What Are the Ethical Issues Surrounding Gene Therapy?*, U.S. NAT'L LIBR. MED. (Feb. 7, 2017), https://ghr.nlm.nih.gov/primer/therapy/ethics [https://perma.cc/B5HY-R83D].

95 Chengzu Long et al., *Prevention of Muscular Dystrophy in Mice by CRISPR/Cas9–Mediated Editing of Germline* DNA, 345 SCIENCE 1184, 1184 (2014).

96 Yuxuan Wu et al., *Correction of a Genetic Disease in Mouse via Use of CRISPR-Cas9*, 13 CELL STEM CELL 659, 659, 662 (2013).

97 *Mitochondrial DNA*, GENETICS HOME REFERENCE (Feb. 7, 2017), http://ghr.nlm.nih.gov/mitochondrial-dna [https://perma.cc/A3DW-4TL4].

98 Pradeep Reddy et al., *Selective Elimination of Mitochondrial Mutations in the Germline by Genome Editing*, 161 CELL 459, 459 (2015).

99 Lukasz Swiech et al., *In Vivo Interrogation of Gene Function in the Mammalian Brain Using CRISPR-Cas9*, 33 NATURE BIOTECHNOLOGY 102, 102 (2015).

100 Haoyi Wang et al., *One-Step Generation of Mice Carrying Mutations in Multiple Genes by CRISPR/Cas-Mediated Genome Engineering*, 153 CELL 910, 910 (2013). *See generally* Wataru Fujii et al., *Efficient Generation of Large-Scale Genome-Modified Mice Using gRNA and CAS9 Endonuclease*, 41 NUCLEIC ACIDS RES. e187 (2013).

101 Chung et al., *supra* note 92, at 201.

102 *Id.*; *see also* Dalgaard, *supra* note 91 (discussing comparative pharmacology and toxicology in humans and other large mammals).

103 J. A. Potashkin et al., *Limitations of Animal Models of Parkinson's Disease*, 2011 PARKINSON'S DISEASE art. ID 658083, at 5 (2011).

104 Xiao-Jiang Li & Shihua Li, *Large Animal Models of Huntington's Disease, in* BEHAVIORAL NEUROBIOLOGY OF HUNTINGTON'S DISEASE & PARKINSON'S DISEASE 149 (2013).

105 Karen Duff & Faraha Suleman, *Transgenic Mouse Models of Alzheimer's Disease: How Useful Have They Been for Therapeutic Development?*, 3 BRIEFINGS FUNCTIONAL GENOMICS & PROTEOMICS 47, 49–50 (2004).

106 Isabel Carvalho-Oliveira, *What Have We Learned from Mouse Models for Cystic Fibrosis?*, 7 EXPERT REV. MOLECULAR DIAGNOSTICS 407 (2007).

107 Chao-Liang Wu & David W. Melton, Production of a Model for Lesch–Nyhan Syndrome in Hypoxanthine Phosphoribosyltransferase–Deficient Mice, 3 NATURE GENETICS 235 (1993).

108 D. R. Howlett, *APP Transgenic Mice and their Application to Drug Discovery*, 26 HISTOLOGY & HISTOPATHOLOGY 1611 (2011).

109 *See, e.g.*, Ashish R. Pinnapureddy et al., *Large Animal Models of Rare Genetic Disorders: Sheep as Phenotypically Relevant Models of Human Genetic Disease*, 10 ORPHANET J. RARE DISEASES 107 (2015).

110 *Compare* Allyson J. Bennett, *Animal Research: The Bigger Picture and Why We Need Psychologists to Speak out*, AM. PSYCHOL. ASS'N, (Apr. 2012), http://www.apa.org/science/about/psa/2012/04/animal-research.aspx, *with Animal Testing Is Bad Science: Point/Counterpoint*, PETA, http://www.peta.org/issues/animals-used-for-experimentation/animal-testing-bad-science/ [https://perma.cc/2JLH-SAH3] (last visited Feb. 12, 2017).

111 Meg M. Sleeper et al., *Gene Therapy in Large Animal Models of Human Cardiovascular Genetic Disease*, 50 INST. FOR LABORATORY ANIMAL RES. J. 199, 200–01 (2009).

112 *Id.*

113 Nana Fan & Liangxue Lai, *Genetically Modified Pig Models for Human Diseases*, 40 J. GENETICS & GENOMICS 67 (2013).
114 Pinnapureddy et al., *supra* note 109.
115 V. Duranthon et al., *On the Emerging Role of Rabbit as Human Disease Model and the Instrumental Role of Novel Transgenic Tools*, 21 TRANSGENIC RES. 699 (2012).
116 E. J. Olivier ten Hallers et al., *The Saanen Goat as an Animal Model for Post-Laryngectomy Research: Practical Implications*, 41 LABORATORY ANIMALS 270 (2007).
117 C. W. McIlwraith et al., *The Horse as a Model of Naturally Occurring Osteoarthritis*, 1 BONE & JOINT RES. 297 (2012).
118 David T. Evans & Guido Silvestri, *Non-Human Primate Models in AIDS Research*, 8 CURRENT OPINIONS HIV & AIDS 255 (2013).
119 Li & Li, *supra* note 104, at 157.
120 Amy Harmon, *Open Season Is Seen in Gene Editing of Animals*, N.Y. TIMES, Nov. 27, 2015, at A1.
121 Kankan Wang et al., *Efficient Generation of Myostatin Mutations in Pigs Using the CRISPR/Cas9 System*, 5 SCI. REP. 16623 (2015).
122 Qingjian Zou et al., *Generation of Gene-Target Dogs Using CRISPR/Cas9 System*, 7 J. MOLECULAR CELL BIOLOGY 580 (2015).
123 *See* Alexandra C. McPherron et al., *Regulation of Skeletal Muscle Mass in Mice by a New TGF-beta Superfamily Member*, 387 NATURE 83 (1997).
124 *See generally* Dongshan Yang et al., *Effective Gene Targeting in Rabbits Using RNA-Guided Cas9 Nucleases*, 6 J. MOLECULAR CELL BIOLOGY 97 (2014).
125 *What Is Von Willebrand Disease?*, NAT'L HEART, BLOOD, & LUNG INST., http://www.nhlbi.nih.gov/health/health-topics/topics/vwd [https://perma.cc/4R7N-WC6G] (last updated June 1, 2011).
126 Tang Hai et al., *One-Step Generation of Knockout Pigs by Zygote Injection of CRISPR/Cas System*, 24 CELL RES. 372, 374 (2014).
127 *Id.* at 372.
128 *See, e.g.*, Eric W. F. W. Alton et al., *The Safety Profile of a Cationic Lipid-Mediated Cystic Fibrosis Gene Transfer Agent Following Repeated Monthly Aerosol Administration to Sheep*, 34 BIOMATERIALS 10267, 10276 (2013).
129 *See, e.g.*, Bernhardt G. Zeiher et al., A *Mouse Model for the ΔF508 Allele of Cystic Fibrosis*, 96 J. CLINICAL INVESTIGATION 2051, 2062 (1996) (introducing the most common CF-associated mutation of *CFTR* into transgenic mice without accurately replicating the CF pathology).
130 *See, e.g.*, Xingshen Sun et al., *Disease Phenotype of a Ferret CFTR-Knockout Model of Cystic Fibrosis*, 120 J. CLINICAL INVESTIGATION 3149 (2010).
131 *See, e.g.*, Zeiher et al., *supra* note 129, at 2062.
132 *See, e.g.*, Lynda S. Ostedgaard et al., *The ΔF508 Mutation Causes CFTR Misprocessing and Cystic Fibrosis–Like Disease in Pigs*, 3 SCI. TRANSLATIONAL

MED. 74ra24 (2011) (engineering pigs carrying the same mutation—ΔF508—as was done in the mouse, but observing a range of human CF pathology); Christopher S. Rogers et al., *Disruption of the CFTR Gene Produces a Model of Cystic Fibrosis in Newborn Pigs*, 321 SCIENCE 1837 (2008) (disrupting the *CFTR* gene in pigs led to development of human CF clinical manifestations).

133 *See* Huaqiang Yang et al., *Species-Dependent Neuropathology in Transgenic SOD1 Pigs*, 24 CELL RES. 464 (2014) (engineering transgenic pigs that showed nuclear accumulation and ubiquitinated nuclear aggregates in the brain, as seen in some human ALS patient brains, but not in ALS mouse models).

134 Yuyu Niu et al., *Generation of Gene-Modified Cynomolgus Monkey via Cas9/RNA-Mediated Gene Targeting in One-Cell Embryos*, 156 CELL 836 (2014).

135 Hailiang Liu et al., *TALEN-Mediated Gene Mutagenesis in Rhesus and Cynomolgus Monkeys*, 14 CELL STEM CELL 323 (2014).

136 Yongchang Chen et al., *Functional Disruption of the Dystrophin Gene in Rhesus Monkey Using CRISPR/Cas9*, 24 HUM. MOLECULAR GENETICS 3764 (2015); Yongchang Chen et al., *Germline Acquisition of Cas9/RNA-Mediated Gene Modifications in Monkeys*, 25 CELL RES. 262 (2015).

137 Haifeng Wan et al., *One-Step Generation of p53 Gene Biallelic Mutant Cynomolgus Monkey via the CRISPR/Cas System*, 25 CELL RES. 258 (2015).

138 Zhen Liu et al., *Autism-Like Behaviours and Germline Transmission in Transgenic Monkeys Overexpressing MeCP2*, 530 NATURE 98 (2016).

139 Jon H. Kaas, *The Evolution of Brains from Early Mammals to Humans*, 4 WILEY INTERDISC. REVS. 33 (2013).

140 *See Xenotransplantation*, WORLD HEALTH ORG. (May 2, 2005), http://www.who.int/transplantation/xeno/en/ [https://perma.cc/V65A-FZW5].

141 C. Rudge et al., *International Practices of Organ Donation*, 108 BRITISH J. ANAESTHESIA i48 (2012).

142 *Donation and Transplantation*, U.S. DEP'T HEALTH & HUM. SERVS., http://www.organdonor.gov/about/data.html [https://perma.cc/R77B-YBP6] (updated Mar. 31, 2015).

143 *See* Shruti Saxena, *Organ Donation: Does India Lack Will?*, INDILENS, (Aug. 7, 2014), http://indilens.com/57441-world-organ-donation-day-does-india-lack-will/ [https://perma.cc/LJM5-JPHV].

144 *See* Wang Yan, *Still Waiting*, NEWS CHINA, (July 2011), http://old.newschinamag.com/magazine/still-waiting [https://perma.cc/XM33-2PT8].

145 *See Final Numbers 2013*, INT'L REGISTRY ORGAN DONATION & TRANSPLANTATION 2 (Dec. 2014), http://www.irodat.org/img/database/pdf/IRODaT %20Newsletter%202013%20.pdf [https://perma.cc/7Q2Y-C7A7].

146 *See Map: Global Observatory on Donation and Transplantation, Global Transplantation Activities of Solid Organs, 2013*, WORLD HEALTH ORG., (2015), http://www.transplant-observatory.org/report-2013/ [https://perma.cc/4MTP-BGCU].

147 U.S. Dep't Health & Hum. Servs., *supra* note 142; *Facts and Myths*, Am. Transplant Found., http://www.americantransplantfoundation.org/about-transplant/facts-and-myths/ [https://perma.cc/4WS7-TP22] (last visited Feb. 12, 2017).

148 *Id.*

149 *See, e.g.*, L. P. Wong, *Factors Limiting Deceased Organ Donation: Focus Groups' Perspective from Culturally Diverse Community*, 42 Transplantation Proc. 1439 (2010).

150 *See* Yan, *supra* note 144.

151 *See* Saxena, *supra* note 143.

152 *See* Bruce Watson, *How Corrupt Governments Make a Killing on Human Organs*, Daily Fin. (Jan. 7, 2011), http://www.dailyfinance.com/2011/01/07/human-organ-trafficking-is-big-business-in-kosovo-china/ [https://perma.cc/ZS64-R9LC].

153 *See The Gap Continues to Widen*, U.S. Dep't Health & Hum. Servs., https://www.organdonor.gov/statistics-stories/statistics/data.html [https://perma.cc/22B7-XCYJ] (last visited Feb. 12, 2017).

154 *Id.*

155 David K. C. Cooper, *A Brief History of Cross-Species Organ Transplantation*, 25 Baylor U. Med. Ctr. Proc. 49, 51–52 (2012).

156 *Id.*

157 Muhammad M. Mohiuddin et al., *Genetically Engineered Pigs and Target-Specific Immunomodulation Provide Significant Graft Survival and Hope for Clinical Cardiac Xenotransplantation*, 148 J. Thoracic & Cardiovascular Surgery 1106 (2014).

158 Hayato Iwase et al., *Pig Kidney Graft Survival in a Baboon for 136 Days: Longest Life-Supporting Organ Graft Survival to Date*, 22 Xenotransplantation 302 (2015).

159 Luhan Yang et al., *Genome-Wide Inactivation of Porcine Endogenous Retroviruses (PERVs)*, 350 Science 1101 (2015). *See also*, Sara Reardon, *Gene-Editing Record Smashed in Pigs*, Nature (Oct. 6, 2015), http://www.nature.com/news/gene-editing-record-smashed-in-pigs-1.18525 [https://perma.cc/B379-BDKX].

160 Dong Niu et al., *Inactivation of Porcine Endogenous Retrovirus in Pigs Using CRISPR-Cas9*, 357 Science 1303 (2017).

161 *See, e.g.*, Press Release, United Therapeutics, Synthetic Genomics Inc. Signs Collaborative Research and Development Agreement with Lung Biotechnology Inc., a Subsidiary of United Therapeutics Corporation, to Develop Humanized Pig Organs to Revolutionize Transplantation Field (May 4, 2014), http://ir.unither.com/releasedetail.cfm?releaseid=845454 [https://perma.cc/C2G8-6G23] (announcing a $50 million equity investment to develop humanized pig organs); Douglas W. House, *United Therapeutics Subsidiary Expands R&D Agreement to Develop Transplant-Ready Pig Organs*, Seeking Alpha News (Sept. 22, 2015),

http://seekingalpha.com/news/2792636-united-therapeutics-subsidiary-expands-r-and-d-agreement-to-develop-transplant-ready-pig-organs [https://perma.cc/682T-UZGX] (expanding the multi-year agreement with an additional $50 million investment); *About Us*, EGENESIS, http://www.egenesisbio.com/about-us.html [https://perma.cc/KRR5-4XE5] (last visited Feb. 26, 2017).

162 *See, e.g.*, Shelly Banjo, *The Highest-Paid Woman in America Is Working on Robot Clones and Pigs with Human DNA*, QUARTZ (Mar. 16, 2015), http://qz.com/362933 [https://perma.cc/GJ95-CZX4] (reporting on America's highest-paid female and transgender executive and her goal to produce transgenic pig organs to meet the demands for human organ transplantation); Jason Koebler, *Martine Rothblatt Wants to Grow Human Organs in Pigs at This Farm*, MOTHERBOARD (June 14, 2015), http://motherboard.vice.com/read/martine-rothblatt-wants-to-grow-human-organs-in-pigs-at-this-farm [https://perma.cc/HG8M-6TTY] (describing United Therapeutics CEO's goal of building a farm where production of 100,000 lungs, hearts, and other transplantable organs can grow inside transgenic pigs by 2020).

163 David K. C. & Richard N. Pierson, *Genetically-Engineered Pig Organ Transplantation into Non-Human Primates*, GRANTOME, http://grantome.com/grant/NIH/U19-AI090959-06 [https://perma.cc/HR63-RWAN] (last visited Feb. 13, 2017).

164 Jing Yang, *Seeing the World Through Pig's Eyes: Chinese Firm to Launch Artificial Cornea*, S. CHINA MORNING POST (July 29, 2015, 7:12 PM), http://www.scmp.com/business/china-business/article/1844830/seeing-world-through-pigs-eyes-chinese-firm-launch [https://perma.cc/3LFB-G54J].

165 *Doctors Conduct 'Animal-Human' Cornea Transplant*, CHINA.ORG.CN (Dec. 22, 2015), http://www.china.org.cn/china/2015–12/22/content_37370047.htm [https://perma.cc/VH6R-VC53].

166 *See* Tianyu Lu et al., *Xenotransplantation: Current Status in Preclinical Research*, 10 FRONTIERS IN IMMUNOLOGY art. 3060 (2020).

167 *Population Projected to Reach 9.6 Billion by 2050*, U.N. DEP'T ECON. & SOC. AFF., (June 13, 2013), https://www.un.org/development/desa/en/news/population/un-report-world-population-projected-to-reach-9–6-billion-by-2050.html [https://perma.cc/3C4E-32H6].

168 Elliot M. Berry et al., *Food Security and Sustainability: Can One Exist Without the Other?*, 18 PUB. HEALTH NUTRITION 2293, 2300 (2015).

169 *Id.*

170 David Tilman et al., *Global Food Demand and the Sustainable Intensification of Agriculture*, 108 PROC. NAT'L ACAD. SCI. U.S. 20260 (2011).

171 *See, e.g.*, Anurag Chaurasia, *India Needs Home-Grown GM Food to Stop Starvation*, 529 NATURE 439 (2016).

172 *See, e.g.*, Found. on Econ. Trends v. Heckler, 756 F.2d 143, 146 (D.C. Cir. 1985) (enjoining the University of California from conducting a "deliberate release

experiment" to delay field testing of genetically altered bacteria on select crops); All. for Bio-Integrity v. Shalala, 116 F. Supp. 2d 166, 181 (D.D.C. 2000) (rejecting a challenge, brought by a coalition group of scientists and religious leaders, to the Food and Drug Administration's policy on genetically engineered foods). *Compare* Ming Zhang et al., *Long-Term Toxicity Study on Transgenic Rice with Cry1Ac and Sck Genes*, 63 FOOD & CHEMICAL TOXICOLOGY 76, 82 (2014) (concluding that insect-resistant GM rice consumption in rodents has no long-term, adverse health effects), *with* Gilles-Eric Séralini et al., *Republished Study: Long-Term Toxicity of a Roundup Herbicide and a Roundup-Tolerant Genetically Modified Maize*, 26 ENVTL. SCI. EUR. 14 (2014) (documenting a series of long-term deleterious effects, including severe hormone-dependent mammary, hepatic, and kidney disturbances, arising from consumption of GM maize treated with Roundup®—the most widely used herbicide worldwide—in rodents). *See also, e.g.*, E.C., A DECADE OF EU-FUNDED GMO RESEARCH 2001–2010, at 15–17 (2010) (compiling results from research studies on the safety of GM organisms funded by the European Union); Allison Kopicki, *Strong Support for Labeling Modified Foods*, N.Y. TIMES (July 27, 2013), http://www.nytimes.com/2013/07/28/science/strong-support-for-labeling-modified-foods.html?_r=1 [https://perma.cc/JE9Z-NGJL] (citing a *New York Times* poll that shows 93 percent of American respondents support labeling GM foods and 75 percent harbor concerns about eating GM foodstuff); *Millions March Against GM Crops*, GUARDIAN (May 25, 2013, 8:26 PM), http://www.theguardian.com/environment/2013/may/26/millions-march-against-monsanto [https://perma.cc/V9XR-HCAU] (reporting on protest rallies organized in the United States and globally against Monsanto); Lee R. Morisy, *Report on the Council for Public Health: Biomedical Engineering*, AM. MED. ASS'N (2012), https://web.archive.org/web/20120907023039/http://www.ama-assn.org/resources/doc/csaph/a12-csaph2-bioengineeredfoods.pdf [https://perma.cc/DM6U-BS2A] (recommending that mandatory labeling of GM foods is not consistent with the FDA's science-based labeling policies despite strong consumer interest in labeling); Lynne Peeples, *GMO Debate Heats up: Critics Say Biotech Industry Manipulating Genes, and Science*, HUFFINGTON POST (Sept. 21, 2012, 8:30 PM), http://www.huffingtonpost.com/2012/09/21/gmo-proposition-37-study-funding-research_n_1904535.html [https://perma.cc/6UZJ-ZY8P] (commenting on California's 2012 Proposition 37, which sought to require labeling of GM foods).

173 *See* Séralini et al., *supra* note 172 and accompanying text.

174 Matin Qaim & Shahzad Kouser, *Genetically Modified Crops and Food Security*, 8 PLOS ONE e64879 (2013).

175 Robert T. Fraley et al., *Expression of Bacterial Genes in Plant Cells*, 80 PROC. NAT'L ACAD. SCI. U.S. 4803 (1983).

176 G. Bruening and J. M. Lyons, *The Case of the FLAVR SAVR Tomato*, 54 CAL. AGRIC. 6 (2000).

177 *GM Crop Events Approved in United States of America*, ISAAA, http://www.isaaa.org/gmapprovaldatabase/approvedeventsin/default.asp?CountryID=US&Country=United%20States%20of%20America [https://perma.cc/RD7C-6WG3] (last visited Feb. 13, 2017).

178 ISAAA, 50 BIOTECH BITES 60 (International Service for the Acquisition of Agri-Biotech Applications ed., 2015), https://www.isaaa.org/resources/publications/50biotechbites /download/50_Biotech_Bites.pdf [https://perma.cc/4AF7-64FL].

179 *Id.*

180 Tilman et al., *supra* note 170.

181 Qiwei Shan et al., *Targeted Genome Modification of Crop Plants Using a CRISPR-Cas System*, 31 NATURE BIOTECHNOLOGY 686 (2013).

182 *Id.*; Zhengyan Feng et al., *Efficient Genome Editing in Plants Using a CRISPR/Cas System*, 23 CELL RES. 1229 (2013); Jin Miao et al., *Targeted Mutagenesis in Rice Using CRISPR-Cas System*, 23 CELL RES. 1233 (2013); Rong-Fang Xu et al., *Generation of Inheritable and "Transgene Clean" Targeted Genome-Modified Rice in Later Generations Using the CRISPR/Cas9 System*, 5 SCI. REP. 11491 (2015).

183 Friedrich Fauser et al., *Both CRISPR/Cas-Based Nucleases and Nickases Can Be Used Efficiently for Genome Engineering in Arabidopsis thaliana*, 79 PLANT J. 348 (2014); Feng et al., *supra* note 182, at 1229; Jian-Feng Li et al., *Multiplex and Homologous Recombination-Mediated Genome Editing in Arabidopsis and Nicotiana benthamiana Using Guide RNA and Cas9*, 31 NATURE BIOTECHNOLOGY 688 (2013).

184 Li et al., *supra* note 183, at 688–89; Vladimir Nekrasov et al., *Targeted Mutagenesis in the Model Plant Nicotiana benthamiana Using Cas9 RNA-Guided Endonuclease*, 31 NATURE BIOTECHNOLOGY 691 (2013).

185 Hongge Jia & Nian Wang, *Targeted Genome Editing of Sweet Orange Using Cas9/sgRNA*, 9 PLoS ONE e93806 (2014).

186 Wenzhi Jiang et al., *Demonstration of CRISPR/Cas9/sgRNA-Mediated Targeted Gene Modification in Arabidopsis, Tobacco, Sorghum and Rice*, 41 NUCLEIC ACIDS RES. e188 (2013).

187 Sergei Svitashev et al., *Targeted Mutagenesis, Precise Gene Editing, and Site-Specific Gene Insertion in Maize Using Cas9 and Guide RNA*, 169 PLANT PHYSIOLOGY 931 (2015); Hui-Li Xing et al., *A CRISPR/Cas9 Toolkit for Multiplex Genome Editing in Plants*, 14 BMC PLANT BIOLOGY 327 (2014).

188 Tom Lawrenson et al., *Induction of Targeted, Heritable Mutations in Barley and Brassica oleracea Using RNA-Guided Cas9 Nuclease*, 16 GENOME BIOLOGY 258 (2015).

189 *Id.*

190 Christopher Brooks et al., *Efficient Gene Editing in Tomato in the First Generation Using the CRISPR/Cas9 System*, 166 PLANT PHYSIOLOGY 1292 (2014).

191 Xianjun Sun et al., *Targeted Mutagenesis in Soybean Using the CRISPR-Cas9 System*, 5 SCI. REP. 10342 (2015).

192 Shigeo S. Sugano et al., *CRISPR/Cas9-Mediated Targeted Mutagenesis in the Liverwort Marchantia polymorpha L.*, 55 PLANT & CELL PHYSIOLOGY 475 (2014).

193 Shaohui Wang et al., *Efficient Targeted Mutagenesis in Potato by the CRISPR/Cas9 System*, 34 PLANT CELL REP. 1473 (2015).

194 Yasuhiro Ito et al., *CRISPR/Cas9-Mediated Mutagenesis of the RIN Locus That Regulates Tomato Fruit Ripening*, 467 BIOCHEMICAL & BIOPHYSICAL RES. COMM. 76 (2015).

195 Yanpeng Wang et al., *Simultaneous Editing of Three Homoeoalleles in Hexaploid Bread Wheat Confers Heritable Resistance to Powdery Mildew*, 32 NATURE BIOTECHNOLOGY 947 (2014).

196 *See, e.g.*, Press Release, Caribou Biosciences, Caribou Biosciences and DuPont Announce Strategic Alliance (Oct. 8, 2015), http://cariboubio.com/in-the-news/press-releases/caribou-biosciences-and-dupont-announce-strategic-alliance [https://perma.cc/H9CW-F5TF].

197 *Cf.* Abdul Rashid War et al., *Mechanisms of Plant Defense Against Insect Herbivores*, 7 PLANT SIGNALING & BEHAV. 1306 (2012).

198 *See, e.g.*, Lei Ma et al., *TALEN-Based Mutagenesis of Lipoxygenase LOX3 Enhances the Storage Tolerance of Rice (Oryza sativa) Seeds*, 10 PLoS ONE e0143877 (2015).

199 *Cf.* Maria Gallo & Richard Sayre, *Removing Allergens and Reducing Toxins from Food Crops*, 20 CURRENT OPINION BIOTECHNOLOGY 191 (2009) (suggesting use of earlier biotechnologies to remove or reduce allergens and toxic cyanogens from food crops); Lena Y. C. Soo et al., *Using Genome-Enabled Technologies to Address Allergens in Seeds of Crop Plants: Legumes as a Case Study*, *in* SEED DEVELOPMENT: OMICS TECHNOLOGIES TOWARD IMPROVEMENT OF SEED QUALITY AND CROP YIELD 503 (2012).

200 *See, e.g.*, Edward P. Glenn et al., *Salicornia igelovii Torr.: An Oilseed Halophyte for Seawater Irrigation*, 251 SCIENCE 1065 (1991); Stuart J. Roy et al., *Salt Resistant Crop Plants*, 26 CURRENT OPINION BIOTECHNOLOGY 115 (2014).

201 *See, e.g.*, Honghong Hu & Lizhong Xiong, *Genetic Engineering and Breeding of Drought-Resistant Crops*, 65 ANN. REV. PLANT BIOLOGY 715 (2014).

202 *See* DAN KOEPPEL, BANANA: THE FATE OF THE FRUIT THAT CHANGED THE WORLD xiv (2008) (chronicling the alarming destruction of banana plantations around the globe and current efforts to save the world's most beloved fruit); *see also* Dan Charles, *Our Favorite Banana May Be Doomed; Can New Varieties Replace It?*, NPR (Jan. 11, 2016), http://www.npr.org/sections/thesalt/2016/01/11/462375558/our-favorite-banana-may-be-doomed-can-new-varieties-replace-it [https://perma.cc/H2KE-CRTK].

203 *See, e.g.*, John Sheehan et al., *Overview of Biodiesel and Petroleum Diesel Life Cycles* 18 (1998), http://www.nrel.gov/docs/legosti/fy98/24772.pdf [https://perma.cc/8MEG-L2KU]; A. Fröhlich & B. Rice, *Evaluation of Camelina sativa Oil as a Feedstock for Biodiesel Production*, 21 INDUS. CROPS & PRODUCTS 25 (2005).

204 Bryan R. Moser, *Camelina (Camelina sativa L.) Oil as a Biofuels Feedstock: Golden Opportunity or False Hope?*, 22 LIPID TECH. 270, 273 (2010); Mark Matsunaga, Navy Looks to Biofuels to Sail the Great Green Fleet in 2016, U.S. DEP'T NAVY (July 3, 2014), http://www.navy.mil/submit/display.asp?story_id=82044 [https://perma.cc/LM3R-YAZA]; Terry Maxon, Southwest Airlines to Use Biofuels Made from 'Forest Residues' Beginning in 2016, DALLAS MORNING NEWS (Sept. 24, 2014), http://aviationblog.dallasnews.com/2014/09/southwest-airlines-to-use-biofuels-made-from-forest-residues-beginning-in-2016.html/ [https://perma.cc/K3SS-A5ZR].

205 Sheehan et al., *supra* note 203, at iii–iv.

206 *How to Feed the World in 2050*, FOOD & AGRIC. ORG. U.N. 8, http://www.fao.org/fileadmin/templates/wsfs/docs/expert_paper/How_to_Feed_the_World_in_2050.pdf [https://perma.cc/2P82-6FNK] (last visited Feb. 25, 2017).

207 According to the USDA, red meat includes beef, veal, pork, lamb, and mutton. USDA REP. 0499–0544, *National Agricultural Statistics Service, Livestock Slaughter 2014 Summary* 6 (2015).

208 *Id.* at 8.

209 USDA REP. NO. 1949–1573, *National Agricultural Statistics Service, Poultry—Production and Value 2014 Summary* 5 (2015).

210 Anthony J. McMichael et al., *Food, Livestock Production, Energy, Climate Change, and Health*, 370 LANCET 1253 (2007).

211 T. F. Randolph et al., *Role of Livestock in Human Nutrition and Health for Poverty Reduction in Developing Countries*, 85 J. ANIMAL SCI. 2788 (2007).

212 Linda L. Lowry, *Niche Markets for Natural Fibers: Strategies for Connecting Farmers Who Raise Fiber Animals with Textile Artists—A New England Perspective*, 52 J. EXTENSION 6FEA6 (2014).

213 *See, e.g.*, LEWIS FALLEY ALLEN, AMERICAN CATTLE: THEIR HISTORY, BREEDING AND MANAGEMENT 56–58 (1868).

214 *See, e.g.*, Junjie Luo et al., *Efficient Generation of Myostatin (MSTN) Biallelic Mutations in Cattle Using Zinc Finger Nucleases*, 9 PLOS ONE e95225 (2014).

215 Ravi Kambadur et al., *Mutations in Myostatin (GDF8) in Double-Muscled Belgian Blue and Piedmontese Cattle*, 7 GENOME RES. 910, 910 (1997); Alexandra C. McPherron & Se-Jin Lee, *Double Muscling in Cattle Due to Mutations in the Myostatin Gene*, 94 PROC. NAT'L ACAD. SCI. U.S. 12457 (1997).

216 Wang et al., *supra* note 121.

217 Luo et al., *supra* note 214.

218 Wei Ni et al., *Efficient Gene Knockout in Goats Using CRISPR/Cas9 System*, 9 PLoS ONE e106718 (2014).

219 M. Crispo et al., *Efficient Generation of Myostatin Knock-Out Sheep Using CRISPR/Cas9 Technology and Microinjection into Zygotes*, 10 PLoS ONE e0136690 (2015).

220 Bernadette M. Dunham, *AquAdvantage Salmon Approval Letter and Appendix*, FDA (Nov. 19, 2015), http://www.fda.gov/AnimalVeterinary/DevelopmentApprovalProcess /GeneticEngineering/GeneticallyEngineeredAnimals/ucm466214.htm [https://perma.cc/Q5ZS -QTGV].

221 *See* Andrew Pollack, *Genetically Engineered Salmon Approved for Consumption*, N.Y. Times, Nov. 20, 2015, at A1.

222 Kristin M. Whitworth et al., *Gene Edited Pigs Are Protected from Porcine Reproductive and Respiratory Syndrome Virus*, 34 Nature Biotechnology 20 (2016).

223 Simon G. Lillico et al., *Live Pigs Produced from Genome Edited Zygotes*, 3 Sci. Rep. 2847 (2013).

224 Paul Wigley et al., *In Vivo and in Vitro Studies of Genetic Resistance to Systemic Salmonellosis in the Chicken Encoded by the SAL1 Locus*, 4 Microbes & Infection 1111 (2002).

225 *C.f., e.g.*, Elizabeth Weise, *Salmonella Outbreaks Lead to Food-Safety Changes*, USA Today (Apr. 2, 2009), http://usatoday30.usatoday.com/news/health/2009–04-01-nuts-salmonella-food-safety_N.htm [https://perma.cc /WQ75-N32G] (reporting on food-related salmonella outbreaks that caused millions of dollars in economic losses).

226 Fibroblast growth factor 5.

227 Xiaolong Wang et al., *Generation of Gene-Modified Goats Targeting MSTN and FGF5 via Zygote Injection of CRISPR/Cas9 System*, 5 Sci. Rep. 13878 (2015).

228 *See, e.g.*, Xu Liu et al., *Generation of Mastitis Resistance in Cows by Targeting Human Lysozyme Gene to β-Casein Locus Using Zinc-Finger Nucleases*, 81 Proc. Royal Soc. B 20133368 (2014); Xu Liu et al., *Zinc-Finger Nickase-Mediated Insertion of the Lysostaphin Gene into the Beta-Casein Locus in Cloned Cows*, 4 Nature Commc'ns 2565 (2013) (generating gene-edited cows—though via a transgene—with the ability to secrete milk that kills Staphylococcus aureus bacteria).

229 Wenfang Tan et al., *Efficient Nonmeiotic Allele Introgression in Livestock Using Custom Endonucleases*, 110 Proc. Nat'l Acad. Sci. U.S. 16526 (2013).

230 A flurry of patent applications has followed many of the scientific findings discussed throughout this paper. *See, e.g.*, Hornless Livestock, U.S. Patent Application No. 14/154,906 (filed Jan. 14, 2014); Control of Sexual Maturation in Animals, U.S. Patent Application No. 13/067,502 (filed Oct. 30, 2013); Genetically Edited Animal, U.S. Patent Application No. 14/427,776 (filed Mar. 1, 2013).

231 Puping Liang et al., *CRISPR/Cas9-Mediated Gene Editing in Human Tripronuclear Zygotes*, 6 PROTEIN & CELL 363 (2015).
232 *Id.* at 366–67.
233 *Id.*
234 *Id.* at 368.
235 *Compare, e.g.*, Benjamin P. Kleinstiver et al., *Engineered CRISPR-Cas9 Nucleases with Altered PAM Specificities*, 523 NATURE 481 (2015) (improving DNA target specificity by a variant Cas9 that reduces off-target effects), *with* Yanfang Fu et al., *High-Frequency Off-Target Mutagenesis Induced by CRISPR-Cas Nucleases in Human Cells*, 31 NATURE BIOTECHNOLOGY 822 (2013) (reporting high frequency of off-target mutations using an older version of the CRISPR system).
236 Jocelyn Kaiser & Dennis Normile, *Embryo Engineering Study Splits Scientific Community*, 348 SCIENCE 486, 487 (2015).
237 *Id.* Not a single study coming out of Junjiu Huang's laboratory in Sun Yat-sen University, Guangzhou, China describes the use of CRISPR-Cas9 predating the tripronuclear zygote study published in *Protein & Cell*, suggesting the investigation marked the first time the laboratory had worked with CRISPR-Cas9. *See Junjiu Huang*, PUBMED.GOV, http://www.ncbi.nlm.nih.gov/pubmed/?term=junjiu+huang[author] [https://perma.cc/5HNF-3MFE] (last visited Feb. 13, 2019).
238 *See, e.g.*, Jean-Baptiste Renaud et al., *Improved Genome Editing Efficiency and Flexibility Using Modified Oligonucleotides with TALEN and CRISPR-Cas9 Nucleases*, 14 CELL REP. 1 (2016).
239 Liang et al., *supra* note 231, at 364–66.
240 Kaiser & Normile, *supra* note 236, at 486. Neither *Nature* nor *Science* confirmed the review or rejection of the manuscript. *Id.* at 487.
241 *See* Edward Lanphier et al., *Don't Edit the Human Germ Line*, 519 NATURE 410 (2015).
242 David Baltimore et al., *A Prudent Path Forward for Genomic Engineering and Germline Gene Modification*, 348 SCIENCE 36 (2015).
243 *See generally* RUTH DEECH & ANNA SMAJDOR, FROM IVF TO IMMORTALITY: CONTROVERSY IN THE ERA OF REPRODUCTIVE TECHNOLOGY (2007).
244 K. H. S. Campbell et al., *Sheep Cloned by Nuclear Transfer from a Cultured Cell Line*, 380 NATURE 64 (1996).
245 *See, e.g.*, Sophie Hutchinson, *Controversy and the Cloning Race*, BBC NEWS (Jan. 17, 2004), http://news.bbc.co.uk/2/hi/uk_news/3406027.stm [https://perma.cc/2X93-WHF9]; Michael Cook, *A Decade of Debate over Dolly*, MERCATORNET (Feb. 27, 2007), http://www.mercatornet.com/articles/view/a_decade_of_debate_over_dolly/1479 [https://perma.cc/7628-ZDLR].
246 *Public Interest Group Calls for Strengthening Global Policies Against Human Germline Modification*, CTR. GENETICS & SOC'Y (Apr. 22, 2015), http://www.geneticsandsociety.org/article.php?id=8528 [https://perma.cc/QM3N-DD54].

247 Kaiser & Normile, *supra* note 236, at 486.

248 Nicholas Wade, *Scientists Seek Ban on Method of Editing the Human Genome*, N.Y. TIMES, Mar. 20, 2015, at A1.

249 *Id.*

250 Nicholas Wade, *Scientists Seek Moratorium on Edits to Human Genome That Could Be Inherited*, N.Y. TIMES, Dec. 3, 2015, at A1.

251 Ewen Callaway, *Embryo Editing Gets Green Light*, 530 NATURE 18 (2016).

252 *See* Angelina Jolie, *My Medical Choice*, N.Y. TIMES, May 14, 2013, at A25.

253 *See* Angelina Jolie Pitt, *Diary of a Surgery*, N.Y. TIMES, Mar. 24, 2015, at A23.

254 Prostate cancer was the third most common type of cancer in the United States in 2016, causing an estimated 26,120 deaths. *SEER Stat Fact Sheets: Prostate Cancer*, NAT'L CANCER INST., http://seer.cancer.gov/statfacts/html/prost.html [https://perma.cc/LN6M-QNLB] (last visited Feb. 14, 2017).

255 An estimated 8,720 new cases of testicular cancer were reported in 2016. *SEER Stat Fact Sheets: Testis Cancer*, NAT'L CANCER INST., http://seer.cancer.gov/statfacts/html/testis.html [https://perma.cc/NKW2-VZEJ] (last visited Feb. 14, 2017).

256 *See Cancer: Fact Sheet No.* 297, WORLD HEALTH ORG. (Feb. 2015), http://www.who.int/mediacentre/factsheets/fs297/en/ [https://perma.cc/A6J3-KLQD]. In 2012, approximately 14 million new cases of cancer and 8.2 million cancer-related deaths were reported worldwide. *Id.*

257 *See id.*

258 *See, e.g.*, Cook, *supra* note 245 (commenting on the media's perception that cloning research might give rise to "armies of Adolf Hitlers"); Robert Pollack, *Eugenics Lurk in the Shadow of CRISPR*, 348 SCIENCE 871 (2015) (analogizing the introduction of germline modification with a return to an agenda of eugenics that aims to select "good" traits and weed out "bad" ones).

259 *See, e.g.*, Antonio Regalado, *Engineering the Perfect Baby*, MIT TECH. REV. (Mar. 5, 2015), https://www.technologyreview.com/s/535661/engineering-the-perfect-baby/ [https://perma.cc/G46W-BQ3N].

260 *See, e.g.*, Lanphier et al, *supra* note 241, at 410 (providing a pulpit to Sangamo BioSciences executives from which to argue that germline, but not somatic, genome editing should be banned). Sangamo BioSciences holds key patents in ZFN technology directed at somatic cell editing. Newer CRISPR-based technologies could negatively impact Sangamo's business strategies. *Id.*

261 *See, e.g.*, HyunJun Kang et al., *CCR5 Disruption in Induced Pluripotent Stem Cells Using CRISPR/Cas9 Provides Selective Resistance of Immune Cells to CCR5-tropic HIV-1 Virus*, 4 MOLECULAR THERAPY NUCLEIC ACIDS e268 (2015).

262 *See, e.g.*, Kristin M. Whitworth et al., *Gene-Edited Pigs Are Protected from Porcine Reproductive and Respiratory Syndrome Virus*, 34 NATURE BIOTECHNOLOGY 20 (2016).

263 *See, e.g.*, Yang et al., *supra* note 159, at 1101; Niu et al., *supra* note 160, at 1303.

264 Erik De Clercq & Guangdi Li, *Approved Antiviral Drugs over the Past 50 Years*, 29 Clinical Microbiology Reviews 695, 732 (2016).

265 *See, e.g.*, Zhong Zou et al., *Construction of a Highly Efficient CRISPR/Cas9-Mediated Duck Enteritis Virus-Based Vaccine Against H5N1 Avian Influenza Virus and Duck Tembusu Virus Infection*, 7 Scientific Reports Art. No. 1478 (2017).

266 *See* World Health Organization, Statement on the Second Meeting of the International Health Regulations (2005) Emergency Committee Regarding the Outbreak of Novel Coronavirus (2019-nCoV), Jan. 30, 2020, https://www.who.int/news-room/detail/30–01-2020-statement-on-the-second-meeting-of-the-international-health-regulations-(2005)-emergency-committee-regarding-the-outbreak-of-novel-coronavirus-(2019-ncov).

267 *See* World Health Organization, WHO Director-General's Opening Remarks at the Media Briefing on COVID-19 – 11 March 2020, Mar. 11, 2020, https://www.who.int/dg/speeches/detail/who-director-general-s-opening-remarks-at-the-media-briefing-on-covid-19–11-march-2020.

268 *See An Incalculable Loss*, N.Y. Times (May 27, 2020), https://www.nytimes.com/interactive/2020/05/24/us/us-coronavirus-deaths-100000.html.

269 *See* Worldometer, *Coronavirus Death Toll*, last visited May 31, 2020, available at https://www.worldometers.info/coronavirus/coronavirus-death-toll/.

270 *See* Worldometer, *Coronavirus Cases*, last visited May 31, 2020, available at https://www.worldometers.info/coronavirus/coronavirus-cases/.

271 *See* Timothy R. Abbott et al., *Development of CRISPR as an Antiviral Strategy to Combat SARS-CoV-2 and Influenza*, 181 Cell 865 (2020).

272 *See* Catherine A. Freije et al., *Programmable Inhibition and Detection of RNA Viruses Using Cas13*, 76 Molecular Cell 826 (2019).

273 *See* Jonathan S. Gootenberg et al., *Nucleic Acid Detection with CRISPR-Cas13a/C2c2*, 356 Science 438 (2017).

274 *See* James P. Broughton et al., *CRISPR–Cas12-Based Detection of SARS-CoV-2*, 38 Nature Biotechnology 870 (2020), https://www.nature.com/articles/s41587-020–0513-4.

275 *See* Julia Joung et al., *Point-of-Care Testing for COVID-19 Using SHERLOCK Diagnostics*, MedRxiv (May 8, 2020), https://www.medrxiv.org/content/10.1101/2020.05.04.20091231v1.full.pdf+html.

276 *See* Sherlock Biosciences, *Sherlock Biosciences Receives FDA Emergency Use Authorization for CRISPR SARS-CoV-2 Rapid Diagnostic* (May 7, 2020), https://sherlock.bio/sherlock-biosciences-receives-fda-emergency-use-authorization-for-crispr-sars-cov-2-rapid-diagnostic/.

277 Paul Enríquez, *Epigenome Editing in* Chromatin and Epigenetics 146 (2020).

278 *See Histone/Histones*, Scitable, https://www.nature.com/scitable/definition/histones-57/ (last visited May 20, 2020).

279 *See* Paul Enríquez, *CRISPR-Mediated Epigenome Editing*, 89 Yale J. Biology & Med. 471 (2016).

280 *See* Seth L. Shipman et al., *CRISPR–Cas Encoding of a Digital Movie into the Genomes of a Population of Living Bacteria*, 547 Nature 345 (2017).

281 Eadweard Muybridge, Animal Locomotion: An Electro-Photographic Investigation of Consecutive Phases of Animal Movements. 1872–1885, Plate 626 Animals and Movements, Horses, *Gallop, Thoroughbred Bay Mare, Annie G.* (1887). The image used to encode the motion picture into the bacterial living cells can be accessed at https://www.loc.gov/pictures/resource/cph.3b00681/.

282 *See, e.g.*, David Bikard et al., *Exploiting CRISPR-Cas Nucleases to Produce Sequence-Specific Antimicrobials*, 32 Nature Biotechnology 1146 (2014); Robert J. Citorik et al., *Sequence-Specific Antimicrobials Using Efficiently Delivered RNA-Guided Nucleases*, 32 Nature Biotechnology 1141 (2014); Ido Yosef et al., *Temperate and Lytic Bacteriophages Programmed to Sensitize and Kill Antibiotic-Resistant Bacteria*, 112 Proc. Nat'l Acad. Sci. U.S. 7267 (2015); Kotaro Kiga et al., *Development of CRISPR-Cas13a-based antimicrobials capable of Sequence-Specific Killing of Target Bacteria*, 11 Nature Commc'ns Art. 2934 (2020). Some concerns of biosecurity and bioterrorism have been associated with applications of CRISPR-based biotechnologies such as gene drives. *See, e.g.*, Kozminski, *supra* note 67, at 3896–97; Rhodi Lee, *Government Experts Concerned About Possible Bioterrorism Using GM Organisms*, Tech Times (Aug. 5, 2015), http://www.techtimes.com/articles/74121/20150805/government-experts-concerned-about-possible-bioterrorism-using-gm-organisms.htm [https://perma.cc/PY3Y-WN3B]; Webber et al., *supra* note 67, at 10565–67. Similar concerns may be raised in the future regarding the ability to manipulate deadly bacteria and viruses. *See* Catherine Jefferson et al., *Synthetic Biology and Biosecurity: How Scared Should We Be?*, King's College London 1, 9 (2014), http://www.kcl.ac.uk/newsevents/news/newsrecords/docs/Jefferson-et-al-2014-Synthetic-Biology-and-Biosecurity.pdf [https://perma.cc/5WHA-YTXX] (recounting how anthrax was used as a bioweapon during the attacks of September 11, 2001).

283 *See, e.g.*, Junwei Shi et al., *Discovery of Cancer Drug Targets by CRISPR-Cas9 Screening of Protein Domains*, 33 Nature Biotechnology 661 (2015).

284 *See, e.g.*, Alan S.L. Wong et al., *Multiplexed Barcoded CRISPR-Cas9 Screening Enabled by CombiGEM*, 113 Proc. Nat'l Acad. Sci. U.S. 2544 (2016).

285 *See, e.g.*, Baohui Chen et al., *Dynamic Imaging of Genomic Loci in Living Human Cells by an Optimized CRISPR/Cas System*, 155 Cell 1479 (2013).

286 *See, e.g.*, Aaron McKenna et al., *Whole Organism Lineage Tracing by Combinatorial and Cumulative Genome Editing*, 353 Science aaf7907 (2016).

287 *See, e.g.*, Andrew B. Lane et al., *Enzymatically Generated CRISPR Libraries for Genome Labeling and Screening*, 34 Developmental Cell 373 (2015).

288 *See* Michael M. Kaminski et al., *A CRISPR-Based Assay for the Detection of Opportunistic Infections Post-Transplantation and for the Monitoring of Transplant Rejection*, 4 Nature Biomedical Engineering 601 (2020).

289 *See, e.g.*, Miles W. Gander et al., *Digital Logic Circuits in Yeast with CRISPR-dCas9 NOR Gates*, 8 Nature Commc'ns Art. 15459 (2017).

290 *See* Hyojim Kim et al., *A CRISPR/Cas9-based central processing unit to Program Complex Logic Computation in Human Cells*, 116 Proc. Nat'l Acad. Sci. U.S. 7214 (2019).

291 *See, e.g.*, Lukas E. Dow et al., *Inducible in Vivo Genome Editing with CRISPR-Cas9*, 33 Nature Biotechnology 390 (2015) (describing a tool for inducible genome editing); Luke A. Gilbert et al., *CRISPR-Mediated Modular RNA-Guided Regulation of Transcription in Eukaryotes*, 154 Cell 442 (2013) (introducing a platform to regulate transcriptional activation or repression in cells); Andrew A. Horwitz et al., *Efficient Multiplexed Integration of Synergistic Alleles and Metabolic Pathways in Yeasts via CRISPR-Cas*, 1 Cell Sys. 88 (2015) (explaining a technique to promote identification of biosynthetic pathways); Silvana Konermann et al., *Optical Control of Mammalian Endogenous Transcription and Epigenetic States*, 500 Nature 472 (2013) (establishing a method for the optogenetic control of epigenetic chromatin modifications); Morgan L. Maeder et al., *Targeted DNA Demethylation and Activation of Endogenous Genes Using Programmable TALE-TET1 Fusion Proteins*, 31 Nature Biotechnology 1137 (2013) (exploring targeted demethylation and its functional significance in cells); Lei S. Qi et al., *Repurposing CRISPR as an RNA-Guided Platform for Sequence-Specific Control of Gene Expression*, 152 Cell 1173 (2013) (introducing a platform to regulate transcriptional activation or repression in cells); Owen W. Ryan et al., *Selection of Chromosomal DNA Libraries Using a Multiplex CRISPR System*, 3 eLife 03703 (2014) (developing a CRISPR-based approach to facilitate directed evolution of biomolecules); Yuexin Zhou et al., *High-Throughput Screening of a CRISPR/Cas9 Library for Functional Genomics in Human Cells*, 509 Nature 487 (2014) (unveiling a large-scale genetic library screen for functional genomics).

6

Redesigning Food

Millions of years ago, world history changed course when our hominid ancestors concocted the Oldowan toolkit. Now, for the first time in the history of civilization, humans have developed another set of specialized tools. Only this time, the tools bring the previously unimaginable prospect of changing the very essence of life—by making intended modifications at specific sites of any organism's genome—within the realm of possibility. The discovery of highly precise and programmable enzymes that function as macromolecular machines capable of shearing DNA has made that feat possible and is democratizing scientists' access to new tools requisite for uncovering future significant medical and scientific advances. At the same time, the emerging technology in the realm of genome editing is challenging long-held conventions of how humans view life and the incipient power to control and alter the genetic destiny of every living creature.

More than four decades have passed since the era of recombinant DNA gave rise to modern biotechnology. During that time, humans have innovated ways to address complex challenges in fields ranging from synthetic biology to medicine and agriculture. The impact of biotechnology on agriculture, for example, has been remarkable.[1] Today, agrobiotechnology is tackling broad issues such as improving human health and nutrition,[2] as well as feeding an ever-increasing world population.[3]

Feeding the world and achieving food security have become major goals of biotechnology, and with good reason. The United Nations estimates that the world population will rise from nearly seven billion to approximately ten billion in the next thirty years.[4] Global crop demand is expected to more than double.[5] Limited arable land and water available for irrigation will pose great impediments in global efforts to foster food security.[6]

To confront the challenges of transforming global agriculture and improving crop yields, scientists have devised ways of using biotechnology to manipulate the genetic material of crop plants to engineer pest, chemical, and drought resistance, improve nutritional content, optimize yields, and minimize the adverse effects of suboptimal environmental conditions.[7]

Unfortunately, good intentions and finite scientific knowledge often translate into imperfect technologies. Early attempts to address modern agricultural problems involved the use of traditional breeding coupled with artificial selection—an often tedious and laborious combination of methods—and what is now known as transgenesis, a process that refers to the artificial introduction of genetic material—namely, transgenic[8] DNA—from one organism into the genome of another unrelated organism. Remarkably, scientists proved that the latter approach could be used to create pest-resistant,[9] drought-tolerant,[10] herbicide-resistant,[11] and other varieties of plants to ameliorate agricultural challenges through biotechnological innovation.

Notwithstanding the scientific progress, the practice of adjoining native and foreign DNAs generated controversy and opposition to genetic engineering. A primary objection has been that genetic modification of living organisms is "unnatural" and, therefore, in some sense, wrong.[12] Some opponents of modern genetic modification techniques have conjured up parallels to *Frankenstein; or, the Modern Prometheus*,[13] the famed fictional novel.[14] Despite the lack of logical resemblance, such flawed comparisons have permeated social discourse surrounding genetic engineering. Public perceptions of genetically modified organisms (GMOs) have become so distorted that foods derived from genetically modified (GM) crops are frequently referred to as "Frankenfoods."[15] Some opponents of genetic engineering "have [even] likened [an] inevitable backlash of GMO technology to the destruction and muderous [sic] rampage of Frankenstein's monster."[16] It is no surprise that the use of genetically modified organisms in agriculture has become one of the most controversial and impassioned topics in modern times.

I A COORDINATED FRAMEWORK

While the use of biotechnology for agricultural purposes has been the subject of scientific research for decades, CRISPR biotechnologies mark a new turning point in the current GMO narrative. CRISPR-based genome editing technologies and their progeny are poised to raise challenging problems that our legal system will be forced to address sooner rather than later. The current GM crop regulatory scheme in the United States—namely, the 1986 Coordinated Framework for the Regulation of Biotechnology (Coordinated Framework)[17]—is largely limited in scope by older genetic engineering methods that rely on recombinant DNA technology. Specifically, the regulatory calculus focuses heavily on the introduction of transgenic DNA, from foreign organisms—such as viruses or bacteria that may be considered plant pests under current law—into GM crops by virtue of human intervention.

At the time the Coordinated Framework went into effect, it would have been impossible for scientists—let alone law and policy makers—to predict all of the technologies by which humans are now able to alter the genetic composition of whole organisms at will. The scientific research and industry communities have, for some time, expressed discontent with the status quo, and calls for the modernization of the Coordinated Framework have grown louder by the day. To answer those calls, the Obama Administration launched an initiative to modernize the Coordinated Framework.[18] The Executive Branch's directive to modernize the US regulatory system for biotechnology aimed to improve transparency, efficiency, predictability, and public confidence in the federal government's ability to develop sound health and environmental policy.

The September 2016 National Strategy for Modernizing the Regulatory System for Biotechnology Products and the January 2017 Update to the Coordinated Framework for the Regulation of Biotechnology led to several recommendations to clarify federal regulatory policies related to agricultural biotechnology. The Trump Administration continued to build upon those recommendations by issuing directives to promote innovation in agrobiotechnology and encourage increased coordination among regulatory agencies with overlapping jurisdictions.[19] In 2019, an Executive Order spelled out the federal government's policy "to protect public health and the environment by adopting regulatory approaches for the products of agricultural biotechnology that are proportionate responses to the risks such products pose, and … avoid arbitrary or unjustifiable distinctions across like products developed through different technologies."[20] The directive mandates that regulatory decisions on agricultural biotechnology products be based "on scientific and technical evidence, and take into account, as appropriate and consistent with applicable law, economic factors."[21]

To understand the need for an overhaul of the current regulatory scheme, an understanding of how the system discriminates between products in terms of risk and process is essential. A high degree of dissonance exists between the ways in which GM crops derived through recombinant DNA technology are regulated relative to those derived through conventional hybridization and plant breeding methods.

On one hand, GM crops developed through nonrecombinant DNA techniques—for example, intergeneric hybridization, induced mutagenesis, and other techniques that we will discuss in this chapter—for cross-breeding *unrelated*[22] crop species or exposing crops to mutagens are largely overlooked under the Coordinated Framework. This lack of regulatory oversight exists despite the fact that genetic modifications in many nonrecombinant DNA crops are, in theory, more likely to result in significant reshuffling of parental genes,[23] which can lead to unexpected phenotypic or compositional changes in GM food.

On the other hand, GM crops developed with recombinant DNA technology, using either *unrelated* or *related* crop species, trigger immediate regulatory scrutiny because, despite being more precise than nonrecombinant methods, the techniques used to introduce DNA could, in theory, also lead to unexpected phenotypic or compositional changes in GM food.

Three decades of scientific research suggest that present-day controversies surrounding GM crops and food are not grounded in scientific fact. A scientific consensus has now formed to support that proposition. From a strict risk-based standpoint, it seems logical that some level of deregulation of GM crops should proceed. Indeed, many in the scientific community have argued on behalf of a risk-based approach to replace the current process-based approach to biotechnology.[24]

The Executive Branch's directive to modernize the US regulatory system for biotechnology coupled with findings in the most recent report by the National Academies of Sciences, Engineering, and Medicine (NASEM) on the status of GM crops suggest that the future regulatory landscape for GM crops will be less restrictive than its current incarnation. However, if the new approach to biotechnology is risk-based, how will CRISPR-mediated genome-edited crops be regulated? In the near future, it will likely be increasingly cumbersome to make meaningful and enforceable regulatory distinctions between genome-edited and naturally occurring crops. Blurring the lines that mark what is natural or not is likely to challenge the very essence of what constitutes a GMO. And, if that is the effect of technological advances in genome editing, should the law regulate CRISPR GM crops at all?

II MAPPING THE ROAD AHEAD

Chapters 6 and 7 explore some of the complex issues raised by new genome-editing technologies—particularly CRISPR-based genome editing—on the legal status of GMOs.

Before we embark on a discussion of law and policy, however, it is imperative to frame that discussion within the bounds of scientific facts, so that the discussion will be productive. Accordingly, this chapter provides an overview of GMOs and how humans have manipulated living organisms to fit their needs since the dawn of civilization. It introduces evidence of domestication-induced crop genetic modification over the past few millennia to point out that arguments that humans ought not to interfere with nature's course have little merit. We will also discuss key scientific discoveries that ushered in the age of evolutionary and molecular biology, which collectively sparked an agricultural transformation that led to global commercialization of the first GM crops.

This chapter will also guide you through a detailed account of numerous techniques used by scientists to make a GMO. It intentionally divides methods to produce GMOs in two categories: (1) nonrecombinant DNA methods, which often rely on artificial selection of desirable plant traits, and (2) genetic engineering methods, which depend on recombinant DNA technologies. Importantly, this chapter examines the advantages, limitations, and potential risks associated with each technique, and airs common misperceptions concerning the false natural status often ascribed to nonrecombinant DNA methods.

Importantly, this chapter also examines the controversies generated by GMOs over the past two decades and anchors the discussion under the framework of a jurisprudence of scientific empiricism.[25] This theoretical foundation is critical to properly address rising legal and policy questions related to GMOs that are firmly grounded in reason and scientific facts. Accordingly, we will undertake a comprehensive examination of the current state of the primary scientific literature related to the potential health and environmental concerns surrounding GMO biotechnology. The primary goal is to give you, the reader, a succinct resource to render dense scientific information accessible and to share that information with law and policy makers.

As part of our conversation, we will analyze the distinct rationales behind fervid opposition to GMOs, which have contributed to making regulation of GMO biotechnologies a "global problem."[26] Evidence suggests that opposition to GMOs is not exclusively related to technological aversion on ethical, health, or environmental grounds, but centers on economic, financial, and political concerns instead.

Consider, for instance, Scotland's 2015 ban on GMOs. The Scotland Rural Affairs Secretary indicated, at the time, that the impetus behind the ban was to "protect and further enhance [the country's] clean, green status."[27] The Cabinet Secretary was concerned that allowing cultivation of GM crops in Scotland "would damage [its] clean and green brand, thereby gambling with the future of [the country's] £14 billion food and drink sector," which "attracts a premium price" around the world based on a perception of being natural and of high quality. Critics point out that potential consumer backlash and a desire to preserve an image of producing high-quality goods, as opposed to scientific facts, are the primary factors behind Scotland's decision to ban GMOs.[28] Similarly, some have argued that the European Commission's opposition to GMOs has been based on "blatant trade protectionism," and that European Union (EU) policies have influenced developing countries in Africa to oppose GMOs for fear of trade restrictions to EU markets.[29]

As a result, many opponents of GMO technologies have been criticized as hypocritical.[30] For instance, although a majority of European countries currently ban production of GM crops, Europe "imports over 30 million tons" of corn and soy-based animal feed every year—mostly derived from GM crops—for its livestock industry because they are cheaper than non-GM crops.[31]

It is interesting to note—although we need not dive into a detailed exposition for purposes of this chapter—the geographical dissonance between the United States and the European Union when it comes to GM crops and global climate change. Although a scientific consensus has formed to support both the safety of GM crops and the anthropogenic contributions to global climate change, the US and the EU have different general approaches to these issues.[32] The EU has seemingly chosen to embrace scientific evidence and lead the world in progressive climate policies, but often blatantly ignores scientific evidence vis-à-vis GM crops.[33] In contrast, the US takes a more liberal approach to cultivation and consumption of GM crops, but frequently ignores the scientific consensus on the dangers posed by global climate change, and has failed to address global climate change at the federal level.[34]

III GENETICALLY MODIFIED ORGANISMS

The term genetically modified organism, colloquially known as GMO, refers broadly to any living organism comprising artificially altered genetic material, which is intended to produce a desired phenotype (trait).[35] On occasion, other terms, such as living modified organism (LMO)[36] or genetically engineered organism (GEO),[37] have been used to refer to the same concept, but none have become as pervasive as GMO.[38] Although many definitions do not specify the type of species encompassed by GMO, the term is applicable to microbes, fungi, plants, and animals, but not human beings.[39]

The striking diversity of microbes,[40] fungi,[41] plants,[42] and animals[43] amenable to genetic manipulation has facilitated the evolution of a wide range of connotations elicited by the term GMO in different biotechnological contexts. A common thread, however, is the notion that GMOs can be used in the production of genetically modified food[44] intended for human consumption.[45] Accordingly, it is no surprise that many GMOs have collectively made their way into our food supply[46] as humans have availed themselves of myriad living organisms on Earth for agriculture and food-processing purposes.

Thus, in the case of plants, which are the focus of this chapter,[47] the manipulation of GM crops through biotechnology seeks to improve agricultural practices and outcomes in any number of ways,[48] such as by conferring pest and chemical resistance, enhancing nutritional content, reducing susceptibility to disease, increasing tolerance to drought and other suboptimal environmental conditions, optimizing yields, improving storage tolerance, and more.[49]

A *Domestication to Tame the Wild*

From times immemorial, humans have utilized domestication as a strategy for altering, taming, or influencing wild living organisms to suit particular needs. The transition of ancient wolves into domestic dogs, for example, is thought to date as far back as 33,000 years ago.[50] Breeding and nonnatural selection[51] of docile behavior—and other traits—eventually led to striking genetic changes,[52] critical for domestication,[53] that facilitated the evolution of wolves into an entirely novel species;[54] one which did not naturally occur, and would not exist today, but for human intervention.

From an evolutionary standpoint, domestication has proven to be remarkable. It can exert substantial pressure to induce rapid phenotypic evolution that yields great variation from a limited genetic pool.[55] What was done with the wolf is not a unique historical or anthropological anomaly. Roughly 10,000 years ago, domestication of all major crop plants occurred through ancient agricultural practices,[56] which led to allele fixation of desired agronomic traits over the span of several hundred years.[57]

Among the first crops to undergo artificial, or nonnatural, selection[58] resulting in genetic alterations was a domesticated version of the wild Mexican grass Balsas teosinte, the progenitor of modern-day maize (corn).[59] Molecular evidence demonstrates that maize and teosinte are strikingly similar. Indeed, they share identical centromere positions and chromosome arm lengths.[60] They also possess an equal number of chromosomes and knobs at the same chromosomal positions, which occur at similar frequencies. Furthermore, modern maize varieties can be crossed with teosinte to form hybrids that exhibit complete chromosomal pairing and fertility.

Despite their genetic similitude, maize and teosinte are not only drastically different in appearance, but also in terms of utility. For instance, the teosinte ear (Figure 6.1) features between five and twelve kernels, each tightly sealed in a stony casing that is impervious to the digestive tract environment of birds and mammals.[61] In contrast, the maize ear bears over 500 naked kernels that are easily digested by any animal that ingests them.[62] These and other significant differences between maize and teosinte have been empirically linked to a mere five genes.[63] Thus, maize is a vivid illustration of the principle that few naturally occurring mutations, derived through artificial selection of rare and desirable characteristics, can exert combinatorial effects that account for a wide array of seemingly complex phenotypes.[64]

More importantly, although the transformation of modern crops from their ancient progenitors is thought to have occurred within a period of several hundreds of years,[65] our current understanding of systematic breeding practices followed by artificial selection has revealed that such drastic genetic transformations can successfully take place within just a few generations. For instance, artificial selection in dog breeds—namely, the systematic breeding practices involving crosses between different breeds, followed by selection of specific traits—over the past 200 years is primarily responsible for the dramatic diversification of traits—body size, coat color, hair texture, etc.—observed in modern canines.[66]

Other crops have undergone similar artificial selection in their path toward domestication. Modern-day wheat (*Triticum aestivum*) originates from the hybridization of a wild wheat grass (*Aegilops tauschii*) and an ancient tetraploid[67] wheat hybrid (*Tritricum turgidum*),[68] which led to the creation of the vastly popular hexaploid wheat species[69] that are produced and consumed all over the world today.[70] Rice, arguably the world's most important crop to human nutrition and caloric intake,[71] has experienced drastic transformations. Wild rice species often display long awns and severe shattering, which are important for seed dispersal.[72] In contrast, domestic rice species have evolved to contain short awns, if any, and reduced shattering, thereby resulting in maximum seed count for harvesting.[73]

Human-dependent selection has not been limited to grain crops throughout history. The wild progenitors of present-day tomatoes (Figure 6.1) had very small fruit designed for species propagation rather than human consumption.[74] However, artificial selection of large fruit size and shape transformed the wild species, once endogenous to the South American Andes, into today's prized tomato cultivars.[75]

FIGURE 6.1 Human-induced evolution of crops via artificial selection

Juxtaposition of select crops genetically modified through artificial selection and their unmodified wild progenitors. (A) Fruit of wild bananas (left) featuring large and hard seeds compared to the cultivated Cavendish banana (right), the most popular fruit in the world. (B) Fruit of domesticated tomatoes (left) relative to the fruit of their wild progenitors (right). (C) Wild strawberry fruit (left) and modern, cultivated strawberry fruit (right). (D) Fruit of a domestic eggplant cultivar (left) and the small, bitter fruit from its wild progenitor species (right). (E) The evolution of modern-day maize (corn) cobs and kernels from teosinte, maize's wild ancestor. The figure contrasts the ears of teosinte (left), a teosinte-maize hybrid (middle), and domestic maize (right).

The modern strawberry (Figure 6.1) was derived from hybrids between two octoploid Native American species that were subsequently selected for fruit size and firmness.[76] Numerous similar fates have been reported for the evolution of other fruits and crops (see, for example, Figure 6.1), including the potato,[77] banana,[78] broccoli,[79] and a vast list of others,[80] all of which have been selected for size, taste, shape, nutritional content, and a variety of other desirable agronomic traits.

The evolution—from wild ancestor to domestic progeny—of various agriculturally important crops sheds light on the crucial role that artificial selection driven by humans has played in the development of agriculture. The overwhelming evidence related to domestication-induced genetic modification of crops, which has accrued over the past few millennia, provides strong support against arguments that humans ought not to interfere with nature's course. Without human intervention, none of these important crops, which collectively feed the world, would exist today. Indeed, human intervention is vital for the survival of many of today's staple crops, which could not grow and reproduce in the wild without human assistance.[81]

B *The Age of Molecular Manipulation*

For millennia, genetic modification of organisms via domestication constituted the primary method of manipulating the genetic composition of crop plants. That all changed with the dawn of the age of evolutionary and molecular biology. Alfred Russel Wallace and Charles Darwin's codiscovery[82] of natural selection,[83] which prompted Darwin to publish his book *On the Origin of Species*,[84] and Gregor Mendel's discovery of "discrete inherited units"[85]—better known today as genes—laid the foundation for the genetics-based era of modern plant breeding.

Farming practices before the nineteenth century involved cross-breeding, domestication, and artificial selection of traits. Insights from Mendel's pea-plant hybridization experiments of how traits were passed down from parents to progeny,[86] which ultimately led to conceptualization of Mendel's Laws of Inheritance[87]—namely, the Law of Segregation and the Law of Independent Assortment—opened the door for subsequent researchers to apply the dual principles of heredity and natural selection in plant breeding for purposes of increasing genetic diversity. In time, these principles had a combined lasting effect on conventional farming, transforming it from an agricultural practice into a bona fide agricultural science.

Scientific discoveries throughout the twentieth century involving DNA and the molecular mechanisms of genetic inheritance helped promote the advent of recombinant DNA technology.[88] By 1972, breakthrough discoveries—in restriction enzyme[89] and DNA double-stranded repair mechanisms—allowed scientists to produce the first recombinant DNA molecules by fusing DNA fragments from two viruses.[90] Within a year, the first genetically modified organism created through modern genetic engineering was reported in the literature, after a team of researchers introduced recombinant DNA into bacterial cells.[91]

The science progressed rapidly after those proof-of-concept studies were established. In 1974, the world's first transgenic—a term that refers to the artificial introduction of genetic material from one organism into the genome of another unrelated organism[92]—animal was reported.[93] The first genetically engineered plants were developed by inserting antibiotic resistance genes into tobacco plant cells in 1983.[94] A genetically modified bacterium capable of breaking down crude oil for bioremediation purposes became the first patented GMO.[95] And the Supreme Court's decision to endorse intellectual property rights for living microorganisms—in *Diamond v. Chakrabarty*[96]—spawned a multibillion dollar biotechnology industry.

Soon thereafter, global commercialization of the first GM crops got under way. In 1992, a virus-resistant tobacco plant produced by Chinese researchers became the world's first commercial GM crop.[97] In the United States, a California-based firm brought the first GM food—the FLAVR SAVR tomato—to market in 1994.[98] The first insect- and herbicide-resistant crops were approved in the mid-1990s,[99] and marked a turning point in agriculture. By 1996, a total of thirty-five approvals had been granted for the commercialization of a variety of transgenic crops worldwide.[100] Genetic engineering also began to be used in the production of biofortified crops.[101]

The new age of recombinant DNA technology and molecular genetics has ushered in a revolution in crop agricultural science the world has never before seen. In 2014, a reported eighteen million farmers in twenty-eight countries across the world devoted 181.5 million hectares (448 million acres) of arable land to cultivation of GM crops.[102] This marked a 107-fold increase in global hectarage devoted to GM crops compared to the 1.7 million hectares reported in 1996—the year in which commercialization of GM crops began.[103] As of 2014, the global market value of GM crops was estimated at $15.7 billion[104] and continues in an upward trend.

IV MAKING GMOS

As pointed out in Section I, genetic modification of crops can be achieved through artificial (nonnatural) selection of desirable agronomic traits. As a result, domestication-induced genetic modification technically also leads to the creation of GMOs, even though propagation of these crops does not involve genetic engineering.[105] This is an important and common misperception regarding GMOs, namely that (1) intentional breeding followed by selection is a natural process—it is not; absent human intervention, such breeding and selection would be extremely unlikely to occur—and (2) genetic engineering is the only method available to produce GMOs—it is not; other methods exist to introduce new alleles and increase genetic diversity.

This section discusses two main categories of methods that have been, and continue to be, used in GMO production: (1) nonrecombinant DNA methods, which do not involve genetic engineering, and (2) genetic-engineering methods. A third category involving genome-editing technologies will be discussed in Chapter 7.

A *Nonrecombinant DNA Methods*

Improving crops by modifying plant genetic makeup has been a long-standing goal throughout the history of human agriculture.[106] The most basic way to introduce genetic modifications involves traditional plant breeding, which is inherently a human-directed, discriminatory process. In traditional breeding, a heterogeneous population of plants undergoes inspection to determine the presence of individuals that exhibit a trait deemed desirable. Once those particular individuals have been identified, their seeds are collected and sown for continuous propagation. Over a period of many years, the iterative dissemination of genes belonging to the parental line—coupled with intercrossing the most valuable individuals from different populations of the same species—leads to a shift in the gene pool, thereby ensuring fixation of the desirable trait.

Another traditional way to increase biodiversity involves cross-breeding of plants that are sexually compatible. This method has proven useful for plant breeders wishing to produce a hybrid that exhibits desirable traits from each parent. Cross-breeding sexually compatible plants can successfully generate desirable hybrids, but getting there requires substantial time and resource commitment. This is mainly because of the physical and biological limitations of natural genetic recombination, which is sometimes commonly described as the process of gene shuffling that increases genetic variation. By genetic recombination, we refer to the exchange of DNA between multiple chromosomes or different regions of the same chromosome.[107]

Ensuring the recombination of only one particular gene from the parental lines during a cross, while leaving all other genes undisturbed, is simply not possible through natural means. One hybrid may inherit an intended trait—for example, bigger fruit—from one of the parents, but it may also inherit other traits, some of which could make the plant undesirable to breeders—such as a hybrid that produces bigger fruit but is susceptible to pests. Although back-crossing to the parental line followed by multiple rounds of artificial selection can breed out potential undesirable traits and maintain advantageous characteristics, the process is time-consuming and inefficient. Simply put, cross-breeding requires screening hundreds, or even thousands,[108] of hybrid progeny to identify offspring that have the desired traits.

It bears noting that these processes are human-centric, that is, the shift in the genetic population of the plants is driven exclusively by human desire. What is most beneficial in a plant from a human perspective, may not necessarily promote the plant's fitness from an evolutionary perspective. For instance, bigger fruit size and sweet flavor are likely to be important agronomic traits for humans, but having those traits might render the plant more susceptible to prey, pests, or even reduce its ability to propagate the species.

Scientific advances in the last century now offer plant breeders a wide array of alternatives to these laborious and time-consuming approaches for increasing genetic diversity beyond natural means. The following nonrecombinant DNA methods have been routinely performed in human agriculture for decades to expand the biodiversity of crops.

1 Interspecific and Intergeneric Hybridization

This type of hybridization technique involves wide crosses between different plant species (interspecific) or genera (intergeneric). The goal is to develop novel hybrid cultivars that feature traits—for example, improved biotic and abiotic stress tolerance—that do not occur within a single species.[109] Both types of hybridization have been established with multiple cultivars and wild relatives in flowering plants,[110] trees,[111] tomato plants,[112] cereals,[113] and other grasses.[114] However, cross incompatibility in interspecific and intergeneric hybridizations has prevented widespread development of these hybrids. Comparable sterility, susceptibility to shattering,[115] low seed set, and poor germination rates[116] pose great limitations for this technique. Even when the distant species are sufficiently compatible to reproduce, abnormal endosperm development and other aberrations often lead to abortion of hybrid embryos.[117]

Importantly, it should be noted that these types of hybridization lead to reshuffling of parental genes,[118] which may result in myriad changes to chromatin structure of unknown and unpredictable function.

2 Embryo Rescue

Embryo rescue is an in vitro technique developed in the 1920s to address the problem of interspecific and intergeneric hybridization that leads to embryonic abortion.[119] An immature or weak embryo is excised from its natural growing environment before it stops growing, and moved directly into culture media.[120] The wide-cross embryo continues to develop in vitro, and then it is inserted into the removed endosperm of a compatible species.[121] Eventually, the nursed embryo develops into a plant. This method has proven successful at overcoming hybrid embryo inviability and halting abortion of starving embryos. Several embryo-rescue techniques have been devised to mediate completion of gene transfer between unrelated species of plants, including embryo, ovary, ovule, and placenta cultures.[122]

3 Chromosome Engineering

Chromosome engineering[123] refers to the use of artificial "mini chromosomes" for gene transfer via recombination.[124] This method comprises a chromosome-based vector system[125] that allows the transformation of large fragments of DNA encoding one or more genes alongside regulatory elements.[126] It seeks to overcome some of the limitations associated with other gene transfer methods that allow insertion of one or a few genes. Site-specific recombination between a minichromosome and a normal chromosome has been established in plant cells.[127] Overall, chromosome engineering aims to mediate safe, controlled, and persistent expression of the genes intended for transfer, and to avoid chromosomal rearrangements often linked with insertion events.[128] This method is, however, limited by the low efficiency rates of plant homologous recombination.

4 Induced Mutagenesis

Induced mutagenesis refers to the practice of exposing plants or seeds to a physical or chemical mutagen—a mutation-inducing agent—with the intent to trigger random changes in the plant's genetic composition.[129] The technique, as applicable to plants, was first reported in the scientific literature in 1928, when it was shown that irradiation with x-rays was capable of inducing mutations in maize plants.[130] To date, several physical (x-rays, gamma rays, UV light) and chemical (ethyl methanesulfonate (EMS), diethyl sulfate (dES), ethyleneimine (EI), etc.) mutagens have been characterized as capable of inducing mutations in plants.[131] Progeny from induced mutants must be subsequently screened for the presence of potential desirable traits.[132]

Notably, mutagenesis of plant cells using this technique results in random mutation events throughout the plant cell's genome. This means that even if a mutagen-induced GMO plant exhibits a desirable trait, there is a strong likelihood that mutations other than those responsible for said trait are present. Such mutations could, in theory, lead to unknown and unpredictable effects. Without sequencing the entire mutant plant's genome, it would be impossible to know the exact location and frequency of mutation events.

Despite the potential risks associated with random mutagenesis, this type of breeding method is wildly successful as a tool for increasing genetic diversity in plants. A partnership between the United Nations Food and Agricultural Organization and the International Atomic Energy Agency has implemented, for nearly half a century, plant breeding and genetics programs that led to the official release of over 3,200 mutant varieties from 214 different plant species in more than sixty countries.[133]

5 Somaclonal Variation

Somaclonal variation refers to the genetic differences observed among progeny of plants regenerated from somatic cells[134] cultured in vitro.[135] Until the early 1980s, it was generally accepted that plants regenerated from tissue culture should be genetically identical to the somatic-cell source from which they were derived.[136] However, trait differences were commonly observed in these types of regenerated plants.[137]

The discrepancy was eventually explained by proposing that somaclonal variation was not merely a tissue-culture technique, but also a new source of genetic variability.[138] A number of processes have been associated with the molecular basis for this phenomenon, including changes in chromosome number, point mutations, chromosomal rearrangements, epigenetics,[139] and others.[140] Although somaclonal variation is considered a nuisance from a micropropagation perspective, it nevertheless has become a convenient alternative for breeders seeking to introduce genetic variability without the need for expensive equipment.[141]

B *Genetic-Engineering Methods*

1 *Agrobacterium tumefaciens*-Based Plant Transformation

Gene transfer via *Rhizobium radiobacter*, formally known as *Agrobacterium tumefaciens*,[142] is the most common method used in plant transformation for genetic engineering.[143] This naturally occurring, Gram-negative, rod-shaped bacterium was discovered over one hundred years ago,[144] when it was first identified as the causal agent for particular types of plant tumors or galls.[145]

Nearly seven decades would pass before researchers realized that a large plasmid —a circular, double-stranded DNA molecule that is not part of the cell's chromosomal DNA[146]—carried within the bacterium was responsible for the tumors observed in crown-gall disease.[147] An explosion of interest related to the molecular basis of tumor induction by A. *tumefaciens* ensued in the late 1970s and early 1980s.[148] The combined research efforts led to a surprising breakthrough in 1983, when various research teams almost simultaneously reported the ability to genetically engineer plants by co-opting the A. *tumefaciens* tumor-inducing system.

The mechanism by which A. *tumefaciens* modifies a plant's genetic makeup is now well characterized. When plant tissue sustains injury—such as when a wound occurs—the plant releases a series of compounds[149] that trigger recruitment of A. *tumefaciens* to the injury site via chemotaxis. Chemotaxis is the process by which the organism—in this case, A. *tumefaciens*—moves in the direction corresponding to a concentration gradient of a specific substance or set of substances.[150] The chemical interaction between the bacterium and plant cells induces expression of virulence genes within a plasmid in A. *tumefaciens* known as the tumor-inducing (Ti) plasmid.[151] The bacterium's Ti plasmid encodes the genetic information for a fragment of DNA known as transfer DNA (T-DNA), which is the segment that ultimately integrates into the genome of the plant host cell and induces proliferation of crown-gall disease.[152] T-DNA is flanked by short "border" sequences at opposite ends of the fragment[153] that serve as cleavage sites, which are in turn recognized by proteins expressed from the Ti virulence genes. Once the T-DNA is excised from the Ti plasmid, other virulence proteins mediate transfer—and random integration—of the T-DNA into the nuclear genome of the host cell.[154]

Initially, A. *tumefaciens*-mediated transformation was thought to be limited to dicot plant species only (the term dicot refers to plants that have a pair of leaves, or "cotyledons," in the embryo of the seed[155]). However, it is now well established that transformation can be achieved in a wide range of plant hosts, including monocots (plants having only one seed leaf in the embryo[156])—such as rice,[157] banana,[158] wheat,[159] and others—and gymnosperms,[160] as well as other unrelated organisms, such as fungi[161] and even human cells.[162] Moreover, although A. *tumefaciens* has become the most popular method of plant transformation for genetic engineering, other *Rhizobium* species have now been shown capable of shuttling DNA of interest into plant hosts.[163] Alternative methods of plant transformation based on other *Rhizobium* species could become important open-source biological tools that allow researchers to circumvent intellectual property restrictions imposed by current *Agrobacterium*-related patents.[164]

The key insight that paved the way for transgenic plants was the realization that the tumor-inducing T-DNA fragment flanked by border sequences could be entirely replaced with any DNA piece of interest; one that would in theory produce a desirable trait. By co-opting this bacterial tumor-inducing system in plants, scientists figured out a way to mediate the transfer of any DNA fragment—regardless of whether the DNA belonged to the same plant species or not—from a bacterial plasmid into a plant host using bacteria as the shuttle.

There are a few major unresolved issues related to A. *tumefaciens* transformation. One concern is that scientists cannot control the site of T-DNA integration and, therefore, a transgene may theoretically be inserted into a site that could interfere with the function of other plant genes. Additionally, duplications, translocations,[165] and transfer of genetic material other than the T-DNA—such as bacterial chromosomal and Ti plasmid fragments—have been shown to occur,[166] which has prompted concerns for greater scrutiny of transgenic plants. These, in a nutshell, are the two major limitations of transgenic plants created via genetic engineering.

2 Particle-Bombardment Transformation

Another common technique to generate GM crops is the particle-bombardment method, also known as biolistics, microprojectile bombardment, or gene gun.[167] This technique was developed to circumvent gene transfer limitations that existed at the early stages of A. *tumefaciens* transformation research. The method comprises an acceleration device that can deliver micron-sized tungsten or gold particles coated with desired DNA molecules for plant-cell transformation.[168] The technique literally involves firing metal-complexed DNA microprojectiles into a cell. The particles penetrate thousands of cell walls and membranes simultaneously without inducing cell lethality.[169] Once delivered inside the cell, the DNA comes off the metal particles and may subsequently be integrated into the host genome.[170]

Particle-bombardment transformation has been used to transform many economically important crops[171] that were initially recalcitrant to A. *tumefaciens*-mediated gene transfer. However, now that A. *tumefaciens* transformation has been firmly established in a long list of plant species, particle bombardment may be used with less frequency. This is particularly because particle bombardment-mediated plant transformation requires specialized equipment and often leads to insertion of many copies of a transgene at multiple sites of the host genome,[172] which can potentially lead to altered patterns of gene expression or even gene silencing.[173]

3 Polyethylene Glycol- and Electroporation-Based Protoplast Transformation

The direct transfer of genetic material using polyethylene glycol (PEG) or electroporation for protoplast[174] transformation has also been established in plant genetic engineering. The mechanism for PEG-mediated DNA uptake is not very well understood, but the technique is very simple and relatively inexpensive to implement.[175] Electroporation involves polarity changes on the cell membrane that trigger the formation of membrane pores upon exposure to an electrical field.[176] Both methods induce changes in cell-membrane permeability, thereby allowing the entry of the foreign DNA of interest. Although relatively simple to perform, these techniques are not very popular due to reported marginally low transformation-efficiency rates,[177] which require burdensome protocol-optimization strategies to increase transformation efficiencies.

4 Microinjection

Microinjection-based plant transformation is a direct physical approach that relies on glass micro-capillary injection pipettes to directly deliver DNA of interest into the plant cell.[178] The technique requires specialized equipment and is labor-intensive and relatively inefficient compared to other methods.[179]

5 Other Methods

Aside from the techniques detailed above, other less common methods have been used to mediate plant-cell transformation of recombinant DNA molecules including, but not limited to, liposome encapsulation,[180] laser microbeams, vacuum infiltration, ultrasound, electrophoresis, and agrolistic transformation.[181] An additional category of tools for targeted genome editing has also been developed. These tools, which include CRISPR systems and will be discussed in more detail in Chapter 7, could fundamentally change the way we think about GMOs.

V HEALTH AND ENVIRONMENTAL GMO SAFETY CONCERNS

Over the last two decades, frequent and arduous contention as to the development and commercialization of GMOs for human consumption has pitted numerous groups among the general public, industry, governmental organizations, and the scientific and legal communities against one another. Ill-tempered disputes have fomented rapid deterioration of the quality of discourse and public attitudes pertinent to the use of biotechnology in this realm. As a result, it is no surprise that GMOs have become one of the most controversial socio-technological topics in modern times.

When it comes to bioengineered foods, the controversy can be divided into two main categories. The first concerns the view that GM food poses grave risk to human health. The second links GM crops to potential detrimental environmental effects.[182]

In this section, we explore those concerns and discuss their merits primarily from a scientific standpoint. The motivation for doing so stems from the view that law and policy makers must proactively strive to grasp core scientific elements associated with that which they must regulate. Accordingly, the discussion about GM crops in this section applies a jurisprudence of scientific empiricism as a structural framework to address questions of science in law and combat the deleterious effects of scientific illiteracy.[183] The objective here is to provide a succinct resource concerning the current scientific literature on the potential health and environmental effects of GM crops.

A *Human and Animal Health*

To date, the totality of institutional, governmental, and international organizations, as well as the scientific literature analyzing the safety of GM crops, have concluded that consuming GM-derived foodstuff poses no more a threat to human health than foodstuff derived from conventional breeding methods.[184]

1 Institutional Authorities and International Organizations

In 2016, the National Academies of Science, Engineering, and Medicine tasked its Committee on Genetically Engineered Crops: Past Experience and Future Prospects to assess the purported negative effects and benefits of GM crops and publish its findings in a detailed report.[185]

Over a period of eight months, the Committee heard over eighty presentations from speakers all over the world, read more than 700 comments and documents submitted from diverse members of the public and organizations, and carefully examined peer- and non-peer-reviewed literature relevant to the risks and benefits of GM crops in the United States and abroad.[186] The Committee found that, on the basis of comparisons between GM and non-GM food in compositional analysis, animal toxicity tests, long-term research data on the health of livestock fed GM food diets, and human epidemiological data, there is no evidence to suggest that consuming GM food is any riskier than consuming non-GM food.[187]

The NASEM's assessment mirrors findings of other independent authoritative agencies, international organizations, and scientific panels. The American Association for the Advancement of Science stated that it is "quite clear" that scientific evidence corroborates the safety of GM crops developed through biotechnology.[188] The European Commission too has published an extensive report presenting findings from hundreds of research groups funded by European research grants totaling over 300 million euros.[189] The Commission declared that "[t]he main conclusion to be drawn from the efforts of more than 130 research projects, covering a period of more than 25 years of research, and involving more than 500 independent research groups, is that biotechnology, and in particular GMOs, are not *per se* more risky" than non-GM crops.[190]

The Commission's endorsement of GM crop safety came despite the fact that a number of European countries currently ban production of GM crops in their territories. For instance, Russia enacted Federal Law 358-FZ, which was signed into law by Vladimir Putin on July 3, 2016, and prohibits cultivation and breeding of GMOs in the Russian Federation territory for all purposes, except scientific research.[191] Scotland banned GMOs in order to "protect and further enhance [its] clean, green status."[192] And similar prohibitions have occurred in France,[193] Germany, Poland, Slovenia, Serbia, and other European countries.[194] The enactment of national bans against GMO products has come even despite the European Union Parliament's disagreement with EU-member states on the enactment of such legislation.[195]

The American Medical Association (AMA) conducted a broad appraisal of peer-reviewed, published scientific literature and found that although bioengineered foods have been consumed for nearly two decades, no overt consequences on human health have been substantiated in the peer-reviewed literature.[196] The AMA further urged government, industry, consumer advocacy groups, and the scientific community to educate the general public and increase access to unbiased information on GM food.[197] At the same time, the AMA indicated that, with respect to GM foods, "a small potential for adverse events exists, due mainly to horizontal gene transfer, allergenicity, and toxicity."[198]

In similar fashion, the United Nations Food and Agriculture Organization (FAO) has proclaimed that foods derived from transgenic crops "have been judged safe to eat and the methods used to test their safety have been deemed appropriate."[199] Despite human consumption of GM food by millions of people, "no verifiable untoward toxic or nutritionally deleterious effects . . . have been discovered anywhere in the world."[200] The Union of the German Academies of Science and Humanities also published a report stating that scientific evidence suggests it is "most unlikely that the consumption of the well-characterised transgenic DNA from approved GMO food harbours any recognisable health risk."[201] The Royal Society of the United Kingdom, the International Council for Science, various National Academies of Science in Brazil, Australia, China, France, India, and the United Kingdom, the World Health Organization, and other institutions have all concurred in that judgment.[202]

2 Scientific Literature

The vast majority of the relevant published scientific literature on the topic of GMO safety spanning the last two decades has reached the consensus that GM crops and human health hazards are not linked or correlated.[203] Published animal feeding studies have provided evidence that GM crops are as safe and nutritional as conventional breeding crops.[204] Long-term and multigenerational studies on the effects of diets containing GM maize, potato, soybean, rice, or triticale on animal health have found no health hazards,[205] and concluded that GM crops are nutritionally equivalent to non-GM crops.[206] Lifelong studies have (1) found no long-term structural alterations of the lining of the small or large intestines in animals fed GM food, and (2) reported that aging affects animals in similar ways—regardless of whether they are fed GM food or not.[207]

GM crops have been reported to exert no significant influence on the health and performance of animals—such as livestock[208] and poultry[209]—grown for human consumption. This includes no adverse effects on the quality of meat, eggs, or milk production and no evidence that any DNA from GM crops was transferred to animals fed GM food. A study performed on publicly available field data sets over a period of almost thirty years (thirteen years before, and fifteen years after the introduction of GM crops), representing more than 100 billion animals, "did not reveal unfavorable or perturbed trends in livestock health and productivity."[210] Although nucleic acids—such as DNA—and proteins are common macromolecular components of all diets, no study has revealed detectable or reliably quantifiable traces—at least using today's standard methods of detection—of GM foreign DNA in dairy products and meat, or any differences in the nutritional profile of products derived from GM crop-fed animals.[211]

With respect to cancer, the scientific literature predominantly agrees that GM-food consumption does not induce, or substantially contribute to the incidence of, cancer.[212] For example, a study that examined breast and cervical cancer incidence and mortality rates in 187 countries between 1980 and 2010[213] found similar patterns in the prevalence of these cancers in North America, where GM foods are commercialized, and Europe, where GM foods are typically not consumed. These observations are important because they dispel the notion that GMOs are directly associated with cancer.

If consumption of GM foods were directly linked to higher occurrence of cancer, a disparity in cancer rates between the two populations (a control, Europe, and an experimental, North America) would be expected. Yet, the data do not show such a disparity. Likewise, data available from the United States National Cancer Institute on trends of cancer incidence among men and women show no obvious differences in the patterns of several types of cancers when compared to corresponding data from the United Kingdom's Cancer Research UK organization—at least none that could be attributed to the increase in consumption of food derived from GM crops.[214] This lack of correlation was also noted by the NASEM's 2016 report on GM crops.[215]

Data on the onset of type II diabetes rates over the past four decades,[216] as well as obesity rates between 1984 and 2013,[217] also seem to reject the hypothesis that GM food consumption is contributing to the obesity and diabetes epidemics in the United States. Incidence for both diseases appears to have steadily increased before GM crops were introduced and continued to increase at a steady pace throughout the 1990s and 2000s. Yet, type II diabetes and obesity rates appear to have reached a plateau in the last decade.[218]

The NASEM's 2016 report on GM crops also considered public comments for a number of other chronic conditions, including chronic kidney disease, Celiac disease, food allergies, autism spectrum disorders, and more. The report determined, after examining the relevant scientific literature and government statistics on the prevalence of these conditions, that no palpable link exists between them and consumption of GM crops.[219]

On the topic of exposure to plant chemicals—such as pesticides—produced by GM crops and the potential adverse effects to human health, the scientific literature reveals that both natural and synthetic compounds found in all plants could be harmful to humans depending on the amount of exposure. For instance, an investigation of naturally occurring pesticides in a laundry list of common human foods—fruits, legumes, vegetables, herbs, and even coffee, chocolate, and honey—found that all contained natural pesticides that induced carcinogenicity in rodents.[220] Although a big focus of GM-food products lies in testing for toxicity of newly introduced proteins or compounds in rodents, it appears that the administration of chemicals at the maximum-tolerated dose (MTD) in standard animal cancer tests may not be the most robust method to assess toxicity.[221] More than 99.9 percent of the chemicals ingested by humans are naturally occurring, and of the small proportion of natural pesticides tested for carcinogenicity, more than half have been found to be rodent carcinogens.[222]

During conventional cross-breeding, gene recombination gives rise to a great number of novel gene arrangements and interactions, which have not been associated with hazardous effects on human health and nutrition, despite the lack of review by regulatory agencies.[223] Likewise, of the hundreds of thousands of GM plant varieties that have been created through nongenetic engineering methods, the emergence of any novel toxin or allergen has never been documented either.[224] The emergence of predictable toxins among crops generated through nongenetic engineering methods, however, has been documented at least three times in the past few decades in potato, lima bean, and canola plants, all of which involved toxins that were already known to be endogenous to the crop and were detected through screenings mandated by regulatory agencies.[225] Thus, because changes in GM crops derived through genetic engineering are more precise than those created via nongenetic engineering methods, the number of potential novel gene recombination events and interactions is likely to be incredibly miniscule.

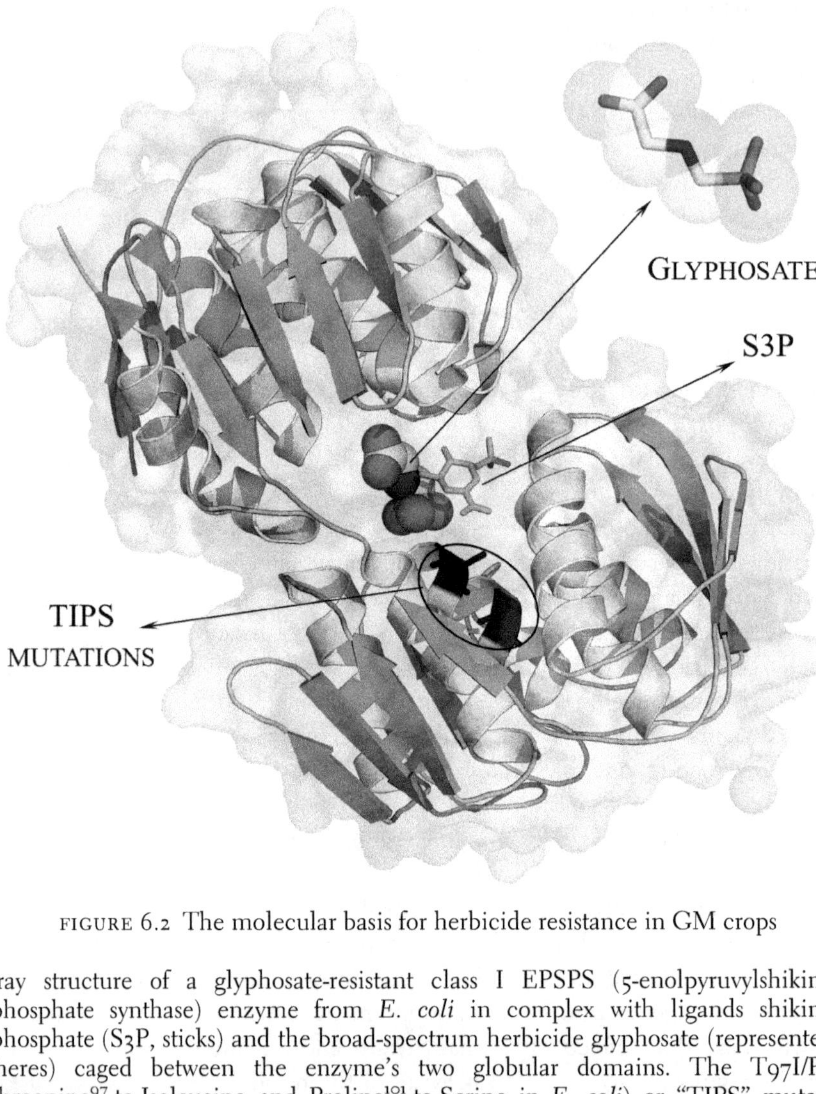

FIGURE 6.2 The molecular basis for herbicide resistance in GM crops

X-ray structure of a glyphosate-resistant class I EPSPS (5-enolpyruvylshikimate-3-phosphate synthase) enzyme from *E. coli* in complex with ligands shikimate-3-phosphate (S3P, sticks) and the broad-spectrum herbicide glyphosate (represented by spheres) caged between the enzyme's two globular domains. The T97I/P101S (Threonine[97]-to-Isoleucine and Proline[101]-to-Serine in *E. coli*) or "TIPS" mutations confer glyphosate resistance by causing fine structural changes within the enzyme's active site (center). The structural changes inhibit optimal glyphosate binding without substantially compromising EPSPS catalytic efficiency.[229] [PDB 3FK1].

Some studies have also investigated potential effects of exposure to glyphosate, the main broad-spectrum herbicide (Figure 6.2) used to treat many GM—as well as non-GM[226]—crops, and found no evidence of a pattern of positive associations linking a number of non-cancer outcomes with glyphosate exposure.[227] Lastly, a public database of peer-reviewed research on the relative risks of GM crops run by an independent, tax-exempt, nonprofit organization focusing on plant genetics and genetic engineering in agriculture has been created.[228] The database, called GENERA, features over 400 publications on GMO research including feeding studies, toxicology, efficacy, and other topics and lists funding information for each study where it is available.

As is evident from this section, there is widespread concord in the scientific community regarding the safety of GM crops. However, although this section is comprehensive and representative of the scientific consensus, I would be remiss to claim it is wholly exhaustive, particularly given the thousands of studies performed over the last two decades related to this topic. Furthermore, no discussion of the safety of GM crops would be complete without highlighting the few dissenting—and loud—voices in select scientific niches that have departed from the general scientific consensus to argue that GM crops pose grave hazards to human health.

3 Dissenting Voices—Opposition to the Scientific Consensus

Notwithstanding the scientific consensus that has crystallized on the topic of safety of GM crops, there are few dissenting voices that have spawned one of the most impassionate controversies in modern times.

Of those voices, perhaps the most prominent is that of Gilles-Eric Séralini, a French scientist and anti-GMO activist, who has published a series of reports in the last decade[230] warning about the health dangers of GMOs. Séralini and his colleagues' studies have warned that GM foods can be directly associated with reproductive aberrations,[231] liver and kidney damage,[232] cardiotoxicity,[233] embryonic disturbances,[234] and more.[235]

The most visible—and notorious—report was published in 2012,[236] which documented a series of long-term effects, including the induction of tumors in rats fed GM maize treated with Roundup®, Monsanto's popular glyphosate-based herbicidal formulation. Upon publication, the article was highly criticized by many in the scientific community, which pointed to, among other things, the study's inadequate methods, erroneous conclusions unsupported by empirical data, lack of proper statistical analyses, improper use of animals, and other flaws.[237] One of the most damaging criticisms of this study, for example, involved the use of the Sprague-Dawley rat strain, which is commonly known to develop spontaneous endocrine tumors with aging regardless of whether rats are fed GM food or not.[238]

Initially the Journal stood by the peer-review process and its decision to publish. But, ultimately, the Journal initiated an independent investigation of the study's conclusions and—upon review—decided to retract it due to the inconclusiveness of its results.[239] Séralini then republished the same paper—without peer review and including minor modifications—in another journal.[240] Notably, the NASEM's 2016 review of the study also concluded that the research was "not conclusive and used incorrect statistical analysis."[241]

Opponents of GMOs point to Séralini's republished paper and other studies[242] in support of claims that greedy corporations, lobbyists, and corrupt government officials have conspired against public health by allowing commercialization of GM crops.[243] They also rely on these studies to demand long-term investigations and permanent bans on all GMOs.[244] These demands are often sensationalized and receive a great deal of media attention.[245]

Moreover, anti-GMO scientists and activists routinely point to apparent conflicts of interest arising from the publication of safety studies that are funded by the very industries that will benefit from favorable GMO reports. For instance, one study found that there was a strong correlation between author affiliation to industry and a favorable outcome reported for peer-reviewed journal articles written on the safety of GM foods.[246] That same study reported that slightly less than half of GMO-related articles in the study were published by authors having industry ties.[247] This would give some credence to anti-GMO activists and scientists, except that they too are guilty of the same type of professional conflicts of interests they often decry from proponents of GMOs.

Séralini, for example, has received funding from CRIIGEN, a company he co-founded in 1999 and of which he was President of the Scientific Board,[248] as well as other organizations that oppose GMOs, including Greenpeace and the Sustainable Food Trust.[249] Sevene Pharma, a company that sells homeopathic remedies,[250] has provided Séralini—a consultant of the company—mixtures of "medicinal plant extracts" that purportedly provide some level of protection against GM crop-derived "pollutants."[251] According to an article correction issued by a journal that noted a failure to disclose all conflicts of interest, Séralini received funding from Sevene for five years to study the detoxifying capacity of plant extracts sold by Sevene Pharma, and received payment for a lecture organized by the company.[252] Worse, proponents of GMOs have accused Séralini of profiting from shady science by timing release of his scientific reports to book and documentary film releases, all while forbidding the press to discuss his work with other scientists via bizarre confidentiality agreements during the book and film promotional periods.[253]

Séralini's supporters argue that he has been ostracized by members of the scientific community because he represents a danger to powerful corporate interests[254] and, as a result, his scientific work is often relegated to low-tier journals. But this proposition has little merit, especially given that other scientific research—featuring unfavorable evidence that could impact industry interests[255]—has been published in prominent journals and proven to be controversial.[256] For instance, in 2014, a paper published in *Nature* reported data suggesting that consumption of noncaloric artificial sweeteners—such as those commonly found in sugar-free foods and beverages—is associated with metabolic dysfunction and glucose intolerance.[257] Similarly, the first report of the potentially harmful effects of GM crops on nontarget species, such as the monarch butterfly, was also published in *Nature* back in 1999.[258]

The overwhelming majority of scientists are not keen on hiding, or hindering the advancement and dissemination of, knowledge. A research team capable of showing a clear and convincing link between human health hazards and a commercial GM crop—that is reproducible and backed by rigorous empirical testing—is likely to have access to the most prominent platforms in the scientific world. Instead, Séralini has not helped himself, or the reputation of his research, by publishing studies either without peer review or in obscure journals. In 2016, for example, one of his papers[259] was published in a Nigerian journal, whose website home page features multiple typos.[260]

Many in the scientific community have become frustrated by what they perceive to be baseless obstructionism over the past twenty years. A 2016 letter signed by 107 Nobel Laureates urged Greenpeace to "cease and desist" in its campaign against GM crops, and exhorted the United Nations and other governments across the world to reject Greenpeace's unscientific efforts to oppose modern methods of plant breeding.[261]

Notwithstanding the scientific consensus on GM crops, the debate carries on. For instance, in 2015, a joint statement signed by more than "300 independent researchers"—most, though not all, of whom are scientists—rejected the existence of a scientific consensus concerning the safety of GM crops.[262] Contrary to common sentiments within anti-GMO groups, the 2015 joint statement—which was published in *Environmental Sciences Europe*, the same journal in which Séralini republished his retracted study without peer review—did not "assert that GMOs are unsafe or safe. Rather, the statement conclude[d] that the scarcity and contradictory nature of the scientific evidence published to date prevents conclusive claims of safety, or of lack of safety, of GMOs."[263]

B *The Environment*

With respect to the environmental effects of GM-crop production, the prevailing scientific outlook is that no substantial evidence or causal relationship has been established between the adoption of GM crops and harmful agronomic and environmental impacts.[264] That was the assessment of the NASEM following an extensive review of the global scientific evidence available to date. At the same time, the NASEM underscored the need for sustainable pest management practices, and acknowledged that reaching definitive conclusions can sometimes be challenging in a few, but not all, areas related to long-term evaluation of environmental changes.[265]

1 Crop Yield and Economics

Of all the traits introduced into GM plants, including resistance to herbicides, insects, viruses, antibiotics, and others,[266] a clear pattern has been established in the past twenty years. Insect-[267] and herbicide-resistance[268] are the two most common traits in GM crops worldwide, and account for more than 99 percent of total GM crop area.[269]

Numerous scientific studies have investigated issues related to improved yields stemming from the adoption of GM crops. For instance, a study of forty-nine peer-reviewed publications reporting results from a dozen countries revealed that, with few exceptions, GM crops led to higher crop yields and benefited small farmers in developing countries.[270] Similarly, a statistical analysis of the economic and agronomic performance of GM crops worldwide concluded that GM crops perform better than their conventional counterparts.[271] Another study investigating yield contributions of a GM crop in ten universities across the United States over a thirteen-year period found that the presence of GM traits has been associated with an increase in yields.[272] However, the NASEM found that although some GM crops have contributed to a statistically significant reduction in the gap between actual and potential yield in some contexts, other factors may also play important roles in yield differences.[273]

On the basis of reduced pesticide use, increased crop yields, and increased farmer profits, primary data from farm surveys or field trials demonstrate that GM crops benefit both developing and developed nations.[274] Thus, although transgenic crop biotechnologies have been initially targeted for developed countries, it appears that developing countries have benefited more from the spillover technology.[275]

2 Pest Management

Cumulative benefits have been documented for the use of transgenic *Bacillus thurigiensis* (*Bt*) maize to combat the propagation of its primary pest, the European corn borer.[276] Transgenic maize-based pest suppression has been so effective, that some populations of the European corn borer have declined to historically low levels.[277] Surprisingly, research shows that farmers growing non-GM maize are actually reaping more economic benefits than those planting GM maize.[278] This is largely due to the fact that GM seed costs are higher—thereby lowering profit margins of GM maize farmers—and overall regional populations of the pest have declined, which ultimately has benefited both GM and non-GM crop farmers.[279] Such data has led to recommendations for the maintenance of non-GM crop refuges as a strategy for sustainable pest resistance management.[280]

3 Pesticide Use, Acquired Resistance, and Controversies

Assessments of the potential associations between GM crops and the reduction of pesticide use vary.[281] Overall, the scientific literature points to a reduction of chemical pesticide applications, but the decrease is larger for insect-resistant than herbicide-resistant crops.[282] On one hand, the evidence clearly shows that the use of insecticides has decreased as a result of GM crop cultivation. Data from various countries including India,[283] South Africa,[284] Pakistan,[285] Australia,[286] the United States,[287] and other parts of the world[288] demonstrate that GM-crop technology has helped to shrink down the use of insecticides.

On the other hand, data for the reduction of herbicide use is mixed. Research shows that herbicide use decreased for the first few years after the adoption of GM crops, but then increased modestly in later years.[289] This swing could presumably be explained by the development of herbicide resistance among some weed populations, which may have induced farmers to apply more herbicides to combat glyphosate-resistant weeds.[290] Overreliance on glyphosate and the rise of resistance in some weed species have caused concern in recent years, particularly because some glyphosate substitutes may be more toxic and persistent herbicides.[291] The NASEM acknowledged that weed resistance to glyphosate is a problem, and recommended the use of "integrated weed-management approaches beyond simply spraying mixtures of herbicides."[292]

One controversial study published in 2012 concluded that, contrary to claims that GM crops have reduced pesticide use, the spread of glyphosate-resistant weeds has set off "substantial increases in the number and volume of herbicides applied."[293] Opponents of GMOs have relied on this and other similar reports to argue that GM crops are polluting the planet and, thus, should be banned to protect our health and the environment.[294] Critics of this study claimed it was flawed because the author, among other things, "did not take into account the fact that glyphosate is less toxic than the herbicides it has replaced and, thus, the net toxicity of herbicide use had decreased even as the total herbicide use increased."[295]

However, subsequent peer-reviewed research has turned away from overarching conclusions and, instead, revealed nuanced crop-specific differences related to herbicide use. Consider a report published in 2016, which found that "[w]hen pesticides are weighed by the environmental impact quotient," non-GM and GM crop farmers used about the same amount of soybean herbicides, but roughly 10 percent less maize herbicides.[296] The NASEM also reviewed the 2012 report[297] mentioned in the prior paragraph and concluded that the study's author had failed to perform a statistical analysis.[298] The NASEM also discouraged researchers from publishing data that makes "simple determination of whether total kilograms of herbicide used per hectare per year has gone up or down," because such data "is not useful for assessing changes in human or environmental risks" and could "mislead readers."[299]

4 Nontarget Species and Biodiversity

In the past two decades, the mass production and commercialization of GM crops has raised environmental concerns involving biodiversity and the reduction of nontarget species populations.

The first study to report a possible risk for nontarget organisms that feed on plants producing transgenic *Bt* insecticides (see Figure 6.3) was published in 1999 and focused on the monarch butterfly.[300] Through laboratory assays, the study showed that larvae of monarch butterflies reared on milkweed leaves dusted with pollen from a GM crop exhibited retarded growth and high mortality rates.[301] Following that report, a research collaboration between several scientists in the United States and Canada performed a two-year study to examine *Bt* corn pollen toxicity on the monarch butterfly.[302] The study found that the impact of transgenic pollen was negligible primarily because *Bt* expression in pollen is low, and laboratory and field

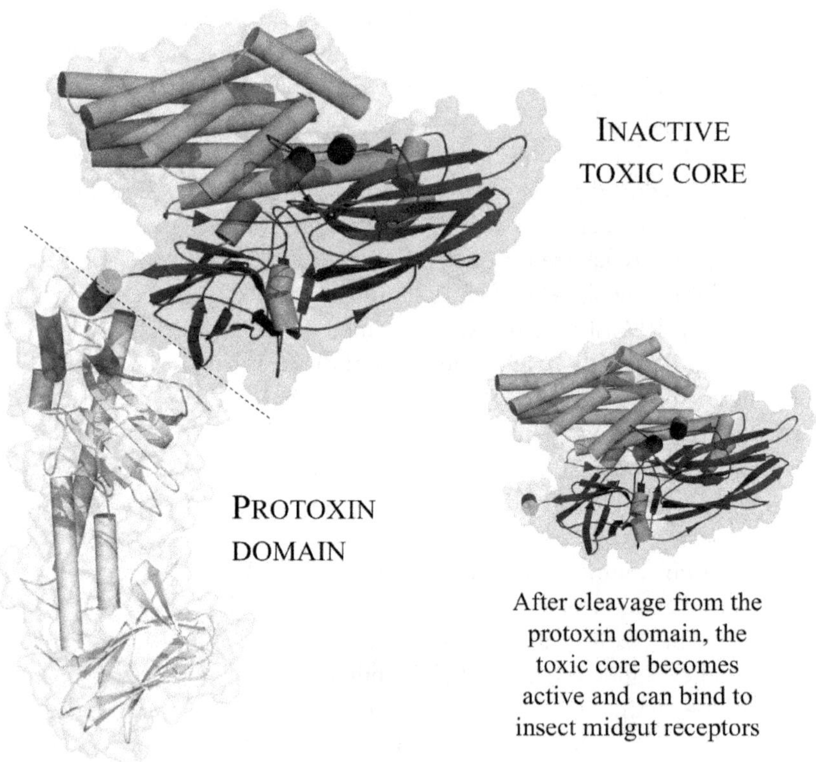

FIGURE 6.3 The molecular basis for insecticide resistance in GM crops

Crystal structure of the *Bt* insecticidal Cry1AC protein from *Bacillus thuringiensis*. After ingestion by a susceptible insect, the inactive full-length protoxin (left) becomes activated via proteolytic cleavage inside the insect's midgut environment. The protoxin domain (light gray) is cleaved off and the toxic core (dark gray) becomes active. The unleashed toxic core (right) is then free to bind specific midgut receptors, thereby creating ion channels or pores in the midgut membrane. Systemic infection resulting from the ulcerated midgut eventually kills the host insect.[305] [PDB 4W8J].

tests failed to establish acute toxic effects at concentrations the insects would likely encounter in the field.[303] The study criticized the 1999 report for not having specified the dose of pollen used in the study.[304]

The potential effects on monarch butterfly fitness arising from the use of glyphosate and other herbicides to control milkweed, the main source of monarch larvae nutrition, has also been studied in recent years. Ample disagreement among researchers can be found in the literature, with some groups arguing that glyphosate-based reduction of milkweeds can be a negative factor in the monarch butterfly's survival,[306] and others claiming no such effect exists.[307] The debate carries on.[308]

Honey bee pollination is vital in agriculture.[309] A concern about the effects of *Bt* crops on honey bees has prompted research into this field. Results from a meta-analysis of twenty-five studies focused on chronic toxicity of *Bt* proteins or plant tissues on honey bee larvae and adults showed that GM crops do not negatively affect the species' survival in laboratory settings, but that additional field environmental stresses could, in theory, lead to indirect effects.[310] Another study concluded that a common *Bt* protein—even at concentrations too high to be found in natural conditions—was not lethal to the bees.[311] However, such high concentrations could likely affect the honey bees' food consumption or learning processes, which in turn could impact honey bee foraging efficiency.[312]

In addition, some studies of the effects of glyphosate on soil, water, and air contamination have determined that, compared to some of the herbicides that glyphosate replaced, the environmental effects are minimal.[313] For example, one meta-analysis of a drought-tolerant GM crop found no impact on yield and shoot or root architecture when grown in moderate- to high-yield environments.[314] Another meta-analysis examining forty-four studies addressing diversity trends associated with eight different field crops demonstrated that overall, in the long run, "no substantial reduction in the regional diversity of crop varieties released by plant breeders has taken place."[315] Comparative risk assessments have found that transgenic crops behave similarly to their non-transgenic counterparts and are not invasive.[316] Other various studies also describe that, overall, currently commercialized GM

FIGURE 6.4 Monarch butterfly and honey bee

crops have reduced the impacts of agriculture on biodiversity primarily through enhanced adoption of conservation tillage practices, reduction of insecticide use, adoption of more benign herbicides, and improved yields that have prevented conversion of additional land for agricultural use.[317]

The NASEM's 2016 report concluded that the bulk of scientific evidence shows that the planting of GM crops tends to result in higher insect biodiversity than the planting of non-GM crops that are treated with synthetic insecticides, and that GM crop fields sprayed with glyphosate have similar or more weed biodiversity than non-GM crop fields.[318] The report concluded that the totality of evidence on the environmental impacts of GM crops currently grown in agriculture shows no cause-and-effect relationships between transgenic crops and environmental harm.[319]

Notes

1 *See generally* Paul Enríquez, *CRISPR GMOs*, 18 N.C. J.L. & TECH. 432 (2017) [hereinafter Enríquez, *CRISPR GMOs*].

2 *E.g.*, Xudong Ye et al., *Engineering the Provitamin A (β-Carotene) Biosynthetic Pathway into (Carotenoid-Free) Rice Endosperm*, 287 SCIENCE 303 (2000) (engineering rice enriched in levels of a Vitamin A precursor).

3 *See generally, e.g.*, NORMAN E. BORLAUG & CHRISTOPHER R. DOWSWELL, FEEDING A WORLD OF TEN BILLION PEOPLE: A 21ST CENTURY CHALLENGE, IN PROCEEDINGS OF THE INTERNATIONAL CONGRESS IN THE WAKE OF THE DOUBLE HELIX: FROM THE GREEN REVOLUTION TO THE GENE REVOLUTION (2003), http://citeseerx.ist.psu.edu/viewdoc/download?doi=10.1.1.462.3105&rep=rep1&type=pdf.

4 United Nations Department of Economic and Social Affairs, *World Population Projected to Reach 9.6 Billion by 2050*, UNITED NATIONS (June 13, 2013), https://www.un.org/development/desa/en/news/population/un-report-world-population-projected-to-reach-9–6-billion-by-2050.html.

5 David Tilman et al., *Global Food Demand and the Sustainable Intensification of Agriculture*, 108 PROC. NAT'L ACAD. SCI. U.S. 20260, 20261 (2011).

6 Elliot M. Berry et al., *Food Security and Sustainability: Can One Exist Without the Other?*, 18 PUBLIC HEALTH NUTRITION 2293, 2300 (2015).

7 It bears noting that genetic modification of plants, including crops, has also been used for other nonfood agricultural purposes beyond the scope of this chapter, such as bioremediation and the production of biofuels and pharmaceutical compounds. *See, e.g.*, Ute Krämer & Agnes N. Chardonnes, *The Use of Transgenic Plants in the Bioremediation of Soils Contaminated with Trace Elements*, 55 APPLIED MICROBIOLOGY & BIOTECHNOLOGY 661 (2001) (bioremediation); Bryan R. Moser, *Camelina (Camelina sativa L.) Oil as a Biofuels Feedstock: Golden Opportunity or False Hope?*, 22 LIPID TECHNOLOGY 270, 273 (2010) (biofuels); Hugh S. Mason et al.,

Expression of Hepatitis B Surface Antigen in Transgenic Plants, 89 PROC. NAT'L ACAD. SCI. U.S. 11745 (1992) (pharmaceuticals).

8 *See Transgene*, SCITABLE, http://www.nature.com/scitable/definition/transgene-223 (last visited Dec. 1, 2016).

9 *See, e.g.*, Ronald L. Meeusen & Gregory Warren, *Insect Control with Genetically Engineered Crops*, 34 ANN. REV. ENTOMOLOGY 373, 373 (1989).

10 *See, e.g.*, Jiyul Chang et al., *Water Stress Impacts on Transgenic Drought-Tolerant Corn in the Northern Great Plains*, 106 AGRONOMY J. 125 (2013).

11 *See, e.g.*, Barbara J. Mazur & S. Carl Falco, *The Development of Herbicide Resistant Crops*, 40 ANN. REV. PLANT PHYSIOLOGY & PLANT MOLECULAR BIOLOGY 441 (1989).

12 *See, e.g.*, 10 *Scary Facts About* GMOs, ONE GREEN PLANET (Mar. 18, 2013), http://www.onegreenplanet.org/vegan-health/10-scary-facts-about-gmos/.

13 MARY SHELLEY, FRANKENSTEIN; OR, THE MODERN PROMETHEUS VOL. I (1818). The novel's first edition was published anonymously in 1818, but Mary Shelley's name appeared on the second edition, which was published in 1823. *See Frankenstein*, WIKIPEDIA, https://en.wikipedia.org/wiki/Frankenstein (last visited May 10, 2017).

14 *See, e.g.*, Jill Ettinger, *Everything You Absolutely Need to Know About GMOs*, ORGANIC AUTHORITY (Feb. 20, 2012), http://www.organicauthority.com/foodie-buzz/what-are-gmos-genetically-modified-crops-foods.html ("The practice of introducing new DNA and chemicals to seeds or animals . . . is similar to how Mary Shelly's Frankenstein created his monster—through piecing together lots of different organisms.").

15 *See, e.g.*, *Watch Out New Frankenfood Arriving Soon: GMO Potatoes*, THE ALTERNATIVE DAILY, (http://www.thealternativedaily.com/watch-new-frankenfood-arriving-soon-gmo-potatoes/ (last visited May 10, 2017); Ettinger, *supra* note 14; Catherine Guthrie, *Frankenfood = Genetically Modified Food*, EXPERIENCE LIFE (June 2013), https://experiencelife.com/article/frankenfood-genetically-modified-foods/.

16 Ettinger, *supra* note 14.

17 Coordinated Framework for the Regulation of Biotechnology, 51 Fed. Reg. 23,302 (June 26, 1986).

18 *See* Memorandum for Heads of Food and Drug Administration, Environmental Protection Agency, and Department of Agriculture: Modernizing the Regulatory System for Biotechnology Products, (July 2, 2015), https://obamawhitehouse.archives.gov/sites/default/files/microsites/ostp/modernizing_the_reg_system_for_biotech_products_memo_final.pdf [hereinafter Modernizing the Regulatory System for Biotechnology Products].

19 *See* Executive Order on Modernizing the Regulatory Framework for Agricultural Biotechnology Products, June 11, 2019, https://www.whitehouse.gov/presidential-actions/executive-order-modernizing-regulatory-framework-agricultural-biotechnology-products/.

20 *Id.* at § 3.

21 *Id.* at § 3(a).

22 It is important to distinguish cross-breeding between unrelated or related plant species. Although both types are deemed not to fall under the regulatory oversight of the Coordinated Framework, crosses between plants of the same species are less likely to lead to unexpected phenotypic or compositional changes in crops.

23 *See* Irving W. Knobloch, *Intergeneric Hybridization in Flowering Plants*, 21 TAXON 97 (1972).

24 *See, e.g.*, Gregory Conko et al., *A Risk-Based Approach to the Regulation of Genetically Engineered Organisms*, 34 NATURE BIOTECHNOLOGY 493 (2016).

25 *See* Paul Enríquez, *Genome Editing and the Jurisprudence of Scientific Empiricism*, 19 VAND. J. ENT. & TECH. L. 603, 611–14 (2017) [hereinafter Enríquez, *Genome Editing*].

26 Paul Enríquez, *Deconstructing Transnationalism: Conceptualizing Metanationalism as a Putative Model of Evolving Jurisprudence*, 43 VAND. J. TRANSNAT'L L. 1265, 1269, 1336 (2010). For instance, several European countries have banned GMOs in recent years. *See infra* Section V.A.1. The bans raise complex legal issues concerning international trade, intellectual property rights, and the future regulation of genome-edited crops in the European Union and around the world.

27 *GM Crop Ban*, SCOTTISH GOV'T RIAGHALTAS NA H-ALBA GOV.SCOT (Aug. 9, 2015), http://news.gov.scot/news/gm-crop-ban.

28 Natasha Geiling, *Scotland Bans Genetically Modified Crops*, THINKPROGRESS (Aug. 10, 2015), https://thinkprogress.org/scotland-bans-genetically-modified-crops-8d6ac8849259.

29 Laurence A. Kogan, *Trade Protectionism: Ducking the Truth About Europe's GMO Policy*, N.Y. TIMES (Nov. 27, 2004), http://www.nytimes.com/2004/11/27/opinion/trade-protectionism-ducking-the-truth-about-europes-gmo-policy.html?_r=0.

30 *See* Mark Lynas, *With G.M.O. Policies, Europe Turns Against Science*, N.Y. TIMES (Oct. 24, 2015), https://www.nytimes.com/2015/10/25/opinion/sunday/with-gmo-policies-europe-turns-against-science.html (arguing that European policies on GM crops are hypocritical because Europe imports large amounts of GM crops for animal feed).

31 *Id.*

32 *See, e.g.*, Brian Kennedy & Cary Funk, *Many Americans are Skeptical About Scientific Research on Climate and GM Foods*, PEW RESEARCH CTR. (Dec. 5, 2016), http://www.pewresearch.org/fact-tank/2016/12/05/many-americans-are-skeptical-about-scientific-research-on-climate-and-gm-foods/; CINNAMON PIÑON CARLARNE, CLIMATE CHANGE LAW AND POLICY: EU AND US APPROACHES 348–49, 359–60 (2010).

33 PIÑON CARLARNE, *supra* note 32, at 348–49, 359–60; Lynas, *supra* note 30.

34 Piñon Carlarne, *supra* note 32, at 348–49, 359–60; Lynas, *supra* note 30.

35 *See, e.g., Frequently Asked Questions on Genetically Modified Food*, World Health Org., http://www.who.int/foodsafety/areas_work/food-technology/faq-genetically-modified-food/en/ (last visited Dec. 1, 2018); *Genetically Modified*, Oxford Online Dictionary, https://en.oxforddictionaries.com/definition/genetically_modified (last visited Dec. 1, 2019); Julia M. Diaz & Judith L. Fridovich-Keil, *Genetically Modified Organism*, Encyclopedia Britannica (Nov. 28, 2016), https://www.britannica.com/science/genetically-modified-organism.

36 *See* Secretariat of the Convention on Biological Diversity, The Cartagena Protocol on Biosafety to the Convention on Biological Diversity, Art. 3(g) (2000) ("'Living modified organism' means any living organism that possesses a novel combination of genetic material obtained through the use of modern biotechnology.").

37 *See, e.g., Glossary of Agricultural Biotechnology Terms*, U.S.D.A. (Feb. 27, 2013), https://www.usda.gov/wps/portal/usda/usdahome?contentid=biotech_glossary.html.

38 As articulated earlier, in a narrow sense—particularly in the view of some opponents of GMOs—the term presumably refers mainly to organisms that have been created using recombinant DNA technology to introduce foreign genetic material.

39 *See, e.g., Directive 2001/18/EC of the European Parliament and of the Council on the Deliberate Release into the Environment of Genetically Modified Organisms and Repealing Council Directive 90/220/EEC*, Official Journal of the European Union, L 106, Art. 2 (2001) ("'Genetically modified organism (GMO)' means an organism, *with the exception of human beings*, in which the genetic material has been altered in a way that does not occur naturally by mating and/or natural recombination.") (emphasis added).

40 *E.g.*, V. V. Mistry, *Chymosin in Cheese Making*, *in* Food Biochemistry and Food Processing 223 (Benjamin K. Simpson ed., 2d ed. 2012).

41 *E.g.*, Production of Provitamin A Carotenoids in Mushrooms and Uses Thereof, U.S. Patent No. 8,907,165 (filed Feb. 11, 2010).

42 Robert T. Fraley et al., *Expression of Bacterial Genes in Plant Cells*, 80 Proc. Nat'l Acad. Sci. U.S. 4803 (1983).

43 *E.g.*, Bernadette M. Dunham, *AquAdvantage Salmon Approval Letter and Appendix*, FDA (Nov. 19, 2015), http://www.fda.gov/AnimalVeterinary/DevelopmentApprovalProcess/GeneticEngineering/GeneticallyEngineeredAnimals/ucm466214.htm; Enríquez, *Genome Editing*, *supra* note 25, at 661–64.

44 GM food sources can encompass a wide array of living organisms consumed by humans including edible fungi (e.g., mushrooms), plants, and animals (vertebrate or invertebrate).

45 Other GMO-derived products exist including, but not limited to, drugs, cosmetics, antibodies, and more. *See, e.g.*, *infra* note 49.

46 *See, e.g.*, G. Bruening and J. M. Lyons, *The Case of the FLAVR SAVR Tomato*, 54 CAL. AGRIC. 6 (2000); Enríquez, *CRISPR GMOs*, *supra* note 1, at 446–47; David Johnson & Siobhan O'Connor, *These Charts Show Every Genetically Modified Food People Already Eat in the U.S.*, TIME MAG. (Apr. 30, 2015), http://time.com/3840073/gmo-food-charts/.

47 Although this chapter specifically covers GM plants and crops, foods derived from other GM organisms share many similarities, including the methods with which they are created and—to some extent—how they are regulated. For a brief overview of genome editing and other biotechnological uses of GM animals in agriculture, see Enríquez, *Genome Editing*, *supra* note 25, at 662–64.

48 Enríquez, *Genome Editing*, *supra* note 25, at 654–55, 660–61.

49 It bears noting that genetic modification of plants, including crops, has also been used for other nonfood agricultural purposes beyond the scope of this chapter, such as bioremediation and the production of biofuels and pharmaceutical compounds. *See, e.g.*, Krämer & Chardonnes, *supra* note 7 (bioremediation); Moser, *supra* note 7 (biofuels); Mason et al., *supra* note 7 (pharmaceuticals).

50 Nikolai D. Ovodov et al., A *33,000-Year-Old Incipient Dog from the Altai Mountains of Siberia: Evidence of the Earliest Domestication Disrupted by the Last Glacial Maximum*, 6 PLOS ONE e22821 (2011).

51 Guo-dong Wang et al., *The Genomics of Selection in Dogs and the Parallel Evolution Between Dogs and Humans*, 4 NATURE COMMC'NS 1860 (2013).

52 Pontus Skoglund et al., *Estimation of Population Divergence Times from Non-Overlapping Genomic Sequences: Examples from Dogs and Wolves*, 28 MOLECULAR BIOLOGY & EVOLUTION 1505 (2011).

53 Adam H. Freedman et al., *Genome Sequencing Highlights the Dynamic Early History of Dogs*, 10 PLOS GENETICS e1004016 (2014).

54 Simon J. M. Davis & François R. Valla, *Evidence for Domestication of the Dog 12,000 Years Ago in the Natufian of Israel*, 276 NATURE 608 (1978).

55 Gianni Liti et al., *Population Genomics of Domestic and Wild Yeasts*, 458 NATURE 337 (2009).

56 Rong-Lin Wang et al., *The Limits of Selection During Maize Domestication*, 398 NATURE 236, 236 (1999) (citation omitted).

57 *Id.* at 238.

58 Artificial selection and nonnatural selection are used interchangeably throughout this chapter to denote human-induced crop evolution through selective breeding of sexually compatible or incompatible organisms to produce offspring with specific desirable agronomic characteristics.

59 Wang et al, *supra* note 56, at 236. *See also* George W. Beadle, *Teosinte and the Origin of Maize*, 30 J. HEREDITY 245 (1939) (first proposing the idea that maize descended from teosinte).

60 John Doebley, *The Genetics of Maize Evolution*, 38 ANN. REV. GENETICS 37, 40–41 (2004).

61 *Id.* at 39.
62 *Id.*
63 *See* Allison Weber et al., *Major Regulatory Genes in Maize Contribute to Standing Variation in Teosinte (Zea mays ssp. parviglumis)*, 177 GENETICS 2349 (2007).
64 *Id.* Genome-wide association studies have also provided important evidence of this principle. *See, e.g.*, Edouard Cadieu et al., *Coat Variation in the Domestic Dog Is Governed by Variants in Three Genes*, 326 SCIENCE 150 (2009) (providing evidence from a study of more than 1,000 dogs from 80 breeds, which revealed that distinct mutations in only *three* genes account for the majority of coat characteristics in purebred dogs in the Unites States).
65 *See* Wang et al, *supra* note 56, at 236.
66 *See* Robert K. Wayne & Bridgett M. vonHoldt, *Evolutionary Genomics of Dog Domestication*, 23 MAMMALIAN GENOME 3 (2012).
67 Polyploidy refers to the heritable condition of having more than two complete sets of chromosomes. *See* Margaret Woodhouse et al., *Polyploidy*, SCITABLE (2009), http://www.nature.com/scitable/nated/topicpage/polyploidy-1552814 (last visited Dec. 1, 2016). Accordingly, a tetraploid organism has four sets of chromosomes, and a hexaploid organism has six sets of chromosomes.
68 Moshe Feldman & Mordechai E. Kislev, *Domestication of Emmer Wheat and Evolution of Free-Threshing Tetraploid Wheat*, 55 ISRAEL J. PLANT SCI. 207 (2007).
69 Yoshihiro Matsuoka, *Evolution of Polyploid Triticum Wheats Under Cultivation: The Role of Domestication, Natural Hybridization and Allopolyploid Speciation in Their Diversification*, 52 PLANT CELL PHYSIOLOGY 750, 751 (2011).
70 *Global Crop Production Analysis: Maps*, U.S.D.A. (Dec. 9, 2016), https://www.pecad.fas.usda.gov/ogamaps/Default.aspx?cmdty=Wheat&attribute=Production.
71 Gurdev S. Khush, *Origin, Dispersal, Cultivation and Variation of Rice*, 35 PLANT MOLECULAR BIOLOGY 25 (1997).
72 Megan Sweeney & Susan McCouch, *The Complex History of the Domestication of Rice*, 100 ANNALS BOTANY 951 (2007).
73 *Id.*
74 Yuling Bai & Pim Lindhout, *Domestication and Breeding of Tomatoes: What Have We Gained and What Can We Gain in the Future?*, 100 ANNALS BOTANY 1085, 1087 (2007).
75 *Id.*
76 Jules Janick, *The Origins of Fruit, Fruit Growing, and Fruit Breeding*, 25 PLANT BREEDING REVS. 255, 302 (2005).
77 *See generally* David M. Spooner et al., *A Single Domestication for Potato Based on Multilocus Amplified Fragment Length Polymorphism Genotyping*, 102 PROC. NAT'L ACAD. SCI. U.S. 14694 (2005).
78 *See* Janick, *supra* note 76, at 298–99.
79 *See, e.g.*, *id.* at 258.

80 *See id.* at 272–308 (providing related accounts all over the world for the evolution of papaya, kiwi, peach, grape, plum, pineapple, apricot, avocado, mango, olive, pomegranate, fig, cherry, citrus fruit, and others).

81 *See, e.g.*, Doebley, *supra* note 60, at 39 (affirming that "maize is completely dependent on humans for its survival").

82 Charles Darwin & Alfred Wallace, *On the Tendency of Species to Form Varieties; and on the Perpetuation of Varieties and Species by Natural Means of Selection*, 3 J. PROC. LINNEAN SOC'Y LONDON ZOOLOGY 45 (1858).

83 Over the years, controversy has surrounded the Darwin-Wallace co-discovery of the theory of evolution by natural selection, credit for which has been suggested to belong to Wallace alone. *See, e.g.*, ROY DAVIES, THE DARWIN CONSPIRACY: ORIGINS OF A SCIENTIFIC CRIME (2008); JOHN LANGDON BROOKS, JUST BEFORE THE ORIGIN: ALFRED RUSSEL WALLACE'S THEORY OF EVOLUTION (1984). Among the main accusations against Darwin is the allegation that he plagiarized ideas found in a paper Wallace sent to him in 1858, which prompted Darwin to revise elements of his own theory and rush to publish it in 1859. John van Wyhe & Kees Rookmaaker, *A New Theory to Explain the Receipt of Wallace's Ternate Essay by Darwin in 1858*, 105 BIOLOGICAL J. LINNEAN SOC'Y 249 (2012) (arguing against the same theory).

Wallace sent Darwin the draft of his unpublished essay titled *On The Tendency of Varieties to Depart Indefinitely from the Original Type* in confidence, requesting Darwin to review it and pass it along to Charles Lyell, a close friend of Darwin's, if he found it worthwhile. *Id.* In his essay, Wallace laid out a version of the theory of evolution by natural selection, which Darwin understood to be precisely what he intended to propose in his own theory. *See* Letter from C. Darwin to C. Lyell (June 18, 1858), *in* THE LIFE AND LETTERS OF CHARLES DARWIN, INCLUDING AN AUTOBIOGRAPHICAL CHAPTER VOL. II 116 (Francis Darwin ed., 1887) (publishing Darwin's personal letter to Lyell upon receipt of Wallace's draft in which he wrote: "I never saw a more striking coincidence; if Wallace had my MS. sketch written out in 1842, he could not have made a better short abstract! Even his terms now stand as heads of my chapters.").

Following Wallace's letter, Lyell and Joseph Hooker, another one of Darwin's influential close friends in scientific circles, advised Darwin to publish extracts from his prior work on evolution alongside Wallace's essay at a meeting of the Linnean Society of London. Van Wyhe & Rookmaaker, *supra*, at 249. Lyell and Hooker subsequently submitted Darwin and Wallace's work, without Wallace's knowledge, to the Linnean Society explaining that both men had "independently and unknown to one another, conceived the same very ingenious theory to account for the appearance and perpetuation of varieties and of specific forms on our planet . . . ." Darwin and Wallace, *supra* note 82, at 45. Lyell and Hooker made it known that Darwin thought Wallace's work to be of high value and worthy of prompt publication, which they approved of "provided Mr. Darwin did not withhold from the public" his own work on the same subject. *Id.* at 45–46. Notably, although Lyell and Hooker's letter to the Linnean Society credited both men, it also highlighted and preserved their dear friend's (Darwin) purported priority. *Id.*

Despite the controversy surrounding who rightfully deserves credit for the theory of evolution by natural selection, researchers have not found clear and convincing evidence to corroborate theories that Darwin plagiarized Wallace. *See generally* JOHN VAN WYHE, DISPELLING THE DARKNESS: VOYAGE IN THE MALAY ARCHIPELAGO AND THE DISCOVERY OF EVOLUTION BY WALLACE AND DARWIN (2013); van Wyhe & Rookmaaker, *supra*. Indeed, Darwin's own writings reveal he was ethically torn vis-à-vis Wallace's disclosure and did not wish to minimize Wallace's contribution. *See* Letter from C. Darwin to C. Lyell (June 25, 1858), *in* THE LIFE AND LETTERS OF CHARLES DARWIN, INCLUDING AN AUTOBIOGRAPHICAL CHAPTER VOL. II 117 (Francis Darwin ed., 1887) ("as I had not intended to publish any sketch, can I do so honourably [sic], because Wallace has sent me an outline of his doctrine? I would far rather burn my whole book, than that he or any other man should think that I had behaved in a paltry spirit. Do you not think his having sent me this sketch ties my hands?").

Nevertheless, the circumstances surrounding Lyell and Hooker's decision to help their friend Darwin hang on to a slice of glory in world history by making Wallace a codiscoverer remain questionable, particularly when Darwin himself realized that his priority had been shattered by Wallace's 1858 essay. *See* Letter from C. Darwin to C. Lyell (June 18, 1858), *in* THE LIFE AND LETTERS OF CHARLES DARWIN, INCLUDING AN AUTOBIOGRAPHICAL CHAPTER VOL. II 116–17 (Francis Darwin ed., 1887) (documenting Darwin's mourning of his loss of priority when he wrote: "So all my originality, whatever it may amount to, will be smashed [by Wallace's essay], though my book, if it will ever have any value, will not be deteriorated; as all the labour [sic] consists in the application of the theory."). Whatever the case may be concerning Darwin and Wallace's contributions, there is no question that Wallace's essay triggered prompt publication of the theory of evolution in 1858 and Darwin's own book nearly a year later in 1859.

84 CHARLES DARWIN, ON THE ORIGIN OF SPECIES BY MEANS OF NATURAL SELECTION, OR THE PRESERVATION OF FAVOURED RACES IN THE STRUGGLE FOR LIFE (1859).

85 Gregor Mendel, *Versuche über Plflanzenhybriden* [*Experiments in Plant Hybridization*], ABHANDLUNGEN 3–47 (1866), Read at Meetings of the Brünn Natural History Society (Feb. 8 & Mar. 8, 1865), *reprinted in* GREGOR MENDEL, EXPERIMENTS IN PLANT HYBRIDIZATION 33–41 (1963).

86 *Id.*

87 The Laws of Inheritance originated from Mendel's observations of how traits were passed down from parents to progeny. His studies helped him to introduce the Law of Segregation and the Law of Independent Assortment, which together

form the bulk of his Laws of Inheritance. Ilona Miko, *Gregor Mendel and the Principles of Inheritance*, 1 NATURE EDUC. 134 (2008).

88 Enríquez, *Genome Editing*, *supra* note 25, at 621–22.

89 Restriction enzymes, also known as restriction endonucleases, are proteins capable of cutting DNA at or near specific nucleotide sequences. *See* Richard J. Roberts & Kenneth Murray, *Restriction Endonucleases*, 4 CRITICAL REVS. BIOCHEMISTRY 123 (1976).

90 David A. Jackson, Robert H. Symons & Paul Berg, *Biochemical Method for Inserting New Genetic Information into DNA of Simian Virus 40: Circular SV40 DNA Molecules Containing Lambda Phage Genes and the Galactose Operon of Escherichia Coli*, 69 PROC. NAT'L ACAD. SCI. U.S. 2904 (1972).

91 Stanley N. Cohen et al., *Construction of Biologically Functional Bacterial Plasmids in Vitro*, 70 PROC. NAT'L ACAD. SCI. U.S. 3240 (1973).

92 *See Transgene*, SCITABLE, http://www.nature.com/scitable/definition/transgene-223 (last visited Dec. 1, 2018).

93 Rudolf Jaenisch & Beatrice Mintz, *Simian Virus 40 DNA Sequences in DNA of Healthy Adult Mice Derived from Preimplantation Blastocysts Injected with Viral DNA*, 71 PROC. NAT'L ACAD. U.S. 1250 (1974).

94 Luis Herrera-Estrella et al., *Expression of Chimaeric Genes Transferred into Plant Cells Using a Ti-Plasmid-Derived Vector*, 303 NATURE 209 (1983); Michael W. Bevan & Richard B. Flavell, *A Chimaeric Antibiotic Resistance Gene as a Selectable Marker for Plant Cell Transformation*, 304 NATURE 184 (1983); R. T. Fraley et al., *Expression of Bacterial Genes in Plant Cells*, 80 PROC. NAT'L ACAD. SCI. U.S. 4803 (1983).

95 U.S. Patent No. 4,259,444 (filed June 7, 1972).

96 447 U.S. 303, 318 (1980) (holding that certain genetically modified microorganisms meet the patent eligibility requirements set forth in 35 U.S.C. § 101).

97 VALEIRE J. KARPLUS & XING WANG DENG, AGRICULTURAL BIOTECHNOLOGY IN CHINA: ORIGINS AND PROSPECTS 62 (2008).

98 G. Bruening & J. M. Lyons, *The Case of the FLAVR SAVR Tomato*, 54 CAL. AGRIC. 6 (2000).

99 Charles M. Benbrook, *Impacts of Genetically Engineered Crops on Pesticide Use in the U.S.—The First Sixteen Years*, 24 ENVTL. SCIS. EUR. art. 24, at 4 (2012).

100 Clive James & Anatole F. Krattiger, *Global Review of the Field Testing and Commercialization of Transgenic Plants: 1986 to 1995: The First Decade of Crop Biotechnology* 23 (1996).

101 *E.g.*, Ye et al., *supra* note 2, at 303 (engineering rice enriched in levels of a Vitamin A precursor).

102 CLIVE JAMES, ISAAA BRIEF NO. 49, GLOBAL STATUS OF COMMERCIALIZED BIOTECH/GM CROPS: 2014, 1 (2014).

103 *Id.* at 2.

104 *Id.* at 12.

105 Although domestication-induced genetic modification is not a "natural" process by any means, there are some opponents of GMOs who selectively consider only organisms derived though recombinant DNA technologies to be genetically modified.
106 *See supra* Section III.B.
107 *See* Suzanne Clancy, *Genetic Recombination*, 1 NATURE EDUC. 40 (2008).
108 J. R. Witcombe & D. S. Virk, *Number of Crosses and Population Size for Participatory and Classical Plant Breeding*, 122 EUPHYTICA 451, 460 (2001).
109 *See, e.g.*, Jaap M. Van Tuyl & Ki-Byung Lim, *Interspecific Hybridisation and Polyploidisation as Tools in Ornamental Plant Breeding*, 612 ACTA HORTICULTURAE 13 (2003).
110 *See, e.g.*, Knobloch, *supra* note 23, at 97–102.
111 *See, e.g.*, Susan M. Hawkins et al., *Interspecific and Intergeneric Hybridization in Dissotis and Tibouchina*, 51 HORTSCIENCE 325 (2016).
112 *See, e.g.*, G. Kalloo, *Interspecific and Intergeneric Hybridization in Tomato, in* GENETIC IMPROVEMENT OF TOMATO, 14 MONOGRAPHS ON THEORETICAL AND APPLIED GENETICS 73 (1991).
113 *See, e.g.*, Arne Müntzing, *Triple Hybrids Between Rye and Two Wheat Species*, 20 HEREDITAS 137 (1935).
114 *See, e.g.*, D. C. Smith, *Intergeneric Hybridization of Cereals and Other Grasses*, 64 J. AGRIC. RES. 33 (1942).
115 *See id.* at 33.
116 *See* Hawkins et al., *supra* note 111, at 325–28.
117 Yukio Kaneko & Sang Woo Bang, *Interspecific and Intergeneric Hybridization and Chromosomal Engineering of Brassicaceae Crops*, 64 BREEDING SCI. 14, 16 (2014).
118 Knobloch, *supra* note 23, at 97.
119 F. Laibach, *Ectogenesis in Plants: Methods and Genetic Possibilities of Propagating Embryos Otherwise Dying in the Seed*, 20 J. HEREDITY 201 (1929).
120 Sandra M. Reed, *Embryo Rescue, in* PLANT DEVELOPMENT AND BIOTECHNOLOGY 237 (2005).
121 *Id.*
122 *See* Kaneko & Woo Bang, *supra* note 117, at 16 (citations omitted).
123 For a detailed exposition of a wide range of aspects related to chromosome engineering research in plants, see generally, CHROMOSOME ENGINEERING IN PLANTS: GENETICS, BREEDING, EVOLUTION, VOLS. I & II (P. K. Gupta & T. Tsuchiya eds., 1991).
124 *See* Weichang Yu et al., *Plant Artificial Chromosome Technology and its Potential Application in Genetic Engineering*, 14 PLANT BIOTECHNOLOGY J. 1175 (2016).
125 It should be noted that, although plant minichromosomes have been used for gene transfer with nonrecombinant DNA methods, chromosome engineering in

plants is now also used with recombinant DNA technology to manipulate plant genomes. *See, e.g.*, *id.* at 1177 (citations omitted) (stating that minichromosomes have been used for genetic engineering in maize, rice, barley, and other crops).

126 Andreas Houben & Ingo Schubert, *Engineering Plant Minichromosomes: A Resurrection of B Chromosomes?*, 19 PLANT CELL 2323 (2007).

127 *See, e.g.*, W. Yu et al., *Construction and Behavior of Engineered Minichromosomes in Maize*, 104 PROC. NAT'L ACAD. SCI. U.S. 8924 (2007).

128 Houben & Schubert, *supra* note 126.

129 M. C. Kharkwal, *A Brief History of Plant Mutagenesis*, *in* PLANT MUTATION BREEDING AND BIOTECHNOLOGY 22 (Q. Y. Shu, et al., eds., 2011).

130 L. J. Stadler, *Genetic Effects of X-Rays in Maize*, 14 PROC. NAT'L ACAD. SCI. U.S. 69 (1928).

131 Souleymane Bado et al., *Plant Mutation Breeding: Current Progress and Future Assessment*, 39 PLANT BREEDING REVS. 23, 37 (2015).

132 *See, e.g.*, L. J. Stadler and G. F. Sprague, *Genetic Effects of Ultra-Violet Radiation in Maize. I. Unfiltered Radiation*, 22 PROC. NAT'L ACAD. SCI. U.S. 572 (1936).

133 JOINT FAO/IAEA PROGRAMME, *Plant Breeding and Genetics*, http://www-naweb.iaea.org/nafa/Pbg/, (last visited Dec. 1, 2016).

134 Somatic cells are all of the body's cells except the reproductive cells. BIOLOGY ONLINE, *Somatic Cells*, http://www.biology-online.org/dictionary/Somatic_cells, (last visited Dec. 1, 2016).

135 Robert A. Morrison et al., *Somaclonal Variation: Its Genetic Basis and Prospects for Crop Improvement*, *in* OPPORTUNITIES FOR PHYTOCHEMISTRY IN PLANT BIOTECHNOLOGY, 22 RECENT ADVANCES IN PHYTOCHEMISTRY 1 (1988).

136 P. J. Larkin & W. R. Scowcroft, *Somaclonal Variation – A Novel Source of Variability from Cell Cultures for Plant Improvement*, 60 THEORETICAL & APPLIED GENETICS 197, 198 (1981).

137 *Id.*

138 *Id.* at 197.

139 Epigenetics refers to the field of scientific research that studies the role of histone post-translational modifications, DNA modifications, and noncoding RNA molecules in the regulation of gene expression and chromatin structure that occur without altering DNA sequences. Paul Enríquez, *CRISPR-Mediated Epigenome Editing*, 89 YALE J. BIOLOGY & MED. 471, 471 (2016).

140 *See* Hare Krishna et al., *Somaclonal Variations and Their Applications in Horticultural Crops Improvement*, 6 3 BIOTECH 54 (2016).

141 *Id.*

142 *Rhizobium radiobacter* or *Agrobacterium radiobacter* have, in recent years, been proposed as more appropriate names to replace *Agrobacterium tumefaciens*, which was used throughout most of the 20th century. *See, e.g.*, H. Sawada et al., *Proposal for Rejection of Agrobacterium tumefaciens and Revised Descriptions for the Genus*

Agrobacterium and for Agrobacterium radiobacter and Agrobacterium rhizogenes, 43 INT'L J. SYSTEMATIC BACTERIOLOGY 694 (1993); J. M. Young et al., *A Revision of Rhizobium Frank 1889, with an Emended Description of the Genus, and the Inclusion of all Species of Agrobacterium Conn 1942 and Allorhizobium undicola de Lajudie et al. 1998 as New Combinations: Rhizobium radiobacter, R. rhizogenes, R. rubi, R. undicola and R. vitis*, 51 INT'L J. SYSTEMATIC & EVOLUTIONARY MICROBIOLOGY 89 (2001); J. M. Young et al., *Proposal that Agrobacterium radiobacter Has Priority over Agrobacterium tumefaciens. Request for an Opinion*, 56 INT'L J. SYSTEMATIC & EVOLUTIONARY MICROBIOLOGY 491 (2006). Although the new name has been proposed, I use both names interchangeably in this chapter, mainly because of the systemically widespread use of the term *Agrobacterium tumefaciens* in the scientific literature.

143 *See, e.g.*, Sang-Min Chung et al., *Agrobacterium is Not Alone: Gene Transfer to Plants by Viruses and Other Bacteria*, 11 TRENDS PLANT SCI. 1 (2006).

144 The original name proposed for this organism was *Bacterium tumefaciens*. Erwin F. Smith & C. O. Townsend, *A Plant-Tumor of Bacterial Origin*, 25 SCIENCE 671, 672 (1907).

145 *Id.* at 672.

146 *Plasmid / plasmids*, SCITABLE, http://www.nature.com/scitable/definition/plasmid-plasmids-28 (last visited Dec. 1, 2016).

147 I. Zaenen et al., *Supercoiled Circular DNA in Crown Gall Inducing Agrobacterium Strains*, 86 J. MOLECULAR BIOLOGY 109 (1974).

148 *E.g.*, Mary-Dell Chilton et al., *Stable Incorporation of Plasmid DNA into Higher Plant Cells: The Molecular Basis of Crown Gall Tumorigenesis*, 11 CELL 263 (1977); P. Zambryski et al., *Tumor DNA Structure in Plant Cells Transformed by A. tumefaciens*, 209 SCIENCE 1385 (1980).

149 One such compound is the phenolic molecule acetosyringone, which induces expression of virulence genes in A. *tumefaciens*. *See* Charles H. Shaw, *virA and virG Are the Ti-Plasmid Functions Required for Chemotaxis of Agrobacterium tumefaciens Towards Acetosyringone*, 2 MOLECULAR MICROBIOLOGY 413 (1988) (investigating acetosyringone chemotaxis).

150 *See* Charles H. Shaw, *Swimming Against The Tide: Chemotaxis in Agrobacterium*, 13 BIOESSAYS 25 (1991) (discussing chemotaxis related to A. *tumefaciens*).

151 *Id.*

152 Chilton et al., *supra* note 148.

153 Narendra S. Yadav et al., *Short Direct Repeats Flank the T-DNA on a Nopaline Ti Plasmid*, 79 PROC. NAT'L ACAD. SCI. U.S. 6322 (1982).

154 For a more detailed exposition of the molecular mechanisms by which A. *tumefaciens* mediates plant transformation, see Stanton B. Gelvin, *Agrobacterium-Mediated Plant Transformation: The Biology Behind the "Gene-Jockeying" Tool*, 67 MICROBIOLOGY & MOLECULAR BIOLOGY REVS. 16 (2003).

155 *Dicotyledon*, ENCYCLOPEDIA BRITANNICA, https://www.britannica.com/plant/dicotyledon (last visited Dec. 1, 2016).

156 *See Monocotyledon*, ENCYCLOPEDIA BRITANNICA, https://www.britannica.com/plant/monocotyledon (last visited Dec. 1, 2019) (indicating that monocots can be distinguished from dicots by the presence of only one seed leaf, or cotyledon, in the embryo of the seed).

157 Y. Hiei et al., *Efficient Transformation of Rice (Oriza sativa) Mediated by Agrobacterium and Sequence Analysis of the Boundaries of the T-DNA*, 6 PLANT J. 271 (1994).

158 Gregory D. May et al., *Generations of Transgenic Banana (Musa acuminata) Plants via Agrobacterium-Mediated Transformation*, 13 NATURE BIOTECHNOLOGY 486 (1995).

159 M Cheng, et al., *Genetic Transformation of Wheat Mediated by Agrobacterium tumefaciens*, 115 PLANT PHYSIOLOGY 971 (1997).

160 Anne-Marie Stomp, *Extended Host Range of Agrobacterium tumefaciens in the Genus Pinus*, 92 PLANT PHYSIOLOGY 1226 (1990).

161 P. Bundock et al., *Trans-kingdom T-DNA Transfer from Agrobacterium tumefaciens to Saccharomyces cerevisiae*, 14 EMBO J. 3206 (1995).

162 T. Kunik et al., *Genetic Transformation of HeLa Cells by Agrobacterium*, 98 PROC. NAT'L ACAD. SCI. U.S. 1871 (2001).

163 *See, e.g.*, Urmi Patel & Sarika Sinha, *Rhizobia Species: A Boon for "Plant Genetic Engineering,"* 51 INDIAN J. MICROBIOLOGY 521, 521 (2011).

164 For a review of some *Agrobacterium*-related patents, see Benoît Lacroix et al., *Recent Patents on Agrobacterium-Mediated Gene and Protein Transfer, for Research and Biotechnology*, 2 RECENT PATS. ON DNA & GENE SEQUENCES 69 (2008).

165 *See, e.g.*, Frans E. Tax & Daniel M. Vernon, *T-DNA-Associated Duplication/Translocations in Arabidopsis. Implications for Mutant Analysis and Functional Genomics*, 126 PLANT PHYSIOLOGY 1527 (2001).

166 *See, e.g.*, B. Ulker et al., *T-DNA-Mediated Transfer of Agrobacterium tumefaciens Chromosomal DNA into Plants*, 26 NATURE BIOTECHNOLOGY 1015 (2008) (documenting transfer of unexpectedly large fragments of A. *tumefaciens* genic chromosomal DNA during plant transformation).

167 John C. Sanford et al., *Delivery of Substances into Cells and Tissues Using a Particle Bombardment Process*, 5 PARTICULATE SCI. & TECH. 27 (1987).

168 Julie R. Kikkert et al., *Stable Transformation of Plant Cells by Particle Bombardment/Biolistics*, *in* TRANSGENIC PLANTS: METHODS AND PROTOCOLS, 286 METHODS MOLECULAR BIOLOGY 61 (2004).

169 Sanford et al., *supra* note 167, at 27.

170 Kikkert et al., *supra* note 168, at 62.

171 *See, e.g.*, Isabel Dupuis & Gary M. Pace, *Gene Transfer to Maize Male Reproductive Structure by Particle Bombardment of Tassel Primordial*, 12 PLANT CELL REP. 607 (1993) (using particle bombardment to transform maize).

172 *See, e.g.*, H. Shou et al., *Assessment of Transgenic Maize Events Produced by Particle Bombardment or Agrobacterium-Mediated Transformation*, 13 MOLECULAR BREEDING 201 (2004); W. P. Pawlowski et al., *Transgenic DNA Integrated into the Oat Genome Is Frequently Interspersed by Host DNA*, 95 PROC. NAT'L ACAD. SCI. U.S. 12106 (1998).

173 *See, e.g.*, Ana Leonor Rivera et al., *Physical Methods for Genetic Plant Transformation*, 9 PHYSICS LIFE REVS. 308 (2012).

174 A plant protoplast refers to a plant cell from which the cell wall has been removed.

175 *See* Zhaohui Liu & Timothy L. Friesen, *Polyethylene Glycol (PEG)-Mediated Transformation in Filamentous Fungal Pathogens, in* PLANT FUNGAL PATHOGENS: METHODS AND PROTOCOLS, 835 METHODS IN MOLECULAR BIOLOGY 366 (Melvin D. Bolton & Bart P. H. J. Thomma eds., 2012) (describing protocol for PEG-mediated genetic transformation).

176 *See, e.g.*, George W. Bates, *Fusion of Plant Protoplasts by Electric Fields*, 72 PLANT PHYSIOLOGY 1110 (1983); Ariel Arencibia et al., *Production of Transgenic Sugarcane (Saccharum officinarum L.) Plants by Intact Cell Electroporation*, 14 PLANT CELL REP. 305 (1995).

177 *See, e.g.*, Carl Rathus & Robert G. Birch, *Stable Transformation of Callus from Electroporated Sugarcane Protoplasts*, 82 PLANT SCI. 81 (1992); A. P. Sorokin et al., *Production of Fertile Wheat Plants via Tissue Electroporation*, 156 PLANT SCI. 227 (2000); Hiromufi Uchimiya et al., *Expression of a Foreign Gene in Callus Derived from DNA-Treated Protoplasts of Rice (Oryza sativa L.)*, 204 MOLECULAR & GENERAL GENETICS 204 (1986).

178 A. de la Peña, et al., *Transgenic Rye Plants Obtained by Injecting DNA into Young Floral Tillers*, 325 NATURE 274 (1987).

179 Gunther Neuhaus and German Spangenberg, *Plant Transformation by Microinjection Techniques*, 79 PHYSIOLOGIA PLANTARUM 213 (1990).

180 Alain Deshayes et al., *Liposome-mediated Transformation of Tobacco Mesophyll Protoplasts by an Escherichia coli Plasmid*, 4 EMBO J. 2731 (1985).

181 For a detailed review of some of these less common plant transformation techniques, see Ana Leonor Rivera et al., *Physical Methods for Genetic Plant Transformation*, 9 PHYSICS LIFE REVS. 308 (2012).

182 Other concerns exist, but human health and the environment dominate the public's familiarity with GM food. *See, e.g.*, Gary Null, *44 Reasons to Ban or Label GMOs*, PROGRESSIVE RADIO NETWORK (Nov. 6, 2015), http://prn.fm/44-reasons-to-ban-or-label-gmos/.

183 *See* Enríquez, *Genome Editing*, *supra* note 25, at 611–14.

184 *See infra* Sections V.A.1–2 and accompanying notes.

185 COMMITTEE ON GENETICALLY ENGINEERED CROPS: PAST EXPERIENCE AND FUTURE PROSPECTS; BOARD ON AGRICULTURE AND NATURAL RESOURCES; DIVISION ON EARTH AND LIFE STUDIES; NATIONAL ACADEMIES OF SCIENCES, ENGINEERING,

AND MEDICINE, GENETICALLY ENGINEERED CROPS: EXPERIENCES AND PROSPECTS 7 (2016) [hereinafter NASEM REPORT].

186 *Id.* at 39–42.

187 *Id.* at 225.

188 AM. ASS'N FOR THE ADVANCEMENT OF SCI., STATEMENT BY THE AAAS BOARD OF DIRECTORS ON LABELING OF GENETICALLY MODIFIED FOODS (Oct. 20, 2012), http://www.aaas.org/sites/default/files/AAAS_GM_statement.pdf.

189 EUROPEAN COMM'N, A DECADE OF EU-FUNDED GMO RESEARCH (2001–2010) 15 (2010), http://ec.europa.eu/research/biosociety/pdf/a_decade_of_eu-funded_gmo_research.pdf.

190 *Id.* at 16.

191 *See, e.g.*, U.S.D.A., FAS REPORT, RUSSIAN BANS CULTIVATION AND BREEDING OF GE CROPS AND ANIMALS (2016), https://gain.fas.usda.gov/Recent%20GAIN%20Publications/Russia%20Bans%20Cultivation%20and%20Breeding%20of%20GE%20Crops%20and%20Animal_Moscow_Russian%20Federation_7–12-2016.pdf (providing an account of the enactment of Russia's Federal Law 358-FZ, which was signed into law by Vladimir Putin on July 3, 2016, and prohibits cultivation and breeding of GMOs on the Russian Federation territory for all purposes, except scientific research).

192 *GM Crop Ban*, *supra* note 27 (announcing Scotland's recent ban of GMOs).

193 *See France Joins Green Wave of GM Crop Bans in Europe*, SUSTAINABLE PULSE (Sept. 17, 2015, 6:40 PM), http://sustainablepulse.com/2015/09/17/france-joins-green-wave-of-gm-crop-bans-in-europe/#.WL1bRXe-Jn4 (reporting on France's recent decision to ban GMOs).

194 *See Germany and Poland Join Green Wave of EU GM Crop Bans*, SUSTAINABLE PULSE (Sept. 30, 2015, 10:27 PM), http://sustainablepulse.com/2015/09/30/germany-and-poland-join-green-wave-of-eu-gm-crop-bans/#.WL1b_Xe-Jn4 (covering news on GMO bans in Germany, Poland, Slovenia, and Serbia).

195 *See, e.g.*, Jonathan Stearns, *European Parliament Opposes National Bans on GMO-Food Imports*, BLOOMBERG (Oct. 28, 2015, 8:46 AM) https://www.bloomberg.com/news/articles/2015–10-28/european-parliament-opposes-national-bans-on-gmo-food-imports.

196 AM. MED. ASS'N, REPORT 2 OF THE COUNCIL ON SCIENCE AND PUBLIC HEALTH (A-12): LABELING OF BIOENGINEERED FOODS (2012), https://web.archive.org/web/20120907023039/http://www.ama-assn.org/resources/doc/csaph/a12-csaph2-bioengineeredfoods.pdf.

197 *Id.* at 9.

198 *Id.* at 1.

199 FOOD AND AGRIC. ORG. OF THE UNITED NATIONS, THE STATE OF FOOD AND AGRICULTURE: AGRICULTURAL BIOTECHNOLOGY MEETING THE NEEDS OF THE POOR? 58 (2004), fao.org/tempref/docrep/fao/006/y5160e/y5160e.pdf.

200 *Id.*

201 Union of the German Acads. of Sci. and Humanities, Are There Health Hazards for the Consumer from Eating Genetically Modified Food? (2006), http://www.interacademies.net/File.aspx?id=6749.

202 *See id.*; Am. Ass'n for the Advancement of Sci., *supra* note 188.

203 *See, e.g.*, Alessandro Nicolia et al., *An Overview of the Last 10 Years of Genetically Engineered Crop Safety Research*, 34 Critical Revs. Biotechnology 1 (2013); Rod A. Herman & William D. Price, *Unintended Compositional Changes in Genetically Modified (GM) Crops: 20 Years of Research*, 61 J. Agric. & Food Chemistry 11695 (2013); José L. Domingo, *Safety Assessment of GM plants: An Updated Review of the Scientific Literature*, 95 Food & Chemical Toxicology 12 (2016).

204 *See, e.g.*, P. Liu et al., *A 90-day Subchronic Feeding Study of Genetically Modified Maize Expressing Cry1Ac-M Protein in Sprague–Dawley Rats*, 50 Food & Chemical Toxicology 3215 (2012); X. He et al., *A 90-day Toxicology Study of Transgenic Lysine-Rich Maize Grain (Y642) in Sprague-Dawley Rats*, 47 Food & Chemical Toxicology 425 (2009).

205 Although some small differences have been documented between animals fed GM and non-GM foods, studies have indicated that the differences fall within the normal variation parameters and, thus, had no biological or toxicological significance. *See, e.g.*, Chelsea Snell et al., *Assessment of the Health Impact of GM Plant Diets in Long-Term and Multigenerational Animal Feeding Trials: A Literature Review*, 50 Food & Chemical Toxicology 1134 (2012).

206 *See id.*

207 *See, e.g.*, S. Battistelli et al., *Histochemical and Morpho-Metrical Study of Mouse Intestine Epithelium After a Long Term Diet Containing Genetically Modified Soybean*, 54 European J. Histochemistry e36 (2010).

208 *See, e.g.*, Patrick Guertler et al., *Long-Term Feeding of Genetically Modified Corn (MON810)—Fate of cry1Ab DNA and Recombinant Protein During the Metabolism of the Dairy Cow*, 131 Livestock Sci. 250 (2010); K. Steinke et al., *Effects of Long-Term Feeding of Genetically Modified Corn (event MON810) on the Performance of Lactating Dairy Cows*, 94 Animal Physiology & Animal Nutrition e185 (2010).

209 *See, e.g.*, Gerhard Flachowsky et al., *Long Term Feeding of Bt-Corn—A Ten-Generation Study With Quails*, 59 Archives Animal Nutrition 449 (2005).

210 A. L. Van Eenennaam & A. E. Young, *Prevalence and Impacts of Genetically Engineered Feedstuffs on Livestock Populations*, 92 J. Animal Sci. 4255 (2014).

211 *See id.* at 4255. To the contrary, the data available show that US livestock health and feed-conversion efficiency rates actually improved over time despite widespread adoption of GM crops in US agriculture and livestock diets. *Id.* at 4259, 4262. However, the increase in productivity and animal health could not be directly attributed to the use of GM crops for dietary intake because improved

rates continued in an upward trend observed before and after introduction of GM crops.

212 *See, e.g.*, Pamela J. Mink et al., *Epidemiologic Studies of Glyphosate and Cancer: A Review*, 63 Reg. Toxicology & Pharmacology 440 (2012). It should be noted that, although the studies analyzed in this publication came from a variety of independent, government, and industry-funded research groups, the researchers who published this review received financial support from Monsanto, Inc. The authors themselves disclosed funding for this research. *Id.* at 451.

213 Mohammad H. Forouzanfar et al., *Breast and Cervical Cancer in 187 Countries Between 1980 and 2010: A Systematic Analysis*, 378 Lancet 1461 (2011).

214 NASEM Report, *supra* note 185, at 208–11 (citations omitted).

215 *Id.*

216 Tobin M. Abraham et al., *Trends in Diabetes Incidence: The Framingham Heart Study*, 38 Diabetes Care 482 (2015).

217 Ruopeng An, *Educational Disparity in Obesity Among U.S. Adults, 1984–2013*, 25 Annals Epidemiology 637 (2015).

218 *See supra* notes 216–17 and accompanying text.

219 NASEM Report, *supra* note 185, at 213–14, 217–21 (citations omitted).

220 Lois Swirsky Gold et al., *Pesticide Residues in Food and Cancer Risk: A Critical Analysis*, *in* Handbook of Pesticide Toxicology 801 (R. Krieger ed., 2d ed. 2001).

221 Bruce N. Ames & Lois Swirsky Gold, *Chemical Carcinogenesis: Too Many Rodent Carcinogens*, 87 Proc. Nat'l Acad. Sci. U.S. 7772 (1990).

222 Gold et al., *supra* note 220, at 801.

223 Henry-York Steiner et al., *Evaluating the Potential for Adverse Interactions Within Genetically Engineered Breeding Stacks*, 161 Plant Physiology 1587, 1589 (2013).

224 *Id.* at 1588.

225 *Id.*

226 Glyphosate has also been used as a ripening agent or pseudo-desiccant on crops. *See, e.g.*, *Clarification of Pre-harvest Uses of Glyphosate, The Advantages, Best Practices, and Residue Monitoring*, Glyphosate, http://www.glyphosate.eu/system/files/sidebox-files/clarification_of_pre-harvest_uses_of_glyphsate_en_0.pdf.

227 *See, e.g.*, Pamela J. Mink et al., *Epidemiologic Studies of Glyphosate and Non-cancer Health Outcomes: A Review*, 61 Reg. Toxicology & Pharmacology 172 (2011).

228 Genetic Engineering Risk Atlas [GENERA], http://genera.biofortified.org/viewall.php (last visited Dec. 1, 2016). The database is currently in beta testing and plans to add more than a thousand additional peer-reviewed reports on GMOs.

229 Structural and biochemical details of the TIPS mutations as well as their impact on EPSPS efficiency and glyphosate resistance are discussed in Todd

Funke et al., *Structural Basis of Glyphosate Resistance Resulting from the Double Mutation Thr^{97} → Ile and Pro^{101} → Ser in 5-Enolpyruvylshikimate-3-phosphate Synthase from Escherichia coli*, 284 J. Biological Chemistry 9854 (2009).

230 For a list of research papers published by Séralini and his colleagues, see Gilles-Eric Séralini, *Relevant Research*, GMOSeralini, http://www.gmoseralini.org/research-papers/.

231 Estelle Cassault-Meyer et al., *An Acute Exposure to Glyphosate-Based Herbicide Alters Aromatase Levels in Testis and Sperm Nuclear Quality*, 38 Envtl. Toxicology & Pharmacology 131, 138–39 (2014).

232 Robin Mesnage et al., *Transcriptome Profile Analysis Reflects Rat Liver and Kidney Damage Following Chronic Ultra-Low Dose Roundup Exposure*, 14 Envtl. Health 70 (2015).

233 Steeve Gress et al., *Cardiotoxic Electrophysiological Effects of the Herbicide Roundup® in Rat and Rabbit Ventricular Myocardium in Vitro*, 15 Cardiovascular Toxicity 324 (2015).

234 Nora Benachour & Gilles-Eric Séralini, *Time- and Dose-Dependent Effects of Roundup on Human Embryonic and Placental Cells*, 53 Archives Envtl. Contamination & Toxicology 126 (2007).

235 *See Relevant Research*, *supra* note 230 (providing a compilation of research published by Séralini and colleagues purportedly linking GMOs, or the use of GMO-related chemicals, to a range of deleterious cellular and physiological outcomes in animal in vitro and in vivo studies).

236 Gilles-Eric Séralini et al., *RETRACTED: Long-Term Toxicity of a Roundup Herbicide and a Roundup-Tolerant Genetically Modified Maize*, 50 Food & Chemical Toxicology 4221 (2012).

237 Many of these criticisms were subsequently published by the journal. *See* Enríquez, *CRISPR GMOs*, *supra* note 1, at 482–83.

238 *See* H. Suzuki et al., *Spontaneous Endocrine Tumors in Sprague-Dawley Rats*, 95 J. Cancer Res. & Clinical Oncology 187 (1979) (finding a high occurrence of spontaneous endocrine tumors in Sprague-Dawley rats, particularly those two years of age and older).

239 *Id.*

240 *See* Gilles-Eric Séralini et al., *Republished Study: Long-Term Toxicity of a Roundup Herbicide and a Roundup-Tolerant Genetically Modified Maize*, 26 Envtl. Scis. Eur. 14 (2014).

241 NASEM Report, *supra* note 185, at 212.

242 For instance, the International Agency for Research on Cancer (IARC) for the World Health Organization published a report in 2015 stating that despite "limited evidence of carcinogenicity in humans," there is "convincing evidence that glyphosate" can cause cancer in laboratory animals. International Agency for Research on Cancer, IARC Monographs Volume 112: evaluation of five

ORGANOPHOSPHATE INSECTICIDES AND HERBICIDES, 1, 2 (Mar. 20, 2015), http://www.iarc.fr/en/media-centre/iarcnews/pdf/MonographVolume112.pdf.; *see also*, I. M. Zdziarski et al., *GM Crops and the Rat Digestive Tract: A Critical Review*, 73 ENV'T INT'L 423, 432 (2014) (arguing that a majority of published long-term GM crop feeding studies concerning histopathological investigations of rat digestive tracts lack transparent methodologies and results and, thus, provide incomplete information regarding the safety and toxicity of GM foodstuff consumed by humans and animals).

However, the European Food Safety Authority (EFSA) and Canada's federal health regulatory agency evaluated glyphosate following the IARC's report and dismissed the IARC's hypothesis of probable glyphosate carcinogenicity. The Canadian health regulatory agency found the WHO had not taken into consideration "the level of human exposure, which determines actual risk." *See* HEALTH CANADA, PROPOSED RE-EVALUATION DECISION PRVD2015-01: GLYPHOSATE, 3 (Apr. 13, 2015), http://publications.gc.ca/collections/collection_2015/sc-hc/H113-27–2015-1-eng.pdf. Similarly, the EFSA concluded "glyphosate is unlikely to pose a carcinogenicity risk to humans." *See* European Food Safety Authority, *Conclusion on the Peer Review of the Pesticide Risk Assessment of the Active Substance Glyphosate*, 13 EUR. FOOD SAFETY AUTHORITY J. 4302 (2015).

243 *See, e.g.*, Mel Gurtov, *Food Politics: The GMO Conspiracy*, PEACEVOICE (Dec. 3, 2016), http://www.peacevoice.info/2016/12/03/food-politics-the-gmo-conspiracy/; Barbara H. Peterson, *Monsanto's Wheat Conspiracy Theory*, FARM WARS (June 24, 2013), http://farmwars.info/?p=10908; *cf.* Mark Lynas, *Time to Call Out the Anti-GMO Conspiracy Theory*, ENVTL. NEWS & COMMENT (Apr. 29, 2013), http://www.marklynas.org/2013/04/time-to-call-out-the-anti-gmo-conspiracy-theory/ (recounting the reversal of a former anti-GMO activist).

244 *See, e.g.*, Null, *supra* note 182.

245 *See, e.g.*, Mike Adams, *The Evil of Monsanto and GMOs Explained: Bad Technology, Endless Greed and the Destruction of Humanity*, NAT. NEWS (Sept. 23, 2012), http://www.naturalnews.com/037289_Monsanto_corporations_ethics.html#ixzz4VEmt6BPM; Donald L. Barlett & James B. Steele, *Monsanto's Harvest of Fear*, VANITY FAIR (May 2008), http://www.vanityfair.com/news/2008/05/monsanto200805.

246 Johan Diels et al., *Association of Financial or Professional Conflict of Interest to Research Outcomes on Health Risks or Nutritional Assessment Studies of Genetically Modified Products*, 36 FOOD POL'Y 197 (2011).

247 *Id.* at 201–02.

248 Gilles-Eric Séralini, *We Can Depollute Ourselves: The Film*, http://nous.depolluer.free.fr/gilles-eric-seralini-cv.html (last visited Dec. 1, 2016).

249 David Despain, *Organic Industry and Other Funders Behind Séralini's Anti-GMO Studies*, GENETIC LITERACY PROJECT (June 18, 2015), https://www.genet

icliteracyproject.org/2015/06/18/organic-industry-and-other-funders-behind-ser alinis-anti-gmo-studies/. *See also supra* notes 230–36.

250 Sevene Pharma, *15 Homeopathic Medicines: A Range of Products To Relieve Common Pains*, http://www.sevenepharma.com/medicines/ (last visited Dec. 1, 2016).

251 *See* Céline Gasnier et al., *Dig1 Protects Against Cell Death Provoked By Glyphosate-Based Herbicides in Human Liver Cell Lines*, 5 J. Occupational Med. & Toxicology 29 (2010); Steeve Gress et al., *Dig1 Protects Against Locomotor and Biochemical Dysfunctions Provoked by Roundup*, 16 BMC Complementary & Alternative Med. 234 (2016).

252 The PLoS ONE Staff, *Correction: Laboratory Rodent Diets Contain Toxic Levels of Environmental Contaminants: Implications for Regulatory Tests*, 10 PLoS ONE e0135542 (2015).

253 *E.g.*, Declan Butler, *Hyped GM Maize Study Faces Growing Scrutiny*, 490 Nature 158 (2012).

254 *See, e.g.*, Federation of German Scientists, *2015 Whistleblower Award* (Sept. 17, 2015), http://neu.vdw-ev.de/wp-content/uploads/2015/10/Presseinformation-Whistleblower-Preisverleihung-2015_150917_eng.pdf (awarding the Whistleblower Award to Séralini for revealing alleged health risks associated with GMOs and standing up to "'interested circles' from the chemical industry as well as the industry-financed British Science Media Centre").

255 *See* Jotham Suez et al., *Artificial Sweeteners Induce Glucose Intolerance by Altering the Gut Microbiota*, 514 Nature 181 (2014).

256 Kai Kupferschmidt, *Artificial Sweeteners May Contribute to Diabetes, Controversial Study Finds*, Science (Sept. 17, 2014), http://www.sciencemag .org/news/2014/09/artificial-sweeteners-may-contribute-diabetes-controver sial-study-finds.

257 Suez et al., *supra* note 255.

258 John E. Losey et al., *Transgenic Pollen Harms Monarch Larvae*, 399 Nature 214 (1999).

259 Gilles-Eric Séralini, *The Experience of One of the First GM Crop Farmers in Europe*, 6 Scholarly J. Agric. Sci. 9 (2016).

260 *See* Scholarly J. Agric. Sci., http://www.scholarly-journals.com/sjas/archive/ 2016/January/toc.htm, (last visited Jan. 9, 2017) (showing the Journal's logo on the home page as "Scholarly Joural [sic] of Agricultural Science," and providing a link for "Instruction for Authors").

261 Support Precision Agric., *Laureates Letter Supporting Precision Agriculture (GMOs)* (Jan. 29, 2016), http://supportprecisionagriculture.org/nobel-laureate-gmo-letter_rjr.html.

262 Angelika Hilbeck et al., *No Scientific Consensus on GMO Safety*, 27 Envtl. Scis. Eur. 4 (2015).

263 *Id.*

264 *See e.g.*, NASEM REPORT, *supra* note 185, at 154–55; Philip J. Dale et al., *Potential For The Environmental Impact of Transgenic Crops*, 20 NATURE BIOTECHNOLOGY 567 (2002) ("From the current state of knowledge, the impact of free DNA of transgenic origin is likely to be negligible compared with the large amount of total free DNA. We can find no compelling scientific arguments to demonstrate that GM crops are innately different from non-GM crops.").

265 NASEM REPORT, *supra* note 185, at 154–55.

266 For a representative, though incomplete, list of GM traits currently studied, see INT'L SERVICE FOR THE ACQUISITION OF AGRI-BIOTECH APPLICATIONS, http://www.isaaa.org/gmapprovaldatabase/gmtraitslist/default.asp (last visited Dec. 1, 2016).

267 Genes transferred from the *Bacillus thuringiensis* (*Bt*) soil bacterium confer insect resistance in GM plants. *See* Richard L. Hellmich & Kristina Allyse Hellmich, *Use and Impact of Bt Maize*, 3 NATURE EDUC. KNOWLEDGE 4 (2012). This species of bacteria produces unique proteins that are toxic to some insects and has been used as a natural insecticide in organic farming for over half a century. *Id.*

268 Glyphosate (N-phosphonomethyl-glycine), the active ingredient in Roundup® and other herbicide products, confers herbicide resistance in GM crops. *See* Loredano Pollegioni et al., *Molecular Basis of Glyphosate Resistance: Different Approaches Through Protein Engineering*, 278 FEBS J. 2753 (2011). This chemical compound kills plants by disturbing the shikimate biochemical pathway, which is pivotal for the synthesis of some essential aromatic amino acids. Glyphosate is a competitive inhibitor of the enzyme 5-enolpyruvylshikimate-3-phosphate synthase (EPSPS), which binds more tightly to glyphosate than its natural substrate. *Id.*; *see also supra* Figure 6.2.

269 Janet E. Carpenter, *Peer-Reviewed Surveys Indicate Positive Impact of Commercialized GM Crops*, 28 NATURE BIOTECHNOLOGY 319 (2010). Interestingly, some evidence alludes that "stacking" of GM traits in the same hybrid crop does not lead to additive gains of the combined traits. *See* Elizabeth Nolan & Paulo Santos, *The Contribution of Genetic Modification to Changes in Corn Yield in the United States*, 94 AM. J. AGRIC. ECON. 1171 (2012).

270 Carpenter, *supra* note 269, at 319.

271 F. J. Areal et al., *Economic and Agronomic Impact of Commercialized GM Crops: A Meta-Analysis*, 151 J. AGRIC. SCI. 7 (2013).

272 Nolan & Santos, *supra* note 269, at 1172.

273 *See* NASEM REPORT, *supra* note 185, at 115–16.

274 Wilhelm Klümper & Matin Qaim, *A Meta-Analysis of the Impacts of Genetically Modified Crops*, 9 PLoS ONE e111629 (2014).

275 Julian Witjaksono et al., *Yield and Economic Performance of the Use of GM Cotton Worldwide Over Time: A Review and Meta-Analysis*, 6 CHINA AGRIC. ECON. REV. 616 (2014).

276 W. D. Hutchison et al., *Areawide Suppression of European Corn Borer with Bt Maize Reaps Savings to Non-Bt Maize Growers*, 330 SCIENCE 222 (2010).
277 Eric W. Bohnenblust et al., *Current European Corn Borer, Ostrinia nubilalis, Injury Levels in the Northeastern United States and the Value of Bt Field Corn*, 70 PEST MGMT. SCI. 1711 (2014).
278 *Id.*
279 *See supra* notes 276–78 and accompanying text.
280 Hutchison et al., *supra* note 276.
281 *See infra* discussion Section V.B.3.
282 Klümper and Qaim, *supra* note 274.
283 *See, e.g.*, Shahzad Kouser & Matin Qaim, *Impact of Bt Cotton on Pesticide Poisoning in Smallholder Agriculture: A Panel Data Analysis*, 70 ECOLOGICAL ECON. 2105 (2011).
284 *See, e.g.*, Bhavani Shankar et al., *Production risk, pesticide use and GM crop technology in South Africa*, 40 APPLIED ECONOMICS 2489 (2008).
285 Shahzad Kouser & Matin Qaim, *Bt Cotton, Damage Control and Optimal Levels of Pesticide Use in Pakistan*, 19 ENV'T & DEV. ECON. 704 (2014).
286 *See, e.g.*, Lewis Wilson et al., *IPM in the Transgenic Era: A Review of the Challenges from Emerging Pests in Australian Cotton Systems*, 64 CROP & PASTURE SCI. 737 (2013).
287 Edward D. Perry et al., *Genetically Engineered Crops and Pesticide Use in U.S. Maize and Soybeans*, 2 SCI. ADVANCES e1600850 (2016).
288 *See* Klümper & Qaim, *supra* note 274, at e111629.
289 Jose Fernandez-Cornejo et al., *Genetically Engineered Crops in the United States*, ERR-162 U.S.D.A., Economic Research Service, at 24 (2014), http://www.beyondpesticides.org/assets/media/documents/USDA_GE[smallpdf.com].pdf.
290 *Id.*
291 *Id.* at 24–25.
292 NASEM REPORT, *supra* note 185, at 15.
293 Benbrook, *supra* note 99.
294 *See, e.g.*, Andrew Kimbrell, *New Report: GMOs Causing Massive Pesticide Pollution*, HUFFINGTON POST (Mar. 18, 2010, updated May 25, 2011), http://www.huffingtonpost.com/andrew-kimbrell/new-report-gmos-causing-m_b_362888.html; Tom Laskawy, *GMOs, Pesticides, and the New Scientific Deadlock*, GRIST (Oct. 5, 2012), http://grist.org/food/superweeds-story/.
295 GENETIC LITERACY PROJECT, *Charles Benbrook: Former Washington State Adjunct Consultant for Organic Industry* (Aug. 10, 2016), https://www.geneticliteracyproject.org/glp-facts/charles-benbrook-former-washington-state-adjunct-consultant-organic-industry/.
296 Perry et al., *supra* note 287, at e1600850.

297 The study, Benbrook, *supra* note 99, was published in *Environmental Sciences Europe*, the same journal that republished Séralini's controversial 2012 retracted paper.
298 NASEM REPORT, *supra* note 185, at 139.
299 *Id.*
300 Losey et al., *supra* note 258, at 214.
301 *Id.*
302 Mark K. Spears et al., *Impact of Bt Corn Pollen on Monarch Butterfly Populations: A Risk Assessment*, 98 PROC. NAT'L ACAD. SCI. U.S. 11937, 11937 (2001).
303 *Id.*
304 *Id.*
305 For a more detailed exposition of various *Bt* pesticidal proteins, see generally E. Schnepf et al., *Bacillus thuringiensis and Its Pesticidal Crystal Proteins*, 62 MICROBIOLOGY & MOLECULAR BIOLOGY REVS. 775 (1998).
306 *See, e.g.*, John M. Pleasants & Karen S. Oberhauser, *Milkweed Loss in Agricultural Fields Because of Herbicide Use: Effect on the Monarch Butterfly Population*, 6 INSECT CONSERVATION & DIVERSITY 135 (2012).
307 *See, e.g.*, Leslie Ries et al., *The Disconnect Between Summer and Winter Monarch Trends for the Eastern Migratory Population: Possible Links to Differing Drivers*, 108 ANNALS ENTOMOLOGICAL SOC'Y AM. 691, 691 (2015) (attributing certain regional declines to factors other than milkweed loss).
308 *Compare* John M. Pleasants et al., *Conclusion of No Decline in Summer Monarch Population Not Supported*, 109 ANNALS ENTOMOLOGICAL SOC'Y AM. 169 (2016) (pointing to evidence that the key driver of monarch butterfly population decline is a massive loss of milkweeds), *with* Hidetoshi Inamine et al., *Linking the Continental Migratory Cycle of the Monarch Butterfly to Understand its Population Decline*, 125 OIKOS 1081(2016) (rejecting the milkweed limitation hypothesis).
309 Jian J. Duan et al., *A Meta-Analysis of Effects of Bt Crops on Honey Bees (Hymenoptera: Apidae)*, 3 PLoS ONE e1415, e1415 (2008).
310 *Id.*
311 R. Ramirez-Romero et al., *Does Cry1Ab Protein Affect Learning Performances of the Honey Bee Apis mellifera L. (Hymenoptera, Apidae)?*, 70 ECOTOXICOLOGY & ENVTL. SAFETY 327, 332 (2008).
312 *Id.* at 332.
313 Antonio L. Cerdeira et al., *The Current Status and Environmental Impacts of Glyphosate-Resistant Crops: A Review*, 35 J. ENVTL. QUALITY 1633 (2006).
314 Chang et al., *supra* note 10, at 125.

315 Mark van de Wouw et al., *Genetic Diversity Trends in Twentieth Century Crop Cultivars: A Meta Analysis*, 120 THEORETICAL & APPLIED GENETICS 1241, 1241 (2010).

316 Alan Raybould et al., *Assessing the Ecological Risks from the Persistence and Spread of Feral Populations of Insect-Resistant Transgenic Maize*, 21 TRANSGENIC RES. 655 (2012).

317 *See, e.g.*, Janet E. Carpenter, *Impacts of GM Crops on Biodiversity*, 2 GM CROPS & FOOD 1 (2011).

318 NASEM REPORT, *supra* note 185, at 146.

319 *Id.* at 154–55.

7

Regulating Bioengineered Food

The advent, and swift progress, of recombinant DNA technologies throughout the 1970s and 1980s signaled the start of a new era. Public health and environmental concerns about the prospects of new biotechnologies surfaced. And legislative and judicial developments in the early to mid-1980s began to exert pressure on the executive branch to act.

On one front, Congress held hearings and entertained the possibility of enacting legislation to deal specifically with new technological developments.[1] Around the same time, an activist environmental organization filed a lawsuit in the US District Court for the District of Columbia against federal officials in charge of supervising scientific research performed at the National Institutes of Health (NIH).[2] The complaint alleged violations of the National Environmental Policy Act of 1969 (NEPA)[3] and the Administrative Procedure Act (APA),[4] and sought a preliminary injunction to enjoin a deliberate release experiment involving genetically modified bacteria.[5]

The Reagan Administration's response to congressional and judicial pressures was to task a group of the White House Office of Science and Technology Policy (OSTP) with outlining a federal framework for the regulation of biotechnology. The OSTP published a proposal draft on the last day of 1984.[6] The proposal was subsequently finalized in 1986 and gave rise to a new "Coordinated Framework for the Regulation of Biotechnology."[7] This policy document avowed that, for the most part, current laws would adequately address regulatory needs related to products derived from traditional genetic-manipulation techniques.[8] Thus, the OSTP argued successfully that "existing health and safety laws . . . could provide more immediate regulatory protection and certainty for the industry than . . . new legislation."[9]

I THE REGULATORY LANDSCAPE — A COORDINATED FRAMEWORK

The Coordinated Framework assigned broad federal jurisdiction over biotechnology products to three federal agencies: the United States Department of Agriculture (USDA), the Food and Drug Administration (FDA), and the Environmental

Protection Agency (EPA).[10] Significantly, the new regulatory scheme made it clear that biotechnology products should be reviewed by the pertinent agencies in "essentially the same manner for safety and efficacy as products obtained by other techniques."[11] Accordingly, US policy would primarily follow a product-based, rather than a process-based, approach as had been the case for products derived without genetic engineering techniques. Where needed, the OSTP recommended that "[a]n independent review of potential risks should be conducted on a case-by-case basis . . . ."[12]

The OSTP further declared that the new Coordinated Framework would be expected to evolve and could be modified via administrative or legislative action.[13] Clarifications to the scope of the biotechnological regulatory scheme were delineated in a 1992 policy statement, which reaffirmed that federal oversight should be confined to a science-based risk assessment with emphasis on the characteristics, risks, and applications of a biotechnological product, rather than the process by which it was created.[14] The policy was based on the OSTP's view that "[p]roducts developed through biotechnology processes do not *per se* pose risks to human health and the environment; risk depends instead on the characteristics and use of individual products."[15] Those products posing little to no risk ought not to be subject to onerous regulation during testing and commercialization.[16]

A *The United States Department of Agriculture*

The Coordinated Framework co-commissioned the USDA as one of the agencies with jurisdiction over GM crops. The USDA derives its authority to regulate biotechnology primarily via the Plant Protection Act (PPA).[17] The PPA vests the Secretary of Agriculture with power to restrict the interstate commerce of plants, plant pests, noxious weeds, and other articles that could harm US agriculture, so as to avoid their dissemination.[18]

Pursuant to that authority, the Animal and Plant Health Inspection Service (APHIS) promulgated regulations that, in effect, created a presumption that categorized GM crops as "regulated articles"[19] or "plant pests"[20] simply because they are derived through genetic-engineering techniques. Under 7 C.F.R. § 360.100, a GM crop may also be deemed a "noxious weed,"[21] if the APHIS believes it is capable of causing injury or damage to any agricultural interest, such as crops or livestock. Accordingly, under current law, GM crops fall within the purview of the PPA and are subject to regulations issued by the APHIS.[22]

A developer may receive authorization to use and commercialize a GM crop by (1) a notification procedure, (2) a permit for release into the environment, or (3) a petition for determination of nonregulated status.[23] The first category is difficult for a GM crop to overcome because it excludes plants with genetic material from animal or human pathogens, and requires any such foreign genetic material in the plant to be of known function, not result in plant disease, and lack substances that can be toxic to nontarget species that may feed on the plant.[24] In essence, this forecloses the authorization by a notification procedure of any crop that produces *Bt* insecticides and has herbicide resistance—virtually all GM crops.[25]

The second category delineates the rules for applying for a permit to introduce a regulated article.[26] The APHIS takes into consideration information ranging from the intended use and distribution to the article's composition and molecular biology of the system by which it was produced.[27] If the APHIS grants the permit, rules related to containment and other measures to prevent dissemination come into force.[28] Such a permit can be rescinded for noncompliance of any APHIS regulations issued pursuant to the PPA.[29]

The third category involves a process of consultation by which the APHIS determines whether the GM crop should or should not be regulated. "Any person may submit . . . a petition to seek a determination that an article should not be regulated" because it does not present a plant pest risk.[30] The petition must include all relevant published and unpublished scientific studies, data from tests performed, and information deemed to contain trade secrets or confidential business information (CBI), which must be marked "CBI."[31] The promulgations also impose a duty of disclosure by requiring that a petitioner include any information known which would be unfavorable to the petition, or state that no such unfavorable information is known at the time of the petition.[32]

B *The Food and Drug Administration*

The Coordinated Framework empowers the FDA to, among other things, protect the public health and ensure the safety of our nation's food supply.[33] The agency has jurisdiction over GM crops through the Federal Food, Drug, and Cosmetic Act (FFDCA)[34] and its food adulteration (§ 402) and additive (§ 409) provisions.[35]

Under the FFDCA, a foodstuff is deemed to have been "adulterated" "[i]f it bears or contains any poisonous or deleterious substance which may render it injurious to health."[36] The law prohibits introduction, or delivery for introduction, of any adulterated food in interstate commerce.[37] The adulterated provision grants the FDA power to impose sanctions—including injunctive relief, fines, imprisonment, and seizures—on violators,[38] and to remove any food from interstate commerce that could pose injury to health by virtue of either (1) its adulterated status or (2) the presence of large quantities of an inherent constituent of the food that renders it injurious to health.[39]

A GM crop is also subject to review if the FDA determines that it contains a "food additive," which has been defined as any substance that can potentially become "a component or otherwise affect[] the characteristics of any food."[40] The FFDCA mandates that plants containing food additives must undergo a safety review prior to market release, regardless of how the additive found its way into the food.[41]

A petitioner wishing to bring said food to market must establish with reasonable scientific certainty that the food additive is not harmful.[42]

Importantly, the law acknowledges that establishing complete certainty of absolute lack of harm may be impossible given the current state of scientific knowledge.[43] In any event, safety must be established by a series of "scientific procedures"[44] aimed at studying stability, purity, potential toxicity, potency, and performance of the food additive.[45] If the food additive is not approved following a formal petition, the item is deemed unsafe and subject to the adulterated provision.[46] Alternatively, if a substance added to food is generally recognized as safe (GRAS) "among experts qualified by scientific training and experience to evaluate its safety,"[47] it is exempt from the food additive provision and no market preapproval is warranted.

The new FDA authority under the Coordinated Framework guidelines gave rise to numerous inquiries from industry, government agencies, academia, and the public concerning the regulatory status of new plant varieties, including those derived from recombinant DNA technologies.[48] As a result, the FDA published a policy statement in 1992 to clarify its interpretation of the FFDCA regarding the extent of the agency's jurisdictional reach vis-à-vis GM crops.[49] In it, the FDA made three important remarks.

First, the FDA reiterated the position that the process by which food is produced or developed should bear no adverse impact on a safety calculus.[50] The key factors for a determination of safety ought to be the characteristics of the food product, rather than the method used to produce it.[51]

Second, the agency declared that materials derived from nucleic acids are presumed to be GRAS because they can be found in every living organism, including all animals and plants used for human consumption, and do not raise safety concerns as food components.[52] Thus, transferred genetic material is not likely to call into question the safety of GRAS substances or trigger the need for increased regulatory scrutiny.

Third, the agency introduced a policy of informal, voluntary consultation to determine the regulatory status of new GM crop varieties. This policy was based on the recognition that expression of nucleic acids introduced via genetic engineering could, in theory, lead to production of proteins, carbohydrates, metabolites, and other materials not substantially equivalent to those found in non-GM food.[53] The FDA refrained from making the consultation process a legal requirement, but it explicitly stated that each food producer is responsible for assuring the safety of products introduced in interstate commerce.[54]

Although the consultation process instituted by the FDA is not compulsory, in practice, it has become a de facto premarket approval mandate. To date, the FDA has completed 187 consultations related to GM plants under its 1992 voluntary consultation policy.[55] A possible explanation for this phenomenon is that developers wish to minimize their exposure to stringent product liability laws.[56] Indeed, because each developer is charged with ensuring the safety of its food product,[57] it is hard to conceive, from a risk-management perspective, that developers would be willing to invest considerable resources to introduce a product that could be later recalled by the FDA.

C The Environmental Protection Agency

The EPA is the federal agency in charge of enforcing environmentally conscious federal statutes concerning human health and the environment. The agency's authority to develop and promulgate rules to ensure the safety of GM plants, and pesticides thereof, stems primarily from two statutes. Jurisdiction over pesticides and plant-incorporated protectants (PIPs)[58] comes from the Federal Insecticide, Fungicide, and Rodenticide Act (FIFRA).[59] In contrast, authority over pesticide residues in foodstuff flows from § 408 of the FFDCA.[60]

Under the FIFRA, it is unlawful for any person to sell or distribute pesticides without a proper registration from the federal government.[61] A pesticide within the meaning of the Act refers to "any substance, or mixtures thereof, intended for (1) the prevention, destruction, or mitigation of any pest; or (2) use as a plant regulator, defoliant, or desiccant."[62]

The law aims to prevent "unreasonable adverse effects on the environment,"[63] which encompass "any unreasonable risk to man or the environment."[64] The analysis for establishing the unreasonable adverse effects of this provision is twofold. First, the EPA's determination cannot be solely based on scientific data; it warrants a cost-benefit analysis that takes into consideration relevant economic, social, and environmental factors connected with the pesticide's use.[65] Second, the risks associated with residues in foodstuff resulting from pesticide use must be consistent with the safety standards outlined in § 408 of the FFDCA.[66] Consequently, registration of a pesticide substance is only warranted if both prongs of the unreasonable adverse effect test are satisfied.

In addition, registration may be granted only after the petitioner submits sufficient scientific information to demonstrate adequate testing and safety of the pesticide.[67] This helps to ensure that "when used in accordance with widespread and commonly recognized practice[,] [the pesticide] will not generally cause unreasonable adverse effects on the environment."[68] Prior to commercialization, the EPA exercises authority over field tests via Experimental Use Permits (EUPs), which sanction the limited use of pesticides on a set number of acres of land or surface water under controlled conditions.[69] Minimum-risk pesticides—substances that pose little to no risk to human and animal health, plants, or the environment—are exempt from the registration requirements under the FIFRA.[70]

Pesticides, or chemical residues thereof, that may find their way into foodstuff fall within the purview of the EPA's authority under the FFDCA. As discussed earlier, a food is deemed "adulterated" under the FFDCA when it contains a substance that could be potentially injurious to health.[71] Thus, the EPA has determined that pesticides are a type of substances covered under the FFDCA's adulterated food provision. Furthermore, the FFDCA grants the EPA authority to set tolerance levels for a pesticide chemical residue in or on food if the agency determines it is safe to do so.[72]

A pesticide substance or residue is safe within the meaning of 21 U.S.C. § 342 if (1) a tolerance pronouncement is in effect and the quantity of the residue is within the limits of said tolerance, or (2) the EPA has carved out an exemption for the pesticide chemical residue.[73] Safety, insofar as tolerance concerns, is established when there is "a reasonable certainty that no harm will result from aggregate exposure to the pesticide[,]" which includes all foreseeable dietary exposures.[74] When contemplating whether to grant an exemption for a pesticide in food under the FIFRA, the EPA uses the FFDCA "reasonable certainty" safety standard.[75] Tolerance determinations and exemptions are dynamic. They can be modified or revoked on the basis on available information related to several safety factors.[76]

II CRISPR GMOS—NEW FOOD OR JUST GMOS 2.0?

The Coordinated Framework for the regulation of biotechnology has now been in force for over three decades. During that time, biotechnology and basic scientific knowledge about diverse mechanisms to accomplish genetic manipulation in cells and whole organisms has progressed immensely. Compared to previous generations, modern-day scientists and plant breeders have at their disposal more powerful and precise tools to manipulate nucleotide sequences at will. Few, if any, scientists—let alone law and policy makers—could have predicted, at the time the Coordinated Framework went into effect, all the ways in which humans are now able to alter the genetic composition of living organisms.

The era of recombinant DNA is in the past. A genome-editing revolution is now underway.[77] This revolution, led by macromolecular machines that enable DNA modification with tremendous precision, is challenging long-held conventions of how humans view life and the incipient power to control and alter the genetic destiny of every living organism.

In the last few years, new methods of genetic manipulation involving programmable nucleases such as Zinc-Finger Nucleases (ZFNs), Transcription Activator-Like Effector Nucleases (TALENs), and CRISPR systems have emerged and taken root in laboratories around the world with remarkable speed.[78] Of these, CRISPR systems are the most renowned due to their ease of use, efficiency, and modular nature.

Genetic manipulation via modern genome-editing technologies, such as CRISPR systems, is strikingly different—in a few, but significant areas—from older genetic engineering methods based on recombinant DNA technology. With respect to GM crops, the primary difference rests on the fact that older methods of plant transformation are limited by the random integration of foreign DNA sequences into the target plant species. Simply put, it is impossible to control where, and with what frequency, insertion of foreign DNA occurs via older genetic-engineering techniques. In contrast, modern genome-editing technologies are precise and need not rely on the insertion of foreign DNA sequences at all to carry out intended genetic manipulations.

The most important implication, for purposes of this discussion, is that modern genome-editing methods extend previously unavailable opportunities to help allay controversies surrounding GM crops.[79]

Consider the case of Arctic® apples[80] and Innate® potatoes,[81] which the FDA cleared for human consumption in 2015 after five- and two-year review periods, respectively. The apples, for example, are engineered to resist browning associated with cuts and bruises via introduction of foreign nucleotide sequences to suppress endogenous genes and the addition of a selectable marker gene (*nptII*) for antibiotic resistance.[82] This is precisely one of the most unacceptable aspects of GM crops for critics: the transfer of genetic material from an unrelated species—bacteria, fungi, animals, etc.—into the genome of a crop plant, which would not otherwise occur in nature.[83]

But what if a non-browning apple cultivar could be grown without introducing any foreign DNA or selectable markers, and instead possessed modifications that were no different from a naturally occurring crop? What if there was an alternative method to locally suppress the endogenous genes that contribute to browning?

Prior to 2016, inquiries to the USDA APHIS led the agency to issue determinations that a GM crop modified using earlier genome-editing technologies—such as ZFNs and TALENs—does not fall within the purview of its regulatory oversight because it is not deemed a regulated article.[84] As discussed in Section I.A, USDA authority over GM crops is warranted if the genetically engineered organism or product is, or there is a reason to believe it is, a "plant pest."[85] However, the crop's own DNA is not considered to be plant pest material within the purview of the PPA.[86]

In 2016, the USDA issued back-to-back responses to the first two inquiries regarding the regulatory status of GM crops modified using the CRISPR–Cas9 system[87] The first inquiry came from researchers at the Pennsylvania State University regarding anti-browning, genome-edited mushrooms designed to produce less melanin—brown pigment—and improve the mushroom's appearance and shelf life.[88] The second inquiry came from DuPont Pioneer concerning a type of waxy corn edited to possess an altered starch composition.[89] In letters issued five days apart, the USDA declared that, based on the information provided by the researchers, neither crop fell under APHIS jurisdiction pursuant to 7 C.F.R. § 340.[90]

The USDA's decision to decline jurisdiction to regulate these GM crops marks a significant first that will likely open the gates for some level of deregulation of CRISPR-based crops. Unlike older genetic engineering methods, CRISPR-mediated genome editing does not require the introduction of foreign DNA into a crop's genome—unless a researcher so desires—as a prerequisite for proper function. Furthermore, the system can target select genes in their native genomic loci. These are fundamental distinctions that may eventually transform, alleviate, or even further complicate, culture wars concerning GMOs.

One important note is that, although it appears that some crops generated using modern genome-editing technologies are not within the USDA's jurisdiction, they may still face regulation by the FDA and the EPA. In any event, opponents of GMOs decry the current regulatory scheme—including the USDA's decision not to regulate CRISPR GM crops—and argue that conglomerates are circumventing regulation through technical loopholes in outdated regulations.[91]

III A REGULATORY PATH FOR GENOME-EDITED CROPS

CRISPR-based genome-editing technologies and their progeny are poised to raise challenging problems that our legal system will be forced to address. The current GM crop regulatory scheme concocted by the Coordinated Framework is largely driven by the realities and limitations of genetic engineering methods that rely on recombinant DNA technology. In particular, the regulatory calculus focuses heavily on the introduction of transgenic DNA, from viruses or bacteria considered to be plant pests, into GM crops by virtue of human intervention.

There is a high degree of dissonance between the ways in which GM crops derived through transgenesis or conventional hybridization and plant breeding are regulated. On one hand, GM crops developed with nonrecombinant DNA techniques (such as intergeneric hybridization, induced mutagenesis, and others discussed in Chapter 6) for cross-breeding *unrelated* crop species are largely overlooked under the Coordinated Framework. This is true even though these types of modifications are, in theory, more likely to result in significant reshuffling of parental genes,[92] which can lead to unexpected phenotypic or compositional changes in GM crops.

On the other hand, GM crops developed with recombinant DNA technology, using either unrelated or related crop species, trigger immediate regulatory scrutiny because—despite being more precise than nonrecombinant methods—the techniques used to introduce DNA could also, in theory, lead to unexpected phenotypic or compositional changes in GM crops.

It is apparent that making a GM crop, using a myriad number of techniques outlined in the previous chapter, may in theory lead to unforeseeable changes in foodstuff derived from it. It is also clear that, despite the congruent likelihood of changes that could arise from all GM-crop methods, only recombinant DNA-based methods have been associated with GMO controversies. The question, therefore, is one of risk. Namely, are the health and environmental risks associated with recombinant DNA-derived GM crops greater than those from their nonrecombinant counterparts?

Three decades of scientific research suggest that the answer to that question is no, and a scientific consensus has now formed to support that proposition.[93] From a strict risk-based standpoint, it seems logical that some level of deregulation of GM crops would be prudent. Indeed, many in the scientific community have recently argued on behalf of a risk-based approach to replace the current process-based approach to biotechnology.[94]

Calls for risk-based deregulation intensified as updates to modernize the Coordinated Framework were initiated by the Obama Administration in 2015.[95] The Executive Branch's directive to modernize the US regulatory system for biotechnology aimed to improve transparency, efficiency, predictability, and public confidence in the federal government's ability to develop sound health and environmental policy.[96] The initiative explicitly aspired to ensure that biotechnology product evaluations adhere to a "risk-based" system that is grounded in the "best science available."[97] In January 2017, the federal government published the final version of the updates to the Coordinated Framework.[98]

The White House initiative coupled with the findings in the most recent report by the National Academies of Science, Engineering, and Medicine on the status of GM crops[99] suggests that the future regulatory landscape for GM crops will likely be less restrictive than it has been over the last three decades. However, if the new approach to biotechnology is risk-based, how will CRISPR-mediated genome-edited crops be regulated? In the near future, it will likely be increasingly cumbersome to distinguish between a genome-edited crop and a naturally occurring crop. Therefore, technological advances in genome editing are likely to challenge the very essence of what constitutes a GMO. And, if that is where the technology is headed, should CRISPR GM crops be regulated at all? To shed some light on these questions, let's consider a hypothetical involving bananas and a fungus.

A *Banana versus Fungus—a Hypothetical*

Suppose a group of researchers is deeply concerned about bananas and their susceptibility to a crippling fungus.[100] After many years of study, the researchers have finally discovered that the fungus secretes factors with epitopes that bind to a small site on a receptor of the plant's cell membrane. Upon binding, a series of conformational changes occur in the receptor that make it easy for the pathogen to perforate the membrane and cause cell lysis, eventually leading to cell death. The researchers have further discovered that resistance to this deadly fungus occurs naturally in some populations of a distantly related crop.

Using the latest technologies on high-throughput sequencing, bioinformatics, functional genomics, and molecular biology, the researchers have discovered that the receptor in banana cells is conserved across all plant species. Structural and biochemical information has revealed that the epitope binding site is less than five ångströms—an ångström (Å) is a unit of length equal to 10^{-10} meters—away from the active site of the receptor's catalytic domain, and that mutating or deleting only one residue[101] in the receptor protein prevents binding of the fungus factor altogether, thereby sparing the fate of the crop.

The researchers transfected preassembled complexes of purified CRISPR–Cas9 and an sgRNA into banana protoplasts to target the gene that encodes the receptor.[102] The CRISPR–Cas9 complexes induced recombinant DNA-free genome editing that introduced small insertions or deletions in the receptor gene and led to three types of genetic modifications. The mutations either (1) deleted the receptor's lone residue essential for binding of the fungus factor, (2) caused a point mutation that triggers misfolding and premature degradation of the receptor protein, or (3) introduced a stop codon that resulted in a truncated version of the receptor protein.

With the exception of plants harboring the second type of mutation that causes receptor misfolding and premature degradation—all of which exhibited arrested development—all other plants developed to maturity and are indistinguishable from wildtype (a term that refers to the most common phenotype for an organism in a natural breeding population)[103] plants. Furthermore, all the banana plants developed from the CRISPR–Cas9 genome-editing experiment are immune to the fungus. Whole-genome sequencing of the new mutants revealed that the only change in the entire banana genome was at the intended site (the gene encoding the receptor), and that the mutations were the same as those found naturally in the distant crop that is resistant to the fungus.

In summary, the researchers used CRISPR–Cas9 to introduce a point mutation in the banana receptor, which conferred resistance to the fungus. The mutant banana has zero foreign DNA, is genetically identical to all other bananas—but for the single amino-acid residue mutation or truncation of the receptor protein—and contains mutations that have already been found to occur in nature and confer natural resistance to the fungus in another crop species. How should this new banana be regulated?

B *The Coordinated Framework and Regulatory Gaps*

Under a broad interpretation of the Coordinated Framework, the new banana crop arguably falls under the jurisdiction of the USDA, FDA, and EPA because it involves the genetic modification of a crop used in agriculture, is grown with the expectation that it will be sold across interstate lines for human consumption, and comprises a substance that, in effect, acts as a pesticide against the fungus.

However, because the crop was produced without addition of foreign DNA and introduced only a small insertion or deletion in the target gene, the USDA is likely to determine that the crop is not a regulated article or plant pest—pursuant to 7 C.F.R. § 340—as it has done with other CRISPR GM crops.[104] Furthermore, because the mutation is naturally occurring in a distant plant, the APHIS may declare that there is a miniscule risk for harm to US agriculture that could justify impediments for transit of the crop through interstate commerce.

An argument could be made that the crop should not be considered safe because it contains a mutation that, while found in nature in distant species, is novel in bananas. Accordingly, the researchers should seek a permit and a safety assessment should be performed on the new gene-edited banana. But this argument falters[105] because the new banana mutation is of known function and does not result in plant disease.[106]

Similarly, it would be unlikely that the FDA would determine that the new banana is an adulterated food product within the meaning of the FFDCA.[107] The single-point mutation, which already occurs in nature and was characterized in the distantly related crop, is probably not going to trigger compositional changes in the food that would qualify it as a food additive that is injurious to human health.[108] Given the (1) lack of foreign DNA sequences, (2) genome-wide similarities between the unmodified and the mutant bananas, (3) presumed lack of off-target effects from CRISPR–Cas9 genome editing,[109] and (4) well-established status of the banana as a nutritious crop, it would be difficult to imagine that the FDA would impose roadblocks in the path to commercialization.

The EPA could decide that the point mutation in the receptor is a plant-incorporated protectant or pesticide.[110] However, because the genetic material needed to produce the purported pesticidal substance is endogenous to the plant and can be found in nature, the agency would likely determine that the crop does not represent an "unreasonable adverse effect on the environment."[111] Moreover, under this specific scenario, the fungus is exclusively acting as a pest and its eradication would presumably only bring benefits and pose no threat to the ecosystem. If the targeted species was an insect instead of a fungus, it may be necessary to assess the potential unreasonable adverse effects on the environment.[112]

An additional factor that may favor deregulation of the banana crop comes from the unique requirement that, under the FIFRA, the EPA's determination cannot be solely based on scientific data, but also on other economic, social, and environmental factors.[113] This standard might strengthen the argument for deregulation given that the mutation is highly specific, characterized, already found in nature, and could potentially save an extremely important agricultural crop from the brink of extinction. The EPA would probably issue an exemption to the registration requirements because the banana mutation poses a minimal risk to human and animal health, plants, or the environment.[114]

The foregoing analysis would change slightly if the truncation (the third type of mutation in our hypothetical), and not the point mutation (the first type of mutation), were the dominant effect from genome editing in the banana. It is possible that a nonfunctional, truncated receptor in a cell membrane could theoretically interfere with cellular pathways and other functional roles. If the truncation leads to accumulation of a particular protein that has allergenic potential, for example, it could represent a potential danger to human health or the environment. The problem under this scenario would be predicting such adverse effects, which are unlikely to occur.

C *Genome Editing and Food Labeling*

Another area of the law for which genome editing will likely pose regulatory challenges is bioengineered-food labeling.[115] Recall our discussion in Chapter 3 concerning the new federal requirement for a National Bioengineered Food Disclosure Standard (NBFDS), as mandated by amendments to the Agricultural Marketing Act of 1946, which went into effect in July 2016.[116] The NBFDS requires the Secretary of the Department of Agriculture to establish disclosure standards for bioengineered food. The law sought to preempt the rise of a potential patchwork of conflicting state or local GMO-labeling laws,[117] such as Vermont's Act 120, which mandated stringent labeling laws for all food produced via genetic-engineering technologies.[118] By enacting the NBFDS, Congress aimed to ensure national uniformity of labeling laws for food derived from genetically engineered crops.

In the context of genome editing, however, the NBFDS is ambiguous, contains many gaps, and only partially addresses the issue of labeling bioengineered foods. For instance, the definition of bioengineered food under the NBFDS is narrow and applies only to foodstuff containing "genetic material that has been modified through in vitro recombinant [DNA] techniques."[119] If the term "genetic material" means "DNA" under the statute—as it likely would—then most packaged products that contain ingredients derived from genetically engineered crops, which are sold at supermarkets everywhere, would not be considered bioengineered because they actually have no detectable DNA. The same would be true for food derived from gene-edited crops.

The recombinant DNA limitation in the definition of bioengineered food is even more problematic. Let's refer back to the banana hypothetical in Section III.A. Recall that researchers used CRISPR–Cas9 to introduce a single amino-acid mutation in the banana receptor, which conferred resistance to the fungus. No foreign DNA was used in the making of the banana. And the mutation induced by the CRISPR–Cas9 system was actually already found in another crop that is naturally resistant to the fugus.

Under the NBFDS statutory constraints, some food derived via CRISPR-based gene-editing technology would be subject to mandatory labeling disclosures depending on how the genome-editing experiments were carried out. If the genome editing occurred with the use of a DNA construct that is incorporated directly into the DNA of the plant cells, the banana would fall under the definition of bioengineered food. But if the genome editing occurred via the use of transient, preassembled sgRNA and Cas9 protein complexes (as in the hypothetical in this chapter), the banana would likely not be subject to the NBFDS labelling requirements because the modification does not involve use of any recombinant DNA material that could be integrated into the plant cell's DNA, and the CRISPR–Cas9–sgRNA complexes would be degraded shortly after the gene editing takes place. Thus, the law facilitates a potential scenario under which one gene-edited crop must be labelled as bioengineered food, while another gene-edited crop is exempt from the NBFDS mandatory disclosure requirements.

The nuances of ever-evolving biotechnological innovation highlight the complexities that regulatory systems will face in the context of genome editing. As jurisdictions around the world weigh in on the legal status of gene-edited crops, such complexities will only exacerbate tensions between advocates and opponents of the use of biotechnology in agriculture. Unlike the US, which has decided not to regulate at least some CRISPR-based crops under the framework applicable to genetically engineered crops,[120] the EU has chosen to regulate all gene-edited crops under more stringent laws applicable to GM crops derived with transgenic DNA material. In July 2018, the Court of Justice of the European Union held that organisms obtained by "new directed mutagenesis techniques" constitute GMOs within the meaning Article 2(2) of Directive 2001/18,[121] which defines GMOs as "an organism . . . in which the genetic material has been altered in a way that does not occur naturally by mating and/or natural recombination."[122] CRISPR-mediated genome editing falls under the category of new mutagenesis techniques that are not exempt under the court's ruling.

Rules establishing bioengineered food disclosures should be coherent and science-based. At the very least, gene editing that uses no foreign DNA, is more precise than conventional breeding methods, and causes genetic modifications already found in nature should not be subject to onerous regulations and disclosure standards. We will discuss law- and science-based policy recommendations related to GM crops in more detail in Chapter 11.

Notes

1 *Biotechnology Regulation: Hearing Before the Subcomm. on Oversight and Investigations of the House Comm. on Energy and Commerce*, 98th Cong. 98–193 (1984); *Environmental Implications of Genetic Engineering: Hearing Before the Subcomm. on Investigations and Oversight and the Subcomm. on Science, Research and Technology of the House Comm. on Science and Technology*, 98th Cong. 2–3 (1983).

2 Found. on Econ. Trends v. Heckler (*Heckler I*), 587 F. Supp. 753, 754 (D.D.C. 1984), *aff'd*, 756 F.2d 143 (D.C. Cir. 1985).

3 42 U.S.C. §§ 4321–70 (2012).

4 5 U.S.C. § 706 (2012).

5 *Heckler I*, 587 F. Supp. at 754.

6 *See* Proposal for a Coordinated Framework for Regulation of Biotechnology, 49 Fed. Reg. 50,856 (proposed Dec. 31, 1984).
7 Coordinated Framework for the Regulation of Biotechnology, 51 Fed. Reg. 23,302 (June 26, 1986).
8 *Id.*
9 *Id.*
10 The 1986 final policy draft followed the 1984 proposal's vision, which stated that

> [T]he Food and Drug Administration (FDA) would regulate genetic engineering products no differently that those achieved through traditional techniques. The Environmental Protection Agency (EPA) described existing and proposed new policies for regulating pesticidal and nonpesticidal microorganisms. The Department of Agriculture (USDA) stated that under its different legislative authorities it could broadly regulate genetically engineered plants and animals, and plant and animal pathogens.

Id.
11 *Id.*
12 *Id.*
13 Coordinated Framework for the Regulation of Biotechnology, 51 Fed. Reg. 23,302 (proposed June 26, 1986).
14 *Exercise of Federal Oversight Within Scope of Statutory Authority: Planned Introductions of Biotechnology Products into the Environment*, 57 Fed. Reg. 6753 (proposed Feb. 27, 1992).
15 *Id.* at 6760. The opinion mirrors the findings of an extensive review performed by the National Research Council (NRC) on the potential risks of introductions of organisms made from new biotechnology processes. The NRC found that "the nature of the process is not a useful criterion for determining whether [a] product requires less or more oversight ... [and] [n]o conceptual distinction exists between genetic modification of plants and microorganisms by classical methods or by molecular techniques that modify DNA and transfer genes." *Id.* at 6755.
16 *Id.* at 6760.
17 *See* 7 U.S.C. §§ 7701–86 (2012). Before the PPA was enacted, the USDA derived authority in this realm from the Federal Plant Pest Act. *See infra* note 22.
18 Section 7712(a) states that, in general,

> The Secretary may prohibit or restrict the importation, entry, exportation, or movement in interstate commerce of any plant, plant product, biological control organism, noxious weed, article, or means of conveyance, if the Secretary determines that the prohibition or restriction is necessary to prevent the introduction into the United States or the dissemination of a plant pest or noxious weed within the United States.

Id.

19 7 C.F.R. § 340.0(a)(2), n.1 (1997). A regulated article is defined as

> Any organism which has been altered or produced through genetic engineering, if the donor organism, recipient organism, or vector or vector agent belongs to any genera or taxa designated in § 340.2 and meets the definition of plant pest, or is an unclassified organism and/or an organism whose classification is unknown, or any product which contains such an organism, or any other organism or product altered or produced through genetic engineering which the Administrator determines is a plant pest or has reason to believe is a plant pest. Excluded are recipient microorganisms which are not plant pests and which have resulted from the addition of genetic material from a donor organism where the material is well characterized and contains only noncoding regulatory regions.

Id. § 340.1.

20 7 C.F.R. § 340.1 defines a plant pest as

> Any living stage (including active and dormant forms) of insects, mites, nematodes, slugs, snails, protozoa, or other invertebrate animals, bacteria, fungi, other parasitic plants or reproductive parts thereof; viruses; or any organisms similar to or allied with any of the foregoing; or any infectious agents or substances, which can directly or indirectly injure or cause disease or damage in or to any plants or parts thereof, or any processed, manufactured, or other products of plants.

Id.

21 7 C.F.R. § 360.100 defines a noxious weed as "[a]ny plant or plant product that can directly or indirectly injure or cause damage to crops (including nursery stock or plant products), livestock, poultry, or other interests of agriculture, irrigation, navigation, the natural resources of the United States, the public health, or the environment."

22 Prior to the enactment of the PPA, the USDA derived its authority to regulate the movement of "plant pests," from the Federal Plant Pest Act, which was repealed in 2000. *See* 7 U.S.C. § 150aa–jj (repealed 2000).

23 7 C.F.R. §§ 340.3, 340.4, 340.6 (2016).

24 *See* §§ 340.3(b–c) (stating that regulated articles must meet six requirements and performance standards to be eligible for introduction under the notification procedure).

25 Nearly 100 percent of GM crops sold are genetically engineered with either herbicide tolerance or insect resistance, or both. Those traits account for almost all of the GM crops grown commercially over the past twenty years. Canadian Biotechnology Action Network (CBAN), *Where in the World are GM Crops and Foods?*, 1, 2 (2015), http://gefreekamloops.org/wp-content/uploads/2015/07/where-in-the-world-gm-crops-foods.pdf.

26 7 C.F.R. § 340.4 (2016).

27 *See* §§ 340.4(b)(1–12).

28 §§ 340.4(f)(1–11).

29 § 340.4 (g).
30 § 340.6.
31 § 340.6(b).
32 7 C.F.R. § 340.6(b) (2016).
33 U.S. FOOD & DRUG ADMIN., *FDA Mission*, http://www.fda.gov/AboutFDA/WhatWeDo/ (last updated Oct. 24, 2016).
34 *See* 21 U.S.C. § 301 (2012).
35 It bears noting that other statutes, such as the Public Health Service Act, 42 U.S.C. §§ 201–300mm-61 (2012), also grant the FDA jurisdiction over certain aspects related to GM crops, including the regulation of drugs and biological products derived from GM plants, which are outside the scope of this chapter.
36 21 U.S.C. § 342(a)(1).
37 § 331.
38 *See* §§ 331–35.
39 *See* § 342.
40 § 321(s).
41 21 U.S.C. § 348 (2012).
42 21 C.F.R. § 170.3(i) (2016).
43 *Id.*
44 *Id.*
45 § 171.1(c) (2016).
46 *See* 21 U.S.C. § 342(a)(2)(c).
47 § 321(s).
48 *See* U.S. Food & Drug Administration, Statement of Policy: Foods Derived From New Plant Varieties, 57 Fed. Reg. 22,984 (proposed May 29, 1992).
49 *Id.*
50 *Id.* at 22,984–85.
51 *Id.*
52 *Id.* at 22,989–90.
53 U.S. Food & Drug Administration, Statement of Policy: Foods Derived From New Plant Varieties, 57 Fed. Reg. 22,990.
54 *Id.*
55 U.S. FOOD & DRUG ADMIN. *Biotechnology Consultations on Food from GE Plant Varieties*, http://www.accessdata.fda.gov/scripts/fdcc/?set=Biocon (last visited Sept. 1, 2020).
56 *See, e.g.*, GRANT ISAAC, AGRICULTURAL BIOTECHNOLOGY AND TRANSATLANTIC TRADE: REGULATORY BARRIERS TO GM CROPS 186 (2002).
57 57 Fed. Reg. 22,984.
58 A plant-incorporated protectant is "a pesticidal substance that is intended to be produced and used in a living plant, or in the produce thereof, and the genetic material necessary for production of such a pesticidal substance. It also includes

any inert ingredient contained in the plant, or produce thereof." 40 C.F.R. § 152.3 (2016).

59 Federal Insecticide, Fungicide, and Rodenticide Act, 7 U.S.C. §§ 136–136y (2012).

60 Federal Food, Drug, and Cosmetic Act, 21 U.S.C. §§ 301–399h (2012).

61 7 U.S.C. § 136a(a).

62 § 136(u).

63 § 136a(a).

64 § 136(bb).

65 *Id.*

66 *Id.*

67 *See, e.g.*, 7 U.S.C. § 136a(c)(5) (2012); 40 U.S.C. §§ 152.50, 152.170, 158.70, 158.130 (2012).

68 7 U.S.C. § 136a(c)(5).

69 § 136c.

70 40 U.S.C. § 152.25(f) (2012).

71 21 U.S.C. § 342(a)(1) (2012).

72 § 346a(b)(2)(A).

73 §§ 342(a)(2)(A)–(B).

74 § 346a(b)(2)(A)(ii).

75 *Id.*

76 § 346a(b)(2)(D).

77 For a detailed exposition of the history of genome editing, as well as some of its applications and implications for science and law, see generally Paul Enríquez, *Genome Editing and the Jurisprudence of Scientific Empiricism*, 19 Vand. J. Ent. & Tech. L. 603 (2017).

78 Other tools for genome editing exist. *See* Enríquez *supra* note 77, at 622–33.

79 The opportunities referred to in this section may not be entirely adequate or meaningful for some people who oppose GMOs from a purist perspective. That is, some anti-GMO people believe that any type of genetic engineering, no matter what the approach or end point, is inherently inappropriate because nature must be allowed to take its course without human intervention. For those who hold that view, modern genome-editing technologies are not likely to help minimize the controversies surrounding GMOs.

80 U.S. Food & Drug Admin., *Biotechnology Consultation Agency Response Letter BNF 000132* (Mar. 20, 2015), http://www.fda.gov/Food/FoodScienceResearch/GEPlants/Submissions/ucm436163.htm.

81 U.S. Food & Drug Admin., *Biotechnology Consultation Agency Response Letter BNF 000141* (Mar. 20, 2015), http://www.fda.gov/Food/FoodScienceResearch/GEPlants/Submissions/ucm436169.htm.

82 *Biotechnology Consultation Agency Response Letter BNF 000132, supra* note 80.

83 Center for Food Safety, *About Genetically Engineered Foods*, http://www.centerforfoodsafety.org/issues/311/ge-foods/about-ge-foods# (last visited Dec. 1, 2016).
84 *See, e.g.*, Michael Gregoire, *APHIS Review as to Whether Zea mays Plants with the IPK1 Gene Deleted Using Zinc Nuclease Technology is Regulated by APHIS* 2 (May 26, 2010), https://www.aphis.usda.gov/biotechnology/downloads/reg_loi/DOW_ZFN_IPK1_052610.pdf.
85 7 C.F.R. § 340.0(a)(2), n.1 (1997).
86 *See* § 340.1.
87 *See* Yinong Yang, United States Department of Agriculture, Request for Confirmation that Transgene-Free, CRISPR-Edited Mushroom Is not a Regulated Article (Apr. 4, 2016), https://www.aphis.usda.gov/biotechnology/downloads/reg_loi/15–321–01_air_response_signed.pdf; Daria H. Schmidt, United States Department of Agriculture, Confirmation of Regulatory Status of Waxy Corn Developed by CRISPR-Cas Technology (Apr. 18, 2016), https://www.aphis.usda.gov/biotechnology/downloads/reg_loi/15–352–01_air_response_signed.pdf.
88 Yang, *supra* note 87.
89 Schmidt, *supra* note 87.
90 *See* Yang, *supra* note 87; Schmidt, *supra* note 87.
91 Andrew Pollack, *By 'Editing' Plant Genes, Companies Avoid Regulation*, N.Y. Times, Jan. 2, 2015, at B1.
92 *See* Irving W. Knobloch, *Intergeneric Hybridization in Flowering Plants*, 21 Taxon 97 (1972).
93 *See generally* Chapter 6, Sections V.A–B.
94 *See, e.g.*, Gregory Conko et al., A *Risk-Based Approach to the Regulation of Genetically Engineered Organisms*, 34 Nature Biotechnology 493 (2016).
95 *See* Executive Office of the President, *Memorandum for Heads of Food and Drug Administration, Environmental Protection Agency, and Department of Agriculture: Modernizing the Regulatory System for Biotechnology Products* (July 2, 2015), https://www.whitehouse.gov/sites/default/files/microsites/ostp/modernizing_the_reg_system_for_biotech_products_memo_final.pdf.
96 *Id.* at 4.
97 *Id.*
98 *See* Modernizing the Regulatory System for Biotechnology Products: Final Version of the 2017 Update to the Coordinated Framework for the Regulation of Biotechnology, https://obamawhitehouse.archives.gov/sites/default/files/microsites/ostp/2017_coordinated_framework_update.pdf.
99 *See generally* Committee on Genetically Engineered Crops: Past Experience and Future Prospects; Board on Agriculture and Natural Resources; Division on Earth and Life Studies; National Academies of Sciences, Engineering, and Medicine, Genetically Engineered Crops: Experiences and Prospects (2016).

100 In fact, the Cavendish banana, the most popular fruit in the world, is currently in danger of extinction in some parts of the world due to its susceptibility to the *Fusarium oxysporum* f.sp. *cubense* Tropical Race 4 (TR4) fungus. *See generally* DAN KOEPPEL, BANANA: THE FATE OF THE FRUIT THAT CHANGED THE WORLD 109, 159, 229–30 (2008); Dan Charles, *Our Favorite Banana May Be Doomed; Can New Varieties Replace It?* NPR (Jan. 11, 2016), http://www.npr.org/sections/thesalt/2016/01/11/462375558/our-favorite-banana-may-be-doomed-can-new-varieties-replace-it. The hypothetical presented is not reflective of the actual pathophysiology of the TR4 fungus disease and is merely based on the banana's susceptibility to the disease for illustrative purposes.

101 Mutations of only a few nucleotides in a gene can potentially lead to dramatic phenotypes. For instance, a naturally occurring mutation of only two amino acids (T102I and P106S) in the 5-enolpyruvylshikimate-3-phosphate synthase (*EPSPS*) gene confers resistance to glyphosate in *Eleusine indica*, a type of Indian grass. *See* Q. Yu et al., *Evolution of a Double Amino Acid Substitution in the 5-enolpyruvylshikimate-3-phosphate Synthase in Eleusine indica Conferring High-Level Glyphosate Resistance*, 167 PLANT PHYSIOLOGY 1440 (2015). This phenomenon is not unique to plants. For instance, a single-point mutation in human cells is responsible for the most common form of Cystic Fibrosis, which has been corrected using CRISPR–Cas9 genome editing in stem cells in vitro. *See* Gerald Schwank et al., *Functional Repair of CFTR by CRISPR/Cas9 in Intestinal Stem Cell Organoids of Cystic Fibrosis Patients*, 13 CELL STEM CELL 653 (2013).

102 *See* KOEPPEL, *supra* note 100. A similar DNA-free genome editing approach was recently reported to introduce targeted mutations in various genes in *Arabidopsis thaliana*, tobacco, lettuce, and rice plants without using any recombinant DNA. *See* Je Wook Woo et al., *DNA-Free Genome Editing in Plants with Preassembled CRISPR-Cas9 Ribonucleoproteins*, 33 NATURE BIOTECHNOLOGY 1162 (2015).

103 BIOLOGY ONLINE, *Wildtype*, http://www.biology-online.org/dictionary/Wildtype (last visited March 7, 2017).

104 *See* Yang, *supra* note 87; Schmidt, *supra* note 87.

105 Suppose that the researchers subsequently find a region of the world in which the banana evolved natural resistance to the fungus resulting from the same mutation that was introduced with CRISPR-Cas9. Such a discovery would seriously undermine any arguments in favor of restrictions based on safety.

106 *See* 7 C.F.R. § 340.3(b) (2016).

107 21 U.S.C. § 342(a)(1) (2012).

108 § 321(s).

109 Off-target activity of CRISPR-based genome editing is an active field of scientific research. Significant improvements in this area have been made in the past three years. *See, e.g.*, Seung Woo Cho et al., *Analysis of Off-Target Effects of*

CRISPR/Cas-Derived RNA-Guided Endonucleases and Nickases, 24 GENOME RESEARCH 132 (2014).

110 *See* 40 C.F.R. § 152.3 (2016); 7 U.S.C. § 136 (2012).

111 7 U.S.C. § 136a(a).

112 *Id.*

113 *See* § 136(bb).

114 *See* 40 C.F.R. § 152.25(f) (2016).

115 *See, e.g.*, Paul Enríquez, *Genetically Modified Food Is too Advanced for Its Out-of-Date Regulations*, THE HILL (July 8, 2017), https://thehill.com/blogs/pundits-blog/energy-environment/341115-genetically-modified-food-is-too-advanced-for-its-out.

116 *See* Pub. L. No. 114–216, 130 Stat. 834 (2016). A prior version of the bill had been introduced in 2015 as the Safe and Accurate Food Labeling Act of 2015 but failed in Congress.

117 Report of the Committee on Agriculture, U.S. House of Representatives, H.R. Rep. No. 114-896, 114th Cong., 2d Sess., at 24, Dec. 27, 2016.

118 9 V.S.A. § 3041–48 (2014). An Act Relating to the Labeling of Food Produced with Genetic Engineering, No. 120, 2014 Vermont Acts.

119 National Bioengineered Food Disclosure Standard, 7 U.S.C. § 1639(1) (2016).

120 *See* Yang, *supra* note 87; Schmidt, *supra* note 87.

121 Case C-528/16, Confédération Paysanne v. Premier Ministre, ECLI:EU:C:2018:583, ¶¶ 24, 38 (July 25, 2018).

122 Directive 2001/18/EC, art. 2(2), 2001 O.J. L (106), 4 (EC).

8

Redesigning Humanity

On the eve of the Second International Summit on Human Genome Editing in November 2018, news broke about the first reported live births of human twins whose genomes had been edited. At the Summit, He Jiankui, a researcher from the Southern University of Science and Technology in Shenzhen, China, confirmed reports that he had performed genome editing on viable human embryos using CRISPR–Cas9.[1] The experiments, which led to the birth of the world's first gene-edited babies, sought to edit a fragment of the *CCR5* locus that encodes a protein receptor involved in HIV resistance in humans.[2] He Jiankui performed the clinical trial in virtually complete secrecy, and his subsequent disclosure sent shock waves throughout the world.[3]

To be clear, as we discussed previously in Chapter 5, He Jiankui's experiments to edit human embryos for clinical use were largely predictable. Another Chinese study published three years earlier amid similar controversy reported the first instance of human embryo editing to correct a genetic mutation.[4] The distinction between that study and the one conducted by He Jiankui primarily concerns the quality of the embryos used. The former had experimented with embryos incapable of leading to a pregnancy, whereas the latter edited healthy embryos that ultimately led to implantation in a woman's uterus and the live birth of twins.

The logical leap between the two Chinese experiments was not large. After all, the same type of experiments had already been reported in monkeys and numerous other animal species.[5] Indeed, the birth of a genetically edited human had been a forgone conclusion[6] since 2012, following the debut of CRISPR–Cas9 as a molecular tool repurposed for programmable genome editing.[7] Predictability and inevitability, however, did not soften the blow generated by the realization that it took humans only six years from the advent of an emerging technology to achieve what had been impossible for thousands of years before.[8]

I TO BAN OR NOT TO BAN

In the aftermath of the births of the first gene-edited babies, calls for permanent or temporary bans on the use of technologies intended for genome editing have surfaced.[9] Critics of the experiments claim that editing the human germline—sperm, eggs, zygotes, and embryos—is immoral, unethical, and will lead humans down a dangerous path.[10] At the same time, gene editing of somatic cells—differentiated cells, not including the germline—is underway to address various unmet needs in human therapeutics.[11] But criticisms of the potential use of human germline genome editing (GGE) clinical applications vastly overlook the advantages of germline modification, especially when compared to interventions for somatic genome editing.[12]

A panel of the US National Academies of Sciences, Engineering, and Medicine (NASEM) recently published a report outlining certain recommendations for genome editing in the human germline.[13] The report recommended that human germline editing clinical trials should proceed only if they seek to prevent serious diseases or conditions for which no reasonable alternatives exist, and the trials are subject to rigorous oversight and transparency regarding their safety and efficacy.[14]

Although the NASEM recommendations outline a potential path forward for translating human GGE technologies to the clinical setting, they are not without potential flaws. For instance, the panel recommended that there should be "ongoing, rigorous oversight during clinical trials of the effects of the procedure on the health and safety of the research participants" as well as "comprehensive plans for long-term, multigenerational follow-up that still respect personal autonomy."[15] However, long-term and multigenerational monitoring can be achieved only with the consent of participants, who may wish to revoke consent at any point following the birth of gene-edited offspring.

In a study involving the birth of a human baby via mitochondrial replacement therapy, which is colloquially known as an intervention involving "three-parent embryos,"[16] the parents decided not to submit their child for mitochondrial DNA load retesting after the initial testing performed at birth "unless there [would be] a clinical benefit."[17] The researchers' goals of monitoring the baby every three months in the first year, every six months in the second year, and every year after the third year of age depend largely on the parents' willingness to permit such monitoring. And the goal of assessing the baby's "fertility function" after age eighteen will depend on the consent of the adult individual at that point.[18]

The birth of the first gene-edited babies brings much uncertainty to an emerging field of the law. Questions regarding how technologies that facilitate editing human genomes will be regulated, allowed to develop, or prohibited abound, particularly given that the technology exists in the context of an increasingly globalized and interconnected world where cultures do not always share the same values.[19] For example, laws related to the genetic modification of the human germline are permissive in Mexico, Japan, and China and slightly more restrictive in the United States and the United Kingdom.[20] Meanwhile, other countries like Canada and Germany have instituted broad bans on human germline manipulations.[21]

The uncertainty is further compounded by the lack of general consensus about what it means to edit human genomes and a lack of general knowledge about technologically feasible outcomes. In the case of genome editing, one common concern advanced by some is that genome-editing technologies are inherently insidious because they will eventually lead to creation of "designer babies" with a panoply of artificial traits, such as superior intelligence, remarkable athleticism, or even enhanced beauty.

Much ink has been spilled in popular media, science fiction, and even scholarly literature entertaining hypotheticals of "made-to-order boutique babies"[22] to genetically modify traits such as eye, hair, and skin color,[23] or even more subjective ones like sexual orientation,[24] beauty, charm, and intelligence.[25] Such a world of "designer genes" would purportedly give parents a menu of choices "from any genes imaginable, *human or not*."[26] But let us not fall into the trap of entertaining such dangerous hypotheticals. Prior to embarking on a discussion about the wisdom of banning or permitting human gene-editing technologies to develop, let's first adhere to the book's theme of grounding the conversation on scientific facts. So doing will help us elucidate the extent of what is technologically possible, which will, in turn, assist us in becoming better at distinguishing between reality and sensationalism in a subject that is so often prone to acrimonious polemic.

II THE LEGENDARY TALES OF DESIGNER BABIES

Three decades ago, advances in assisted reproductive technology pioneered the emergence of an unusual set of human pregnancies.[27] Scientists had figured out an innovative approach to couple IVF and a novel way of screening fertilized embryos derived from couples at risk of transmitting genetic diseases to their offspring.

The revolutionary method, called preimplantation genetic diagnosis (PGD), involved screening for the presence of the Y chromosome in cells biopsied from fertilized embryos. Embryos carrying the Y chromosome are male[28] and, thus, susceptible to inheriting recessive X-linked diseases such as X-linked mental retardation, Lesch-Nyhan syndrome, and Duchenne muscular dystrophy (DMD).[29] PGD proved scientists could successfully screen embryos from X-linked, disease-carrier parents on the basis of gender. Consequently, the technique was presented as an alternative to abortion for couples whose only path to becoming parents to a healthy child had been to get pregnant, wait to find out the sex of the fetus—or do prenatal testing—and then decide to terminate the pregnancy if the fetus turned out to be genetically "defective" or male.

A *Playing God?*

It was not long before a debate on the social and ethical implications of PGD commenced. Some immediate concerns regarding PGD technologies initially focused on eliminating certain genetic diseases, family balancing,[30] and the prospect of gender discrimination arising from embryonic sex selection,[31] all of which were legitimate considerations raised by the technology at the time. However, other more dubious concerns—such as commercialization of children, dehumanization of childbirth, and "playing god"—piggybacked on the discussion.[32]

Unfounded claims predicted the inevitable use of PGD to essentially make people "smarter" or increase brain capacity, "eventually lead[ing] to the entire human race becoming increasingly intelligent."[33] Allegations that PGD was the first step in the creation of a "designer baby" as a way to "use money and technology to fulfill superficial desires" began to circulate.[34] Alluring declarations that parents could choose to endow their children with beautiful features and athletic prowess became normalized.[35] Soon thereafter, PGD became associated with a radical expansion of the old eugenics movement in which parents would be able to select offspring based on nonpathological characteristics in a free-market form of eugenics.[36]

These sensational perceptions of technological uses to create designer babies who are genetically enhanced to be "more intelligent, athletic, musically talented, and the like"[37] has become an emblem of misinformation in areas of reproductive technology, and now genome editing.[38] Regardless of why some perpetuate the designer-baby canard—whether due to misinformation, intent to deceive, or a desire to sensationalize—the inherent inaccuracies they are promulgating have taken root in the culture and severely interfere with the ability to have a reasoned debate on true issues.

B *The Gap between Public Opinion and Scientific Fact*

Consider a STAT-Harvard poll on public opinion of genetic editing, testing, and therapy published in early 2016.[39] Results revealed that 83 percent of Americans believe modifying "unborn babies" to improve their "intelligence or physical characteristics" should be illegal. Likewise, 65 percent believe genetic modifications should be illegal even to reduce the risk of developing serious diseases.

Polling, of course, is not quite a science and certainly is not an exact one. In fact, it is highly vulnerable to the use of specific terminology and ambiguity in framing the questions asked. For instance, there is likelihood of bias in the STAT-Harvard poll's reference to "changing genes of *unborn babies*"[40] as opposed to the more technically accurate terms "embryo," "zygote," or "germ cells" (sperm and eggs), particularly given the respondents' probable lack of knowledge that genome editing in a fetus or near full-term baby is not likely to be a viable clinical option for quite some time.

Other polls over the years reflect similar views regarding genetic enhancement to boost intelligence or athletic ability of "designer babies,"[41] but conflict with the STAT-Harvard poll in regard to the legality of using genetic modifications to prevent or reduce the risk of serious diseases in offspring or embryos.[42]

Yet, nothing in these observations detracts from the surprising revelation that, according to this poll, a majority of Americans apparently believe that genome modifications can actually be used for altering inherently polygenic (determined by more than one gene) traits such as intelligence, eye color, athletic ability, and beauty—many of which are intrinsically subjective.

Indeed, even discounting the bias in the premise of the poll questions, namely, that the potential for improving intelligence, athletic ability, or appearance is true, the data suggest that the public is largely unaware of what is technologically feasible or not. More importantly, the poll results suggest that the general population cannot recognize, and is highly susceptible to, technological deceptive simplicity.

Contemplate the claim that genetic modifications can be used to create a superhuman race of geniuses. This claim was precisely the subject matter of an article with a cheeky headline[43] featured in a popular magazine[44] pseudo-reporting on BGI,[45] a Chinese biotechnology firm partly funded by the Chinese government, and its Cognitive Genomics Research (CGR) project.[46] According to BGI, the goal of the CGR branch is to study human cognition and use next-generation DNA sequencing technologies to interrogate the relationships between genes, the environment, and cognitive ability in the human brain.[47]

There is no doubt that BGI's Gene-Trait Association Study of Intelligence suffers from cohort methodological flaws related to recruitment of "cognitively gifted" volunteer subjects who meet peculiar—to say the least—qualifying criteria. For instance, automatic qualifying volunteer criteria include obtaining high scores in select standardized tests such as the SAT, ACT, and GRE; having "performed well" in academic competitions such as the Math, Physics, or Informatics Olympiads, the William Lowell Putnam Mathematical Competition, and TopCoder; and earning a PhD degree from a "top" US program in physics, math, electrical engineering, or theoretical computer science.[48] A volunteer may also qualify by demonstration of "exceptional academic credentials or technical accomplishments."[49] Regardless of the flawed qualifying criteria for the study, BGI's approach to human cognition research appears to have nothing in common with the bombastic claims made against it. Indeed, over the past two decades, some BGI-sponsored research has been featured in many of the most prominent scientific journals.[50] And there is simply no evidence to suggest that the Chinese government is trying, or even would be able, to create an army of geniuses born out of basic research into human cognition. Unfortunately, that has not prevented the dissemination of misinformation, which is eagerly picked up by diverse media and spreads like wildfire in a dry deciduous forest.[51]

Even more disheartening is the fact that this kind of deceptive simplicity surrounding designer babies has permeated scholarly fields, including legal scholarship.[52] Many have entertained hypotheticals of "made-to-order boutique babies"[53] to genetically modify traits such as eye, hair, and skin color,[54] or even more subjective ones like sexual orientation,[55] beauty, charm, and intelligence.[56] Such world of "designer genes" would purportedly give parents a menu of choices "from any genes imaginable, *human or not*."[57] It is time to adhere to higher standards in this regard. Let's examine the scientific basis for the claim that scientists are now able to engineer superhuman geniuses with extraordinary intelligence. Our discussion of this particular trait can help to illuminate the scientific basis for many other similar traits associated with so-called designer babies.

III CAN INTELLIGENCE REALLY BE ENGINEERED IN A TEST TUBE?

The source of human intelligence and cognition has been the subject of study for well over a century.[58] Francis Galton first proposed in the 1860s that genius and mental ability are as heritable as physical traits.[59] Evidence to support his thesis consisted of "showing how large is the number of instances in which men who are more or less illustrious have eminent kinsfolk."[60] The "laws" of heredity with respect to genius were thus initially laid out by surveying men of high reputation—judges of England, statesmen, literary men, men of science, poets, musicians, etc.—within hierarchies.[61]

A *The Racist and the Dubious Genius*

From the start, the field of study concerning the heritability of human intelligence was destined for controversy and prone to racial animus masquerading as science. Galton, the founding father of the field, sponsored racial hierarchies, affirmed the superiority of the ancient Greek race, and professed "the average intellectual standard of the negro race is some two grades below [his] own."[62]

Galton's vitriol had few limits. He even expressed that he often felt ashamed of being human when flagrantly pondering about the "idiocy among the negroes."[63] Galton's ideology cemented racial contempt into the foundation of the pseudoscience surrounding hereditable human intelligence and mental cognitive ability.

General cognitive ability (GCA), also known as general intelligence, or *g*, was first formally introduced in 1904.[64] Research on familial[65] and twin[66] studies in the early twentieth century cemented the notion of the heritability of intelligence. Adoption studies contributed a layer of complexity by concluding that the environment has some considerable effect on a child's intelligence quotient (IQ).[67] Current estimates of g heritability—that is, the proportion of the variance attributable to genetic factors—range from 0.5 to 0.7,[68] and to as high as 0.8.[69] Studies over decades have consistently shown that g is a highly heritable trait.[70] Although the extent of the range of g heritability estimates has been contested,[71] the bulk of literature demonstrates that g is at least reasonably heritable.[72]

Empirical evidence for g heritability provided by quantitative genetics highlights the issue of whether there are specific genes and Single-Nucleotide Polymorphisms (SNP)—variations in single nucleotides at specific positions in the genome—responsible for intelligence and GCA. Thanks to the advent of DNA sequencing technology in the twenty-first century, attempts to identify the "intelligence" gene(s) at the molecular level are underway. The search, however, has proved the gene(s) to be incredibly elusive.

B *Hunting for Elusive Genes*

To date, several Genome-Wide Association Studies (GWAS) have interrogated potential connections between various SNPs and g. For instance, a GWAS of intelligence in middle to older adulthood probing nearly 600,000 SNPs in approximately 3,500 individuals found no specific genetic variants robustly associated with human intelligence.[73] Although a prior published gene-based test for association had found one genome-wide significant association with the gene *FNBP1L*,[74] which is highly expressed in neurons in developing brains, the GWAS failed to replicate that result using an independent sample.[75]

Members of the same team followed up with another GWAS, this time focusing on childhood intelligence from nearly 18,000 individuals (ages six to eighteen) in six discovery and three replication samples.[76] Again, the study failed to identify individual SNPs associated with childhood intelligence.[77] Gene-based analysis revealed that SNP rs236330, located in *FNBP1L*, was strongly associated with childhood intelligence.[78] Yet, not even this SNP could explain more than 0.24 percent of the total phenotypic variation, suggesting that the largest effects of such SNPs are so minuscule that other smaller-effect SNPs are virtually undetectable. Both studies concluded that intelligence is highly heritable and polygenic, yet GWAS results are consistent with a model of intelligence under which many genetic variants have very small additive effects.

Another independent group attempted to replicate the findings related to general cognitive ability and *FNBP1L* via a more robust method (GWAS Plus) using nearly 2.6 million SNPs.[79] Results could not corroborate the aforementioned findings and no gene reached statistical genome-wide significance using the same methodology of the prior report.[80] Polygenic scores from all SNPs considered could not even account for 1 percent of the total variance (0.7 percent).[81]

A GWAS meta-analysis of more than 125,000 individuals identified ten SNPs associated with increased educational attainment, three of which had genome-wide significant associations.[82] However, the contribution of each genetic locus was incredibly small and the largest estimated effect was 0.02 percent of the variance.[83] The findings hint that the genetic basis of complex behavioral phenotypes—such as intelligence—is far more diffuse than that of complex physical traits.[84] Three additional SNPs associated with cognitive performance, as well as other SNPs near loci across the *KCNMA1*, *NRXN1*, *POU3F2*, and *SCRT* genes—which are predicted to be involved in a glutamate neurotransmission pathway and synaptic plasticity—were identified in a subsequent study.[85] The estimated effect for each SNP statistically associated with cognitive performance in the cohort was also negligible (0.02 percent of the phenotypic variance).[86]

The heritability of fluid general cognitive function in middle and older age was studied in a large meta-analysis GWAS of nearly 2.5 million SNPs in approximately 54,000 individuals.[87] Genome-wide significant SNP associations were identified in three genomic regions comprising thirteen SNP variants, associated with, inter alia, *MIR2113*, *AKAP6*, *NPAS3*, *TOMM40*, and *APOE*.[88] Gene-based tests of association yielded one genome-wide significant result for *HMGN1*, a gene that has been linked to some neurodevelopmental disorders.[89] Together, all SNPs identified barely accounted for 1 percent of the total variance, corroborating the conclusion that general cognitive function is heritable and highly polygenic as others have shown before.[90]

Conflicting research and the manifest failure to reproduce GWAS results connecting specific genes with human cognition have prompted some scientists to call into question the validity of nearly a decade's worth of research. For instance, a study published in 2012 sought to replicate findings related to a dozen other genes reported to be associated with g.[91] Using data sets from three large, independent, and well-characterized longitudinal studies, the group found only one SNP associated with g that was nominally significant, despite expectations of finding ten to fifteen significant associations.[92] The failure to identify unequivocal correlations prompted the group to conclude that most reported genetic associations with GCA are likely false positives.[93]

C *Heritable, Yes. Simple, Definitely Not*

Given the existing body of literature in quantitative and molecular genetics concerning general cognitive ability, it is not surprising that, to date, "[n]o single SNP has yet been replicably associated with human intelligence at genome-wide significance levels."[94] Although there is consensus regarding the heritability of GCA, the hunt for the "intelligence gene(s)" has largely proved to be an exercise in futility.

The molecular underpinnings of intelligence may ultimately be a question that science will wrestle with for some time. The genetics-based view that mere SNPs account for highly complex and polygenic traits such as intelligence may very well be a gross underestimation of the unknown truth. The missing heritability of intelligence may be due to uncommon polymorphisms our current technologies cannot detect or Copy Number Variations (CNVs)—deletions or duplications of large sections of DNA.[95] In other words, entire sections of DNA, as opposed to SNPs, could be responsible for a large proportion of human genetic variation.[96] On this point, several CNV regions have been shown to carry genes related to development and cognitive ability.[97]

Alternatively, the basis for intelligence may rest in epigenetic mechanisms. In contrast to genetics, which focus on the four nucleotides (A, C, G, T) of the DNA alphabet, epigenetics is far more complex in nature.[98] Epigenetic mechanisms are capable of altering gene expression without ever changing DNA sequences and comprise post-translational modifications of histones and other proteins,[99] DNA modifications—for example, methylation[100]—and regulatory RNA molecules.[101] Collectively, these epigenetic processes add an incredible degree of complexity to gene regulation that takes into consideration dietary, nutritional, social, cultural, pharmacological, and environmental exposures.[102]

Yet another basis for GCA heritability could rest on principles of pleiotropy (one gene affects many traits) and epistasis (one gene affects expression of one or more genes). An article published in 2016 performed a systems-level analysis of genome-wide expression data to reveal the existence of conserved gene-regulatory networks enriched with genetic variants linked to human cognitive abilities.[103] One such network comprises up to 150 genes with tight coexpression relationships.[104] It may be the case that hundreds or thousands of genes clustered into networks contribute to genetic associations and heritability of GCA. It has been proposed that human intelligence is not unitary, but rather rises from multiple cognitive components organized into functionally specialized brain networks.[105]

As detailed in this chapter, the potential complexity for highly polygenic traits such as intelligence is remarkable. The take-home message is that deceptively simplistic notions of "gene X is responsible for trait Y" breed mass misperceptions about the role genetic associations play in trait formation and development. In the case of genome editing, one common concern advanced by some is that genome-editing technologies are inherently insidious because they will eventually lead to creation of "designer babies" with a panoply of artificial traits—high intelligence being purportedly one of them.[106] However, as documented throughout this chapter, anyone who claims that gene-editing technology is at the verge of enabling the creation of genius designer babies has simply fallen prey to, or wishes to distract others with, deceptive simplicity.

This chapter used intelligence as a model for confronting deceptive simplicity. The same principles, however, apply to other designer baby polygenic traits. At least 180 genetic variants, for instance, have been reported to influence height in humans.[107] Thus, it is preposterous to claim that, at this time or any time in the near future, genome-editing technologies will allow humans to engineer a world-class basketball player in a petri dish.[108] Simply put, human knowledge is vastly incomplete concerning the genetics of these complex polygenic traits. And the lack of knowledge does not justify entertaining far-fetched hypotheticals in public discourse related to genome-editing technologies. It is imperative that people become better informed about scientific principles before advocating any given position about scientific matters. That is the only way to elevate the level and quality of discourse in society.

IV LETTING REALITY SINK IN

So what, then, can be successfully achieved using the genome-editing technology that is available to researchers now and, more importantly, the technology that is likely going to be available in the short- and long-term? The answer is, quite a lot!

To start, all of the applications and potential uses discussed in Chapter 5 are feasible, some in the near-term, others in the long-term. For all those purposes, the issues that need to be addressed going forward concern planning, executing carefully thought-out strategies, closing gaps in technological development, and—above all—elucidating the molecular roles and mechanisms underlying genomic targets of interest—all of which can be addressed and sorted out as genome-edited technologies mature. That all, however, takes considerable time.

A *A Slipshod Plan Gone Awry*

To illustrate the complexity of clinical uses of genome editing in humans, contemplate, for example, the experiments performed by He Jiankui mentioned at the beginning of this chapter. His experiments aimed to engineer a human genome via DNA modifications at an embryonic stage, so as to confer prophylactic lifetime resistance to the HIV virus. The strategy involved blocking the molecular gateway by which the virus enters human cells. Let us dive deeper into the rationale for that molecular strategy by understanding more about how the HIV virus infects cells.

1 HIV—an Opportunistic Virus

To invade the cells of the immune system, the HIV-1—the most common form of HIV—virus must fuse its viral membrane with the host target-cell membrane. The process of membrane fusion occurs in multiple stages, and requires an intricate series of protein interactions between the HIV-1 virion and the host cell. One pivotal protein-protein interaction involves the formation of a CCR5–gp120 complex, which has been proposed to be the most crucial interaction that induces viral and target-cell membrane fusion.[109] The gp120 protein is a glycoprotein of the HIV envelope that is exposed on the surface of the HIV-1 virion and plays an essential role in HIV-1 binding to host cell-surface receptors called Cluster of Differentiation 4 (CD4) receptors (you may recall our discussion of CD4 receptors in Chapter 5, Section I.A).

HIV-1 viral entry into $CD4^+$ cells—a type of white blood cells bearing surface CD4 glycoproteins that are important for the function of the immune system—occurs as follows. First, the HIV-1 virion encounters CD4 glycoproteins on the host-cell surface. CD4 then binds to a region of the gp120 viral protein. The CD4–gp120 interaction induces conformational changes in a fragment of gp120 called the hypervariable region 3 (V3) loop,[110] which assumes a hook-like shape that docks inside a nearby CCR5 coreceptor as shown in Figure 8.1 below.

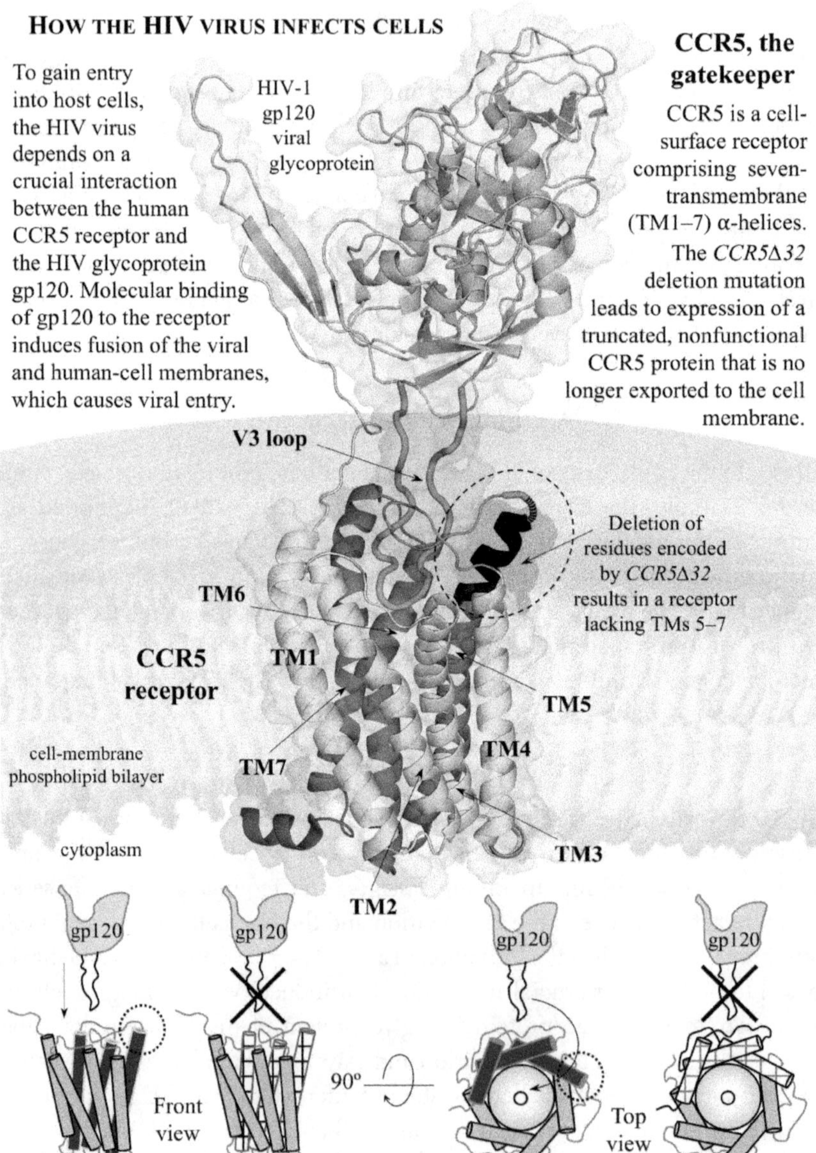

FIGURE 8.1 HIV-1 gp120 viral glycoprotein in complex with a CCR5 receptor (prior to membrane fusion)

The *CCR5Δ32* mutation precludes HIV entry into human cells. [PDB 6MEO].

This crucial molecular "docking" of the gp120 viral protein to the human CCR5 coreceptor allows the mature HIV-1 envelope spike—comprised of the gp120 protein and gp41 fusion peptides (gp41 is another subunit of the HIV-1 envelope)—to undergo further conformational changes that bring the virion closer to the cell membrane, so that the viral and human cell membranes can fuse together. Upon membrane fusion, the virus gains entry into the cell, where it can then replicate.[111]

2 Exploiting Natural Resistance

One important point for purposes of our discussion here is that a small population of humans carries a mutant version of the CCR5 receptor, involving deletion of thirty-two base pairs in the *CCR5* gene (*CCR5Δ32*). The CCR5 receptor encoded by this naturally occurring mutant gene generates a truncated and nonfunctional protein that disrupts the manner in which the entire receptor folds and functions in cell membranes. Figure 8.1 shows the residues that are deleted in the mutant protein. The CCR5 receptor consists of seven integral transmembrane α-helices that are indispensable to maintain the structural integrity of the protein receptor, including the shape of the receptor's "pocket." Deletion of the residues encoded in *CCR5Δ32* precludes the proper formation of the fifth, sixth, and seventh α-helices in the receptor, which results in a CCR5 that can no longer be exported to the cell membrane.

The *CCR5Δ32* mutation has been shown to mediate resistance to the HIV-1 virus in humans in part because the gp120 viral protein cannot bind to the nonfunctional CCR5 mutant protein, which is absent from the cell surface. It is that particular *CCR5*-altering mutation that He Jiankui attempted to generate in the embryos that led to the birth of the twin girls in China. But questions loom large as to whether the genome editing performed in the embryos led to precise targeting of the *CCR5* locus without off-target effects. In other words, because previous experiments have shown that some CRISPR–Cas9 complexes can sometimes cut DNA at the target site *and* also at unintended sites, we cannot know with substantial certainty that the gene-editing experiments induced mutations in other genes or DNA regions that might lead to harmful health consequences.[112]

He Jiankui intended to introduce changes to a specific gene (*CCR5*), which was known to play a specific role in human disease (resistance to HIV infection). The intended genetic changes, therefore, were targeted to a specific site in one gene and had a specific purpose—to introduce mutations that would lead to a truncation in the CCR5 receptor.

The problem with He Jiankui's experiments did not rest in the ability of CRISPR gene-editing technology to trigger the intended genetic changes. After all, targeting of *CCR5* in human cells had already been established in the scientific literature. Rather, the problem stemmed from He Jiankui's (1) inability to properly plan for what could go wrong, including the high probability of off-target genome editing given the early state of technological development; (2) poor choice of a genetic target, namely, one for which extensive research had not yet been performed to elucidate complete biological and physiological roles in vivo; and (3) failure to consider alternative means to achieve the goal of helping an HIV-positive male conceive children without transmitting the HIV virus. In essence, He Jiankui's experiments in human embryos were premature, posed risks that were not outweighed by potential benefits, and were ripe with challenges that could have, but had not, been anticipated.

B *Appreciating Nature's Complexity*

The problems associated with the type of *CCR5* gene editing performed by He Jiankui shed light on why alluring and frivolous claims that reproductive technologies will inevitably be used to create tall, beautiful, highly intelligent, and athletic "designer babies" are simply beyond what is technologically feasible at this point in time – and perhaps ever. As has been explored throughout this chapter, the molecular basis for these highly complex traits reflects the contribution of hundreds – and perhaps, in some instances, thousands – of genes. We do not know how, or the extent to which, one gene like *CCR5* might interact with numerous other genes. Nor do we know how a multitude of genes might interact with each other.

Even if we perfected genome-editing technologies, we would still need to unravel genetic relationships and associations through basic research before targeted clinical trials may proceed. Clinical testing and experimentation involving genes or genetic loci for which known functional and biological roles do not yet exist are simply too premature, unethical, and unlawful to conduct. For context, recall from Chapter 2 that there are approximately 19,000 to 22,000 protein-coding genes and 22,000 non-coding genes in the human genome.[113] Testing and characterization of genetic relationships and associations among multiple genetic targets constitutes a laborious endeavor. That kind of research requires considerable time and resource expenditure.

Furthermore, many of the aforementioned complex polygenic traits are not exclusively genetic in nature. Although genetics certainly contributes to traits such as intelligence and beauty, there are numerous epigenetic, socioeconomical, cultural, ethical, and other factors that may affect, and contribute to, the expression of those traits. That is why a child who grows up poor, without adequate nutrition, and does not attend school may never fully reach her intellectual potential, no matter how cognitively gifted her parents might be. It is also why an individual suffering from severe addiction and substance abuse may have health complications, damaged skin, dull hair, or appear unattractive regardless of how symmetrical her bone structure may be.

Lastly, we must remember that technological advances do not occur in a vacuum. Public acceptance and other policy considerations often play significant roles in the development of any given technology. A heightened risk to health arising from performing perfunctory experiments to manipulate human genomes may lead to public opposition to gene-editing technologies for clinical purposes. Similarly, despite having the technology to introduce a gene drive in a given population, releasing modified organisms without contemplating the proper implications of such deployment on the environment may lead to negative consequences and public opposition to technological development. We will discuss the role of public opinion in some gene-editing technologies in the next chapters.

Notes

1 Statement, Francis S. Collins, Dir., Nat'l Insts. of Health, Statement on Claim of First Gene-Edited Babies by Chinese Researcher (Nov. 28, 2018), https://www.nih.gov/about-nih/who-we-are/nih-director/statements/statement-claim-first-gene-edited-babies-chinese-researcher [https://perma.cc/RW3Q-BWDV].

2 *Id.*; Jon Cohen, *After Last Week's Shock, Scientists Scramble to Prevent More Gene-Edited Babies*, SCIENCE (Dec. 4, 2018), https://www.sciencemag.org/news/2018/12/after-last-weeks-shock-scientists-scramble-prevent-more-gene-edited-babies [https://perma.cc/2KQC-PU7C]; *see also infra* Figure 8.1.

3 *See* Statement, Francis S. Collins, *supra* note 1; Cohen, *supra* note 2.

4 Puping Liang et al., *CRISPR/Cas9-Mediated Gene Editing in Human Tripronuclear Zygotes*, 6 PROTEIN & CELL 363, 363–64 (2015). For an overview of the results of the study as well as its implications, see Paul Enríquez, *Genome Editing and the Jurisprudence of Scientific Empiricism*, 19 VAND. J. ENT. & TECH. L. 603, 664–67 (2017).

5 *See, e.g.*, Yuyu Niu et al., *Generation of Gene-Modified Cynomolgus Monkey via Cas9/RNA-Mediated Gene Targeting in One-Cell Embryos*, 156 CELL 836, 836–37 (2014).

6 *See* Paul Enríquez, *Genome Editing and the Jurisprudence of Scientific Empiricism*, 19 VAND. J. ENT. & TECH. L. 603, 664 (2017) ("Genome editing in human germ cells was largely predictable in light of the successes of germline editing in a plethora of animal and plant species [in recent] years. . . . In principle, manipulation of the human germline is not much different than germline manipulation in other species."); *see also* Edward Lanphier et al., *Don't Edit the Human Germline*, 519 NATURE 410, 410 (2015) (advocating for a complete ban on human GGE in response to news about the study Liang and colleagues performed on nonviable human embryos in China); Liang et al., *supra* note 4, at 363–64 (reporting results from the first experiments to edit nonviable human embryos); Lichun Tang et al., *CRISPR/Cas9-Mediated Gene Editing in Human Zygotes Using Cas9 Protein*, 292 MOLECULAR GENETICS & GENOMICS 525, 525 (2017) (presenting results from experiments to edit viable human embryos).

7 *See* Martin Jinek et al., *A Programmable Dual-RNA–Guided DNA Endonuclease in Adaptive Bacterial Immunity*, 337 SCIENCE 816, 820 (2012) (concluding that CRISPR–Cas9 "could offer considerable potential for gene-targeting and genome-editing applications").

8 *See* Enríquez, *supra* note 4, at 607 ("A quantum leap in genome editing capabilities has led us to the Rubicon of precise, endogenous, genetic manipulation—one originally envisioned decades ago, yet methodologically beyond reach for prior generations of scientists." (footnote omitted)).

9 *See, e.g.*, *UNESCO Panel of Experts Calls for Ban on "Editing" of Human DNA to Avoid Unethical Tampering with Hereditary Traits*, UNESCO, https://en.unesco.org/news/unesco-panel-experts-calls-ban-editing-human-dna-avoid-unethical-tampering-hereditary-traits [https://perma.cc/Y6JJ-54W8].

10 *See, e.g.*, Marc A. Thiessen, *Gene Editing Is Here. It's an Enormous Threat.*, Wash. Post (Nov. 29, 2018), https://www.washingtonpost.com/opinions/gene-editing-is-here-its-an-enormous-threat/2018/11/29/78190c96-f401-11e8-bc79-68604ed88993_story.html?noredirect=on&utm_term=.d949dc81d002 [https://perma.cc/S85U-KB24].

11 *See* Damian Garde, *FDA Signs Off on Editas CRISPR Study on Patients with a Rare Genetic Disorder*, STAT (Nov. 30, 2018), https://www.statnews.com/2018/11/30/editas-crispr-trial/ [https://perma.cc/6B92-6AZU].

12 *See* Enríquez, *supra* note 4, at 668 (pointing out that human GGE offers "greater prospects for human health and welfare than somatic" interventions because GGE can be used to correct genetic aberrations and prevent their transmission to an individual's progeny); *see also* Nat'l Acads. Scis., Eng'g & Med., Human Genome Editing: Science, Ethics, & Governance 111, 113–16 (Rona Briere & Helaine Resnick eds., 2017) [hereinafter NASEM Report] (stating that human GGE can potentially alleviate emotional, financial, and other types of burdens that families experience as a result of the transmission of serious genetic diseases).

13 *See generally* NASEM Report, *supra* note 12 (considering critical questions regarding genome editing in the human germline, providing conclusions on the need for public education and engagement on that issue, and recommending principles for governing human genome editing).

14 *Id.* at 7–8.

15 *Id.* at 8.

16 *See* Françoise Baylis, *The Ethics of Creating Children with Three Genetic Parents*, 26 Reprod. Biomedicine Online 531, 532 (2013).

17 *See* John Zhang et al., *Live Birth Derived from Oocyte Spindle Transfer to Prevent Mitochondrial Disease*, 34 Reprod. Biomedicine Online 361, 367 (2017) (reporting the first live birth of a human baby via mitochondrial replacement therapy—a type of germline intervention—to prevent transmission of mutations in mitochondrial DNA).

18 *See id.*

19 *See* Paul Enríquez, *Deconstructing Transnationalism: Conceptualizing Metanationalism as a Putative Model of Evolving Jurisprudence*, 43 Vand. J. Transnat'l L. 1265, 1289–91, 1336 (2010).

20 *See, e.g.*, R. Isasi, E. Kleiderman & B. M. Knoppers, *Editing Policy to Fit the Genome?*, 351 SCIENCE 337, 337–38 (2016); Cohen, *supra* note 2; David Cyranoski, *Japan Set to Allow Gene Editing in Human Embryos*, NATURE (Oct. 3, 2018), https://www.nature.com/articles/d41586-018–06847-7 [https://perma.cc/UA9Y-BYJ2].

21 *Id*. at 337.

22 Peter H. Huang, *Herd Behavior in Designer Genes*, 34 WAKE FOREST L. REV. 639, 659 (1999).

23 *See, e.g.*, *id*. at 642 (arguing that in the near future, genetic selection of hair color, skin color, intellectual ability, or behavior predispositions may be feasible); Joan Mahoney, *Genome Mapping and Designer Babies*, 79 UMKC L. Rev. 309, 313 (2010) (citing not a single primary scientific source for the proposition that new technology may presumably allow parents to decide eye color and sexual orientation of designed babies).

24 Mahoney, *supra* note 23, at 313.

25 *See, e.g.*, Jason T. Corsover, *The Logical Next Step? An International Perspective on the Issues of Human Cloning and Genetic Technology*, 4 ILSA J. INT'L & COMP. L. 697, 744 (1998) ("One can imagine menus offering a price list of particularly desirable traits. . . . For the right price, one may have the option to purchase the DNA of a world class athlete, award winning actor, or a beautiful supermodel."); Sarah M. Markwood, Comment, *Creating a Perfect Human Is Not So Perfect: The Case for Restricting Genetic Enhancement Research*, 110 PENN. ST. L. REV. 473, 473–74 (2005) (proposing a scenario where genetic enhancement will lead to producing "athletically gifted," "physically attractive" children, or "a theatrical prodigy, a strong wrestling champion, or a mathematical genius"); Maxwell J. Mehlman, *The Law of Above Averages: Leveling the New Genetic Enhancement Playing Field*, 85 IOWA L. REV. 517, 528–29 (2000) (entertaining the possibility that new technologies may allow genetic manipulation of traits such as beauty, strength, stamina, charm, cheerfulness, confidence, memory, intelligence, and creativity); Daniel L. Tobey, *What's Really Wrong with Genetic Enhancement: A Second Look at Our Posthuman Future*, 6 YALE J.L. & TECH. 54, 56 n.1 (2003) (asserting that "[g]enetic enhancement will, in the short run, be more concerned with improving present traits such as intelligence, personality, and strength"); Lindsey A. Vacco, Comment, *Preimplantation Genetic Diagnosis: From Preventing Genetic Disease to Customizing Children. Can the Technology Be Regulated Based on the Parents' Intent?*, 49 ST. LOUIS U. L.J. 1181, 1183 (2005) (stating a scenario where PGD will be used "to select for traits such as intelligence, athletic ability, or musical inclination").

26 Huang, *supra* note 22, at 658 (emphasis added).

27 The first human pregnancies derived from this approach were reported in 1990. *See* A. H. Handyside et al., *Pregnancies from Biopsied Human Preimplantation Embryos Sexed by Y-Specific DNA Amplification*, 344 NATURE 768, 768 (1990).

28 *Id.*; Whitney Akchurin & Ryan Kartzke, *The Ethics of Gender Selection, in* The Ethical Imperative in the Context of Evolving Technologies 33 (Dan McIntosh, et al. eds., 1996), http://www.ethicapublishing.com/3CH2.htm [https://perma.cc/Z4U3-6NNM] (wildtype human embryos are diploid and inherit one sex-determining chromosome from each parent; embryos carrying X and Y chromosomes are male, while those carrying two sets of X chromosomes are female).

29 Handyside et al., *supra* note 27, at 768.

30 Family balancing is a term for the use of PGD in families with one or more children of one gender seeking to "balance" the offspring gender ratio by ensuring the next child is of the opposite gender. *See* Akchurin & Kartzke, *supra* note 28, at 33.

31 *See, e.g.*, Blake Rodgers & Brandon Peterson, *The Ethics of Stem Cell Research and Prenatal Genetic Alteration, in* The Ethical Imperative in the Context of Evolving Technologies 47 (Dan McIntosh et al. eds., 1996), http://www.ethicapublishing.com/3CH3.htm [https://perma.cc/D5ZU-XBJF]; Akchurin & Kartzke, *supra* note 28, at 32–33.

32 *See, e.g.*, Rodgers & Peterson, *supra* note 31, at 46–48.

33 *Id.* at 48.

34 *See, e.g.*, Akchurin & Kartzke, *supra* note 28, at 35.

35 Rodgers & Peterson, *supra* note 31, at 47.

36 *See, e.g.*, David S. King, *Preimplantation Genetic Diagnosis and the 'New' Eugenics*, 25 J. Med. Ethics 176, 176, 179–80 (1999).

37 Marcy Darnovsky, *Genetically Modified Babies*, N.Y. Times, Feb. 25, 2014, at A25.

38 *See, e.g.*, Michael D. Lemonick, *Designer Babies,* Time Mag., Jan. 11, 1999, at 64 (arguing—back in 1999—that "[w]ithin a decade or two, it may be possible to screen kids . . . for an enormous range of attributes, such as" height, body type, hair and eye color, intelligence, personality type, etc.). *Accord* James Gallagher, *Is It Time to Make Designer Babies?*, BBC News (Sept. 10, 2015), http://www.bbc.com/news/health-34207470 [https://perma.cc/R8GC-Y96V]; Antonio Michele Grygotis, *Higher Level of Embryo Testing Raises Questions About Possibility of Creating "Designer Babies"*, Transplant News, June 30, 2001, at 12; Rubanath Karuthedath, *Biotech Nightmare: Science Fiction Dystopian Visions of Human Genetic Engineering and Cloning with Special Reference to the Boys from Brazil and Beggars in Spain*, 2 Res. J. Eng. Language & Literature 1 (2014), http://www.rjelal.com/2.4.14/RUBANATH%20KARUTHEDATH%201–6.pdf [https://perma.cc/5SSU-YQ2Y]; Gautam Naik, *A Genetic Code for Genius?*, Wall St. J. (Feb. 15, 2013), https://www.wsj.com/articles/SB10001424127887324162304578303992108696034 [https://perma.cc/FA4L-KRUV]; Antonio Regalado, *Engineering the Perfect Baby*, MIT Tech. Rev. (Mar. 5, 2015), https://www.technologyreview.com/s/535661/engineering-the-perfect-baby/; Antonio Regalado, *Scientists Call for a Summit on Gene-Edited Babies*, MIT Tech. Rev.

(Mar. 19, 2015), https://www.technologyreview.com/s/536021/scientists-call-for-a-summit-on-gene-edited-babies/ [https://perma.cc/4D53-3AX9]; *"Designer Babies" on the Way? In China, Scientists Attempt to Unravel Human Intelligence*, CBS NEWS (Mar. 5, 2014), http://www.cbsnews.com/news/designer-babies-on-the-way-in-china-scientists-attempt-to-unravel-human-intelligence/ [https://perma.cc/W3GE-3Z6B].

39 *The Public and Genetic Editing, Testing, and Therapy*, STAT & HARV. T.H. CHAN SCH. PUB. HEALTH 1 (Jan. 2016), https://cdn1.sph.harvard.edu/wp -content /uploads/sites/94/2016/01/STAT-Harvard-Poll-Jan-2016-Genetic-Technology.pdf [https://perma.cc/GK6F-MVGN].

40 *Id.* (emphasis added).

41 *See, e.g.*, *United Kingdom: Reproductive and Research Cloning, Genetic Modification and Selection, Sex Selection*, YOUGOV®, at 6 (Aug. 19, 2005) [hereinafter UK Poll], http://iis.yougov.co.uk/extranets/ygarchives/content/pdf/TEL050101042_1.pdf [https://perma.cc/ZBD6-2ARY] (reporting that only 4 percent of total respondents approve of using genetic modification to improve a child's academic or sporting abilities); *VCU Life Sciences Survey: Public Values Science but Concerned About Biotechnology*, VCU CTR. PUB. POL'Y 4, 10 (2003), http://lifesciences.vcu.edu/media/life-sciences/docs/survey2003.pdf [https://perma.cc/MB2A-LJJ2] (94 percent of respondents opined that "changing a baby's characteristics for cosmetic purposes such as eye or hair color … is taking medical advances too far").

42 Biotechnology Australia, *Increasing Public Support for Stem Cell Research* 1–2 (July 7, 2003), http://www.geneticsandsociety.org/downloads/20030707_Biotechnology_Australia.pdf [https://perma.cc/HZ65-96UX] (reporting 61 percent support for genetic testing of unborn children and 79 percent support for gene therapy to correct any genetic disorders that may be diagnosed); Antonio Regalado, *Patients Favor Changing the Genes of the Next Generation with CRISPR*, MIT TECH. REV. (Dec. 2, 2015), https://www.technologyreview.com/s/544141/patients-favor-changing-the-genes-of-the-next-generation-with-crispr/ [https://perma.cc/U7LB-FQ3Y]; UK Poll, *supra* note 41, at 6 (noting that 57 percent and 43 percent of respondents approve using genetic modifications to "prevent children from suffering serious genetic diseases" or to reduce the risk of developing diseases such as cancer, Alzheimer's disease, and heart disease, respectively); *see also id.* (reporting that 51 percent of respondents believe that it should be legal for parents and doctors to "carry out genetic tests on embryos created during IVF treatment in order to select those with the lowest chances of developing [serious] diseases … later in life," while only 30 percent believe that such testing should be illegal).

43 The article appears in *Vice Magazine*. It features a picture of school-age Chinese children lined up in a formation that stretches as far as the camera lens can capture and gives the appearance that China is trying to build an army of homogeneous, little human robots. Aleks Eror, *China Is Engineering Genius*

Babies, VICE MAG. (Mar. 15, 2013), http://www.vice.com/read/chinas-taking-over-the-world-with-a-massive-genetic-engineering-program [https://perma.cc/4BSB-5Z7S].

44 *Vice* is a print magazine and website focused on popular culture, news, and entertainment. *See Vice (Magazine)*, WIKIPEDIA, https://en.wikipedia.org/wiki/Vice_(magazine) [https://perma.cc/HGH5-GF6C] (last visited Feb. 25, 2017). The magazine expanded into Vice Media LLC, a company that now operates the magazine and a multimedia network including several digital channels, *Vice News*, a record label, a film production studio, and book publishing division. *Vice Media*, WIKIPEDIA, https://en.wikipedia.org/wiki/Vice_Media [https://perma.cc/S36E-JF3U] (last visited Feb. 25, 2017). Vice is the media company that funded Dennis Rodman's—the former NBA player—2013 trip to meet North Korea's dictator. Lindsay Silberman, *Rodman's Revelations*, DUJOUR, http://dujour.com/culture/dennis-rodman-north-korea-kim-jong-un-interview/ [https://perma.cc/35XY-Q6EV] (last visited Feb. 25, 2017). In recent years, Vice Media has been valued at more than $2.5 billion following investments from Technology Crossover Ventures ($250 million), A&E Networks ($250 million), and Rupert Murdock's Twenty-First Century Fox ($70 million). Emily Steel, *Vice Gets 2nd Investment, to Aid Expansion*, N.Y. TIMES, Sept. 4, 2014, at B1.

45 For more information on BGI, see BGI, http://bgi-international.com/us/about-us/introduction/ [https://perma.cc/8KE5-U5EA] (last visited Feb. 25, 2017).

46 For more information on BGI's Cognitive Genomics Research group, see BGI, https://www.cog-genomics.org/ [https://perma.cc/2N2V-DVBL] (last visited Feb. 13, 2017).

47 Christopher C. Change et al., *BGI Cognitive Genomics Lab: Proposal for Gene-Trait Association Study of* g, BGI 2, https://www.cog-genomics.org/static/pdf/bgi_g_proposal.pdf [https://perma.cc/VZJ2-BU5H] (last visited Feb. 25, 2017).

48 *See id.*

49 *See How to Qualify*, BGI, https://www.cog-genomics.org/volunteer [https://perma.cc/787Y-L8HK] (last visited Feb. 13, 2017).

50 *See Our Publications*, BGI, http://bgi-international.com/us/about-us/our-publications/ [https://perma.cc/7MTV-8G39] (last visited Feb. 25, 2017) (providing a list of scientific articles published in various high-quality, peer-reviewed journals).

51 *See, e.g.*, Eror, *supra* note 43; *republished in Chinese Company Attempts to Engineer Genius Babies*, GENETIC LITERACY PROJECT (Mar. 22, 2013), https://www.geneticliteracyproject.org/2013/03/22/chinese-company-attempts-to-engineer-genius-babies/ [https://perma.cc/5ZZW-TSLF]; *also republished in How China Is Trying to Engineer Genius Babies*, REAL CLEAR POLITICS (Mar. 17, 2003), http://www.realclearpolitics.com/2013/03/17/how_china_is_trying_to_engineer_genius_babies_304097.html [https://perma.cc/GZ9A-MPLW]; *referred to in, e.g.*, George Dvorsky, *Is China Selectively Breeding a New Generation of Genius Babies?*, IO9

(Mar. 18, 2013), http://io9.gizmodo.com/is-china-selectively-breeding-a-new-generation-of-geniu-455634018 [https://perma.cc/72WA-A5RK]; Roy Klabin, *Chinese Labs Are Engineering Genius Babies, Should the U.S. Follow Suit?*, POLICY.MIC (Mar. 18, 2013), http://mic.com/articles/30111/chinese-labs-are-engineering-genius-babies-should-the-u-s-follow-suit#.Q5X5YENgb [https://perma.cc/XM3W-3E4R]; *China to Begin Producing 'Designer Babies' in Horrific Scheme*, CATHOLIC ONLINE (Jan. 16, 2014), http://www.catholic.org/news/technology/story.php?id=53890 [https://perma.cc/B9A9-K7K5].

52 *See* discussion *supra* notes 22–26.

53 Huang, *supra* note 22 at 659.

54 *See, e.g.*, *id.* at 642 (arguing that in the near future, genetic selection of hair color, skin color, intellectual ability, or behavior predispositions may be feasible); Mahoney, *supra* note 23, at 313 (proposing that new technology may presumably allow parents to decide eye color and sexual orientation of designed babies).

55 Mahoney, *supra* note 23, at 313.

56 *See, e.g.*, sources cited *supra* note 25.

57 Huang, *supra* note 22, at 658 (emphasis added).

58 *See generally* FRANCIS GALTON, HEREDITARY GENIUS: AN INQUIRY INTO ITS LAWS AND CONSEQUENCES (1st ed. 1869) [hereinafter GALTON 1st ed.], http://galton.org/books/hereditary-genius/galton-1869-Hereditary_Genius.pdf [https://perma.cc/82YP-SRMF]. For the second edition published in 1892, see FRANCIS GALTON, HEREDITARY GENIUS: AN INQUIRY INTO ITS LAWS AND CONSEQUENCES (2d ed. 1892), http://galton.org/books/hereditary-genius/text/pdf/galton-1869-genius-v3.pdf [https://perma.cc/LM6D-WNMU].

59 GALTON 1st ed., *supra* note 58, at 1.

60 *Id.* at 6.

61 *See id.* at 2.

62 *Id.* at 338, 340.

63 *Id.* at 339.

> [T]he number among the negroes of those whom we should call half-witted men, is very large. . . . The mistakes the negroes made in their own matters, were so childish, stupid, and simpleton-like, as frequently to make me ashamed of my own species. . . . I have no information as to actual idiocy among the negroes—I mean, of course, of that class of idiocy which is not due to disease.

Id.

64 *See* C. Spearman, *"General Intelligence", Objectively Determined and Measured*, 15 AM. J. PSYCHOL. 201, 268–72 (1904).

65 *See, e.g.*, HENRY HERBERT GODDARD, FEEBLE-MINDEDNESS: ITS CAUSES AND CONSEQUENCES vii (1914); HENRY HERBERT GODDARD, THE KALLIKAK FAMILY: A STUDY IN THE HEREDITY OF FEEBLE-MINDEDNESS viii (1912); Daniel Starch, *The Similarity of Brothers and Sisters in Mental Traits*, 24 PSYCHOL. REV. 235, 237

(1917) (concluding that mental traits resemblance among siblings is as great as that of physical traits).

66 *See, e.g.*, Curtis Merriman, *The Intellectual Resemblance of Twins*, 33 Psychol. Monographs 1, 16–18 (1924) (studying the intellectual level of a population of twin children ages five to fourteen).

67 *See, e.g.*, Frank N. Freeman et al., *The Influence of Environment on the Intelligence, School Achievement, and Conduct of Foster Children*, *in* The Twenty-Seventh Yearbook of the National Society for the Study of Education 103, 106 (Guy Montrose Whipple ed., 1928) (using foster children as a cohort to test whether residence in a foster home environment can influence intellectual capacity).

68 Thomas J. Bouchard & Matthew McGue, *Familial Studies of Intelligence: A Review*, 212 Science 1055, 1056 (1981).

69 Thomas J. Bouchard, Jr., *Genetic Influence on Human Intelligence (Spearman's g): How Much?*, 36 Annals Hum. Biology 527, 533 (2009).

70 *See, e.g.*, Beben Benyamin et al., *Large, Consistent Estimates of the Heritability of Cognitive Ability in Two Entire Populations of 11-Year-Old Twins from Scottish Mental Surveys of 1932 and 1947*, 35 Behav. Genetics 525 (2005).

71 *See, e.g.*, B. Devlin et al., *The Heritability of IQ*, 388 Nature 468, 470 (1997) (arguing that, in addition to genes and environments, the heritability of IQ also depends on maternal effects).

72 *Contra* Mae-Wan Ho, *No Genes for Intelligence in the Fluid Genome*, 45 Advances Child Dev. & Behav. 67, 70 (2013) (pointing out that some scientists and popular media tend to mistakenly assume that highly heritable traits are predominantly genetically determined).

73 G. Davies et al., *Genome-Wide Association Studies Establish That Human Intelligence Is Highly Heritable and Polygenic*, 16 Molecular Psychiatry 996, 1001 (2011).

74 *Id.* at 999 (citing Jimmy Z. Liu et al., A *Versatile Gene-Based Test for Genome-Wide Association Studies*, 87 Am. J. Hum. Genetics 139 (2010)).

75 *Id.*

76 B. Benyamin et al., *Childhood Intelligence Is Heritable, Highly Polygenic and Associated with FNBP1L*, 19 Molecular Psychiatry 253 (2014).

77 *Id.* at 257.

78 *See id.* at supp. fig. 6, https://genepi.qimr.edu.au/contents/p/staff/BENYAMIN_FNBPIL_MOLPSYCH_OSI.pdf [https://perma.cc/QF6H-DYPZ].

79 Robert M. Kirkpatrick et al., *Results of a "GWAS Plus": General Cognitive Ability Is Substantially Heritable and Massively Polygenic*, 9 PLoS ONE e112390, 4 (Nov. 10, 2014), http://journals.plos.org/plosone/article/file?id=10.1371/journal.pone.0112390&type=printable [https://perma.cc/TP2S-KKY6].

80 *Id.* at 10.

81 *Id.*

82 Cornelius A. Rietveld et al., *GWAS of 126,559 Individuals Identifies Genetic Variants Associated with Educational Attainment*, 340 SCIENCE 1467, 1468 (2013).
83 *Id.* at 1469.
84 *Id.*
85 Cornelius A. Rietveld et al., *Common Genetic Variants Associated with Cognitive Performance Identified Using the Proxy-Phenotype Method*, 111 PROC. NAT'L ACAD. SCI. U.S. 13790, 13793 (2014), *corrected in* 112 PROC. NAT'L ACAD. SCI. U.S. E380 (2015).
86 *Id.* at 13792.
87 G. Davies et al., *Genetic Contributions to Variation in General Cognitive Function: A Meta-Analysis of Genome-Wide Association Studies in the CHARGE Consortium (N=53 949)*, 20 MOLECULAR PSYCHIATRY 183, 185 (2015).
88 *Id.* at 186–87.
89 *Id.* at 189.
90 *Id.* at 187.
91 Christopher F. Chabris et al., *Most Reported Genetic Associations with General Intelligence Are Probably False Positives*, 23 PSYCHOL. SCI. 1314 (2012).
92 *Id.* at 1319.
93 *Id.* at 1314.
94 Kirkpatrick et al., *supra* note 79, at 10.
95 *Id.* at 11.
96 *See* Andrew T. M. Bagshaw et al., *No Effect of Genome-Wide Copy Number Variation on Measures of Intelligence in a New Zealand Birth Cohort*, 8 PLoS ONE e55208 (2013).
97 *Id.* (citations omitted).
98 *See* Paul Enríquez, *CRISPR-Mediated Epigenome Editing*, 89 YALE J. BIOLOGY & MED. 471 (2016).
99 *See, e.g.*, Andre Fischer et al., *Recovery of Learning and Memory Is Associated with Chromatin Remodelling*, 447 NATURE 178 (2007) (studying the role of histone acetylation and chromatin remodeling on learning and memory access).
100 *See, e.g.*, Swati Gupta et al., *Histone Methylation Regulates Memory Formation*, 30 J. NEUROSCIENCE 3589 (2010) (investigating the role of the H3K4me3 epigenetic mark in memory formation).
101 *See* Enríquez, *supra* note 98, at 471.
102 *See id.*
103 Michael R. Johnson et al., *Systems Genetics Identifies a Convergent Gene Network for Cognition and Neurodevelopmental Disease*, 19 NATURE NEUROSCIENCE 223 (2016).
104 *Id.*

105 Adam Hampshire et al., *Fractionating Human Intelligence*, 76 NEURON 1225, 1233 (2012).
106 *See, e.g.*, discussion *supra* note 25 and accompanying text.
107 Hana Lango Allen et al., *Hundreds of Variants Clustered in Genomic Loci and Biological Pathways Affect Human Height*, 467 NATURE 832 (2010).
108 *See, e.g.*, Corsover, *supra* note 25, at 744.
109 Md Munan Shaik et al., *Structural Basis of Coreceptor Recognition by HIV-1 Envelope Spike*, 565 NATURE 318, 318 (2019).
110 Wei-Kung Wang et al., *Hypervariable Region 3 Residues of HIV Type 1 gp120 Involved in CCR5 Coreceptor Utilization: Therapeutic and Prophylactic Implications*, 96 PROC. NAT'L ACAD. SCI. U.S. 4558, 4558 (1999).
111 For an overview of the mechanisms of HIV entry into human cells, see, for example, Craig B. Wilen, John C. Tilton & Robert W. Doms, *HIV: Cell Binding and Entry*, 2 COLD SPRING HARBOR PERSP. MED., no. a006866, Aug. 2012, at 1, 1–3, 5–6.
112 *See* Paul Enríquez, *Editing Humanity: On the Precise Manipulation of DNA in Human Embryos*, 97 N.C. L. REV. 1147, 1231 (2019).
113 *See* Mihaela Pertea et al., *CHESS: A New Human Gene Catalog Curated from Thousands of Large-Scale RNA Sequencing Experiments Reveals Extensive Transcriptional Noise*, 19 GENOME BIOLOGY art. 208, at 1 (2018); *see also* Human Genome Project Information Archive 1990–2003, *About the Human Genome Project*, https://web.ornl.gov/sci/techresources/Human_Genome/project/index.shtml (noting earlier estimates that the human genome has approximately 20,000 to 25,000 genes).

9

DNA and the Administrative State

Human genome editing has become a reality. Now that humanity faces the inevitable use of such a transformative technology, one logical question that arises is whether the government should regulate the technology and, if so, what precise measures should be followed. This chapter focuses on those questions and navigates the intersection of human genome editing—specifically germline genome editing (GGE)—and administrative law, primarily in the context of executive authority under existing law to regulate GGE technological advances. Importantly, the chapter focuses on the Food and Drug Administration's (FDA) jurisdictional powers as the agency in charge of "protecting the public health by ensuring the safety, efficacy, and security of human . . . drugs, biological products, and medical devices,"[1] and its current role in shepherding scientific discoveries into the clinical realm.

We begin by recounting a brief history of federal public-health and consumer-protection laws in the United States, which led to the establishment and expansion of the FDA's jurisdiction over various aspects of public health. Because the issue of GGE regulation is one of first impression for the administrative legal system, the chapter looks to somatic-cell gene therapy and the emergence of FDA oversight in this field, which has established precedents that are potentially applicable to GGE. By examining existing laws applicable to gene therapy, the chapter identifies potential regulatory gaps that could be viewed as rendering some types of GGE beyond the FDA's regulatory reach. At the same time, the chapter contends that any such gaps are the product of the FDA's forbearance in claiming jurisdiction over GGE.

The chapter then proposes a novel regulatory path for GGE that flows from the US Court of Appeals for the District of Columbia Circuit's ruling in *United States v. Regenerative Sciences LLC* (*Regenerative Sciences*), which held that specific stem-cell mixtures can be regulated as drugs or biological products within the meaning of the Federal Food, Drug, and Cosmetic Act (FDCA) and the Public Health Service Act (PHSA).[2] The approach identifies potential classifications for GGE products and reinforces FDA jurisdiction over GGE products and therapies. It is important to note that our discussion of how GGE should be regulated at some point in the near future comes at the heels of a current de facto legislative ban on GGE clinical applications, which prohibits making intentional genetic modifications in human embryos. As we will examine in the next pages, such a ban is likely unnecessary because it creates more societal costs than benefits and prevents the FDA from (1) carrying out its mission to protect the public health by ensuring the safety and efficacy of drugs, biological products, and medical devices; and (2) exercising full jurisdictional power over an area that is a mere extension of what has traditionally been subject to regulation by the Agency. Taken as a whole, this chapter provides a legal foundation to demonstrate that the FDA is well equipped to address the challenges of regulating emerging technologies intended for GGE—including GGE products and therapies, particularly from safety and efficacy standpoints—that fall within the scope of its jurisdiction.

At the outset, it is important to note that GGE research involving human embryos is currently susceptible to regulation pursuant to the Dickey-Wicker Amendment, the oversight of the National Institutes of Health (NIH), and other regulations related to assisted reproductive technologies (ART).[3]

The Dickey-Wicker Amendment, for example, prohibits the Department of Health and Human Services (DHHS) from using appropriated funds on "research in which a human embryo or embryos are destroyed, discarded, or knowingly subjected to risk of injury or death greater than that allowed for research on fetuses in utero."[4] The Amendment was passed by Congress in 1996 and signed into law by President Clinton. It has exerted a significant inhibitory effect on the generation of new stem-cell lines despite continuous funding for research on already-existing cell lines.[5] For its part, NIH oversight over federally funded research has, in the past, occurred via its Recombinant DNA Advisory Committee (RAC) and the use of local Institutional Review Boards and Institutional Biosafety Committees.[6] In August 2018, the NIH announced it "will no longer accept new human gene transfer protocols for the protocol registration process under the *NIH Guidelines for Research Involving Recombinant or Synthetic Nucleic Acid Molecules* (*NIH Guidelines*), or convene the RAC to review individual human gene transfer protocols."[7] The NIH's reduced involvement in this area makes FDA jurisdiction all the more relevant.

I THE FOOD AND DRUG ADMINISTRATION

The FDA is the federal agency within the US Department of Health and Human Services "responsible for protecting the public health by ensuring the safety, efficacy, and security of human . . . drugs, biological products, and medical devices."[8] It is the "oldest comprehensive [federal] consumer protection agency" in the United States.[9] The history of the Agency is replete with important lessons relevant to the discussion of GGE and other emerging technologies. The Agency's past highlights the significance of balancing the federal government's goal of ensuring consumer protection in the marketplace and the private sector's opposition to regulatory reform in various contexts. It also brings into focus the pivotal role of public opinion in shifting the fulcrum when government or corporate malfeasance disturbs such balance. On this point, the effects induced by public outrage during the 1906 meat-packing scandal[10] and the 1937 Elixir of Sulfanilamide drug scandal[11] led to an increase in jurisdictional powers of the FDA.

Above all, the FDA's history showcases, in principle, the separation of powers in our democratic system. Over the past century, Congress has enacted laws that granted new and broad regulatory powers to the administrative agency. The executive agency has then promulgated rules[12] under its statutory mandates and sought to enforce perceived violations of the laws. And the judiciary has either endorsed or checked the Agency's power by interpreting the regulations in the context of cases or controversies under Article III of the Constitution.[13]

Setting the proper historical context provides an opportunity to learn from past mistakes and take proactive steps toward adequate regulation of emerging technologies. Accordingly, this chapter examines why Congress has consolidated federal oversight within the FDA to regulate the food and drug industries, and how the FDA has become one of the quintessential consumer-protection watchdog agencies. This backdrop of the FDA's status as the consumer-protection federal agency tasked with ensuring the safety and efficacy of drugs, biological products, and medical devices underscores the notion that the FDA is well suited to regulate GGE and GGE-related emerging technologies.

A *Rising Power*

The FDA's inception can be traced back to 1839 when Congress appropriated funds to the Patent Office for agricultural purposes, including the "collection of agricultural statistics."[14] The congressional appropriations subsequently led to the creation of a chemical laboratory within the Agricultural Division of the Patent Office in 1848.[15] Since then, the federal government has continuously used chemical analysis to monitor the safety of products available to consumers.[16]

Over the next decade, calls for an independent department to oversee agricultural matters led to legislation that established the US Department of Agriculture (USDA) in May of 1862.[17] President Abraham Lincoln then appointed a chemist to head a new USDA Chemical Division,[18] which comprised what was formerly known as the Chemical Laboratory of the Agricultural Division of the Patent Office.[19] Under the leadership of Harvey W. Wiley, who was appointed chief chemist in 1883,[20] the Division of Chemistry[21] began to undertake seminal studies on food analysis, particularly pertaining to the detection of food adulteration.[22] The research was published in a series of ten reports summarizing the best current methods of detecting and analyzing adulteration in foods.[23]

Wiley's reports aroused public attention and led to the introduction of a food inspection bill in 1887,[24] as well as the first pure food bill in 1889.[25] By the turn of the twentieth century, Wiley's advocacy[26] for food and drug safety had contributed to the introduction of nearly one hundred bills that sought to address pervasive abuses in the consumer product marketplace.[27] Each of those bills succumbed to the influence of powerful industry and manufacturing groups that strongly opposed regulatory reform.[28]

But in 1906, the release of Upton Sinclair's novel *The Jungle*,[29] which chronicled the exploitation of immigrant workers and a litany of repugnant and unsanitary practices characteristic of the meat-packing industry of the early twentieth century, stoked massive public fear and uproar.[30] Sinclair's primary impetus for writing the novel was to promote a socialist movement in the United States. Accordingly, he expressed discontent that the novel's focus on the plight and injustice experienced by immigrant workers at the hands of the meat-packing industry, along with its political message, took a backseat to the public uproar engendered by his relatively brief depictions of unsanitary conditions at the Chicago stockyards. Indeed, after his novel had become a commercial success, Sinclair published an essay in Cosmopolitan Magazine, in which he candidly stated,

> I wished to frighten the country by a picture of what its industrial masters were doing to their victims; entirely by chance I had stumbled on another discovery—what they were doing to the meat supply of the civilized world. In other words, *I aimed at the public's heart, and by accident I hit it in the stomach*.[31]

Within weeks of the novel's publication, President Theodore Roosevelt appointed a Special Committee to investigate practices at the meat-packing houses of the Chicago stockyards.[32] The findings of the investigation, which lasted more than two weeks, documented a long list of food handling and preparation methods deemed dangerous to human health.[33] The Special Committee's report lent support to Roosevelt's urgent call to enact laws sanctioning the power of the federal government to inspect, supervise the preparation methods of, and establish sanitation norms for meat and meat food products entering into interstate commerce.[34]

B A *Federal System of Consumer Protection*

Public clamor concerning the meat-packing exposé coupled with Wiley's longstanding advocacy for the institutionalization of food and drug safety eventually paved the road for regulatory reform. On June 30, 1906, the Pure Food and Drug Act (PFDA) was enacted into law.[35] It sought to prevent "the manufacture, sale, or transportation of adulterated or misbranded or poisonous or deleterious foods, drugs, medicines, and liquors."[36] The landmark legislation—signed into law on the same day as the Federal Meat Inspection Act[37]—left an indelible mark during the formative years of what would eventually become the FDA.

FIGURE 9.1 Chicago stockyards (Alpha Stock / Alamy Stock Photo)

The PFDA had several notable provisions. First, the Act made it unlawful to manufacture[38] and introduce into interstate commerce[39] any article of food or drug that was deemed "adulterated"[40] or "misbranded"[41] within the meaning of the law, and it prescribed fines or imprisonment as penalty for such violations.[42] Second, the legislation assigned authority to the USDA to make rules and regulations to implement provisions of the Act.[43] Third, the law granted enforcement powers to the Bureau of Chemistry,[44] including the power to examine specimens of foods and drugs manufactured or sold in interstate commerce.[45] Fourth, the Act outlined due process provisions applicable in the event that testing by the Bureau of Chemistry revealed adulteration or misbranding of food and drugs within the meaning of the PFDA.[46] Lastly, the law introduced the antecedent of the modern definition of "drug" as "any substance or mixture . . . intended to be used for the cure, mitigation, or prevention of disease" and recognized the US Pharmacœpeia and National Formulary as authoritative drug entities.[47]

The PFDA was the first of more than two hundred laws that constitute the backbone of our federal public-health and consumer-protection system.[48] It represented an unprecedented expansion of federal oversight over food and drug law, and consolidated federal jurisdiction over food and drug products intended for interstate commerce into a single federal agency with broad regulatory powers. Thus, the PFDA essentially established the FDA's modern regulatory functions, which laid the groundwork for building the basic elements of consumer protection that stand to this day.[49]

Following the PFDA's enactment, the Bureau of Chemistry undertook the task of enforcing the new law.[50] Under Wiley's leadership, the Bureau gained strength and stature as an administrative body.[51] Its appropriations more than sextupled, the staff expanded, and a new building was set aside for operations.[52] Soon thereafter, however, Wiley encountered strong opposition from business and manufacturing interests that sought to curtail the Bureau's new regulatory powers.[53]

Litigation ensued and led to a string of judicial decisions that stymied the Bureau's enforcement mechanisms and constricted the regulatory scope of the PFDA, often in perplexing ways that ran contrary to the advancement of public welfare.[54] For instance, *United States v. Johnson* held that the PFDA applied only to false or misleading statements about the ingredients or identity of a drug, and did not prohibit false curative claims.[55] Shortly thereafter, *United States v. Lexington Mill & Elevator Co.* astoundingly held that the government had the burden to establish that a poisonous or deleterious food additive may render a food article injurious to health before it can be condemned, and that the mere presence of such an additive is not sufficient to render the article of food illegal.[56] These and other decisions undermining public welfare laws ignited fierce controversy among the government branches. Congress sought to overcome the Supreme Court's narrowing of the scope and power of the Bureau of Chemistry by enacting the Sherley Amendment, which was enacted to prohibit the type of false and fraudulent curative or therapeutic claims of health benefits that had been upheld in *Johnson*.[57] Subsequent judicial interpretation, however, made enforcing the Sherley Amendment problematic because of the high threshold required to establish fraudulent intent.[58]

When law and science-based policies threatened their economic interests, powerful businesses often engaged in carefully orchestrated attacks to sabotage progress in the discovery and dissemination of scientific knowledge. The Chief of the Office of Interstate Supervision at the Division of Food and Drug Administration within the USDA, for example, recounted how in one case defense counsel for a ketchup company delegitimized effective methods of determining food spoilage by characterizing them as "encroachments of mendaciously meddling bureaucracy" threatening "[t]raditional American freedom[s]."[59] The so-called encroachments of American freedom decried by the manufacturer concerned government seizures of shipments of ketchup prepared from rotten tomatoes using dirty utensils, tanks, and pipe lines. The government had seized the product after microscopists and food technicians inspected several bottles and established the presence of mold filaments and yeast cells when samples were examined under the microscope. During trial, counsel sowed doubts about the extent of contamination in the product and persuaded the jury to find for the manufacturer by asking: "Should a whole carload of this splendid food product be destroyed on what an impractical scientist thought he saw in a few drops through a high powered microscope?"[60]

The apparent influence of business interests over the execution of the PFDA was deeply troubling to advocates of increased regulation. Wiley, for example, articulated his concern as follows:

> There is a distinct tendency to put regulations and rules for the enforcement of the law into the hands of the industries engaged in the food and drug activities. I consider this one of the most pernicious threats to pure food and drugs.... When we permit business in general to regulate the quality and character of our food and drug supplies, we are treading upon very dangerous ground.... It is never advisable to surrender entirely food and drug control to business interests. There is much to be done yet before we can point to a food and drug control that is wholly interested in the welfare of the consumer.[61]

The chief law responsible for launching the FDA into the modern era of health and consumer protection was far from perfect. Indeed, Wiley, the PFDA's author and chief enforcer, lamented the gradual decrease of enthusiasm in the years after the bill was signed into law. He contemporaneously expressed that "[the PFDA] is regarded as established and in perfect operation. This is a great mistake. There are practises [sic] which are permitted under the present administration of the law that are in direct opposition to fundamental principles."[62] In the end, despite the enforcement hurdles associated with the PFDA, the landmark legislation succeeded in establishing foundations and a preliminary framework for the system of food and drug law that has prevailed for more than a century.

C *Expanding the Core of Modern Food and Drug Law*

The late 1920s and early 1930s marked a turning point in the history of the FDA.[63] Pressure began to mount to address a long list of inherent shortcomings that rendered the PFDA toothless against flagrant abuses and misdeeds in the marketplace.[64] The FDA recommended a complete overhaul of the 1906 law[65] and advocated for stronger legislation. For instance, in the aftermath of the New Deal, the FDA engaged in a public-relations campaign to underscore the need for new, stronger federal laws to adequately enforce food and drug safety and protect consumers from dangerous products that were marketed legally. To reach a wide range of audiences in government, the press, and the general public, the Agency assembled a collection of graphic depictions and turned it into an exhibit that became known as the "Chamber of Horrors."[66] The exhibit consisted of a series of ghastly images depicting harmful effects caused by various unsafe products, which were lawfully marketed to consumers at the time.[67] Despite the FDA's efforts, the proposed bill stalled in Congress and triggered a five-year legislative battle.[68] Progress on enacting a new law stagnated until a public tragedy involving a so-called Elixir of Sulfanilamide drug became publicized in 1937.[69]

FIGURE 9.2 Elixir of sulfanilamide (Science Photo Library)

The Elixir of Sulfanilamide contained diethylene glycol, a toxic and untested organic solvent commonly used in a wide range of industrial products.[70] As the drug hit the market, reports of mass poisonings, including the death of 107 people—mostly children—highlighted the pressing need to enact a more robust food and drug law to protect consumers.[71] Thus, it took a wave of public outrage—much like the meat-packing scandals leading up to the enactment of the PFDA in 1906[72]—to break congressional gridlock and pass the legislation through Congress.

On June 25, 1938, Congress enacted the FDCA.[73] The legislation aimed to "prohibit the movement in interstate commerce of adulterated and misbranded food, drugs, devices, and cosmetics."[74] It repealed the PFDA of 1906 and replaced it with a sweeping statute that constitutes the core of today's food and drug law. The FDCA addressed many of the weaknesses of the PFDA, expanded the FDA's jurisdictional powers over new areas, and closed loopholes derived from judicial interpretations of the antecedent regulatory scheme.

For instance, under the FDCA, the FDA assumed authority to regulate therapeutic claims on drug labels,[75] thereby repealing the Sherley Amendment requirement that one must prove intent to defraud or mislead in a misbranding case.[76]

The Act expanded the FDA's jurisdiction to encompass regulation of cosmetics and medical devices.[77] It broadened the scope and definition of terms including food,[78] drug,[79] label,[80] and misbranded article.[81] The law further specified the FDA's authority to conduct inspections of any "factory, warehouse, or establishment in which food, drugs, devices, or cosmetics are manufactured, processed, packed, or held."[82] The FDCA also charged the FDA with promulgating rules to set tolerance limits for unavoidable poisonous ingredients in foods.[83] Drug labels were now required to indicate, in language likely to be read and understood by an ordinary individual, whether the drug contained any habit-forming substances or derivatives.[84]

Importantly, the FDCA instituted a mandatory premarket approval scheme for new drugs. No drug manufacturer could introduce a new drug into interstate commerce without first filing an application that contained sufficient information to establish the drug's safety before the FDA.[85] Had this feature been in place prior to 1938, the Elixir of Sulfanilamide crisis might have been averted.

Armed with an arsenal of new jurisdictional powers, the FDA began to enforce provisions of the FDCA. Predictably, the Agency faced litigation challenges. But as courts began to examine and interpret the FDCA, the Agency's authority was upheld in pivotal cases that ultimately strengthened the FDA's jurisdiction over public-health and consumer-protection matters.[86]

Further expansion of that authority came with the enactment of the PHSA,[87] another legislative milestone that consolidated and updated laws related to the administration of the Public Health Service. The PHSA addressed a broad spectrum of health concerns, including the establishment of the federal government's quarantine powers to prevent the spread of communicable diseases,[88] the government's duty to promote and coordinate research and investigations into the causes and treatment of disease,[89] and the regulation of biological products applicable to the prevention, treatment, or cure of diseases.[90]

Another key legislative achievement for consumer protections came in 1962 with the enactment of the Kefauver-Harris Amendments.[91] Prior to this landmark legislation, drug manufacturers merely had to establish safety before introducing a drug into interstate commerce.[92] But the Kefauver-Harris Amendments "established a framework that required drug manufacturers to prove scientifically that a medication was not only safe, but effective."[93] The law significantly enhanced the FDA's authority over drugs, although it also increased the cost of developing new drugs by imposing premarket review, effectiveness, and other requirements on the drug industry.[94]

In the decades since their enactment, both the FDCA and the PHSA—alongside other laws related to public health and consumer protection—have undergone numerous amendments that have amplified the scope of FDA jurisdiction over health care in the United States.[95] Today, the FDA regulates more than $2.5 trillion worth of food, medical products, and tobacco.[96] It exercises jurisdiction over food safety, drug safety and efficacy, biological products ranging from blood to vaccines, cosmetics, medical devices, consumer products that emit radiation, veterinary products, and tobacco products.[97] Products regulated by the FDA constitute roughly twenty cents of every dollar spent by American consumers.[98] The FDA has become one of the most powerful and effective agencies in the federal government. Despite its sheer size and power, the FDA has earned a favorable reputation among the public,[99] with consumers reporting higher levels of trust in the FDA than the federal government as a whole.[100]

In addition to protecting consumers, the FDA strives to (1) advance "the public health by helping to speed innovations that make medical products more effective, safer, and more affordable"[101] and (2) educate the public by providing access to "accurate, science-based information" needed for consumers to make choices about the use of "medical products and foods to maintain and improve their health."[102] Moreover, the Agency plays a significant role in the federal government's counter-terrorism capabilities by ensuring the security of the food supply and developing strategies to respond to public-health threats.[103]

As is evident from its historical antecedents, the FDA has become what it is today due largely to its pivotal function of protecting consumers from systemic abuses perpetrated by select industry and manufacturing groups. The FDCA, the PHSA, and other laws related to public health and consumer protection have been the statutory means through which the Agency has fulfilled that broad policy goal. The FDA's long-standing history of consumer protection is significant for purposes of this discussion because it has laid a legal foundation to support the view that the FDA is well equipped to address the challenges of regulating emerging technologies—particularly from safety and efficacy standpoints—that fall within the scope of its jurisdiction. Indeed, the FDA has already paved ample groundwork in the once-emerging fields of recombinant DNA technology and gene therapy, which have set precedents in many respects analogous to the issue of GGE.

II LESSONS FROM GENE THERAPY

During the 1970s, the discovery of restriction enzymes capable of triggering sequence-specific cleavage of DNA molecules triggered a scientific revolution of colossal proportions.[104] In a matter of a few years, research into new recombinant DNA techniques ushered in the era of modern biotechnology that has changed the world.[105] In the midst of this molecular enlightenment, which suddenly brought genetic engineering within the realm of possibility, scientists began to posit whether genetic manipulation in humans could be used for genetic therapies to treat, cure, or ameliorate heritable diseases[106] and other conditions.[107] Less than twenty years later, results from the first approved nuclear gene transfer in a group of five patients with metastatic melanoma—an advanced cancer—established proof of concept for this novel approach to human gene therapy.[108]

This modern-medicine breakthrough raised questions regarding how human gene therapy would be regulated. Soon, manufacturers of products intended for use in emerging gene therapies sought regulatory status clarifications from the federal government.[109] The FDA answered that call in a statement published in 1993.[110] Pursuant to its jurisdictional authority under the FDCA[111] and the PHSA,[112] the FDA asserted jurisdiction to regulate human somatic-cell[113] and gene-therapy products.[114]

In the late 1990s, gene therapy experienced severe setbacks after the unfortunate death of Jesse Gelsinger, an eighteen-year-old patient suffering from partial ornithine transcarbamylase (OTC) deficiency[115] who died from a gene-therapy treatment in a clinical trial in 1999.[116] However, following improvements in nonviral and viral gene-transfer vectors over the last two decades, gene therapy is now viewed as a viable tool to address a wide range of diseases.[117] Two gene-therapy treatments—Glybera® and Strimvelis®—have already gained approval in Europe,[118] and in 2017, Kymriah® became the first FDA-approved gene-therapy product in the United States.[119]

A *What Is Gene Therapy?*

The concept of gene therapy can be traced back nearly a half century ago. Scientific progress in methods of genetic manipulation gave rise to the notion that exogenous, or so-called "good," DNA could be used to replace defective DNA material found in the cells of individuals suffering from genetic diseases.[120] This novel therapeutic strategy, if successful, could presumably provide cures for thousands of genetic-based disorders.

The FDA originally defined human gene therapy as "a medical intervention based on modification of the genetic material of living cells . . . intended to *prevent, treat, cure, diagnose, or mitigate disease* or injuries in humans."[121] Today, it also refers to "a technique that modifies a person's genes to *treat or cure* disease" via manipulation of gene expression or the alteration of biological properties of living cells.[122] The cells may be modified *in vivo*, which refers to a process, experimentation, or occurrence that takes place directly inside the body of a living organism. Thus, an in vivo cell modification refers to a change that occurs in a cell that is directly inside the body of a living organism. Alternatively, cells may also be modified *ex vivo* for subsequent administration to humans.[123] In this context, ex vivo refers to a process, experimentation, or occurrence that takes place outside of the body of a living organism. Accordingly, an ex vivo cell modification refers to a change that occurs in a cell that is outside of the body of a living organism.

Genetic modifications performed in vivo or ex vivo may constitute a form of somatic-cell therapy, which refers to the administration of autologous, allogeneic, or xenogeneic "living non-germline cells . . . for *therapeutic*, diagnostic, or preventive purposes."[124]

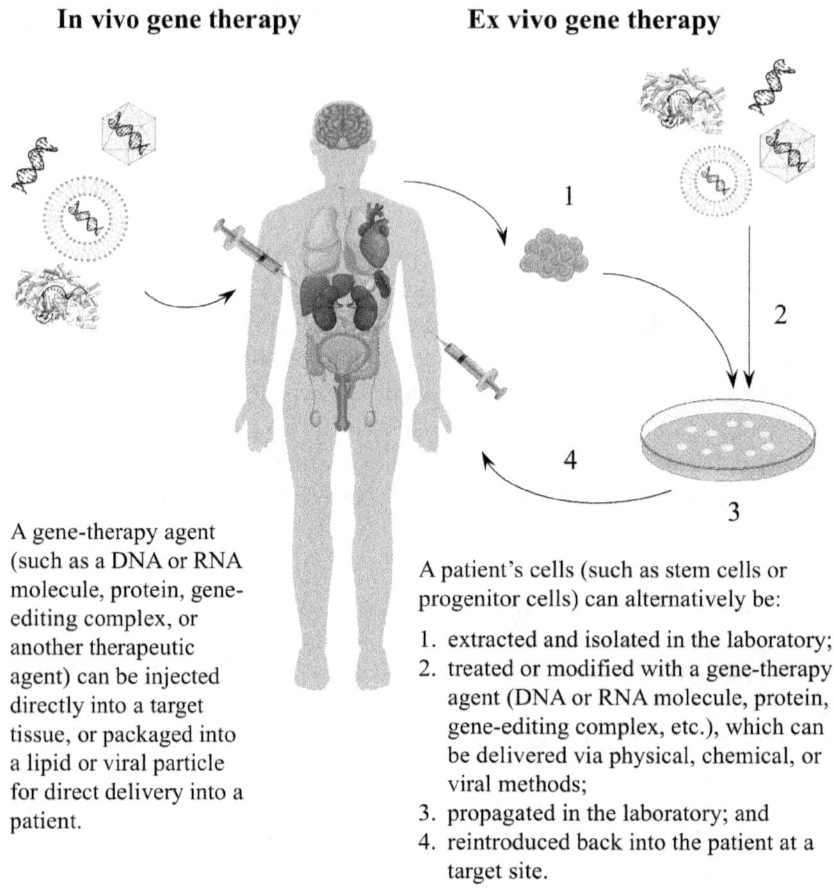

FIGURE 9.3 In vivo and ex vivo gene therapy

The term *autologous* refers to cells or tissues derived from the same individual. The risk of rejection of autologous cells and tissues in gene therapies is low because your body will recognize such cells or tissues as its own.

Conversely, the term *allogeneic* refers to cells or tissues derived from a different individual of the same species. Allogeneic cells or tissues, therefore, may or may not be immunologically compatible. Consider the use of human allogeneic cells from a donor individual in gene therapies. If the cells from the donor are not immunologically compatible with the recipient's immune system, the recipient's body will reject the allogeneic cells and trigger an allogeneic immune response that can lead to life-threatening complications.

In contrast to autologous and allogeneic biological material, the term *xenogeneic* refers to cells or tissues derived from individuals of different species such as, for example, the transfer of porcine biological material into primates.[125] Due to salient biological differences between members of different species, the use of xenogeneic cells or tissues in gene therapies carries a substantial risk of triggering a xenogeneic immune response that can be quite severe and life-threatening. This risk exists despite the use of genetically engineered xenogeneic cells and immunosuppressive drugs to suppress the recipient immune response. Recent advances in genome editing, however, have shown some promising strides in reducing the likelihood of rejection of xenogeneic material among species, including pigs and humans.[126]

Regardless of whether a gene therapy uses autologous, allogeneic, or xenogeneic cells or tissues, all "[c]ellular products intended for use as somatic[-]cell therapy are biological products subject to regulation pursuant to the PHS[A] . . . and also fall within the definition of drugs in the [FDCA]."[127]

Among current gene-therapy products within the purview of the FDA authority are plasmid DNA molecules, viral and bacterial vectors, human gene-editing technology, and patient-derived cellular gene-therapy products.[128] These products are deemed to be biological products subject to regulation by the FDA's Center for Biologics Evaluation and Research (CBER).[129] In 2017, Kymriah® became the first FDA-approved gene-therapy product in the United States for the treatment of "certain pediatric and young adult patients with a form of acute lymphoblastic leukemia."[130]

Notwithstanding the FDA's long-established jurisdiction over gene therapies aimed at somatic-cell modification, to date the Agency has remained silent regarding its authority to regulate products intended to modify the human germline. The FDA recently expressed views that technologies for human genome editing can be regulated under the gene-therapy framework. On January 18, 2017, the then FDA Commissioner, Robert Califf, published a statement asserting that the FDA intends to regulate genome-editing products using a product-specific, risk- and science-based approach.[131] On the issue of human medical products that feature gene-editing components of therapeutic nature, the FDA indicated that regulation would proceed under the existing gene-therapy framework.[132] At the same time, the FDA clarified that the statement regarding gene-editing products applies only to nonheritable somatic-cell gene therapy and not to germline gene therapy.[133] In July 2018, the Agency published proposed draft regulations asserting jurisdiction over gene-therapy products involving genome editing.[134] However, such authority explicitly applies to somatic cell-based gene therapies and excludes GGE interventions.[135]

B *One Therapy Does Not Fit All*

The FDA's clear intent to regulate technologies for human genome editing under the gene-therapy framework coupled with its silence vis-à-vis gene therapies involving GGE brings uncertainty to a new field of law. Although both somatic and germline treatments could be used for gene therapy and other therapeutic applications, the current gene-therapy model simply does not fit GGE intervention.

Two important points reveal large gaps in the gene-therapy regulatory scheme and deserve special attention. First, the Agency has explicitly excluded modification of germline cells from its definition of gene therapy over the last three decades.[136] This is significant because it is unclear whether the FDA intends to regulate GGE differently—presumably because it is fully cognizant of the limitations inherent in the current gene-therapy framework that render it inapplicable toward GGE modifications—or whether the Agency believes it lacks the authority to regulate such technologies at all, which is unlikely.

The methods used to achieve GGE therapies are likely to overlap extensively with those used in modern-day gene-therapy approaches that are in preapproval stages or have already been approved. Thus, assuming that a particular type of gene therapy warrants approval because it is safe and effective, the dispositive distinction between somatic-cell and GGE interventions appears to turn on the intended results of the therapy—namely, whether the modification remains confined to the individual patient or has the potential to be inherited by the individual's progeny. A focus on discriminating among somatic-cell and germ-cell gene therapies raises many legal issues that go beyond the scope of administrative law. For instance, in Chapters 10 and 11, we will explore constitutional issues related to whether a fundamental right to edit the human germline—or even an individual's own germ cells—exists.

Second, the FDA's explicit narrowing of the scope of gene therapy to treat or cure disease could create a deep regulatory void.[137] The Agency's circumscription to therapeutic applications means that nontherapeutic GGE interventions would, in theory, fall beyond the Agency's regulatory reach. In practice, however, it is difficult to imagine that the FDA would declare it lacks authority to regulate some human genetic interventions simply because they involve aesthetic, enhancement, or any other nontherapeutic purposes. Failure to broaden the scope of GGE past the therapeutic realm might enable an alternate system of deregulation in which the potential modification of traits for cosmetic or enhancement purposes is not sufficiently scrutinized.

III ASSERTING AUTHORITY FOR GERMLINE GENOME EDITING

As noted above, the establishment of FDA jurisdiction over GGE under the current gene-therapy framework is problematic. Therefore, this chapter proposes that the FDA should instead assert authority over the regulation of *all* types of GGE products —regardless of whether they are intended for therapeutic uses—as drugs and biological products within the meaning of the FDCA and the PHSA. In so doing, the chapter outlines a new regulatory path for GGE that flows from the DC Circuit's ruling in *Regenerative Sciences*, which held that the FDA can regulate specific stem-cell mixtures as drugs or biological products within the meaning of the FDCA and the PHSA.

A Regenerative Sciences—*You Shall Not Proliferate Cells, for Too Long*

In *Regenerative Sciences*, a Colorado clinic operated by two physicians marketed Regenexx-C, a procedure involving a cultured stem-cell mixture, as part of a medical therapy for treatment of arthritis and other orthopedic conditions.[138] The procedure involved the use of mesenchymal stem cells (MSC), which are a type of multipotent stem cells capable of differentiating into various cell lineages, including fat, muscle, bone, cartilage, and other cells.[139] MSCs are of clinical interest because they can be easily isolated from bone marrow and expanded in vitro. The first step in the Regenexx-C protocol concerned the extraction of MSCs from a patient's bone marrow. The MSCs would then be allowed to differentiate and proliferate via a culturing process of approximately two weeks,[140] which included the addition of an antibiotic to prevent bacterial contamination of the cells.[141] Following in vitro expansion, the mixture was subsequently injected back into the patient's body at a target site.[142]

The Regenexx-C procedure became the subject of FDA scrutiny when stem-cell therapies were increasingly identified as being part of an unregulated, Wild West-like cottage industry. Despite the promise of stem-cell medicine and its potential to eradicate many diseases, the uncertain risks and efficacy of stem-cell therapies,[143] which by default rendered them premature for clinical use, cautioned against their broad and unregulated use. Dangerous side effects had already been reported for some of these unregulated stem-cell therapies, which were not subject to traditional clinical-trial protocols.[144] Private clinics began to thrive in an environment of little to no regulation by marketing therapies directly to consumers, often via the internet.[145]

Providers of stem-cell therapies generally portrayed stem-cell medicine as safe and frequently made unsubstantiated and false claims about the efficacy of costly stem-cell procedures for a broad range of aesthetic and medical conditions, including aging, skin care, diabetes, orthopedic injuries, Parkinson's Disease, spinal cord injuries, osteoarthritis, stroke, autism, hair loss, erectile dysfunction, pain, and many others.[146] Even today, many private clinics that constitute the backbone of the stem-cell therapy industry remain largely underregulated, have spread globally, and are no longer confined to developing countries where weak laws or lax enforcement has enabled the clinics to operate with relative impunity.[147]

In a span of just a few years, US stem-cell businesses engaged in direct-to-consumer marketing have expanded to offer procedures at nearly six hundred clinics as of 2016,[148] a trend that is consistent in other developed countries.[149] In a globalized world, clinics now compete for a share of the so-called stem-cell tourism pie.[150]

Against a backdrop of public-health concerns surrounding overoptimistic and unsubstantiated stem-cell interventions, which thwart adequate patient-informed

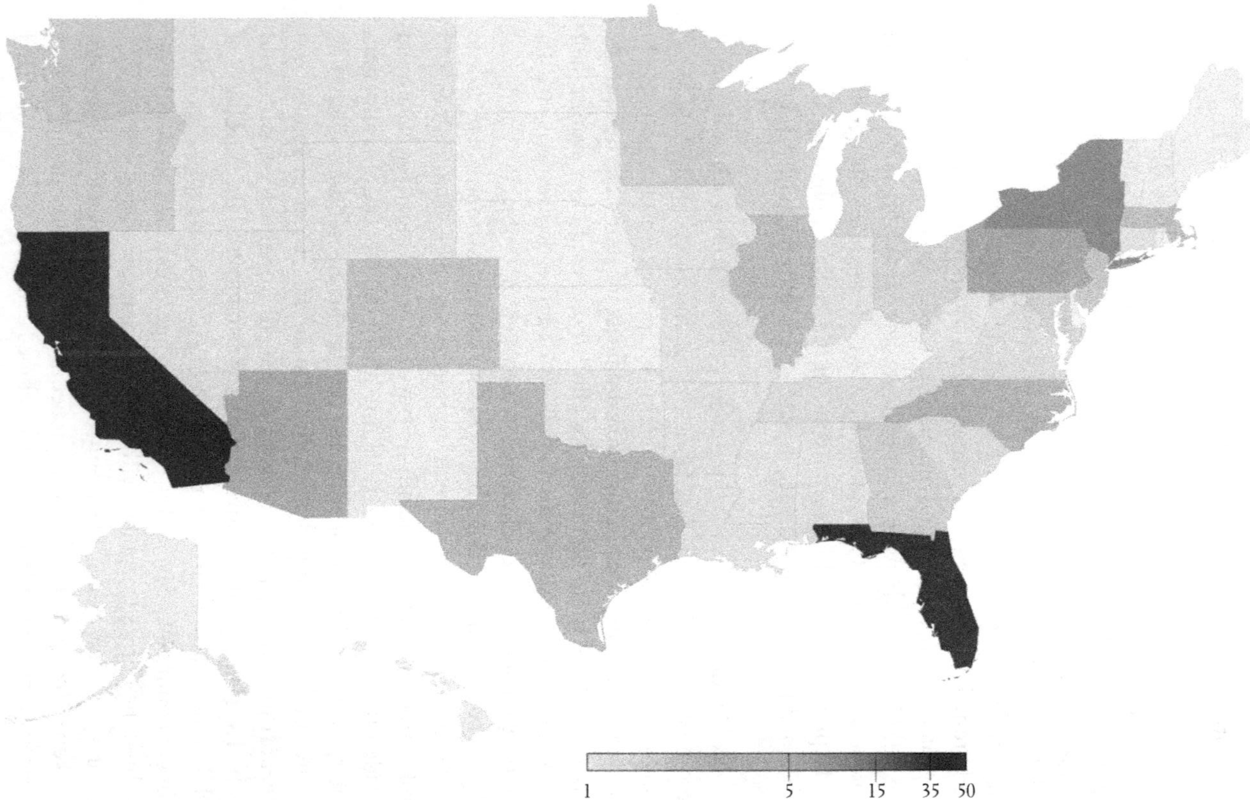

FIGURE 9.4 Stem-cell clinics offering direct-to-consumer marketing of stem cell-based interventions in the United States

The choropleth map shows the number of stem-cell clinics per state. California (49), Florida (35), and New York (15) have the highest number of clinics in the country.

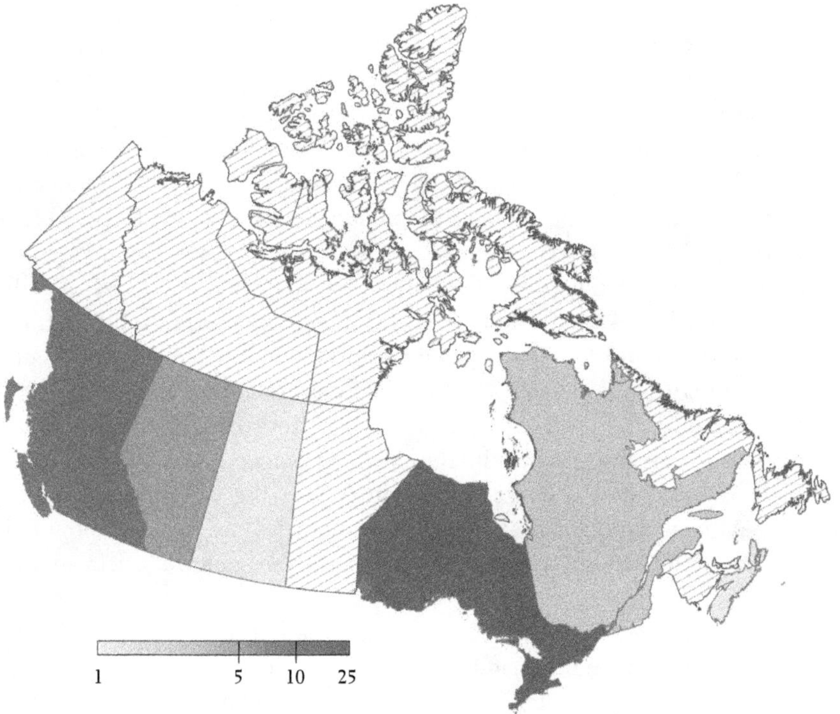

FIGURE 9.5 Stem-cell clinics offering direct-to-consumer marketing of stem cell-based interventions in Canada

Ontario (24), British Columbia (8), and Alberta (6) have the highest number of clinics in Canada (no data available for provinces and territories shown with linear hatching).

consent and examination of clinical outcomes, the federal government intervened. The FDA filed a request to permanently enjoin the Colorado clinic from administering the Regenexx-C cell mixture as part of a medical procedure.[151] The FDA argued that the mixture was a drug and biological product subject to FDA jurisdiction.[152] The defendants countered the FDA's position by arguing that the Agency lacked jurisdiction to regulate its mixture because it was not a drug or biological product, but rather a medical procedure that was part of the practice of medicine,[153] which is an area governed by states and not the federal government.[154] The district court ruled in favor of the FDA,[155] and the DC Circuit affirmed that ruling.[156]

In reaching its decision, the DC Circuit considered the definitions of "drug" and "biological product."[157] Under the FDCA, a drug is an "article[] intended for use in the diagnosis, cure, mitigation, treatment, or prevention of disease" or "intended to affect the structure or any function of the body."[158] A biological product under section 351 of the PHSA as it is currently codified is any "virus, therapeutic serum, toxin, antitoxin, vaccine, blood, blood component or derivative, allergenic product, protein (except any chemically synthesized polypeptide), or analogous product . . . applicable to the prevention, treatment, or cure of a disease or condition of human beings."[159] The appellate panel held that these two statutory definitions clearly applied to the stem-cell mixture under review.[160] Moreover, the panel rejected the practice-of-medicine claims because the FDA had focused on the mixture itself—and its safety in human use—as opposed to the medical procedure in which the mixture was utilized.[161] In essence, the mixture was considered a drug or biological product regardless of whether or not it was used in conjunction with a medical procedure.[162]

The panel also agreed with the FDA's position that the mixture was a cellular product intended for somatic-cell therapy.[163] Cellular products fall within the definition of drugs and biological products subject to FDA regulation[164] unless they are minimally manipulated.[165] "Minimal manipulation" means "processing that does not alter the relevant biological characteristics."[166] The court determined that the mixture at issue in *Regenerative Sciences* had been more than minimally manipulated because, for example, (1) the culturing process can "determine the growth and biological characteristics" of the cell population, and (2) the addition of certain substances to the culture affect stem-cell differentiation.[167]

Some have criticized the FDA's actions against the Regenexx-C stem cell-mixture on various grounds, including statutory and policy principles.[168] Professor Richard A. Epstein, for example, has argued that the FDA lacks authority to regulate the stem-cell procedure because the *statutory* definition of interstate commerce under the FDCA is not as expansive as Congress's *constitutional* authority to regulate interstate commerce under the Supreme Court's decision in *Wickard v. Filburn*, 317 U.S. 111 (1942).[169] Epstein acknowledged that under modern law the FDA has authority to regulate a business engaging in the type of interstate commerce at issue in *Regenerative Sciences* but argued instead that the FDCA, which was enacted before *Wickard*, does not grant the federal government power to apply constitutional authority where only statutory authority exists.[170] Regardless of whether such an argument has potential merit, *Regenerative Sciences* explicitly held that the stem-cell clinic's marketing reach, clientele, and other interstate activities collectively warrant the exercise of FDA jurisdiction under the Commerce Clause power. The court held that the mixture used in the Regenexx-C procedure, which contained the antibiotic doxycycline—a regulated article shipped in interstate commerce—"undoubtedly ha[s] effects on interstate markets for orthopedic care."[171] Accordingly, "[t]he Commerce Clause poses no obstacle to regulating the [m]ixture under the FDCA."[172]

Yet the most significant blind spot in criticisms of the *Regenerative Sciences* decision concerns the unexplored link between the law, science, and policy underlying the case. Indeed, the culturing process and its effects on the safety of MSCs intended for clinical use, as well as the FDA's focus on protecting consumer safety by regulating private clinics that market therapies with unsubstantiated claims, have been largely overlooked by critics.

FIGURE 9.6 Stem-cell clinics offering direct-to-consumer marketing of stem cell-based interventions globally

The choropleth map shows the number of clinics per country. The US (187), India (35), Mexico (28), China (23), Australia (19), England (16), Thailand (14), Malaysia (12), and Germany (11) have more than 10 stem-cell clinics in operation.

Consider the claims that FDA interference in *Regenerative Sciences* was unjustified because (1) use of autologous donor stem cells eliminates the risk of transmitting infectious or genetic diseases, and (2) stem-cell processing under locally controlled circumstances is no riskier than other standard laboratory procedures that lie outside FDA jurisdiction.[173] Such claims overlook the vast empirical scientific evidence associated with documented changes in stem-cell characteristics following prolonged in vitro expansion of MSCs and other types of stem cells.

Similarly, the view that "extracting and re-injecting a patient's own cells is not that different from other reparative or surgical procedures," such as coronary artery bypass graft surgery (in which the saphenous vein from a patient's leg is removed and transferred to the site of an occluded artery) or spinal surgery (in which a piece of bone from a patient's pelvis or rib is used to fuse vertebrae) is not at all accurate.[174] That view confounds the level of invasiveness associated with (1) the transfer of a patient's *differentiated* autologous tissue to another site of the patient's body with (2) the transfer of autologous *multipotent stem cells* to another site following in vitro expansion. The first involves tissue that cannot differentiate into other subtypes—in other words, vein tissue cannot suddenly become heart tissue; a piece of bone cannot magically turn into muscle or fat tissue. Conversely, the second involves stem cells that can proliferate and differentiate on their own into multiple tissue types.

The distinction is both scientifically and legally significant. Declaring that the autologous transfer of differentiated tissues and stem cells is "not that different," from a clinical perspective, is akin to analogizing the transfer of an inert piece of wood into a small garden enclosure—for purposes of straightening out a crooked plant—with the transfer of a tomato plant that can grow and proliferate in the small garden enclosure over time. The two could not be more different.

To be clear, issues surrounding the decentralization of medical research, the impact of overregulation on innovation, and the role of administrative agencies in the advancement of emerging technologies that can benefit humankind are interesting, multifaceted, and worthy of discussion. Those topics, however, are beyond the central scope of *Regenerative Sciences*. Simply put, the stem-cell procedure at issue in that case, which involved the expansion of stem cells in vitro over a period of approximately two weeks, should *absolutely* be regulated by the FDA because of the serious potential safety issues associated with in vitro stem-cell expansion.

Under a jurisprudence of scientific empiricism,[175] the type of therapy at issue in *Regenerative Sciences* should fall within the FDA's regulatory jurisdiction because prolonged in vitro expansion and culture of stem cells has been shown to induce genomic instability, spontaneous malignant transformation (cancer), chromosomal abnormalities, loss of multipotency, and aberrant patterns of gene expression.[176] The progressive accumulation of DNA damage in stem cells increases with time of culture and can ultimately lead to loss of stemness[177] and differentiation potential.[178]

It bears noting that, in the aftermath of *Regenerative Sciences*, Regenexx clinics began to market Regenexx-SD, or "same-day," stem-cell procedures in the United

States.[179] During the SD procedures, a "patient's cells are harvested in the morning, isolated and processed, then re-injected into the patient's injured area —all within a period of a few hours."[180] Thus, unlike Regenexx-C, the Regenexx-SD procedures fall within the Same Surgical Procedure Exception for human cells, tissues, and cellular and tissue-based products (HCT/Ps) outlined under 21 C.F.R. § 1271.15(b), which permits the removal and implantation of autologous HCT/Ps so long as they are performed within the same surgical procedure.[181] Because the risks associated with prolonged stem-cell in vitro expansion are not present in same-day, stem-cell procedures, the FDA has not asserted jurisdiction over them.[182] Thus, critics' claims that the "aggressive expansion" of FDA authority and its "aggressive legal maneuverings" against select, private, stem-cell clinics will exert a chilling effect on the industry have not materialized.[183] In fact, private stem-cell clinics and their direct-to-consumer marketing methods have increased dramatically over the last decade.[184]

Although scientists continue to research the causes underlying the above phenomena related to in vitro intracellular and extracellular influences on stem cells, private clinics have continued to profit from unapproved therapies that are costly and may have little to no therapeutic effect.[185] In 2018, the FDA filed requests for permanent injunctions against two stem-cell clinics—US Stem Cell Clinic LLC of Sunrise, Florida, and California Stem Cell Treatment Center, Inc.—to enjoin them "from marketing stem cell products without FDA approval and for significant deviations from current good manufacturing practice requirements."[186]

B *Making Product Classifications*

Although *Regenerative Sciences* applies to somatic stem-cell therapies and is silent on the status of germ cells, the stem-cell procedures examined in that case are relevant to GGE in many ways, particularly because the safety and efficacy of GGE interventions have yet to be proven. Accordingly, *Regenerative Sciences* establishes a firm regulatory path for the oversight of GGE by the FDA. The following classifications may apply to the regulation of GGE technologies.

1 Drug

Products intended for genome editing meet the FDCA's definition of drug. Under the FDCA, a drug is an article "intended for use in the diagnosis, cure, mitigation, treatment, or prevention of disease" or "intended to affect the structure of any function of the body."[187] GGE techniques will most likely require extraction or collection of germ-cell samples from patients, followed by a culturing process and the addition of a CRISPR-based or other product that enables genome editing directly to gametes, zygotes, or human embryos.[188] For purposes of in vitro fertilization, the modified germ cells will be used during fertilization and subsequent implantation into a patient's uterus with the intent of causing a pregnancy. Implantation of genetically modified embryos to induce a pregnancy has, for example, already been achieved in cynomolgus monkeys [189] and, more recently, in humans.[190]

The product aimed at genome editing may or may not be used for therapeutic purposes, but it will certainly affect the structure and function of the target cells as it will trigger cuts on DNA and introduce changes that are intended to affect the wildtype[191] characteristics of the target genetic locus.[192] Whether a genome-editing product ends up being used in therapeutic or nontherapeutic applications is significant—from a legal perspective—because the statute specifies that a drug is an "article[] intended for use in the diagnosis, cure, mitigation, treatment, or prevention of disease,"[193] and thereby excludes nontherapeutic GGE purposes as outlined earlier in Section II of this chapter. Furthermore, the Supreme Court has shown deference to the FDA and held that the statutory definition of drug under the FDCA is a term of art that is broader than the strict medical definition of the word.[194] For purposes of the FDCA, the interpretation of the term hinges on the article's intended use, rather than its technical properties.[195] Accordingly, the product for genome editing would squarely fit the definition of a drug under the FDCA.[196]

2 Biological Product

Depending on its intended use and method of delivery, a product intended for genome editing may also fit the definition of a biological product under section 351 of the PHSA for purposes of GGE.[197]

The statute specifies that biological products may encompass viruses or sera with therapeutic applications.[198] Technological advances have recently enabled GGE via delivery of large fragments of DNA into zygotes using adeno-associated virus (AAV) vectors.[199] An AAV is a nonpathogenic virus that infects humans—as well as nonhuman primates—and carries a relatively small, linear, single-stranded DNA genome.[200] The AAV's small size and nonpathogenic properties have enabled the development of AAV-based vector biotechnologies for use in gene-therapy clinical trials to treat a diverse range of human diseases.[201] The prospective use of AAV vectors, therefore, potentially extend FDA jurisdiction to this type of GGE intervention. Biological products within the meaning of the PHSA also include vaccines intended for therapeutic purposes.[202] Thus, GGE products for prophylactic uses would also likely fit the statutory definition of a biological product subject to FDA jurisdiction.

Interestingly, proteins for therapeutic use are included in the statutory definition of a biological product, which would encompass all modern protein-based tools for genome editing—including zinc finger-, TALEN-, and CRISPR-based systems—*so long as* they are not "chemically synthesized."[203] In theory, this exception creates a loophole in the statute, whereby a researcher using a purified, recombinant protein to trigger genome editing for GGE purposes is subject to regulation under the PHSA, but another researcher using a chemically synthesized version of the same protein is not. From a biochemical perspective, the purified and chemically synthesized versions of the same protein would be indistinguishable; both proteins would comprise the same amino-acid sequence regardless of the origin source. Lastly, unless Congress amends the definition of biological products under the PHSA, it should be noted that the statutory text, in its current incarnation, precludes regulation of any GGE products intended for nontherapeutic uses as biological products subject to FDA oversight.[204]

3 Medical Device

Under section 201(h) of the FDCA, as it is currently codified, a medical "device" is

> an instrument, apparatus, implement, machine, contrivance, implant, in vitro reagent, or other similar or related article, including any component, part, or accessory . . . intended for use in the diagnosis of disease or other conditions, or in the cure, mitigation, treatment, or prevention of disease, in man . . . or intended to affect the structure or any function of the body . . . and which does not achieve its primary intended purposes through chemical action . . . and which is not dependent upon being metabolized for the achievement of its primary intended purpose.[205]

GGE products intended for therapeutic use are likely to be classified as contrivances or in vitro reagents that affect the structure or function of their targets. However, as it applies to GGE, in which the primary purpose is to modify a target nucleotide sequence, the chemical action clause of the statutory text would render GGE products beyond the meaning of a medical device under the FDCA, primarily because effectors that catalyze DNA double-stranded breaks for genome editing achieve their primary goal through enzymatic—namely, chemical—action.[206] Accordingly, GGE products are not likely to constitute medical devices under the statute.

4 Combination Product

A combination product is a product comprised of two or more different types of regulated components.[207] A GGE product may be a combination product if it is both a drug and a biological product within the meaning of section 503(g) of the FDCA.[208] Combination products are assigned to an FDA center with primary jurisdiction for its premarket review and regulation based on a determination of the product's "primary mode of action."[209] Therefore, the Center for Drug Evaluation and Research (CDER) would have primary jurisdiction over a drug-biological GGE product, while the CBER would have primary jurisdiction of a biological-drug GGE product.

C *Minimal Manipulation*

Germ cells undergoing modification during GGE interventions will likely be deemed more than minimally manipulated under both the FDA rules and the *Regenerative Sciences* standard. As noted above, any processing that alters the relevant characteristics of cells or tissues cannot constitute minimal manipulation.[210] The alteration of specific biological characteristics of germ cells is at the core of GGE and, thus, the addition of products that enable genome editing would be deemed to affect not merely how the germ cell differentiates but also the cell's own genetic identity. The modified germ cells would not qualify as section 361 products subject to minimal FDA oversight because GGE interventions would likely involve microinjections, viral-based delivery of packaged molecules to activate genome editing, and other types of micromanipulations.[211] In essence, the germ cells would be considered more than minimally manipulated and GGE would involve "combination of the [germ] cells or tissues with another article,"[212] namely an effector that catalyzes genome editing.

The aforementioned analysis of the potential classifications for GGE regulation, coupled with the current lack of scientific evidence to establish the safety and efficacy of genome editing—in both somatic and germ cells—provides the FDA strong footing to assert its jurisdiction over GGE.[213]

D *Congress Can Get No Satisfaction*

The FDA stands on a strong legal foundation to assert jurisdiction over GGE and should do so promptly to restrict the rise of a premature industry aimed at engineering genetically modified humans. The safety and efficacy of GGE technologies must be adequately addressed from a scientific perspective before clinical GGE interventions can proceed. At the same time, robust public debate must focus on the potential social and ethical benefits and risks of GGE interventions.

Once jurisdictional hurdles are cleared, any manufacturer of products intended for use in clinical applications of GGE would be required to submit an Investigational New Drug Application (IND)[214] and a Biologics License Application (BLA),[215] which must be approved prior to marketing GGE interventions. However, the FDA is currently prohibited from reviewing any IND or BLA under a provision in the Consolidated Appropriations Act (CAA) of 2016,[216] which Congress has since renewed.[217] The provision states that

> None of the funds made available by this Act may be used to notify a sponsor or otherwise acknowledge receipt of a submission for an exemption for investigational use of a drug or biological product . . . in research in which a human embryo is intentionally created or modified to include a heritable genetic modification. Any such submission shall be deemed to have not been received by the Secretary, and the exemption may not go into effect.[218]

To be clear, there currently is no law explicitly banning human GGE. Although no federal funds may be used to perform research on human embryos since passage of the Dickey-Wicker Amendment,[219] such research is legal in the United States, so long as it is privately funded. The rider provision of the CAA merely restricts the FDA's ability to acknowledge receipt of—in other words, to *review*—an application for clinical use of GGE technology in an embryo. However, that limitation is significant because all drugs and biological products, including gene therapies, must be approved by the FDA before they can be marketed and used in clinical settings. Such approval cannot occur if the Agency cannot review INDs and BLAs for GGE purposes.

In essence, because Congress would likely find it difficult to enact a law that directly bans GGE[220]—particularly given increasingly favorable public attitudes toward the use of technologies for genome editing[221]—it has used its power of the purse to achieve a similar policy result.[222]

With the rider provision of the CAA, Congress introduced a de facto ban on any clinical applications of GGE and prohibited the FDA from assessing and evaluating the safety and efficacy of any GGE clinical intervention. Such a legislative ban is unnecessary and counterintuitive as it prevents the FDA from carrying out its mission to protect the public health by ensuring the safety and efficacy of drugs, biological products, and medical devices.[223]

By restricting the FDA's oversight over GGE INDs, Congress is also interfering with the Agency's "responsib[ility] to advance the public health by helping to speed innovations that make medical products more effective, safer, and more affordable and by helping the public get the accurate, science-based information they need to use medical products . . . and improve their health."[224] Indeed, the FDA's role within the regulatory system is not limited to its consumer-protection responsibilities. The Agency also plays an important role in incentivizing the creation of robust scientific information about products.[225] By foreclosing FDA review of GGE technologies, Congress is hindering efforts to develop robust scientific data on GGE applications.

Furthermore, Congress has not presented evidence to demonstrate that the FDA would be unable to fulfill its regulatory duties concerning GGE technologies. Simply put, the current ban is unnecessary because, given the FDA's long record of enforcing regulations aimed at consumer protection, no evidence suggests that the FDA would approve any GGE intervention without first subjecting it to the long and rigorous process required to establish its safety and efficacy. To the contrary, the FDA has discretion to apply clinical holds, which refer to orders that delay or suspend an ongoing clinical investigation due to unreasonable risks to research subjects or discovery of information that undermines confidence in the investigators or the study protocols.[226] Indeed, the FDA availed itself of this authority by instituting a clinical hold on a CRISPR-based therapy in 2018.[227]

Lastly, the current ban increases the likelihood that GGE technologies will be pushed to develop in other jurisdictions,[228] where regulations may be inadequate from social and ethical standpoints. Some commentators posit that stringent FDA regulations are one major reason why clinical trials move to low- and middle-income countries. [229] Emerging reproductive technologies can, therefore, present difficult social and ethical challenges related to patient informed consent, confidentiality, access to information, long-term follow-up, and adequate access to justice when things go wrong.[230]

Consider, for instance, the case of He Jiankui and the November 2018 birth of the Chinese twin girls whose genomes were edited at the *CCR5* locus (recall our discussion throughout Chapter 8). To obtain informed consent from parents enrolling in the clinical trial, He Jiankui described the research as an "AIDS vaccine development project" that would bestow upon "gene editing [sic] babies . . . the genotype of the Northern European to naturally immunize against the HIV-1 virus."[231] The consent form was a twenty-three-page document filled with technical jargon and underscores the question of whether patients were able to provide adequate informed consent to the research that would be performed on embryos intended for subsequent implantation and pregnancy.

One striking aspect of the consent form is the disclaimer of risks associated with off-target effects, which were identified as "[t]he primary risk of gene editing" without actually disclosing the deleterious consequences of genomic mutations that could arise from potential targeting of unintended DNA sites.[232] Assuming that patients thoroughly understood the implications of off-target genome editing, the waiver of liability clause disclaiming responsibility for off-target effects is dubious from ethical and legal perspectives. The consent form's acknowledgment that the risks associated with the clinical trial are "beyond the risk consequences of the existing medical science and technology,"[233] arguably establishes prima facie evidence that safety and efficacy concerns are substantial enough to warrant halting the trial. In the United States, for example, proceeding with such a trial at the early stages of technological development before safety and efficacy issues have been addressed from a scientific perspective likely constitutes a reckless or grossly negligent act, which would automatically void the waiver of liability.[234] It also bears noting that although the consent form loosely mentions the risk of off-target effects, it does not inform patients of potential unintended *on-target* effects that could arise from editing the *CCR5* locus on embryos, including susceptibility to other diseases that might be relevant in the patients' geographic location or unknown cognitive outcomes. We will explore some of these potential on-target effects in Chapter 11.

Lastly, He Jiankui admitted "he obtained consent from the couples himself, rather than having a trained, uninvolved professional do it."[235] And despite He Jiankui's claim that he explained the meaning of the consent form "to each family line by line and paragraph by paragraph,"[236] it is hard to imagine that all patients enrolled in the clinical trial provided informed consent. Similar to the problems associated with obtaining informed consent in the case of the Chinese twin girls outlined above—which stemmed from clear institutional failures and gaps in the Chinese regulatory system—other issues that fall within social and ethical ambits may be inadequately addressed in jurisdictions that lack robust regulatory systems with clear and established rules to ensure patient protections.

As this chapter shows, the kind of legislative ban currently in place for GGE provides fertile ground for the proliferation of unethical human experimentation in jurisdictions lacking robust legal systems aimed at protecting consumers. Simply put, the legislative ban imposes higher scientific, research, and social costs that are not outweighed by their potential benefits.

Notes

1 *What We Do*, FDA, https://www.fda.gov/aboutfda/whatwedo/default.htm [https://perma.cc/8H8A-6SK9].

2 United States v. Regenerative Scis., LLC, 741 F.3d 1314, 1317 (D.C. Cir. 2014).

3 The FDA may also regulate GGE under provisions applicable to assisted reproductive technologies (ART), which relate to the handling of gametes and embryos. *See* 42 U.S.C. § 263a-1(a)–(c) (2012). For a general overview of ART regulations in the United States, see generally David Adamson, *Regulation of Assisted Reproductive Technologies in the United States*, 78 Fertility & Sterility 932 (2002).

4 Balanced Budget Downpayment Act, Pub. L. No. 104–99, § 128, 110 Stat. 26, 34 (1996).

5 *See* Russell A. Spivak, I. Glenn Cohen & Eli Y. Adashi, *Germ-Line Gene Editing and Congressional Reaction in Context: Learning from Almost 50 Years of Congressional Reactions to Biomedical Breakthroughs*, 30 J.L. & Health 20, 30 (2017).

6 *See, e.g.*, Nat'l Acads. Scis., Eng'g & Med., Human Genome Editing: Science, Ethics, & Governance 130–31 (Rona Briere & Helaine Resnick eds., 2017) [hereinafter NASEM Report]. *See also generally* Nat'l Insts. of Health, NIH Guidelines for Research Involving Recombinant or Synthetic Nucleic Acid Molecules (2016), https://osp.od.nih.gov/wp-content/uploads/2013/06/NIH_Guidelines.pdf [https://perma.cc/HX4L-JT9F] (outlining the safety considerations, experimental protocols, and responsibilities required for conducting clinical investigations under the NIH guidelines).

7 Statement, Francis S. Collins, Dir., Nat'l Insts. of Health, Statement on Modernizing Human Gene Therapy Oversight (Aug. 16, 2018), https://www.nih.gov/about-nih/who-we-are/nih-director/statements/statement-modernizing-human-gene-therapy-oversight [https://perma.cc/37TG-GGK8]; *see also Amendments to Streamline Review of Gene Therapy Trials and Transform the RAC to NExTRAC – April 2019*, Nat'l Institutes Health, https://osp.od.nih.gov/biotechnology/nih-guidelines/ [https://perma.cc/JUS9-DDTT].

8 *What We Do*, *supra* note 1.

9 *The History of FDA's Fight for Consumer Protection and Public Health*, FDA, https://www.fda.gov/AboutFDA/History/default.htm [https://perma.cc/HDK9-RXJV] [hereinafter *Fight for Consumer Protection*].

10 *See generally*, *e.g.*, Carol Ballentine, *Taste of Raspberries, Taste of Death: The 1937 Elixir Sulfanilamide Incident*, FDA Consumer, June 1981, *reprinted in* Sulfanilamide Disaster, https://www.fda.gov/media/110479/download [https://perma.cc/DZR4-UCJT] (noting that the 1937 Elixir of Sulfanilamide drug scandal increased the jurisdictional powers of the FDA).

11 *See* Michelle Meadows, *A Century of Ensuring Safe Foods and Cosmetics*, FDA Consumer, Jan.–Feb. 2006, at 6 (chronicling the effects induced by public outrage in the 1906 meat-packing scandal on the jurisdictional powers of the FDA).

12 It bears pointing out that some scholars have noted—with light discomfort—that administrative agencies, including the FDA, are increasingly relying on the issuance of nonbinding guidance documents and other less formal administrative tools to implement their statutory authority, while shifting away from the promulgation of binding rules. *See, e.g.*, Lars Noah, *Governance by the Backdoor: Administrative Law(lessness?) at the FDA*, 93 Neb. L. Rev. 89, 90 (2014).

13 It should be noted that, in general, the decisions of administrative agencies are subject to the *Auer* and *Chevron* doctrines of judicial deference. *See* Auer v. Robbins, 519 U.S. 452, 459 (1997) (endorsing deference to an agency's nonsubstantive interpretation of its own regulations); Chevron U.S.A. Inc. v. Nat. Res. Def. Council, Inc., 467 U.S. 837, 842–45 (1984) (reflecting deference to an agency's interpretation of its governing statute).

14 Peter Barton Hutt, *Historical Themes and Developments at FDA over the Past Fifty Years*, *in* FDA in the Twenty-First Century: The Challenges of Regulating Drugs and New Technologies 17, 17 (Holly Fernandez Lynch & I. Glenn Cohen eds., 2015).

15 *Id.*; *When and Why Was FDA Formed?*, FDA, https://www.fda.gov/aboutfda/transparency/basics/ucm214403.htm [https://perma.cc/4H89-JBCA].

16 Chemical analysis was initially used to monitor the safety of agricultural products, but the scope expanded in subsequent decades to encompass other types of consumer products. *Fight for Consumer Protection*, *supra* note 9.

17 Act of May 15, 1862, ch. 72, 12 Stat. 387. The Act charged the newly formed USDA with duties "to acquire and to diffuse . . . useful information on subjects connected with agriculture . . . and to procure, propagate, and distribute . . . new and valuable seeds and plants." *Id.* § 1, 12 Stat. at 387.

18 FDA History Office, *A Guide to Resources on the History of the Food and Drug Administration*, *in* The Food and Drug Administration (FDA) 149, 149 (Meredith A. Hickmann ed., 2003).

19 Hutt, *supra* note 14, at 17–18.

20 *See* Dr. Harvey W. Wiley, *of Indiana, Class of 1871 of the Indiana Medical College*, 25 IND. MED. J. 446, 447 (1907) [hereinafter Dr. Harvey W. Wiley].
21 The Chemical Division of the USDA became the USDA Division of Chemistry in 1890. Hutt, *supra* note 14, at 18.
22 *See* Dr. Harvey W. Wiley, *supra* note 20, at 446–47. Before undertaking his role as chief of the Division of Chemistry, Wiley was the State Chemist of Indiana. *Id.*
23 The first report, for example, examined consumer dairy products. *See* USDA, DIV. OF CHEMISTRY, BULLETIN NO. 13, FOODS AND FOOD ADULTERANTS. PART FIRST: DAIRY PRODUCTS 3 (1887). Subsequent reports were published over the span of the next fifteen years. W. D. Bigelow, *Obituary: Harvey Washington Wiley*, 72 SCIENCE 311, 311 (1930).
24 Dr. Harvey W. Wiley, *supra* note 20, at 447.
25 Bigelow, *supra* note 23, at 311. For additional accounts of the history of the FDA in the late nineteenth and early twentieth centuries, see Lewis A. Grossman, *Food, Drugs, and Droods: A Historical Consideration of Definitions and Categories in American Food and Drug Law*, 93 CORNELL L. REV. 1091, 1098–111 (2008); Patricia J. Zettler, *Pharmaceutical Federalism*, 92 IND. L.J. 845, 854–56 (2017).
26 *See* Mary K. Bruch & Elaine Larson, *An Early Historical Perspective on the FDA's Regulation of OTC Drugs*, 10 INFECTION CONTROL & HOSP. EPIDEMIOLOGY 527, 527–28 (1989). For his leadership and contributions to the promotion of food and drug safety during his nearly thirty-year career, Wiley became widely known as the "Father of the FDA." *See, e.g.*, WILLIAM H. EAGLSTEIN, THE FDA FOR DOCTORS 89 (2014).
27 *When and Why Was FDA Formed?*, *supra* note 15.
28 Bigelow, *supra* note 23, at 311; *see also* Dale A. Stirling, *Profiles in Toxicology: Harvey W. Wiley*, 67 TOXICOLOGICAL SCI. 157, 157 (2002) (noting that attempts at passing food-safety legislation had failed until the enactment of the Pure Food and Drug Act of 1906).
29 UPTON SINCLAIR, THE JUNGLE (1906).
30 Daniel E. Slotnik, *Upton Sinclair, Whose Muckraking Changed the Meat Industry*, N.Y. TIMES (June 30, 2016), https://www.nytimes.com/interactive/projects/cp/obituaries/archives/upton-sinclair-meat-industry [https://perma.cc/M3D5-4NYF].
31 Upton Sinclair, *What Life Means to Me*, COSMOPOLITAN, May–Oct. 1906, at 591, 594 (emphasis added).
32 *See* Message from President Theodore Roosevelt to the Senate and House of Representatives on Conditions in Chicago Stock Yards (June 4, 1906), *republished in Report on Chicago Stock Yards*, HIST. ART & ARCHIVES, https://history.house.gov/Records-and-Research/Listing/c_042/ [https://perma.cc/E4A9-AMYT].
33 *Id.*

34 *Id.*
35 Pure Food and Drug Act of 1906, ch. 3915, 34 Stat. 768, *repealed by* Federal Food, Drug, and Cosmetic Act, ch. 675, 52 Stat. 1040 (1938) (codified as amended at 21 U.S.C. §§ 301–399 (2012 & Supp. 2017)).
36 *Id.* § 1, 34 Stat. at 768.
37 Federal Meat Inspection Act, ch. 2907, 34 Stat. 1256 (1907) (codified as amended at 21 U.S.C. §§ 601–695 (2012)); *see also* Meadows, *supra* note 11, at 8 (noting that the PFDA and Federal Meat Inspection Act became law on the same day).
38 Pure Food and Drug Act of 1906, § 1, 34 Stat. at 768.
39 *See id.* § 2, 34 Stat. at 768.
40 *Id.* § 7, 34 Stat. at 769–70. The PFDA defined adulterated articles, for the first time, as (1) drugs that differed from recognized standards of strength, quality, or purity; (2) confectionery with ingredients that were deleterious or detrimental to health; or (3) food that contained injurious mixtures or substitutes, had constituent parts abstracted, featured addition of poisonous or deleterious ingredients, concealed damage or inferior quality, or consisted of a decomposed animal or vegetable substance. *Id.*
41 *Id.* § 8, 34 Stat. at 770–71. Misbranded articles were also defined, for the first time, as (1) drugs that bore a false name, featured false contents, failed to include a label that lacked the quantity or proportion of specific numerated substances; or (2) food that was an imitation of another article, contained misleading labels, failed to include a label that lacked the quantity or proportion of specific numerated substances, did not state its weight or measure, or contained a label with misleading ingredients. *Id.*
42 *Id.* § 1, 34 Stat. at 768.
43 The Department of the Treasury and the Department of Commerce and Labor also shared authority to make rules and regulations to carry out the provisions of the Act. *Id.* § 3, 34 Stat. at 768–69.
44 The USDA Division of Chemistry became the USDA Bureau of Chemistry in 1901. Hutt, *supra* note 14, at 17.
45 Pure Food and Drug Act of 1906, § 4, 34 Stat. at 769.
46 *Id.* §§ 4–5, 34 Stat. at 769.
47 *Id.* § 6, 34 Stat. at 769. Compare the definition of drug under the PFDA with that of the FDCA. *See infra* note 79 and accompanying text.
48 *Laws Enforced by FDA*, FDA, https://www.fda.gov/RegulatoryInformation/LawsEnforcedbyFDA/default.htm [https://perma.cc/F2DZ-DEGD].
49 *See id.*
50 *See* Harvey W. Wiley, An Autobiography 288 (1930).
51 *Harvey Washington Wiley, M.D.*, FDA, https://www.fda.gov/AboutFDA/History/FOrgsHistory/Leaders/ucm093765.htm [https://perma.cc/C8TS-FBG4].
52 *Id.*

53 *See, e.g.*, WILEY, *supra* note 50, at 261–73 (recounting select legal battles stemming from prosecution of PFDA violations).

54 *See, e.g.*, C. W. Crawford, *Technical Problems in Food and Drug Law Enforcement*, 1 LAW & CONTEMP. PROBS. 36, 36 (1933) ("It has been rightly said that the policy of the Federal Food and Drugs Act regarding added poisonous substances in food is an inverted one since the law places the obligation on the Government to show that the contaminated food may be harmful to health, rather than on the manufacturer to show that it will not.").

55 221 U.S. 488, 497–98 (1911).

56 232 U.S. 399, 411 (1914).

57 Sherley Amendment to the Pure Food and Drugs Act, ch. 352, 37 Stat. 416 (1912), *repealed by* Federal Food, Drug, and Cosmetic Act, ch. 675, § 902(a), 52 Stat. 1040, 1059 (1938) (codified as amended at 21 U.S.C. § 387b (2012)).

58 *See* STEPHEN WILSON, FOOD & DRUG REGULATION 81–82 (1942).

59 Crawford, *supra* note 54, at 41 (1933).

60 *Id.*

61 WILEY, *supra* note 50, at 273.

62 *Id.* at 272–73.

63 By 1927, the Bureau of Chemistry underwent reorganization to separate its regulatory and research branches. *Milestones in U.S. Food and Drug Law History*, FDA, https://www.fda.gov/aboutfda/history/forgshistory/evolvingpowers/ucm2007256.htm [https://perma.cc/QP8M-4KTL] [hereinafter *Milestones*]. The regulatory division of the Bureau became the Food, Drug, and Insecticide Administration, which was subsequently abbreviated to Food and Drug Administration in 1930. *Id.* Although the FDA was baptized with its current name in 1930, it was still part of the USDA. Then in 1940, it was transferred to the Federal Security Agency, which was twice renamed as the Department of Health Education and Welfare in 1953 and the Department of Health and Human Services in 1979. *History of FDA's Internal Organization*, FDA, https://www.fda.gov/AboutFDA/History/FOrgsHistory/default.htm [https://perma.cc/2LNU-WUGZ]. The FDA currently resides within the DHHS. *Id.*

64 For a brief account of said shortcomings, including the lack of oversight over cosmetics, patent medicines, false advertising, food preservatives, etc., and vagueness vis-à-vis food adulteration, see CHARLES O. JACKSON, FOOD AND DRUG LEGISLATION IN THE NEW DEAL 3–8 (1970).

65 *Milestones*, *supra* note 63.

66 John P. Swann, *How Chemists Pushed for Consumer Protection: The Food and Drugs Act of 1906*, CHEMICAL HERITAGE, Summer 2006, at 6, *reprinted in* HOW CHEMISTS PUSHED FOR CONSUMER PROTECTION: THE FOOD AND DRUGS ACT OF 1906, https://www.fda.gov/media/110307/download [https://perma.cc/PT4D-H8SQ].

67 *Id.*

68 *Milestones*, *supra* note 63.

69 *Id.*; FDA History Office, *supra* note 18, at 151.
70 *See* Leo J. Schep et al., *Diethylene Glycol Poisoning*, 47 Clinical Toxicology 525, 525 (2009).
71 *Milestones*, *supra* note 63.
72 *See supra* notes 29–34 and accompanying text.
73 Federal Food, Drug, and Cosmetic Act, ch. 675, 52 Stat. 1040 (1938) (codified as amended at 21 U.S.C. §§ 301–399 (2012 & Supp. 2017)).
74 *Id.* (quoting the long title of the Act).
75 *Id.* § 502(a), (i)(1), 52 Stat. at 1050–51.
76 *See supra* notes 58–60 and accompanying text.
77 *See* Federal Food, Drug, and Cosmetic Act, § 201(h)–(i), 52 Stat. at 1041.
78 *Id.* § 201(f), 52 Stat. at 1040. The definition of "food" explicitly included chewing gum. *Id.*
79 *Id.* § 201(g), 52 Stat. at 1041. The term "drug" under the FDCA of 1938 meant "articles intended for use in the diagnosis, cure, mitigation, treatment, or prevention of disease in man or other animals; and . . . articles (other than food) intended to affect the structure or any function of the body of man or other animals." *Id.*
80 *Id.* § 201(k), 52 Stat. at 1041.
81 *Id.* § 201(n), 52 Stat. at 1041.
82 *Id.* § 704, 52 Stat. at 1057. The FDCA also authorized inspectors "to enter any vehicle being used to transport or hold such food, drugs, devices, or cosmetics." *Id.*
83 *Id.* § 406(a), 52 Stat. at 1049.
84 *Id.* § 502(c)–(d), 52 Stat. at 1050.
85 *Id.* § 505(a), 52 Stat. at 1052.
86 *See, e.g.*, United States v. Sullivan, 332 U.S. 689, 697–98 (1948) (holding that the FDCA did not exceed its constitutional authority under the Commerce Clause when a retailer was charged with performing acts that resulted in a drug being misbranded while held for sale after shipment in interstate commerce); Alberty Food Prods. v. United States, 194 F.2d 463, 464 (9th Cir. 1952) (affirming a lower court's ruling that the drugs in question were misbranded under the FDCA because the label lacked adequate directions for use). *But see* United States v. Cardiff, 344 U.S. 174, 176–77 (1952) (holding that refusal to grant permission to inspect a factory pursuant to the FDCA cannot constitute a crime because the Act is too vague to be enforced under criminal law).
87 Public Health Service Act, ch. 373, 58 Stat. 682 (1944) (codified as amended at 42 U.S.C. §§ 201–300mm (2012)).
88 *See id.* § 311, 58 Stat. at 693; *id.* § 361(a), 58 Stat. at 703.
89 *Id.* § 301, 58 Stat. at 691–92.
90 *Id.* § 351, 58 Stat. at 702–03.
91 Kefauver-Harris Drug Amendments of 1962, Pub. L. No. 87–781, 76 Stat. 780 (codified as amended in scattered sections of 21 U.S.C.).

92 Federal Food, Drug, and Cosmetic Act, ch. 675, § 505, 52 Stat. 1040, 1052 (1938) (codified as amended at 21 U.S.C. § 355 (Supp. 2017)).

93 *Kefauver-Harris Amendments Revolutionized Drug Development*, FDA, https://www.fda.gov/ForConsumers/ConsumerUpdates/ucm322856.htm [https://perma.cc/BC2L-AKJY].

94 *See* Grossman, *supra* note 25, at 1129–30.

95 *See, e.g.*, 21st Century Cures Act, Pub. L. No. 114–255, 130 Stat. 1033 (2016) (codified in scattered sections of Titles 21, 34, 38 & 42 of the U.S.C.); Drug Quality and Security Act, Pub. L. No. 113–54, 127 Stat. 587 (2013) (codified as amended at 21 U.S.C. §§ 353, 353b, 360eee, 379j (Supp. 2017)); Biologics Price Competition and Innovation Act of 2009, Pub. L. No. 111–148, §§ 7001–7003, 124 Stat. 119, 804–21 (codified as amended in scattered sections of Titles 21, 28, 35 & 42 of the U.S.C.); Family Smoking Prevention and Tobacco Control Act, Pub. L. No. 111–31, 123 Stat. 1776 (2009) (codified at 21 U.S.C. § 387 (2012)).

96 *Fact Sheet: FDA at a Glance*, FDA, https://www.fda.gov/AboutFDA/Transparency/Basics/ucm553038.htm [https://perma.cc/5Q4J-T9Z2].

97 *What Does FDA Regulate?*, FDA, https://www.fda.gov/AboutFDA/Transparency/Basics/ucm194879.htm [https://perma.cc/R94E-UU98].

98 *Fact Sheet*, *supra* note 96. The Agency also employs over 18,000 individuals, *see* FDA, 2020 JUSTIFICATION OF ESTIMATES FOR APPROPRIATIONS COMMITTEES 343 (2020), https://www.fda.gov/media/121408/download [https://perma.cc/SHV8-AUF5], and for fiscal year 2020 requested a federal budget of $6.1 billion, *id.* at 8.

99 *Cf.* Seok-Eun Kim, *The Role of Trust in the Modern Administrative State: An Integrative Model*, 37 ADMIN. & SOC'Y 611, 613 (2005) ("American political theories are often quite explicit in their inherent distaste for strong bureaucratic powers because of concern about ensuring accountability.").

100 *See, e.g.*, Sarah D. Kowitt et al., *Awareness and Trust of the FDA and CDC: Results from a National Sample of US Adults and Adolescents*, 12 PLOS ONE, no. e0177546, May 16, 2017, at 1, 4–6 (reporting results of a study that found 79 percent of adolescents and 63 percent of adults have high levels of trust in the FDA compared to 43 percent of adults with a "[g]reat deal or a fair amount of trust in the federal [government]"); *see also* PEW RESEARCH CTR., BEYOND DISTRUST: HOW AMERICANS VIEW THEIR GOVERNMENT 58 (2015) (reporting a 51 percent favorable rating of the FDA among the public compared to Congress's 27 percent favorable rating).

101 *What We Do*, *supra* note 1.

102 *Id.*

103 *Id.*

104 *See* Paul Enríquez, *Genome Editing and the Jurisprudence of Scientific Empiricism*, 19 VAND. J. ENT. & TECH. L. 619–21 (2017).

105 *Id.* at 621.

106 A heritable disease refers to a genetic disorder—namely, a type of genetic abnormality giving rise to a medical condition—that is passed down from

one generation to the next via the germline. *See Specific Genetic Disorders*, NAT'L HUM. GENOME RES. INST., https://www.genome.gov/10001204/specific-genetic-disorders/ [https://perma.cc/39XZ-GUS7]. For a list of some common heritable diseases, see *id.* (including, for example, achondroplasia, some forms of hereditary breast cancer, hemophilia, Cystic Fibrosis, familial Parkinson's disease, phenylketonuria, Marfan syndrome, and Tay-Sachs disease).

107 *See, e.g.*, Theodore Friedmann & Richard Roblin, *Genetic Therapy for Human Genetic Disease?*, 175 SCIENCE 949, 949 (1972).

108 *See* Steven A. Rosenberg et al., *Gene Transfer into Humans—Immunotherapy of Patients with Advanced Melanoma, Using Tumor-Infiltrating Lymphocytes Modified by Retroviral Gene Transduction*, 323 NEW ENG. J. MED. 570, 571 (1990).

109 *See* Application of Current Statutory Authorities to Human Somatic Cell Therapy Products and Gene Therapy Products, 58 Fed. Reg. 53,248, 53,248 (Oct. 14, 1993).

110 *See id.*

111 Federal Food, Drug, and Cosmetic Act, 21 U.S.C. §§ 301–399 (2012 & Supp. 2017).

112 Public Health Service Act, 42 U.S.C. §§ 201–300 (2012 & Supp. 2017).

113 "Somatic cells are all of the body's cells except the reproductive cells." Enríquez, *supra* note 104, at 633 n.178.

114 *See* Application of Current Statutory Authorities to Human Somatic Cell Therapy Products and Gene Therapy Products, 58 Fed. Reg. at 53,249–51.

115 OTC is "a rare metabolic disease that can cause a dangerous build-up of ammonia in the body." Sally Lehrman, *Virus Treatment Questioned After Gene Therapy Death*, 401 NATURE 517, 517 (1999).

116 *See id.*

117 *See, e.g.*, Michael Gross, *New Hopes for Gene Therapy*, 24 CURRENT BIOLOGY R983, R983 (2014); A. M. Keeler, M. K. ElMallah & T. R. Flotte, *Gene Therapy 2017: Progress and Future Directions*, 10 CLINICAL & TRANSLATIONAL SCI. 242, 242 (2017).

118 *See* Keeler et al., *supra* note 117, at 242.

119 *See infra* note 130 and accompanying text.

120 Theodore Friedmann & Richard Roblin, *Gene Therapy for Human Genetic Disease?*, 175 SCIENCE 949, 949 (1972).

121 Application of Current Statutory Authorities to Human Somatic Cell Therapy Products and Gene Therapy Products, 58 Fed. Reg. 53,248, 53,251 (Oct. 14, 1993) (emphasis added); CTR. FOR BIOLOGICS EVALUATION & RESEARCH, FDA, GUIDANCE FOR INDUSTRY: GUIDANCE FOR HUMAN SOMATIC CELL THERAPY AND GENE THERAPY 3 (1998) (emphasis added) [hereinafter GUIDANCE FOR SOMATIC CELL THERAPY], https://www.fda.gov/media/72402/download [https://perma.cc/G7ZS-88P7].

122 *What Is Gene Therapy?*, FDA, https://www.fda.gov/biologicsbloodvaccines/cellulargenetherapyproducts/ucm573960.htm [https://perma.cc/KEH3-TJ790] (emphasis added).

123 Guidance for Somatic Cell Therapy, *supra* note 121, at 3.

124 Guidance for Somatic Cell Therapy, *supra* note 121, at 3 (emphasis added).

125 *See, e.g.*, David H. Adams et al., *Human Membrane Cofactor Protein (MCP, CD 46) Protects Transgenic Pig Hearts from Hyperacute Rejection in Primates*, 8 Xenotransplantation 36 (2001).

126 *See, e.g.*, Megan Sykes & David H. Sachs, *Transplanting Organs from Pigs to Humans*, 4 Science Immunology Art. eaau6298 (2019).

127 Application of Current Statutory Authorities to Human Somatic Cell Therapy Products and Gene Therapy Products, 58 Fed. Reg. 53,248, 53,249 (Oct. 14, 1993) (citations omitted).

128 *What Is Gene Therapy?*, *supra* note 122.

129 *Id.*

130 *FDA Approval Brings First Gene Therapy to the United States*, FDA (Aug. 30, 2017), https://www.fda.gov/newsevents/newsroom/pressannouncements/ucm574058.htm [https://perma.cc/V2M3-QKYH]. Kymriah® is a genetically modified, autologous, somatic cell–based, gene-therapy product sold by Novartis Pharmaceuticals Corporation. *Id.*

131 *See* Robert M. Califf & Ritu Nalubola, *FDA's Science-Based Approach to Genome Edited Products*, FDA Voice (Jan. 18, 2017), https://perma.cc/X936-U9JJ, *reprinted in* Robert M. Califf & Ritu Nalubola, *FDA's Science-Based Approach to Genome Edited Products*, Check Orphan (Jan. 19, 2017), http://www.checkorphan.org/news/fda2019s-science-based-approach-to-genome-edited-products [https://perma.cc/C7H3-QDG7].

132 *See id.*

133 *Id.* The statement appeared on FDA Voice, the FDA's official blog. *Id.* Interestingly, the statement on the FDA's intended approach toward the regulation of genome-edited products was taken down from the FDA website on or around October 3, 2018, and replaced with a collection of perspectives from FDA experts. *See FDA Voices: Perspectives from FDA Experts*, FDA, https://www.fda.gov/newsevents/newsroom/fdavoices/default.htm [https://perma.cc/6XS4-ESJK]. It is not clear whether removal of the policy statement signals that the FDA intended to proceed with a different approach under the direction of Scott Gottlieb, the new FDA Commissioner appointed by the Trump Administration who, unexpectedly, resigned from his post in March 2019, *see* Sheila Kaplan & Jan Hoffman, *F.D.A. Commissioner Scott Gottlieb, Who Fought Teenage Vaping, Resigns*, N.Y. Times (Mar. 5, 2019), https://www.nytimes.com/2019/03/05/health/scott-gottlieb-resigns-fda.html [https://perma.cc/74CR-FLXL], or merely that the FDA's blog was reorganized.

134 *See* Ctr. for Biologics Evaluation & Research, FDA, Long Term Follow-Up After Administration of Human Gene Therapy Products 4, 26 (2018) [hereinafter Long Term Follow-Up], https://www.fda.gov/downloads/BiologicsBloodVaccines/GuidanceComplianceRegulatoryInformation/Guidances/CellularandGeneTherapy/UCM610797.pdf [https://perma.cc/KG7E-9HFY]; *see also* Long Term Follow-Up After Administration of Human Gene Therapy Products; Draft Guidance for Industry; Availability, 83 Fed. Reg. 32,311, 32,311–12 (July 12, 2018) (announcing the availability of draft guidance).

135 *See, e.g.*, Ctr. for Biologics Evaluation & Research, FDA, Guidance for Industry: Gene Therapy Clinical Trials – Observing Subjects for Delayed Adverse Events 1 n.1 (2006), https://www.fda.gov/media/72225/download [https://perma.cc/LP9D-CWQH]; Long Term Follow-Up, *supra* note 134, at 28; *see also* Guidance for Industry: Gene Therapy Clinical Trials—Observing Subjects for Delayed Adverse Events; Availability, 71 Fed. Reg. 68,821, 68,821–22 (Nov. 28, 2006) (announcing the availability of draft guidance); Guidance for Somatic Cell Therapy, *supra* note 121, at 3.

136 *See* sources cited *supra* notes 114, 121–22, 134–35 and accompanying text.

137 *See What Is Gene Therapy?*, *supra* note 122.

138 United States v. Regenerative Scis., LLC, 878 F. Supp. 2d 248, 251, 256 (D.D.C. 2012), *aff'd*, 741 F.3d 1314 (D.C. Cir. 2014).

139 *See* Umberto Galderisi, Antonio Giordano & Marco G. Paggi, *The Bad and the Good of Mesenchymal Stem Cells in Cancer: Boosters of Tumor Growth and Vehicles for Targeted Delivery of Anticancer Agents*, World J. Stem Cells, Feb. 26, 2010, at 5, 6.

140 *Regenerative Scis.*, 878 F. Supp. 2d at 251–52; *see also Are the Regenexx Procedures Performed in the U.S. Approved by the FDA?*, Regenexx, https://www.regenexx.com/resources/faqs/4/are-the-regenexx-procedures-performed-in-the-us-approved-by-the-fda/ [https://perma.cc/QG87-99TS] [hereinafter *Regenexx Procedures*] (describing the Regenexx culturing process).

141 *Regenerative Scis.*, 878 F. Supp. 2d at 259.

142 *Id.* at 251–52.

143 *See generally* Chris E. P. Goldring et al., *Assessing the Safety of Stem Cell Therapeutics*, 8 Cell Stem Cell 618 (2011) (describing safety issues and knowledge gaps in novel stem-cell treatments); Hans Lassmann, *Stem Cell and Progenitor Cell Transplantation in Multiple Sclerosis: The Discrepancy Between Neurobiological Attraction and Clinical Feasibility*, 233 J. Neurological Sci. 83 (2005) (commenting that despite progress in stem-cell research, the feasibility and safety of stem-cell therapies remain unresolved).

144 *See, e.g.*, Bruce H. Dobkin, Armin Curt & James Guest, *Cellular Transplants in China: Observational Study from the Largest Human Experiment in Chronic Spinal Cord Injury*, 20 Neurorehabilitation & Neural Repair 5, 5 (2006).

145 Darren Lau et al., *Stem Cell Clinics Online: The Direct-to-Consumer Portrayal of Stem Cell Medicine*, 3 CELL STEM CELL 591, 591 (2008).

146 *See, e.g.*, Israel Berger et al., *Global Distribution of Businesses Marketing Stem Cell-Based Interventions*, 19 CELL STEM CELL 158, 158, 160 (2016) (analyzing the content of hundreds of websites marketing stem cell–based interventions and finding that many made vague therapeutic claims unsupported by data generated in randomized, controlled, and independent clinical trials); Lau et al., *supra* note 145, at 593 ("We therefore find that the treatments offered on stem-cell websites are generally unsupported by clinical evidence.").

147 Berger et al., *supra* note 146, at 158; Lau et al., *supra* note 145, at 591.

148 Leigh Turner & Paul Knoepfler, *Selling Stem Cells in the USA: Assessing the Direct-to-Consumer Industry*, 19 CELL STEM CELL 154, 154 (2016); *cf.* Berger et al., *supra* note 146, at 158 ("[Berger and colleagues] identified 187 unique websites in the US offering interventions at 215 clinics, while Turner and Knoepfler found 351 distinct businesses offering interventions at 570 physical locations. Due to differences in search strategy stringency, inclusion and exclusion criteria, and search engines used, it is not possible to make direct comparisons between these analyses, but the implication is that growth of the industry in the US has been rapid and pronounced.").

149 *See* Berger et al., *supra* note 146, at 158–59; Leigh Turner, *Direct-to-Consumer Marketing of Stem Cell Interventions by Canadian Businesses*, 13 REGENERATIVE MED. 643, 643 (2018).

150 Berger et al., *supra* note 146, at 158; *see also* Ruairi Connolly, Timothy O'Brien & Gerard Flaherty, *Stem Cell Tourism – A Web-Based Analysis of Clinical Services Available to International Travellers*, 12 TRAVEL MED. & INFECTIOUS DISEASE 695, 696 (2014) (referring to "stem cell tourism" as an expanding category of medical tourism).

151 United States v. Regenerative Scis., LLC, 878 F. Supp. 2d 248, 262–63 (D.D.C. 2012), *aff'd*, 741 F.3d 1314 (D.C. Cir. 2014).

152 *Id.* at 254.

153 A body of literature has examined in recent years the extent to which the FDA regulates the practice of medicine, which has been traditionally recognized as a matter of state jurisdiction. *See, e.g.*, Lars Noah, *Ambivalent Commitments to Federalism in Controlling the Practice of Medicine*, 53 KAN. L. REV. 149, 150–51 (2004); Zettler, *supra* note 25, at 849–50.

154 *Regenerative Scis.*, 878 F. Supp. 2d at 254–55.

155 *Id.* at 263.

156 United States v. Regenerative Scis., LLC, 741 F.3d 1314, 1326 (D.C. Cir. 2014).

157 *Id.* at 1319.

158 21 U.S.C. § 321(g)(1)(B)–(C) (Supp. 2017).

159 42 U.S.C. § 262(i)(1) (Supp. 2017).

160 *Regenerative Scis.*, 741 F.3d at 1319.

161 *Id. But see* Lars Noah, *Growing Organs in the Lab: Tissue Engineers Confront Institutional "Immune" Responses*, 55 JURIMETRICS 297, 315–17 (2015) (questioning the court's reasoning on that point).
162 *See Regenerative Scis.*, 741 F.3d at 1319.
163 *Id.* at 1321–22; *see also* 21 C.F.R. § 1271.3(d)(4) (2018).
164 Application of Current Statutory Authorities to Human Somatic Cell Therapy Products and Gene Therapy Products, 58 Fed. Reg. 53,248, 53,249 (Oct. 14, 1993).
165 *Regenerative Scis.*, 741 F.3d at 1321. It should be noted, however, that minimal manipulation is not the only criterion under which cellular products fall within the definition of drugs or biological products.
166 21 C.F.R. § 1271.3(f)(2) (2018).
167 *Regenerative Scis.*, 741 F.3d at 1322.
168 *See, e.g.*, RICHARD A. EPSTEIN, MANHATTAN INST., THE FDA'S MISGUIDED REGULATION OF STEM-CELL PROCEDURES: HOW ADMINISTRATIVE OVERREACH BLOCKS MEDICAL INNOVATION 4–7 (2013) (arguing the stem-cell procedure in *Regenerative Sciences* is not interstate commerce or a drug under the FDCA); Mary Ann Chirba & Stephanie M. Garfield, *FDA Oversight of Autologous Stem Cell Therapies: Legitimate Regulation of Drugs and Devices or Groundless Interference with the Practice of Medicine?*, 7 J. HEALTH & BIOMEDICAL L. 233, 238 (2011) (arguing that the FDA's position "impedes medical advances").
169 *See* EPSTEIN, *supra* note 168, at 5–6.
170 *See id.* at 5.
171 *See Regenerative Scis.*, 741 F.3d at 1320.
172 *Id.*
173 *See* EPSTEIN, *supra* note 168, at 17.
174 *See* Chirba & Garfield, *supra* note 168, at 235.
175 *See* discussion in Chapter 1, Section II.B; Enríquez, *supra* note 104, at 611–14 (defining a jurisprudence of scientific empiricism as "a normative structural legal framework . . . that is broadly adaptable to addressing questions of science in law").
176 Flora Clément et al., *Stem Cell Manipulation, Gene Therapy and the Risk of Cancer Stem Cell Emergence*, 4 STEM CELL INVESTIGATION, no. 67, July 25, 2017, at 1, 9; Sven Geißler et al., *Functional Comparison of Chronological and in Vitro Aging: Differential Role of the Cytoskeleton and Mitochondria in Mesenchymal Stromal Cells*, 7 PLOS ONE, no. e52700, Dec. 28, 2012, at 1, 10; Carla A. Herberts, Marcel S.G. Kwa & Harm P.H. Hermsen, *Risk Factors in the Development of Stem Cell Therapy*, 9 J. TRANSLATIONAL MED., no. 29, Mar. 22, 2011, at 1, 6; Myungshin Kim et al., *Passage-Dependent Accumulation of Somatic Mutations in Mesenchymal Stromal Cells During in Vitro Culture Revealed by Whole Genome Sequencing*, 7 SCI. REP., no. 14508, Nov. 6, 2017, at 1, 2; Masako Miura et al., *Accumulated Chromosomal Instability in Murine*

Bone Marrow Mesenchymal Stem Cells Leads to Malignant Transformation, 24 STEM CELLS 1095, 1095 (2006); Fatemeh Norozi et al., *Mesenchymal Stem Cells as a Double-Edged Sword in Suppression or Progression of Solid Tumor Cells*, 37 TUMOR BIOLOGY 11, 679, 11,679 (2016).

177 In general, the term "stemness" refers to stem cells' ability to self-renew and differentiate into other cell types. *See* Pedro M. Aponte & Andrés Caicedo, *Stemness in Cancer: Stem Cells, Cancer Stem Cells, and Their Microenvironment*, STEM CELLS INT'L, Apr. 4, 2017, at 1, 1; Douglas Melton, *'Stemness': Definitions, Criteria, and Standards*, *in* ESSENTIALS OF STEM CELL BIOLOGY 7, 14–15 (Robert Lanza & Anthony Atala eds., 3d ed. 2014).

178 *See, e.g.*, Hugo Alves et al., *A Link Between the Accumulation of DNA Damage and Loss of Multi-Potency of Human Mesenchymal Stromal Cells*, 14 J. CELLULAR & MOLECULAR MED. 2729, 2729 (2010).

179 *See Regenexx Procedures*, *supra* note 140.

180 *Id.*

181 21 C.F.R. § 1271.15(b) (2018); *see also* CTR. FOR BIOLOGICS EVALUATION & RESEARCH, FDA, GUIDANCE FOR INDUSTRY: SAME SURGICAL PROCEDURE EXCEPTION UNDER 21 CFR 1271.15(b): QUESTIONS AND ANSWERS REGARDING THE SCOPE OF THE EXCEPTION 2 (2017) [hereinafter GUIDANCE FOR SAME SURGICAL PROCEDURE EXCEPTION], https://www.fda.gov/downloads/biologicsbloodvaccines/guidancecomplianceregulatoryinformation/guidances/tissue/ucm419926.pdf [https://perma.cc/58YY-9FC4].

182 *See* GUIDANCE FOR SAME SURGICAL PROCEDURE EXCEPTION, supra note 181, at 2–3.

183 *See* EPSTEIN, *supra* note 168, at 4; Chirba & Garfield, *supra* note 168, at 268 n.210.

184 *See, e.g.*, Berger et al., *supra* note 146, at 158–59; *supra* Figures 9.4, 9.5, and 9.6.

185 *See* Berger et al., *supra* note 146, at 158–59; Turner & Knoepfler, *supra* note 148, at 154–55.

186 *See FDA Seeks Permanent Injunctions Against Two Stem Cell Clinics*, FDA (May 9, 2018), https://www.fda.gov/newsevents/newsroom/pressannouncements/ucm607257.htm [https://perma.cc/G75W-LJCT].

187 21 U.S.C. § 321(g)(1) (Supp. 2017).

188 *See, e.g.*, Xiangjin Kang et al., *Introducing Precise Genetic Modifications into Human 3PN Embryos by CRISPR/Cas-Mediated Genome Editing*, 33 J. ASSISTED REPROD. & GENETICS 581, 581 (2016); Puping Liang et al., *CRISPR/Cas9-Mediated Gene Editing in Human Tripronuclear Zygotes*, 6 PROTEIN & CELL 363, 364 (2015); Hong Ma et al., *Correction of a Pathogenic Gene Mutation in Human Embryos*, 548 NATURE 413, 413 (2017); Lichun Tang et al., *CRISPR/Cas9-Mediated Gene Editing in Human Zygotes Using Cas9 Protein*, 292 MOLECULAR GENETICS & GENOMICS 525, 525 (2017).

189 *See* Yuyu Niu et al., *Generation of Gene-Modified Cynomolgus Monkey via Cas9/RNA-Mediated Gene Targeting in One-Cell Embryos*, 156 CELL 836 (2014).

190 *See* David Cyranoski & Heidi Ledford, *International Outcry over Genome-Edited Baby Claim*, 563 NATURE 607, 607–08 (2018).

191 The term "wildtype" refers to the most common phenotype—observable characteristics or traits—for an organism in a natural breeding population. *See Wildtype*, BIOLOGY ONLINE DICTIONARY, biology-online.org/dictionary/wildtype [https://perma.cc/R9SL-SPFK].

192 The "target genetic locus" in this context means the particular chromosomal position—the DNA site within the genome—to which a genome-editing enzyme is recruited to cut DNA.

193 21 U.S.C. § 321(g)(1)(B) (Supp. 2017).

194 United States v. An Article of Drug . . . Bacto-Unidisk . . . , 394 U.S. 784, 792–93 (1969).

195 *See id.*

196 *See* 21 U.S.C. § 321(g)(1)(c) (Supp. 2017) (defining drugs as "articles (other than food) intended to affect the structure or any function of the body of man or other animals," which, when read broadly, includes genome editing).

197 *See* 42 U.S.C. § 262(i)(1) (Supp. 2017).

198 *See id.*

199 Naoaki Mizuno et al., *Intra-Embryo Gene Cassette Knockin by CRISPR/Cas9-Mediated Genome Editing with Adeno-Associated Viral Vector*, 9 ISCIENCE 286, 286 (2018).

200 Shyam Daya & Kenneth I. Berns, *Gene Therapy Using Adeno-Associated Virus Vectors*, 21 CLINICAL MICROBIOLOGY REVIEWS 583, 583 (2008).

201 *See id.* at 586, 588–90.

202 *See* § 262(i)(1).

203 *See id.* ("'The term 'biological product' means a . . . protein (except any chemically synthesized polypeptide) . . . applicable to the prevention, treatment, or cure of a disease or condition of human beings.").

204 *See* § 262(i)(1) (requiring explicitly that biological products be "applicable to the prevention, treatment, or cure of a disease or condition of human beings").

205 *See* 21 U.S.C § 321(h) (Supp. 2017).

206 Interestingly, a distinction could theoretically be made between GGE that relies on programmable base-editing enzymes—as opposed to genome-editing enzymes—and somatic epigenome editing to control patterns of gene expression. Although both methods rely on the use of a deactivated genome-editing enzyme, such as dCas9, the former utilizes a base-editing enzyme that mediates a chemical reaction to achieve its primary purpose, *see, e.g.*, Nicole M. Gaudelli et al., *Programmable Base Editing of A•T to G•C in Genomic DNA Without DNA Cleavage*, 551 NATURE 464, 464 (2017) (using adenine base editors to mediate A•T to G•C conversion); Yanting Zeng et al., *Correction of the Marfan Syndrome Pathogenic FBN1 Mutation by Base Editing in Human Cells and Heterozygous Embryos*, 26

MOLECULAR THERAPY 2631, 2631–32 (2018) (discussing the use of base editors to solve "genetic diseases at the embryo stage"), whereas the latter merely relies on physical interactions between the deactivated genome-editing enzyme and its target molecule to activate or inhibit gene expression, *see, e.g.*, Luke A. Gilbert et al., *Genome-Scale CRISPR-Mediated Control of Gene Repression and Activation*, 159 CELL 647, 647–48 (2014). In other words, each method achieves its primary intended purpose either via chemical action—in the base-editing GGE case—or physical action—in the epigenome-editing case. Only the somatic epigenome-editing product would thus constitute a medical device under the law.

The aforementioned analysis would depend largely on how the FDA interprets the term "chemical action." The Agency recently published a guidance document that describes the FDA's position that chemical action should be interpreted consistently with the term "pharmacological action" as that term is generally understood in the medical field. *See* FDA, CLASSIFICATION OF PRODUCTS AS DRUGS AND DEVICES & ADDITIONAL PRODUCT CLASSIFICATION ISSUES: GUIDANCE FOR INDUSTRY AND FDA STAFF 7 (2017), https://www.fda.gov/downloads/RegulatoryInformation/Guidances/UCM258957.pdf [https://perma.cc/AA6F-TT7R]. The guidance is not legally binding but offers the Agency's current thinking on the topic. Because the term "pharmacological action" in the medical field includes the mere binding of molecules through electrostatic, hydrophobic, and other types of interactions without the need for catalytic activity, *see id.* at 7 n.4, the somatic epigenome-editing product would no longer constitute a medical device under the guidance interpretation of the FDCA.

207 *See* 21 C.F.R. § 3.2(e) (2018).

208 *See* 21 U.S.C. § 353(g) (Supp. 2017).

209 *See id.* § 353(g)(1).

210 *See* 21 C.F.R. § 1271.3(f) (2018).

211 *See id.* § 1271.10(a)(1)–(4).

212 *Id.*

213 In addition to regulation under the gene-therapy framework and the *Regenerative Sciences* standard, the FDA may also regulate GGE under provisions applicable to assisted reproductive technologies, which relate to the handling of gametes and embryos. *See* 42 U.S.C. § 263a-1(a)–(c) (2012).

214 *See* 21 C.F.R. § 312.20 (2018).

215 *See* 42 U.S.C. § 262(a)(3) (Supp. 2017).

216 Consolidated Appropriations Act of 2016, Pub. L. No. 114–113, § 749, 129 Stat. 2242, 2283 (2015).

217 Consolidated Appropriations Act of 2019, Pub. L. No. 116–6, § 731, 133 Stat. 13; Consolidated Appropriations Act of 2018, Pub. L. No. 115–141, § 734, 132 Stat. 348, 389; Consolidated Appropriations Act of 2017, Pub. L. No. 115–31, § 743, 131 Stat. 135, 175.

218 Consolidated Appropriations Act of 2016, § 749, 129 Stat. at 2283.
219 *See supra* note 4 and accompanying text.
220 *See, e.g.*, Spivak et al., *supra* note 5, at 38, app. tbls.1–4 (compiling data over the last few decades on bills related to then-controversial technologies with reproductive applications to demonstrate that, despite widespread concerns and contentious debate among members of Congress, the vast majority of proposed prohibitions never became law).
221 *See* discussion in Chapter 10, Section VII nn.196–99.
222 *See* Spivak et al., *supra* note 5, at 37.
223 *See What We Do*, *supra* note 1.
224 *Id.*
225 *See generally, e.g.*, Rebecca S. Eisenberg, *The Role of the FDA in Innovation Policy*, 13 MICH. TELECOMM. TECH. L. REV. 345 (2007) (reexamining "the role of FDA regulation in motivating investment in biopharmaceutical innovation").
226 *See* 21 C.F.R. § 312.42 (2018).
227 *See* Alexander Burik, *FDA Puts Clinical Trial for CRISPR Therapy on Hold*, LABIOTECH (Jan. 6, 2018), https://labiotech.eu/medical/crispr-therapeutics-fda/ [https://perma.cc/52Y8-TNH7]. The FDA removed the hold on the clinical trial in October 2018. *See* Allison DeAngelis, *FDA Lifts Hold on First-Ever CRISPR/Cas9 Gene-Editing Trial*, MEM. BUS. J. (Oct. 12, 2018, 11:48 AM), https://www.bizjournals.com/memphis/news/2018/10/12/fda-lifts-hold-on-first-ever-crispr-cas9-gene.html [https://perma.cc/K4BT-PBHB].
228 *See, e.g.*, John Zhang et al., *First Live Birth Using Human Oocytes Reconstituted by Spindle Nuclear Transfer for Mitochondrial DNA Mutation Causing Leigh Syndrome*, 106 FERTILITY & STERILITY (ISSUE 3 SUPP.) e375, e375–76 (2016) (reporting the birth of a baby conceived via mitochondrial replacement therapy in Mexico aided by an American physician from New York who could not perform the procedure in the United States); John Zhang et al., *Live Birth Derived from Oocyte Spindle Transfer to Prevent Mitochondrial Disease*, 34 REPROD. BIOMEDICINE ONLINE 361, 365 (2017) (same); *see also* Rob Stein, *Clinic Claims Success in Making Babies with 3 Parents' DNA*, NPR (June 6, 2018, 5:11 AM), https://www.npr.org/sections/health-shots/2018/06/06/615909572/inside-the-ukrainian-clinic-making-3-parent-babies-for-women-who-are-infertile [https://perma.cc/L9T9-56YF] (noting that a Ukrainian clinic is currently marketing in the United States a $15,000 procedure involving the use of DNA from three different people to help infertile women—who are willing to travel to Ukraine—conceive a biological child).
229 *See* Katrin Weigmann, *The Ethics of Global Clinical Trials*, 16 EMBO REP. 566, 567 (2015).
230 *See generally, e.g.*, Jonathan M. Breslin et al., *Top 10 Health Care Ethics Challenges Facing the Public: Views of Toronto Bioethicists*, 6 BMC MED.

ETHICS, no. 5, June 26, 2005, at 1 (discussing various ethical challenges posed by innovation in the medical profession).

231 He Jiankui, Informed Consent Version: Female 3.0, at 1 (unpublished consent form), http://web.archive.org/web/20181126212007/http:/www.sustc-genome.org.cn/source/pdf/Informed-consent-women-English.pdf [https://perma.cc/RR9Y-54DX].

232 *See id.* at 4.

233 *See id.*

234 *See* 45 C.F.R. § 46.116(a)(6) (2018) ("No informed consent may include any exculpatory language through which the subject . . . is made to waive or appear to waive any of the subject's legal rights, or releases or appears to release the investigator, the sponsor, the institution, or its agents from liability for negligence."); Step 3: Clinical Research, FDA, https://www.fda.gov/patients/drug-development-process/step-3-clinical-research [https://perma.cc/49MM-Y4XX] (describing the safety and efficacy information, which must be reviewed by the FDA before clinical trials can legally begin).

235 Sharon Begley, *Amid Uproar, Chinese Scientist Defends Creating Gene-Edited Babies*, STAT (Nov. 28, 2018), https://www.statnews.com/2018/11/28/chinese-scientist-defends-creating-gene-edited-babies/ [https://perma.cc/SFF7-96YP].

236 *See id.*

10

Constitutional Predicaments

Administrative law, as the previous chapter demonstrated, is pivotal to delineating the limits of governmental regulation of technological advances. Indeed, courts grant administrative agencies vast deference on matters related to the agencies' expertise and jurisdiction. The administrative state, however, is not the sole source of law in our democratic system. A particular set of rights come from the constitutional structure that supports our system of governance itself. These rights, called fundamental rights, involve human liberties considered so important that the government can only infringe them if it has a truly compelling interest in doing so. Fundamental rights, therefore, are examined under a doctrine called *strict scrutiny*, which mandates that governmental action that curtails any fundamental right be examined under the most rigorous standards permitted by the law. To pass constitutional muster under strict scrutiny, the government must not only articulate a compelling purpose for enforcing the law, but also prove that the means by which it seeks to accomplish said purpose are narrowly tailored—in other words, that there are no less restrictive means to accomplish the law's purpose.

Some fundamental rights are enumerated in the text of the Constitution, while others are not. For instance, the right to vote—at least insofar as it relates to the prohibition of the abridgment of the right to vote on account of race, gender, age, failure to pay poll taxes, or previous condition of servitude—is enumerated in the Constitution (protected explicitly under the Fifteenth, Nineteenth, Twenty-Fourth, and Twenty-Sixth Amendments, and implicitly under the Fourteenth Amendment). The First Amendment, likewise, protects the fundamental rights to freedom of speech, freedom of the press, and the free exercise of religion.

Other fundamental rights, however, are not explicitly found in the text of the Constitution. Instead, many of these unenumerated fundamental rights have been recognized by the Supreme Court as integral components of our constitutional democracy. These fundamental rights include, for example, the liberty to procreate, engage in consensual sexual activity among adults, travel, exercise autonomy in parental decisions, be free to make medical care decisions, marry, use contraception, express a sexual orientation, and have custody of one's children.

This chapter explores novel issues related to human germline genome editing (GGE) introduced in earlier chapters and the Constitution. We will discuss in greater detail the dangers of misinterpreting science and spreading misinformation, which may appear benign at first glance, but often lead to catastrophic societal consequences. To illustrate this point, the chapter analyzes *Buck v. Bell*, which astonishingly legalized the involuntary sterilization of people deemed mentally "defective." The chapter then pivots to survey the due process and equal protection landscape through a—mostly—descriptive lens to identify whether a cognizable fundamental right to select uses of GGE may exist under the Constitution. The chapter, therefore, builds upon existing case law and scholarship, and presents an interpretive model for this body of jurisprudence in the GGE context, which promotes extrapolation of applicable legal principles that can guide and promote coherent public policy.

I PRECEDENTS SET THE LIMITS

As the foregoing preamble indicates, this chapter examines whether a fundamental right to select uses of GGE may exist under the Constitution. Such a right would flow from precedents and jurisprudence in the areas of procreative, parental autonomy, and—to some extent—privacy rights, but it would not be absolute.[1]

At the outset, it is important to note that, in addition to law in the realm of fundamental rights and liberties, another set of precedents applicable to the discussion in the pages that follow concerns the ability of individuals to access certain therapies or technological advances, for which safety and efficacy are not yet established. A putative fundamental right to perform select GGE interventions as articulated in this chapter should not be confused with the unrecognized rights of terminally ill patients to access (1) unapproved drugs that are not recognized as safe and effective under *United States v. Rutherford*,[2] or (2) potentially toxic drugs that have no proven therapeutic benefit under *Abigail Alliance for Better Access to Developmental Drugs v. von Eschenbach*.[3] In *Abigail*, for example, a court rejected a presumptive right of a terminally ill patient desperately in need of a curative treatment to use a drug that could potentially hasten death.[4]

Limiting access to unproven therapies is rooted in the precept of primum non nocere, which is latin for "first, do no harm" and is perhaps better adapted to our discussion as "do no more harm than good." Given the current state of emerging genome-editing technologies, including potential experimental GGE interventions, the primum non nocere principle poses appropriate limitations on an individual's access to GGE treatments. And this chapter does not at all advocate that certain parents should assert a so-called "right to try" GGE interventions because of a purported lack of alternatives to conceiving a healthy child. To the contrary, this chapter extensively links the discussion in the previous chapter about the FDA's role in establishing the safety and efficacy of drugs and biological products to the GGE context. The chapter argues, however, that once safety and efficacy of select GGE interventions are established, which probably will occur at some point in the near future, the government likely cannot categorically ban access to the technology.

Unlike the distribution of unapproved drugs, research in human embryos is legal — at least when performed without the use of public funds. Drug manufacturers may not legally test unapproved drugs without FDA oversight, but little currently prevents geneticists, fertility specialists, and other researchers from continuing to test, refine, and develop GGE technologies for use in early-stage embryos.[5] This marks a fundamental distinction between the right-to-try cases and GGE technologies. Scientists in the United States and abroad are conducting research in human and animal embryos to address current limitations of genome-editing technologies, which will lead to more precise genome-editing tools to make GGE safe and effective. Thus, at some point in the future, the only impediment to clinical uses of GGE may be the current legislative ban on FDA review of Investigational New Drug Applications and Biologics License Applications for GGE purposes. But such a ban may not withstand the pressures of strict scrutiny or the rapid and continuous scientific advances that may lead to precise, safe, and effective GGE.

II INSTITUTIONAL UNCONSTITUTIONALISM

A *Injustice and the Imbeciles Who Must Endure It*

Buck v. Bell[6] is among the most horrid illustrations of deceptive simplicity in the exercise of American jurisprudence. In a surreal series of events, government-sanctioned sterilization arrived at the US Supreme Court, the most powerful court in the world. Learned judges heard arguments in favor of involuntary sterilizations and endorsed the practice without a single word in opposition. A near unanimous Court upheld, eight to one — Justice Pierce Butler dissented from the Court's decision, but filed no opinion of his own[7] — the constitutionality of a Virginia statute that legalized the involuntary sterilization of individuals deemed "mental defectives" in state institutions, provided it was in "the best interest of the patients and of society."[8]

Writing for the Court, Oliver Wendell Holmes, Jr. infamously memorialized what is arguably among the most incendiary and ignorant language ever published in the United States Reports. "It is better for all the world, if instead of waiting to execute degenerate offspring for crime, or to let them starve for their imbecility, society can prevent those who are manifestly unfit from continuing their kind. . . . *Three generations of imbeciles are enough.*"[9]

The question presented in *Buck* was whether a statute authorizing compulsory sterilization of the "feeble-minded" violated the Due Process and Equal Protection clauses of the Fourteenth Amendment.[10] The Court belabored — in one-third of its nearly three-page decision—the argument that Carrie Buck had sufficient procedural Due Process at law.[11] Yet, the Court virtually ignored the Equal Protection challenge, ridiculing it as a desperate "last resort" argument for defending individual rights.[12]

The entirety of the opinion cited no constitutional authorities, save for *Jacobson v. Massachusetts*,[13] an inapposite case that sanctioned the exercise of State police powers to authorize compulsory vaccination statutes. At the same time, the Court ignored a series of cases brought in state and federal courts in Massachusetts,[14] Michigan,[15] New Jersey,[16] and Iowa[17] dealing squarely with the Equal Protection question. Applying a primitive form of modern rational basis review, the Court determined the State had a legitimate legal and policy justification to sterilize Buck and promote the welfare of society by severing her fallopian tubes.[18] Notably, the decision did not examine any scientific evidence to support its assertion that mental deficiencies are congenital.

Appellant Carrie Elizabeth Buck, a *teenager* who had been raped[19] and institutionalized was characterized by the Court as "a feeble-minded white woman . . . daughter of a feeble-minded mother . . . , and the mother of an illegitimate feeble-minded child."[20] Reporters and scholars who met Buck before her death in 1983 all agreed that she was not "feeble-minded" as the Court had stated, but appeared to be a woman of normal intelligence.[21] Vivian, Carrie Buck's daughter who lived until the age of eight, had been an average student in school and was not mentally disabled—a social worker had diagnosed her with purported developmental deficiencies when she was seven months old.[22] Some have argued that the case itself was fraudulently pursued.[23] In any event, one can hardly disagree with the view that what was done to Carrie Buck was gravely unjust and remains a stark blemish on American law.

Many have chronicled the history and legal implications of *Buck* in books[24] and legal scholarship.[25] Consequently, this chapter will not belabor and rehash what has already been said about the case.[26] The conventional view is that *Buck*'s holding is illegitimate because it rests on false science[27] and incorrect moral and ethical principles.[28] But an analysis of the case through an alternative and overlooked prism underscores the need to reject that conventional view. *Buck* was not the result of false science. Rather, it was the product of *deceptive simplicity*. In fact, as this chapter argues below, *Buck*'s ruling is grounded more on deceptive simplicity than on the "science" of the time, which was greatly void of empiricism, reproducibility, adequate statistical methodology, and did not even come close to establishing the heredity and genetic contributions of intelligence.

B *Of Blinded Justice and Hollow Reasoning*

To support the proposition that *Buck* was not the product of false science, consider first and foremost the substantively porous decision published by the Supreme Court. Holmes cited not a single scientific source for the Court's lending of credence to the precarious notion that "heredity plays an important part in the transmission of insanity, imbecility, etc."[29] The Supreme Court did not even bother to consider the existing science of the time. Instead, it wholly deferred to the state legislature and treated the heredity of insanity and imbecility as a foregone conclusion. In fact, the Court was blatantly clear that its decision relied on "general declarations of the Legislature"[30] and "experience"[31] showing the heritability of traits related to cognitive deficiencies.

The "experience" Holmes referred to was quite probably the direct derivation of Francis Galton's eugenic pseudoscientific research showing numerous purported instances in which "illustrious" men engendered illustrious kindred.[32] Indeed, Galton's dubious and racist research methodologies on human cognition and intelligence in the mid to late nineteenth century partly garnered support among elite circles with the help of his half cousin, Charles Darwin, who effused about Galton's theories and helped to disseminate them to judges in his social network. Darwin, for example, wrote Galton a letter to praise his *Hereditary Genius* volume, stating in part:

> I have only read 50 pages of your book (to Judges), but I must exhale myself, else something will go wrong with my inside. I do not think I ever in all of my life read anything more interesting and original—and how well and clearly you put every point! ... I congratulate you on producing what I am convinced will prove a memorable work.[33]

The notion that *Buck*'s holding was based on false science rests on an analytically precarious foundation. Simply put, *Buck* relied on *no* science at all.

Buck epitomizes an instance where the Supreme Court allowed a State's erroneous scientific assertions to go unchallenged and ruled on the basis of those faulty assertions. Although the Court is not required to cross-examine every statement made by a legislative branch before properly ruling on a given issue, it ought to consider, at the very least, whether "general declarations" and "anecdotal experience" constitute unequivocal evidence that withstands constitutional scrutiny. Such analysis is imperative, more so in cases where fundamental rights may be curtailed. In light of its blank endorsement of compulsory sexual sterilization for mentally defective and undesirable individuals—all justified by public welfare pretenses—the *Buck* Court might as well have been acting as a lifeless extension of a State's legislative branch.

Had the Court bothered to critically examine and analyze the state of the science, it would have discovered that, contrary to popular belief at the time, heredity's role in cognition and other traits was highly inconclusive, contentious, and likely supported by flawed methodologies. On this point, perhaps one of the most prominent examples was the discovery of inheritance-independent genetic mutations by Thomas H. Morgan, the late Nobel Laureate, in 1910.[34] Morgan observed that one white-eyed fruit fly had inexplicably appeared from a contained stock of wildtype[35] red-eyed flies in his laboratory.[36] The implications of this realization were that certain traits are not merely inherited, but rather appear spontaneously as a result of biological and molecular mechanisms—for example, mutations—other than Mendelian genetics.

Morgan's observation and subsequent experiments using the white-eyed mutant fly provided the foundations for the establishment of the modern theory of the gene, which expanded and challenged the simple model of Mendelian inheritance[37]—recall our earlier discussion in Chapter 2—established at the turn of the twentieth century.[38]

Morgan, who initially supported but later renounced the eugenics movement[39] after uncovering empirical scientific truth through his research, eloquently presented the problem of the modern interpretation of Mendelian inheritance when he stated:

> [F]acts are being transformed into factors at a rapid rate. . . . The superior jugglery sometimes necessary to account for the result, may blind us, if taken too naïvely, to the common-place that the results are often so excellently "explained" because the explanation was invented to explain them. We work backwards from the facts to the factors, and then, presto! explain the facts by the very factors that we invented to account for them . . . yet I cannot but fear that we are rapidly developing a sort of Mendelian ritual by which to explain the extraordinary facts of alternative inheritance. . . . [I]t is only fair to state that those who are doing the actual work of progress along Mendelian lines are aware of the hypothetical nature of the factor-assumption. *But those who know the results at second hand and hear the explanations given, almost invariably in terms of factors, are likely to exaggerate the importance of the interpretations and to minimize the importance of the facts.*[40]

In time, others too began to publicly oppose eugenics,[41] along with its racist and classist undertones,[42] as a pseudoscience.[43] However, despite the shouts of a few dissenting voices, eugenics became deeply rooted in American culture, garnering support from elites, scholars, and several institutions, including the Supreme Court.[44] Between 1907, when the first sterilization statute passed in Indiana, and 1930, a total of twenty-three states had enacted eugenical sterilization laws.[45] By 1933, four years after *Buck*, twenty-two states introduced new sterilization laws.[46] During the span of seven decades (1907–1979), a total of more than 65,000 sterilizations in thirty-two states took place in the United States.[47]

* * *

Morgan's conceptualization of second-hand explanations that lead to exaggeration, oversimplification, and a poor understanding of scientific progress is precisely the deleterious essence of deceptive simplicity, which is broader and more damaging than mere pseudoscience.

The distinction is crucial. Whereas false, or pseudo, science refers to a system of theories and rules configured to give the appearance of being grounded in scientific methodology,[48] deceptive simplicity dangles from vague intuition derived from reductive explanations that strip logic beyond a bare minimum.

Accordingly, Galton's elaborate, hyperbolic, cognitive hereditability theses and explanations, which worked backwards "from the facts to the factors," were so "excellently explained"[49] because he created a counterfeit theoretical basis to support his unscrupulous racist ideology. It was false science.

In contrast, Holmes' opinion in *Buck* did not even attempt to embellish its reasoning with false science. *Buck* institutionalized compulsory sterilization using vague intuition born out of second-, third-, and fourth-hand reductive explanations that diminished heredity to a deceptively simple catchphrase *popularized by* false science: Imbecility is a heritable disease. For these reasons, *Buck* embodies a conclusory ruling bereft of legal or scientific reasoning. It was deceptive simplicity, bred to be more dangerous than false science. Indeed, the Nazi party relied on *Buck* and its deceptive simplicity to legitimize its eugenic agenda.[50]

Pseudointellectual hogwash became the deceptive simplicity that propelled, maintained, and expanded the eugenics agenda. The historical account is crystal clear: *Buck* did not rely on false science; it was the product of pervasive deceptive simplicity concerning a rationale for the heritability of human cognitive abilities and mental deficiencies. No legitimate scientific debate existed regarding the simplistic pre-twentieth century view of Mendelian inheritance adopted by the Court in 1927.

At the time *Buck* made its way into the Supreme Court, eugenics was not a real scientific movement,[51] but rather a reductive political and social fad that fed off of outdated scientific theories, misinformation, and gossip. The propaganda had been de facto codified into popular culture by deceptive merchants with ulterior motives and dangerous agendas. And Justices of the US Supreme Court, despite all their education and intellect, proved to be highly susceptible to it.

Given the fact that *Buck* lacked any constitutional[52] or scientific support for its holding and came thickly veiled with deceptive simplicity, the decision amounts to no more than institutionalized legal quackery built upon social and scientific quackery.

Buck is a stern cautionary tale. It warns that we must ground legal- and policy-based determinations firmly on scientific facts, especially when those determinations concern issues for which substantive scientific principles or elements may be dispositive. Had a robust system to address questions of science in law existed at the time, *Buck* may have been decided much differently.

The next section will lay out a doctrinal foundation of constitutional jurisprudence in areas of parental, family, procreative, and reproductive autonomy. The discussion helps to frame the unexplored issue of transgenerational human genome editing and sets the stage for exploring normative considerations for genome editing in the context of law- and science-based policy that constitute the remainder of this book.

III FUNDAMENTAL RIGHTS—WHERE DO THEY COME FROM?

The current de facto legislative ban on GGE clinical applications may be lawful for now, but it is merely a temporary fix that cannot adequately address many legal challenges that are looming on the horizon. Although human GGE technologies are not quite "ready for primetime,"[53] fundamental research to address current technological limitations of genome editing, including the identification and reduction of off-target effects,[54] prevention of mosaicism,[55] and improvements in target efficiency,[56] specificity,[57] delivery,[58] and other areas[59] constitute active and prolific fields of scientific inquiry. Collectively, the results from today's research will pave the road to overcome current obstacles in genome editing.

As has been discussed throughout this book, at some point in the near future, genome-editing technology will become primed for clinical applications,[60] which in turn will likely lead to claims brought by parents wishing to use GGE technologies. This chapter contends that permanent legislative or administrative bans on select uses of GGE cannot withstand constitutional scrutiny and, thus, will likely succumb to litigation because they impinge on a cognizable fundamental right that protects select uses of GGE. This fundamental right flows from jurisprudence in the areas of procreative, family autonomy, and—to some extent—privacy rights, but it is not absolute.

To determine whether a fundamental right exists under substantive due process, the Supreme Court articulated a two-prong test in *Washington v. Glucksberg*.[61] First, the asserted right must be "objectively, 'deeply rooted in this Nation's history and tradition.'"[62] Second, the party must articulate a "'careful description' of the asserted fundamental liberty interest."[63] If the right is deemed fundamental, strict scrutiny applies, "which forbids the government to infringe certain 'fundamental' liberty interests *at all*, no matter what process is provided, unless the infringement is narrowly tailored to serve a compelling state interest."[64] If the right in question is not fundamental, "[t]he general rule is that legislation is presumed to be valid and will be sustained if the classification drawn by the statute is rationally related to a legitimate state interest."[65]

A narrow interpretation of *Glucksberg* could, at first glance, appear to foreclose the emergence of a right to perform select GGE interventions because modern GGE is a nascent biotechnology and no deeply rooted history exists that chronicles GGE uses. Under a broader interpretation of *Glucksberg*, however, the right might be articulated as the right to bear healthy offspring, make offspring health determinations, guarantee the success of biological procreation, be free from government interference in procreative decisions related to GGE, or a combination thereof—all of which derive from already-existing fundamental rights.

Although *Glucksberg* outlined the modern test to determine fundamental rights, subsequent case law has abandoned its rigid interpretation. Notably, the Supreme Court has indicated that "[h]istory and tradition are the starting point but not in all cases the ending point of the substantive due process inquiry."[66] For instance, the Court explained in *Obergefell v. Hodges* that the definition of rights "in a most circumscribed manner, with central reference to specific historical practices, . . . may have been appropriate for the asserted right" of physician-assisted suicide at issue in *Glucksberg* but is not the approach the Court has "used in discussing other fundamental rights, including marriage and intimacy."[67] Thus, history can guide the analysis of certain constitutional questions, but "rights come not from ancient sources alone. They rise, too, from a better-informed understanding of how constitutional imperatives define a liberty that remains urgent in our own era."[68]

In essence, *Lawrence* and *Obergefell* jointly abrogate *Glucksberg*'s rigid approach to determining fundamental rights. And just as "*Loving* did not ask about a 'right to interracial marriage,'" the right to perform select uses of GGE articulated in this chapter may encompass a right "in its comprehensive sense,"[69] that fits within the rights of procreation, parental autonomy, and—to some extent—privacy.

An analytical checkpoint is indispensable at this juncture. Although this chapter examines an issue that has never before been the subject of judicial review, it does so in the context of an enduring, and often contentious, debate regarding the methodological framework under which the Constitution should be interpreted. At the outset, it is imperative to note that the invocation of the Due Process Clauses of the Fifth and Fourteenth Amendments[70] to adjudicate cases and controversies under Article III of the Constitution has "at times been a treacherous field for [the Supreme] Court."[71] The doctrine has spawned a litany of controversial decisions, many of which are discussed below.

At its core, the doctrine of substantive due process concerns the inquiry "of whether the government's deprivation of a person's life, liberty or property is justified by a sufficient purpose."[72] The term "liberty" in the clause has been interpreted broadly to encompass protection of certain fundamental rights unenumerated in the Constitution.[73] Supporters of the doctrine state that it has been used to safeguard some of the "most precious liberties" found in modern constitutional law.[74] Yet critics of that interpretive method have gone as far as labeling it "the most anticonstitutional branch of constitutional law."[75]

This chapter acknowledges the interpretive dichotomy of this area of constitutional law. Whether the extant body of substantive due process jurisprudence is proper when viewed through the lenses of originalism and nonoriginalism, however, is beyond the scope of this chapter, or even this book. And no position on the issue is taken herein. With this context as a backdrop, this part undertakes a—mostly—descriptive, rather than normative, analysis of the existing jurisprudence in this area of the law. The chapter concludes that the current substantive due process precedents, collectively, pave a potential path for the recognition of a right to perform GGE in select contexts.[76]

IV FAMILIAL RIGHTS

A *Liberty and Parental Autonomy*

The origins of a constitutional doctrine of autonomy involving parental choice and the family-unit sphere trace back to the 1920s.[77] In *Meyer v. Nebraska*,[78] the Supreme Court recognized the core of what is now a parent's fundamental right to make child-rearing decisions.

Meyer involved a challenge to a Nebraska statute that prohibited teaching in any language except English at public or private schools.[79] Under that law, foreign languages could be taught only beyond the eighth grade.[80] A parochial-school teacher was tried and convicted for unlawfully teaching a ten-year-old child to read in the German language,[81] and the Nebraska Supreme Court affirmed his conviction.[82]

Understanding the wider historical context is essential to appreciate why *Meyer* arrived at the Supreme Court. After the United States entered World War I by declaring war against Germany in 1917,[83] a wave of anti-German sentiment swept the nation. Many school districts stopped teaching German as a foreign language as nationalism and blinded patriotism replaced melting-pot philosophies.[84] German books were burned, operas and symphonies banned German music, and acts of violence or intimidation toward German-Americans occurred.[85] Even German-derived vernacular terms changed temporarily. Hamburgers, sauerkraut, frankfurters, dachshunds, hamburger steaks, and German measles suddenly became "liberty sandwiches," "liberty cabbage," "liberty sausages," "liberty dogs," "Salisbury steaks," and "liberty measles," respectively.[86]

Animus toward German culture among government and private actors led to the breakdown of civil liberties. Americans were encouraged to spy on and report individuals who displayed disloyalty, spoke critically of the war, taught German language at schools, or supported pacifism.[87] And government officials publicly averred that the freedom of speech in the federal and state constitutions did not guarantee the right to speak in any language other than English. The governor of Iowa, for instance, issued a proclamation that prohibited conversations in non-English languages in public places, along with statements to declare English as the only official language of the United States and Iowa.[88]

By 1923, thirty-four states – including Nebraska – had enacted legislation mandating English-only instruction at public and private elementary schools.[89] Meanwhile, the pseudoscientific eugenics movement had gained vast popularity,[90] and the assimilation of immigrants in America had become a major concern.[91]

Operating in front of this historical backdrop, the Supreme Court examined the constitutionality of the Nebraska statute, which the Nebraska Supreme Court had ruled reasonable and duly enacted within the state's police powers.[92] The state court had held that allowing foreigners to rear and educate their children in a foreign language was not only contrary to the country's best interests but also inimical to American safety.[93]

In a landmark ruling, the Supreme Court reversed the state court's judgment and held that the Due Process Clause of the Fourteenth Amendment, "without doubt," protected the liberty "to marry, establish a home and bring up children . . . and generally to enjoy those privileges long recognized at common law as essential to the orderly pursuit of happiness by free men."[94] In so doing, it interpreted the term "liberty" broadly and endorsed the concept that "the individual has certain fundamental rights which must be respected."[95] Thus, an instructor has a constitutional right to teach a foreign language to a child whose parents "engage him so to instruct their [child]."[96] The liberty guaranteed by the Fourteenth Amendment "may not be interfered with, under the guise of protecting the public interest, by legislative action which is arbitrary or without reasonable relation to some purpose within the competency of the state to effect."[97]

Two years later, in *Pierce v. Society of Sisters*,[98] the Court extended the newly minted *Meyer* principle of fundamental familial rights to another family context.[99] *Pierce* concerned amendments to the Oregon Compulsory Education Act of 1922,[100] which compelled parents to send their children to public schools.[101] Enforcement of the Act posed a threat to the existence of the primary private-school model.[102] In a unanimous decision, the Court struck down Oregon's statute as unconstitutional[103] because it "unreasonably interfere[d] with the liberty of parents and guardians to direct the upbringing and education of children under their control."[104]

Under the *Meyer* doctrine, the Constitution's "fundamental theory of liberty . . . excludes any general power of the state to standardize its children by forcing them to accept instruction from public teachers only."[105] More significantly, *Meyer* memorialized the constitutionally established principle that "[*t*]*he child is not the mere creature of the state*; those who nurture him and direct his destiny have the right, coupled with the high duty, to recognize and prepare him for additional obligations."[106] The doctrinal consequences of the substantive due process applied in *Meyer* and *Pierce* have had long-lasting effects on American jurisprudence. The liberty involving family and parental autonomy remains relevant a century later[107] and has laid a foundation for the application of substantive due process—albeit controversially—in the context of other personal liberties.

B *Broad, But Not Absolute*

Despite the broad liberties vis-à-vis the family-unit sphere and parental autonomy predicated in *Meyer* and *Pierce*, the judiciary has recognized that the right to make parental decisions about the rearing of one's children is not absolute and may be limited by governmental action in certain contexts.

The Court endorsed such restrictions on parental autonomy in *Prince v. Massachusetts*,[108] in which the Commonwealth demonstrated a cognizable interest in protecting the welfare of children.[109] *Prince* dealt with a challenge to a Massachusetts child-labor law that forbade individuals from furnishing or selling articles to any minor with the knowledge that the minor intended to sell the article in contravention of the law.[110] The government convicted Sarah Prince, a Jehovah's Witness and guardian of her nine-year-old niece, of violating child-labor laws when she allowed her niece to distribute religious literature in exchange for voluntary contributions while Prince was preaching on a public street.[111]

The *Prince* Court acknowledged the parental autonomy enshrined in the substantive due process rulings of *Meyer* and *Pierce*.[112] However, it also noted "the family itself is not beyond regulation in the public interest, as against a claim of religious liberty. And neither rights of religion nor rights of parenthood are beyond limitation."[113] The Court further articulated activities that could overcome the constitutional bar of parental autonomy, such as compelling parents to send children to school, regulating child labor, and mandating compulsory vaccination so as not to expose the community or the child to preventable disease or death.[114] Thus, *Prince* signaled an inclination to restrict the scope of *Meyer* and *Pierce* in certain contexts.

But *Prince* appears to be an outlier case that is incongruous to subsequent seminal cases examining the bundle of parental and family autonomy rights. Indeed, Justice Murphy's persuasive dissent in *Prince* appears to have laid the foundation for broadening the scope of parental rights decades later. "[P]arents or guardians [cannot] be subjected to criminal liability because of vague possibilities that their religious teachings might cause injury to the child. The evils must be grave, immediate, substantial."[115] Murphy denounced the lack of evidentiary support—in either the record or sources subject to judicial notice—for the proposition "that children engaged in distributing literature pursuant to their religious beliefs have been or are likely to be subject to any [health or moral harms]."[116] Restrictions on parental autonomy rights would, thus, apply only to instances where "grave, immediate, [or] substantial" harm to the child were under consideration.[117]

In *Wisconsin v. Yoder*,[118] the Court ruled that Amish parents have a constitutional right under the First and Fourteenth Amendments to refuse to comply with state laws that mandate children attend school beyond the eighth grade.[119] Although states may lawfully regulate the duration of children's education, the governmental interest of ensuring an educated citizenry "is not totally free from a balancing process when it impinges on fundamental rights and interests, such as those specifically protected by the Free Exercise Clause of the First Amendment, and the traditional interest of parents with respect to the religious upbringing of their children."[120]

The argument that enforcement of Wisconsin's law compelling education beyond the eighth grade would "gravely endanger if not destroy the free exercise of [Amish] religious beliefs" persuaded the Court.[121] Curiously, the *Yoder* Court emphasized that the decision to terminate primary instruction at an early age does not perpetrate "any harm to the physical or mental health of the child or to the public safety, peace, order, or welfare."[122] Yet, this emphasis creates tension with *Prince*, in which distribution of religious literature and preaching on a public street led to the conclusion that children would be exposed to potential emotional, psychological, or physical harm and injury.[123]

Another case that highlights the Supreme Court's expansion of broad deference to parental autonomy rights is *Parham v. J.R.*[124] The *Parham* Court held that the power to make choices related to child rearing does not automatically transfer from parents to a governmental agency simply because it involves certain risks or is not agreeable to a child.[125] Beyond the broad scope of parental discretion in the educational context, *Parham* held that the authority to make decisions concerning medical procedures also lies within the liberty rights afforded to parents because "[m]ost children, even in adolescence, simply are not able to make sound judgments concerning many decisions, including their need for medical care or treatment."[126] Thus, even when it comes to commitment of a child in a mental institution, parents "retain a substantial, if not the dominant, role in the decision, absent a finding of neglect or abuse."[127] The rationale underlying such wide discretion stems from the historical presumption that parents often act in the best interest of their children.[128] "For centuries it has been a canon of the common law that parents speak for their minor children. So deeply imbedded in our traditions is this principle of law that the Constitution itself may compel a State to respect it."[129]

The foregoing cases establish great parental latitude over the control of a child's upbringing. The interest of parents in directing a child's upbringing "is perhaps the oldest of the fundamental liberty interests recognized" by the Supreme Court.[130] Rights concerning the family-unit sphere and parental autonomy can be limited by a state's interest in protecting children against parental decisions that "jeopardize the health or safety of the child, or have a potential for significant social burdens."[131] However, the substantive due process liberty rights in this area are fairly broad in scope, such that parents may institutionalize their offspring or even curtail educational opportunities at an early age without government intervention.

V PROCREATE AWAY

The fundamental right of individuals to procreate was first articulated in *Skinner v. Oklahoma*.[132] The case involved the Oklahoma Habitual Criminal Sterilization Act,[133] which allowed the compulsory sterilization of individuals convicted of crimes amounting to felonies involving moral turpitude.[134] Compulsory sterilizations had been legitimized in American society for decades prior to *Skinner* as a convenient method to propel eugenical laws and policies.[135] Indeed, in 1927, the Supreme Court in *Buck v. Bell*[136] had upheld the constitutionality of sexual sterilization practices targeting the mentally disabled.[137]

From a procedural standpoint, *Skinner* extended an opportunity for the Court to answer whether (1) the State exceeded the lawful exercise of its police powers in view of scant scientific evidence to buttress a theory of heritability of criminal behavior,[138] (2) due process was lacking due to inadequate review of a prisoner's purported genetic predisposition to father undesirable offspring, and (3) the sterilization provisions of the Act constituted cruel and unusual punishment under the Fourteenth Amendment.[139] The Court overlooked all those issues and instead chose to focus on whether the Act violated the Equal Protection Clause of the Fourteenth Amendment.[140]

The *Skinner* Court held that Oklahoma's sterilization law violated principles of equal protection under the Fourteenth Amendment because it discriminated on the basis of seemingly arbitrary distinctions between felonies of the same type.[141] Thus, individuals convicted of grand larceny or embezzlement—both felonies—were subject to unequal treatment under the law; the larcenist could be subject to sterilization, while the embezzler could not.[142]

More importantly, *Skinner* explicitly articulated the fundamental status of human procreation by framing the issue presented as one concerning a basic right "to the perpetuation of a race—the right to have offspring."[143] According to the Court, individuals have fundamental civil rights to marry and procreate, which are crucial to the survival of our species.[144] "The power to sterilize, if exercised, may have subtle, far-reaching and devastating effects. . . . There is no redemption for the individual whom the law touches. Any experiment which the State conducts is to his irreparable injury. He is forever deprived of a basic liberty."[145]

Because of the delicate nature of the right to procreate, the Court emphasized that strict scrutiny is the only judicial standard of review that could apply to state action encroaching on the ability of humans to reproduce.[146] The irreversibility of sterilization procedures, as well as the social and biological implications of reproduction, provided an analytical foundation to promote the majority's view that the sort of sterilization provisions under Oklahoma's Habitual Criminal Sterilization Act should be held to the highest scrutiny possible.[147]

Interestingly, Justice Jackson filed a brief concurrence in *Skinner* in which he stated that the eugenic purpose of the Oklahoma statute raised "other constitutional questions of gravity" because the state of scientific knowledge at the time was uncertain as to the heritability of select behavioral traits.[148] Thus, Jackson's concurrence suggests that, under a slightly different fact pattern, he likely would have examined the merits of whether the state exceeded its constitutional authority by exercising police powers to undertake actions unsupported by scientific evidence—precisely the type of question that a jurisprudence of scientific empiricism would seek to address.

Although *Skinner* applied only to punitive sterilizations and failed to overturn *Buck*,[149] it nevertheless stands as a landmark decision that conceptualized the guarantee of procreative rights under the Constitution.

VI PRIVACY

The fundamental rights elucidated in *Meyer, Pierce, Skinner,* and other cases related to parental choice, procreation, and the family-unit sphere had a lasting impact on early twentieth-century American jurisprudence. Collectively, these cases caused a tectonic shift in the interpretation of equal protection and due process law. As time passed, it became clear that such precedents could, and would, ultimately support a revolution that marked the dawn of the right of privacy and other reproductive rights.[150]

Griswold v. Connecticut[151] was the landmark case that unveiled a right to privacy under the Constitution.[152] The case involved a challenge to a Connecticut statute that prohibited (1) the use of "any drug, medicinal article or instrument for the purpose of preventing conception" and (2) individuals to assist, abet, counsel, cause, or command others to violate the law.[153]

Griswold's arrival at the Court was anything but stochastic. The Connecticut anticontraception statute under review had been enacted nearly a century earlier in 1879.[154] It came at the heels of what became known as the Comstock Laws, a set of federal and state statutes enacted in the 1870s designed to punish obscene behavior, providers of abortion, and the use of contraception.[155] The Comstock Act of 1873 criminalized the act of knowingly sending "obscene, lewd, or lascivious" materials through the mail.[156] It was named after Anthony Comstock, founder of the New York Society for the Suppression of Vice and special agent of the US Postal Service, who had, for years, engaged in a series of anti-obscenity campaigns aimed at ridding society of all masturbation, pornography, contraceptives, and nonreproductive sexual activity.[157] The Comstock Act, however, was not the first piece of legislation that aimed to regulate the distribution of obscene materials in the United States.[158] Indeed, throughout the late nineteenth century nearly half the states enacted statutes to criminalize obscene acts, birth control, and "perversions of the human mind."[159] And laws banning pornography had been enacted as early as 1821 at the state level, and 1842 at the federal level with the passage of the US Customs Act.[160]

By the mid-1930s, with no progress made to repeal the Connecticut law, some physicians began to quietly open birth control clinics throughout the state.[161] At first, the clinics thrived due to low enforcement of the anticontraception law.[162] Poor women gained access to birth control advice previously available only to those who could afford private physicians.[163] With time, however, enforcement of the law led to the prosecution and conviction of physicians who distributed contraceptives at the birth control clinics.[164]

On November 1961, Estelle Griswold, the Executive Director of the Planned Parenthood League of Connecticut, and Lee Buxton, a licensed physician and professor at the Yale Medical School, were arrested after they opened a birth control clinic in New Haven.[165] Connecticut prosecuted and convicted them for providing information and medical advice to married people with the intent that the information would prevent conception.[166] Griswold and Buxton appealed their convictions, and the Supreme Court granted certiorari to consider the constitutionality of the anticontraception statute.[167]

The *Griswold* majority found that the "Framers did not intend that the first eight amendments be construed to exhaust the basic and fundamental rights which the Constitution guaranteed to the people."[168] Accordingly, the majority identified a "zone of privacy" created by the fundamental constitutional guarantees of the Bill of Rights.[169] The privacy right articulated by the Court concerned the right to be free from governmental intrusion, which arose from the "penumbras" and "emanations" of other constitutional guarantees.[170] In the contraceptive context at bar, the majority opined that the idea of government intrusion into "the sacred precincts of marital bedrooms" was "repulsive to the notions of privacy surrounding the marriage relationship."[171]

The right to marital privacy with respect to intimate conduct born out of *Griswold* subsequently led to the conceptualization of a right to reproductive and procreative autonomy enshrined in *Eisenstadt v. Baird*.[172] In *Eisenstadt*, the Court extended *Griswold*'s holding outside the marital context to rule that unmarried couples also have a right to use contraception.[173] Significantly, the Court famously noted that "[i]f the right of privacy means *anything*, it is the right of the *individual*, married or single, to be free from unwarranted governmental intrusion into matters so fundamentally affecting a person as the decision whether to bear or beget a child."[174] The Court further expanded this privacy-based right against government intrusion into matters of procreation in *Carey v. Population Services International*.[175] In *Carey*, the Court ruled that the right to privacy extends to decisions affecting procreation not only for adults but for minors as well.[176] Thus, these cases establish a robust fundamental right for individuals to make decisions about how and when to procreate.

In 1973, the Supreme Court held in *Roe v. Wade*[177] that the liberty protected under substantive due process includes a right to privacy that supports a woman's constitutional right to terminate her pregnancy.[178] That constitutional right, however, has been restricted in recent decades with the introduction of the "undue burden" standard articulated in *Planned Parenthood of Southeastern Pennsylvania v. Casey*.[179] Undue burden refers to governmental action that "has the purpose or effect of placing a substantial obstacle in the path of a woman seeking an abortion of a nonviable fetus."[180] Although *Roe* and *Casey* held that women have a fundamental right to an abortion, the cases have, to some extent, confounded the privacy-based substantive due process jurisprudence. For instance, *Roe* held that strict scrutiny applied, but *Casey*'s joint opinion failed to articulate a level of scrutiny and instead concocted the new undue burden standard.[181]

Issues related to abortion and GGE may appear intertwined at first glance. Both involve questions of reproductive liberties. However, *Roe*'s brand of substantive due process may be less significant in the GGE realm, particularly when it comes to therapeutic GGE interventions. As will be discussed in Chapter 11, clinical interventions to cure or ameliorate disease in an embryo—with the intent to save a child from premature death—are at the opposite end of what abortion achieves. In the former case, a parent wishes to conceive a child without a harmful genetic mutation, whereas in the latter, the parent does not wish to bring the embryo to term. Similarly, therapeutic GGE brings into focus the prospect of eliminating the need to create dozens of embryos during IVF, which ultimately get discarded or frozen and stored indefinitely.[182]

The one area related to abortion that is presumably more relevant to GGE than the type of substantive due process applied in *Roe* and its progeny is related to cases involving government restrictions on public funding for abortion.[183] Thus, restrictions on the use of government funds to perform GGE interventions are likely constitutional.

VII IT ALL DEPENDS HOW YOU ASK

A final pivotal consideration in the discussion of whether a fundamental right to GGE might exist under the Constitution is the ultimate framing of the issue. Consider, for example, the arrival of *Bowers v. Hardwick*[184] at the Court. In that case, the issue presented was "whether the Federal Constitution confers a fundamental right upon *homosexuals to engage in sodomy*," which had been illegal "for a very long time."[185] *Bowers* was also decided at a crucial point of social unrest and anxiety during the AIDS epidemic and, thus, framing the issue as a right of homosexuals to engage in sexual conduct undoubtedly played an outcome-determining role. Nearly two decades after *Bowers*, the Court reviewed virtually the same question in *Lawrence v. Texas*,[186] except that it was framed as whether "two persons of the same sex [can] engage in certain intimate sexual conduct."[187] Unsurprisingly, the *Bowers* Court did not find a liberty right to engage in homosexual sodomy under the Constitution,[188] whereas the *Lawrence* Court ruled that consenting adults of the same sex have a constitutionally protected liberty right to engage in intimate sexual conduct.[189]

Similarly, in *Washington v. Glucksberg*,[190] the Court reviewed whether a "prohibition against "caus[ing]" or "aid[ing]" a suicide offends the . . . Constitution."[191] This framing stands in contrast to alternative phrasing in concurring opinions in that case, which articulated other possible versions such as the "merciful termination of suffering,"[192] "the narrower question whether a mentally competent person who is experiencing great suffering has a constitutionally cognizable interest in controlling the circumstances of his or her imminent death,"[193] and "the avoidance of severe physical pain (connected with death)."[194]

Carefully framing an issue for judicial review has many parallels to the design of questions intended for polling and surveys to reveal public attitudes about controversial topics. "Polling, of course, is not quite a science and certainly is not an exact one. . . . [I]t is highly vulnerable to the use of specific terminology and ambiguity in framing the questions asked."[195]

Consider, for instance, recent polls on public attitudes on the use of technologies for genome editing.[196] A greater percentage of respondents in multiple surveys supported the use of gene-editing tools to "cure life-threatening" or "debilitating" diseases.[197] In contrast, one poll reported that a majority of respondents believed that "changing the genes of *unborn babies* . . . to reduce their risk of developing certain serious diseases" should be illegal.[198] "Public sentiment has considerable influence over allocation of resources, political policy, and participation rates in studies, all of which affect the course of research."[199] And just as public sentiment can be influenced by the manner in which a particular issue is presented, so too can judicial sentiment be affected. Undoubtedly, judicial review is anything but impervious to the proverbial anatomy of the question presented before a court.

The foregoing case law and discussion highlight a crucial role for framing a question centered on the right to perform GGE. Different outcomes likely would be associated with questions framed as whether parents have a constitutional right to, among other things, (1) perform GGE to bear a healthy child, (2) genetically modify offspring, (3) engineer "designer babies," (4) prevent life-threatening disease or death by correcting deleterious genetic mutations in their child, (5) use reproductive technology to cure genetic disease, (6) customize traits in their offspring, or (7) bear biological children by treating their germ cells with medicinal advances.

Notes

1 This chapter builds upon the influential scholarship of the late John A. Robertson, who was a pioneer in the fields of law, bioethics, and reproductive rights. Throughout various works, Robertson proposed that "principles of reproductive freedom and family autonomy appear to support a presumptive liberty right to obtain and use genetic information in making reproductive decisions." John A. Robertson, *Genetic Selection of Offspring Characteristics*, 76 B.U. L. REV. 421, 422 (1996) [hereinafter Robertson, *Genetic Selection*]; *see also* John A. Robertson, *Embryos, Families, and Procreative Liberty: The Legal Structure of the New Reproduction*, 59 S. CAL. L. REV. 939, 955–56 (1986). *See generally* JOHN A. ROBERTSON, CHILDREN OF CHOICE: FREEDOM AND THE NEW REPRODUCTIVE TECHNOLOGIES (1994) (examining legal, ethical, and social implications of reproductive technologies through the lens of an individual's procreative liberty); John A. Robertson, *Assisting Reproduction, Choosing Genes, and the Scope of Reproductive Freedom*, 76 GEO. WASH. L. REV. 1490 (2008) (exploring reproductive freedom in genetic and offspring selection); John A. Robertson, *Procreative Liberty in the Era of Genomics*, 29 AM. J.L. & MED. 439 (2003) (discussing

challenges presented by the use of genomic information in reproduction); John A. Robertson, *The Right to Procreate and in Utero Fetal Therapy*, 3 J. LEGAL MED. 333 (1982) (arguing that prenatal gene therapy would be desirable and, in some cases, required under the law).

Robertson believed that the use of genetic technology to make certain prebirth decisions is "an essential aspect of an individual's procreative liberty, and that the harms thought to flow from prebirth selection decisions are insufficient to justify interference with them." Robertson, *Genetic Selection*, *supra*, at 468. "Individuals, not government or third parties, are the best judge of whether [a particular package of reproductive burdens and benefits] is in their own best interest." *Id.* at 469. Robertson's thinking on the fundamental status of reproductive choices has influenced subsequent scholarly works, including this chapter.

Although Robertson's scholarship has helped to pave the road for a potential, cognizable constitutional right to select offspring genetic modifications in some contexts, the bulk of his literature was published well before the advent of genome-editing technologies, which have recently been used to modify the human germline. Accordingly, this chapter helps to reintroduce and adapt some of his scholarship to the modern age of genome editing and expands the literature to the GGE context. More importantly, this chapter goes beyond the existing literature to not only corroborate principles embedded in the Constitution that likely give rise to a fundamental right to perform GGE in select contexts but also to propose the creation of a normative framework that delineates clear and specific limits for such a constitutional right, which is currently lacking in the legal literature. *Cf.* Jason C. Glahn, *I Teach You the Superman: Why Congress Cannot Constitutionally Prohibit Genetic Modification*, 25 WHITTIER L. REV. 409, 433–34 (2003) (making similar constitutional arguments that Robertson articulated in his scholarship without specifying any potential limitations applicable to a right of genetic modification); Tandice Ossareh, Note, *Would You Like Blue Eyes with That? A Fundamental Right to Genetic Modification of Embryos*, 117 COLUM. L. REV. 729, 756, 758 (2017) (arguing that from a constitutional standpoint, a "truly reflective and full description" of a right to genetic modification "should assert a right to privacy against state interference to make decisions central to procreation and to parenting," while noting that "drawing [an] exact line" to mark the limits of a right to genetic modification for therapeutic or enhancement uses was "beyond the scope" of the paper (footnotes omitted)); Robertson, *Genetic Selection*, *supra*, at 475 (arguing that positive alterations to the genetic composition of biological offspring may be protected by the Constitution, while acknowledging—at that point in time—that "as a practical matter [such alterations were] so speculative and so distant in the future that precise predictions about their ultimate status [were] difficult").

2 *See* United States v. Rutherford, 442 U.S. 544, 546 (1979) (finding no constitutional right to try "a drug not recognized as 'safe and effective'").

3 *See* Abigail All. for Better Access to Developmental Drugs v. von Eschenbach, 495 F.3d 695, 713 (D.C. Cir. 2007).
4 *See id.*
5 *See, e.g.*, Hong Ma et al., *Correction of a Pathogenic Gene Mutation in Human Embryos*, 548 NATURE 413, 413 (2017) (correcting pathogenic heritable mutations in human embryos via GGE).
6 Buck v. Bell, 274 U.S. 200 (1927).
7 *Id.* at 200, 208.
8 *Id.* at 205–06.
9 *Id.* at 207 (emphasis added) (internal citation omitted).
10 *Id.* at 205.
11 *Id.* at 206–07.
12 *Id.* at 208.
13 *Id.* at 207 (citing Jacobson v. Massachusetts, 197 U.S. 11 (1905)).
14 *See id.* at 200.
15 *See* Haynes v. Lapeer, 166 N.W. 938, 939, 941 (Mich. 1918) (declaring Michigan's sterilization law unconstitutional).
16 *See* Smith v. Bd. of Exam'rs of Feeble-Minded, 88 A. 963, 964, 967 (N.J. 1913) (striking, on Equal Protection grounds, New Jersey's sterilization law).
17 *See* Davis v. Berry, 216 F. 414, 418 (S.D. Ia. 1914) (prohibiting the enforcement of vasectomies for criminals twice convicted of a felony in Iowa).
18 *Buck*, 274 U.S. at 205.
19 PAUL A. LOMBARDO, THREE GENERATIONS, NO IMBECILES: EUGENICS, THE SUPREME COURT, AND *BUCK V. BELL* 140 (2008).
20 *Buck*, 274 U.S. at 205.
21 *See* Stephen Jay Gould, *Carrie Buck's Daughter*, 2 CONST. COMMENT. 331, 331, 336 (1985).
22 *Id.* at 337–38.
23 LOMBARDO, *supra* note 19, at 154–55.
24 For a detailed historical account of the events leading up to the Supreme Court litigation and the decision's aftermath, see *id.* at 149–55.
25 *See, e.g.*, Robert J. Cynkar, *Buck v. Bell: 'Felt Necessities' v. Fundamental Values?*, 81 COLUM. L. REV. 1418 (1981); James C. Dugan, Note, *Conflict Between 'Disabling' and 'Enabling' Paradigms in Law: Sterilization, the Developmentally Disabled, and the Americans with Disabilities Act of 1990*, 78 CORNELL L. REV. 507 (1993); Paul A. Lombardo, *Disability, Eugenics, and the Culture Wars*, 2 ST. LOUIS J. HEALTH L. & POL'Y 57 (2008).
26 For example, some scholars have discussed *Buck*'s dismissal of the Equal Protection Clause as the "last resort of constitutional arguments," Buck v. Bell, 274 U.S. 200, 208 (1927). *See, e.g.*, Victoria Nourse, *Buck v. Bell: A Constitutional Tragedy from a Lost World*, 39 PEPP. L. REV. 101, 115 (2013). Others contend that Equal Protection in state and lower federal courts preceding *Buck* actually

afforded strong constitutional claims against involuntary sterilization. *See* Stephen A. Siegel, *Justice Holmes, Buck v. Bell, and the History of Equal Protection*, 90 MINN. L. REV. 106, 108 (2005).

27 *See, e.g.*, Lombardo, *supra* note 25, at 69 n.84, 69 n.85, 70–71 n.90 (citing Res. 247, 149th Gen. Assem., Reg. Sess. (Ga. 2007), which referred to the "so-called science of eugenics" as a "pseudo-scientific movement"); Nourse, *supra* note 26, at 107 (arguing *Buck* is not part of constitutional law curricula partly because it "is seen as a case about a false science").

28 *See, e.g.*, Gould, *supra* note 21, at 336, 338–39.

29 *Buck*, 274 U.S. at 206.

30 *Id.* at 207.

31 *Id.* at 206.

32 *See* FRANCIS GALTON, HEREDITARY GENIUS: AN INQUIRY INTO ITS LAWS AND CONSEQUENCES 6 (1st ed. 1869).

33 FRANCIS GALTON, MEMORIES OF MY LIFE 290 (2d ed. 1908).

34 T. H. Morgan, *Sex Limited Inheritance in Drosophila*, 32 SCIENCE 120 (1910).

35 "Wildtype" refers to the most common phenotype for an organism in a natural breeding population. *Wildtype*, BIOLOGY ONLINE http://www.biology-online.org/dictionary/Wildtype [https://perma.cc/2QPV-S5VU] (last modified June 10, 2009).

36 Morgan, *supra* note 34, at 120.

37 Mendel's theory of inheritance was derived from his experiments of pea plants that displayed only one physical trait—for example, seed color (green or yellow), plant height (tall or short), etc. Mendel challenged the existing view that all offspring were a combination of parental traits blended together. Among his scientific contributions are the laws of allele segregation and independent assortment. *See generally* Gregor Mendel, *Versuche über Plflanzenhybriden* [*Experiments in Plant Hybridization*], ABHANDLUNGEN 3–47 (1866). For a more detailed account of Mendel's contributions to science, see the discussion in Chapter 2, Sections I and II.D.

38 *See generally* THOMAS H. MORGAN ET AL., THE MECHANISM OF MENDELIAN HEREDITY 1–2 (1915).

39 *See* Garland E. Allen, *The Eugenics Record Office at Cold Spring Harbor, 1910–1940: An Essay in Institutional History*, 2 OSIRIS 225, 250 (1986).

40 T. H. Morgan, *What Are 'Factors' in Mendelian Explanations?*, 5 J. HEREDITY 365, 365 (1909) (emphasis added).

41 Francis Galton, who is considered to be the father of eugenics, defined it as "the science of improving stock . . . which, especially in the case of man, takes cognisance of all influences that tend . . . to give to the more suitable races or strains of blood a better chance of prevailing speedily over the less suitable." FRANCIS GALTON, INQUIRY INTO HUMAN FACULTY AND ITS DEVELOPMENT 17 n.1 (1883) (internal citation omitted).

42 *See* Paul Popenoe, Applied Eugenics 15–16 (1918) ("The distinguished father is likely to have a distinguished son, while the son of two 'nobodies' has a very small chance of becoming distinguished. . . . [T]he son of a distinguished judge ha[s] about one chance in four of becoming himself distinguished, while the son of a man picked out at random from the population ha[s] about one chance in 4,000.").

43 *See, e.g.*, Lombardo, *supra* note 19, at 155–56 (describing views from a Harvey Wickham book, critical of outdated Mendelian inheritance, that was published just before the announcement of the *Buck* decision).

44 Paul A. Lombardo, *Taking Eugenics Seriously: Three Generations of ??? Are Enough?*, 30 Fla. St. U. L. Rev. 191, 203–07 (2003).

45 Harry H. Laughlin, The Legal Status of Eugenical Sterilization 7, 57 (1930).

46 Nourse, *supra* note 26, at 103 n.18 (quoting Victoria F. Nourse, In Reckless Hands: Skinner v. Oklahoma and the Near Triumph of American Eugenics 24 (2008)).

47 Lombardo, *supra* note 19, at xiii, 294 app. C.

48 Pseudoscience is defined as "a system of theories, assumptions, and methods erroneously regarded as scientific." *Pseudoscience*, Merriam-Webster Online Dictionary, http://www.merriam-webster.com/dictionary/pseudoscience [https://perma.cc/RAT7-SH36] (last visited Feb. 15, 2017).

49 Morgan, *supra* note 40, at 365.

50 *See, e.g.*, Trials of War Criminals Before the Nuremberg Military Tribunals Vol. IV 1158–59 (1950) (publishing an extract from a document entered on behalf of Otto Hofmann, a high ranking SS officer and key contributor to Nazi Germany's eugenics laws, citing *Buck v. Bell*, 274 U.S. 200 (1927), to establish that Nazi eugenic practices during World War II were derived from race protection laws in other European countries and the United States).

51 For instance, during the 1920s, only approximately 10 percent of members of the Advisory Council of the American Eugenics Society were trained geneticists. Cynkar, *supra* note 25, at 1426.

52 *See* discussion *supra* Section II.

53 Paul Enríquez, *Genome Editing and the Jurisprudence of Scientific Empiricism*, 19 Vand. J. Ent. & Tech. L. 603, 666 (2017).

54 *See, e.g.*, Pinar Akcakaya et al., *In Vivo CRISPR Editing with No Detectable Genome-Wide Off-Target Mutations*, 561 Nature 416, 416, 419 (2018).

55 *See, e.g.*, Yetki Aslan et al., *High-Efficiency Non-Mosaic CRISPR-Mediated Knock-In and Indel Mutation in F0 Xenopus*, 144 Development 2852, 2852, 2855 (2017).

56 *See, e.g.*, Jean-Baptiste Renaud et al., *Improved Genome Editing Efficiency and Flexibility Using Modified Oligonucleotides with TALEN and CRISPR-Cas9 Nucleases*, 14 Cell Rep. 2263, 2263–64 (2016).

57 *See, e.g.*, Ian M. Slaymaker et al., *Rationally Engineered Cas9 Nucleases with Improved Specificity*, 351 Science 84, 84 (2016); Josh Tycko, Vic E. Myer &

Patrick D. Hsu, *Methods for Optimizing CRISPR-Cas9 Genome Editing Specificity*, 63 MOLECULAR CELL 355, 355 (2016).

58 *See, e.g.*, Wenhua Zhou et al., *Enhanced Cytosolic Delivery and Release of CRISPR/Cas9 by Black Phosphorus Nanosheets for Genome Editing*, 57 ANGEWANDTE CHEMIE 10, 268, 10,271 (2018).

59 *See, e.g.*, Alejandro Chavez et al., *Precise Cas9 Targeting Enables Genomic Mutation Prevention*, 115 PROC. NAT'L ACAD. SCI. U.S. 3669, 3669–73 (2018); Van Trung Chu et al., *Increasing the Efficiency of Homology-Directed Repair for CRISPR-Cas9-Induced Precise Gene Editing in Mammalian Cells*, 33 NATURE BIOTECHNOLOGY 543, 543 (2015); Paul Enríquez, *CRISPR-Mediated Epigenome Editing*, 89 YALE J. BIOLOGY & MED. 471, 483 (2016); Benjamin P. Kleinstiver et al., *High-Fidelity CRISPR–Cas9 Nucleases with No Detectable Genome-Wide Off-Target Effects*, 529 NATURE 490, 490 (2016) (reducing off-target effects).

60 *See* Marilynn Marchione, *Chinese Researcher Claims Birth of First Gene-Edited Babies – Twin Girls*, STAT (Nov. 25, 2018), https://www.statnews.com/2018/11/25/china-first-gene-edited-babies-born/ [https://perma.cc/5469-LUZQ] (reporting on what is presumably the first birth of humans whose genomes were altered during the embryonic stage). *See generally, e.g.*, Matthew H. Porteus, *Towards a New Era in Medicine: Therapeutic Genome Editing*, 16 GENOME BIOLOGY 286 (2015) (discussing how advances in genome editing have increased the spectrum of diseases that can be treated with therapeutic uses of genome editing). It should be noted that the experiments leading to the birth of the first gene-edited babies in China highlight the use of a faulty gene-editing strategy by an inexperienced researcher but nevertheless demonstrate the feasibility of using gene editing in human embryos. The methods requisite to perform such experiments in the human germline are likely to improve over time.

61 521 U.S. 702, 720–21 (1997).

62 *Id.* (quoting Moore v. City of East Cleveland, 431 U.S. 494, 503 (1977) (plurality opinion)).

63 *Id.*

64 Reno v. Flores, 507 U.S. 292, 302 (1993).

65 City of Cleburne v. Cleburne Living Ctr., Inc., 473 U.S. 432, 440 (1985).

66 Lawrence v. Texas, 539 U.S. 558, 572 (2003) (quoting County of Sacramento v. Lewis, 523 U.S. 833, 857 (1998) (Kennedy, J., concurring)).

67 Obergefell v. Hodges, 576 U.S. 644, 671 (2015).

68 *Id.*

69 *See id.*

70 U.S. CONST. amend. V ("[N]or shall any person . . . be deprived of life, liberty, or property, without due process of law . . . ."); *id.* amend. XIV, § 1 ("[N]or shall any State deprive any person of life, liberty, or property, without due process of law . . . .").

71 Moore v. City of East Cleveland, 431 U.S. 494, 502 (1977) (plurality opinion).

72 Erwin Chemerinsky, *Substantive Due Process*, 15 TOURO L. REV. 1501, 1501 (1999).
73 Daniel O. Conkle, *Three Theories of Substantive Due Process*, 85 N.C. L. REV. 63, 69 (2006).
74 Chemerinsky, *supra* note 72, at 1501.
75 Nelson Lund & John O. McGinnis, *Lawrence v. Texas and Judicial Hubris*, 102 MICH. L. REV. 1555, 1557 (2004).
76 One caveat is that, given the contention in this area of the law, such a path is potentially susceptible to the composition of the Court at a particular point in time, as some Justices have expressed a willingness to discard the doctrine in the past. *See, e.g.*, United States v. Windsor, 570 U.S. 744, 794 (2013) (Scalia, J., dissenting) ("The majority never utters the dread words 'substantive due process,' perhaps sensing the disrepute into which that doctrine has fallen . . . ."); Griswold v. Connecticut, 381 U.S. 479, 530 (1965) (Stewart, J., dissenting) ("I can find no such general right of privacy in the Bill of Rights, in any other part of the Constitution, or in any case ever before decided by this Court.").
77 It bears noting some have argued that the enactment of the Fourteenth Amendment during the Reconstruction era is itself evidence of the existence of the sort of liberty articulated by the Court in the 1920s. *See* Peggy Cooper Davis, *Neglected Stories and the Lawfulness of* Roe v. Wade, 28 HARV. C.R.-C.L. L. REV. 299, 309–10 (1993). This is because the framers of the Reconstruction Amendments had

> vivid impressions of what it meant to be denied rights of family, for the denial of those rights was a hallmark of slavery in the United States . . . that inverted concepts of human dignity, citizenship and natural law. . . . [T]he Fourteenth Amendment [was] the instrument with which to re-enshrine family liberty as an inalienable aspect of national citizenship and natural law.

Id. at 309 (citations omitted).
78 262 U.S. 390 (1923).
79 *Id.* at 397.
80 *Id.*
81 *Id.* at 396.
82 Meyer v. State, 187 N.W. 100, 104 (Neb. 1922), *rev'd*, 262 U.S. 390 (1923).
83 RONALD SCHAFFER, AMERICA IN THE GREAT WAR: THE RISE OF THE WAR WELFARE STATE, at xvi–xvii (1991).
84 Carlos J. Ovando, *Bilingual Education in the United States: Historical Development and Current Issues*, 27 BILINGUAL RES. J. 1, 5 (2003).
85 SCHAFFER, *supra* note 83, at 20–23.
86 H. L. MENCKEN, THE AMERICAN LANGUAGE, SUPPLEMENT I: AN INQUIRY INTO THE DEVELOPMENT OF ENGLISH IN THE UNITED STATES 429 (1988); SCHAFFER, *supra* note 83, at 20.

87 SCHAFFER, *supra* note 83, at 19–20.
88 *See id.* at 20.
89 Ovando, *supra* note 84, at 5.
90 For an examination of the eugenics movement, its pseudoscientific roots, and its rise to legitimacy in the United States in the late 1800s and early 1900s, see Enríquez, *supra* note 53, at 679–80, 687–91.
91 *See* PAUL POPENOE & ROSWELL HILL JOHNSON, APPLIED EUGENICS 298–301 (1918). Popenoe and Johnson, for example, asserted: "It is essential if America is to be strong eugenically that it slow down the flood of immigrants who are not easily assimilable." *Id.* at 306. The rhetoric related to immigration in the early twentieth century bears some resemblance to that of today's anti-immigration debate. *Compare id.* at 303–04 (attributing a rise in crime, pauperism, violence, and alcoholism to the wave of immigration of "inferior" people from southern and eastern European countries), *with* ANN COULTER, ¡ADIOS, AMERICA!: THE LEFT'S PLAN TO TURN OUR COUNTRY INTO A THIRD WORLD HELLHOLE 18 (2015) (arguing that the "mass immigration of the poorest of the poor to America is bad for the whole country" and is responsible for an increase in welfare consumption and crimes such as credit card fraud, human trafficking, child prostitution, and robberies perpetrated by immigrants who are not expected to assimilate into American culture), *and* Amber Phillips, *'They're Rapists.' President Trump's Campaign Launch Speech Two Years Later, Annotated*, WASH. POST (June 16, 2017), https://www.washingtonpost.com/news/the-fix/wp/2017/06/16/theyre-rapists-presidents-trump-campaign-launch-speech-two-years-later-annotated/?noredirect=on&utm_term=.04fb553351cd [https://perma.cc/SQ5T-Q7D5] (memorializing President Donald Trump's remarks during his campaign for the 2016 presidential election in which he stated, "When Mexico sends its people, they're not sending their best. . . . They're sending people that have lots of problems, and they're bringing those problems with [sic] us. They're bringing drugs. They're bringing crime. They're rapists. And some, I assume, are good people.").
92 Meyer v. Nebraska, 262 U.S. 390, 397–98 (1923).
93 *Id.* at 398.
94 *Id.* at 399.
95 *Id.* at 401.
96 *Id.* at 400.
97 *Id.* at 399–400. Justice Holmes, a supporter of the eugenics movement who would go on to author the infamous *Buck v. Bell*, 274 U.S. 200 (1927), decision that legalized forced sterilization of mentally disabled individuals, *see id.* at 207; *see also* Enríquez, *supra* note 53, at 685–86, dissented in *Meyer* and filed a dissenting opinion in another case decided the same day, in which he expressed the view that the case presented a question upon which reasonable people might disagree, particularly because he did not find it unreasonable to require young children to hear and speak only English at school, *see* Bartels

v. Iowa, 262 U.S. 404, 412 (1923) (Holmes, J., dissenting). Thus, Holmes likely would have deferred to the judgment of the legislature when considering the question of whether the means adopted to achieve language homogeneity in elementary education violated an individual's liberty guaranteed by the Fourteenth Amendment. *See id.* (advocating language homogeneity in education). Holmes's brand of deference to the legislative branch also played a key role in *Buck*'s analytically bereft holding, which endorsed a state's erroneous scientific assertions that legalized involuntary sterilizations under the pretense of promoting public welfare. *See Buck*, 274 U.S. at 205–08; *see also* Enríquez, *supra* note 53, at 687–88.

98 268 U.S. 510 (1925).

99 *See id.* at 534–35.

100 Compulsory Education Act, ch. 1, 1923 Or. Laws 9 (1922), *invalidated by* Pierce v. Soc'y of Sisters, 268 U.S. 510 (1925).

101 *Pierce*, 268 U.S. at 531.

102 *Id.* at 533–34.

103 In 2000, Justice Anthony Kennedy indicated that if *Meyer* and *Pierce* had been decided in recent times, they likely would have been grounded upon First Amendment principles that protect the freedom of speech, belief, and religion. *See* Troxel v. Granville, 530 U.S. 57, 95 (2000) (Kennedy, J., dissenting). When *Pierce* was decided, however, the Court had not yet incorporated the First Amendment into the rights and liberties guaranteed by the Due Process Clause of the Fourteenth Amendment as it applied to the states. Such incorporation occurred in a case decided a week after *Pierce*. *See* Gitlow v. New York, 268 U.S. 652, 666 (1925).

104 *Pierce*, 268 U.S. at 534–35.

105 *Id.* at 535.

106 *Id.* (emphasis added).

107 *See* discussion in Sections IV–VI of this chapter.

108 321 U.S. 158 (1944).

109 *Id.* at 165.

110 *Id.* at 161.

111 *Id.* at 161–62.

112 *Id.* at 166.

113 *Id.* (citations omitted).

114 *See id.* at 166–67.

115 *Prince*, 321 U.S. at 175 (Murphy, J., dissenting).

116 *Id.* (citation omitted); *see also* Wisconsin v. Yoder, 406 U.S. 205, 234–36 (1972) (holding that Amish parents have a right to exempt their teenage children from mandatory-school-attendance laws on constitutional grounds related to the right to control child-rearing decisions and the free exercise of religion).

117 *Prince*, 321 U.S. at 175 (Murphy, J., dissenting).

118 406 U.S. 205 (1972).
119 *Id.* at 234.
120 *Id.* at 214.
121 *Id.* at 219.
122 *Id.* at 230.
123 *See* Prince v. Massachusetts, 321 U.S. 158, 170 (1944); *see also supra* notes 113–14 and accompanying text.
124 442 U.S. 584 (1979).
125 *Id.* at 603.
126 *Id.*
127 *Id.* at 604.
128 *Id.* at 602, 604.
129 *Id.* at 621(Stewart, J., concurring).
130 Troxel v. Granville, 530 U.S. 57, 65 (2000).
131 Wisconsin v. Yoder, 406 U.S. 205, 234 (1972).
132 316 U.S. 535 (1942).
133 Act of May 8, 1935, ch. 26, 1935 Okla. Sess. Laws 94, *invalidated by* Skinner v. Oklahoma, 316 U.S. 535 (1942).
134 *Skinner*, 316 U.S. at 536.
135 Between 1907 and 1979, more than 65,000 compulsory sterilizations took place in thirty-two states across America. Enríquez, *supra* note 53, at 689–90.
136 274 U.S. 200 (1927).
137 *See id.* at 207–08.
138 I have, in prior work, explored aspects of the fascinating question surrounding the judiciary's reluctance, if not flagrant antipathy at times, to overcome the false dichotomy frequently associated with mutually exclusive roles for science and law. Enríquez, *supra* note 53, at 679–91. For instance, as outlined earlier in this chapter, I have argued against the conventional view that *Buck*'s holding is illegitimate because it rests on pseudoscience. An examination of the state of scientific knowledge at the time *Buck* was decided reveals that no legitimate scientific debate existed regarding the heritability of human cognitive abilities or mental deficiencies. *Buck* relied on no scientific evidence. Instead, it relied on deceptive propaganda that had been de facto incorporated into popular culture over a period of decades. *See id.* at 685–91.
139 *Skinner*, 316 U.S. at 537–38.
140 *Id.* at 538.
141 *Id.* at 541.
142 *Id.* at 538–39.
143 *Id.* at 536.
144 *See id.* at 541.
145 *Id.*

146 *Id.* In contrast, *Buck* had applied a primitive form of modern rational basis as the standard of review fifteen years earlier. Enríquez, *supra* note 53, at 686; *see also* Buck v. Bell, 274 U.S. 200, 207–08 (1927).
147 *See Skinner*, 316 U.S. at 541.
148 *Id.* at 546 (Jackson, J., concurring).
149 Indeed, the *Skinner* Court distinguished *Buck* by asserting that the latter could be upheld because it applied only to mentally disabled individuals in state custody. *Id.* at 542.
150 *See* Griswold v. Connecticut, 381 U.S. 479, 502–03 (1965) (White, J., concurring) (citing *Meyer*, *Pierce*, *Prince*, *Skinner*, and other cases concerning liberty guarantees under the Fourteenth Amendment).
151 381 U.S. 479 (1965).
152 *Id.* at 479.
153 *Id.* at 480.
154 David J. Garrow, Liberty and Sexuality: The Right to Privacy and the Making of Roe v. Wade 1 (1994).
155 Nicola Beisel, Imperiled Innocents: Anthony Comstock and Family Reproduction in Victorian America 36–38 (1997).
156 Paul R. Abramson & Steven D. Pinkerton, With Pleasure: Thoughts on the Nature of Human Sexuality 177 (rev. ed. 2002).
157 *Id.* at 176–77.
158 *See id.* at 178. Judith Giesberg, Sex and the Civil War: Soldiers, Pornography, and the Making of American Morality 12 (2017).
159 *See* Mary Ware Dennett, Birth Control Laws: Shall We Keep Them Change Them or Abolish Them app. at 268–70 (1926). *See generally* J. C. Ruppenthal, *Criminal Statutes on Birth Control*, 10 J. Am. Inst. Crim. L. & Criminology 48 (1919) (providing a survey of said laws).
160 Abramson & Pinkerton, *supra* note 156, at 178; Judith Giesberg, Sex and the Civil War: Soldiers, Pornography, and the Making of American Morality 12 (2017).
161 Garrow, *supra* note 154, at 1.
162 *Id.*
163 *Id.*
164 *See, e.g.*, Poe v. Ullman, 367 U.S. 497, 508–09 (1961); Tileston v. Ullman, 318 U.S. 44, 46 (1943) (per curiam).
165 Griswold v. Connecticut, 381 U.S. 479, 480 (1965).
166 *Id.*
167 *Id.*
168 *Id.* at 490.
169 *Id.* at 484–85.
170 *Id.* at 483–84.
171 *Id.* at 485–86.

172 405 U.S. 438 (1972).
173 *Id.* at 453.
174 *Id.* (emphasis added).
175 431 U.S. 678 (1977).
176 *Id.* at 693.
177 410 U.S. 113 (1973).
178 *Id.* at 164–67.
179 505 U.S. 833 (1992) (per curiam) (holding certain restrictions on the right to an abortion are constitutional unless they impose an "undue burden").
180 *Id.* at 877.
181 *See id.* at 964 (Rehnquist, C.J., concurring in the judgment in part and dissenting in part) ("[*Roe*] adopted a . . . standard under which state regulations could survive only if they met the requirement of 'strict scrutiny.' . . . The same cannot be said for the 'undue burden' standard, which is created largely out of whole cloth by the authors of the joint opinion. . . . [I]t is a standard which is not built to last.").
182 *See* Julie Steffann et al., *Could Failure in Preimplantation Genetic Diagnosis Justify Editing the Human Embryo Genome?*, 22 Cell Stem Cell 481, 481–82 (2018) (analyzing results from the Preimplantation Genetic Diagnosis (PGD) Centre of Béclère-Necker hospitals in Paris over a five-year period to reveal that PGD aimed at helping couples bear healthy children had a 73 percent failure rate). The study performed by Steffann and colleagues found that out of 3,047 embryos obtained from 358 couples, only 2,038 embryos were successfully diagnosed. *Id.* at 481–82 & app. Of the embryos diagnosed, 53 percent (1,079) were unaffected by genetic disease while 47 percent (959) tested positive for genetic disease and were discarded. *Id.* The unaffected embryos were transferred or cryopreserved and ultimately resulted in only 95 deliveries, in which 118 babies were born. *Id.*
183 *See generally*, *e.g.*, Harris v. McRae, 448 U.S. 297 (1980) (holding that states participating in Medicaid are not obligated to fund medically necessary abortions when the state cannot be reimbursed under federal law); Beal v. Doe, 432 U.S. 438 (1977) (holding that a state's refusal to extend Medicaid coverage to nontherapeutic abortions contravened federal law); Poelker v. Doe, 432 U.S. 519 (1977) (per curiam) (holding that a city was not constitutionally required to provide publicly financed hospital services for elective abortions even if the city provides such services for childbirth).
184 478 U.S. 186 (1986), *overruled by* Lawrence v. Texas, 539 U.S. 558 (2003).
185 *Id.* at 190 (emphasis added).
186 539 U.S. 558 (2003).
187 *Id.* at 562.
188 *Bowers*, 478 U.S. at 189.
189 *Lawrence*, 539 U.S. at 578–79.

190 521 U.S. 702 (1997).
191 *Id.* at 705–06.
192 *Id.* at 754–55 (Souter, J., concurring).
193 *Id.* at 736 (O'Connor, J., concurring).
194 *Id.* at 791 (Breyer, J., concurring).
195 Enríquez, *supra* note 53, at 675.
196 *E.g.*, STAT & HARVARD T.H. CHAN SCH. OF PUB. HEALTH, THE PUBLIC AND GENETIC EDITING, TESTING, AND THERAPY 9 (2016), https://cdn1.sph.harvard.edu/wp-content/uploads/sites/94/2016/01/STAT-Harvard-Poll-Jan-2016-Genetic-Technology.pdf [https://perma.cc/LY3G-CPK3] (compiling results from interviews "conducted with a nationally representative sample of 1,000 randomly selected adults, ages 18 and older, via telephone"); Tristan McCaughey et al., *A Global Social Media Survey of Attitudes to Human Genome Editing*, 18 CELL STEM CELL 569, 569 (2016) (reporting results from "a worldwide online survey of over 12,000 people recruited via social media to gauge attitudes toward" genome-editing technology); Dietram A. Scheufele et al., *U.S. Attitudes on Human Genome Editing*, 357 SCIENCE 553, 553 (2017) (reporting results from "national survey data from 1600 U.S. adults that YouGov collected in December 2016 and January 2017"); Masato Uchiyama, Akiko Nagai & Kaori Muto, *Survey on the Perception of Germline Genome Editing Among the General Public in Japan*, 63 J. HUM. GENETICS 745, 745 (2018) (conducting "a survey of 10,881 general adults and 1,044 patients in Japan who indicated that their disease conditions are related to their genetic makeup").
197 *See, e.g.*, McCaughey et al., *supra* note 196, at 569 (noting that 59.0 percent and 59.4 percent of survey respondents approved the use of gene editing in children and adults to cure life threatening or debilitating diseases, respectively); *accord* Scheufele et al., *supra* note 196, at 553 (finding the use of human genome editing for therapeutic purposes is acceptable to 64 percent of respondents for somatic therapies and 65 percent of respondents for germline therapies); Uchiyama et al., *supra* note 196, at 745 ("[R]esults clearly indicated that the Japanese people generally accepted the use of genome editing for disease-related genes.").
198 *See* STAT & HARVARD T.H. CHAN SCH. OF PUB. HEALTH, *supra* note 196, at 2 (emphasis added) (reporting that 26 percent of respondents believed "changing the genes of unborn babies" should be legal in a therapeutic context, while 65 percent believed it should be illegal to do so). It should be noted that phrasing the question as one involving changing unborn babies to reduce the risk of disease, rather than using a technology to cure disease, may underlie the contrast in the respondents' attitudes toward gene editing among the various polls.
199 McCaughey et al., *supra* note 196, at 571.

11

Science, Law, and Policy

This chapter introduces normative recommendations for developing a law- and science-based policy framework to address many of the genome-editing issues discussed throughout this book. It begins by proposing a normative framework to delineate primordial limits for a putative right to perform germline genome editing (GGE) on the basis of four distinct categories of what the technology may be used for. This conceptual and structural approach outlines a legal blueprint for a path to GGE clinical interventions. It also aims to encourage scholarly and public discussions about whether, and the extent to which, editing the genetic composition of the human germline should be permitted, and in some instances protected—a subject arguably among the most significant and consequential of this generation. The chapter then turns to examine the regulation of new gene-edited crops in the twenty-first century by identifying several obstacles to developing scientific-based public policy in the realm of GMOs. Lastly, the chapter proposes a set of policy recommendations to facilitate the rational regulation of genome-edited crops.

I TO EDIT OR NOT TO EDIT

Chapter 10 laid out a doctrinal foundation of jurisprudence in areas of parental, family, procreative, and reproductive autonomy guaranteed by the Due Process and Equal Protection Clauses of the Constitution. But jurisprudence in this realm must be framed in the context of GGE in order to derive applicable legal principles that can ultimately guide and promote coherent public policy. This section argues that these constitutional underpinnings of jurisprudence in the family-unit sphere serve as the basis for a cognizable fundamental right to perform specific types of GGE. Of course, like many of the rights identified via substantive due process—such as the rights to control a child's upbringing, marry, terminate a pregnancy, and others[1]—the right to perform GGE would not be absolute.

Congressional or judicial fiat may delineate, at some point in the near future, the extent and limitations of a right to perform GGE in select contexts. However, no framework currently exists to draw clear lines that distinguish between permissible and impermissible uses of GGE technologies. This chapter fills that gap and proposes a normative framework that identifies four distinct categories of GGE: (1) therapeutic uses to remedy disease; (2) prophylactic purposes, which may or may not be of therapeutic nature; (3) cosmetic or enhancement purposes; and (4) uses involving modification of traits that raise concerns of unlawful discrimination.

The four-category spectrum proposed here facilitates the creation of initial boundaries for GGE and outlines a putative regulatory and legal blueprint. Furthermore, the approach avoids the squabbles that frequently rise from the conventional tendency to group GGE applications into therapeutic uses on one hand, and enhancements on the other. That outdated model is inefficient and susceptible to analytical derailments stemming from awkward attempts to fit therapeutic, eugenical, and so-called "designer baby" enhancements into a single doctrinal model.

The normative framework proposed here, however, deconstructs the nuances inherent in various applications of GGE. Hence, under Category 1, certain GGE uses are permitted, can withstand strict constitutional scrutiny, and likely constitute a fundamental right. Conversely, Category 4 GGE uses at the opposite end of the spectrum are prohibited because they create a likelihood of unlawful discrimination against specific groups and are not constitutionally justifiable. Lastly, many GGE applications that fall within the sphere of Categories 2 and 3 involve conditions or traits that are polygenic (determined by the contribution of more than one gene), as opposed to monogenic (determined by the effects of a single gene), and are either poorly understood or not characterized at the molecular level. As a result, it is unlikely that the technology to address these GGE interventions will be ready for clinical use in the near future. Because of this fact, premature laws and regulations concerning the sanction or prohibition of GGE prophylactic, cosmetic, and enhancement interventions should be avoided at this point in time.

A *On Therapies and the Law*

The first category of GGE applications concerns therapeutic uses to remedy disease. For parents carrying genetic mutations that increase the likelihood of conceiving a child susceptible to a serious genetic disease,[2] it is quite likely that the awareness of their genetic composition fundamentally affects their decision whether to become parents. The Supreme Court has noted that "[i]f the right of privacy means *anything*, it is the right of the *individual*, married or single, to be free from unwarranted governmental intrusion into matters so fundamentally affecting a person as the decision whether to bear or beget a child."[3]

The prospect of bringing a child into this world to suffer a debilitating, lifelong illness would certainly play a fundamental role in an individual's decision to pursue parenthood within the meaning of our existing substantive due process jurisprudence. After all, what good is the existence of a "right to have offspring" or procreate[4] if that offspring is destined to suffer disease and premature death? Governmental authority aimed at denying parents the ability to perform GGE for therapeutic purposes when their child faces the probability of suffering from an imminent, life-threatening, genetic disease[5] would have overt, "far-reaching[,] and devastating effects" on the health and survival of said child that arguably go beyond the prohibition of the power to sterilize articulated in *Skinner*.[6] Congenital disease may force upon a child, as well as all members of her family unit, "a distressful life and future. Psychological harm may be imminent. Mental and physical health may be taxed by child care."[7] Denial of a fundamental right to perform GGE under this scenario arguably runs contrary to the guarantees found in the Constitution, which protect the right to procreation as crucial to the survival of the species.[8]

1 Procreation and the Meaning of Perpetuating Our Genes

A discussion of the right to procreate calls for deeper analytical exploration of the basis underlying the incorporation of a putative right to rescue one's offspring from imminent illness or death as part of the human procreational prerogative. The core of this argument is that the basic fundamental right to "perpetuat[e] a [human] race" and "have offspring"[9] articulated in *Skinner* pertains specifically to a right rooted in the success of *biological* procreation. This inference must be drawn from *Skinner*'s holding because merely having offspring does not, in and of itself, guarantee the perpetuation of the human race. In order to perpetuate one's genetic composition in the human gene pool, one's offspring must be viable, fertile, and capable of developing to an age at which the individual can procreate and have offspring herself. The right to procreate under *Skinner*'s constitutional structure is, thus, essentially meaningless if one's children are destined to an early death, or substantial impairment, at the hands of genetic disease.

That conceptual exposition is also supported by dicta in *Skinner* noting that the power to sterilize "can cause races or types which are inimical to the dominant group to *wither and disappear*."[10] Again, a reference to favorable or adequate biological procreation appears nowhere explicitly in the opinion. But the majority's concern that specific "races or types"—namely, traits that can be traced to specific genotypes—can "wither and disappear"[11] speaks clearly to the proposition that, without a fundamental right to biological procreation that limits governmental intrusion into procreative matters, some individuals belonging to nondominant groups might find themselves defenseless against invidious government action and will ultimately be unable to pass down their genes to subsequent generations. Procreation in that sense calls for more than just producing offspring; it calls for producing offspring healthy enough to fulfill the biological role of perpetuating one's genotype within the constitutional structure erected by *Skinner*.

One important consideration here relates to the definition of the term "healthy." For instance, does a child with rheumatoid arthritis who is severely crippled and ill but grows up to marry and have children qualify as healthy within the meaning of *Skinner*? Does an individual with Cystic Fibrosis (CF) who grows up to become a parent and dies at a young age from CF-related complications—but nevertheless was able to bear children who also carry CF-associated mutations—qualify as healthy within the meaning of *Skinner*? These questions are more difficult to resolve under a fundamental right to procreate but may be more soluble under the principles embedded in the right to parental autonomy. In any event, at a minimum, *Skinner* arguably endorses a substantive reading of biological procreation in the context of a right to have offspring healthy enough to develop and grow to an age when they will be able to reproduce and pass down their genetic makeup to a new generation.

2 Forever Bonds

Although the Supreme Court has counseled caution and restraint in the application of substantive due process, "it does not counsel abandonment."[12] Parents who must choose between having a child destined to be ill or forgoing the benefits of biological parenthood entirely would be, in essence, abandoned by the Constitution. Accordingly, it is difficult to imagine a more compelling scenario for the application of modern substantive due process. Furthermore, the decision to enter into a marriage relationship has been recognized as the core of family in our society.[13] But what shall we then make of the decision to enter the ultimate relationship that perpetuates the human race—namely, the parent-child relationship—which, unlike marriage, is ever-lasting, not susceptible to divorce,[14] and often becomes more significant and life altering than the decision to marry? Assuming GGE technologies become safe and effective for clinical use,[15] if the rights of procreation, parental autonomy, and privacy mean "*anything at all*,"[16] they must imply some right to enter the parent-child relationship unencumbered by the burdens of disease stemming from random or inherited genetic mutations many individuals bear no responsibility for carrying.

For individuals who carry alleles associated with genetic diseases, the right to be free from state intervention in the decision to bear children without deleterious genetic mutations via GGE intervention likely triggers strict scrutiny. Thus, the government may find it difficult to establish a compelling state interest that would justify wholly prohibiting GGE interventions.[17] After all, bearing healthy children significantly contributes to the pursuit of happiness in the family context.[18] Moreover, the wide latitude afforded to parents in making decisions related to the upbringing of their offspring—including medical decisions that do not endanger the health or safety of the child[19]—support a cognizable right to GGE interventions with therapeutic intent. In fact, the availability of GGE that is proven safe and effective brings into focus the prospect of allowing parents to make medical decisions that will promote and safeguard the health of the child by ensuring offspring will not carry genetic mutations for serious diseases.[20]

Under a strict scrutiny analysis, the government might find it difficult to establish the existence of narrowly tailored measures to further the interest of denying GGE for therapeutic purposes. Indeed, for homozygous individuals carrying deleterious genetic mutations that all but guarantee that offspring will be susceptible to genetic diseases,[21] there are likely few, if any, suitable alternative means[22]—including preimplantation genetic diagnosis (PGD)[23]—to conceive an otherwise healthy child without GGE intervention. For instance, the argument that the risk of transmitting genetic disease can be avoided via PGD coupled with abortion overlooks PGD's financial, medical, and emotional burdens; its low chance of success; and the large number of embryos that are discarded in the process, which some potential parents may object to from ethical or faith-based perspectives.[24] Thus, the right to be free from government intrusion in the decision to pursue GGE for therapeutic purposes is an *extension* of the rights to procreate and exercise parental autonomy under current substantive due process jurisprudence.[25] Once GGE's safety and efficacy are scientifically established, it may be difficult for the government to impose bans on access to the technology for therapeutic uses.

Lastly, there is some validity to the point that banning a technology that may assist deleterious mutation-carrying parents would not violate the right to procreate because they may still choose to conceive and assume the risks of bringing a child who may be susceptible to genetic disease. That some parents may choose not to reproduce because of an awareness of the burdens inherent in their genetic composition is a personal choice, with which the government does not interfere when it denies access to a particular reproductive technology. For instance, *Califano v. Jobst*[26] articulated the principle that a "general rule is not rendered invalid simply because some persons" might be deterred from engaging in certain conduct.[27] But *Jobst* can be clearly distinguished from the GGE context, as it concerned a limitation on the right to marry in the context of a specific program concerning the distribution of government benefits, which would have been lost when the plaintiff remarried and was no longer dependent on government assistance.[28]

As stated earlier, for some parents who carry deleterious genetic mutations, there is no alternative path to have a healthy child. That strikes at the core of the fundamental right to procreate. It also stands in contrast to *Jobst*, which was related to the loss of a government benefit and, thus, did not strike at the core of the fundamental right to marry. In the GGE context, parents contemplate a decision that goes beyond giving up a government benefit. Rather, parents must decide whether they are willing and able to bring a human being into the world who is likely destined to suffer from disease—a decision that carries substantial emotional, social, and financial costs.

As discussed above, the use of GGE intervention—for which scientific evidence exists to establish the safety and efficacy of the desired genetic modification—in the therapeutic context may constitute a fundamental right and could withstand strict constitutional scrutiny. However, the analysis in the foregoing section may be inapplicable to a right to perform GGE for nontherapeutic uses.

B *Preemptive Strikes*

The second category of GGE applications refers to the use of GGE interventions for prophylactic purposes. This category shares many similarities to Category 1, but can be clearly distinguished by noting that prophylactic interventions may or may not be therapeutic in nature.

The use of GGE in this category is likely to be important, but may not be sufficient to withstand the pressures of strict scrutiny that Category 1 uses could. For example, parents may wish to confer immunity to the HIV virus[29] upon an embryo, or protect it against potential risks of cardiovascular disease, diabetes, and some cancers. The parental autonomy highlighted under these scenarios would be weighed against potential state interests derived from access to the technology, fairness, and equality. Parents may have a constitutionally protected right to perform GGE intervention on an embryo to spare it from a life of suffering or premature death, but will they also have a constitutional right to modify the genes of their offspring based on the possibility that a given disease will affect them in the future? HIV immunity, for example, would not be relevant to a genetically modified individual unless, at some point, the person is exposed to the virus. In other words, parents may have a constitutional right to bear healthy children, but may or may not have a constitutional right to bear children who are immune to HIV.

The prophylactic category of GGE interventions also shines a light on the policy challenges presented by medical advances and technologies, which often affect the status of a particular disease in society. Case in point, the US National Academies of Sciences, Engineering, and Medicine (NASEM) recommended restricting GGE interventions to a "*serious* disease or condition" and to "prevent extension" to other uses.[30] But adherence to that recommendation largely depends on a definition of what constitutes a "serious disease or condition" at a particular point in time, and whether extension to other potential uses at some point in the future might be palatable, or even desirable, from social, ethical, and policy perspectives.

Consider the case of HIV infection. During the 1980s and 1990s, when the AIDS epidemic caused a public-health crisis, HIV infection was considered a death sentence and certainly constituted a serious disease or condition that could even be transmitted to an individual's offspring.[31] However, scientific advances in antiretroviral drug therapies in the last two decades have dramatically altered medical outcomes associated with HIV diagnoses in the developed world, and many in the medical profession now consider HIV a chronic infection, on par with other chronic diseases such as diabetes.[32]

In fact, individuals already have access to antiretroviral therapy for prophylactic purposes today.[33] On the other hand, HIV continues to represent a serious threat to public health in poverty-stricken regions of the world,[34] which highlights the spatial and temporal challenges of defining a "serious disease or condition"[35] that should be addressed via GGE interventions.

The semantic problem of limiting GGE to serious diseases also lies beneath the analytical impetus for the recent Chinese GGE experiments. He Jiankui claimed that he edited the *CCR5* gene in human embryos, which led to the birth of twins in China, in order to "show compassion" and help "people in need."[36] But, as pointed out earlier, there is a legitimate question about the compelling nature of He Jiankui's experiments given the availability of alternate means to achieve the goal of helping an HIV-positive male conceive children without transmitting the HIV virus, such as the use of antiretroviral drug therapies or low-cost "semen washing" procedures commonly used to reduce HIV transmission in HIV-discordant couples.[37]

Importantly, He Jiankui claimed that he is "against genome editing for enhancement" and that "he would conduct the experiment on his own unborn daughter if she were at risk with [sic] HIV infection."[38] But his experiments underscore the murkiness inherent in drawing clear distinctions between some prophylactic and enhancement GGE interventions.

Conferring natural immunity to the HIV virus by deleting a fragment of the CCR5 receptor may, at first glance, appear to fit squarely within the confines of prophylactic intervention under Category 2 experiments because the manipulation is meant to prevent HIV infection upon a future exposure event. However, the CCR5 receptor has recently been implicated in diverse functional roles not related to HIV protection, including cognitive function,[39] enhanced recovery following stroke,[40] and increased susceptibility to the West Nile virus.[41] Accordingly, He Jiankui's experiments may very well have unintended consequences for the twin girls born from his experiment. Because the biological and physiological functions of the CCR5 receptor are not yet fully elucidated, the *CCR5* gene is not a prudent target at this point in time, and He Jiankui could theoretically bear responsibility for latent harms brought on by his genetic manipulation[42]—at least in jurisdictions willing to recognize such causes of action. The same principle applies to other potential targets of prophylactic GGE intervention in polygenic diseases for which genetic mechanisms and molecular pathways are not completely understood, such as obesity, cancer, and diabetes, among others.

The takeaway point is that prophylactic intervention ought to apply only to instances where the desired results match the intended purpose. Safety and efficacy must be clearly established, through empirical scientific evidence, for any molecular targets of GGE. This is not to say that researchers must know *everything* there is to know about a gene, or DNA target, before certain GGE interventions are allowed to proceed. Such a standard would be impracticable and could stunt scientific progress that seeks to ameliorate human disease and suffering. As with any medical intervention, the decision to perform GGE would involve many factors, including an assessment of the benefits and risks to the child and family.

Until researchers understand the molecular basis underlying many human diseases and conditions—which will take a substantial amount of time—a robust link cannot exist between intended purpose and actual result in any GGE intervention. Therefore, under a jurisprudence of scientific empiricism, the constitutionally sanctioned assumption that parents can make decisions in the best interests of the child is inapplicable to Category 2 GGE interventions.[43]

In sum, many GGE applications that fall within the sphere of Category 2 are likely to involve polygenic, as opposed to monogenic, conditions. As a result, the technology is unlikely to be ready for clinical use anytime soon. Premature laws and regulations concerning the sanction or prohibition of GGE prophylactic interventions should be avoided at this early time of technological development.

C *Murky Lines*

The third category of GGE applications relates to interventions for cosmetic or enhancement purposes. Interventions under this category might involve genetic modifications associated with traits such as height, musculature, hair color, intellectual ability, and athletic ability, among others.

The issue here is similar to that in Category 2: Parents may have a constitutional right to bear healthy children, but do they have a constitutional right to bear children with brown hair and green eyes? The scope and authority of state intervention under Category 3 GGE uses may be stronger than those in Category 2. But this is not to say that all cosmetic or enhancement GGE applications should be prohibited. After all, parents can lawfully submit their children to cosmetic procedures—such as rhinoplasty, polydactyly reconstructive surgery, among others—without violating the Constitution. Assuming that GGE procedures for cosmetic or enhancement purposes could be performed safely and effectively at the molecular level, the issue then becomes whether or not such procedures should be treated differently merely because they are done at an embryonic stage.

One notable distinction here is that parents who subject their children to some types of cosmetic surgeries will—depending on the child's age at the time of the procedure—receive input from the child as to whether to go forward with said surgery, even when the parents are the ultimate decision makers. In contrast, parents who perform GGE on their embryos are purportedly the sole and final arbiters. This distinction, in a way, strengthens the legal basis for therapeutic GGE under *Parham* and *Yoder* when compared to cosmetic or enhancement GGE interventions. Parental autonomy in matters of child rearing, which includes the decision to subject a child to cosmetic reconstructive surgery, is fairly broad even if "not agreeable to the child."[44] An individual likely could grow up wishing her parents did not choose green eyes or a broad nose for her, but she is unlikely to grow up and decide that she would prefer her parents did nothing to correct a deleterious mutation that would lead to life-threatening disease. Implied consent is almost embedded in a decision to perform therapeutic GGE intervention. Thus, the doctrine of parental autonomy and the presumption that parents generally "act in their child's best interest" collectively strengthen the rationale for therapeutic GGE in cases where scientific evidence exists to establish the safety and efficacy of the desired genetic modification.[45]

Consider traits associated with obesity, smaller breast size, or baldness. Today, individuals may elect to undergo surgical procedures—such as gastric bypass surgery, abdominoplasty (tummy tuck), breast augmentation, or hair transplantation—to alter their physical appearance and improve self-image. If an individual carries certain alleles that predispose her to developing any of those traits—which are at least partly heritable[46]—and wishes to perform GGE to reduce the likelihood of passing those alleles to her offspring, should the law be concerned with such types of GGE interventions? Assuming that safety and efficacy are not part of the equation, reasonable people may disagree about the answer to that question depending on a multitude of factors, including financial, egalitarian, ethical, and moral considerations.

In any event, as laid out above, time currently favors the creation of a rational and robust legal approach to GGE concerning Categories 2 and 3. Because not all prophylactic, cosmetic, and enhancement concerns for GGE uses are scientifically based and their development is not technologically feasible at this time[47]—and perhaps may not be even in the near future—premature laws and regulations concerning the authorization or prohibition of Category 3 GGE interventions should also be avoided.

D *You Shall Not Edit*

The fourth category of GGE applications concerns the potential modification of traits that raise concerns of discrimination already prohibited by the law. Like many of the traits that fall under Categories 2 and 3 of the proposed framework, Category 4 traits are unlikely to be within the realm of clinical possibility in the near future. Nevertheless, a special history of discrimination—against race, gender, sexual orientation, specific disabilities,[48] etc.—counsels against sanctioning modifications of the genetic composition of germ cells related to these traits, regardless of whether or not it ever becomes possible to alter them. Because these traits create a likelihood of unlawful discrimination against specific groups, there is little to no constitutional justification to pursue GGE interventions in this realm.

Although some of these traits cannot currently be engineered, they are routinely selected for or against using modern reproductive technologies without violating any laws. For instance, couples have been free to select the gender of embryos through IVF and PGD for decades. The same is true for parents who are deaf or have achondroplasia and other forms of dwarfism. Sexual orientation, on the other hand, is not a trait that can be screened for because a definitive genetic basis for it —if one even exists—has not been established. Regarding race, humans have, in effect, selected and continue to select for this trait in offspring indirectly by choosing a mate who fits particular preferences.

Selection of all these traits using IVF and PGD is drastically different from modification of the same traits via GGE technologies. The former merely selects an already existing embryo that naturally features all the desired traits, whereas the latter would involve genetic engineering to modify nucleotides in an embryo's genome with the intent that such manipulation would give rise to desired phenotypic characteristics. Genetic engineering of such complex polygenic traits is unlikely to be possible at this point in time, not merely because the technology is not yet capable of producing the intended result but simply because we do not know enough about the genetic basis underlying most of these traits.

Clear lines should be drawn to make Category 4 GGE uses unpalatable to perform in the clinical setting. And the Supreme Court's equal protection and due process jurisprudence can serve as a robust guide that justifies prohibition of GGE interventions intended to modify traits that raise concerns of unlawful discrimination. Indeed, the Supreme Court has at times invoked due process and equal protection principles to strike down precedents and laws that targeted some minorities and disadvantaged groups on the basis of race, gender, or sexual orientation.[49] Thus, the evolution of laws and jurisprudence aimed at protecting minorities from invidious government discrimination throughout US history could serve as a guide to inform law and policy makers on the suitability of select uses of GGE that raise concerns of unlawful discrimination.

Consider the issue of race, which is inextricably linked to eugenics.[50] Due to the sensitive history of racial discrimination and systemic racial inequalities in the United States—as well as abroad—it would be unwise to allow parents to edit genetic sequences associated with changing an embryo's race—even if it were ever technologically feasible to do so. This principle would apply to cases in which parents of a majority group wish to bear offspring of a racial minority group and vice versa.[51] Government restrictions on these types of GGE interventions would almost certainly pass rational basis review because a legitimate government interest likely exists in avoiding the institutionalization of race-conscious reproductive policies that could lead to unlawful discrimination against select discrete and insular groups. Simply put, it is hard to conceive any *constitutional* justification to endorse the use of GGE interventions to edit an embryo's race.

Under the same reasoning, the Constitution would likewise not permit parents to use GGE methods to "edit out" a preexisting disability in a zygote or embryo, particularly because alternative means currently exist—such as contraception,

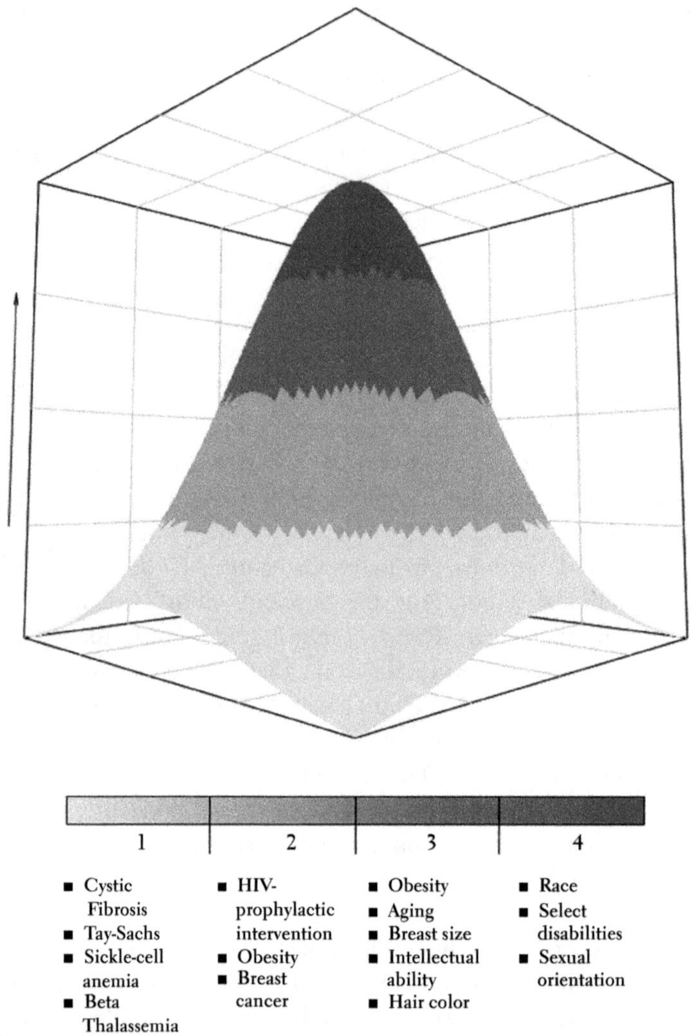

FIGURE 11.1 Taxonomy of select germline genome editing applications

abortion, and PGD—to achieve the ultimate result of not having disabled offspring. Although some might argue that removing a disability from an embryo's genome has a therapeutic purpose, the history of discrimination against particular disabilities embedded in our culture cautions against that proposition. And we must remember that many individuals that society perceives as having a disability do not actually consider themselves disabled and are able to lead meaningful lives. The analysis may change, however, if both parents bear genes that all but guarantee their offspring will be born with a particular type of disability. Under that scenario the parents lack alternative means to achieve their goal of bearing a child without a disability and, thus, could challenge GGE prohibitions under a strict scrutiny standard. Whether the disability at issue overcomes strict scrutiny may depend on how closely linked the disability is to a putative Category 1 purpose.

By the same token, parents should not be allowed to "edit in" disabilities into their embryos. Although members of specific groups with disabilities may sometimes wish to procreate and bear a child who shares their disability—for example, blindness, deafness, etc.—society ought not to endorse bestowing a disability upon human embryos. And the law ought not to be used for such purposes either. Under this scenario, the disabled parents would already have alternative legal and scientific means to select, screen, or discard embryos bearing desirable traits. For instance, a deaf, lesbian couple made headlines when they used a deaf sperm donor with a family history of deafness to increase the likelihood of conceiving a deaf son.[52] The couple, who already had a deaf daughter, expressed a desire to bear children who would be able to share their culture.

In sum, our equal protection and due process jurisprudence supports drawing a line that prohibits individuals to either edit in or edit out traits associated with discrimination already prohibited by the law.[53] Government restrictions on the use of GGE for Category 4 purposes—assuming they will ever become technologically feasible to perform—should be examined under a rational basis standard of review, which only require the government to articulate a legitimate purpose. The proposed framework under Category 4 aims to take eugenics out of the GGE equation. In so doing, it reduces the likelihood that eugenics and "designer babies" will pollute decision making in the GGE context, which would ultimately promote fruitful dialogue and debate about the benefits and risks of availing humanity of the use of technologies for genome editing.[54]

II FOOD POLICY PERSPECTIVES

As is evident from our discussion in Chapters 6 and 7, it is quite probable that certain types of genetically modified crops derived via gene editing will escape regulation under the Coordinated Framework. However, perhaps the most interesting question is not how will gene-edited crops be regulated, but rather *should* they be regulated at all?

If the hypothetical banana in Chapter 7 is nearly identical to a naturally occurring cultivar and the mutation has been found in nature, it is puzzling to imagine the government treating the crop differently than one developed via traditional plant breeding methods. If anything, the banana would presumably be safer because any genomic changes are likely to be very precise and their exact location would be known.

A *Science versus Policy*

For better or worse, issues concerning the contours of regulatory oversight and policy making cannot be resolved in a scientific vacuum, in which the sole and primary considerations necessary to adjudicate controversies orbit the relevant scientific facts and evidence. Quite the contrary, the process of developing policy is inherently complex and dependent on a multitude of factors—legal, economic, social, political, and others.[55] In fact, studies suggest that scientific-based evidence is often eclipsed by other considerations, and those who develop and promote model public health laws—laws or private policies publicly recommended by organizations for adoption by government bodies or private entities—frequently provide scant information about the methods and evidence used in developing such laws.[56] This policy "reality" can be difficult to grasp for many scientists and advocates of strict science-based law and policy making who are routinely dismayed when law and policies eschew scientific evidence.

Consider, for example, a scenario in which the CRISPR banana illustrated in Chapter 7 is commercially viable but threatens local economies because producers are suddenly unshackled from the spending associated with care and maintenance of the natural banana that is susceptible to disease. Technological advances in genome editing may save the banana from extinction, but impose high social costs such as job losses for hundreds or thousands of workers that irrigate fields with pesticides and fungicides, perform labor on the land, and remove individual plants when signs of infection appear.

This scenario is not far from the actual tensions between heeding scientific recommendations or weighing other nonscientific factors. For instance, President Donald Trump signed an Executive Order in 2017 to "review existing regulations that potentially burden the development or use of domestically produced energy resources and appropriately suspend, revise, or rescind those that unduly burden the development of domestic energy resources beyond the degree necessary to protect the public interest or otherwise comply with the law."[57] The Executive Order was seen by many as an effort to roll back climate-change policies implemented during the Obama Administration.[58] Critics of the move to curb such policies argued that the Trump Administration was favoring the coal industry and other energy interest groups over scientists' warnings concerning a "future of severe droughts, floods, rising sea levels and food shortages" as a result of climate change.[59] Trump's comments during the Executive Order's signing ceremony illustrate the significance that nonscientific factors play in developing national policy. At the conclusion of his speech, he addressed a group of coal miners present at the ceremony and remarked: "Come on, fellas. Basically, you know what this is? You know what it says, right? You're going back to work."[60]

Social, economic, and political costs may not rank at the top of scientists' concerns, but considering those costs is likely a pivotal task for elected public officials and other policy makers who must answer to their constituents.

Although scientists and policy makers can sometimes share common interests and goals, they largely operate on a myriad of distinct functional systems of accountability, career development, research methodology, and problem-solving. Scientists—and scholars in general—are typically interested in pushing the boundaries of knowledge and drawn to questions of theoretical or empirical value to them.[61] They are accountable under a system of peer review and advance their careers by publishing work that will impress others in their field.[62] There often is no reward system for scientists to engage in policy development.[63] Involvement in controversial policy debates may actually be detrimental to scientists' careers by making them subject to personal attacks[64]—which, unlike politicians, scientists are not sufficiently inured to—or impacting their ability to secure funding for their work via research grants.[65] Accordingly, it is no surprise that scientists seldom engage in policy development.

Policy makers, on the other hand, have little to no interest in the types of theoretical or empirical inquiries that fuel scientists' endeavors.[66] They value research, but usually only if it serves as a tool to tackle imminent and obvious problems that their constituents face.[67] Policy makers are held accountable at the voting ballot, either directly or indirectly depending on whether they are elected officials or appointed by them. This system of accountability guarantees that individuals in charge of policy development will give great weight to public opinion, particularly when an issue receives considerable attention in the media.[68] Indeed, research suggests that when confronted with a tough policy issue, policy makers seldom turn to published literature.[69] Instead, they often turn to their constituents, a group that may include lobbyists and other interests groups.[70] The end result of this process is that policy makers can adopt a patchwork of policies that exhibit little regard, or even run contrary, to scholarly and scientific-based research.[71]

B *Research- and Science-Based Policy Development*

There are several obstacles to developing science-based public policy in the realm of GMOs. Perhaps the most intractable impediment is overcoming the breed of hyper sensationalism—namely, deceptive simplicity[72]—that can sometimes flourish within public opinion, which flows directly from the public's lack of education about the science concerning GMOs in general, and GM foods in particular. A potentially effective strategy to ameliorate this problem is to develop policies that aim to tackle a range of seemingly peripheral, but fundamentally central, areas surrounding regulation of GMOs and technological advances in general.

1 Transparency Goes a Long Way

The bulk of opposition to GMOs in the public discourse stems primarily from perceptions that corporate conglomerates with ulterior motives control the output of scientific research available on the health and safety risks of GMOs.[73] As pointed out in Chapter 6, evidence suggests that a vast majority of the peer-reviewed studies on the safety of GMOs do not actually corroborate conspiracy theories about insidious links between the research published by scientists all over the world and corporate efforts to undermine public health and the environment. However, it is also true that many peer-reviewed studies—both in favor and in opposition of GMOs—are published by authors with some industry ties.[74]

Given the highly charged controversies surrounding GMOs in recent years, it would be beneficial for industry and government agencies to work together to formulate and implement policies that make more scientific health and testing data public. Publication of these data would involve a careful and delicate balance between (1) protecting intellectual property rights—such as trade secrets—and confidential business information (CBI) of producers of GM crops, and (2) ensuring adequate disclosure of health and safety data to the public.[75]

In general, the law permits companies to avail themselves of the right to claim some or all of the data submitted to regulatory agencies as CBI.[76] However, the 1990 case concerning the use of recombinant bovine growth hormone (rbGH) in dairy cattle[77] set a unique, and presumably limited, precedent for a federal regulatory agency's decision to publish scientific information used in the safety evaluation of a product prior to its approval.[78] In that case, the FDA decided to publish a summary of the relevant health and safety data to address public concerns about potential hazards from the use of rbGH that had been reported in the media.[79] Although the FDA's decision to make the data public did not put to rest all controversies surrounding rbGH,[80] it brought an increased level of transparency to the regulatory process. Industry players and policy makers should consider the rbGH case as a potential precursory model that can be tweaked to educate and allay public concerns surrounding select biotechnologies.

On the topic of transparency, for example, the National Academies of Sciences, Engineering, and Medicine report on genetically engineered crops (NASEM Crop Report) recommended that GM crop producers publicly disclose as much health and safety data submitted to regulatory agencies during the approval process as possible, and that regulatory exemptions from disclosure should be as narrow as possible.[81] However, the NASEM Crop Report did not elaborate or provide guidance regarding what constitutes a narrow exemption, which would ultimately be an issue of law. Furthermore, the amount of information a corporation deems to fall under an "as much as possible" category for purposes of voluntary disclosure is likely to be substantially different from the amount of information that a regulatory agency, or even the public in general, will deem appropriate to disclose. A recommendation without some degree of specificity is, therefore, likely to vanish in rhetorical quicksand. Accordingly, this chapter goes a step further and recognizes that industry and government agencies could use the rbGH case as a starting point to delineate the contours of the relationship between data disclosure and regulatory exemptions that consider the interests of GM crop developers and the public.

2 Liberal Disclosures

The concern engendered by the appearance of deep-seated conflicts of interests as perceived by many who oppose GMOs is not entirely unreasonable. After all, history has shown that in some instances, powerful corporate entities—as well as the individuals who lead them—can act unethically and put financial interests ahead of their social responsibilities to the public. A notorious example is the case of the tobacco industry—circa the early 1950s—and the smear campaign it launched in response to the peer-reviewed scientific evidence and consensus that had crystallized around the deleterious health hazards of smoking.[82]

Interestingly, the case of the tobacco industry involved a powerful lobby deploying an arsenal of strategies designed to undermine the legitimacy of scientific research, engineer controversies about purported conflicts of interest, and generate public skepticism of science by calling for *more research* and offering funding as a public-relations plot.[83] In contrast, GMO-related controversies in the last decade or two have been propelled mainly by activist organizations defying powerful corporations that seek to commercialize the production of GM crops. Although not exactly analogous, the legitimacy of scientific evidence is at the core of both controversies. But unlike the case of the tobacco industry—in which the corporations tried to undermine the science that had accumulated on the health risks of tobacco—biotechnology corporations now seek shelter in the peer-reviewed scientific evidence, while activist entities dismiss the peer-reviewed scientific consensus and promote public skepticism by calling for more research to be performed on the health impacts of GMO consumption.[84]

The more recent infamous Volkswagen affair also comes to mind.[85] In 2017, the auto maker agreed to plead guilty to federal conspiracy charges to defraud the United States government and pay a record $4.6 billion fine for selling vehicles with software designed to cheat pollution laws.[86] Given some high-profile corporate scandals in the last decades, it is no surprise that some segments of the public may distrust powerful interests and corporations.

To mitigate some of the controversies associated with either the existence or appearance of conflicts of interest in scientific research, policy makers and scientific publishers should promote full disclosure of all potential conflicts in scientific publications. Because the appearance of a conflict of interest can damage a journal's reputation, publishers ought to require disclosure of all competing interests—financial, political, institutional, personal, etc.[87]

Journals may enforce this policy by issuing special corrections for inadvertent omissions, and imposing fines or banning repeat offenders from publishing work in the journal and its affiliates. Government agencies should implement strict guidelines outlining compulsory disclosure of any possible conflicts of interest for specified periods of time—for example, sources of funding that may raise conflicts for the three, five, or seven years preceding the published research. The guidelines should further explicitly communicate consequences for failing to disclose conflicts, which could include a mix of penalties, requirements to enroll and attend ethics seminars, or even temporarily banning repeat offenders from applying for government grants.

Adhering to clear and robust conflict-of-interest policies can help scientists defend the integrity of their work. For instance, shortly after the NASEM Crop Report was released, a study criticized some members of the committee for not disclosing apparent financial and institutional conflicts of interest.[88] The study claimed that the NASEM failed to follow disclosure requirements set forth in the Federal Advisory Committee Act.[89] The NASEM quickly responded to the allegations by pointing out that it has "a stringent, well-defined, and transparent conflict-of-interest policy, with which all members of [the] study committee complied[,]" and that "its report underwent the Academies' usual rigorous, external, and anonymous peer-review process before it was approved for publication."[90] The NASEM further characterized the authors of the study and its conclusions as "unfair and disingenuous" for applying "their own perception of conflict of interest ... in place of [the NASEM's] tested and trusted conflict-of-interest policies."[91]

3 Dedicated Grants

Another potential strategy that could impact the advancement of scientific-based policy development in the realm of GMOs is to promote policies that erect a buffer zone between industry and scientific research. Independent researchers at public universities and nonprofit institutions must sometimes rely on private industry players for sources of funding due to scarcity of government funds or programs. This, in turn, leads to perceived or apparent conflicts of interest between the researchers and their funders.

To address this problem, policy makers should consider the use of dedicated grants to encourage independent study of the short- and long-term effects of GM food consumption. For instance, in 2017, the State of Washington appropriated funds for a Dedicated Marijuana Account to study the short- and long-term health effects of marijuana use as part of Initiative 502 (I-502).[92] I-502 provides research funds for proposals awarded under a peer-review process on the basis of scientific merit.[93]

The National Institute of Food and Agriculture and the USDA also jointly administer the Biotechnology Risk Assessment Research Grants (BRAG) program.[94] The BRAG program was created to "support the generation of new information that will assist Federal regulatory agencies in making science-based decisions about the environmental effects of introducing organisms genetically engineered [] by recombinant nucleic acid techniques."[95] However, the BRAG program is limited in reach due to funding limitations—$4.5 million in fiscal year (FY) 2020, up from $4 million in FY 2017.[96] Similar programs of dedicated grants could be instituted by other federal and state agencies to support increased independent research on the potential long-term effects of GMO consumption.

Admittedly, developing such policies can be difficult in an ever-increasing political environment of budgetary cuts to scientific research.[97] However, from a science-based policy perspective, it may be worthwhile in the long run for policy makers to consider all avenues to develop policies to support independent scientific research.

For instance, to pay for its dedicated grants program, the State of Washington designated the Liquor and Cannabis Board as the regulatory entity in charge of collecting "marijuana excise taxes, license fees, penalties, forfeitures, and all other moneys including income, or revenue received [from] marijuana-related activities."[98]

4 Keeping Up with the Technology

A fundamental question regarding crops developed via traditional breeding methods and transgenic crops containing recombinant DNA material is the degree to which changes in the crop's genome may ultimately render the plant hazardous to humans.[99] As detailed in Chapter 6, GMOs are produced using nonrecombinant, as well as recombinant, DNA methods.[100] However, the current regulatory scheme under the Coordinated Framework only requires health and safety testing of crops produced through recombinant DNA technology, despite the fact that both categories of making GMOs can lead to unintended changes in the plant's genome.

As laid out in Chapter 6, a large body of peer-reviewed literature concerning the health and environmental safety of GMOs has accumulated in the past two decades. But it is important to recognize that human knowledge is not absolute. We may continue to learn more about the science behind GM crops as technological improvements in methods of detection and statistical analysis in the realm of "omics"[101] disciplines occur. The field of omics specifically concerns the large-scale interactions, relationships, and networks within biological systems. Thus, for example, genomics is the large-scale study of the genomes of organisms, proteomics is the large-scale study of proteins produced by organisms, and metabolomics is the large-scale study of metabolites produced from cellular processes.[102]

Already, a wealth of information has been compiled about the equivalence of GM crops compared to their near isogenic[103] non-GM counterparts.[104] Many of the omics assessments performed to date reveal that GM crops do not raise safety concerns relative to non-GM crops, even when some compositional differences, which are within the range of expected natural variation due to environmental growth conditions, are detected.[105] Despite the advantages and potential uses of emerging omics technologies as powerful research tools, mandatory requirements of omics safety assessments of GM crops are not appropriate at this point in time given the early stage of some omics tools, which can be susceptible to bias, experimental design flaws, and statistical errors.[106]

As technological advances in omics disciplines accrue and gaps in methodology and statistical analysis begin to close, policy makers ought to develop policies that encourage researchers and GM crop developers to incorporate modern technologies—including high-throughput whole-genome sequencing (WGS), mass spectrometry, chromatin immunoprecipitation followed by sequencing (ChIP-Seq), Bisulfite sequencing, RNA sequencing, and others—in their research, so long as these tools do not pose undue financial burdens.[107] Fortunately, the use of modern technologies is unlikely to be a burden on all major GM crop producers.

Consider the downward trend in genome-sequencing costs over the past two decades. Estimates of the total cost to sequence the first human genome at the dawn of the twenty first century range from half a billion to one billion dollars.[108] By 2006, the cost had dropped to roughly between twenty and twenty-five million dollars.[109] Today, that figure has dropped to approximately 1,000 to 1,500 dollars.[110]

Given the increasing accessibility of these technologies, it may be prudent, in the near future, to require GM crop producers to submit omics data to corroborate their products' "substantial equivalence" to crops developed via traditional breeding methods when seeking approval before regulatory agencies. Substantial equivalence in this context refers to the concept that "an assessment of a novel food, in particular one that is genetically modified, should demonstrate that the food is as safe as its traditional counterpart."[111] Policy makers should weight the benefits and costs of imposing such a requirement, which would inevitably add a regulatory burden on developers in the short-term,[112] but may help to allay the type of fervid controversies concerning GM products in recent times. It may also be in the interest of GM crop producers to make that information publicly available to demonstrate to the general public that GM crops are indeed virtually indistinguishable from traditional crops.

Lastly, it is important to point out that promoting policies for omics technology development could present new opportunities to reassess what constitutes "substantial equivalence," and whether the concept in its current incarnation is an adequate standard for GM crop production safety assessments.[113]

Case in point, a recent omics study of GM maize and its isogenic non-GM counterpart reported that the nutritional and compositional contents of the two crops were not substantially equivalent and, thus, argued that the commonly used standard should not be used as proof of safety.[114] Of course, finding a compositional difference in a food or crop is not prima facie evidence of a safety risk.[115] Although the study indicated that a clear mechanistic link between food compositional differences and deleterious health effects of long-term consumption of the GM crop have not been established,[116] anti-GMO outlets rushed to sensationalize the report by claiming it reveals "serious safety implications" related to the toxic and carcinogenic effects of GMOs.[117] The study was promptly criticized by many in the scientific community for, among other things, having inadequate statistical modeling, including flawed experimental designs, and confusing statistically significant with biologically significant differences.[118]

Without clear guidance on precisely what constitutes substantial equivalence[119] among crop varieties, and necessary improvements in omics technologies discussed earlier in this section, growing controversies over the complex meaning of substantial equivalence could ultimately fuel litigation. Accordingly, technological progress in omics tools could lead to significant developments for the implementation of the substantial equivalence standard.

* * *

The intersection of science, law, and policy is dynamic and multidimensional. This chapter has intertwined many of the concepts and ideas discussed throughout the book to introduce normative recommendations for developing legal and science-based policy in select areas of genome editing. The take-home message is that policy development is an inherently complex process that depends not only on strict science-based evidence, but on a multitude of legal, economic, social, political, and other factors that ultimately shape law and science. It is imperative to take these ancillary factors into account as genome-editing technologies continue to develop and mature.

Notes

1 Indeed, other fundamental rights enumerated by the Supreme Court are not absolute and could be subject to governmental restrictions. *See, e.g.*, Obergefell v. Hodges, 576 U.S. 644, 666 (2015) (implicitly restricting the fundamental right to marry only to "*couples*" or individuals in a "*two-person* union" (emphasis added)); Planned Parenthood of Se. Pa. v. Casey, 505 U.S. 833, 876 (1992) (per curiam) (holding certain restrictions on the right to have an abortion are constitutional unless they impose an "undue burden"); Wisconsin v. Yoder, 406 U.S. 205, 234 (1972) (articulating limits to parental autonomy when a child's safety or health are at risk). Accordingly, a fundamental right to perform GGE in certain contexts most likely would still be subject to some level of governmental interference that meets the burden of strict scrutiny. *See* Paul Enríquez, *Editing Humanity: On the Precise Manipulation of DNA in Human Embryos*, 97 N.C. L. REV. 1147, 1223–25 (2019) [hereinafter Enríquez, *Editing Humanity*].

2 The discussion in this section applies broadly to a myriad of congenital conditions of all types. At the same time, it focalizes on monogenic diseases because they are currently better characterized and studied than complex polygenic diseases. Monogenic conditions are, therefore, likely to be the main focus of early genome-editing therapies in the near future, but that will change as more knowledge accrues about the molecular foundations of polygenic conditions. *See* Paul Enríquez, *Genome Editing and the Jurisprudence of Scientific Empiricism*, 19 VAND. J. ENT. & TECH. L. 603, 636 (2017) [hereinafter Enríquez, *Genome Editing*]; Enríquez, *Editing Humanity*, *supra* note 1, at 1232.

3 *See* Eisenstadt v. Baird, 405 U.S. 438, 453 (1972) (emphasis added).

4 Skinner v. Oklahoma, 316 U.S. 535, 536 (1942).

5 The probability of developing a genetic disease depends on many factors, including patterns of inheritance. *See, e.g.*, *If a Genetic Disorder Runs in My Family,*

What Are the Chances that My Children Will Have the Condition?, GENETICS HOME REFERENCE, https://ghr.nlm.nih.gov/primer/inheritance/riskassessment [https://perma.cc/V2S2-5CFT]. In general, children are most at risk of inheriting a serious genetic condition when both parents are homozygous for particular mutations that can lead to certain diseases.

6 *Cf. Skinner*, 316 U.S. at 541 (holding that "[t]he power to sterilize, if exercised, may have subtle, far-reaching and devastating effects" on individuals affected by the law).

7 Roe v. Wade, 410 U.S. 113, 153 (1973).

8 *Id.*

9 *Skinner*, 316 U.S. at 536.

10 *Id.* at 541 (emphasis added).

11 *Id.*

12 *Moore* v. City of East Cleveland, 431 U.S. 494, 502 (1977) (plurality opinion).

13 Zablocki v. Redhail, 434 U.S. 374, 386 (1978).

14 Although the legal status of the parent-child relationship is unaffected by divorce between two parents, it should be noted that the law recognizes circumstances under which the parent-child bond can be severed. *See, e.g.*, Adoptive Couple v. Baby Girl, 570 U.S. 637, 641–42 (2013) (terminating paternal rights of a biological father who never had custody of his child); Michael H. v. Gerald D., 491 U.S. 110, 131–32 (1989) (restricting parental rights of unmarried fathers); Diamond v. Diamond, 283 P.3d 260, 261 (N.M. 2012) (addressing the issue of child emancipation); *In re* Moore, 306 N.C. 394, 405–06, 293 S.E.2d 127, 134 (1982) (terminating parental rights in response to child abuse or neglect). However, termination of parental rights, emancipation of minors, and other related principles are *legal* constructs. From a purely *biological* perspective, which encompasses the ambit of the fundamental right to "perpetuat[e] a [human] race . . . [and] have offspring" articulated in *Skinner*, *see Skinner*, 316 U.S. at 537, the parent-child genetic link is permanent.

15 Safety and efficacy are relative terms—"no technology is ever completely safe, or completely efficacious." OFFICE OF TECH. ASSESSMENT, ASSESSING THE EFFICACY AND SAFETY OF MEDICAL TECHNOLOGIES 17 (1978), https://ota.fas.org/reports/7805.pdf [https://perma.cc/M6VU-ZJ4A]. "Efficacy is defined in terms of a benefit; safety, in terms of a risk. . . . Neither efficacy nor safety is absolute. Both are discussed in terms of probability and magnitude of benefit or harm." *Id.* at 18 (emphasis omitted). Thus, for example, the FDA's determination that a drug is safe does not indicate a complete absence of risk or potential harm. Safety means that the therapeutic "benefits of the drug outweigh the risks." 21 U.S.C. § 355–1(a)(1) (Supp. 2017).

16 *Zablocki*, 434 U.S. at 386 (emphasis added).

17 Indeed, it is not difficult to imagine the opposite scenario in which the government might begin to mandate GGE intervention for prospective parents

carrying deleterious genetic mutations, so as to promote a myriad of governmental interests related to the protection of children and the reduction of social costs associated with health care and management of diseases. *See* Jacobson v. Massachusetts, 197 U.S. 11, 11–12 (1905) (upholding the authority of states to enforce compulsory vaccination statutes).

18 *See* Meyer v. Nebraska, 262 U.S. 390, 399 (1923).

19 *See* Parham v. J.R., 442 U.S. 584, 603 (1979) ("Most children, even in adolescence, simply are not able to make sound judgments concerning many decisions, including their need for medical care or treatment.").

20 The prospect of using GGE for benign, therapeutic purposes actually overcomes one of the possible limitations outlined in Chapter 10 relating to the protection of children from harm and exploitation articulated in *Prince*. *See* Prince v. Massachusetts, 321 U.S. 158, 166 (1944).

21 Several patterns of inheritance exist by which an individual may inherit a genetic condition, including, for example, autosomal dominant, autosomal recessive, codominant, and mitochondrial inheritance. For a brief explanation of each pattern, see, for example, *What Are the Different Ways in Which a Genetic Condition Can Be Inherited?*, GENETICS HOME REFERENCE, https://ghr.nlm.nih.gov/primer/inheritance/inheritancepatterns [https://perma.cc/Z3YJ-7Q6F]. The probability of inheriting a particular genetic disease varies depending on the pattern of inheritance and whether the parents are homozygous or heterozygous for a particular allele associated with genetic disease. Cases in which both parents are homozygous for a particular genetic disease are very rare, but they can occur. And potential arguments that GGE should be banned because only a small minority of couples would be affected by such prohibitions are likely to crumble before legal challenges brought by individuals asserting the principle that the Constitution protects the rights of individuals rather than the collective rights of groups. *See* District of Columbia v. Heller, 554 U.S. 570, 579 (2008) (explaining that "the right of the people" refers to individual and not "collective" rights).

22 The parents could elect to receive sperm, egg, or embryo donations from other individuals or decide to have an abortion as possible alternatives. Neither of these options, however, offers a path toward biological parenthood and, thus, cannot truly be considered alternatives within the general purview of the right to have biological offspring articulated in *Skinner*. *See* Skinner v. Oklahoma, 316 U.S. 535, 541 (1942).

23 Preimplantation genetic diagnosis refers to an ART technique that facilitates genetic profiling of human embryos—obtained through IVF—for the purpose of testing for genetic abnormalities. Peter Braude et al., *Preimplantation Genetic Diagnosis*, 3 NATURE REVIEWS: GENETICS 941, 941 (2002). The screening takes place prior to implantation in a woman's uterus and, therefore, can be

distinguished from in utero prenatal diagnosis or screening of an embryo or fetus. *See id.* PGD is often used as an alternative to abortion for parents with substantial risk of transmitting genetic disorders to their progeny by preventing a pregnancy from occurring in the first place. *Id.* at 942.

24 *See* Julie Steffann et al., *Could Failure in Preimplantation Genetic Diagnosis Justify Editing the Human Embryo Genome?*, 22 CELL STEM CELL 481, 481 (2018) ("In weighing the risks and benefits of [GGE], one needs to consider the potential of genome editing to cure genetic diseases at an early stage of life, and the concept that we have a moral duty to cure affected human embryos instead of discarding them.").

25 An alternative legal path would be to identify a de novo fundamental right to GGE for therapeutic purposes under *Glucksberg*'s two-prong test. *See* Washington v. Glucksberg, 521 U.S. 702, 703 (1997). It appears, however, that extending already-established rights affords the best strategy to crystallize a right to perform GGE for therapeutic purposes under procreative- and parental-autonomy principles. *See, e.g.*, Obergefell v. Hodges, 576 U.S. 644, 665 (2015) (extending an already existing right to marry for opposite-sex couples to same-sex couples); Carey v. Population Servs. Int'l, 431 U.S. 678, 681–82 (1977) (extending an already-existing right to purchase and use contraception for adults to minors under age sixteen); *see also* discussion in Chapter 10, Section III.

26 434 U.S. 47 (1977).

27 *Id.* at 54.

28 *Id.* at 48–50.

29 Roughly 1 percent of the world's Caucasian population carries a genetic mutation in the *CCR5* gene that confers immunity against the HIV virus. Enríquez, *Genome Editing*, *supra* note 2, at 633–34. Clinical trials are currently underway to explore possible cures for HIV using genome-editing technologies. *Id.* at 634.

30 NAT'L ACADS. SCIS., ENG'G & MED., HUMAN GENOME EDITING: SCIENCE, ETHICS, & GOVERNANCE 7–8 (Rona Briere & Helaine Resnick eds., 2017) [hereinafter NASEM REPORT] (emphasis added).

31 *See* Kevin M. De Cock, Harold W. Jaffe & James W. Curran, *Reflections on 30 Years of AIDS*, 17 EMERGING INFECTIOUS DISEASES 1044, 1044 (2011) (describing AIDS as an "inevitably fatal disease" when it was first documented in the early 1980s, while noting that the disease would go on to cause approximately 30 million deaths).

32 *See, e.g.*, AM. DIABETES ASS'N, FAST FACTS: DATA AND STATISTICS ABOUT DIABETES, https://professional.diabetes.org/sites/professional.diabetes.org/files/media/sci_2019_diabetes_fast_facts_sheet.pdf [https://perma.cc/3DRS-2YU5] (noting that "[d]iabetes kills more Americans every year than AIDS and breast cancer combined"); Mandy Freeman, *'I Believe It's Easier to Live with HIV than Being Diabetic'*, HEALTH24 (May 29, 2017), https://www.health24.com/Medical/HIV-AIDS/Real-life-story/i-believe-its-easier-to-live-with-hiv-than-being-dia

betic-20170526 [https://perma.cc/R5DY-VL2K]; Max Pemberton, *As a Doctor, I'd Rather Have HIV than Diabetes*, SPECTATOR (Apr. 19, 2014), https://www.spectator.co.uk/2014/04/why-id-rather-have-hiv-than-diabetes/# [https://perma.cc/F62Z-UJHS] ("As a doctor I can tell you that, medically speaking, I'd rather have HIV than diabetes. . . . [T]he prognosis for those with type 2 diabetes is much worse than for those with HIV. . . . For those with HIV, providing [sic] they take their medication, there are very few problems.").

33 Gilead Sciences, Inc. markets "TRUVADA for PrEP® (preexposure prophylaxis) [as] a prescription medicine that can help reduce the risk of getting HIV-1 through sex, when taken every day and used together with safer sex practices." TRUVADA, https://www.truvada.com/ [https://perma.cc/2ZX9-87RN].

34 *See, e.g.*, Siobhan O'Grady, *Every Day, 170 Young People Are Infected with HIV in West and Central Africa, and Many Can't Afford Treatment*, L.A. TIMES (Apr. 2, 2018), https://www.latimes.com/world/la-fg-africa-aids-20180402-story.html [https://perma.cc/V3HD-4CV2].

35 NASEM REPORT, *supra* note 30, at 7.

36 *See* Gerry Shih & Carolyn Y. Johnson, *Chinese Genomics Scientist Defends His Gene-Editing Research in First Public Appearance*, WASH. POST (Nov. 28, 2018), https://www.washingtonpost.com/world/chinese-genomics-scientist-defends-his-gene-editing-research-in-first-public-appearance/2018/11/28/b99b5eba-f2e1-11e8-9240-e8028a62c722_story.html?noredirect=on&utm_term=.b1f843707a20 [https://perma.cc/YTS4-XJ54].

37 *See* Maryam Zafer et al., *Effectiveness of Semen Washing to Prevent Human Immunodeficiency Virus (HIV) Transmission and Assist Pregnancy in HIV-Discordant Couples: A Systematic Review and Meta-Analysis*, 105 FERTILITY & STERILITY 645, 646 (2016).

38 *See* Shih & Johnson, *supra* note 36.

39 Miou Zhou et al., *CCR5 Is a Suppressor for Cortical Plasticity and Hippocampal Learning and Memory*, 5 ELIFE, no. e20985, Dec. 20, 2016, at 1, 2 (reporting a previously unknown role for CCR5 in cognitive function).

40 Mary T. Joy et al., *CCR5 Is a Therapeutic Target for Recovery After Stroke and Traumatic Brain Injury*, 176 CELL 1143, 1143 (2019) (reporting findings that CCR5 inhibition or knockdown in mice and CCR5 loss of function in humans induce enhanced recovery of neurological impairments, motor control, and cognitive function after stroke and traumatic brain injury).

41 *See, e.g.*, William G. Glass et al., *CCR5 Deficiency Increases Risk of Symptomatic West Nile Virus Infection*, 203 J. EXPERIMENTAL MED. 35, 35 (2006) ("We conclude that CCR5 mediates resistance to symptomatic WNV infection.").

42 *See* Dov Fox, *Reproductive Negligence*, 117 COLUM. L. REV. 149, 161 (2017) (advocating reproductive negligence as a cause of action in cases where reproductive professionals engage in negligent acts).

43 *See* Parham v. J.R., 442 U.S. 584, 604 (1979) (noting that "the traditional presumption that the parents act in the best interests of their child should apply" absent evidence of neglect or abuse).
44 *See id.* at 603.
45 *See id.* at 602–03.
46 *See, e.g.*, Nicola Pirastu et al., *GWAS for Male-Pattern Baldness Identifies 71 Susceptibility Loci Explaining 38% of the Risk*, 8 NATURE COMMC'NS Art. no. 1584, Nov. 17, 2017, at 1, 7 (reporting data that suggest baldness is among the most heritable complex traits); Tracey D. Wade, Gu Zhu & Nicholas G. Martin, *Body Mass Index and Breast Size in Women: Same or Different Genes?*, 13 TWIN RES. & HUM. GENETICS 450, 450 (2010) (finding breast size is moderately heritable).
47 *See, e.g.*, Enríquez, *Genome Editing*, *supra* note 2, at 679–85 (providing a detailed outline of the current state of empirical scientific knowledge, vis-à-vis the molecular and genetic basis of human intelligence and cognition, to highlight the inherent complexity of polygenic traits and contrast it to widespread public misperceptions about genetic associations in trait formation and development); *see also* Hana Lango Allen et al., *Hundreds of Variants Clustered in Genomic Loci and Biological Pathways Affect Human Height*, 467 NATURE 832, 832 (2010) (reporting the existence of hundreds of genetic variants in at least 180 genetic loci that influence height in humans); Loic Yengo et al., *Meta-Analysis of Genome-Wide Association Studies for Height and Body Mass Index in ~700000 Individuals of European Ancestry*, 27 HUMAN MOLECULAR GENETICS 3641 (2018) (reporting 1,185 previously unidentified, height-associated, single-nucleotide polymorphisms).
48 Current legislation and jurisprudence interpreting the Americans with Disabilities Act of 1990 might be used to inform what qualifies as a disability that ought to be shielded from GGE interventions. *See* 42 U.S.C. §§ 12101–12102 (2012).
49 *See, e.g.*, Bowers v. Hardwick, 478 U.S. 186, 196 (1986) (upholding the constitutionality of a statute that criminalized sexual activity among homosexual individuals), *overruled by* Lawrence v. Texas, 539 U.S. 558 (2003); Goesaert v. Cleary, 335 U.S. 464, 467 (1948) (upholding a state statute that prohibited women from being licensed as bartenders unless their father or husband owned the establishment), *overruled by* Craig v. Boren, 429 U.S. 190 (1976); Plessy v. Ferguson, 163 U.S. 537, 540 (1896) (upholding the constitutionality of a Louisiana statute that required "equal but separate accommodations for the white, and colored races"), *overruled by* Brown v. Bd. of Educ., 347 U.S. 483 (1954). Likewise, the Constitution has been amended to remedy institutional discrimination endorsed by the Supreme Court in the past. *See* Dred Scott v. Sandford, 60 U.S. (19 How.) 393, 452–54 (1857) (holding that persons of African descent could never lawfully become US citizens), *superseded by constitutional amendments*, U.S. CONST. amend. XIII; *id.* amend. XIV.

50 *See, e.g.*, Marius Turda, *Race, Science, and Eugenics in the Twentieth Century*, *in* THE OXFORD HANDBOOK OF THE HISTORY OF EUGENICS 62, 62–63 (Alison Bashford & Philippa Levine eds., 2010) (discussing the relationship between race and eugenics).

51 Suppose that, in order to save their offspring from what some may consider social "disabilities" rooted in racial inequality and injustice, *see generally* Kimani Paul-Emile, *Blackness as Disability?*, 106 GEO. L.J. 293 (2018) (arguing it may be appropriate to think of being black as disabling in the United States), some minority parents choose to bear offspring with features that resemble a racial majority group. Government endorsement of such GGE purposes could lead to pervasive abuses and discriminatory practices that go far beyond the limits of a putative fundamental right to perform GGE articulated earlier in this chapter.

52 M. Spriggs, *Lesbian Couple Create a Child Who Is Deaf like Them*, 28 J. MEDICAL ETHICS 283, 283 (2002).

53 *Cf.* Tandice Ossareh, Note, *Would You Like Blue Eyes with That? A Fundamental Right to Genetic Modification of Embryos*, 117 COLUM. L. REV. 729, 766 (2017) ("[T]here may be strong ethical motivations to limit certain types of modifications. However, in most cases, there is no principled legal reason to ban or restrict access to genetic modification . . . ."). In contrast, this chapter demonstrates that existing jurisprudence can guide the conception of limits on a putative right to GGE interventions.

54 *See* Enríquez, *Genome Editing*, *supra* note 2, at 613, 694.

55 *See, e.g.*, MASON A. CARPENTER & SANJYOT P. DUNUNG, CHALLENGES AND OPPORTUNITIES IN INTERNATIONAL BUSINESS V. 1.0 67, 73 (2012), http://2012books.lardbucket.org/pdfs/challenges-and-opportunities-in-international-business.pdf (linking some of these factors to global trade); Andy Norton & Diane Elson, *What's Behind the Budget? Politics, Rights and Accountability in the Budget Process* 5 (2002), https://www.odi.org/sites/odi.org.uk/files/odi-assets/publications-opinion-files/2422.pdf (connecting similar factors to budgetary policy).

56 *See, e.g.*, DeKeely Hartsfield et al., *A Review of Model Public Health Laws*, 97 AM. J. PUB. HEALTH S56, S59 (2007) (revealing findings from a study of 107 model public health laws published between 1907 and 2004 in which only 7 (6.5 percent) of the 107 sponsors provided scientific information to support the laws).

57 Exec. Order No. 13,782, 82 Fed. Reg. 16,093 (Mar. 27, 2017).

58 *See, e.g.*, Doral Davenport & Alissa J. Rubin, *Trump Signs Executive Order Unwinding Obama Climate Policies* (Mar. 28, 2017), https://www.nytimes.com/2017/03/28/climate/trump-executive-order-climate-change.html?_r=0.

59 *Id.*

60 Donald Trump, US President, Remarks at Signing of Executive Order to Create Energy Independence (Mar. 28, 2017), https://www.whitehouse.gov/the-press-

office/2017/03/28/remarks-president-trump-signing-executive-order-create-energy.

61 David N. Plank & Debbi Harris, *Minding the Gap Between Research and Policymaking, in* THE SAGE HANDBOOK FOR RESEARCH IN EDUCATION: ENGAGING IDEAS AND ENRICHING 38 (Clifton F. Conrad & Ronald C. Serlin eds., 2006).

62 *Id.*

63 Ross C. Brownson et al., *Researchers and Policymakers: Travelers in Parallel Universes*, 30 AM. J. PREVENTIVE MED. 164, 167 (2006).

64 *Id.*

65 *See, e.g.*, Keelie Lyn Elektra Murdock & *David Koepsell, Principals, Agents, and the Intersection Between Scientists and Policy-Makers: Reflections on the H5N1 Controversy*, 2 FRONTIERS IN PUB. HEALTH art. 109, at 3 (2014).

66 Plank & Harris, *supra* note 61, at 38.

67 *Id.*

68 *Id.*

69 *See, e.g.*, Richard Sorian & Terry Baugh, *Power of Information: Closing The Gap Between Research and Policy*, 21 HEALTH AFF. 264, 269 (2002).

70 *Id.*

71 Plank & Harris, *supra* note 61, at 39.

72 "Deceptive simplicity" is as an umbrella term used to refer to common substantive impediments to constructive debate that consist of impractical and often sensationalist claims about issues raised by scientific and technological advances. *See* Enríquez, *Genome Editing*, *supra* note 2, at 614–16.

73 *See* discussion in Chapter 6.

74 *See* Chapter 6, Section V.A.3.

75 Rena Steinzor & Matthew Shudtz, *Sequestered Science: Secrets Threatening Public Health*, CTR. FOR PROGRESSIVE REFORM 1 (Apr. 2007), http://www.progressivereform.org/articles/Secrecy_703.pdf.

76 *Id.* at 5.

77 *See generally* Judith C. Juskevich & C. Greg Guyer, *Bovine Growth Hormone: Human Food Safety Evaluation*, 249 SCIENCE 875 (1990).

78 Paul Enríquez, *GM-Food Regulations: Engage the Public*, 548 NATURE 31, 31 (2017).

79 *Id.*

80 *See* Richard Raymond et al., *Recombinant Bovine Somatotropin (rbST): A Safety Assessment*, NAT'L ANIMAL INTEREST ALL. 14–15 (Mar. 22, 2010), http://www.naiaonline.org/uploads/WhitePapers/RecombinantSomatotropinASafetyAssessment2010.pdf.

81 COMMITTEE ON GENETICALLY ENGINEERED CROPS: PAST EXPERIENCE AND FUTURE PROSPECTS; BOARD ON AGRICULTURE AND NATURAL RESOURCES; DIVISION ON EARTH AND LIFE STUDIES; NATIONAL ACADEMIES OF SCIENCES, ENGINEERING, AND

MEDICINE, GENETICALLY ENGINEERED CROPS: EXPERIENCES AND PROSPECTS 506 (2016) [hereinafter NASEM CROP REPORT].

82 *See* Allan M. Brandt, *Inventing Conflicts of Interest: A History of Tobacco Industry Tactics*, 102 AM. J. PUB. HEALTH 63 (2012).

83 *Id.*

84 *See* discussion in Chapter 6, Section V.A.3.

85 Nathan Bomey, *VW Pleads Guilty to Conspiracy, Obstruction of Justice; 6 Execs Charged*, USA TODAY (Jan. 11, 2017, 6:26 PM), https://www.usatoday.com/story/money/cars/2017/01/11/volkswagen-epa-doj-department-of-justice-settlement/96439678/.

86 *Id.*

87 *Conflict of Interest in Peer-Reviewed Medical Journals*, WORLD ASS'N OF MEDICAL EDITORS (Jul. 25, 2009), http://www.wame.org/about/conflict-of-interest-in-peer-reviewed-medical.

88 Sheldon Krimsky & Tim Schwab, *Conflicts of Interest Among Committee Members in the National Academies' Genetically Engineered Crop Study*, 12 PLoS ONE e0172317 (2017).

89 *Id.*

90 *Statement by the National Academies of Sciences, Engineering, and Medicine Regarding PLOS ONE Article on Our Study of Genetically Engineered Crops*, NAT'L ACADS. SCIS., ENG'G & MED. (Mar. 1, 2017), http://www8.nationalacademies.org/onpinews/newsitem.aspx?RecordID=312017b&utm_source=NASEM+News+and+Publications&utm_campaign=049bfc0b62-NAP_mail_new_2017–03-06&utm_medium=email&utm_term=0_96101de015-049bfc0b62-101937173&goal=0_96101de015-049bfc0b62-101937173&mc_cid=049bfc0b62&mc_eid=d85449f0d7.

91 *Id.*

92 *Guidelines for ADAI Small Grants with I-502 Marijuana*, ALCOHOL & DRUG ABUSE INST., http://adai.uw.edu/grants/Small%20Grants%20Guidelines%20Marijuana%20FINAL.pdf (last visited Apr. 14, 2017).

93 *Id.*

94 *Biotechnology Risk Assessment Research Grants Program*, U.S.D.A., https://nifa.usda.gov/sites/default/files/rfa/FY2017%20Biotechnology%20Risk%20Assessment%20Research%20Grants%20Program%20%28BRAG%29%20RFA.pdf.

95 *Id.* at 4.

96 *Id.* at 12.

97 *See, e.g.*, *NIH, DOE Office of Science Face Deep Cuts in Trump's First Budget*, SCIENCE (Mar. 16, 2017), http://www.sciencemag.org/news/2017/03/nih-doe-office-science-face-deep-cuts-trumps-first-budget.

98 H.B. 2136, 2015 Leg. 2d Spec. Sess. (Wash. 2015).

99 *See* discussion in Chapter 6, Sections IV–V.

100 *Id.*

101 Omics is a term that refers to the study of "the collective characterization and quantification of pools of biological molecules that translate into the structure, function, and dynamics of an organism or organisms." *Omics*, WIKIPEDIA, https://en.wikipedia.org/wiki/Omics.

102 *Id.*

103 A near isogenic line refers to a strain of an organism—for example, a plant—that has a near identical genetic composition, but for a few specific differences at certain genomic loci. Guangdi Yuang et al., *Development of Near-Isogenic Lines in a Parthenogenetically Reproduced Thrips Species, Frankliniella occidentalis*, 8 FRONTIERS PHYSIOLOGY art. 130, at 1 (2017) (citations omitted).

104 *See, e.g.*, Agnès E. Ricroch et al., *Evaluation of Genetically Engineered Crops Using Transcriptomic, Proteomic, and Metabolomic Profiling Techniques*, 155 PLANT PHYSIOLOGY 1752, 1753–57 (2011). *But cf.* Robin Mesnage et al., *An Integrated Multi-Omics Analysis of the NK603 Roundup-Tolerant GM Maize Reveals Metabolism Disturbances Caused by the Transformation Process*, 6 SCIENTIFIC REPS. art. no. 37855, at 1 (2016) (using a multi-omics approach to compare a widely commercialized GM crop and its non-GM isogenic line, and concluding that the two lines are not "substantially equivalent" in terms of nutritional and compositional content).

105 Ricroch et al., *supra* note 104, at 1755, 1757–59.

106 *See generally* Jackson O. Lay Jr. et al., *Problems with the "Omics"*, 25 TRENDS ANALYTICAL CHEMISTRY 1046 (2006); Ricroch et al., *supra* note 104, at 1757–58. *See also* NASEM CROP REPORT, *supra* note 81, at 395 (stating that, in order to realize the full potential of omics technologies, "a more comprehensive knowledge base of plant biology at the systems level (DNA, RNA, protein, and metabolites) should be constructed for the range of variation inherent in both conventionally bred and genetically engineered crop species.").

107 Note that some in the scientific community have criticized the idea of introducing policy proposals that require the use of high-throughput "omics" technologies in GM crop regulation because the state of the technology is not fully developed, and there is not enough information as of yet to correlate omics patterns to specific traits. *See* L. Val Giddings & Henry Miller, *US National Academies Report Misses the Mark*, 34 NATURE BIOTECHNOLOGY 1226, 1227 (2017).

108 *The Cost of Sequencing a Human Genome*, NAT'L HUMAN GENOME RES. INST. (Jul. 6, 2016), https://www.genome.gov/sequencingcosts/.

109 *Id.*

110 *Id.*

111 *Substantial Equivalence*, OECD, https://stats.oecd.org/glossary/detail.asp?ID=2604. The concept was first introduced in 1993 by the Organization for Economic Co-Operation and Development. *Id.* The concept has since been

adopted as a global standard for GM-food safety assessment by many national and international agencies, including the United States FDA. *Substantial Equivalence in Food Safety Assessment*, COUNCIL FOR BIOTECHNOLOGY INFORMATION (2001), http://thebeuselaer.weebly.com/uploads/6/3/8/4/6384873/substantial_equivalence.pdf.

112 Policy makers must also weigh the potential effects of those regulatory burdens on small businesses and farmers, which may not be able to compete with corporate conglomerates in an undue regulatory environment.

113 For instance, some critics have characterized the concept of substantial equivalence as unscientific, arbitrary, and intentionally vague. *Compare* Erik Millstone et al., *Beyond 'Substantial Equivalence,'* 401 NATURE 525, 525–26 (1999) (arguing that "substantial equivalence has never been properly defined" and "is a pseudo-scientific concept because it is a commercial and political judgment masquerading as if it were scientific."), *and* Mae-Wan Ho & Ricarda A. Steinbrecher, *Fatal Flaws in Food Safety Assessment: Critique of the Joint FAO/WHO Biotechnology and Food Safety Report*, THIRD WORLD NETWORK, 1, 23 (2002), http://www.twn.my/title2/biosafety/pdf/bio01.pdf (characterizing the principle as "unscientific," "arbitrary," and "intentionally vague and ill-defined so as to be as flexible, malleable and open to interpretation as possible"), *with* Harry A. Kuiper et al., *Substantial Equivalence—An Appropriate Paradigm for the Safety Assessment of Genetically Modified Foods?*, 181 82 TOXICOLOGY 427, 430 (2002) (opining that "[t]he concept of substantial equivalence is an adequate tool in order to identify safety issues related to genetically modified products that have a traditional counterpart. It is not a safety assessment procedure per se.").

114 *See* Mesnage et al., *supra* note 104, at 6. The study was coauthored by Gilles-Eric Séralini, who has published a string of anti-GMO reports in recent years. *See* Gilles-Eric Séralini, *Relevant Research*, GMOSERALINI, http://www.gmoseralini.org/research-papers/ (providing a compilation of research published by Séralini and colleagues purportedly linking GMOs, or the use of GMO-related chemicals, to a range of deleterious cellular and physiological outcomes in animal in vitro and in vivo studies).

115 *See* NASEM CROP REPORT, *supra* note 81, at 511.

116 Mesnage et al., *supra* note 104, at 10.

117 *See, e.g., Why You Should Really Think Twice About Eating GMO Corn*, ALTERNET, http://www.alternet.org/food/new-study-raises-questions-about-safety-eating-gmo-corn.

118 *See, e.g., Expert Reaction to Multiomics Analysis of NK603 GM Maize*, SCIENCE MEDIA CENTRE, http://www.sciencemediacentre.org/expert-reaction-to-multiomics-analysis-of-nk603-gm-maize/; *Séralini Paper: Molecular Analysis Shows GMO Corn Differs from Non-GMO—Is Difference Meaningful?*, GENETIC LITERARY PROJECT, https://geneticliteracyproject.org/2016/12/21/sera

lini-paper-molecular-analysis-shows-gmo-corn-differs-non-gmo-difference-meaningful/.

119 Although the FDA has broad discretion to make determinations about the safety and effectiveness of products under its regulatory oversight, courts have not always been "entirely comfortable with the FDA's interpretation of 'substantial equivalence.'" General Medical Co. v. FDA, 770 F.2d 214, 217 n.1 (D.C. Cir. 1985). In *General Medical*, a case involving a petition of reclassification of an antiperspirant device, the US Court of Appeals for the District of Columbia Circuit acknowledged that "[t]he determinations of safety and effectiveness are clearly crucial considerations in the classification of devices," but expressed concerns that the FDA's arguments may "require [the court] to make a hop and a skip of faith from the safety-and-effectiveness provisions to the classification provisions to the substantial-equivalence provisions." *Id.*

12

Epilogue

As we meet at the end of this journey, and before you and I embark on separate paths, let us reflect on the overarching theme of this book. My sincere hope is that you have gained a deeper understanding and appreciation of genome editing. This technology holds the power to fundamentally change the world, perhaps in ways we cannot yet begin to comprehend. How exciting it is that you and I are both alive at this time, when we can attest to having witnessed the world before and after the advent of genome editing!

Exciting as these times may be, they too carry heavy responsibilities, demand leadership and accountability, and call for resolute and sage action. We must not become distracted from those tasks. Scientists and interdisciplinary experts on genome editing bear a substantial burden to communicate properly and engage effectively with law and policy makers, as well as general audiences. Law and policy makers, in turn, have a responsibility to become informed, heed the advice of scientists and other experts, and engage openly and transparently with experts and the general public when conflicting laws and policies that are inconsistent with science-based principles become instituted. And the public has a civic duty to become better educated about issues related to genome editing—as with other important scientific breakthroughs of widespread significance—so that it is less susceptible to being duped by deceptive merchants with ulterior motives and dubious political, economic, and social agendas.

Cooperation among lawyers, scientists, and policy makers will be pivotal as genome-editing technologies continue to develop and mature in an increasingly globalized and interconnected world.[1] Genome editing has made it possible for scientists all over the world to modify the genetic composition of virtually every living organism—including humans—in ways that were previously unimaginable. Each passing day, researchers continue to develop and refine the tools that are steadily inching humankind closer and closer to unlocking the powers of genome editing. This will change the course of human history.

Despite the accrual of steady scientific advances, however, significant and complex issues surrounding genome-editing technologies are looming on the horizon. Global problems related to the national and international governance of genome editing are likely to exert effects on current intellectual property, international trade, and foreign investment regimes. Regulatory agencies will decide whether statutory authority grants them jurisdiction to develop and promulgate rules to regulate products and technologies derived from genome editing. Novel issues of statutory interpretation and construction may soon be the subject of litigation.

Scientists are not well equipped or positioned to address these problems on their own. Case in point, the birth of the first gene-edited babies in China in November 2018 underscored the urgency with which the world needs to address the issue of germline interventions. Self-regulation in the scientific community fell short of any acceptable standards. Admittedly, scientists have failed to preempt premature use of the technology despite international efforts to build principles of governance for human genome editing. Unfortunately, the shortcomings of self-regulation are not limited to a particular field of science and technology.[2] There is much the legal, scientific, and policy communities can—collectively—contribute to the emerging field of genome editing.

The fate of genome editing on a wide range of areas cannot rest on éminence grise scientists, or any powerful insular group for that matter. And society must be wary of the monopolization and concentration of power by a few who seek to control the technology. No exclusive group of corporate entities should control it. No government should control it. No cadre of scientists or individual investors should control it. This technology belongs to all of humankind and must be nurtured and developed in ways that will serve future generations as an agent for good.

This book has examined the prospective benefits and risks associated with the use of select genome-editing technologies from statutory, regulatory, constitutional, international, ethical, egalitarian, scientific, policy, and other standpoints. In so doing, it encourages a broad debate and highlights the pivotal synergistic roles that law, science, and public policy will play on the development of this truly exceptional and transformative emerging technology. My goals in writing this volume have been to (1) jumpstart a dialogue about how genetic engineering in general, and genome editing in particular, can be used to the benefit or detriment of society; (2) highlight the crucial roles that law, science, and public policy will play in the development of this emerging technology; and (3) encourage debate grounded in reason rather than baseless conjecture.

As the book argues, issues concerning oversight and policy making cannot be resolved in a scientific vacuum, in which the sole and primary considerations necessary to adjudicate controversies orbit the relevant scientific facts and evidence. Sociopolitical, economical, and legal concerns are pivotal in shaping policy. It is in the interest of scientists and developers of genome-editing products to recognize how these factors can play crucial roles in promoting science-based public policy.

Science is not suasible. Nor is it democratic. It does not care about social media trends, public opinion, or the state of any given culture humans live in. Scientific truths may not be readily visible or perceptible to us, but they exist. The truth and principles upon which science stands are immutable. Scientific facts simply do not change. And scientific principles are only modified because humans must amend their beliefs to comport with scientific truths that were previously undiscovered and unappreciated.

The truth about established *scientific facts* is neither susceptible to, nor dependent on, public referenda. Much of the scientific research around the world, however, takes place in countries where democracy guarantees the right to vote, even for people who are not well educated in scientific matters. As a result, *scientific progress* —regardless of whether it is meritorious and seeks to address human problems—depends heavily on societal support and can be stifled by undue public concerns.[3] Opposition to scientific advances based on public misperceptions about scientific facts can suppress or even halt progress altogether. Legal challenges can cripple entire industries and make it difficult to develop, refine, and bring technologies to market. Thus, failure to meaningfully engage the public through education while dismissing opposing viewpoints can be very costly for the development of science-based policies.[4]

Within a cloud of uncertainty surrounding the future of genome-editing technologies, this book marks a step toward bringing clarity to an emerging new discipline. By addressing significant gaps between science, law, and policy, the book seeks to foster an interdisciplinary dialogue among lawyers, scientists, policy makers, and, more importantly, contribute to increasing public education and engagement of issues raised by scientific advances in genome editing. Robust and substantive discussions are more important than ever in this watershed era of genetic manipulation and genome editing.

In this book, I have further argued that a uniform doctrinal structure is sorely needed to address future questions that will be raised by the ensuing application of scientific advances to come—including genome-editing technologies—and proposed a jurisprudence of scientific empiricism as a normative legal framework to broadly address questions of science in law. This paradigm builds upon the interdependence of law and science and expands the scope of scientific evidence in the legal system. It also seeks to promote the creation of institutional standards through which lawyers can fuse scientific empiricism and jurisprudence to combat scientific illiteracy, as well as the oversimplification and misinterpretation of scientific advances, which are all common substantive impediments to constructive debate. Above all, the book seeks to spur a conversation about the future of genome editing, its role in society and, more broadly, about how science and technology can influence the world.

* * *

I hope this book ignites a passion within you and inspires you to embark on many other independent journeys, especially those that will allow you to share the knowledge you have gained here and contribute to important, timely conversations that we, as a society, ought to have as genome editing continues to develop. This generation will shape the future of genome editing. We owe it to ourselves—and, even more so, to future generations—to treat this remarkable technology with the gravitas it deserves.

Society has come a long way since Copernicus sparked the scientific revolution. But, as ever, the pursuit of knowledge faces challenges. Misinformation and alternative facts in the era of so-called fake news are undermining scientific progress and even democracy itself. We cannot stand idly as we face these growing threats. We must empower ourselves and others to become allies of truth and leaders in the fight against misinformation. Let transparency, education, public outreach, interdisciplinary cooperation and communication, and a willingness to set aside our implicit biases be our weaponry in these epoch-making times.

But make no mistake. Time does not summon leaders. It is the pressures of times that forge few, ordinary humans of grit gradually and steadily into tenacious leaders. May you become both ally and leader of reasoned and fruitful conversations, grounded and guided by the light of facts.

Notes

1 *See* Paul Enríquez, *Deconstructing Transnationalism: Conceptualizing Metanationalism as a Putative Model of Evolving Jurisprudence*, 43 VAND. J. TRANSNAT'L L. 1265, 1269, 1336 (2010).

2 *See* Davide Castelvecchi, Interview, *AI Pioneer: 'The Dangers of Abuse Are Very Real'*, NATURE (Apr. 4, 2019), https://www.nature.com/articles/d41586-019–00505-2?utm_source=Nature+Briefing&utm_campaign=ffc684d4ec-briefing-dy-20190405&utm_medium=email&utm_term=0_c9dfd39373-ffc684d4ec-43359693 [https://perma.cc/FE9H-59FH] (interviewing "Yoshua Bengio, winner of the prestigious Turing award for his work on deep learning," who expressed the following: "Self-regulation [in artificial intelligence] is not going to work. Do you think that voluntary taxation works? It doesn't."); Nina Jankowicz, *It's Time to Start Regulating Facebook*, WASH. POST (Nov. 15, 2018), https://www.washingtonpost.com/news/democracy-post/wp/2018/11/15/its-time-to-start-regulating-facebook/?utm_term=.9bf5b6aaaa50 [https://perma.cc/PE6G-ZU36] (arguing that self-regulation in the social media sphere has failed).

3 *See, e.g.*, Found. on Econ. Trends v. Heckler, 756 F.2d 143, 146 (D.C. Cir. 1985) (enjoining the University of California from conducting a "deliberate release experiment" to delay field testing of genetically altered bacteria on select crops after environmental groups filed suit against federal officials for alleged NEPA violations).

4 *See* Paul Enríquez, *GM-Food Regulations: Engage the Public*, 548 NATURE 31, 31 (2017).

Index

For EU product safety concerns, contact us at Calle de José Abascal, 56–1°,
28003 Madrid, Spain or eugpsr@cambridge.org.

www.ingramcontent.com/pod-product-compliance
Lightning Source LLC
Chambersburg PA
CBHW071322180926
51611CB00002B/26
9781108468794